THE OXFORD HISTORY OF
ENGLISH LITERATURE

Edited by

BONAMY DOBRÉE *and* NORMAN DAVIS

THE OXFORD HISTORY OF
ENGLISH LITERATURE

ENGLISH LITERATURE
OF THE LATE
SEVENTEENTH
CENTURY

BY

JAMES SUTHERLAND

1969
OXFORD UNIVERSITY PRESS
New York and Oxford

PRINTED IN THE UNITED STATES OF AMERICA

PREFACE

THIS volume was originally planned as a joint work by the late Hugh Macdonald and myself. At a later stage it was agreed that I should be solely responsible for the text, and that Mr. Macdonald should compile the bibliography. When he died, in 1958, the notes that he had made for the bibliography came into my possession; but few of his general or individual bibliographies were complete, and most of them were in a fragmentary and unchecked state. I therefore thought it best to begin again from the beginning, and although I have been able to make some use of Mr. Macdonald's notes, I must accept responsibility for the bibliography as it now stands. In any case, something approaching half of the entries are to books and articles published since his death.

Since considerable latitude has been allowed to the writers of these volumes, I have felt free to discuss a number of the lesser known authors of my period with some fullness. The body of critical comment on Dryden is now formidable, and has increased notably in the past two decades; and the same is true, to a smaller extent, of Bunyan and Locke. Among the writers of Restoration drama, Etherege, Wycherley, and Congreve have all been studied and discussed in considerable detail. But with the other dramatists, such as Shadwell, Lee, Otway, Southerne—and still more with such authors as John Banks, Mrs. Behn, Crowne, Durfey, or Ravenscroft—it is a very different story; and one is driven to conclude that their work is virtually ignored by most critics of Restoration drama. So, too, with the notable Restoration preachers, the writers of history and biography, the essayists, poets of the calibre of Cotton or Oldham (there is a distinct revival of interest in Rochester), and delightful eccentrics like John Aubrey and Walter Pope. It has seemed to me that, while it is not the business of a literary historian to seek to reanimate the dead, it is part of his function to call attention to writers who are being unduly neglected, and whose writing still has life and individuality. The late seventeenth century is also a period of several new and important developments, and I therefore thought it necessary to say something about the men of science, the political and economic

writers, the preachers and religious controversialists, the growth
of periodical journalism, the development of literary criticism,
and even the tentative advances made in prose fiction. On some
of those subjects I have inevitably had to depend on writers
better equipped than myself, but I have tried always to remember that I was writing a history of English literature, and not a
history of science or political economy or religion.

Texts are normally quoted from first or authoritative early
editions, but unemphatic italics have not been retained. Titles
are given in their original form in the bibliography and modernized in the text and chronological tables. In the two chapters on
Drama the dates given for plays are those of their earliest known
performance; in the bibliography they are those of publication.

I have read for this volume in so many different places that
it is difficult to recall all the libraries and their staffs to which
I am indebted. In England I have made most frequent use of
the libraries of the British Museum, the University of London,
University College, London, and the Dr. Williams Library,
conveniently situated round the corner in Gordon Square, and
especially rich in the literature of my period. In America I have
worked mainly at the Widener and Houghton Libraries, at
the Huntington Library (to which I am grateful for a grant
awarded in 1955), at the U.C.L.A. Library, and, above all, at
the William Andrews Clark Memorial Library. My appointment as Clark Library Fellow for 1962–3 enabled me to spend
several months there reading uninterruptedly and in the
greatest comfort. Without that halcyon period, free from teaching and administration, I would have found it difficult to bring
this volume to completion.

The late Professor F. P. Wilson read a few sections of my
manuscript, and gave me constant help and encouragement;
and I owe much to the careful reading and friendly criticism of
the present general editors, Professor Bonamy Dobrée and
Professor Norman Davis. I am also indebted to my colleague,
Mr. Basil Greenslade, who read the whole manuscript and
made many valuable suggestions. For help on the bibliography (for which it is only right that I should acknowledge
what I owe to Professor Douglas Bush's example, and to the
admirable 'Current Bibliography' published annually by the
Philological Quarterly), I am indebted to Professor Curt A.

Zimansky, Professor Donald F. Bond, and Professor Earl Miner. For other advice and criticism I have to thank the late Professor Douglas McKie, Professor Irène Simon, Dr. F. W. Sternfeld, and Professor William Matthews. Among much that I have learnt from Professor Bush is the usefulness of the phrase *et al.*', and I must use it now to refer to the many other friends who have helped me in one way or another, but whose names are not entered in this list of acknowledgements.

J. S.

CONTENTS

I

THE BACKGROUND OF THE AGE

(1)

For the literary historian the year 1660 marks a clearer break with the past than he is usually able to find. The reigns of Charles II, James II, and William and Mary form a well-defined period; and although social and political developments of the greatest importance were taking place after the Revolution of 1688, it was some time before their effects became seriously felt in literature, except to some extent in the drama, and in the rapid development of the newspaper. With the reign of Queen Anne, however, those changes in the moral, political, and social temper had begun to spread through all classes of society, and the results were soon apparent in the changing culture of the new period. Whether 'tis well or not, it is certainly clear that by 1700

an Old Age is out,
And time to begin a New.

At this distance of time many of the controversies that divided Englishmen in the closing decades of the seventeenth century seem strangely remote, but underneath some of the other disputes and national upheavals the ashes are still glowing hot. It may be questioned, indeed, whether even yet the modern reader is able to approach some of the more controversial figures of the period with that detachment which the passage of centuries usually brings. The critical estimate of Bishop Burnet, for example, both as a man and a writer, is probably still biased by the modern equivalent of Whig or Tory sympathies; and on such issues as the Popish Plot or the Exclusion Bill, and on the interpretation of the characters and motives of the chief actors in them, notably Shaftesbury and Halifax, informed opinion is still apt to be deeply divided or at least uncertain. Similarly, the literature of this period will almost certainly make a mixed impression of modernity and antiquity on the twentieth-century reader; it will sound 'at once far off and near'. He will find it hard, too, to define the spirit of an age that produced such diverse writers as Bunyan and Etherege, Butler and Locke, Evelyn and Rochester, Halifax and Nathaniel Lee, Robert South and William Penn. Diversity meets us wherever we look: 1667 is the year of *Paradise Lost* and *The Indian Emperor*; 1671 of *Samson Agonistes* and *An Evening's Love*; 1682 of *The Holy War*, *The London Cuckolds*, *Religio Laici*, *Venice Preserved*, Creech's translation of Lucretius, Nehemiah Grew's *Anatomy of Plants*, and of H. Playford's *Wit and Mirth*. *Quot homines, tot sententiae*, no doubt; but what helps to distinguish this period is the absolute difference between one attitude to life and another. No one man, therefore, not even Dryden, is fully representative of the age; it speaks with many voices, and with an irreconcilable diversity of thought and expression. It will only conform to the conventional notion of the Restoration age if we confine our attention to such fields as the drama and poetry, and forget about some of its greatest writers, such as Bunyan and South, Clarendon and Halifax, and its greatest thinkers, such as Newton and Locke.

To a large extent the explanation of this wide diversity is to be found in the political, social, economic, and religious situation that existed when Charles II returned to his throne. Although the political and religious storm that had broken out in the reign of his father had now largely blown itself out, the commotion which it had caused was still being felt all through English society; for

> whan the storm is all ago,
> Yet wol the water quappe a day or two.

The sharp division of opinion that flared up at one political-religious crisis after another pointed to the existence of two nations, not merely in Disraeli's sense of the rich and the poor (although that was part of the total situation), but in the still smouldering antagonism of those who had been displaced from power and privilege towards the Cavaliers and the adventurers who had stepped so gladly into their places. The very way in which the Restoration came about left most of the fundamental questions unresolved. During the last months of the Commonwealth there appears to have been one of those silent revolutions of public opinion, so widespread and, within the central body of neutral opinion, so general that at first it proved irresistible. The Puritans, who had split up into many mutually antagonistic sects, found themselves discredited and on the defensive, and their military government detested. A majority of Englishmen of all classes were now weary of their particular brand of well-doing, and hostile to the graft and hypocrisy that had often gone with it. Even among those who were still undecided, many felt insufficiently interested in their aims and ideals to give any active support towards prolonging the life of the Commonwealth. Some who were no doubt unwilling to see a restoration of the monarchy were prepared to stay their judgement and let things take their course; the alternative, another civil war, was too hideous to contemplate. If there was not, therefore, a desire for change on all sides, there was no great determination to prevent it. To many, indeed, the Restoration seemed to be an act of God. In one of those numerous pindaric odes written on the death of Charles II, Sir Francis Fane looked back to the wonderful spring of 1660: just when it seemed that 'our dying hopes could ebb no more', God by 'a turn miraculous' restored the King to his loyal subjects—

> To bring which blessed work to pass,
> Neither Man's Pow'r nor Policy had place;
> No Contract made, nor blows were given;
> The astonish'd World saw 'twas the mighty work of Heav'n.

That the return of the King to his throne should have passed off without a single serious incident was also a triumph for the political astuteness of General Monck, and for the tact and charm of the King himself. The clemency of Charles II—one of his most genuine virtues—made the restoration of the monarchy easier to accept by those who had no sort of enthusiasm for the Stuarts, and a general sense of good times come again gave the new regime a promising start. There ensued a short honeymoon period when large numbers of Englishmen got gloriously drunk tossing off loyal bumpers to the King's health, when everything that reminded them of the Good Old Cause was contemptuously ridiculed, and when decency and piety were discredited as sure signs of hypocrisy and fanaticism. In the first decade after the Restoration, and for some time after that, a stock theme for the new comedy was the satirizing of Puritans, who were almost invariably represented as hypocrites and timeservers. Many even of those who had supported the Commonwealth now felt that the best way for them to work their passage home was, in the words of Burnet, 'by going into the stream, and laughing at all religion, telling or making stories to expose both themselves and their party as impious and ridiculous'. The slightly shocked acquiescence of Samuel Pepys in the excesses of England's new masters, and his willingness to wait upon events, must have been typical of many.

The young King was welcomed with a shower of verse panegyrics by Davenant, Waller, Cowley, Dryden, Charles Cotton, and other of his equally loyal but more obscure subjects. Although those poems naturally varied in content, they tended to stress the redemption of England from bondage, the binding up of her old wounds, the restoration of order and authority, and the willing consent of a loyal and expectant nation to the coming reign of its lawful king, with all the promise of future greatness:

> And now Time's whiter Series is begun
> Which in soft Centuries shall smoothly run;
> Those Clouds that overcast your Morne shall fly
> Dispell'd to farthest corners of the sky.
> Our Nation with united Int'rest blest
> Not now content to poize, shall sway the rest.

Dryden went on to prophesy the future growth of empire, the development of English trade, and the conversion of the factious and discontented by 'the life and blest example' of the King. Above all, the panegyrists stressed the heroic and magnanimous qualities of the young King, his suffering in exile for his people following upon the martyrdom of his royal father, and his own divine right to the throne. Throughout the reign of Charles II and the brief reign of his brother James the deification of kingship remained a constant theme of the Tory poets, and was perhaps the chief reason for their rather uneasy search for a heroic style that would sustain the myth of regal dominion. The King, too, was not only the absolute father of his national family, but, by reason of his heroic virtue, a pattern to his subjects. No doubt the deliberate building up of the last two Stuart kings into a species of sun-gods was one of the reasons for the unreality of much heroic poetry in this period: the truth was as different from the pretence as Restoration comedy from the heroic play.

Although from the first new forces were at work, the Restoration began with an understandable attempt to restore as much as possible from the shattered past; and the King, who was a more moderate and more modern man than most of his subjects, was forced to comply with severe and reactionary measures that he would almost certainly not have taken on his own initiative. In the first hours of triumph such episodes as the exhumation of Cromwell's body and the hanging of it in his coffin at Tyburn, together with the execution of some of the surviving regicides with all the barbarous circumstances of drawing and quartering, were no doubt the inevitable consequences of public excitement and of a general desire to remove all traces of the hated past. Such public spectacles and sacrifices satisfied many, and must have seemed to others no less than just. But if old scores could be settled in this spectacular fashion, old grievances remained, and new ones were developing all the time. The danger of discontent and disaffection lay especially in the inevitable transfer of power and property that followed upon the Restoration. The return of sequestrated lands involved legal proceedings of the most complicated kind; and a compromise was eventually reached which provided for the return of Crown and Church lands to their former owners, but allowed those who had purchased private estates in the open market to remain in undisturbed possession. This rough justice left many loyal Cavaliers with a genuine grievance; and such men could very fairly apply to themselves Samuel Butler's bitter observation that 'all Acts of Oblivion have, of late times, been found to extend rather to loyal and faithful services done than rebellion and treason committed'. Equally exasperated, of course, were those who had been unlucky enough to purchase Crown or Church lands.

A similar problem faced the Convention Parliament when it came to deal with those ministers who had now, with the re-establishment of the Church of England, become Dissenters. Some sort of compromise with the Presbyterians appeared feasible in the early discussions which took place in 1660. An Act was passed providing for the reinstatement of evicted Anglican clergymen to their livings, but it was designed to cause as little hardship as possible to 'intruded' ministers. When the new Parliament met in 1661, however, the spirit of compromise had almost evaporated, and while the Savoy conference was still sitting (from April to July) the prospects for the Presbyterians and other Dissenters rapidly worsened. Indeed, it soon became almost a matter of principle that the Presbyterians were more responsible than any other party for the outbreak of the Civil War and all the subsequent troubles. Here, too, Charles II's recollection of his treatment in 1650 by the godly Scots still rankled; and he once told Lauderdale that presbyterianism was not a religion for gentlemen. The Act of Uniformity, which was placed on the statute book in May 1662, finally deprived of his benefice any minister who had not been ordained by a bishop of the Church of England; and in 1673 the Test Act made it obligatory on the holder of any office, civil or military, to take the sacrament of the Lord's Supper according to the usage of the Church of England. Although the fortunes of the Dissenters fluctuated in the years that followed, they could never count on more than a grudging toleration for the rest of the century, or indeed for a long time after that.

The uncompromising treatment of the Dissenters was extended to all who could be suspected of favouring the old regime, and a series of Acts increased the royal powers for dealing with suspects. Early in the new reign various malcontents were convicted of speaking treasonable words, or of 'compassing and imagining' the death of the King, and were sentenced to be hanged, drawn, and quartered. One of the first measures of the new reign was a Licensing Act (1662) designed to keep the press under strict control; and early in 1664 John Twyn, a printer, was hanged for printing a 'seditious, poisonous and scandalous book' entitled *A Treatise of the Execution of Justice.* He had been arrested through the vigilance of Roger L'Estrange, who had recently been appointed 'Surveyor of the Imprimery'. Four years later fifteen London prentices were indicted for 'tumultuously assembling themselves in Moorfields under colour of pulling down bawdy-houses', and four of them were hanged. In addressing the jury the Lord Chief Justice made it clear what lay behind prosecutions of this sort:

If every Man may reform what he will, no Man is safe: therefore this thing is of desperate Consequence, we must make this for a publick Example. There is reason we should be very cautious, we are but newly delivered from Rebellion, and we know that that Rebellion first began under the Pretence of Religion and the Law. . . . Therefore we have great Reason to be very wary that we fall not again into the same Error.

The long shadow of the Commonwealth fell across the first two decades of the new reign, and as late as 1681 Shaftesbury and the Whigs came near to destroying for a second time the existing monarchy.

It would be far from true to say that Charles II went in danger of his life all through the twenty-four years of his reign; and yet, for all his personal charm, he was left with a permanent minority of discontented subjects, and in times of crisis the old republican spirit smouldered dangerously. Tact and bonhomie are all very well, but with Charles they led only to papering over the cracks, rather than to removing the causes of discontent. Among the King's subjects there must have been many who wondered

> why, so long, they had obey'd
> An Idoll Monarch which their hands had made;

but it was true (as Dryden went on to point out) that

> David's mildness manag'd it so well,
> The Bad found no occasion to Rebell.

As the King once put it to the Earl of Essex, thinking of all the trouble that his various parliaments had given him, he 'did not wish to be like a Grand Signior, with some mutes about him, and bags of bow-strings to strangle men as he had a mind to it; but he did not think he was a king as long as a company of fellows were looking into all his actions, and examining his ministers as well as his accounts'. Towards the close of his reign, after he had successfully weathered the storms of the Popish Plot and the Exclusion Bill, he came nearer than ever before to ruling absolutely, but he was a schemer and a politician to the last. Courage, political adroitness, and a genius for postponement kept Charles II on his throne, but left the nation divided in politics and religion, its conflicts unresolved and the national energy dissipated in faction. The King did not give the nation a lead: he was either too lazy to bother, or too concerned with adapting his policy from day to day to his own precarious situation, or too busy attending to his own idle pleasures.

The short reign of his more forthright and much less politic brother had at least the advantage of bringing differences into the light, and to some extent united the nation in a determined opposition to Roman Catholicism and absolute government.

The triumph of the Protestant cause with the landing of William of Orange at Torbay, on 5 November 1688, was ultimately a triumph for the Whigs and the City; but if the reign of William and Mary did not make for a merry England, it had the merit (if it is a merit) of carrying the English people forward into the modern world, and releasing forces of social and economic progress that had hitherto been partially frustrated by political reaction. The full effect of the Revolution, however, was not felt until the next century.

(ii)

The view we take of England in the later seventeenth century will necessarily depend to a large extent on what we are looking at. There is plenty of evidence of profligacy and spiritual apathy, but there are equally obvious signs of spiritual zeal and intellectual curiosity. The religious temper of the age is not easy to assess. If we do not readily think of it as an age of martyrdom, it was none the less one in which large numbers of men were prepared to suffer stubbornly and without compromise for their religious, and sometimes for their political, beliefs. The fanaticism of the previous age did not disappear all at once. In January 1661 a wine-cooper called Thomas Venner led a party of about fifty Fifth-Monarchy men into the streets of London to overthrow the Government. They were all killed or captured, and Venner himself was hanged opposite his meeting-house in Coleman Street. This fantastic episode, of no great importance in itself, was made the excuse for imposing harsher measures on all who could be suspected of fanaticism, and the Quakers especially suffered severely. The Quakers Act of 1662 prohibited their meeting together for worship, the penalty for a third offence being transportation. In 1662 about 1,300 Quakers were lying in prison; only about 500 of those were still alive in 1672, when the Declaration of Indulgence set them free. Among the other Nonconformists who were liberated on that occasion was John Bunyan, who had spent all but a few months since November 1660 as a prisoner in Bedford Gaol. Although the Presbyterians were in general subjected to less severe penalties, they too suffered for conscience' sake in the loss of civil rights and other deprivations. Even the Toleration Act of 1689, welcome though it was to the harassed

Dissenters, perpetuated some of the existing restrictions and penalties.

With such a formidable body of Dissenters, and such a prolonged tale of persecution, it is impossible to dismiss the age as lacking in spiritual fervour. But the Dissenters amounted to only a large minority of the total population: if we are to form a true estimate of the religious temper of the age we must obviously pay particular attention to the Church of England. A church which subjected Nonconformists to severe penalties ought to have been actuated by a zeal for religion, or at any rate by a strong conviction that the doctrine and discipline of the Established Church came as near to perfection as was possible in an imperfect world. Most Anglicans did believe this. In the words of one of their own apologists, Simon Patrick, they had

a deep veneration of her Government, which they stedfastly beleive to be in it self the best, and the same that was practised in the times of the Apostles. They did alwayes abhor both the Usurpation of Scottish Presbytery, and the confusion of Independent Anarchy; and do esteem it one of the methods which the Prince of Darkness useth to overthrow the Church and Religion, by bringing the Clergy into contempt. . . .

It has been very properly observed that loyalty to the Church of England is as genuine a thing as sectarian conviction, and that 'the desire to find shelter and emotional stability in a dignified well-regulated community', such as the Church of England gave to its communicants, is quite as authentic a sign of true religion as an intense care for personal salvation.

None the less, it is difficult to avoid the conclusion that the attitude of many among the clergy towards the Nonconformists was governed as much by considerations of prestige as by religious conviction. Anything that weakened the authority of their Church undermined their security and their importance in the community, just as anything short of universal military service lowers the prestige of the Army. Dissenters, because they dissented, drained away some of the Church's strength. No doubt, too, the mere fact of dissent carries with it an implied insult to those who have remained within the Establishment. If men break away from the Church it is because the Church is not good enough for them; they are protesting inside Protestantism, and can hardly expect to be loved by those from whom they have deliberately sought separation. The attitude of the laity to the Nonconformists was for the most part more simple and less interested: they tended to equate dissent with fanaticism and excess of zeal, and they associated it with shopkeepers and artisans. To give any encouragement to the Dissenters was therefore to encourage the subversion of authority, and the surest way of bringing back the rule of the saints. Such feelings were fully expressed in the sermons of Robert South, and in Butler's *Hudibras*, which was perhaps as frequently quoted in Anglican circles as the English Bible.

The Revolution of 1688 distressed the Church of England in another way, by causing an unhappy schism within its own ranks. At the Restoration it was not only the monarchy that was restored, it was also the Church of England; and ever since 1660 the Church had preached up the doctrine of non-resistance to the hereditary king. When, therefore, William of Orange was called to the throne by the Convention Parliament of 1689, every Englishman had to examine his own conscience and decide whether to accept him as the lawful King of England or reject him as a usurper while James II was still alive. For Churchmen, and more especially for High Churchmen, the choice was a peculiarly difficult one. The aged William Sancroft, Archbishop of Canterbury, six other bishops, and some four hundred of the clergy, sticking bravely to the doctrine of non-resistance which they had always upheld, refused to take the oath of allegiance to the new King and Queen. In the country at large there was little admiration, or even approval, for what was in some ways a gallant stand; the doctrine of the divine right of kings had been silently abandoned by most of the laity, and in so far as the Church of England still taught that doctrine, it was preaching what almost all of the Whigs, and (as events suggest) most of the Tories, felt to be a mere superstition. On the other hand, the main body of the clergy, who, like the Vicar of Bray, 'set conscience at a distance', and decided that

> Passive obedience is a joke,
> A jest is Non-resistance,

threw themselves open to the charge, especially if they belonged to the High Church party, of having betrayed their own principles. Either way, the Church was bound to suffer from the unprecedented turn of events, and some loss of prestige was inevitable.

This loss of prestige was the more distressing because the Church had rarely stood higher in popular esteem than in the tense weeks that preceded the Revolution. The firm resistance offered by the Seven Bishops when they refused to allow their clergy to read James II's declaration of liberty of conscience, their trial, and their eventual acquittal, were the occasion for a remarkable demonstration of loyalty and spontaneous emotion. The issue in 1688 was as much political as religious, and in so far as it was religious it was a question of making a stand against Popery and a Papist king. The feelings aroused on that tremendous occasion were certainly genuine, but among many good Englishmen they were perhaps not altogether different in kind from those which Defoe heard expressed by a gentleman of very high quality to his footman, after the debate in the House of Lords which resulted in William of Orange's being voted on to the throne: 'Jack (says he) God damn ye, Jack, go home to your Lady, and tell her we have got a Protestant King and Queen, and go make a Bonfire as big as a House, and bid the Butler make ye all Drunk, ye Dog.' At all events, a deep-seated hatred of Popery was one of the few emotions that could unite almost the whole nation, and it could make ordinary Englishmen rally to the defence of the Church in an hour of danger.

A church which could number among its prelates and thinkers many of the best minds of the day, such as Barrow, South, Stillingfleet, Simon Patrick, Sprat, Tillotson, Ken, Collier, and Burnet should have been able to command widespread respect. Yet at least some of the evidence points in the opposite direction. Edward Chamberlayne, writing in 1669 what purports to be an impartial account of 'the present state of England', has this to say about the Anglican clergy:

It hath been observed, even by strangers, that the iniquity of the present Times in England is such, that the English Clergy are not only hated by the Romanists on the one side, and maligned by the Presbyterians on the other . . ., but also that, of all the Christian Clergy of Europe, whether Romish, Lutheran, or Calvinistic, none are so little respected, beloved, obeyed, or rewarded, as the present pious, learned, loyal clergy of the Church of England, even by those who always professed themselves of that Communion.

It may be that the need to fill so many benefices after the passing of the Act of Uniformity led to a temporary lowering of intellectual standards among the Anglican clergy; but their private lives too were not always such as to command the respect of their parishioners. Reasonable men like John Eachard found that among the grounds and occasions for the contempt of the clergy was the fact that they were often 'idle, intemperate, and scandalous'. Eachard was willing to attribute most of their backsliding to poverty. So many of the country parsons were struggling to bring up a family and maintain their professional position on twenty or thirty pounds a year that the temptation to the depressed incumbent to accept local hospitality, and 'to forsake his own study of a few scurvy books, and his own habitation of darkness where there is seldom eating and drinking, for a good lightsome one where there is bountiful provision of both', must often have been overwhelming. Yet by accepting such invitations the poor parson often placed himself in an equivocal position: he had to listen without protest to the Squire's broad jokes and profane conversation, knowing that if he made any attempt to 'damp a frolic' he would no longer be welcome at the manor house. In his own humbler sphere he had to face the same situation as Burnet faced at Court when Charles II embarked on one of his bawdy stories. Again, when the Squire passed the bottle and gave a toast, he expected his guests to drink. Defoe, who was far from being a strict Puritan, was significantly fond of reflecting upon the lack of sobriety among the Anglican clergy: 'The Parson preaches a thundering Sermon against Drunkenness, and the Justice of the Peace sets my poor Neighbour in the Stocks, and I am like to be much the better for either, when I know perhaps that this same Parson, and this same Justice, were both drunk together the Night before.'

Yet with all its faults, the influence of the Church on the community was beyond question. It should not be forgotten that, in an age when churchgoing was still almost universal outside the large cities, the clergy exercised a powerful effect on the minds of their humbler parishioners. The liturgy of the Church helped to maintain the *status quo*, and to strengthen the Restoration settlement; and the political influence of the country clergy, almost unchallenged in a community still largely illiterate, was one of the main supports of the Tory party after the historical division into Whigs and Tories became established. In a troubled age they helped to give the nation stability, at the price of some bigotry and stupidity, and of resistance to change, good as well as bad.

When the Restoration clergyman climbed into his pulpit, his discourse was normally in accordance with the two principles of preaching that were later to be laid down by Swift: he endeavoured 'to tell the people what is their duty, and then to convince them that it is so'. On 24 February 1661 Pepys listened to the most excellent sermon against drunkenness that ever he heard in his life; and rather more than a year later he heard 'a very honest sermon' preached at Court before the King by a Canon of Christ Church, who 'did much insist upon the sin of adultery; which methought might touch the King, and the more because he forced it into his sermon, besides his text'. In 1673 the intrepid Burnet (then aged 30) had a long private audience with the King, and seized the chance to tackle him about the immoral course of his life. The King 'bore it very well', freely admitting that it would be wrong to live with another man's wife, but expressing the belief that 'God would not damn a man for a little irregular pleasure'. Although a few of the Anglican clergy were of the sort 'who never mention hell to ears polite', most of them—and some of their greatest preachers, like Robert South—were ready enough to speak out and rebuke immorality. It is a common mistake to assume that Restoration comedy gives us a reliable (or, at any rate, a fully representative) picture of the life of the time; if we keep all classes in view, we get a very different impression. A glance at the Verney Papers, or at the diaries of Robert Hooke and John Evelyn, or a consideration of the vast output of religious literature between 1660 and 1700 should be enough to convince any fairminded person that the conventional picture of an age of immorality and profaneness is much overdrawn.

Yet there are too many disquieting features in the public life of the time not to suggest that among certain sections of the community the moral thermometer was standing at an abnormally low level. In the smaller England of 1660 the Court exerted a greater influence for good or evil than it could ever do in the next century. Charles II must be held at least partly responsible for the immorality that pervaded so much of the upper class during his reign; for the example he gave his subjects was in some ways deplorable. Not too much need be made of his mistresses, since several of his successors indulged in similar freedoms without seriously affecting the moral tone of the nation. Yet the amours of Charles II were so openly paraded before his people, and they had, as Halifax observed, 'so little of the seraphic part' in them, that they were the common talk of the town; so that even his own Poet Laureate could refer with casual amusement to his 'vigorous warmth' and to the way in which he had 'scattered his Maker's image through the land'. We can hardly imagine Nicholas Rowe or Laurence Eusden complimenting George I on his extra-matrimonial virility. But although the King's example may have encouraged gentlemen of fashion, if encouragement was needed, to keep mistresses, it was much more his general attitude to life that adversely influenced the Court, and so, less directly, the greater part of upper-class society. Burnet found that the King had a low opinion of men and women, and thought that the world was 'governed wholly by interest'. This sceptical, realistic (and, as many would have said, Hobbesian) temper was characteristic of the whole period, and may perhaps have been partly due to what Halifax called 'the hypocrisy of the former times', which 'inclined men to think they could not show too great an aversion to it'. This aversion is frequently expressed in the comedies of the period; and Shadwell's Bruce put it characteristically in *The Virtuoso* when comparing his own generation with that of 'the last age': 'I believe there was the same Wenching then: only they dissembled it. They added Hypocrisie to Fornication, and so made two Sins of what we make but one.' Frankness and an absence of pretence gave to the upper class an undeniable consistency of outlook and an unshakeable self-confidence, but predisposed it to cynicism, or turned the minds of its more thoughtful members towards an Epicureanism that is one of the genuine intellectual currents of the period. One of the reasons why Pepys is such an endearing character in a hard-bitten age which showed little interest in natural human feeling is that he continually speaks the language of the heart. On 28 December 1667 he saw Hart and Nell Gwyn in *The Mad Couple* of James Howard, in which the hero is confronted by a series of his mistresses presenting him with his illegitimate children: 'It pleased us mightily to see the natural affection of a poor woman, the mother of one of the children brought upon the stage: the child crying, she by force got upon the stage, and took up her child and carried it away off of the stage from Hart. Many fine faces here today.' Many fine faces; but how many of them showed the same human interest as that of Pepys?

One of the King's personal habits, that of making 'broad allusions', seems to have spread pretty generally through the Court, and may have done something to encourage the startling indecency of so many passages in Restoration comedy, and in the prologues and epilogues that accompanied the plays. One December evening in 1668 Pepys went on to Whitehall after the play, and there found himself listening to 'the silly discourse of the King', who was entertaining a group of courtiers with 'a story of my Lord Rochester's having of his clothes stole while he was with a wench; and his gold all gone, but his clothes found afterwards, stuffed into a feather bed by the wench that stole them'. No book gives a clearer picture of this side of Restoration life than Anthony Hamilton's *Memoirs of the Count de Grammont*: if this work were not fully authenticated one might suspect it of being a fabrication by someone well versed in Restoration comedy, so frequently are its situations and intrigues paralleled by those in contemporary plays. When the King could be so free in his conversation, it is hardly surprising that so many indecent poems were circulating in manuscript and eventually found their way into print. Lord Roscommon was not, perhaps, the only poet of the period who could boast 'unspotted bays', but his decency is certainly exceptional. The fine gentleman of the Restoration was often, indeed, a person of very dubious culture. A university education was so far from conferring gentility that it was generally held to breed pedants; the academic rust had to be scoured off by conversation with men of fashion. The half-educated young lords and gentlemen who returned from exile in 1660 and set the tone of the Restoration Court were more likely to know French than Latin, and more about the flavour of a ragout than the conjugation of an irregular verb. Even men of a very different stamp such as the Earl of Essex, whose education had been interrupted by the Civil War, bore through life the marks of a displaced person: Evelyn found him to be 'a sober, wise, judicious, and pondering person', but added significantly, 'not illiterate beyond the rate of most noblemen in this age'.

With such an educational background the emphasis tended to fall on those accomplishments which could be naturally acquired by merely living in affluence among one's social equals: on easy deportment and gay, unforced conversation; on dress; on the ability to manage an intrigue or fight a duel; on the authority that could command the instant compliance and respect of coachmen, chairmen, drawers, watchmen, and the lower orders in general. The gentleman's dress, varying from one decade (and even one year) to another, but always distinctive; his Chedreux wig, his laced ruffles, his gloves, his right to carry a sword—all such things defined his social standing unmistakably and separated him from the common herd. His conversation, too, marked him out from his social inferiors by its characteristic drawl, by his command of fashionable oaths, and by the delicate turn he gave (or liked to think he gave) to his obscenities. To be obscene with an air was part of the fine gentleman's equipment. The Earl of Mulgrave made it clear that while

> . . . obscene words, too gross to move desire,
> Like heaps of Fuel do but choak the Fire,

he had no objection to obscenity that was well turned. Roscommon, as we should expect, warns writers against using immodest words; yet even he seems to be unable to make his point without having recourse to a sexual metaphor typical of the whole period:

> What mod'rate *Fop* would rake the *Park* or *Stews*,
> Who among Troops of *faultless Nymphs* may chuse?

So much emphasis has been laid since the days of Jeremy Collier on the libertinism of Restoration comedy that we are apt to overlook other and more serious signs of moral indifference. One of the most disquieting indications of the low state of public morality in the years preceding the Revolution was the venality and corruption of the judges. During the Commonwealth they had held office *dum bene gesserint*, but after the Restoration their tenure of office was dependent on the approval of the Crown. Both Charles and James got rid of judges who failed to obtain verdicts satisfactory to the Crown, and promoted men who were prepared to direct the jury to bring in a verdict contrary to the weight of the evidence. Even so, there were a few incorruptible judges such as Sir Matthew

Hale; but Hale, like Clarendon, was rather a survivor from the past than a man of the new age. Although a few of the new men resisted the pressure that was constantly brought to bear upon them and maintained an honourable impartiality, others like Scroggs and Jeffreys resorted to such practices as browbeating prisoners and witnesses, refusing to hear the evidence for the defence, and misdirecting and threatening juries. A corrupt judicature makes the way easy for a general lowering of moral standards, and encourages cynicism in all classes of society. Another form of corruption that became distressingly common was the false evidence that informers and others so often tendered on oath. The perjured testimony of Titus Oates is only the most flagrant example of a practice that was widespread at the time, and that sent many innocent men to the gallows.

The times were no doubt abnormally difficult for public men; and the highly personal and unpredictable policy of Charles II and James II made a certain easiness of principle obligatory on statesmen who wished to stay in office. If, like Sir William Temple, they remained true to their principles, they were driven into retirement. Twice within a few years— in 1685 and 1688—the national policy underwent an abrupt and radical change, and placemen and office-seekers were compelled to adjust their loyalties to entirely altered circumstances. The Vicar of Bray is indeed a symbolic figure for the whole period, and his ecclesiastical tergiversations were repeated by many cautious and practical Englishmen in the secular sphere. In the circumstances Charles II and James II often got the sort of servants they deserved, and they were fortunate to have one or two—notably the Marquis of Halifax— far better than they deserved. Looking back in 1693 at the world he had known, Dryden reflected sadly, and with an unfamiliar touch of bitterness, on the standards of honesty and decency in public life: 'No Government has ever been, or ever can be, wherein Time-servers and Blockheads, will not be uppermost. The Persons are only chang'd, but the same juglings in State, the same Hypocrisie in Religion, the same Self-interest and Mis-mannagement, will remain for ever. Blood and Mony will be lavish'd in all Ages, only for the Preferment of new Faces, with old Consciences.' Those may be the words of a veteran grown superfluous on the stage, but they do not come from a saint or a sentimentalist. No less disillusioned are some observations by Samuel Butler about perjury: the immediate context is probably the Test Act of 1673, but Butler's remarks have a wider relevance to the whole period:

As soon as a Man has taken an Oath against his Conscience and done his Endeavour to damn himself, he is capable of any Trust or Employment in the Government; so excellent a Quality is Perjury to render the most perfidious of Men most fit and proper for publick Charges of the greatest Consequence, and such as have ever so little restraint laid upon them by Conscience, or Religion or Natural Integrity are declared insufficient and unable to hold any Office of publick Trust in the Nation.

The Revolution of 1688 did not immediately raise the standards of public life, nor did it effect a universal reformation of manners and morals among the upper class. Young peers continued to abuse their privileges; rakes and bullies still beat the watch and terrorized the citizens. The seventh Earl of Pembroke, who had filled his thirty useless years with riot and debauchery, scouring the Town with his drunken companions, killing one man in a tavern quarrel, and another, a watchman, on his way home from a night's hard drinking, died in his bed in 1683. But Nature was prodigal of her rakes, and about 1690 the young Lord Mohun came upon the Town. His career was marked by the same brutal unconcern for order and decency, and the same patrician contempt for the lower orders; he died appropriately enough in Hyde Park in 1712, after fighting a duel with the Duke of Hamilton and giving his opponent a fatal wound. Such men were a law to themselves, and had an unassailable belief that their rank gave them special privileges. The type is seen to perfection in Colonel Christopher Vratz, a soldier of fortune who was hanged in 1682 for the murder of Thomas Thynne. To the clergyman (probably Burnet) who accompanied him to the gallows and administered spiritual advice, Vratz said stoutly that 'dying he did not value a rush, and hoped and believed God would deale with him like a Gentleman'.

By 1690, however, England was becoming a little less safe for the Pembrokes and the Mohuns. William of Orange had a vested interest in law and order, and his wife was a woman of genuine piety. The growth, during the last decade of the century, of the Societies for the Reformation of Manners must be attributed to a widespread reaction from the moral laxity of the 1670s and 1680s. Burnet traces the origin of those societies to the short reign of James II, when many good people in and around London were alarmed by the spread of Popery, and began to meet in small groups for devotional purposes and for their mutual instruction and improvement. After the Revolution those societies increased in numbers and influence, partly through the encouragement of Queen Mary, and partly because they reflected a new seriousness and to some extent a revived puritanism. They now began to organize a determined attack on immorality and profaneness, working by means of informers who reported any cases of swearing, blasphemy, or drunkenness that came to their notice, and the existence of bawdy-houses and other places of ill fame. By those unattractive methods they undoubtedly did some good; but, as Defoe was to complain, the laws were cobweb laws 'in which the small flies are catched, and great ones break through'. A few scandalous whores might be sent to Bridewell, and some alehouse-keepers and vintners fined for opening on a Sunday, but the rich offender escaped unpunished: 'The Man with a Gold Ring, and Gay Cloaths, may Swear before the Justice, or at the Justice, may reel home through the open Streets, and no Man take any notice of it; but if a poor Man get drunk, or swears an Oath, he must to the Stocks without Remedy.' All the same, public life was slowly becoming more decent. The publication in 1698 of Jeremy Collier's *Short View of the Immorality and Profaneness of the English Stage*, although it may have had little immediate effect on the theatres, was at least symptomatic of a change that was coming over public morals. To 'swear like a gentleman', to be 'as drunk as a lord', had rather less relevance in 1700 than in 1660. In the second number of *The Gentleman's Journal*, 1692, Motteux relates how a young spark turned over a copy of the first number in a bookseller's shop, and found nothing in it to his taste. 'At last, "Here, take your Book, Mister," said he, "there is not a word of Bawdy in't: how the Devil can it be a Journal fit for a Gentleman?" ' Motteux is inviting his readers to laugh at a young rake who has been overtaken by time, and who is not so fashionable as he supposes. Twenty years later the reaction from Restoration manners and morals has gone much further; and Steele is able to tell the readers of the *Spectator* that Etherege's celebrated

comedy *The Man of Mode* is 'a perfect Contradiction to good
Manners, good Sense, and common Honesty'.

The attempt to reform society found another practical expression in the Society for the Promotion of Christian Knowledge.
By means of its charity schools the Society gave to considerable
numbers of poor children an education which was secular as
well as religious. Three years later, in 1701, the Society for the
Propagation of the Gospel in Foreign Parts began its work.
These and other philanthropic movements were mainly of
middle-class origin, supported by both Anglicans and Nonconformists; they give clear indications of a widespread kindliness
and piety, and of that practical Christianity which a more sober
generation was substituting for the hot-headed doctrinal zeal of
its grandfathers.

(III)

The upper class may have given only a faint example of
moral virtue to the rest of the nation, but as patrons and
employers of artists and craftsmen the great families did much to
enrich the culture of the period. Here Charles II, who had his
own dreams of glory and sometimes saw himself as an English
Louis XIV, gave a genuine lead to his subjects. Besides taking
an active interest in the rebuilding of London after the Great
Fire of 1666, the King (so far as his chronically impoverished
exchequer would allow) launched into several grandiose building projects of his own. Two new palaces were begun, but never
completed: the first at Greenwich by John Webb, and the
second at Winchester by Wren. Thomas Bruce, afterwards
Earl of Ailesbury, who was a Gentleman of the Bedchamber,
has recorded that on the last Sunday of the King's life he was in
an unusually good humour, and talked gaily and longingly
about the palace he was building at Winchester, 'ending with
the fatal expression, "I shall be most happy this week, for my
building will be covered with lead"'. Charles II's most successful
architectural ventures (most of which were destroyed in the
reigns of George III and George IV) were the extensive alterations and developments carried out with a baroque magnificence at Windsor by Hugh May, with carvings by Grinling
Gibbons and murals by Antonio Verrio.

Writing about 1664, Sprat had observed that whereas the

French nobility tended to live close to each other in their cities and in well-built streets, the English nobility, preferring the pleasures of the field to those of the town, were scattered in their country-houses, and that English cities were less well designed for the amenities of a civilized life. By the end of the century this was no longer so true. The great country-houses, both old and new—Audley End, Badminton, Cassiobury Park (where Gibbons and Verrio were again employed), Cliveden, Knole, Euston, and the rest—continued to exist as self-supporting communities employing large numbers of people; but their owners were normally spending more of their time in London, where there was now a recognized season, followed in the summer months by a shorter season at a fashionable resort such as Bath or Tunbridge Wells. The persons of quality were to be found in the handsome new streets to the north and to the immediate south of Piccadilly, and in the new squares— Soho Square, Golden Square, Southampton (later Bloomsbury) Square, and, in the late 1690s, Berkeley Square. To this day the names of the streets in the neighbourhood of St. James's and Mayfair—Jermyn, Sackville, Albemarle, Dover, Arlington Street, and the rest—are almost a roll-call of the Restoration peerage.

After the Great Fire the City was rapidly rebuilt; and although Wren's original designs proved to be impractical and the old narrow-street plan was largely retained, there was some widening of the main thoroughfares, and the burnt-out timber houses were (by an Act of 1667) replaced by substantial buildings of brick or stone. Wren's fifty-two churches were beginning to change the London skyline, his Dorset Garden theatre was completed in 1671, his Royal Hospital in Chelsea about 1690, and in 1697 the choir of his new cathedral was opened for services. The speed and determination with which the City was rebuilt says much for the vigour and wealth of the trading community. 'As for Housing,' Petty wrote about 1676, '. . . I conceive it is double in value in that City to what it was forty years since.' Similar developments were taking place at Newcastle, Norwich, and other provincial cities, and in the Oxford and Cambridge colleges, and the effect of all this planned building must have been at once stimulating and a source of pride. As Wren wisely remarked, 'Architecture has its political use, publick buildings being the ornament of a country; it establishes a nation, draws people and commerce; makes the people love their native country. . . .' Various inventions and technological advances, due partly to the activities of the Royal Society, were making life more comfortable for the well-to-do, and in London more luxurious. Coaches were better sprung, and were now being fitted with glass windows. In the winter of 1668 Pepys acquired an important status symbol when he bought his first chariot, complete with two horses and a coachman in livery. After the Restoration, hackney coaches in London and Westminster multiplied so fast that in 1674 an Act was passed limiting the number to four hundred. There was little real advance in street lighting, but some progress was made in the provision of sewers and in keeping the streets clear of refuse. Coffee-houses, which had made their first appearance only a few years before the Restoration, quickly increased in number; indeed, they became such popular centres of gossip and political discussion that in 1675 an ineffectual royal proclamation was issued for their suppression. For the men of quality there were expensive eating-houses such as Locket's, where, as Lord Foppington was to discover, you could be so nicely and delicately served that 'they can compose you a dish, no bigger than a saucer, shall come to fifty shillings'.

London, indeed, was now a modern capital, with most of the recognized facilities for amusement and dissipation and the cultivation of the arts. Although the theatres were supported by a flourishing national drama, the English still relied to a considerable extent on foreigners, such as Lely and Kneller, for their best painting, and on men like Grinling Gibbons (a Dutchman) and Caius Gabriel Cibber (a Dane) for their sculpture. The industrious Lely seems to have painted almost everyone of note from Pepys to Lady Castlemaine; and his portraits of languishing Restoration ladies with 'the sleepy eye that spoke the melting soul' are among the most familiar exhibits of the period. Foreigners, again, provided a good deal of the music given at Court or in the theatres, but there was one native composer, Henry Purcell, of the first rank, and several others of undoubted competence, such as John Blow. That there was a very widespread and informed interest in music is suggested by such amateur composers as Pepys and such talented amateur performers as Roger North and L'Estrange, by the annual celebrations held from 1683 on

St. Cecilia's day, by the fashionable throng that gathered for weekly concerts of vocal and instrumental music in the loft of Thomas Britton, the small-coal man, and by the popularity of the *Choice Airs* and *The English Dancing Master* of John Playford, the leading music publisher of the period.

In spite of much political uncertainty at home, the City was growing steadily in power and importance. Commercial rivalry with the Dutch and the French led to several wars, but also stimulated the growth of trade and the development of joint-stock companies and stockjobbing. All this in turn led to the foundation in 1694 of the Bank of England, and in 1696 to the important Council of Trade and Plantations, whose business it was to devise and suggest measures to promote trade and commerce. The establishment in 1680 by William Dockwra of an efficient penny post for London and the suburbs is one of those straws that show how the wind was blowing, and the rapid development of newspapers after the lapse of the Licensing Act in 1695 is another. By 1700, too, the English countryside was becoming a good deal more than a playground for the fox-hunting and beer-swilling squires pictured in Restoration comedies: enclosures were modifying the old and relatively unproductive open-field system of agriculture, drainage schemes in the Fens and elsewhere were bringing many more acres under cultivation, and some new crops were introduced. The effective modernization of English agriculture, however, belongs rather to the next century. There were some developments in afforestation and in mining; and the range and quality of English manufactured goods were considerably increased and improved by the settlement in England of large numbers of Huguenot and other refugees. Some improvements, too, in the road system were slowly beginning; but for the most part the traveller still had to put up with appalling conditions— of dust in the summer, of deep mud and ruts in the winter. Progress, then, was uneven, and varied in its extent from one field of activity to another; but there was much skill and enterprise among craftsmen, manufacturers, and merchants, aided (and sometimes frustrated) by government planning and organization. By 1700, at all events, England was well on its way to becoming the leading commercial nation in Europe, and therefore in the world.

In his reply (1665) to M. de Sorbière's rather acid account of

England, Sprat was already able to point proudly to the great progress now being made by the English in science and technology:

The Arts that now prevail amongst us are not only all the usefull Sciences of Antiquity, but more especially all the late discoveries of this Age in the reall knowledge of mankind and nature. For the improvement of this kind of light, the English disposition is of all others the fittest. And an universal zeal towards the advancement of such designs has not only overspread our Court and Universities, but the Shops of our Mechanicks, the fields of our Gentlemen, the Cottages of our Farmers, and the Ships of our Merchants.

What was already noticeable in 1665 became more remarkable in the next few decades. In mathematics, and in the chemical, physical, and biological sciences, the last forty years of the seventeenth century must be reckoned a period of quite exceptional development in England, affording the clearest possible evidence of the inquiring and sceptical spirit of the age, and the forward-looking tendency of so many of its best minds. Boyle and Newton were only the most famous of a group of men who were contributing (mostly outside the universities) to the advancement of scientific knowledge by experiment, hypothesis, and classification. Not only were those English scientists men of intellectual distinction, but, almost without exception, they were men of noble character; a surprising number of them were in holy orders, or, like Boyle and Newton, amateur theologians. What also distinguished such men as Boyle, Petty, Hooke, and Wren, or, in his more amateur status, Evelyn, was the extraordinarily wide range of their scientific knowledge, and their ability to make contributions of value in many different fields. Charles II took an affable interest in the Royal Society to which he had granted his charter in 1662, and he threw what weight he had on the side of applied science and technology. He was himself unusually well informed on naval architecture, and the bias of his mind may be seen in the encouragement he gave to John Graunt the statistician, whose observations on the Bills of Mortality were of immediate practical concern. His recommendation that Graunt, a shopkeeper, should be made a Fellow, and that 'if they found any more such tradesmen, they should be sure to admit them all without any more adoe', is no doubt characteristic of the King, but typical too of the democratic temper of the new science. Here it was not just a question of gentlemen, but of 'gentlemen and others', and the others were respected for their special knowledge and technical skills. 'He deserves not the knowledge of Nature', wrote the Hon. Robert Boyle, 'that scorns to converse even with mean persons that have the opportunity to be very conversant with her.' The discoveries of the men of science percolated through the consciousness of the age and led in time to fundamental changes of attitude in many spheres of thought; but (as in all ages) the process was gradual, and the advancing stream of knowledge left behind it many islands of resistance or indifference. Dryden, a lapsed Fellow of the Royal Society, continued to believe in astrology; and Glanvill, another Fellow, in witchcraft. It was no doubt to support the mystique of royalty that Charles II continued the practice of touching for the King's Evil, but a majority of his subjects probably still believed in the efficacy of this cure: on 28 March 1684 Evelyn recorded 'so greate and eager a concourse of people with their children, to be touch'd of the *Evil*', that six or seven 'were crush'd to *death* by pressing at the Chirurgion's doore for Tickets'.

Although the most remarkable intellectual advances of the period were those made in science, there was a corresponding activity in many other fields of thought. When we take into account the antiquarians and the historians, when we remember that classical scholarship was represented by Richard Bentley, medical diagnosis by Thomas Sydenham, and (in their very different ways) political thought by Locke and Halifax, we have little excuse for assuming that the achievements of the age can be measured, or its intellectual temper adequately assessed, by the standards of Restoration comedy or *Covent Garden Drollery*.

(IV)

Yet the greater part of Restoration literature that is still widely read today was the work of the small upper class which wrote most of the poetry and drama of the period, or of educated middle-class writers who had access to it, accepted its standards, and successfully imitated its mode of writing. The most obvious exceptions are Bunyan and Milton, who, although they belonged to two very different worlds, would have agreed at least in condemning 'the sons of Belial, flown with insolence and wine', in whose ranks so many of their fellow authors were to be found. At no other period has that class which Matthew Arnold was to call 'Barbarians'—a class marked by 'high spirits, choice manners, and distinguished bearing', but also (Arnold thought) by 'an insufficiency of light'—played such a dominant part in the creation and control of English literature. Its authors ranged from noblemen like the Duke of Buckingham, the Earl of Roscommon, and the Earl of Dorset to gentlemen of fashion like Sir George Etherege, Wycherley, and Congreve, and to the sons of country gentlemen or professional men like Dryden and Shadwell. How are we to account for the simultaneous appearance of such a mob of gentlemen who wrote, not only with ease, but often with distinction, and sometimes with genius? Something must be allowed for the operation of mere chance, but more to the effect of a favourable environment. This was one of the only periods in which the English Court had a genuine influence on literature. Charles II, it is true, gave little practical encouragement to his poets and dramatists; but more important than any financial rewards he could afford them was the fact that they could really please him, that he took an intelligent interest in what they wrote— most obviously when they wrote plays. In the early years after his return to the throne there was almost an obligation for noblemen and gentlemen, if they had the requisite talents, to write for the stage; for only they were likely to have the necessary experience of that high society and fashionable life in which contemporary tragedy and comedy dealt.

Since the drama was the dominant literary form all through the period, it was almost certainly the most important single factor in establishing a compact and conscious literary world in London. The members of the fashionable audiences who patronized the two theatres were well known to one another, meeting socially at Court and elsewhere; and at the first night of a new play they would see the same familiar group of critics in the pit. Before the play began the audience was addressed, with varying degrees of familiarity, in a prologue, and again, when the play was finished, in an epilogue; when the play was printed it would be dedicated, if it was the work of a professional writer, to some member of this same upper class, and there might also be a Preface discussing in an easy conversational style some points in the play, or criticizing the plays of other dramatists. Most of the playwrights were almost as well known to the audience as were the leading players, and they might also be on terms of friendship with such men as the Duke of Newcastle, or the Earl of Rochester, or Sir Charles Sedley. Not only did such noblemen and gentlemen write themselves, but they helped professional authors like Dryden and Shadwell with criticism and advice, and by giving them an entrée into that polite and fashionable world they mirrored in their plays. It was one of Dryden's objections to the Elizabethan dramatists that 'they wanted the benefit of converse' with upper-class society. 'Greatness', he explained, 'was not then so easy of access, nor conversation so free as it now is.' Shadwell was fond of mentioning his familiarity with the great. The Duke of Newcastle invited him to stay at Welbeck, encouraged him to write *The Virtuoso*, and admitted him to his 'more retired conversation, when I alone enjoyed the honour'. He was proud, too, of having sometimes enjoyed the conversation of the Duke of Buckingham, 'the most charming in the world'; he had been received by the Earl of Dorset as one of the family at Copt-Hall, where he wrote the first Act of *The Squire of Alsatia*; and when he had completed *A True Widow*, he submitted the play to Sir Charles Sedley, who gave him the benefit of his correction and alteration. Such ready access to the arbiters of contemporary elegance undoubtedly refined the manners of much Restoration literature. When circumstances made such access difficult, as with Mrs. Behn, we can at once feel the difference of tone: Mrs. Behn is happiest with her aldermen and landladies, but her young men about town are such boisterous rakes as her own not very fortunate experience probably threw in her way.

For one reason or another, therefore, the literary world of the Restoration period was more closely organized than it had ever been before. Patronage, publishers, coffee-houses, and, by 1700, literary periodicals all played their part. The conditions were especially favourable for satire: in this compact society such a satirical exposure as Buckingham's *Rehearsal* could count on an immediate and informed response, for almost everyone who saw his famous skit knew the plays that were being satirized, and so knew at once who and what was under attack. Outside the theatre, similar conditions naturally produced the lampoon, the epigram, the private joke, and such outbursts of satirical wit as the numerous verses on the Hon. Edward Howard at one end of the period and on Sir Richard Blackmore at the other. In the Preface to *King Arthur*, Blackmore asserts that he was not at all surprised when his *Prince Arthur* was attacked, since he had never 'made the least Court to the Committee that sits in Covent Garden'. It was therefore only natural to expect that

the Gentlemen who by Assisting, Crying up, Excusing and Complementing one another, carry on their Poetical Trade in a Joynt-stock, would certainly do what they could to sink and ruin an unlicens'd Adventurer. . . . I knew that I ran a very great Risk while I was so hardy to venture abroad Naked and Unguarded, when none of the *Company* went out without a notable Convoy of Criticks and Applauders who were constantly in their Service.

Poetical miscellanies, often predominantly satirical, point to the existence of literary coteries, as do the letters of wits which were beginning to appear in various collections. On this plane of personality it was natural that literary controversy should flourish, with Dryden, Shadwell, Settle, and others quarrelling in public and scoring off one another, so that, as the author of *Raillerie à la Mode* put it, '. . . as one *ill word* begets *another*, so (we see) doth one *abusive* Book another. . . . One Book beares the Bell away one while, and then presently comes out *Reflections*, *Observations*, *Answers*, *Replications*, and *Exceptions* upon it, till the Press is . . . bepestred with them.'

Whether it was carried on controversially or not, the discussion of literature was now becoming a common pursuit; and the emergence of men like Rymer and Dennis, who were primarily critics rather than creative writers stooping to criticism, is a significant development. England was now so far from being, in Rymer's words, 'as free from Criticks as it is from Wolves', that the critic was well on the way to matching the creative writer in importance. Most of the recognized signs of an organized literary market had become evident before the close of the century: anthologies, dictionaries, encyclopaedias, literary guidebooks and gossip about writers, biographical collections, books of popular knowledge, pocket editions of famous authors, illustrated books, the Term Catalogues, book-sellers' lists and advertisements, publication by subscription, auction sales of libraries, and even the first beginnings of book reviewing. At one end of the period writers of verse are catered for by Joshua Poole's *The English Parnassus: or a Help to English Poesie* (1657), 'with all the chiefest epithets and phrases' and 'with some general forms upon all occasions, subjects and themes'; and at the other, by Edward Bysshe's *The Art of English Poetry* (1702), with its 'rules for making verses; a dictionary of rhymes; a collection of the most natural, agreeable, and noble thoughts, *viz.* allusions, similes, descriptions, and characters of persons and things that are to be found in the best English poets'. By 1700 the hackney author had come into his own, abridging the works of his betters, making potted collections of history, or vamping biographies from other men's materials. One of the more reputable of those hack writers was Nathaniel Crouch, who (as John Dunton put it) 'melted down the best of our English histories into twelve-penny books, which are filled with wonders, rarities, and curiosities'. Of another of those hacks, John Shirley, who published 'at least a hundred bound books', Dunton observes: 'His great talent lies at collection, and he will do it for you at six shillings a sheet. He knows how to disguise an author that you shall not know him, and yet keep the sense and the main scope entire.'

With such journeyman writers as Crouch and Shirley we have left the smaller world of *belles lettres*, and reached that wider and more popular public which was increasing in numbers with every decade. So far as the booksellers were concerned, the works that sold best were predominantly religious. When Dunton set up in business as a bookseller in 1682, the first piece he ventured to publish was one on the sufferings of Christ by the Revd. Thomas Doolittle; and this proved so successful that by exchanging it through the trade he was able to build up a good general stock of books for his shop. His second venture, *Daniel in the Den*, was a political pamphlet on Shaftesbury's release from prison, and this too had a good sale. For his third publication he chose a funeral sermon by the Revd. John Shower, and 'the growing reputation of the author made the Sermon move very well'. Dunton also tells us that he printed 10,000 copies of Henry Lukin's *Practice of Godliness*, which had first appeared in 1658; but his outstanding success was with Richard Sault's *The Second Spira*, a horrific account of an atheist who dies in despair, which sold 30,000 copies in six weeks. As for Benjamin Keach's *War with the Devil* and *Travels of True Godliness* (of which he printed 10,000 copies), he thought they would both sell 'till the end of time'.

Most of Dunton's authors were Dissenters; but although the devotional literature of the Anglicans was in general more sedate, it too reached a very large public. The sermons of such popular preachers as Tillotson, books on cases of conscience like Jeremy Taylor's *Ductor Dubitantium* (1660), Sherlock's *Practical Discourse concerning Death*, controversial works like Simon Patrick's *Friendly Debate between a Conformist and a Nonconformist*, all sold in great numbers. Jeremy Taylor's *Holy Living* and *Holy Dying* were frequently reprinted after the Restoration, and John Rawlet's *The Christian Monitor* (1686), which also dealt with holy dying 'in a very plain and easy style for all sorts of people', had reached its twenty-fifth edition by 1699. Perhaps the favourite reading of many devout Anglicans between 1660 and 1700 is to be found in three substantial works which all laid a stress on sound morality: *The Whole Duty of Man* (1658), *The Gentleman's Calling* (1660), and *The Ladies Calling* (1673). The first of these was in a twenty-fifth edition by 1700, the second in a seventeenth, and the last had reached an eighth edition. It is significant, too, that while few of Robert Boyle's scientific works went into a second edition, his *Considerations touching the Style of the Holy Scriptures* reached four editions, and *Some Motives and Incentives to the Love of God* ran into ten.

Such sales are quite abnormal for the poetry and drama of the period. New plays were normally published in quarto, and when they were in demand, like *The Conquest of Granada*, *The Plain Dealer*, *The Rival Queens*, *The Orphan*, or *Love for Love*, they might run to five or six editions or even more, which would represent a very considerable sale. But not all the plays of even Dryden reached a second quarto edition, and about half of those by such second-flight dramatists as Mrs. Behn, Crowne, Ravenscroft, or Durfey had only one printing, which would mean a sale of perhaps 1,000 copies in all. The popularity of a play often depended on political rather than literary considerations: what else could account for three reprints in 1689 of Settle's wretched anti-Catholic piece *The Female Prelate*? Dryden's poetry sold comparatively well, but perhaps less well than might have been expected; and again, the popularity of his most frequently reprinted poems, *Absalom and Achitophel* and *The Hind and the Panther*, must be partly accounted for by their relevance to the political and religious controversy of the time. It is a significant comment on the taste of the reading public that while Cotton's volume of *Poems on Several Occasions* was only once reprinted, his *Scarronides: or, Virgile Travestie* (1664) had run through nine editions by 1700.

It would be a mistake to set aside the verdict of posterity, or to deny that most of the permanent contributions to literature made during this period were the work of the wits and gentleman-writers. To that small class we are indebted for a new kind of English comedy; for a new kind of poetry that came increasingly under the influence of neo-classical standards, but still retained something of the spontaneity of an earlier day; and for the firm establishment of an urbane and unacademic sort of literary criticism suited to the capacity of the intelligent reader. Above all, we are indebted to it for a tradition of easy, polite, familiar discourse that left many delightful traces in the verse of the period, and that created a prose style beautifully poised between the natural and the artificial, enabling the writer to address the reader as an equal, and to express his own thoughts and feelings with accuracy and elegance. Yet outside the world of Dryden and Rochester and Congreve there are many other writers with different claims to our attention. On the fringes of that world, but not really of it, are Clarendon and Burnet, Halifax and Temple, Evelyn and Pepys and Aubrey, poets like Samuel Butler and Charles Cotton, and a political journalist and translator like L'Estrange. Further off, in intellectual worlds of their own, are the great scholar Richard Bentley, churchmen like Robert South or Richard Baxter, lonely republicans like Ludlow and Algernon Sidney, all the men of science, and those, like Sprat and Glanvill, who wrote about it. And still more remote from the vain world of Will's and Locket's, of *MacFlecknoe* and *The Country Wife*, are Bunyan, Fox, Penn, Barclay, and the many other dissenting men and women who lived and thought and wrote with a forthright-ness and urgency that expressed one side of this divided and transitional period, and who produced in John Bunyan the greatest imaginative writer of the age.

II

DRAMA (I)

(1)

THE drama was one of the first things to be restored at the Restoration. Charles II, who had a natural taste for plays, and who knew well that a flourishing national drama was essential to the prestige of a Court and capital city, lost little time in re-establishing the London theatres, closed since 1642. On 21 August 1660 patents were issued to 'our trusty and well-beloved Thomas Killigrew, Esq., one of the Grooms of our Bedchamber, and Sir William Davenant, knight', to form two companies of players and erect two playhouses. Killigrew thereupon took over the management of a group of experienced actors, including Michael Mohun and Charles Hart, who had appeared on the London stage before the closing of the theatres, and Davenant formed his company from a group of younger men, including Thomas Betterton, Cave Underhill, and James Nokes, who had been acting immediately before the Restoration under the management of John Rhodes. Davenant and Killigrew also made theatrical history by engaging a number of actresses to play women's parts for the first time on a public stage.

Killigrew's company, which came to be known as the King's Players, opened with a performance of *Henry IV* on 8 November 1660, in a makeshift theatre converted from Gibbon's Tennis Court in Vere Street, Clare Market. Pepys, who saw *The Beggar's Bush* acted there on 20 November, observed that it was 'the finest play-house, I believe, that ever was in England'. On 15 November Davenant's company, the Duke of York's Servants, opened at the old theatre in Salisbury Court. Although it had been made clear in their patents that no other company should be allowed to act in the City of London, plays continued to be performed for some time at the Red Bull and the Cockpit theatres. Pepys saw Rowley's *All's Lost by Lust* at the Red Bull on 23 March 1661, sitting 'in the pit, where I think there was not above ten more than myself, and not one hundred in the whole house'; and again, on 26 May 1661, at the same theatre he saw *Dr. Faustus*, 'but so wretchedly and poorly done that we were sick of it'. On 9 September 1661, at the Salisbury Court theatre (after Davenant had moved with his company to their new house in Lincoln's Inn Fields), Pepys saw *'Tis Pity she's a Whore*, 'a simple play, and ill acted', but was so fortunate as to be sitting 'by a most pretty and most ingenious lady, which pleased me much'. The two offending managers who were thus defying the patentees were George Jolly and John Rhodes. They were finally snuffed out by being given licences to act in the provinces, and Davenant and Killigrew were left, as had always been intended, with a monopoly for the production of plays in London.

Of the two companies Davenant's appears to have been the better managed, and in the young Thomas Betterton it had the Roscius of the Restoration theatre. In June 1661 Davenant moved with his company of young actors to their new theatre in Lincoln's Inn Fields, the Duke's Theatre, and opened with his own 'opera', *The Siege of Rhodes*. Some days later, when Pepys went to see a play at the other house, he remarked on the meagre attendance at a theatre 'that used to be so thronged, now empty since the Opera began'. Part of the attraction at the Duke's Theatre was undoubtedly the elaborate scenes which Davenant had provided, and which London playgoers were now seeing for the first time. In 1671, a few years after Davenant's death, the Duke's Players moved to their second new theatre in Dorset Garden. Designed by Wren, and costing £9,000, it had a river frontage and could therefore be reached by playgoers arriving by boat at Dorset Stairs. Both outside and inside it achieved a new standard of magnificence.

Killigrew's company, who had been acting without scenery at their Vere Street theatre, opened on 7 May 1663 at their new house, the Theatre Royal in Drury Lane. When this was burnt in 1672, a new Theatre Royal designed by Wren was built on the same site and opened in 1674. In the early years of the company Killigrew was in the fortunate position of having the best of the older actors at his disposal, and those were later joined by some lively young actors and actresses, notably Nell Gwyn. Killigrew was a man of pleasure and a 'merry droll', but as a manager and business man he had his shortcomings.

In the 1670s he was at loggerheads with his actors, and the Lord Chamberlain had to step in and hand over the control to some of the leading members of the company. Later, his son Charles was given control, but things went from bad to worse, and in 1682 the Duke's Players and the King's Players were united, making the Theatre Royal their headquarters. Even so, the united company was often in serious difficulties; and although its troubles were partly due to mismanagement, and more particularly to the greed and dishonesty of one of the managers, there is little reason to doubt that public support of the theatre had, for one reason or another, sensibly declined. When, in 1695, there were again two companies, it was not because of a public demand but because Betterton, at the head of a number of disgruntled players, including Elizabeth Barry and Anne Bracegirdle, had obtained a licence from the Lord Chamberlain to form a separate company. They moved back to Lincoln's Inn Fields, and on 30 April Betterton opened, propitiously enough, with Congreve's *Love for Love*, creating the part of Valentine himself and giving Angelica to Mrs. Bracegirdle. In a decade which saw the production of Congreve's and Vanbrugh's comedies and the best plays of Southerne, it may seem misleading to talk of the decline of the theatre; but with tragedy mainly in the hands of such dreary exponents as Mrs. Pix, Catherine Trotter, Charles Hopkins, John Dennis, and Charles Gildon, and with comedy often degenerating to farce, and Rich and Skipwirth trying to attract audiences to Drury Lane with rope-dancing, tumbling, and buffoonery, the condition of the theatre in 1700 was neither healthy nor hopeful.

During the forty years from the return of Charles II to the close of the century well over four hundred plays were written, and most of them were acted on the London stage. If an average of ten new plays a year seems low for two theatres, it must be remembered that the managers constantly revived stock plays from the Elizabethan and Jacobean periods, as well as many of their own recent successes, and that the effective season for the London theatres was rather less than nine months in the year. The evidence, however, tends to show that the two playhouses were rarely filled to capacity and that their most habitual supporters formed only a small segment of the population: the men and women of fashion who adorned or had an entrée to the Court, army officers, Inns-of-Court men, wits, critics, beaux and fops, sparks and bullies, kept mistresses and women of the town, the odd squire up from the country, together with some solid citizens who went to see a play at holiday time especially, and enjoyed the spectacular effects at the Dorset Garden theatre. 'Men of figure and consideration', wrote Tom Brown, 'are known by seldom being there, and men of wisdom and business by being always absent.' But Brown was almost certainly exaggerating a little. It is true that John Evelyn was seldom to be seen at a play, but Samuel Pepys went to the theatre, alone or with his wife, pretty frequently; and one is driven to conclude that the Restoration audience could not have supported a drama which is sometimes highly intelligent and at least intermittently serious if it had been as bad as it is sometimes painted. Contemporary comedy was not exclusively a matter of cuckolding and farce; and when it is remembered that tragedy was very nearly as popular as comedy with the playgoers, it is clear that there was a sufficient number of serious-minded spectators to encourage a dramatist to give them such plays as *All for Love* and *Venice Preserved*.

Yet when we have made every allowance for the presence in the audience of men and women of wit and intelligence, we cannot ignore the frequent complaints of the dramatists, from Dryden to Congreve, that the taste of the Restoration playgoer was in general crude, and that his attention was gained with difficulty, and easily lost. The Restoration playhouse, indeed, was only one of a number of places, like the Mulberry Garden or Locket's, where men of fashion were regularly to be found; they went to one or other of the two theatres partly because the players were acting 'some confounded play or other', but mainly perhaps to show themselves and meet their friends and acquaintances. As Miss Gatty put it in *She Wou'd if she Cou'd*, the young sparks were accustomed to ramble 'from one Play-house to the other Play-house, and if they like neither the Play nor the Women, they seldom stay any longer than the combing of their Perriwigs, or a whisper or two with a Friend; and then cock their Caps, and out they strut again'. Not all playgoers treated the play and actors in so cavalier a fashion, but many did, and their presence was at best an irrelevance, and at the worst a source of distraction from the play. When we reflect that those casual, flippant, bored, and frequently intoxicated and insolent young men invariably formed a considerable part of the Restoration audience, we may well wonder that the plays of the period were as subtle and delicate as, at their best, they often are, and we need wonder the less at the coarseness and childishness of much of the comedy, and the rant and absurdity in the heroic drama. Satirical references in plays, prologues, and epilogues to the noisy behaviour of theatregoers are so frequent that they point unmistakably to a state of affairs ranging from chronic inattention to near-pandemonium. Gentlemen had dined before going to the theatre, and it needed only the arrival of one or two who had dined too well to start the trouble. (In the reign of Charles II half-past three seems to have been the usual hour for performances to begin. By the end of the century the hour had advanced to four o'clock, or even later.) The theatre was a magnet for the worst elements in fashionable society, and fatal quarrels in and around the playhouses were common: there seems to be little doubt that Elizabethan gentlemen were, as a class, better behaved than their grandsons.

Even when the play was not stopped by actual rioting, it was often difficult to hear the players on account of the chatter going on in the pit and boxes. The wits were there upon their mettle, and determined to show, like Lord Foppington, that their audible pleasantries were more entertaining than 'the forced products of another man's brain', or the labours of professional actors. 'Gad,' says Sparkish in *The Country Wife*, 'I go to a Play as to a Country-treat, I carry my own wine to one, and my own wit to t'other, or else I'm sure I shou'd not be merry at either; and the reason why we are so often lowder than the Players, is because we think we speak more wit, and so become the Poet's Rivals in his audience.' On this occasion it is possible to check literature by reference to life: some seven years earlier Pepys had apparently come to the conclusion that 'the upper bench [of the pit] next the boxes' was the right place for him. 'I find it do pretty well,' he writes, 'and have the advantage of seeing and hearing the great people, which may be pleasant when there is good store.' As playgoers went in the 1660s Pepys was probably well above the average in intelligence and in his liking for a good play; but his eyes and ears seem to have been equally divided between the stage and the auditorium. It is only fair to add that he hardly ever complains of being unable to hear the actors, and he records only

one or two disturbances in the theatre, once when an outraged lady of fashion had hired some people to hiss and throw
oranges (one of the recurring disorders in the theatres), and
on another occasion when the players had not learnt their
parts. This last trouble is one that Pepys found reason to
complain about fairly often, and in view of the frequent change
of plays it is not surprising that the actors were sometimes at
fault. On one occasion he attended a performance of a new
play in which one of the actors, Beeston, was compelled to
read his part from a book, 'and thereby spoils the part, and
almost the play, it being one of the best parts in it'. This was
not Beeston's fault; he had been given the part at a few hours'
notice to replace his fellow actor Kynaston, who had been
severely beaten by a bravo hired by Sir Charles Sedley.

When circumstances were ideal—the players word-perfect,
the theatre quiet, and the audience attentive—the dramatist
was still at the mercy of those who had little relish for high
comedy or true tragedy. The repeated complaints from Dryden
about the low intelligence of the playhouse audience come, not
from an unsuccessful dramatist trying to find an excuse for his
failure, but from a successful one apologizing for the steps he had
necessarily taken to ensure success. In 1671 he notes how an
audience will laugh just as much at the ridiculous dress and
grimaces of an antic as at a genuine stroke of wit, and confesses
that he is often 'vexed to hear the people laugh and clap, as
they perpetually do, where I intended 'em no jest; while they
let pass the better things without taking notice of them'. In
his *Essay of Dramatic Poesy* Lisideius makes an observation,
quite incidentally, that throws a disconcerting shaft of light
on the mentality of a typical audience at the performance of
tragedy: 'I have observ'd that in all our Tragedies the Audience
cannot forbear laughing when the Actors are to die; 'tis the
most Comick part of the whole Play.' Equally significant are
the words that Shadwell addressed to Sedley in the Dedication
of *A True Widow*. Referring to 'the little poetasters of the fourth
rate' who have condemned his plays, he retorts that 'the putting
out of candles, kicking down of tables, falling over joynt-stools,
impossible accidents, and unnatural mistakes (which they most
absurdly call plot) are the poor things they rely upon'. This, it
must be admitted, comes a little oddly from Shadwell, who
relies a good deal on such poor things himself; but in view of

his protest it is only fair to suppose that he was driven to include
such farcical stuff in his comedies to satisfy the immature minds
which predominated in his audience.

It may be wondered how such an audience could ever bring
itself to sit out a tragedy. That something was required to make
tragedy palatable to the regular frequenters of the playhouse
may be seen from the tendency to spend large sums of money
on the dresses and machines for tragic plays. In the epilogue to
the first part of *The Destruction of Jerusalem* (1677) Crowne
alludes sarcastically to those plays that rely for their effect on
'shew and great machines' and 'on ropes instead of raptures',
but the third act of his own tragedy called for several spectacular effects, including an angel which descends over the altar,
and we happen to know from a petition of the players that they
were at 'a vast expense in scenes and cloathes' for this play. In
sneering at scenic effects, and in asserting that

> These tricks upon our stage will never hit,
> Our company is for the old way of wit,

Crowne was not so much speaking his own mind as making the
best of a bad job: his play, refused by the Duke's company at
Dorset Garden, was being produced by the King's company at
the Theatre Royal, and the King's company was in straitened
circumstances owing to the expense of building a new theatre
in Drury Lane, and could not afford to stage its productions so
elaborately as those of the rival company. From 1670 onwards
it was at Dorset Garden that most of the spectacular productions
took place. It was there that Settle's *The Empress of Morocco* was
produced in 1673, and the gorgeousness of the costumes and
scenes was carried over into the printed version of the play,
which, as Pope noted in *The Dunciad*, was 'the first that was ever
printed with cuts'. Such spectacular productions must often
have reconciled the more empty-headed part of the audience to
what would otherwise have proved a boring afternoon. Indeed,
a bare stage and the rigour of the tragic game could only result
in a half-empty theatre. In the prologue to *The Albion Queens*
John Banks discounted his chances of success on the grounds
that he was offering no

> Song, Show, nor Dance, these Scenes to recommend:
> And, Sirs, full well you know where that must end.

The popularity of heroic plays must also be associated with the
opportunities they gave to satisfy a taste for the spectacular.
The writers of those plays were fond of setting the action in
remote and picturesque countries—Peru, Mexico, India, China,
Persia, Morocco, and so on—and the exotic scenes and bizarre
costumes must have given the same sort of 'joy, innocent of
thought' as that afforded by the glories of technicolour in modern
film re-creations of Babylon or ancient Egypt. It must not
be forgotten, too, that many of the Restoration actresses were
lovely women, and that actors like Charles Hart (the original
of Dryden's Almanzor) and William Mountfort in the next
generation were men of fine presence, who graced a tragedy
so effectively that, as was said of Hart in the role of Alexander
the Great, they 'might teach any king on earth how to comport
himself'. If words are thrown away on the dull and unimagina-
tive, the eloquence that lies in a look or a gesture, in poise
and movement, in the rhythm and harmony of a controlled
voice, will penetrate to all but the sub-human. We have it
on the testimony of Downes the prompter that if, in his later
years as an actor, Hart appeared in one of his favourite
tragic roles, 'the house was filled as at a new play'. Such
facts are reassuring, and they may be set in the balance against
that other body of evidence which tends to suggest that the
Restoration theatre was sometimes little better than a bear-
garden.

In accounting for the continuing vogue of tragedy, in many
ways so antipathetic to the genius of the period, there is one
other factor to be taken into account. Whatever the fops and
bullies may have thought of it, tragedy had a special appeal to
the ladies. Paying his addresses to Leonora in *Sir Courtly Nice*,
the hero of that play explains that he has constantly sought for
her at tragedies, never at comedies, 'for I presum'd your
Ladyship nauseates Comedys'. Encouraged by Leonora's
assenting 'Oh! foh!' he goes on to explain that comedies 'are
always cram'd with our odious Sex. . . . Now, at Tragedies, the
House is all lin'd with Beauty, and then a Gentleman may
endure it.' The partiality of women for tragedy seems to have
been well understood by the dramatists, and by none more profitably than Otway and John Banks, and (in the next generation)
Rowe, who gave them not merely tragedy, but their own speci-
ality of 'she-tragedy'. Women seem also to have found a good

deal of enjoyment in the heroic drama. In the epilogue to *The Virtuoso* Shadwell notes their preference for 'a dull romantick whining play' in which 'woman's made a deity'. Pushing his analysis a stage further, he remarks upon how much they are flattered by a hero who beats armies single-handed from the field, huffs kings, and rants at the gods, only to fall in abject submission at some lady's feet ('Yet if the Dame once chides, the Milk-sop Heroe swoons').

It would be pleasant to suppose that with an increasing experience of the theatre the audience gradually became better educated; but the evidence points rather in the opposite direction. If we are to believe John Dennis, the fate of plays in the reign of Charles II was not left entirely to the chance of their hitting the taste of the pit. The Town might easily go wrong in its judgement, either because of 'the enchanting performance' of a Hart or a Mohun, or because the play was by some celebrated author who had given delight before.

But then there were several extraordinary men at Court who wanted neither Zeal nor Capacity, nor Authority to sett them right again. There was Villers Duke of Buckingham, Wilmot Earl of Rochester, the late Earl of Dorsett, the Earl of Mulgrave who was afterwards Duke of Buckinghamshire, Mr. Savil, Mr. Buckley, Sir John Denham, Mr. Waller etc. When these or the Majority of them Declard themselves upon any new Dramatick performance, the Town fell Immediately in with them, as the rest of the pack does with the eager cry of the stanch and the Trusty Beagles.

Dennis was something of a *laudator temporis acti*, and he is here speaking of a time when he was himself little more than a boy; but there can be no doubt that this little senate of peers and men of wit did exercise some influence on the stage. Dennis reminds us of how Buckingham's *Rehearsal* helped to laugh the heroic drama off the stage, and he tells us, on the authority of the author himself, that *The Plain Dealer* looked like being a failure at its first performance until 'the formention'd gentlemen by their loud approbation of it, gave it both a sudden and a lasting reputation'. Such efforts might save a good play and enable it to gain a hearing, but they could not furnish an audience with an understanding. Whether Dennis is right in his further contention (he is writing about 1725) that the audience of those days was greatly superior in taste and education to the playgoers of later generations, who had grown rich quickly, 'some in the Armies, some in the Fleets, and some in the wrecks of the fraudulent Pacifique Ocean', is perhaps more doubtful. Yet here again he is able to point out that at the Restoration the theatres were in the hands of gentlemen who 'had Honour, learning, breeding, Discernment, Integrity, Impartiality and generosity'; and their influence must have counted for a good deal. Dennis might have added that some of those discerning lords and gentlemen whose judgement he praises also wrote for the theatre themselves. In one way or another they undoubtedly exercised a considerable, and on the whole favourable, control over the drama for at least two decades after the King's return. By the late 1670s, however, farce was growing more frequent; and by 1700 the theatre had become much more commercialized; the playwrights were repeating the old formulas over and over again, and the drama was drifting towards that Sargasso Sea in which it was to wallow for nearly two centuries.

(II)

When Davenant and Killigrew began to produce their first plays on the Restoration stage, they were necessarily compelled to rely mainly on the best comedies and tragedies of the pre-Restoration theatre. It might have been expected that both patentees would have been equally free to draw upon the plays of Shakespeare, Beaumont and Fletcher, Jonson, and the rest, but in the event Killigrew emerged with a lion's share of the old drama. The explanation appears to be that the acting rights in the old plays were vested in the surviving players of the Eliza-bethan-Jacobean companies, and since Killigrew had taken over the older men he had also acquired the sole right to perform their plays, including almost all those of Jonson and of Beaumont and Fletcher. In this extremity Davenant success-fully petitioned in December 1660 for the right to perform nine of Shakespeare's plays and Webster's *The White Devil*, to which otherwise he would presumably have had no title; and in August 1668 he was granted the right to perform a further twenty-five plays by Shakespeare, Beaumont and Fletcher, Chapman, Ford, and others. Although Davenant's slender claim to the older drama must have proved to be initially an em-barrassment, it led him to look for successful new playwrights

like Roger Boyle, Earl of Orrery, Sir Samuel Tuke, and
Etherege. The comedies of Ben Jonson and the comedies
and tragedies of Beaumont and Fletcher were frequently and
profitably revived by Killigrew, but Shakespeare kept the
stage mainly through his tragedies. Among the early revivals
of Elizabethan, Jacobean, and Caroline plays were *The Merry
Devil of Edmonton*, Heywood's *Love's Mistress*, Webster's *The
Duchess of Malfi*, Massinger's *The Bondman*, Middleton's *The
Changeling*, Brome's *The Jovial Crew*, Shirley's *The Cardinal*, and
also Suckling's *Aglaura* and *Brennoralt*, with their still not entirely
unfashionable Platonic sentiment. On the whole, the best
dramatists of 'the last age' were represented by their best plays;
and if we overlook the under-emphasis on Shakespeare and
the over-emphasis on Beaumont and Fletcher, we have little
reason to condemn the taste of Davenant and Killigrew, who
appear to have known what their audience ought to like, and
to have given them at least the best of those plays which they
were likely to like.

But 1660 was not 1640, and still less was it 1600. A new age,
so acutely conscious of its own modernity, had to write its own
plays. Among the first who tried to meet the need were a number
of middle-aged Cavaliers, most of whom had followed the
King into exile. There must have been some rummaging in
desks and cabinets for plays that had been written in the interregnum, but never performed, or that had been performed before
the closing of the theatres and might now be revised for the
Restoration stage. Thomas Killigrew revived his own *Claracilla*
in December 1660, a tragi-comedy in prose of the Beaumont and
Fletcher kind, with a plot of considerable complexity, involving
two usurpers, various lords in revolt, and a group of virtuous
pirates, and largely motivated by the actions of the rival
suitors for the hand of the King's lovely daughter Claracilla.
The second time that Pepys saw it he thought it 'a poor play',
and after seeing it for a third time he recorded: 'It do not please
me almost at all, though there are some good things in it.'
Killigrew's *Claracilla* was clearly not the answer to the theatre's
problems. Nor were the rather similar plays of his elder brother
any better. Sir William Killigrew's *Selindra* (March 1662),
a tragi-comedy in which disguise played a considerable part, had
a large cast and a plot of some ingenuity; but, like *Claracilla*, it
looked back to the theatrical past. The tone of those plays is

eminently decent. Sir Robert Stapleton's *The Slighted Maid*
(1663)—'acted with great applause', as the title-page informs
us—is another of those over-ingenious and rather old-fashioned
tragi-comedies, depending for most of its effects upon disguise
and mistaken identity; the tone is, again, decent, even improving. Unlike the Killigrews, Stapleton writes in an easy and
colloquial blank verse; but at one point, remarking that she
will 'answer, like an Oracle, in Heroicks', one of the characters reels off sixteen lines of rhyming couplets—a significant
reference to an innovation that was already on its way. *The
Slighted Maid* is a 'serious' play, with comic scenes, although
what it is being serious about is not of the least consequence.
By 1668 it was competing with other plays that were just as
empty of content, but that had in their tone and manners more
of the spirit of the new age.

Among these was Sir Robert Howard's[1] tragi-comedy, *The
Surprisal* (April 1662). This play, with its hired villain Villeroto,
who is working for himself as well as for the man who has
hired him, comes near to tragedy in the fourth act, where the
suspense is well contrived. Elsewhere, in the attempt of old
Castruccio to marry his niece Samira to the rich Brancodoro
(she is already in love with the noble but impoverished Cialto),
and in Samira's protest to her uncle—

> Marriage you know admits no separation,
> And if Affections shou'd not be united,
> The Persons must be miserable—

Howard is interesting himself in what was to be one of the
recurring themes of Restoration comedy. In Brancodoro, too,
he has created a prototype of the rich fop who was to flower
more fully in such finished examples as Sir Courtly Nice and
Sir Fopling Flutter. In this mainly romantic play Brancodoro
is consistently and confidently anti-romantic; he is not an

---

[1] Sir Robert Howard (1626–98), sixth son of the first Earl of Berkshire, was
the brother of the dramatists Edward and James Howard, and had a sister Elizabeth who became the wife of John Dryden. He collaborated with Dryden in *The
Indian Queen* (1664), and his own most successful play was his comedy *The Committee*
(1662). Howard soon left writing plays for the more serious business of politics.
He had been elected to Parliament in 1660, was made Auditor of the Receipt in
the Exchequer in 1673, and subsequently held various other employments connected with the public finance. Shadwell's ridicule of him in *The Sullen Lovers* as
Sir Positive At-All stuck to him for the rest of his life.

arrant coward, but he is not prepared to risk what is, for him,
a very satisfactory life in needless affairs of honour:

> I'le not fight
> With any man that hath a less Estate
> Than my self; such a one ventures nothing.

Since Sir Robert Howard has had rather a hard deal from
posterity, it is only fair to say that he writes like a man who has
a lively mind, and that his images are often fresh and unconventional. When he makes one of his characters speak of fear
being 'Gentleman-Usher to Conscience' he has not wholly
freed himself from the clotted metaphorical manner of an
earlier generation; but when his Miranzo cries:

> How my thoughts work,
> Heaving like labouring moles within the Earth!

he is giving a Restoration audience the sort of figurative writing that they could still digest, although as the years passed
they were to have fewer opportunities of doing so.

Some early attempts were made to introduce French tragedy
to the English stage, notably in the version of Pierre Corneille's
Pompée (1664) which was made by 'certain persons of honour',
including Waller, Dorset, and Sedley. This translation, in
rhymed couplets that have more enjambment than those normally used in the heroic play, reproduces some of the dignity
and controlled passion of the original. (Another version, by
Katherine Philips, had been produced at the Smock Alley
theatre, Dublin, in the previous year.) Pepys, who read the
Waller version one day in the summer of 1666, while being
ferried down the river to Deptford, thought it 'but a mean play,
and the words and sense not very extraordinary', but by this
time he was growing accustomed to the more flamboyant
style of plays like *The Indian Queen* by Dryden and Howard. He
was, it is true, delighted with a performance of Corneille's
Heraclius which he had seen two years earlier, and saw a
second time, to his 'extraordinary content', in 1667; but what
seems to have pleased him most was the scenic effects. On the
whole, the objections offered by Dryden's Neander to French
tragedy almost certainly expressed the views of the average
playgoer. To Neander the speeches were so many declamations which 'tire us with the length; so that instead of

perswading us to grieve for their imaginary Heroes, we are concern'd for our own trouble, as we are in the tedious visits of bad
company'. As for the action, in their desire for regularity of
plot and the integrity of scenes the French dramatists had
'brought on themselves that dearth of plot, and narrowness of
imagination, which may be observed in all their plays'.

In those first uncertain years after the Restoration, when
English dramatists were still searching for the form of drama
which would express the sensibility of the new age, tragedy was
not, perhaps, the appropriate mode. Yet some interesting
work was done. Thomas Porter[1] wrote one genuine tragedy,
The Villain (1662), which looks back to the earlier drama, but
which in some of its scenes is a good deal more modern. The
villain, Maligni, is an Iago whose machinations result in the
deaths of three men and two women, one of them, Charlotte,
going mad in the Ophelia fashion. But while there are such
clear debts to Shakespeare, and the brisk and spirited dialogue
of the young officers is sometimes reminiscent of Fletcher, the
gay life of a garrison town, with the soldiers and the girls, could
almost be contemporary. What is significant, however, is that
Porter has written not a tragi-comedy of the conventional type,
with a tragic and a comic plot, but a tragedy in which the
comedy is simply a momentary lifting of the tragic atmosphere.
In this, and in such songs as that beginning

> See where Calisto wheels about
> The Northern Axle-tree of Heav'n—

he has more in common with the age of Shakespeare than with
the Restoration. *The Vestal Virgin* (c. 1664), by Sir Robert
Howard, written mainly in rhyming couplets, and dealing in
love and honour and physical horror, was perhaps a more
fashionable tragedy than *The Villain*, but it is much inferior to
it. The fifth act is a blood bath. With only Sulpitius and Emilius
left alive, Sulpitius is removed for execution, and Emilius promises us that as soon as he has had his revenge he means to die
too. How much Howard cared about what he was doing may

---

[1] Thomas Porter (1636–80), fourth son of Endymion Porter, became an army
officer, and lived an erratic life. At the age of 19 he was imprisoned for a short time
for abducting a daughter of the Earl of Newport, and shortly afterwards he
killed a soldier and was found guilty of manslaughter. In 1667 he killed one of
his best friends, Sir Henry Bellasis, in a duel. Porter's plays are much more intelligent than his life.

be seen from the fact that he provided his play with an alternative happy ending. His brother James was to deal similarly with Shakespeare's *Romeo and Juliet*. Sir Robert Howard's last play, *The Great Favourite, Or, the Duke of Lerma*, is one of the best tragedies of the period, but it was based (as Howard himself admitted) on an earlier play, perhaps by Ford. At all events, the rival Dukes of Lerma and Medina are powerful characters, whose motives are intelligible and real, and Maria is a heroine of nobility and some subtlety. The play is written in a mixture of blank verse and rhymed couplets, and it has often a largeness and simplicity of utterance easier to associate with the years before the Civil War than with those following the Restoration. It was surely the unknown dramatist, rather than Howard, who wrote such lines as

> The memories of Princes are but graves
> Where Beauty and where Merit lie forgotten.

Above all, this tragedy does not turn upon the artificial dilemmas of love and honour, but is based on issues that we can recognize as real and important. There is little reason to believe that it hit the taste of the town.

Few, if any, of the plays so far considered would have offended Jeremy Collier; in manners and morals they are unexceptionable almost throughout. The moral tone is even more noticeable in Richard Flecknoe's[1] romantic-pastoral-tragi-comedy *Love's Kingdom*. This play, first published as *Love's Dominion* in 1654, and then described by its author as 'a Dramatique Piece, Full of Excellent Moralitie; Written as a Pattern for the Reformed Stage', was revised by Flecknoe and produced in 1664. The 'excellent morality' is abundantly apparent; and even such comedy as is provided by the amorous Pamphilius, persistently pursuing the chaste maidens of Flecknoe's Arcadian world, is entirely decorous. But Flecknoe was living in the past. Something new was needed, and it came with the heroic play.

---

[1] Richard Flecknoe (d. 1678?) is thought to have been an Irish priest. He travelled extensively, and gave some account of his experiences in *A Relation of Ten Years' Travels in Europe, Asia, Affrique and America* (1656). He wrote some ineffective plays, but his characters and a few of his poems are considerably better than one would expect from the man ridiculed in Dryden's *MacFlecknoe*.

(III)

In the drama of the period the rhymed heroic play is a comparatively short-lived kind. Like Brown's famous *Estimate*, it 'rose like a paper-kite and charmed the town'; but after a few years of mounting absurdity the craze for heroic drama came to an end, not so much, perhaps, because of the brilliant satire of *The Rehearsal* (1671) as on account of its own suicidal extravagance. But although there was a temporary revulsion from rant and heroics, it would be wrong to suppose that the change was permanent or at any time pronounced. When the first flush of novelty and excitement had died away Dryden's heroic plays were not very often revived on the stage, but they continued to be reprinted at fairly frequent intervals, and so too were those of Settle and Lee; and long after rhyming couplets had gone out of fashion in the theatre some of the other characteristic features of the heroic play survived in later tragedy.

For a definition of the English heroic play we need go no further than to Dryden, who set himself the task of legislating, in his Preface to *The Conquest of Granada* (1672), for what was now recognized as a new form of drama. 'An Heroick Play', he decided, 'ought to be an imitation, in little, of an Heroick Poem; and consequently . . . Love and Valour ought to be the Subject of it.' If a heroic play is the dramatic counterpart of epic poetry, it follows that the characters and actions and language can all be 'raised . . . to a greater height', and that the author may safely indulge in 'a further liberty of Fancy, and of drawing all things as far above the ordinary proportion of the Stage, as that is beyond the common words and actions of humane life'. All Dryden's thinking about the heroic play is governed by his conviction that the world of the theatre is far from being the world of ordinary life; and when once that idea has taken firm hold of an author's mind, it becomes a virtue to go beyond the normal and the reasonable and the expected. The more theatrical the theatre becomes, the more completely is it fulfilling its function. On no other grounds can we account for the extravagance and romantic hyperbole, not only of the heroic drama, but of most of the tragedy of the period. When the Restoration playgoer went to the theatre to see a tragedy or a heroic play he sat down in his seat knowing that he was about to take leave of the real world; that the characters would be kings and queens, intriguing statesmen, and bloody, treacherous villains; that the action would be remote in time, or place, or both; and that the dramatist had no intention whatever 'to imitate, and, as far as possible, to adopt the very language of men', but that his characters would address each other in blank verse or rhymed couplets, and in a poetic diction at once exclamatory, declamatory, and grandiloquent. That the author of *Tyrannic Love* should also be the poet of *MacFlecknoe* and *Religio Laici* shows what Dryden thought of the theatre, and ultimately, perhaps, how he thought of epic poetry. The shrewd, critical, sensible mind of the satirical and discursive poet could not be entirely submerged even when he was writing a heroic play, but Dryden often seems to be doing his unhappy best to run amok emotionally and intellectually, because he believed that was what was required of him. Quoting in 1677 Horace's *si vis me flere, dolendum est primum ipsi tibi*, Dryden makes the ominous comment: 'The Poet must put on the Passion he endeavours to represent: a man in such an occasion is not cool enough, either to reason rightly, or to talk calmly.' A self-induced excitement no doubt accounts for some of the most frigid ardours of the heroic drama; but the underlying reason for most of the rant and extravagance is the belief that the heroic poet must go far beyond a bare imitation of nature. In Dryden's heroic plays we can see what is apt to happen when a mind that is naturally classical chooses to be romantic.

Even in the Restoration period there were some for whom the unreality of heroic drama was intolerable. That the implications which lay behind Dryden's definition of the heroic play were not acceptable to all playgoers may be seen not merely from the ridicule of it in *The Rehearsal* and elsewhere, but from Dryden's complaints about the literal-mindedness of those people who objected to all heroic elements in literature. 'Are all the flights of Heroique Poetry', he asked, 'to be concluded bombast, unnatural, and mere madness, because *they* are not affected with their Excellencies?' To overcome such unwillingness to co-operate on the part of the playgoer Dryden saw that the dramatist must make use of any means available to stampede an audience into accepting what its good sense would lead it to resist or reject. Among such means were the drums and trumpets and stage battles in which the heroic play abounds: all those were necessary 'to raise the imagination of the Audience, and to perswade them, for the time, that what they behold on the Theatre is really perform'd'. Such effects are, of course, inoperative for the reader; and the heroic drama has less than justice done to it if it is not seen and heard on the stage. With all the aids that sound and spectacle can give, the verbal drums and trumpets of Dryden's rhetoric would have at least the merit of being in consonance with the kind of entertainment being offered. But surely Dryden has already given his case away; the audience is to be stupefied into acquiescence, so that it may respond to any sort of effect that the dramatist chooses to put across. The poet, Dryden argues, is 'to endeavour an absolute dominion over the minds of the Spectators; for, though our fancy will contribute to its own deceipt, yet a Writer ought to help its operation'. Dryden admits that such an argument might be used to justify the worst extravagances of the popular theatre (he cites the *Red Bull*), but he has his answer ready: it would be absurd for a physician 'to forbear an approv'd medicine, because a Mountebank has us'd it with success'. Such a defence, however, is open to question. It is not merely that there is an element of the mountebank even in Dryden's best heroic plays, but that his whole justification rests upon the assumption that on the one hand there is the dramatist, and on the other hand the audience, and that the business of the dramatist is to play upon the feelings of the audience as an orator plays upon those of a crowd. But can we accept this assumption? The first thought of a dramatist must surely be for his play; and though acting, scenery, stage effects, and so on will all contribute to the effect, the play should generate its own energy and contain within itself the power to persuade and satisfy. If the dramatist has his mind fixed all the time on the audience, he will probably, and, if he thinks as little of the intelligence of the audience as Dryden did, he will inevitably, come to believe that the end always justifies the means, and the end will be popular success. The basis of the heroic drama is therefore rhetoric, and the tropes and figures of rhetoric persuade because, as Dryden himself says, 'it was observed they had such and such effect upon the audience'.

Those features, then, of the heroic play which strike us today as least defensible—the bragging and blaspheming heroes, the extravagant action, the artificially sustained excitement, the hyperbole, and so on—can nearly all be traced to the dramatist's thinking too much of his audience. And if Dryden could stoop to such crude effects, how much more easily could Settle. It is only fair to remember that Dryden looked back at his own contributions to this delirious drama with regret, and even with a sense of shame. 'All I can say for those passages, which are I hope not many, is, that I knew they were bad enough to please, even when I writ them; but I repent of them amongst my Sins. . . . I draw a stroke over all those Dalilahs of the Theatre; and am resolv'd I will settle[1] my self no reputation by the applause of fools.' In return for this handsome apology, we may acknowledge that in all Dryden's heroic plays there are passages of good sense and of dramatic argument as thoughtful as anything that he ever wrote.

Since the subject of a heroic play was love and valour, intellectual qualities in a hero were usually suspect; it was normally the villain or the coward (often the same man) who showed cunning. The hero was cast on simple lines: intrepid, passionate, daring, the conqueror of his foes and yet a slave to love. Between the opposite poles of war and love, roughness and tenderness, self-sufficiency and amorous dependence, insolence and compliance, he oscillated dangerously, carrying all things to an extreme, and existing almost exclusively on the plane of feeling. If the modern reader is apt to find the Maximins and Almanzors rather stupid, the reason lies no doubt in the fact that he never has a chance of meeting them in a quiet moment, but always in a state of rage or despair or amorous ecstasy. Almanzor, indeed, uses his brain a good deal less than, say, the Lone Ranger of the western film, and so far as we take any interest in him at all it is the sort of interest we have in a dangerous animal, or, at the most, in a noble savage. Yet for the exciting and spectacular kind of play the writers of heroic drama had in mind, that all-but-impossible-he is undeniably effective; he is rarely static, he is the main source of the action, and with his unpredictable and conflicting passions the outcome is in doubt until the closing scene. When, as was in fact usual, the action turns not so much upon love and valour as upon love and honour, the conflict in the soul of the hero is intensified; he vacillates, he is on the horns of a dilemma, and

---

[1] Perhaps in *O.E.D.*'s sense 24: 'to ensure the stability or permanence of'. But it is possible that Dryden was punning on Elkanah Settle's name here.

those of Dryden; its absurdities are of a lofty and innocent kind.

The heroic play is not such an exotic, therefore, as it has sometimes been said to be. But we may still wonder why it made such a powerful appeal in the early years of the Restoration period. Something must be allowed for the preferences of the King and those of his Court who had followed him into exile, and who had become accustomed to French rhymed tragedy. For less travelled Englishmen, who were not yet accustomed to rhymed plays (Pepys found *The Indian Queen* 'good, but spoiled with the rhyme, which breaks the sense'), there was still the attraction of spectacle, and, once the first shock of unfamiliarity had worn off, the interest of seeing each new heroic play outdo all the others in rodomontade and violence, and in the gorgeousness of its scenes and costumes. But the main reason for the vogue of the heroic play is almost certainly that it pleased the upper-class playgoer. Davenant, as we have seen, considered that a heroic play was the proper entertainment of 'the gentry', and there is a good deal of contemporary evidence to show that they were the chief supporters of this type of drama. Settle, for example, in the Dedication to *Cambyses*, thought it only right that he should offer 'the heroick stories of past ages to their hands who are the ornaments of the present'; and Dryden, in the Dedicatory Epistle of *The Indian Emperor*, stated categorically that 'the favour which heroic plays have lately found upon our theatres has been wholly derived to them from the countenance and approbation they have received at Court'.

Whether we can go on to say, with some modern critics, that the heroic play was the natural drama of an unheroic age is perhaps doubtful. The Restoration courtier (so the argument runs) could not face up to genuine tragedy on the stage, but he got some kind of satisfaction from romantic plays that were so obviously unreal and remote from the world in which he lived that, although they gave him a mild thrill and even a sense of exaltation, they did not compel him to come to terms with life or with his own unheroic existence. If the Restoration Court is fairly represented in such books as *Memoirs of the Count de Grammont*, it was unheroic enough; but the men of pleasure could also be men of action, and many of them were ready enough to leave Locket's and the Mall and the Playhouse to

fight for their country. On the summer day in 1665 when
Dryden and his friends, rowing on the Thames near Greenwich,
heard the sound of naval guns 'like the noise of distant thunder,
or swallows in a chimney', the Duke of York was engaging the
Dutch in a desperate engagement at Solebay, and among the
young volunteers who distinguished themselves on that occasion were Charles Sackville, afterwards Earl of Dorset, and the
sixteen-year-old Duke of Monmouth. In the course of the Dutch
Wars Henry Savile, Rochester, Mulgrave, Wycherley, and
Buckingham all served at sea, and some of them took part in
naval actions which were far from being unheroic. Back on
shore, they no doubt resumed a dissipated round of drinking,
wenching, and beating up the watch; but they had seen enough
not to confuse life with heroic plays. It would be safer to attribute the craze for heroic drama to the uncertain taste and
imperfect education of the upper class. The Court of Charles II
may have been witty and gay, but there are few indications
that its culture was more than superficial; fine clothes rather
than fine feelings, the well-turned phrase rather than the
considered thought.

In the stately but almost lifeless plays of Roger Boyle, Earl
of Orrery,[1] we are in the presence of a culture that is not so
much superficial as quite unreal. Orrery would hardly be
worth more than a brief mention if there were not a good deal
of contemporary evidence to show that his plays were performed
to packed theatres, and if the credit, such as it is, of introducing
the rhymed heroic play to the English stage did not belong
mainly to him. According to his first biographer, it was Charles
II who 'put my lord upon writing plays', because he wished to
see whether the French fashion of rhymed plays could not be
equally successful in English. Some time in 1661 Orrery completed his first rhymed play, *The General*, and sent it to the
King, who passed it on to Thomas Killigrew to be acted. At the
request of Davenant, who felt that he was missing something
good, Orrery next wrote (1661–3?) another rhymed tragi-
comedy, *Henry V*, for the Duke's Players, and Davenant

---

[1] Roger Boyle, Baron Broghill and first Earl of Orrery (1621–79), was the
third son of Richard Boyle, first Earl of Cork, and was a brother of the Hon.
Robert Boyle. He saw active military service, both as a Royalist and afterwards
as a Parliamentarian. In 1660 he declared for Charles II, and helped to bring about
the Restoration. Besides his romance *Parthenissa* and his plays, he published some
poems, and an interesting *Treatise of the Art of War* (1677), dedicated to Charles II.

produced this play in August 1664 before an enthusiastic audience. 'A most notable play', Pepys thought it, '. . . the most full of height and raptures of wit and sense, that ever I heard.' The success of *Henry V* may have reminded Killigrew that he too had an Orrery play stuffed away in a drawer, for on 14 September, at the Theatre Royal, he produced *The General* before a full house and 'with the highest applause imaginable'. Both of these plays had been preceded in January 1664 by *The Indian Queen* of Dryden and Howard. Yet any historical importance that Orrery may have lost through the dilatoriness of his London producer he may be said to have recovered from the fact that he had himself produced *The General* (under the title of *Altemera*) in October 1662 in Dublin. In all, five of Orrery's heroic plays were produced between 1662 and 1668, and he wrote several others which were never acted.

In *The General* the rival claims of Love and Honour are already being debated, and the choice between conflicting modes of action—the characteristic dilemma of heroic drama— is clearly expounded. Clorimun, the general, finds himself torn between his desire for revenge and the commands of his mistress, who asks him to help his rival. 'What a fierce warre is in this narrow roome!' he cries. It was that fierce war in the narrow room of the heart that Orrery, following his French models, was to dramatize in one play after another. The war, we often feel, need never have broken out at all, and is only possible owing to the absurd scruples of honour or the quixotic motives of the characters. In *Henry V* the King and Owen Tudor are rivals for the love of Princess Katherine, and Tudor finds that he must either be false to Honour or false to Love. 'But stay!' he reflects,

> If I her right above my Love prefer,
> In that, by losing, I shall merit her.
> And to obtain, not merit her, will prove
> Less than to lose her and deserve her Love.

The climax of this solemn foolery is reached by the King and Owen Tudor striving to outdo each other in abnegation, the King even commanding Tudor to pursue his courtship, and promising to act as his advocate with Katherine. The two men are still going through these honourable paces in the fifth act, where Tudor tells the Princess that he now pays his debt of friendship to the King by 'resigning what I never had'; and Henry, not to be outdone in courtesy by a subject, assures him:

> Yours is the Nobler, mine the happier share,
> I'm the oblig'd, but you th' obliger are.

In an English King—and English Harry at that—such sophisticated emotions strike like a frost on the spirits; Henry V as a Restoration man of feeling is too much. One touch of nature in those plays, one single reminder of anything or anyone we know and care for, is enough to expose the unreality of the emotions on which their dramatic conflicts are based.

Orrery is seen at his best in *Mustapha*. Here again there is a sufficiency of extravagant sentiments, notably in the love-debate between Mustapha and his brother Zanger. In the scenes between Roxalana and the Queen of Hungary we have two women contending in noble attitudes, nicely considering the claims of honour and their own high station: Orrery here is providing a sort of intellectual ballet. And again, in the name of friendship, the two lovers, Mustapha and Zanger, almost plead each other's cause. Yet in spite of such absurdity and artificiality of feeling there are some strong scenes, such as the poisoning of Solyman's mind (II. iii) by Rustan and Pyrrhus. How quickly those drooping plays revive when the motive force is not love. In construction, too, *Mustapha* is superior to Orrery's earlier plays; the events have, if not inevitability, at least a natural and probable sequence. Inevitability the heroic play rarely has; it depends rather on surprise. Finally, *Mustapha* has all that dignity and gravity which is perhaps Orrery's most characteristic note. In *The General* he had permitted himself one rather Fletcherian scene in which three army officers chattered cynically (in heroic couplets) about such topics as women and platonic love. In his later plays he abandoned such comic relief, and aimed at a uniformly lofty effect. The remoteness of Orrery was perfectly described by Sir Robert Howard when he said that his expression seemed to come from a great height, 'like birds got so high, that use no labouring wings, but only with an easie care preserve a steadiness in motion'.

Dryden's[1] conception of a heroic play was altogether more

---

[1] John Dryden (1631–1700) was the son of a Northamptonshire gentleman, and was educated at Westminster School (under Dr. Busby) and at Trinity Col-

robust, and he seems to have known what he was doing from the very outset. *The Indian Queen* (1662), for which the chief credit should perhaps be given to his brother-in-law, Sir Robert Howard, sprang like Minerva from the head of Jove. The hero Montezuma, who is always flying into a passion, and who fights (as his more famous successor, Almanzor, was to do after him) for both sides in turn, is involved in a plot that presents him with a choice between Love and Honour. Dryden's brother-in-law may have restrained him in this play from the more operatic flights he was afterwards to take on his own, or perhaps with each successive play he wrote Dryden felt bound to go beyond the point of heroic extravagance he had already reached. At all events, there is some reasonable enough debate in *The Indian Queen*, and a vein of strong sense runs through many of the speeches. To the contemporary playgoer the chief attraction probably lay in the spectacular effects, such as the Temple of the Sun (v. i), 'all of gold', with its attendant priests 'in habits of white and red feathers'. Although the two theatres had not been open for much more than three years, the demand for something new was already making itself felt. Dryden's epilogue remarks on the heavy outlay on scenery and costumes for this new American tragedy: if, after all this expense, the play fails to take, ' 'tis a true voyage to the Indies lost'.

It was obviously to recover some of this capital expenditure on scenery that Dryden wrote a sequel, *The Indian Emperor*, which takes up the story of Montezuma some twenty years

lege, Cambridge. What employment he had in the closing years of the Protectorate is not certainly known; but soon after the Restoration he had established himself as a man of letters, with a number of long poems, his early heroic plays and comedies, and, in 1668, his *Essay of Dramatic Poesy*. In that year he succeeded Sir William Davenant as Poet Laureate, and two years later became Historiographer Royal, but he lost those two appointments after the Revolution, since he could not take the oaths to the new King and Queen. In 1663 he had married the eldest daughter of the Earl of Berkshire. In 1668 he had become a shareholder in the Theatre Royal on agreeing to provide the company with three plays a year; and although he was never able to fulfil this exacting contract, he wrote no fewer than twenty-one plays between 1663 and the death of Charles II in 1685, and five more after the Revolution of 1688. The six years from 1681 to 1687 saw the publication of his major political and religious poems. In the last decade of his life he was chiefly engaged in translation, including *The Works of Virgil* (1697) and *Fables Ancient and Modern* (1700), but he also wrote some of his best occasional poems. He was subjected to many critical attacks, especially after 1688, and in 1679 was beaten up by some ruffians (hired, it is usually said, but perhaps wrongly, by the young Earl of Rochester).

later, when Mexico was invaded by the Spaniards. The prologue is entirely frank about the spectacular effects:

> The Scenes are old, the Habits are the same,
> We wore last year, before the Spaniards came.

The play itself, Dryden says, is 'an irregular piece, if com-
par'd with many of Corneille's', and written 'with more
Flame than Art'. There is, in fact, a good deal of Dryden's
rather oily flame in this play. The materials out of which an
English heroic play is constructed are highly inflammable, and
every now and then they break out in a sudden blaze, 'soon
kindled, and soon burnt'. But it may be questioned if the
heroic couplet is a happy medium for such extravagant effects
as Dryden often intends; it is at least partly responsible for his
tendency to hover between the sublime and the ridiculous.
When, in II. i, a Spirit explains how

> A God more strong, who all the Gods commands,
> Drives us to exile from our Native Lands;
> The Air swarms thick with wandering Deities,
> Which drowsily like humming Beetles rise. . . .

the effect is precariously balanced. No doubt the gods would
never have been humming beetles to John Donne, but if Donne
had seen them so, his colloquial rhythms and the prevailing
idiosyncrasy of his thought would have enabled him to make
the comparison without difficulty. But Dryden, with the pronounced rhetorical structure of his verse and the more conventional levels of his normal utterance, subjects the abnormal
comparison to a strain it cannot quite take. Yet this criticism is
perhaps only valid when the words are read. *The Indian Emperor*
is full of fine rhetorical passages (the most celebrated being the
speech of Cortez in III. ii, 'All things are hush'd, as Nature's
self lay dead'), which, spoken to a full house, would enable the
dramatist to obtain that 'absolute dominion' over the minds of
the audience which he invariably attempted. In such an
atmosphere the drama of contending passions, the quixotic
behaviour of the heroes, the elaborate similes and descriptive
passages, the extravagance of

> Moon, slip behind some Cloud, some Tempest rise
> And blow out all the Stars that light the Skies. . . .

—all find their place in a complex effect which may seem
tawdry enough the morning after, but which at the time was no
doubt exciting and even impressive.

With his next heroic play, *Tyrannic Love*, Dryden is crossing
the Niagara Falls on a tight-rope: an abyss of bathos yawns
beneath him, but he staggers precariously across after some
appalling stumbles. Maximin's bluster and blasphemy are
carried about as far as Dryden ever took this particular heroic
effect, except perhaps for some speeches of Almanzor's. How
rapidly the heroic play was acquiring its own clichés may be
seen from a speech of Berenice at the close of Act ii, where
she tells Porphyrio how after she is dead she will come to him
'all soul and spirit', play before him in the sunbeams, peep at
night within the curtains of his bed, and with empty arms
embrace him while he sleeps. Striking a more domestic note in
v. i, she tells her lover that if she dies first, she will

> Stop short of Heav'n, and wait you in a Cloud;
> For fear we lose each other in the crowd.

This assignation with the loved one in the next world re-
appears in Settle's first play, *Cambyses*, where Mandana tells
Osiris that her soul will 'hov'ring fly' and steal into his breast;
sometimes she will 'with gentle whispers flow', and at other
times 'a stormy murmur blow'. Settle was obviously copying
what he regarded as a great beauty in Dryden's play, but the
Berenice passage was very fairly picked out for parody in *The
Rehearsal*. From *Tyrannic Love*, too, Settle may have learnt the
effect upon the Restoration audience of scenes of physical
cruelty, in which he afterwards specialized. In the last act of
Dryden's play 'the scene opens, and shews a wheel': St.
Catherine is not actually tortured in front of our eyes, though
we are led to expect it, but the speech in which Maximin
prescribes the approaching torture in detail is perhaps more
shockingly sadistic than anything even in Jacobean drama. It
is followed by a passage of unusual gentleness, in which St.
Catherine's mother reminds her how she was always her
favourite child:

> About my neck your little arms you spred,
> Nor could you sleep without me in the bed;
> But sought my bosom when you went to rest,
> And all night long would lye across my brest.

Dryden here is quite shamelessly playing an emotional sym-
phony on the nerves of his audience. A few minutes later we
are on tenterhooks for Berenice, who is discovered on a scaffold
about to be executed; and the scene reaches its climax with the
violent death of Maximin. As he sits astride the body of Placidius, stabbing him repeatedly, he utters his famous last words:

> And shoving back this Earth on which I sit,
> I'le mount—and scatter all the Gods I hit.

How could Dryden—how could anyone—come to write such
stuff? It may fairly be answered that it is such stuff as theatrical
dreams are made on. Removed from their context and held
up for ridicule, Maximin's words *are*, of course, ridiculous; but
in the closing stages of a heroic play an audience has become
conditioned by all that has gone before, and this ranting
blasphemy is in keeping with the prevailing atmosphere, and,
incidentally, is entirely characteristic of Maximin. We might
say of Dryden's tyrant-monster what Schlegel said of Caliban:
if there were such monsters, this is how they would speak.
Dryden, in fact, has taken leave of reality before the play
begins; his aim is to arouse admiration by every means at his
command—rhetoric, rant, horror, passion, magnificence,
magniloquence, drums and trumpets, spectacle and costume,
all the emotional stock in trade of the Restoration theatre. He
can be real enough—how delightfully so!—the moment the
play is over. Maximin, Valeria, Placidius lie dead upon the
stage, and the bearers enter according to custom to carry off
the bodies. At this point Nell Gwyn, who has played Valeria,
starts to her feet and cries:

> Hold, are you mad? You damn'd confounded Dog,
> I am to rise, and speak the Epilogue.

This is a different, and no doubt a better, Dryden. With a
single couplet, perfectly timed, he has transported us from his
dream-world of tyrants and Christian martyrs back to the
London of Charles II, the 'dear, damn'd, distracting Town' for
which those astonishing entertainments were composed. But
in the prologue to *Tyrannic Love* he offers some justification of
the extravagant play he had written, and incidentally gives us
an illuminating glimpse of the way he had written it. Poets,
like lovers (so his argument runs), ought not to be too careful;

the writer who 'servilely creeps after sense' will never achieve
much. As for himself, he gives his fancy full scope in these plays
of his; and in this one in particular, having a tyrant for his
theme, 'he loosed the reins, and bid his Muse run mad'. He
knew, of course, what he was about, but he was being hurried
along so rapidly by his thoughts that 'to chuse the ground might
be to lose the race'. This helter-skelter, hit-or-miss writing is
almost the last brave fling of the old Elizabethan fashion before
an age of correctness closes down over English poetry. What was
rapidly becoming impossible in non-dramatic poetry lingered
for some time in the hothouse poetry of the theatre. It flares up
for perhaps the last time in the tragedies of Nathaniel Lee, and
there expires 'like a spent taper, and instantly goes out'.

With *The Conquest of Granada* Dryden brought the heroic
play to the fullest expansion of which it was capable. To blow
any harder would have been to burst the balloon. With this
play, as he tells us himself, he 'swept the stakes'. It appealed
above all to the ladies: John Evelyn's sister, for one, was en-
raptured by it. 'I have seen "The Siege of Grenada",' she
wrote, 'a play so full of ideas that the most refined romance I
ever read is not to compare with it: love is made so pure, and
valour so nice, that one would imagine it designed for an
Utopia rather than our stage. I . . . admire one born in the
decline of morality should be able to feign such exact virtue.'
All that the heroic play had been doing was here consummated:
Almanzor (a compound of Achilles, Rinaldo, and the Artaban
of La Calprenède) is the final development of blustering valour;
Almahide and Lyndaraxa, the apotheosis of lovely woman
whose merest frown reduces the warrior to trembling awe or
passionate pleading. It is here that Dryden's appeal to the fair
sex was so effective; his recipe for a heroic play is to present
the maximum of martial bravery going down in hopeless ruin
before the maximum of feminine charm. As one of Lyndaraxa's
victims put it (in one of Dryden's worst lapses),

> Her voice is like a Syren's of the Land;
> And bloody Hearts lie panting in her hand.

Apart from all this, *The Conquest of Granada* is a stirring play,
full of unexpected turns of fortune, glowing with moral argument and sententious utterance, and (within the limits of the
heroic pattern) enlivened by considerable character interest.

Lyndaraxa, in particular, the gold-digger of Dryden's theatre, is a welcome change from those virtuously yielding maidens who chill whatever they shine upon. *'Exit; but looks smiling back on him'* is one of Dryden's stage directions for Lyndaraxa; he had evidently visualized her completely. In the second part of this ten-act play Dryden maintains the action at the same high pitch of excitement, and with the ghost of Almanzor's mother and the surprising discovery of his unknown father on the field of battle he passes even more completely into the realm of romance.

Five years later he returned for the last time to the rhymed heroic play, and wrote in *Aureng-Zebe* what was on almost every count his best. No further progress was possible along the lines of *The Conquest of Granada*, and Dryden accordingly retreated from the romantic extravagance of that play and was content to proceed along more naturalistic levels. The dialogue, as Johnson noted, is often domestic; but what is more remarkable, it sometimes approaches closely to the idiom of Restoration comedy. In the husband-wife recriminations between the Emperor and Nourmahal, and again in the scene in which Morat repudiates his wife Melesinda with her 'stale domestic face', we have the very accents of contemporary comedy. To Addison the Emperor's treatment of Nourmahal was merely shocking: strip the sentiments of 'the shining dress of words', he complained, and they would be 'too coarse for a scene in Billingsgate'. Possibly so; but a scene in Billingsgate brings us much nearer to the essential passions of the human heart than the stately interchanges of an oriental palace. Most modern readers will probably welcome the passages that Addison deplored; if they do not show us how kings and queens should talk, they come near to showing us how husbands and wives sometimes do talk. Even the heroine, the virtuous Indamora, benefits from the increased naturalism: for almost the first time in these plays Dryden has drawn a young woman who is as intelligent as a heroine in comedy. Indamora's handling of the amorous but ageing Arimant has all the poise and control of a Millamant: 'You can at most', she tells him,

> To an indiff'rent Lover's praise pretend:
> But you would spoil an admirable Friend—

and a moment later she adds that she needs 'just such a friend':

You must perform, not what *you* think is fit:
But to what ever I propose, submit.

Submit Arimant does, grumbling but helpless. To accompany these saner and more natural effects Dryden pulls out a new stop; his verse is at once easier and more varied, his rhymes are less pronounced, and he tends to avoid what Scott called the 'emphatic swell' of his earlier plays. Even the set pieces, such as the famous 'When I consider life, 'tis all a cheat', have more of the rhythm of conversation than of declamation. It is significant that in the prologue to *Aureng-Zebe* Dryden announced to all and sundry that he had now grown weary of 'his long-lov'd mistress, Rhyme'. He had come at last to believe what his brother-in-law had failed to convince him of years before, that

Passion's too fierce to be in Fetters bound,
And Nature flies him like Enchanted Ground.

Elkanah Settle[1] specialized in heroic plays placed in an oriental setting, a wise decision in view of the extravagance that had come to be associated in the English theatre with this kind of drama. The standard of conduct expected of a Cambyses or an Empress of Morocco was obviously much less rational than that considered proper to a European, and Settle was therefore free to portray any sort of arbitrary behaviour and noble or ignoble savagery that commended itself to his own crude tastes. His first play, *Cambyses* (1667), was produced while he was still an undergraduate, and must have been written before he was nineteen. Although the Tragedy of Intrigue has not been recognized as a separate dramatic kind by literary critics, that is in fact the best definition of Settle's first play and of *The Empress of Morocco* that followed about two years later. Settle had worked hard at his plot, complicating it with misunderstandings and frequent disguises that surprise the audience quite as much as the characters on the stage, and colouring it with murders and scenes of horror. *The Empress of Morocco* is a

---

[1] Elkanah Settle (1648–1724) was something of a literary prodigy. According to John Downes the prompter, he wrote, while still at Oxford, his heroic play *Cambyses*, which was successfully produced with Thomas Betterton in the leading part. *The Empress of Morocco* and some of his later plays brought him a high reputation for some years, but he dwindled in later life to being City Poet and devising pageants for the Lord Mayor's Day, and he also wrote drolls for Bartholomew Fair. He died in poverty in the Charterhouse. Besides his plays and some complimentary poems, he wrote political pamphlets, first in the Protestant and then in the Catholic interest, and two interesting rogue biographies.

sort of Restoration *Titus Andronicus*, with its spectacular effects, its hideous cruelties, and its murderous Empress (a female Aaron), who leaves single crimes to 'common hands' and 'scorns to kill less than whole families'. The plot is elaborate and at times ingenious; but plotting is a comparatively easy business when there is no compulsion to preserve any credibility in the characters. The only certainty in these plays is that most of the leading characters will fall violently in love, but when, or with whom, will depend on the requirements of the plot.

It is not difficult to see why Dryden was annoyed with Settle, and why he went out of his way to discredit this highly successful upstart in his *Notes . . . on the Empress of Morocco*. Settle's play was the logical outcome of the heroic style: the cords are all strung tighter, the note is shriller, and the danger of something snapping is correspondingly increased. But Settle was only doing, in a slightly more absurd fashion, the same foolish things that Dryden had already done and was to do again; the deliberate ridicule of *The Rehearsal* must have been less disturbing to Dryden than the unconscious parody (that was scarcely parody) of Settle's only too faithful imitation. Indeed, when Settle came to reply to his critics in *Notes and Observations on the Empress of Morocco Revised*, he was usually able to find a precedent in Dryden's plays for every folly of his own. There is perhaps less sheer nonsense in Settle than Dryden tried to suggest, but there is much absurdity, and, unlike Dryden, he did almost nothing to redeem it. We get little impression of a mind stirring in Settle; he has almost none of Dryden's power of reflecting upon events and circumstances. Dryden's ridicule of his contemporaries often obscured the truth; but when he said of Settle that he 'faggoted his notions as they fell' he came very near the mark.

The Conquest of China (1675) is another exciting play with ingenious plotting, some sadistic scenes, and Settle's usual mixture of sense and nonsense. But *Ibrahim*, written when he was nearing thirty, is a sober enough drama, not without some dignity, and comparing favourably in point of good sense with some of Dryden's heroic plays. Settle's later career as City Poet, deviser of Pope-burning pageants, writer of Smithfield drolls, and finally as an inmate of the Charterhouse, has seemed to confirm the estimate of his abilities given to the world in the satire of Dryden and Pope. Yet the crude violence of so much of his work (seen at its drivelling worst in *The Female Prelate*), and the long years of eclipse during which he was 'reduced at last to hiss in [his] own dragon', should not blind us to the undisciplined promise of his vigorous if not mighty youth, when, as Dennis testifies, he was looked upon by the Town as a formidable rival to Dryden, and even by 'the younger fry' thought to be his superior. His rapid decline was due less perhaps to the ridicule of Dryden and his associates than to his own crude intervention in party politics, to his willingness in his dramatic work to exploit beyond reasonable limits the sensational and the spectacular, and to his tendency to write down whatever came into his head. Dryden's sneer that Mr. Settle 'would persuade us he is a kind of fanatic in poetry, and has a light within him, and writes by an inspiration', is fair enough.

(IV)

Although the rhymed heroic play had gone out of fashion by the close of the 1670s, the heroics and extravagance it engendered and encouraged took much longer to die away. The serious drama, indeed, never quite recovered from the flamboyant decade of the heroic plays; it never, with one or two notable exceptions, became fully serious. Buckingham's witty burlesque, *The Rehearsal* (December 1671), was appreciated by audiences who continued to enjoy the very plays it ridiculed so successfully. Some indication of this is given by the list of plays performed before royalty. In 1674 *The Indian Emperor* and *The Rehearsal* were both given twice; in 1675 there were five command performances of Lee's *Sophonisba* and two of *Aureng-Zebe*, and in 1676 *Tyrannic Love* was performed once, and *Aureng-Zebe* presented at Court. Ten years later James II and his Queen were present at a command performance of *The Rehearsal*, and a few months later they attended a revival of Orrery's *Mustapha*. About the time that Dryden was growing tired of his 'long-lov'd mistress Rhyme', a number of younger dramatists were starting upon their writing careers with one or more rhymed plays. *Nero*, the first of three written by Lee, was produced in 1674; Otway's *Alcibiades* followed in 1675, and his *Don Carlos* a year later. Durfey, who tried his hand at almost everything, produced *The Siege of Memphis* in 1676, John Banks began with *The Rival Kings* (1677), and Mrs. Behn's fourth play, improbably enough, was a heroic tragedy, *Abdelazer, or The Moor's Revenge* (1677). About the same time John Crowne and Samuel Pordage were both writing rhymed tragedies, and Sedley's *Antony and Cleopatra* appeared in 1677.

When Dryden returned to the stage in 1677 with *All for Love*, his version of *Antony and Cleopatra*, he had not wholly shaken off the heroic fever, but he was now entering upon what may be called his neo-classical period. This play, in which he endeavoured 'to follow the practice of the Ancients' in so far as it was compatible with the taste of an English audience, is perhaps the finest example in the English theatre of a neo-classical tragedy. 'I never writ anything for myself but *Antony and Cleopatra*', he observed some years later, and one must regret that he did not more frequently forget his audience. (About the time that *All for Love* was produced he was at work on *Limberham*, in which he deliberately lowered himself to the level of his audience, if not actually below it.) Although *All for Love* has a love-and-honour situation it is wonderfully free from the rant and hyperbole of his heroic plays, and more truly dramatic. The tension is in the situation and in the conflicting characters; and Antony, subjected to alternate pressures from Ventidius and Octavia on the one side and Cleopatra on the other, is so far from being the gyrating weathercock of the heroic drama that the dominating impression he makes is one of a sad dignity. This new restraint is often deeply moving. Dryden, who saw his two chief characters as 'famous patterns of unlawful love' whose crimes were 'wholly voluntary', has given a note of contrition to Antony which is not to be found in Shakespeare, but he has preserved the nobility and generosity of his character. Time, place, and action are all adjusted to neo-classical demands, and the language has been refined to suit contemporary taste. In his version of *Troilus and Cressida* Dryden sometimes 'conformed' his style to Shakespeare's, and in the Preface to that play he expressed a fear that 'the language is not altogether so pure as it is significant'. In *All for Love* the language is both pure and significant; and Dryden's claim that he has not copied his author servilely is no less than the truth. How skilfully he adapted Shakespeare's metaphorical language to the more prosaic taste of a Restoration audience may be seen in the very few passages (most notably the description of Cleopatra's passage

down the River Cydnus) in which he actually makes use of
Shakespeare's words. His own metaphor is normally more
conventional, but it is often both apt and ingenious, as when,
in a scene with Dolabella, Alexas urges Cleopatra to make
Antony jealous, and tells her that jealousy in a lover is like

> A polish'd Glass held to the lips when life's in doubt:
> If there be breath, 'twill catch the damp, and show it.

All for Love also gave Dryden the opportunity to exploit what
was perhaps his greatest excellence as a playwright, the dramatic debate involving persuasion and dissuasion, putting a case
and answering it; and since the chief characters in this tragedy
are all firmly drawn, each argument has the additional interest
of being characteristic of the speaker.

About eighteen months later Dryden's adaptation of *Troilus
and Cressida*, another neo-classical tragedy with traces of the
heroic play, was produced at the Dorset Garden theatre. He
had reduced the number of the characters (but added Andromache), he had 'new-modelled the plot' so as to construct a more
regular play, and he had written a new fifth act in which Cressida, who has *not* been false, dies by her own hand. In this rearranged form he retained a good deal more of Shakespeare
than he had done in *All for Love*: for one thing, the debates of
Shakespeare's Greeks and Trojans provided the sort of dramatic material that Dryden would probably have thought up for
himself. But the more he keeps of Shakespeare, the more conscious we become of impoverishment; for Dryden is so convinced
that Shakespeare's whole style is 'pestered with figurative
expressions' that he everywhere eliminates his rich metaphor,
or reduces it to something more conventional and trite. If we
were not so often reminded of the original, no great harm would
be done; but, like his own Troilus, Shakespeare stalks continually about the background,

> Like a strange soul upon the Stygian banks
> Staying for waftage.

Some months earlier Dryden had collaborated with Lee
in the tragedy of *Oedipus*, which, according to Downes, 'took
prodigiously, being acted ten days together'. This play is a
mixture of Sophocles, Seneca, and Corneille, with occasional
echoes of Jacobean tragedy and the heroic drama. It contains

some good writing, such as the opening description of plague-
stricken Thebes, and a speech of Creon's, 'O 'tis a fearful thing
to be no more' (III. i); but, as Dennis suggested, those who
admired this tragedy 'may have mistaken horror for terror
and pity'. In the summer of 1682 Dryden and Lee had another
tragedy ready for production, *The Duke of Guise*, a play based
on one Dryden had written as early as 1660 and which he now
resuscitated because the conflict of Henry IV of France with the
Holy League offered an apt parallel to Charles II's troubles
with the New Association of the Whigs. Some of the allusions
were so close to the Duke of Monmouth and others that it was
not until November that the Lord Chamberlain released the
play for production. In his 'Vindication' of the play Dryden
asked, 'Am I ty'd in Poetry to the strict rules of History?' But
in fact the chief objection to this tragedy is that the authors did
keep too close to the history of Henry IV and the Duke of
Guise. Dryden had thought of calling his play 'The Parallel',
and that is what it effectively is: a political play in which
events in sixteenth-century Paris are dramatized because of
their relevance to the activities of the English Whigs in 1681–2.
The Duke of Guise is soberly enough written, for either Dryden
restrained Lee's raptures or Lee adapted his style to that of his
collaborator; but it contains some fine lines that could only
have come from Dryden, as, for example, Aumale's reply to
Bussy (I. i):

> What's our Reward? Our Offices are lost,
> Turn'd out like Labour'd Oxen, after Harvest,
> To the bare Commons of the wither'd Field.

When Dryden's next tragedy, *Don Sebastian*, was produced in
the winter of 1689 he had fallen on evil days, and was attempting to restore his shattered fortunes. The play he had written
was much too long and had to be 'judiciously lopped' (to the
extent of 1,200 lines) by Betterton, who, perhaps inevitably,
pared away 'the most poetical parts, which are Descriptions,
Images, Similitudes and Moral Sentences'. Dryden restored
those cuts when the play was printed, and *Don Sebastian*
justifies his claim that 'in the roughness of the numbers and
cadences (which I assure was not casual, but so design'd) you
will see somewhat more masterly arising to view than in most,
if not any of my former Tragedies'. Dryden, in fact, seems to

have had Shakespeare in mind; he deliberately introduced 'some old words . . . for their significance and sound' and consciously attempted 'a more noble daring in the figures', and he brought in some scenes of comic relief. Stylistically, then, this tragedy is interesting. So too is his statement that 'Love and Honour (the mistaken Topicks of Tragedy) were quite worn out'. But in finding a substitute Dryden was not so happy: the abnormal theme of an incestuous love between brother and sister, which seems to have haunted Dryden in his later years, is perhaps, in its unrelieved suffering and in the hopelessness of the outcome, more painful than tragic. It is only fair to add that this tragedy has had many admirers. In Johnson's day it was 'commonly esteemed either the first or the second of his dramatick performances', and Scott had no hesitation in preferring it to *All for Love*. Dryden's last tragedy, *Cleomenes* (with some assistance from Southerne), appeared in 1692, at a time when there seems to have been some revival of interest in plays dealing with the ancient world. Again the first performance was held up for some time because a Spartan king in exile at the Court of the King of Egypt seemed to have too close an application to the situation of James II at the Court of Louis XIV. This is a dignified tragedy; but the manly Cleomenes, who is not passion's slave, who resists without difficulty the allurements of Cassandra, and who adheres throughout to what she calls 'your blunt Laconic way', is a consistent character without ever becoming an interesting one. In spite of the turns and twists that Dryden gives to the course of events, the action moves steadily towards the doom of this Spartan Brutus, not with the inevitability of great tragedy but by a sort of settled misfortune. Dryden had now moved so far from the rant and passion of his early plays that Cleomenes seems rather to be the hero of an epic poem than of a tragedy.

John Crowne,[1] who wrote no fewer than eleven tragedies,

---

[1] The early life of John Crowne (d. 1703?) is obscure, but he appears to have spent some part of his youth in Nova Scotia, to which his father had emigrated. His first published work was his chaotic prose romance, *Pandion and Amphigenia* (1665). He began writing for the stage in 1671, and between that date and 1698 produced eleven tragedies and a few lively comedies, including *Sir Courtly Nice* (1685). Although he was apparently well liked by Charles II, and was invited, through the influence of the Earl of Rochester, to write the Court masque *Calisto* (1675), he had, according to Dennis, 'a mortal aversion to the Court', and according to another contemporary, was known as 'starch Johnny Crowne' from 'the stiff, unalterable primness of his long crevat'.

the last of which, *Caligula* (1698), returned very belatedly to the rhymed verse of his earliest plays, never really abandoned the heroic mode. Most of his tragedies contain a good deal of violence under a thin pretence of classical calm, but (if we forget his *Thyestes*) he wrote less nonsense than most of his contemporaries, and indeed showed a mild hankering after sense. He is seen at his best in *The Destruction of Jerusalem* (1677), a rhymed play in two parts and ten acts, which had a considerable success, partly owing to its spectacular effects, but partly, it may be hoped, on account of its merits. It is generously supplied with lovers (apparently more to comply with the taste of the age than from any preference on Crowne's part), and one of these, Phraartes, who is in love with the religious maiden Clarona, is a character of some originality, entirely without religion himself, but brave and chivalrous. In his 'Epistle to the Reader' Crowne explains that, having provided so much love for the female part of the audience, 'I thought I had given 'em enough for reasonable Women, and might borrow this Hero to entertain the Men for a minute with a little reason'. The 'little reason' that he supplies is Phraartes' outspoken comments on priests and religion, for which in his old age Crowne was to express his regret. When, in the opening scene, Monobazus observes that although we worship only our own gods we reverence those of other nations, Phraartes has his retort ready:

> *Mon.* All own some Power that does the World command:
> Even mighty Rome bows to Celestial Powers.
> *Phraar.* She does—but lower to her Emperors.

In several later scenes between Phraartes and Clarona the argument for and against religion is carried on in a downright fashion which is saved from being offensive by the courtesy and intellectual frankness of Phraartes: we might almost be listening to Rochester arguing with Bishop Burnet. In introducing such intellectual, and at times satirical, passages, Crowne was no doubt influenced by the practice of Dryden; the heroic play at its best accommodated itself to the discussion of ideas, although such discussion was always liable to be swept away by gusts of theatrical passion or disintegrated by the empty ingenuities of repartee. 'Since Love has got the sole possession of the Stage,' Crowne complains to his readers,

'Reason has little to do there.' This was only too true with
many of his contemporaries, and it may be added that the love
is rarely recognizable as love at all. It is therefore to Crowne's
credit that in Phraartes he has created a character who really
seems to be in love, and whose passion has not impaired his
reason. There is little in this hero to remind us of Almanzor
until near the end of Part II, when, as the wounded Clarona
dies in his arms, he goes mad. 'I begin to wander from my sense,'
he cries:

> Where is Clarona gone?
> Aloft!—I see her mounting to the Sun!—
> The flaming Satyr towards her does roul,
> His scorching Lust makes Summer at the Pole.
> Let the hot Planet touch her if he dares!—
> Touch her, and I will cut him into Stars,
> And the bright chips into the Ocean throw!

No doubt most of the contemporary audience found such
ravings more to their liking than all the sense that preceded
them. Crowne could 'give a loose' to his feelings if he thought
the situation or the audience demanded it, and he was prepared,
like Dryden, to defend his poetical licence: 'I love not too much
carefulness in small things. To be exact in trifles is the mark of
a little Genius.' This is a variation of Dryden's willingness 'to
loose the reins, and bid his muse run mad', and this conscious
abandon accounts for most of the extravagance in Restoration
tragedy.

No one has more of it than Nathaniel Lee.[1] Between 1674
and 1683 he saw no less than ten of his tragedies performed,
and two more that he wrote in collaboration with Dryden. He
was always attempting an eagle flight, and he drove himself
hard. The result is what we might expect: when Lee rises he
mounts higher than any of his contemporaries except Dryden
and Otway at their best; when he falls, his descent is sudden,

---

[1] Nathaniel Lee (1649?–92), the son of a clergyman, was educated at Charterhouse and Trinity College, Cambridge. Like Otway, he was an unsuccessful actor
who took to writing plays. With the exception of *The Princess of Cleve* his eleven
plays are tragedies, and based on classical history. His *Lucius Junius Brutus* was
banned after several performances in December 1680 on account of some anti-
monarchical passages. He collaborated with Dryden in *Oedipus* and *The Duke of
Guise*. In 1684 he was confined in Bedlam, where he remained for some years; he
was well enough in 1689 to write a poem on the death of Mrs. Behn. He died, or
was killed by a passing coach, after a drinking bout in May 1692.

and can be disastrous. He was conscious of his faults (the critics saw to that), but impenitently confident that he more than redeemed them by a brave spontaneity. Answering his critics (in the Dedication to *Theodosius*), he admits that his imagination is sometimes ungoverned: 'But I hope the World will pardon the Sallies of Youth; Age, Despondence, and Dulness come too fast of themselves. I discommend no Man for keeping the beaten Road; but I am sure the Noble Hunters that follow the Game must leap Hedges and Ditches sometimes, and run at all, or never come in to the fall of the Quarry.' Whether this is a good defence or not, we may be sure that it was put forward by Lee in all sincerity. His was not a calculated recklessness, nor was it the result of consciously urging on his Pegasus: he had a natural extravagance, and he constantly abandoned himself to the violence of his feelings. Like his own Brutus in *Lucius Junius Brutus*, he allows himself to be hurried away by 'a blood-shot anger and a burst of fury'; and like Titus again in the same play, he could often have said of himself:

> My Thoughts were up in arms,
> All in a Roar, like Seamen in a Storm,
> My Reason and my Faculties were wrack'd,
> The Mast, the Rudder and the Tackling gone. . . .

The effect would be finer if it were not so frequent. Lee carries everything to an extreme: the despairs and melting ecstasies of lovers, the scorn of a Roxana, the cruelties of a Borgia are all given a hysterical emphasis that must have left the audience emotionally exhausted and almost incapable of hearing the voice of natural feeling. Lee, in fact, rarely gives them the chance to hear it; he is hardly ever content to let the situation tell on its own merits, but involves it in his own overcharged emotions. 'Prithee, undo this button' would never have done for Lee; but the earlier ravings of Lear were just the kind of thing that he strove to emulate.

When he began writing for the theatre at about the age of twenty-five, the rhymed heroic tragedy was still in favour, and his first three tragedies were accordingly in heroic couplets. The first of these, *Nero*, a play full of riot, rant, blasphemy, and horror, and, ominously enough, of madness, has some of that terrible energy which he imparted to all that he wrote. It was followed by *Sophonisba*, a favourite tragedy for many years to come, which appealed especially to the ladies. Before the charms of Sophonisba and Rosalinda the men go down like ninepins—Hannibal, Massinissa, Massina, and even for one short scene the stern and virtuous Scipio. It was on such feminine triumphs that much of Lee's popularity was based. With *The Rival Queens* (1677) he passed to blank verse, although there are still some passages in rhyme and the atmosphere is still that of the heroic play. Of many scenes in this tragedy Lee might have said what Dryden came to say of some of his own heroic excesses: 'I knew they were bad enough to please, even when I writ them.' *The Rival Queens* has many of the elements of popular drama: strong scenes (e.g. the altercation between Roxana and Statira; the feast at which Alexander slays honest Clytus), tension, well-defined characters (including the bluff soldier, repeated by Lee in Marcian in *Theodosius*), passion (and especially amorous fury, for Lee can be luscious), and much fine rhetoric. Again the atmosphere is tense with impending madness, as in the outburst of Roxana:

> The storm is up, and my hot bleeding heart
> Splits with the rack, while passions like the winds
> Rise up to Heav'n and put out all the Stars.

The madness is in his characters, but it may also (we begin to feel) be in Lee himself.

Of the later tragedies *Caesar Borgia* is of interest mainly because Lee appears to be trying to portray in Borgia a character who is not a simple monster, but a villain shot through with streaks of nobility. Yet the situation is too full of openings for Lee's inevitable violence, and the effect is one of Elizabethan horror rather than tragedy. *Theodosius; or The Force of Love* is perhaps best summed up in a phrase of Lee's: it is a passionate play dealing with 'Love's melodious ill'. Lee has not learnt to control his extravagance, nor ever will; but there is less rant, more thought, and even some gentleness. From time to time we hear unmistakable echoes of Shakespeare, and also of Beaumont and Fletcher, from whom Lee probably learnt to make his characters dwell on the joys of a simple life free from the responsibilities of their royal blood. There are, too, some fine passages of his characteristically theatrical poetry, notably Varanes' description of the night (v. ii. 1 ff.), with its silence of suspended animation, when even 'the stars, Heav'ns centry, wink and seem to dye'. Lee's next tragedy, *Lucius Junius Brutus*, is in most respects his finest play. Where there is violence there is generally a good dramatic justification of it: Lee is not just injecting it into his play. What chiefly distinguishes this tragedy is a new weight of thought. Lee himself seems to have felt that he had come to a turning point in his dramatic career, for in his Dedication of the play to the Earl of Dorset he observes: 'Nature 'tis believed (if I am not flattered and do not flatter my self) has not been niggardly to me in the Portion of a Genius, tho I have been so far from improving it, that I am half affraid I have lost of the Principle. It behoves me then for the future to look about me to see whether I am Lagg in the Race. . . .' For such a play as he has now written he admits that there must be 'Greatness of Thought without Bombast, . . . speaking out without cracking the Voice or straining the Lungs'. This is a chastened Lee; and although the old fury sometimes hurries him away, he shows a new power to develop a genuinely tragic argument. The new quality in his thought may be seen from an utterance of Brutus:

> Nay, 'tis the hardest task perhaps of life
> To be assur'd of what is Vice or Virtue—

an astonishingly thoughtful observation to come from a hero of Restoration tragedy. *Lucius Junius Brutus* never had a chance to become a popular play; it was suppressed after a few performances for certain 'very scandalous expressions and reflections upon the Government'—in fact, for being anti-monarchical in a number of passages. In the inflammatory political world of 1680 some of the speeches would indeed have been dangerous. Yet Lee had not written a crude Whig play like Settle's *The Female Prelate*; he had written a historical tragedy that had a disquieting relevance to contemporary England, and the seriousness of his intentions comes out not so much in the political parallels as in some passages that have a more general bearing on the England of Charles II. Perhaps one of his 'scandalous expressions' was the fine speech near the end of the play in which Brutus contemplates a purified Rome, where not only is a free-born people not governed by 'partial tyrants', and where 'there's no innovation of Religion', but where there are

No hopes of Pardon for Assassinates,
No rash advancements of the Base or stranger,
For Luxury, for Wit, or glorious Vice;
But on the contrary, a Balanc'd Trade,
Patriots incourag'd, Manufactors cherish'd,
Vagabonds, Walkers, Drones, and Swarming Braves,
The Froth of States, scum'd from the Common-wealth . . .

Lucius Junius Brutus has perhaps too many faults to be called a great tragedy, but unlike most tragedies of the period it is about something that really matters. Lee never reached the same heights again.

So long as the dramatists continued to set their plays in foreign (and more especially oriental) courts, remote both in time and place, the extravagant passion and the rant, together with the generalized excitement independently generated by rhyming couplets, were likely to continue. A change was felt when one or two of the playwrights chose to look homeward and take their themes from English history. One of the earliest of these was John Caryll (1625–1711), whose rhymed tragedy of *The English Princes, or, The Death of Richard III* was produced in 1667. Aware that he was offering none of those exotic effects which the contemporary audience had come to expect, Caryll took pains in his prologue to prepare them for what they were to expect:

> You must to day your Appetites prepare
> For a plain English Treat of homely Fare. . . .
> Nor shall we charm your Ears or feast your Eyes
> With Turkey works, or Indian Rarityes:
> But to plain Hollinshed and down right Stow
> We the coarse web of our Contrivance owe.

The reaction of Pepys to this tragedy was what we might expect: he found it to be 'a most sad, melancholy play, and pretty good; but nothing eminent in it, as some tragedys are'. The modern reader is more likely to think this absence of eminence the play's most attractive quality. Although it is written in rhymed couplets, these are oddly muted, with little of the pounding emphasis of Dryden or Settle, and the effect is one of quiet reasonableness. Edward Ravenscroft's *King Edgar and Alfreda*, produced in 1677, but written, according to the author, at least ten years earlier, is the first play in the period to go back to early English history, and the first in which most of the

emphasis is placed on the heroine. The prologue makes it
clear that this tragi-comedy had not been produced at the time
it was written because 'nothing pleas'd you in those dayes but
Rymes'; but now, he believes, the taste of playgoers has
changed:

> Well he forbore, and well has nick'd the time,
> If Sense may do that is not shodd with Ryme;
> If Heroes too that are no more than men,
> May be allowed to tread the Stage agen;
> If Lovers may be Lovers, yet not by fits
> Rave and discourse like Folk beside their wits.

That at least a partial reaction from heroics was taking place
may be seen from the career of John Banks.[1] Beginning with
two heroic plays, he passed in 1681 to his blank-verse historical tragedy, *The Unhappy Favourite: or The Earl of Essex*. In his
own day and for several generations later this was one of the
most consistently popular tragedies on the London stage. It
has the great merit, singularly lacking in most Restoration
tragedy, of dealing with real situations: real not merely in the
sense that they are based on historical events and characters,
but in their truth to human feelings and human behaviour.
This tragedy is also well constructed, the action turns naturally
and inevitably on comprehensible motives, and in Queen
Elizabeth Banks has drawn a character of some complexity,
whose indecision is credible and at times moving. Dealing with
the actual, Banks was encouraged to avoid the implausible
and the extravagant; the English theme had at once a sobering
and an inspiring influence on his mind. This, then, was another
'English treat of homely fare', and it has the peculiar interest
that while it delighted the audience, and more especially 'the
shining sex' to whom all his 'she-tragedies' were addressed, and
who willingly responded to his appeal to their natural feelings,
its homeliness completely antagonized the critics. Indeed, it
became a critical commonplace to maintain that Banks was
a poor writer. Writing in the *Tatler* a few years after the

---

[1] Little is known of the life of John Banks, except that between 1677 and 1696
he wrote seven plays, and that two of them, *The Island Queens* (Queen Elizabeth
and Mary Queen of Scots) and *The Innocent Usurper* (Lady Jane Grey) were prohibited. He published the first in 1684 (produced in 1704 as *The Albion Queens*), and
the second in 1694. Two of his tragedies, *The Unhappy Favourite* and *Virtue Betrayed*,
remained popular through most of the eighteenth century.

dramatist's death, Steele recommended *The Unhappy Favourite*
as a play which never failed to draw tears from the eyes of an
audience, and which no unprejudiced playgoer could see without being touched with pity. Yet this could happen with a
play 'in which there is not one good line', and in which there
are 'expressions almost ridiculous with respect to propriety'.
For Steele the play was 'a remarkable instance that the soul is
not to be moved by words, but things'. Pope sneered at Banks
in the *Dunciad*, and even Cibber, who knew better than most
what splendid acting parts Banks had given the players,
thought that his plays were written 'in a most barren, barbarous style'. Such judgements may seem hard to account for,
but the explanation is simple enough: Banks was attempting
(with occasional lapses into the heroic) to make his characters
speak the language of the heart, and that was almost never the
language of the Restoration or the eighteenth-century theatre.

In *Virtue Betrayed: or, Anna Bullen* (1682) Banks again succeeded in creating a heroine who has both dignity and emotional integrity; but this play suffers in comparison with *The
Unhappy Favourite* by being too exclusively a tragedy of circumstance, and in consequence the emphasis is on hopeless lament
for what cannot be altered. Since the heart of the tragedy lies
in the conflict in the minds of Anne Boleyn and her lover Piercy,
it is almost inevitable that the presentation of Henry VIII
should be adversely affected; he acts, indeed, like one of the
characters of a heroic play, swept by violent gusts of passion.
When Wolsey tells him that his wife has been reported unfaithful, the King explodes in anger, without waiting for the least
proof:

> Reported, said'st thou! Is not that enough?
> Report? why she is damn'd if she's but thought
> A Whore, much more reported to be so.
> By all the horrid Fiends that punish Lust,
> And by the black Concupiscence of Hell,
> I'll tumble her from the Throne into a Dungeon. . . .

Again, the wicked and unscrupulous Lady Blunt, like the
Countess of Nottingham in the earlier tragedy, resembles the
viragos of the heroic drama, and further traces of that genre
may be found in some exclamatory apostrophes and elaborate
similes. In *The Innocent Usurper*, Lady Jane Grey is again a
victim of circumstance, a woman faced with a cruel dilemma,

and the situation is genuinely tragic. But here we have a sentimental dwelling on the joys of married love, and here too we
have one of Banks's recurring clichés (common also in Dryden,
Lee, and other tragic dramatists), the longing of the great for
the humble and happy lot of the peasant. Lady Jane would
'descend from this disturbed high mountain', and fly with her
husband to blissful obscurity:

> In Shepherds Clothes let thee and I repair,
> To some lone Vale, like Tempe's Golden Bowers,
> To Love away the Day, and Charm the tedious Hours.

The Innocent Usurper, which was written about 1683–4, was
stopped in rehearsal by 'some civil powers of the Stage', no
doubt because the theme of a Protestant usurper was thought
to bear too closely on the Duke of Monmouth and the question
of the succession. Banks was equally unlucky with *The Island
Queens*, which was banned in 1684, presumably because it, too,
raised the question of a Catholic successor. The plot of this
impressive tragedy, in which Queen Elizabeth reluctantly signs
a warrant for the execution of Mary Queen of Scots, bears a
general resemblance to that of *The Innocent Usurper*. Whatever
reservations may be made about Banks as a writer, he had a
true conception of a tragic situation, and a greater ability to
work it out than most of his contemporaries.

Of all the Restoration dramatists Otway[1] went nearest to
obeying consistently the injunction to look into his heart and
write. Dryden was more apt to look into Ovid, and Lee trusted
to a self-engendered excitement to bring along with it a rush of
words. But in *Don Carlos*, *The Orphan*, and *Venice Preserved* it is
evident that Otway proceeded, in Johnson's words, 'by consulting nature in his own breast', and that for the most part he
brought back a true report. Of those three tragedies, all

---

[1] Thomas Otway (1652–85) was born at Trotton in Sussex, where his father
was curate. He was educated at Winchester College and Christ Church, Oxford,
but left the university without taking a degree. After failing as an actor in one of
Mrs. Behn's plays, he began to write for the theatre, and his second play, the
rhymed heroic tragedy *Don Carlos* (1676), was a resounding success. His first
comedy, *Friendship in Fashion* (1678), met with 'general applause', and about this
time Otway fell hopelessly in love with the actress Elizabeth Barry, who was
Rochester's mistress. He now obtained a commission in the army, and in 1678–9
saw some military service in Flanders. When he came back to the stage in 1680
with *The Orphan*, Mrs. Barry had the part of Monimia, and she was to play Belvidera two years later in *Venice Preserved*. Otway died, apparently in poverty, at the
age of 33.

favourite plays in their own day, and the two last surviving to delight many generations of playgoers, only *Venice Preserved* can be put among the enduring English tragedies, and even so, only with some misgivings. The rhymed tragedy of *Don Carlos*, with the amorous king married to the woman whom the son had intended for his own bride (as if the King in *Hamlet* had married Ophelia), suffers to some extent from an improbable situation: Carlos is allowed by his father to take some most unlikely liberties with the young Queen. But the play has dignity and restraint where most of Otway's contemporaries would have had neither, and it has many touches of natural feeling. Otway showed that rhyme did not necessarily lead to rant, and the tone of this tragedy comes nearer to Racine than is usual among English dramatists. If he was already in love with Mrs. Barry the actress, who became the mistress of his patron Rochester, Otway may indeed have consulted his own breast for the feelings of Don Carlos, and in his development of the entire situation. That situation is one in which 'all is to be endured, nothing done', and Otway's tendency to spin out the scenes between Carlos and the Queen ('*Goes to the door, stops, and turns back again*', etc.) makes the feeling of inhibited action even more oppressive.

In *The Orphan* he found, if not a stronger situation, one which had richer possibilities of development. But again the effect is weakened by the excessive demands on our credulity. That two brothers should love the same girl (Monimia) and that one (Castalio) should secretly marry her, is a promising opening for a tragedy. That the other brother (Polydore), not knowing that Castalio is married to Monimia and overhearing him arranging to go to her chamber in the early hours of the morning, should assume that he is making this assignation as a lover and not as a husband, is possible enough; but that he should then succeed in substituting himself for Castalio, and that Castalio on arriving at Monimia's window should be dismissed by her maid, who mistakes him for Polydore, has the sort of implausibility—night and darkness notwithstanding—which no audience should be asked to accept. The early critic who remarked on what a deal of trouble might have been spared by a farthing's worth of candlelight was fully entitled to his sneer. Some of the subsequent developments, too, depend upon the almost sublime stupidity of Monimia's brother Chamont, and in general the plot turns upon a succession of misunderstandings. The effect of this is to make the tragedy at once precarious and painful: precarious, because two or three words would have prevented it from ever happening, and painful, because the characters are helpless victims of circumstance. Otway is rightly praised for his pathos, his power to fill the eyes with tears; yet Hazlitt's objection that in *The Orphan* there is little else than 'this voluptuous effeminacy of sentiment and maw-kish distress, which strikes directly at the root of that mental fortitude and heroic cast of thought which alone makes tragedy endurable', is well founded. Tragedy here is a melo-dious hopelessness, a passionate dwelling upon private griefs, a mournful threnody of broken hearts: its significance is little more than 'Alas, how easily things go wrong!' Yet, when we remember when he wrote and for whom he wrote, Otway may be praised for his touching simplicity, and for his avoidance in general of that declamatory utterance which describes rather than expresses emotion.

The writers of Restoration tragedy continually confront us with emotional conflicts and dilemmas in which we are either not interested, or in which we simply cannot believe. It is an indication of Otway's firmer grasp of reality that the dilemma in which Jaffier finds himself in *Venice Preserved* is both credible and distressingly actual. The seriousness of the conflict is largely due to the permanency of Jaffier's relationships, on the one side with Pierre his old friend, and on the other with Belvidera his faithful and loving wife. With Settle—or, for that matter, with Dryden—we are too often asked to feel con-cern about the hero's passion for some woman he has known for less than twenty-four hours: Otway prefers to deal in hus-bands and wives, and the gain in emotional integrity is in-calculable. Even in this fine play (which reflects the grim political situation of 1681) there are occasional lapses into abject nonsense, as when, near the end, Pierre asks Jaffier to do some justice to his memory, and Jaffier exclaims:

> . . . thy wishes shall be satisfi'd;
> I have a Wife, and she shall bleed, my Child too
> Yield up his little Throat, and all t'appease thee.

No one has ever questioned the power of 'moving Otway' to touch the heart; but his domestic tragedy suffers from the inevitable tendency of its kind to become merely harrowing. He had little of Dryden's intellectual range or of his interest in general ideas; he was interested primarily in personal relationships, and the very closeness with which he clings to his tragic theme, and works it out in the lives of individuals to its sad conclusion, precludes the possibility of relief. (The abject comic scenes in *Venice Preserved*, in which Antonio the senator is a satirical portrait of Shaftesbury, provide not relief, but distraction.) Otway's three other tragedies, *Alcibiades*, a rhymed heroic play, *Titus and Berenice*, an adaptation of Racine's *Bérénice*, and *The History and Fall of Caius Marius*, in which he went to Plutarch for the life of Marius and joined it to *Romeo and Juliet*, hardly added much to his reputation but contributed something to his popularity, more especially with 'the fair ones who in judgment sit'.

The minor tragic drama of the period is a bourne from which the few travellers who venture at all usually return as quickly as possible. When we do find a tragedy that holds the attention, it usually does so by dealing with a theme that had some relevance to contemporary life, so avoiding that air of unreality which hangs like a cloud over the whole genre. One such play is Robert Gould's[1] *The Rival Sisters* (1695), a domestic tragedy in which a young man who is in love with the younger of two daughters is tricked by her father into marrying the elder sister. This play, which is partly in rhyme but singularly free from rant, concentrates upon the disastrous consequences that flow naturally and inevitably from the father's deception. Enforced marriage, either as the main or as a subsidiary theme, appears in many of the more interesting tragedies and comedies of the period, and is clearly related to the contemporary situation in which marriages were normally arranged by parents, with or without the acquiescence of their children. After so many plays in which we are invited to interest ourselves in the problems of oriental tyrants, lustful queens, and ambitious statesmen, a change to the life that the Restoration audience knew is indeed welcome.

Gould's tragedy was almost certainly based on Shirley's

---

[1] Robert Gould (1660?–1709?) was for some time a servant of the Earl of Dorset, and probably held other similar employments. He wrote a good deal of bitter satirical verse, such as *Love Given Over* and *A Satire against the Playhouse*. His tragedy, *The Rival Sisters*, with a prologue and epilogue by Durfey, and some music by Purcell, was produced in the autumn of 1695.

The Maid's Revenge. Other plays of the earlier drama were altered in varying degrees to suit the taste of the new age. Rochester produced a new version of Fletcher's *Valentinian*, Settle altered *Philaster*, and George Powell made *Bonduca* into an opera. Several of Shakespeare's tragedies were similarly adapted and 'regularized' for the Restoration stage: because of their relevance to contemporary politics Tate produced versions of *Richard II* and *Coriolanus*, and Crowne turned *2 Henry VI* into *The Misery of Civil War*. Other adaptations, such as Ravenscroft's *Titus Andronicus* (1678), Shadwell's *Timon of Athens* (1678), and Tate's *King Lear* (1681), were carried out in the honest belief that the original play was susceptible of considerable improvement. Tate, who was worried about the lack of poetic justice in Shakespeare's *Lear*, provided his version with a happy ending, and this gave such general satisfaction that for the next hundred years and more Cordelia, in Johnson's words, 'always retired with victory and felicity'. Shadwell, who took little more from Shakespeare's *Timon* than the basic situation and characters, claimed that he had 'made it into a play'. This provocative remark should not be allowed to conceal the fact that he had written a tragic satire of genuine merit. By adding two female characters, Evandra, the generous and faithful courtesan who comes to Timon's aid when he is ruined, and Melissa, the mercenary lady whom he is about to marry and who promptly deserts him when the crash comes, Shadwell arrived at a typically Restoration satire on the mercenary marriages so frequently contracted among the upper and middle classes of the period. His corresponding glorification of the kept mistress is also in keeping with the spirit of the 1670s.

The one outstanding writer of tragedy in the last decade of the century is Thomas Southerne.[1] His first tragedy, *The Loyal Brother* (1682), was a political play, in which Ismail, 'a villainous favourite', represented Shaftesbury, and the virtuous prince Tachmas, the Duke of York. Southerne, however,

---

[1] Thomas Southerne (1659–1746) was born in Ireland, educated at Trinity College, Dublin, and entered at the Middle Temple, London, in 1678. His first play, a tragedy with an anti-Whig bias, was produced in 1682; it was followed by the much more interesting domestic drama, *The Disappointment*, two years later. In 1685 he obtained a commission in the army, but his military career ended with the abdication of James II in 1688. He now turned again to the stage and wrote several successful comedies and tragedies, his last play, a tragedy, being produced as late as 1726. He died, 'the poets' Nestor', in his 86th year.

was to do much better than this. He was praised by a contemporary for his knowledge of 'the way and disposition of mankind', and that knowledge acted as a steadying influence on
The Fatal Marriage (1694), which he described on the title-page
as 'a play'. With a better tradition behind him Southerne
would almost certainly have been a better dramatist. In the
early acts of this tragedy Isabella suffers with real dignity, and
her gradual yielding to Villeroy in the face of circumstances
is credibly motivated and movingly expressed. It is only when
the final crisis is reached—when, in fact, the tragedy is at its
height—that Southerne loses control and proceeds to give us
the usual lather of rhetoric instead of the words that could
alone convey to us the full tragedy of the situation. This happens again and again in the tragedy of the period: the foot is
fatally placed on the accelerator and the engine merely races.
In the highly capable hands of Mrs. Barry (Southerne admits
that he would despair of ever being able to express what his
play owed to her acting) the ravings of Isabella in the last act
may have been deeply moving; but if so, Southerne had provided no more than a libretto for her operatic effects. In
Oronooko (1696) the sufferings of the noble slave justify his passion and his fine scorn for the devilish Christians who have
betrayed him: we have a sense of listening to an indictment,
based on facts which are adequate to the intense feelings expressed. The mercenary planters, too, provide an effective
contrast with the nobility of Oronooko. But in the last act,
again, the torrent of words tends to drown all natural feeling,
although it is only fair to add that the contemporary critic
already quoted picked out this act for special praise. In both
those plays Southerne supplied a comic sub-plot to comply with
'the present humour of the Town', and Congreve, who wrote
the epilogue for *Oronooko*, made it clear that the comic stuff
was inserted to please the audience, not the dramatist:

> Your different Tastes divide our Poet's Cares:
> One Foot the Sock, t'other the Buskin wears:
> Thus while he strives to please, he's forc'd to do't,
> Like Volscius, hip-hop, in a single Boot.

Yet the comic scenes are not bad of their kind, and do surprisingly little damage to the tragic effect: in both plays Southerne
has finished with comedy when the action begins to move to

its tragic close, and his comedy is often of the Shakespearian kind that merely shifts for the moment our attitude to the tragic events and lets us see them through the eyes of some uninvolved character. This awareness of a neutral world with its own concerns deepens rather than disperses the tragic impression. An earlier play, *The Disappointment* (1684), also styled 'a play', has tragic implications. Dealing with an unsuccessful attempt by a libertine to debauch the chaste Erminia, it can hardly be called a problem play, for there is really no problem; it is, however, a domestic drama with considerable traces of sentimentalism. Here, as in all his work, Southerne's strong hold on reality and his knowledge of the way of the world give the play a psychological interest that is absent from the serious drama of most of his contemporaries.

This interest is certainly not present in *The Mourning Bride* (1697) of Congreve. Dedicated to the future Queen Anne, this once famous play is now no more than the mausoleum of a dead taste; it is more a tragic thriller than a tragedy, curiously mingling Jacobean violence with a neo-classical calm. What can be praised is Congreve's measured yet intelligently varied blank verse, which shows to advantage in the set descriptive passages (including Almeria's speech in ii. i, which Johnson thought 'the most poetical paragraph' in the whole of English poetry), but also stirs the heavy hangings of the dialogue with a faint breath of life. *The Mourning Bride* met with almost universal acclamation, but Congreve brought nothing new to tragedy: in so far as he deserved his great reputation it was because he did rather better what had been done over and over again.

(v)

Davenant's *The Siege of Rhodes* was not only of some importance for the genesis of the heroic play; it was also the first English opera. The entertainment that Davenant mounted in the autumn of 1656 at Rutland House, when stage plays were still banned, was cautiously described by him as 'a Representation by the Art of Prospective in Scenes and the Story sung in Recitative Musick'. The music has not survived, but it seems certain that the whole play was sung from beginning to end, and in this respect it was more completely an opera in the modern sense of the word than almost anything that followed it in the next forty years. For something comparable we must turn to Henry Purcell's *Dido and Aeneas* (the libretto by Nahum Tate), which was written about 1689 for private performance by the girls of a Chelsea boarding-school. The operas of Shadwell, Dryden, Settle, and others were partly spoken and partly sung, and may best be described by the term 'dramatic opera'.

Various factors affected the development of this characteristically English hybrid: the true-born English opera was influenced by the old Court masques and by contemporary French and Italian opera; but it was also to a large extent the haphazard result of introducing more and more songs into comedy, and spectacular chorus scenes of 'zambras' and priests officiating in temples into the heroic play and tragedy. The development of opera in the 1670s owed a good deal to Charles II. While in exile he had acquired a taste for French music, and whether he actually enjoyed opera or not he almost certainly felt that it was a form of entertainment that would give lustre to his Court. He encouraged the French opera players to visit London, he appointed Louis Grabu to be Master of the King's Music, and he patronized such composers as Robert Cambert, who directed the performance of Crowne's *Calisto* when it was acted at Court by ladies and gentlemen in 1675. Most of his subjects, however, were a good deal less well instructed. All through this period the word 'opera' was used in England to designate any play, comic or tragic, which had more than the usual amount of incidental music and songs, dancing, spectacular scenery, and 'machines'; so that in the early eighteenth century we find George Granville protesting that 'to introduce Singing and Dancing, by Head and Shoulders, no way relative to the Action, does not turn a Play into an Opera: though that Title is now promiscuously given to every Farce sprinkled here and there with a Song and a Dance'. Most of the operas of the Restoration period were performed at the Dorset Garden theatre, which became especially associated with plays offering spectacular effects.

For a contemporary definition of opera we can go (as Johnson did when compiling his Dictionary) to Dryden's Preface to his *Albion and Albanius* (1685), where he is consciously laying down the rules for a new 'kind':

An Opera is a poetical Tale or Fiction, represented by Vocal and Instrumental Musick, adorn'd with Scenes, Machines, and Dancing.

The suppos'd Persons of this musical Drama are generally supernatural, as Gods, and Goddesses, and Heroes, which at least are
descended from them, and are in due time to be adopted into
their Number. The Subject therefore being extended beyond the
Limits of Humane Nature, admits of that sort of marvellous and sur-
prizing conduct which is rejected in other Plays.

Here the influence of the Jacobean and Caroline masque is
obvious. With the exception of Albion (Charles II) and
Albanius (James II) all the characters in Dryden's opera are
classical divinities or allegorical figures (Augusta, Thamesis,
Democracy, Chorus of Cities, etc.). Shadwells' *Psyche* (1675—
cleverly travestied by Thomas Duffet), Charles Dávenant's
Circe (1677), and Durfey's *Cinthia and Endimion* (1697) are further examples of the opera based on a classical theme; but
more popular still were the operatic versions of *Macbeth* and
The Tempest, and Settle's pantomime-like entertainment, *The
Fairy Queen*, based on *A Midsummer Night's Dream*, with music
by Purcell. Perhaps the nearest to collaboration between poet
and composer occurred with *King Arthur* (1692); but even there
Dryden grumbles at having had to 'cramp' his verses and 'make
them rugged to the reader' to comply with the musical demands
of his collaborator Purcell. For all his conventional tributes to
music and musicians Dryden could never bring himself to take
opera quite seriously, or even allow that any man of sense could
do so. In the prologue to *Albion and Albanius*, after telling the
audience that in the past they have failed to respond to wit and
satire, he continues:

> Wee now prescribe, like Doctors in despair,
> The Diet your weak appetites can bear.
> Since hearty Beef and Mutton will not do,
> Here's Julep dance, Ptisan of Song and show:
> Give you strong Sense, the Liquor is too heady;
> You're come to Farce, that's Asses milk, already.
> Some hopeful Youths there are, of callow Wit,
> Who one Day may be Men, if Heav'n think fit;
> Sound may serve such, ere they to Sense are grown;
> Like leading strings, till they can walk alone.

In taking this low view of opera Dryden was only being a
typical Englishman, and his attitude differs hardly at all
from that of Lord Chesterfield in the eighteenth century, who
told his son: 'Whenever I go to an opera, I leave my sense and

reason at the door with my half guinea, and deliver myself up
to my eyes and my ears.'

In such circumstances it is not surprising that as literature
most of the operas of Dryden and his contemporaries are almost
unreadable: no doubt they would have been even less readable
if the words and the music had been more closely integrated.
Here and there we come upon a memorable song, such as
Shadwell's 'Arise, ye subterranean winds' in the operatic
Tempest, or Dryden's 'Fairest isle, all isles excelling' in *King
Arthur*; but in between there are stretches of inanity. How far
Dryden was from understanding the nature of opera may be
seen from *The State of Innocence* (1677), a dramatic rendering of
Paradise Lost which never reached the stage. Almost the whole
piece is in rhyming pentameters recalling at times the atmo-
sphere of a heroic play, and Adam has a long and interesting
discussion with Raphael and Gabriel on the problem of free
will and necessity. In Act V there is a domestic quarrel, as
realistic as heroic couplets will allow, between Adam and Eve,
with the doting Adam finally relenting in a manner rather
reminiscent of Fondlewife in *The Old Bachelor*. In some of
Dryden's plays the characters are not real enough; but here
Adam and Eve are superfluously and disconcertingly real, a
London citizen and his wife mixing on familiar terms with
angels and archangels. So far as opera is concerned—for that
is what Dryden called *The State of Innocence*—he seems to have
believed that it could be so described by reason of the incidental
music and of the scenes and machines, which were here so
elaborate that the company at the Theatre Royal may well
have considered them too expensive to mount. By the time
he came to write *King Arthur* Dryden's approach to opera had
become better informed; but so long as the musical education
of English audiences remained as low as it was there could be
little hope for opera as a popular entertainment. For such
audiences, as for those of the 1740s, Pope's words were only too
applicable:

> Others the Syren Sisters warble round,
> And empty heads console with empty sound.

III

DRAMA (II)

ALTHOUGH the comic dramatists of the Restoration took some of their plots from the plays of Plautus and Terence, and many more from the comic drama of Spain and France, it is now well understood that Restoration comedies were in the main a natural development from those (or, more precisely, some of those) written in England before the closing of the theatres. After 1660 the comedies of Shakespeare were comparatively neglected, and had little effect on the new drama; but those of Jonson and of Beaumont and Fletcher were frequently revived, and greatly influenced in their different ways the work of Dryden and most of his contemporaries. Shadwell was the chief admirer and imitator of Jonson, but he made his plays more palatable to Restoration audiences by providing, as best he could, the gay young fashionable couples who were now thought almost essential to a modern comedy, and by not concentrating exclusively on satirical types. In the plays of Beaumont and Fletcher, and in those of Brome and Shirley in the next generation, Restoration dramatists found many proto-types for their gentlemen of pleasure and the witty young women who pleased them. Mirabel, Rosalura, and Lillia-Bianca in *The Wild-Goose Chase*, Don John in *The Chances*, Lord Bonville in Shirley's *Hyde Park*, and Celestina in *The Lady of Pleasure* (to name only a few characters at random) would all have found themselves perfectly at home in a Restoration comedy. We have Dryden's word for it that the plays of Beaumont and Fletcher were 'the most pleasant and frequent entertainments of the Stage; two of theirs being acted through the year for one of Shakespeare's or Jonson's'. The gaiety of their comedies and their flair for reproducing (even in blank verse) the witty and liber-tine conversation of gentlemen had a strong appeal, and the pathos and romantic-heroic sentiments in their serious plays were also suited to the taste of the new age. In contrast, Shakespeare and Jonson seemed to the Restoration playgoer rather old-fashioned, and their language was often obsolete

and frequently 'incorrect'. In his examen of *The Silent Woman*
Dryden expressed the opinion that Jonson had managed 'the
conversation of Gentlemen in the persons of Truewit and his
Friends, with more gayety, ayre, and freedom than in the rest
of his Comedies'; but, as he said of Truewit in his 'Defence of the
Epilogue', 'the best of his discourse is drawn, not from the
knowledge of the Town, but Books; and, in short, he would
be a fine Gentleman, in an University'. Similarly, Shakespeare
'show'd the best of his skill in his Mercutio'; but Dryden,
thinking no doubt of the vastly improved rake of Restoration
comedy who 'stunn'd with his giddy larum half the town',
considered Mercutio to be an 'exceeding harmless' young man.
Not only, then, do we find in the plays of Beaumont and
Fletcher, Brome, Shirley, and others an adumbration of the
typical characters of Restoration comedy, but in their critical
attitude to marriage, to the 'cits', to the boredom of country
life and much else they anticipate most of the points that were
made— so often!—after 1660.

Since comedy is traditionally a Dionysiac revel, expressing
the unrestrained and unregenerate nature of man, it might be
expected that from its first beginnings Restoration comedy
would show that libertine spirit which was to become so characteristic of it, and which reached some sort of climax in the 1670s.
Yet for the first few years, although it was anti-Puritan from the
start, the tone remained for the most part surprisingly decent.
In *Pandora* (1664) Sir William Killigrew aimed to give his
audience 'what he does think will please the present age'; and
his play is largely concerned with platonic love and the reformation of a rake. This is achieved by the virtuous ladies of the
Court taking a wild young man in hand and inducing him to
fall in love with Pandora, who has vowed never to marry. This,
then, is not just a comedy in which the rake reforms in the
fifth act, but one in which his education begins in Act II, and
proceeds (with one notable lapse when he makes his protest
about being 'fool'd into the Platonick pound') to the desired
end. *Pandora* seems to be addressed primarily to the female part
of the audience; and in the sensible and discreet conversation
of the Court ladies we might almost be listening to the voices of
Mrs. Montagu and Hannah More. Killigrew, however, was
rather behind the times with his platonic ladies. Even before
the closing of the theatres, in such plays as Davenant's *The*

Wits and Suckling's *Aglaura*, the platonic mode had been subjected to some good-natured ridicule, and not long after the appearance of *Pandora* Sir William's brother, Thomas Killigrew,[1] produced his anti-platonic and anti-romantic comedy, *The Parson's Wedding*, at his own theatre. Tom Killigrew was not in any sense a modest man, and the fact that he held up his comedy until the autumn of 1664 (when it was also published) may indicate that he had waited until he thought the time was ripe for his ribaldry. Pepys, who had not himself seen it, noted in his diary that a friend had told him 'what an obscene, loose play this "Parson's Wedding" is, that is acted by nothing but women at the King's house'. This comedy of sex antagonism and sex attraction, played out between two young gallants on the one side and a rich young widow and her niece Mistress Pleasant on the other, is not so much salacious as free-spoken. On any reckoning the Parson is a coarse brute, and Lady Love-all, 'an old Stallion-Hunting Widow', is his female counterpart. But the indecency is frank and open; there is no mincing of words, but there is little or no *double entendre*. Yet the effect of such a vigorously bawdy comedy on the play-goer must have been to lower the standards of decency. When such a play establishes itself on the stage, the appetite grows by what it feeds on; restraint and decorum begin to appear insipid, and the next comedy, and the next, must carry the process a step further. Before, and for some years after, *The Parson's Wedding*, however, most of the new comedies remained comparatively innocent. Two dominant types of play emerged between 1660 and 1665: comedy of the humours kind, usually satirizing the Puritans and life during the Commonwealth period, and comedy of intrigue, usually based on plots taken from such Spanish dramatists as Calderón and Moreto, and, to a lesser extent, Lope de Vega.

---

[1] Thomas Killigrew (1612–83) was a brother of Sir William Killigrew and of Dr. Henry Killigrew, D.D. (the father of the young poetess commemorated in Dryden's ode). In 1647 he joined Prince Charles in exile, and remained a favourite of the new King after the Restoration. Besides being granted a patent to form a company of players and erect a playhouse, he was given several minor offices, and in 1673 succeeded Sir Henry Herbert as Master of the Revels. There is no evidence that *The Parson's Wedding* was acted before the closing of the theatres in 1642; but (even in the presumably revised version of 1664) there are enough references to events in 1639–40 to suggest that the play was written about that time.

John Tatham's[1] *The Rump* (1660), 'acted many times with great applause', was perhaps the earliest of those satirical comedies which turned to account the hatred of the old regime. With feelings running high no subtlety was required, and in his virulent attacks on Lambert, Lady Lambert, Fleetwood, Desborough, and Hewson, Tatham has none to offer. In 1660 he could not fail to hit the mark. A more reasonable satire was Cowley's *Cutter of Coleman Street* (1661), a revised and modernized version of *The Guardian*, which he had written in 1641 for the entertainment of the young Prince Charles when he was passing through Cambridge. The indifferent reception this comedy met with in 1661 throws some light on the taste of Cavalier audiences immediately after the Restoration. From the lengthy preface which Cowley wrote in defence of his play, it appears that it had a poor first night, and that it never became popular. It was thought to be 'a piece intended for abuse and satire against the King's party'; and if it was so thought, one can only suppose that the returned Cavaliers expected nothing but eulogy from their playwrights. Objection was taken in particular to Colonel Jolly, 'a gentleman whose estate was confiscated in the late troubles', and who was portrayed as something less than a perfect gentleman in his treatment of his niece, whose estate he, in his turn, tried to appropriate. No doubt he also gave offence by his willingness to marry a rich soap-boiler's widow, the canting Mrs. Barebottle, to repair his shattered fortunes. Well written and ingeniously constructed though it is, *Cutter of Coleman Street* was too much concerned with 'low' characters to please the Restoration audience, and in its meaty dialogue it looks back to *Bartholomew Fair* rather than forward to the indolent and fashionable conversation of Etherege's comedies. In the character of Puny, however, 'a young, rich, brisk fop, pretending to extraordinary wit', and elaborating almost every sentence he utters with a comical simile, Cowley started something that was to have a long life in Restoration comedy.

In *The Committee* (1662) Sir Robert Howard found part of

---

[1] John Tatham (*c.* 1610?–64) probably wrote for the Red Bull playhouse before the closing of the theatres, and composed other dramatic pieces either not meant for production or intended for private performance. *The Rump* was first performed 'at the Private House in Dorset Court' in 1660; Mrs. Behn produced a revised version called *The Roundheads* (*c.* Dec. 1681). Tatham wrote pageants for the Lord Mayor's shows from 1657 to 1664, at which time he was presumably City Poet.

his theme in the activities of a sequestration committee in the Commonwealth period. This play owes much of its vitality to its portrayal of middle-class vulgarity, its Jonsonian types such as Mrs. Day and the clerk Obadaiah, and its comic Irish servant Teague (played to perfection by John Lacy); but its two high-spirited Cavaliers involved with two attractive young women gave this comedy the focus on persons of quality necessary to please a Restoration audience. Howard and his like could afford to be merry in 1662 about the discredited Puritans, but it is to his credit that he should have written such a good-natured play, gay and lively without ever becoming indecent, and satirical without losing its tone of easy contempt. *The Committee* remained popular for many years, as did John Lacy's *The Old Troop* (1663), a farcical romp of a play, more remarkable for its good humour than its wit. The most Jonsonian of the early Restoration satirists was John Wilson.[1] *The Cheats* (1663), with its rogues and gulls, became a stock play, and ran through several editions; it is a ribald satire on cant and hypocrisy, robust rather than subtle in its wit and humour, and verging often on the fantastical. There is no recorded performance of Wilson's other comedy, *The Projectors* (printed in 1665), but it is at least an interesting play to read. It has much of Jonson's learned fooling, and if it failed to obtain performance on the stage that may have been because its erudite and fanciful clap-trap was better fitted to amuse a university or Inns-of-Court audience than the *beau monde* of the London theatre.

The interest taken by Charles II in Spanish drama had undoubtedly some effect on the genesis of the comedy of intrigue on the Restoration stage. The King encouraged Sir Samuel Tuke[2] to produce an English version of Calderón's *Los Empeños de Seis Horas*; and shortly before his death he put into the hands of John Crowne a copy of Moreto's *No puede ser*,

---

[1] John Wilson (1627?–96) was called to the bar, c. 1649, and became Recorder of Londonderry, c. 1681. He published in 1684 *A Discourse on Monarchy*, vindicating the claims of the Duke of York to the succession, and in 1685 a pindaric poem on his coronation. His only popular play, *The Cheats*, went into at least four editions in his lifetime.

[2] Sir Samuel Tuke (d. 1674) fought for Charles I at Marston Moor and elsewhere, and was one of the defenders of Colchester in 1648. He was knighted and made a baronet in 1664. *The Adventures of Five Hours* remained popular on the Restoration stage; it was revived in 1705, when it was said to have been 'not Acted these Six Years'.

already used by Sir Thomas St. Serfe for his comedy of *Tarugo's Wiles* (1667), and now to be the source of Crowne's *Sir Courtly Nice* (1685). Tuke's comedy, *The Adventures of Five Hours*, produced early in 1663, was one of the major successes of the revived theatre. Pepys left the first performance feeling that this play was 'the best, for the variety and the most excellent contrivance of the plot to the very end, that ever I saw, or think I ever shall'. He noted, too, that it did not depend for its effect on ribaldry, an observation which suggests that he was conscious that some of the other comedies he had seen during the past two years did. In his epilogue to *The Adventures of Five Hours* Tuke showed himself to be aware that some, at least, among his audience would find its decency and modesty rather flat:

> A Fopp! in this brave Licentious Age,
> To bring his musty Morals on the Stage!
> .   .   .   .   Why, Vertue now is Impudence;
> And such another modest Play would blast
> Our new Stage, and put your Palates out of Tast.

Although it turns on a series of ingenious and plausible accidents and stratagems, and depends for a good deal of its laughter on the ridiculous antics of the servants, Tuke's comedy shows a willingness to take life seriously that is not often to be found in the more flippant comedies of the 1670s. The undoubted success of this play at the time of its production and for some years to come seems to prove that the Restoration audience did not yet require those 'gross and violent stimulants' and that perpetual search for novelty that became more and more necessary as audiences grew more sophisticated.

The English Monsieur of Dryden's brother-in-law, James Howard, was produced in 1663. Until recently it was thought that this play belonged to the year 1666, and Howard has therefore been denied the little meed of praise that was his due in developing the pattern of Restoration comedy. His humour-type characters (Frenchlove, an Englishman who thinks nothing good that is not French, and Vaine, who 'to gain the reputation of a debauch belies himself and all women he knows') had some novelty in 1663; but the scenes between Wellbred and the gay young widow, Lady Wealthy, have real historical importance, for they precede by almost a year the

similar scenes between Etherege's Sir Frederick Frollick and *his*
widow. Wellbred is something of a rake and an inveterate
gambler, and he and his friend Comely have a pair of kept
mistresses on their hands whom they are trying to marry by a
trick to Frenchlove and Vaine—a recurring situation in later
Restoration comedy. But Wellbred has the easy confidence
and the indolent good manners of a gentleman, and he is not
irreclaimable. *The English Monsieur*, like the plays of Howard's
two brothers, is the work of a talented amateur; the plot is
comparatively simple, and such pleasure as the play affords
comes mainly from the easy conversation and light repartee. The
tone is not indecent, and there is one surprisingly moral development: Comely falls in love with a farmer's pretty daughter and
seems never to think of her in any other terms than those of
marriage (this, of course, may be Howard's joke), but she, in
the broadest west-country dialect, declares that she will remain
faithful to her rustic lover William. The decency of this play
is the more significant in view of Howard's second comedy, *All
Mistaken, or The Mad Couple* (1667?), where a rather foolish
main plot of cross-purposes and misunderstanding is relieved
by the impudent antics and libertine talk of the mad couple,
Philidor and Mirida (acted by Hart and the young Nell Gwyn).
Mirida has a fat lover who is driven by her ridicule to try to
reduce his weight by purging; the consequences need not be
particularized, but at one point a stage direction reads: 'He
runs round and sometimes goes out to untruss.' It has always
been assumed that Philidor and Mirida are a coarsened version
of Dryden's Celadon and Florimel in *Secret Love*; but if, as
there is some reason to suppose, the correct date for Howard's
comedy is 1665, the debt would not be on Howard's side, but
on Dryden's.

Among the innocent comedies of intrigue was *Flora's Vagaries*
(1663), by Richard Rhodes, a student of Christ Church. With
Nell Gwyn taking over the part of the 'mad wench' Flora, it was
frequently revived, and in 1666 was one of the comedies given
at Court. Another early comedy of cross-purposes and
mistakes, with little humour and no indecency, was *Elvira*,
a rendering by George Digby, Earl of Bristol, of Calderón's
No siempre lo Peor es Cierto. According to Downes, Digby was
the author of two other comedies taken from Calderón and
acted between 1662 and 1665, '*Tis Better than it was* and *Worse*

and Worse; but if these were ever printed they have not survived. Spanish influence is to be seen again in Thomas Porter's
The Carnival (*c.* 1663), a high-spirited romantic comedy, with
some farcical elements, and in the irresponsible Don Felices and
Miranda an early example of the gay couple. A serious note
is struck when Ferdinando, betrothed to Beatrice, becomes
temporarily infatuated with Elvira; and Porter's honest handling of this situation—a genuine infatuation, and not an affair
of gallantry—marks him off from the writers of comedy who
were soon to follow.

The Spanish influence was most marked in the first few
years of the Restoration. Much more important and prolonged
was that of Molière, whose first work was produced in Paris
just before 1660. As his comedies became available, they were
continually rifled by English dramatists, who were indebted
to him for many of their plots and characters. But Molière's plots
were rarely complex enough for an English comedy, and the
English dramatists showed their ingenuity by combining the
plots of two, or even three, different plays into one. As for his
characters and his dialogue, they almost always became unmistakably English when they crossed the Channel; but if
much of the spirit of Molière had evaporated, the English
dramatist could hardly fail to profit from his unfailing sense
of dramatic relevance, and to learn from him (as has been said
of Wycherley) 'how to focus his implications'. Although Molière
was the main quarry from which the writers of comedy obtained their material, they also went to the plays of Pierre
Corneille, Thomas Corneille, Philippe Quinault, and several
others, and borrowed freely too from the French writers of
romances. But those Restoration dramatists, who, like Dryden,
were taxed with stealing all their plays, could usually reply in
Dryden's own words:

'Tis true, that where ever I have lik'd any story in a Romance,
Novel, or forreign Play, I have made no difficulty, nor ever shall,
to take the foundation of it, to build it up, and to make it proper
for the English Stage. . . . But these little criticks do not well consider
what is the work of a Poet, and what the graces of a Poem: the Story
is the least part of either: I mean the foundation of it, before it
is modell'd by the art of him who writes it; who formes it with more
care, by exposing only the beautiful parts of it to view, than a skilful
Lapidary sets a Jewel.

By 1665, at all events, the English writers of comedy had laid the foundations for a comedy of humours and a comedy of intrigue that would continue to be written, with variations, for the next forty years or more. Tragi-comedies, too, with a romantic main plot and an anti-romantic sub-plot, remained popular for the rest of the century, and indicate either the conservative tastes of the English playgoer (for whom the world of Beaumont and Fletcher still held some sort of truth), or simply his muddle-headedness.

If we do not immediately associate Dryden with Restoration comedy, the explanation may be found in the wide range of his output, which tends to blur his achievement in any one dramatic species. Yet Dryden, who as a playwright always endeavoured to delight the age he lived in, wrote more than a dozen comedies and tragi-comedies between 1663 and 1694, and some of these were outstandingly successful. This is the more remarkable since he had decided as early as 1668 that he had no special genius for comedy: 'I want that gayety of humour which is required to it. My conversation is slow and dull; my humour Saturnine and reserv'd: In short, I am none of those who endeavour to break Jests in Company, or make reparties.' Yet if he had little wit in company, he could certainly break jests on paper, and if those jests and repartees were the result of deliberation, they have in their context the immediate effect of spontaneous wit. Unlike Etherege or Sedley, however, he stood rather apart from the carefree world of his comic rakes and was consequently portraying a way of life that he never really practised or accepted himself; and this, combined with the fact that he was consciously playing down to contemporary taste and morality, may account for the startling indecencies in some of his comedies.

The first of these was produced in February 1663. Although *The Wild Gallant* is a comedy of intrigue it is of native English growth, owing apparently nothing to Spanish influence, but drawing some of its material from the work of Brome, Fletcher, Shirley, Shakespeare, and Ben Jonson. The original audience appears to have disliked the play, but it was acted at Court, revised by Dryden, and produced again in 1669, and it ran through four printed editions in his lifetime. It was an influential play for the worst of reasons: what is new in this comedy is mainly its indecency and blasphemy. Dryden seems to have intended to shock, and the failure of *The Wild Gallant* in 1663 may have been partly due to the uneasiness of an audience not yet accustomed to the irreligion and libertinism that were later to become common enough, and for some time almost a *sine qua non* in comedy. As for the indecency, it is often of a vulgar kind (Constance stuffing a pillow under her clothes so as to appear pregnant), or of a farcical and fantastic kind (her father being persuaded that *he* is pregnant too). Loveby, again, is a gentleman of rather poor quality (his very name has a bourgeois sound): Dryden was not yet sufficiently familiar with fashionable society. He is much more successful with Loveby's landlady Frances, whose vulgar conversation is thoroughly idiomatic; and he gives us his earliest exercises in effective repartee, and in the airy impudence which so often provides the occasion for it. In Loveby and Constance, too, we have what is perhaps the earliest contemporary example of the gay young couple engaged in the high-spirited love-duel that was to become a permanent feature of Restoration comedy, and also the first example of the 'proviso scene', when Isabella states to Sir Timorous the terms on which she will consent to marry him.

The Rival Ladies, which followed rather more than a year later, is compounded of so many different elements that it is something of a dramatic hybrid. This play probably derives from Calderón's *Novelas ejemplares*, but it is at once romantic and anti-romantic, reminiscent of the tragi-comedy of Fletcher, and symptomatic of the coming of the heroic drama. As a transitional play it has considerable interest; but the old business of two girls disguised as page boys attending the man they both love, and sometimes finding themselves in situations to which their feminine courage is unequal, had grown stale from repetition. Dryden had taken pains over his plot, and had conducted his lovers 'through so many various Intrigues and Chances, as the Labouring Audience shall think them lost under every Billow'; but the characters themselves are so high-minded in their platonic love that we are only faintly concerned about what happens to them. *The Rival Ladies*, indeed, betrays some uncertainty of intention on Dryden's part, and suggests that he was finding it difficult at times to subscribe to the noble sentiments of his romantic lovers.

Three years later, however, he found a new formula, and in

Secret Love, or The Maiden Queen produced a play that not only delighted Charles II, who 'graced it with the title of his play', but also satisfied most contemporary playgoers. Dryden had reached what was for him a happy compromise, and had written a play with a 'serious' main plot of romantic love, and a comic underplot involving two anti-romantic lovers. *The Maiden Queen* is a Restoration version of Fletcherian tragi-comedy, and Dryden was to repeat the formula in two other successful plays, *Marriage-à-la-Mode* and *The Spanish Friar*. The young queen with a hopeless passion for one of her own sub-jects is a character of dignity and touching charm, and her situation gives occasion for several passages of melodious lament in flowing blank verse. The other characters in the 'serious' plot have little interest, and Philocles, torn between his love for Candiope and something very like love for the Queen, is hardly a character at all, but rather that member of the dra-matis personae whose function is to register those conflicting passions which the new heroic drama was making fashionable. The love-debates between the Queen and Philocles and between Philocles and Candiope slide naturally into the rhyming coup-lets of the heroic play, and they provide Dryden with frequent opportunities, which he always enjoys taking, for those general reflections on life that go beyond the immediate context. It was, however, the free-spoken couple, Celadon and Florimel, Dryden's Benedick and Beatrice, who most delighted the Res-toration audience. In his Preface to the play the dramatist paid his tribute to the excellent acting of the chief players, both serious and comic; and for Pepys, the performance of young Nell Gwyn in the part of Florimel was such that he thought he could never hope 'to see the like done again' by man or woman.

Later in the same year Dryden was to have an even greater success with *Sir Martin Mar-all*. Pepys, who saw it on the second night and on many later occasions, thought it 'the most entire piece of mirth . . . that certainly was ever writ'. According to Downes, the Duke of Newcastle handed to Dry-den a translation that he had made of Molière's *L'Étourdi*, and Dryden then adapted it for the English stage, characteristic-ally complicating the action by taking a good deal of additional material (for the theme of feigned innocence) from Quinault's *L'Amant indiscret*. This play owed a great deal to the comedian Nokes, who, as the blundering Sir Martin, created his most celebrated part. *Sir Martin Mar-all* is in the Jonsonian tradition, a comedy of intrigue with a scheming servant, relying more on humour than on wit, and with several well-defined comic characters who spend most of their time gulling or being gulled. As such it is not especially characteristic of Dryden's comedy. Before the year was out he gave the public a very different sort of entertainment, *The Tempest; or, The Enchanted Island,* an adaptation of Shakespeare's comedy he had written in collaboration with Sir William Davenant. Such adaptations have at least the value of showing what was required to satisfy contemporary taste. The parts of Shakespeare's quarrelling sailors were considerably enlarged, and this additional matter was apparently the work of Davenant. Caliban is given a sister whom Trincalo adopts as his wife, and to whom he refers on one occasion as 'my dear blubberlips'; two additional sailors, Mustacho and Ventoso, are introduced, and the parts of Stephano and Trincalo are largely rewritten. In his Preface to the play Dryden tells us that Davenant, 'a man of quick and piercing imagination', had realized that the play could be improved by 'the Counterpart to Shakespeare's Plot, namely, that of a Man who had never seen a Woman'. This brilliant notion was given to Dryden to develop, and it pleased him from the first moment he heard of it. 'I never writ any thing with more delight', he tells us. In order to carry out Davenant's plan the island was given two additional inhabitants, Hippolito, the rightful heir to the Dukedom of Mantua, and Dorinda, a sister to Miranda, whose function it was to fall in love with Hippolito. All three had been brought to the island by Prospero when he was banished from Milan, but he had somehow managed to keep his daughters and Hippolito in ignorance of each other's existence until the play begins. So Dryden has the standard two pairs of lovers which a Restoration audience expected, and he proceeds to exploit, often unpleasantly, their sexual inexperience, and to entangle them in the usual misunderstandings and jealousies. Dryden leering at innocence is in his least attractive vein. However shocking Restoration comedy may sometimes be, its characters are usually honest and outspoken; but here, and elsewhere, Dryden pays lip service to 'pretty innocence' while revelling in innuendo.

In April 1688, on the death of Davenant, Dryden was appointed Poet Laureate. Shortly afterwards he became one of

the shareholders in Killigrew's company, and signed a contract
to supply the Theatre Royal with three new plays a year, an
undertaking which he was never able to keep. But he was now
under pressure to write for the playhouse, and his next comedy,
An Evening's Love (1668), shows some signs of it. This comedy of
intrigue, which Evelyn thought 'very profane' and Pepys 'very
smutty', was based mainly on Thomas Corneille's *Le feint
astrologue*, which in turn derived from Calderón's *El Astrologo
fingindo*. With its two young Englishmen visiting Madrid during
the Carnival, it is the sort of holiday play that Tom Durfey
could have written with as much liveliness and impudence, but
without the occasional distinction of phrase. As a 'gay couple'
Wildblood and Jacintha are inferior to Celadon and Florimel,
and the two rakes are at times rather laboured in their gaiety,
and seem to betray the dramatist's underlying contempt for
their kind. In the wide-ranging Preface to this play Dryden
answers the objection that he has made debauched persons his
protagonists, and, against the laws of comedy, has failed to
punish them at the end of the play. He denies that he had any
intention of making libertinism amiable, and adds on behalf of
himself and his fellow dramatists: 'We make not vicious persons
happy, but only as Heaven makes sinners so; that is, by re-
claiming them from vice. For so 'tis to be suppos'd they are,
when they resolve to marry; for then enjoying what they desire
in one, they cease to pursue the love of many.' Whatever may be
thought of Dryden's defence, it does seem to represent the usual
attitude of Restoration dramatists to the young rake-hero of
their comedies: he sows his wild oats, and then in the last act,
with varying degrees of plausibility, he settles down to married
life. What happens after that is not the dramatist's business
(except occasionally, as in Otway's *The Atheist* and Vanbrugh's
The Relapse); but at least the married state continues throughout
the period to be regarded as the normal one for men and women,
if less tolerable for the men than for the women.

    For the next few years Dryden gave his mind to writing
heroic plays, and when he returned to comedy in 1672 with
Marriage-à-la-Mode, it was tragi-comedy with some admixture
of the heroic drama. Leonidas, for example, convinced that he
is not, after all, of royal birth, reflects that he is better off without
a train of fawning followers, and exclaims in the true heroic
fashion:

'Tis true I am alone;
So was the Godhead ere he made the world.

The serious plot turning upon a palace revolution is no more
absurd than that of Beaumont and Fletcher's *Philaster* and
many other tragi-comedies of the same romantic kind. Polydamas,
who at one point exclaims:

I lie as open to the gusts of passion
As the bare Shore to every beating Surge

is the typical tyrant of Jacobean drama; Argaleon, the wicked
favourite, is another stock type; Leonidas is a better-behaved
Philaster; and poor Amalthea, who loves him in secret, fades
out at the end like Bellario in the same play. This was old-
fashioned stuff in 1672; but if Dryden uses almost all the old
clichés they often shine and glow in the brilliance of his writing.
The passage in rhymed couplets between Leonidas and Palmyra
(II. ii) is based on one of the oldest clichés of all—how happy is
a simple country life, how artificial and frustrating the life of
royal courts!—but it has a lyrical and rhetorical effectiveness
that would still keep a modern audience hushed and attentive.
The comic scenes are beautifully written, and Dryden has taken
care to connect them with the serious plot by a number of
effective links. In the involved relationship between Rhodophil,
Palamede, Doralice, and Melantha his comedy reaches its most
adult level. He writes here, not only with more comic assurance
than ever before, but with one of the most thoughtful treat-
ments of sex and marriage that Restoration comedy can show.
With its witty repartee, its engaging impudence, its critical
precision of phrase, and the comic force of its situations, this
is comedy without any admixture of farce, and it contains what
many would call his finest comic character, the affected and
foolish Melantha. In dedicating the play to the Earl of Rochester, Dryden is willing to give him some of the credit: 'I am
sure, if there be any thing in this Play wherein I have rais'd my
self beyond the ordinary lowness of my Comedies, I ought
wholly to acknowledge it to the favour of being admitted into
your Lordship's Conversation.' This, of course, may be only the
polite compliment often paid on such occasions; and yet it may
be rather more than that. Once or twice in *Marriage-à-la-Mode*
we meet with that uncompromising attitude to life which we

associate with Rochester—in these words of Palamede, for
example:

O Friend, this is not an age to be critical in Beauty: when we had
good store of handsome women, and but few Chapmen, you might
have been more curious in your choice; but now the price is en-
hanc'd upon us, and all Mankind set up for Mistresses, so that poor
little creatures, without beauty, birth, or breeding, but onely
impudence, go off at unreasonable rates: and a man, in these hard
times, snaps at 'em, as he does at Broad-gold, never examines the
weight, but takes light, or heavy, as he can get it.

This is very like the voice of Dorimant, to be heard in *The
Man of Mode* four years later, and both may echo the voice
of Rochester, easily contemptuous, completely detached from
all conventional morality, and making the largest assumptions
about the unregenerate condition of the human race. This
antinomianism is not really natural to Dryden, who never quite
freed himself from his Puritan upbringing, and who had, too,
a vein of idealism that he never suppressed. When he flouts
conventional religion or morality, it is almost always in his
plays; and he is writing then, as often as not, to amuse a
fashionable audience in 'this lubrique and adulterate age'.

Later in the same year Dryden tried again with another
comedy, *The Assignation: or, Love in a Nunnery*, which he admits
'succeeded ill in the representation'. He was already beginning
to repeat himself, notably in the blundering Benito, who is a
poor variant of Sir Martin Mar-all, and there was nothing in
this play that he had not done better before. He was consciously writing down to the intellectual level of his audience,
and in the prologue he said as much. Farce again, but this time
of a peculiarly distasteful kind, was what he had to offer in his
next comedy, *The Kind Keeper: or, Mr. Limberham* (1678).
' 'Twas intended', he says, 'for an honest Satyre against our
crying sin of *Keeping*', and he considers it to be 'of the first
Rank of those which I have written, and that Posterity will be
of my Opinion'. None of those claims appears to be justified:
Dryden has written another farcical comedy of copulation. If
it is a satire on keeping, all that we learn is that an elderly and
impotent roué cannot expect a young mistress to remain
faithful to him, and we do not need five acts to tell us that.
It is true, however, that this play was prohibited after the third
night, and not, if we are to believe Langbaine, on account of its

indecency, but because Dryden had 'exposed the keeping part of the town'. When the play was printed Dryden left out 'those things which offended on the stage', and, as Scott observes, it is hard to guess what he could have deleted when we consider what he retained. What we have is a series of bedroom scenes Dryden's innovation is to have one woman on the bed and another under it), with the usual hasty concealing of the rake when the unexpected husband inevitably returns. Several of the characters are moral imbeciles, headed by the young rake's father, 'an honest, good-natured gentleman of the town', who, too old for the enjoyment of women himself, takes a vicarious pleasure, like Otway's Sir Jolly Jumble, in procuring them for younger men. It may be added that in Brainsick Dryden has created what must be the most boring cuckold in Restoration comedy. In 1680 he returned to his favourite form of tragi-comedy and produced *The Spanish Friar*, with the daughter of a usurper on the throne and the rightful heir coming to claim his own, and with the usual comic intrigue in the sub-plot. Dryden himself was well pleased with this play, on which he claimed to have bestowed more care and pains than on any of his other tragi-comedies. In the Dedication he drew attention to the skill with which he had tacked his two plots together, and later commentators (including Johnson, who praised the play for 'the happy coincidence and coalition of the two plots') have tended to follow this critical lead rather too easily. Dryden's fat friar, the shameless and reprobate Father Dominick, is a sort of Restoration Falstaff, nimble-witted, imperturbable, and infinitely corruptible. The serious plot is no less absurd than Dryden's other exercises in this kind; but the quality of the writing has often a new restraint and precision that amply justify his claim to have taken more care and pains than usual. Dryden had now entered upon his own neo-classical period. It is in the Preface to *The Spanish Friar* that he formally recants from his earlier extravagances, wishes many of the speeches of his Maximin and Almanzor 'in the same fire with Statius and Chapman', and renounces all those 'Delilahs of the theatre'.

It was ten years before Dryden attempted comedy again, and when he did so with *Amphitryon* in 1690, his decision to refurbish a play by Plautus which had already been used by Molière may indicate some weakening at last in his creative

powers. *Amphitryon*, well acted by the players and characteristically plumped out to make an English comedy by the addition of Mercury's intrigue with Phaedra, was deservedly a
success. The ladies in particular were delighted with Purcell's
settings of the three songs, and they could enjoy, too, the love
scenes between Jupiter and Alcmena, which Dryden developed
with all his now slightly old-fashioned charm. Landor's opinion
that Dryden was 'never tender nor sublime' has been so often
cited with approval that it is only fair to point out that in his
own day he was usually associated with tender and moving
love-scenes. The author of *The Tory Poets: A Satyr* (1682) sneers
at him on this very account. Dryden's appeal, he insists, lies
in his amorous passages, which delight 'the feeble Females and
the Fop', and in those 'gentle flourishes' which move 'the weak
admiring Maid, and fire love'. It may be questioned, however,
if his power to inflame the amorous maid is really what is
needed in this comedy: the cool and passionless Congreve might
have exploited more delicately the comic possibilities of the
theme.

On 11 January 1694 Evelyn noted in his diary that he had
dined with Dryden, 'who now intending to write no more
Plays... read to us his Prologue and Epilogue to his last Valedic-
tory Play, now shortly to be Acted'. The prologue was as brilliant as anything Dryden had written of that kind, but the play,
Love Triumphant, another tragi-comedy, was an irretrievable
failure. For the serious action Dryden had saddled himself
with a hopelessly complicated and improbable plot, apparently
of his own devising:

> a Story which no Books relate;
> Coin'd from our own Old Poet's Addle-pate.

As such it was a failure of misplaced ingenuity, turning on
mistaken identity, rapid changes of fortune, and what Coleridge
once called 'virtuous vice'—an *apparently* incestuous relationship which turns out to be innocent. The comic scenes are
feeble and irrelevant, deficient in both wit and humour. It was
time to stop, and only Dryden's necessities had kept him writing
for the stage so long. His contribution to English comedy is not
easy to assess. Much hard work had gone into the writing of his
plays, and much time that might have been better spent. In
1676, in his Dedication of *Aureng-Zebe* to the Earl of Mulgrave,

he had expressed his distaste for playwriting, and more especially for the writing of comedies:

> I am weary with drawing the deformities of Life, and Lazars of the people. . . . I desire to be no longer the Sisyphus of the Stage; to rowl up a Stone with endless Labour. . . . I never thought my self very fit for an Employment, where many of my Predecessors have excell'd me in all kinds; and some of my Contemporaries, even in my own partial Judgement, have out-done me in Comedy.

It is significant that he was usually at his happiest in tragi-comedy. He frequently defends this form, and in the Dedication of *Love Triumphant* returns to his old argument that it is 'agreeable to the English Genius. We love variety more than any other Nation; and so long as the Audience will not be pleas'd without it, the Poet is oblig'd to humour them.' No doubt this was true enough; but it may also be true that Dryden had a personal preference for tragi-comedy because it enabled him to write a play that did not have to be all comic for five acts. He certainly had some success in comedy, but he had no great *vis comica*; and his happiest moments usually occur in the light-hearted exchange of repartee between his lovers. Dryden undoubtedly influenced his contemporaries in a variety of ways, but he was himself too concerned with the reactions of the audience to write a single great comedy, and he never wrote a pure comedy of manners. That was left for his friend Etherege.

The reputation of Sir George Etherege[1] has risen considerably in the present century, and although there is now some danger of his being given an importance that he would have been the first to disown, he undoubtedly stamped his own unemphatic image on the Restoration theatre. The comic world of his first two plays, although it is almost as unreal to the modern play-goer as the world of Edwardian musical comedy, is still young and fresh; it has the cool fragrance of those early mornings in the sixteen-sixties that Etherege knew so well as he went

---

[1] Sir George Etherege (1634?–91). Not much is known of Etherege's early life before the production of the first of his three comedies in 1664. In 1668 he went to Turkey as secretary to Sir Daniel Harvey, returning to England in the summer of 1671. His last and best comedy, *The Man of Mode*, was produced in 1676; and for the next year or two the few hard facts about Etherege are mostly concerned with drunken brawls or fights in the company of one or more of his fellow wits. About 1680 he was knighted, and married a wealthy widow. In 1685 he was sent by James II as English minister to Ratisbon, where he remained until the King's abdication. He died in Paris.

rollicking home after a night of pleasure. *The Comical Revenge; or, Love in a Tub* (1664) and *She wou'd if she cou'd* (1668) are almost his own frolics recollected in tranquillity. His gentlemen never do anything that he and his friends would have been ashamed to do themselves. Whatever his moral standards may be, we have at least the satisfaction of feeling (as we do not with Dryden) that he is not consciously lowering them to make an English comedy.

Yet, for all his air of innocence and irresponsible gaiety, Etherege knew what he was doing; and in the end he succeeded completely in expressing an attitude to life which informs many of the more thoughtful comedies of the time. That attitude is a development from seventeenth-century libertinism. The libertine was anti-rational, holding with Rochester that reason is

> an *Ignis Fatuus* of the Mind,
> Which leaves the light of Nature, Sense behind.

But although he was anti-rational he was eminently reasonable, believing in a reasonable gratification of his senses, and in taking his pleasure where he found it. He was sceptical of conventional beliefs in religion and morality, and the conventional attitudes and behaviour to which they gave rise. In Etherege's plays this libertine attitude is expressed through the young men of fashion who are normally the heroes, and also (though not invariably) through the gay and witty and emancipated young women whom they eventually marry. The conventional attitude is embodied in the various dupes and cullies and country squires and middle-aged ladies who are hurried into crudities of behaviour from their lack of percipience or good breeding or self-control. Since he felt himself to be free and unprejudiced, the Restoration libertine valued frankness of speech and freedom from make-believe. When he is talking to other young men like himself, or to young women of intelligence whom he respects or admires, he is normally truthful and even outspoken; but if he has occasion to deceive a woman in the course of an intrigue, hypocrisy is in order, and if she proves to be frail, no mercy need be shown to the victim. Sir Frederick Frollick in Etherege's first play is more of a playboy than a fully-realized libertine, but in his second comedy Courtall and Freeman (the names are significant) are well on the way to becoming mature examples of the kind. It is Dorimant, how-

ever, who is Etherege's most finished libertine; and in him we
find a further development, a love of conquest for its own sake
and for the sense of power that it gives. It is certainly possible,
and it is now fashionable, to find in such characters the influence of Machiavelli and Hobbes; but in order to create them
Etherege had only to participate in and observe the life of
Restoration London. Much of what nowadays passes for thought
in Restoration comedy is perhaps no more than an intelligent
rationalization of patrician insolence.

Love in a Tub is certainly not the work of a thinker, nor is it a
well-constructed play. Set in London in the last days of the Commonwealth, it is a mixture of farce, humour, wit, fashionable
manners, romantic sentiment, songs and catches, and of
rhymed couplets, blank verse, and prose; it is the play of a
beginner who brings in something of everything. The romantic
plot, with its conflict between love and honour (the unhappy
Aurelia being secretly in love with the brave and unfortunate
Colonel Bruce, who loves her sister Graciana, who in turn
loves Lord Beaufort), is carried on in rhymed couplets, and is
full of generous gestures and heroic sentiment. On a very different level the cheating of Sir Nicholas Cully by Wheadle and
Palmer, and his marriage by a trick to Sir Frederick's cast
mistress Lucy, is in the Jonsonian tradition. The wedging of
the French valet Dufoy in a tub is a piece of purely visual farce,
and its inclusion in the play (not to mention that it gives the
comedy its title) would seem to indicate that Etherege had
made a shrewd assessment of the intellectual capacity of a
large part of the contemporary audience. It was, however,
in the leisurely and uncommitted wooing of the widow by
the easy-going Sir Frederick Frollick that Etherege must have
caught the attention of his more discriminating contemporaries.
Sir Frederick has most of the marks of the Restoration comic
hero in his attitude and behaviour; he makes no moral claims for
himself and he exposes the moral pretensions of others. But he has
hardly reached the point of being a conscious critic of society, as
Dorimant or Mirabell were to be; his indolent good-nature and
tolerance give to his shameless escapades an air of innocent and
Falstaffian frolic. He comes as near as any character in Restoration comedy to Lamb's notion of the 'stage libertine playing his loose pranks of two hours' duration, and of no after
consequence'. It is, of course, part of the ethos of Restoration

comedy that marriage is for the man a last resource, and therefore a sort of comic defeat; but even in his capitulation to the
widow Sir Frederick accepts matrimony as just another adventure which is capable of giving pleasure.

> *Widow.* Now I have receiv'd you into my Family, I hope you
> will let my maids go quietly about their business, Sir.

> *Sir Fred.* Upon condition there be no twits of the good man
> departed; no prescription pleaded for evil customs on the
> Wedding night. Widow, what old doings will be anon!

She wou'd if she cou'd (the title refers to the amorous Lady
Cockwood) is at once wittier and more sophisticated than
Love in a Tub, but the rumbustious Sir Joslin Jolley and Sir
Oliver Cockwood in his penitential suit bring with them a
strong element of humour and farce. In construction Etherege's
second comedy is only a little less off-hand than his first. It was
his ability to reproduce the leisurely conversation of the
fashionable world—heightened, polished, freed from irrelevance
and repetition, and completely up to date—that constituted
his most important technical contribution to Restoration
comedy. No one knew better than Etherege the art of killing
time, and even when the action stands still, and two young men
idle with two young women in the Mulberry Garden, the conversation flows on. Although Congreve's dialogue has sometimes more point, and makes a more consistently thoughtful
comment on men and manners, it has lost some of the unforced
ease and natural rhythm of Etherege's conversation. Both men
were happy, of course, in having for their point of departure a
conversation that was already more studied and mannered than
any we are likely to meet with today. That his own age recognized the superlative quality of his style is indicated by Dryden's
advice to Southerne: 'The standard of thy style let Etherege
be.' Yet Etherege had more to offer than witty conversation.
In Courtall and Gatty, Freeman and Ariana, he created two
intelligent couples, through whose eyes the rest of the comic
world is seen, and by whom it is judged. They have that
awareness which characterizes the Restoration hero and
heroine. Awareness involves being in the mode, dressing fashion-
ably but not (like Sir Fopling) flamboyantly, conversing grace-
fully and intelligently in the latest idiom of the *beau monde*,
being thoroughly familiar with the fashionable diversions of

the town, and knowing what the manners, attitudes, and modes of behaviour of the polite world demand. Awareness also implies an ability to sum up character, motives, and behaviour, as in Courtall's observation that 'whatsoever women say, I am sure they seldom think the worse of a man for running at all; 'tis a sign of youth and high mettal, and makes them rather piquée, who shall tame him'. The young hero, again, will be aware of the underworld of London as represented by Rake-hell, 'a Knight of the Industry', or by such sharpers as Wheadle and Palmer, but will not himself be of it. At a deeper level, the comic hero will be conscious of the difference between appearance and reality, order and disorder, unbridled animal passions and reasonable feelings. Conversely, the unaware are those whom Congreve's Belinda calls 'outlandish creatures, . . . tramontanae and foreigners to the fashion or any thing in practice'; they have usually come up from the country, like Sir Oliver Cockwood and his lady, they are coarse and un-discriminating, and in their lusts and diversions mere animals. Courtall variously describes the amorous Lady Cockwood as 'the longing lady' and 'this ravenous kite'; his own sexual vigour is not in question, but he finds Lady Cockwood alto-gether too much of a good thing. 'She would by her good will', he confides to Freeman, 'give her Lover no more rest, than a young Squire that has newly set up a Coach, does his only pair of Horses.' The woman he does fall in love with is cool, poised, witty, and intelligent; and although, since there is in Restoration comedy a double standard for the sexes, she cannot enjoy the same freedom as he does, she still belongs to his world of free thought and frank acceptance of facts.

In *The Man of Mode* Restoration comedy reached one of its highest achievements. The farce and good-natured fooling of the two earlier comedies have disappeared; the wit remains, and has become consistently adult. This is nowhere better seen than in Sir Fopling Flutter, comic in his self-absorption and preening his gay plumage like some exotic bird, and yet, as Dryden pointed out in the epilogue to the play,

> a Fool so nicely writ,
> The Ladies wou'd mistake him for a Wit.

The tolerant Lady Townley in the same play thinks it a desirable thing to have a universal taste: 'We should love Wit,

but for Variety be able to divert our selves with the Extravagancies of those who want it.' She could certainly have found
ample material for such easy diversion in Restoration comedy,
which, as Congreve was later to complain, had so many and
such gross fools that, in his opinion, 'they should rather disturb
than divert the well-natured and reflecting part of an audience',
and excite our compassion rather than our mirth. But Sir
Fopling, with some natural wit, has misapplied it and studied
to be a fool, as Dorimant and Medley explain to the company.

> *Dor.* He is a person indeed of great acquir'd follies.

> *Med.* He is like many others, beholding to his Education for
> making him so eminent a Coxcomb; many a Fool had been lost
> to the World, had their indulgent Parents wisely bestow'd
> neither Learning nor good breeding on 'em.

Without Sir Fopling, however, *The Man of Mode* would be
almost a dark comedy: whenever he enters he brings with him
a glittering triviality that scents the air and dissipates the
shadows. Etherege has considerably extended his range of
characters in his last comedy: Dorimant the fine gentleman, his
friend Medley (whom the eighteenth century would have called
'an agreeable rattle'); the cast mistress Loveit and the too fond
Bellinda; the conventional young lovers, Bellair and Emilia;
the older generation, represented by Bellair's bustling father,
the fashionable Lady Townley, and the old-fashioned Lady
Woodvill; the cool but lively Harriet, who plays Dorimant as
an angler plays a lightly-hooked trout; and, for good measure,
the lower orders, represented by an orange-woman and by a
shoemaker who stands up for the rights of his class, and
answers Dorimant's reproof that 'Whoring and Swearing are
Vices too gentile for a Shoomaker' with the assertion: ' 'Zbud,
I think you men of quality will grow as unreasonable as the
Women; you wou'd ingross the sins o'the Nation; poor Folks
can no sooner be wicked, but th'are rail'd at by their Betters.'
It is not surprising to learn from John Dennis that when *The
Man of Mode* was first performed it 'was generally believed to
be an agreeable Representation of the Persons of Condition of
both Sexes, both in Court and Town; and that all the World was
charm'd with Dorimant'. It is Dorimant, a Restoration Don
Juan and almost too intense a personality to be the hero of a
comedy, who dominates the play, whether today we find him

charming or not. If, as Dennis reported, Etherege had Rochester
in mind when he drew Dorimant, we have a clue to the powerful and highly individual impression that this formidable
character makes. He never wastes a word, his comments are
devastating, and he has a detachment and self-control that put
all the other characters, except Harriet, at his mercy. Even
Harriet's courage and self-possession occasionally tremble on
the verge of defeat, and the duel between the two generates an
unusual tension. But Dorimant is seen in many different situations. For Dorimant, Harriet is only the next young woman on
his list; but when he discovers that she is not another Loveit
or Bellinda, and that he cannot have her on the same easy
terms, there is an immediate deepening of the relationship.
Dorimant is in love: we are witnessing the comic fall to a state
of grace. It is true that he tells young Bellair:

> The wise will find a difference in our Fate,
> You wed a Woman, I a good Estate.

But we know, and Dorimant knows, that this is only an
attempt to save face; his later declarations to Harriet have all
the marks of a willing convert.

It is often assumed that marriage is invariably held up to
ridicule in Restoration comedy, but this is far from being so.
Two or more young people who are in love, and whose love
normally leads to marriage in the fifth act, are part of the
staple of that comedy: they were the exceptions in real life.
Marriages among people of quality were normally arranged
by the parents of the young couple, and in the late seventeenth century such marriages were increasingly contracted
with a view to augmenting the estate of the family, more
especially in landed property. It would be naïve to suggest that
marriages of this kind were invariably disastrous, but in practice they led to much unhappiness, to marital unfaithfulness,
and to a general scepticism about married life as a satisfactory
human relationship. There is a considerable body of literature
outside the drama to show that the practice of parents' offering
their son or daughter to the highest bidder was one that disturbed some of the most serious minds of the age. What the
dramatists were being cynical about was not so much marriage
itself, but marriage as it too often was in the later decades of
the seventeenth century: the loveless marriage of convenience,

the forced marriage, the elderly knight or baronet or wealthy
man of business joined in matrimony to the young girl who was
already in love with a young man of her own choice—in fact,
the sort of marriage that a large part of the audience of ladies
and gentlemen sitting in the boxes had already contracted. So
far were the dramatists from being cynical about marriage,
that the very persistence with which they allow their young
couples to fall in love, and after outwitting or reconciling
parents or guardians or elderly suitors to get married, could
almost be described as romantic and escapist. The modern
critics of Restoration comedy have sometimes been more
cynical than were the dramatists themselves.

The playwright who appears to have the greatest affinity
with Etherege is his friend Sir Charles Sedley.[1] His first comedy,
The Mulberry Garden (1668), set, like Etherege's first play,
immediately before the Restoration, and with the comic scenes
in prose and the romantic ones in rhymed couplets, is the work
of a writer who knows well the world that he has set out to
portray, and who has a natural turn for witty dialogue. In
Modish and Estridge Sedley has drawn two impudent and
empty-headed sparks, whose conversation has the artificial
gallantry of the fashionable world. Wildish, however, is a man
of sense, who finds himself attracted by the witty and high-
spirited Olivia, plays with her for some time, and eventually
falls in love with her. The final coming to terms of this gay
couple is as good as anything of its kind in Restoration comedy.

> *Oliv.* If I were your Wife, I must board half a year with a Friend
> in the Country, tumble about the other half in most villainous
> Hackneys, lye two pair of Stairs high, and wear black farren-
> dine the whole year about: see you when you had no money
> to play, and then be kist out of a Ring or a Bracelet. . . .
>
> *Wild.* If I make but love to a Chambermaid, I shall be answer'd,
> you have a sweet Lady of your own, and why will you wrong

---

[1] Sir Charles Sedley (1639?–1701) succeeded to the baronetcy in 1656 on the
death of an elder brother. He spent some time at Wadham College, but left without taking a degree. Later, as a member of what Marvell called 'the merry gang',
he became notorious for various drunken exploits in and about London. In 1668 he
became M.P. for Romney, and in his more sober later life in the reign of William
and Mary he took a considerable part in parliamentary debates. He was something
of a patron of men of letters, and appears to have been on terms of genuine friendship with such writers as Dryden and Shadwell, who speak, with apparent sincerity,
of his wit and good taste.

her? If I get acquainted with any young woman, after the
fourth or fifth visit, be look'd upon by her Father and Mother
worse than the Tax-Gatherers in a Country Village; all this
you count nothing!

While the young men in the romantic half of Sedley's play can
and do assert their undying love in extravagant protestations,
the comic hero can remain a hero only if he retains something
of his freedom. Although the audience must be assured that he
is genuinely in love, they must also be left with the feeling that
this marriage is not going to be the end of all liberty and
laughter. Sedley's other comedy, *Bellamira* (1687), based on
The Eunuch of Terence, is one of the most assured plays of the
period, although in 1687 it was perhaps already a little old-
fashioned. Bellamira herself is said to have been a portrait
of Barbara Palmer, Duchess of Cleveland, but she could
equally well have been drawn from Sedley's own daughter
Catherine, who had for some time been the Duke of York's
mistress. At all events, the sureness of the characterization and
the hard and unsparing force of the dialogue come from Sedley's
longstanding intimacy with the world in which his characters
live. Sedley really knew, as Etherege or Rochester knew, but as
Dryden or Shadwell could not, how this world behaved and
talked, what it really thought, what gave it cohesion and the
will to live. On the night of 18 February 1667 Pepys found
himself sitting close to Sedley at a performance of *The Maid's
Tragedy*. Sedley, who was more interested in a lady wearing
a mask than in the play that was being performed, kept up a
running conversation with her; and this lady,

being exceeding witty as ever I heard woman, did talk most pleasantly with him; but was, I believe, a virtuous woman, and of quality.
He would fain know who she was, but she would not tell; yet did
give him many pleasant hints of her knowledge of him, by that
means setting his brains at work to find out who she was, and
did give him leave to use all means to find out who she was but
pulling off her mask. He was mighty witty, and she also making
sport with him very inoffensively, that a more pleasant rencontre I
never heard.

This could be Etherege's Courtall picking up Miss Gatty, or
Sedley's own Wildish meeting with Olivia in the Mulberry
Garden. Etherege and Sedley ought to have known how to
write such scenes, since they had so often lived them.

The career of William Wycherley[1] is rather like a play that has been loosely put together, with the motivation left uncertain and the values by which we are to judge him allowed to remain ambiguous. His own generation clearly regarded him as one of its big men, and tributes to his work and personality come from such different admirers as the Duke of Buckingham, Congreve, and Dennis. Dryden, who thought him equally eminent as a writer of comedy and as a satirist, was proud to call him his friend, and believed that with *The Plain-Dealer* he had 'obliged all honest and virtuous men, by one of the most bold, most general, and most useful satires which has ever been presented on the English theatre'. To Macaulay, however, Wycherley was like the skunk, 'too filthy to handle, and too noisome even to approach'. The modern reader, who has grown well-accustomed to skunks and who is living in an age that in some ways resembles that of Wycherley, may still find it difficult to decide what was really important for this dramatist, and how far his satire was the result of moral indignation, or merely the fashionable attitude of the man of sense. In his younger days at least he seems to have had no great quarrel with the society in which he lived. He could apparently do all the things that were done by a Sir Frederick Frollick, and in fact did them with considerable *réclame*. He would probably have agreed with his own Hippolita that ' 'tis a pleasant — well-bred — complacent — free — frolick — good-natur'd — pretty Age: and if you do not like it, leave it to us that do.' But from the first he reserved the right to disturb its complacency, and although he accepted much, he rejected even more. If the world of Restoration society was on the surface one of

---

[1] William Wycherley (1641–1716) was descended from a family settled in Shropshire from the fifteenth century. At the age of about 15 he went to live in France, but he was back in England before the Restoration, and was for some time a member of the Inner Temple. He served with the fleet in 1664. Wycherley, whose memory failed him in later years, has puzzled his biographers by telling Pope 'over and over' that his first play was written when he was 19, his second when he was 21, and *The Plain-Dealer* when he was 25; but those dates are almost certainly wrong. Charles II offered to make him governor of his son, the Duke of Richmond, at a large salary; but Wycherley chose instead to marry a rich widow, the Countess of Drogheda, in 1679. After her death less than two years later he fell into debt and in consequence spent some months in prison, until (according to Dennis) James II gave an order to have his debts paid. He published a volume of *Miscellany Poems* in 1704, and continued to write much indifferent verse which he sent to Pope for correction. Almost on his deathbed he married again to disinherit his heir.

intelligence and vivacity and good manners, he knew that it rested upon a foundation of sham and hypocrisy; that for every man of sense there were a dozen empty-headed fops, or foolish lords, or money-loving men of business (money is one of Wycherley's obsessions); and that the moral integrity of a Harcourt and an Alithea or the unselfish devotion of a Fidelia were rare indeed. His satirical vision dwells frequently upon the contrast between the imposing outward show and the vulgarity and triviality and sheer animalism that lay beneath. Sometimes, as with Lady Flippant in his first play, he hardly troubles at all to impress us with the outward show; she is, however, no better than 'the relict of a citizen', and a Restoration audience would expect little from that. Like several of Wycherley's characters, she is guilty of indecent exposure of her mind. This may indeed be satire for an age not over-nice in such matters; but, to the modern reader, Lady Flippant running loose at night in St. James's Park, hoping that some 'Burgundy Man or drunken Scourer will reel my way', and lamenting that 'the Rag-Women, and Synder-women, have better luck than I', is a case rather for medical care than for satire.

Wycherley, then, has a sort of love-hate relationship to the world in which he lives. 'The World', as Eliza says in *The Plain-Dealer*, 'is but a constant Keeping Gallant, whom we fail not to quarrel with when any thing crosses us, yet cannot part with't for our hearts.' This seems to have been pretty much Wycherley's own position: he was not the first or the last to love the 'dear damn'd distracting Town', and yet at the same time to be acutely aware of its follies and brutalities. But it would be wrong to suggest that he had a delicate moral sense. His morality is accurately enough described, in Wilde's epigram, as 'the attitude we adopt towards people whom we personally dislike'; it becomes active with him when he contemplates elderly and unattractive widows longing for husbands, or rich citizens leading a double life, or women of the town living by their wits, or canting hypocrites professing friendship to the man they mean to cheat. There are other people, like Dapper-wit, or Novel, or Lord Plausible, more fools than rogues, whom he is prepared to find amusing. The two sides of Wycherley, humorist and satirist, find expression in different degrees in his four plays.

Love in a Wood (1671), with its misunderstandings and mistaken identity, its aimless ramblings and meetings in St. James's Park, and its long conversations between fops and coxcombs on the one side and men of sense on the other, is a mixture of manners, humours, intrigue, wit, and satire. Like Etherege in his first comedy, the young dramatist is trying a little of everything. Wycherley's young men and women are rarely as witty as those of Congreve, and in this comedy they are mainly concerned with the problems arising from love and dalliance. On the other hand, Wycherley's dialogue is sometimes more dramatic than Congreve's; it is used on most occasions to develop some situation or advance the action. Of the three 'young gentlemen of the town' the most attractive is Vincent, who is a sort of still centre in the play, neither in love nor in pursuit of a wench, but obviously Wycherley's idea of a man of sense, and capable of effectively sardonic comment and repartee. In *Love in a Wood* Wycherley is only learning to show his teeth, but the satirical snarl is audible throughout. The tone is often harsh and jeering; it is as if he has convinced himself that ill nature is a sign of strength, and is determined to leave the mark of his fists on his audience no less than on his characters. This is 'manly' Wycherley, not yet come fully to man's estate as an observer of the human scene or as a playwright. Dapperwit (almost a James Boswell in his self-satisfaction and his introspective asides—'That I think was brisk' . . . 'I keep up with her, I think') is allowed to answer Lady Flippant's question why he looks so jealous with the brutal reply: 'If I had met you in Whetstone's Park with a drunken Foot-Soldier, I should not have been jealous of you.' In the fifth act Wycherley contrives a compendious Jonsonian exposure of human weakness and wickedness. Dapperwit has deceived Sir Simon Addlepot and has married Gripe's daughter Martha, but Martha justifies herself to her father by explaining, 'I found myself six months gone with Child, and saw no hopes of your getting me a Husband, or else I had not married a Wit, sir.' The lecherous and frustrated Gripe, determined that not a penny of his money shall go to Dapperwit, decides to marry Lucy ('tis cheaper keeping a wife than a wench'), only to be told a minute later that she has been Dapperwit's wench. And so Wycherley's first comedy hurries to its end in shouts of ill-tempered and brutal laughter.

The Gentleman Dancing-Master (1672), which is at once good-

humoured, amusing, and surprisingly decent, is a beautifully
made play, but it is a masterpiece of farce rather than of
comedy. For the central situation, in which intelligent youth
outwits crabbed and fussy age, Gerrard wooing Hippolita in
the guise of a dancing-master, Wycherley was indebted to
El Maestro de Danzar of Calderón and perhaps to *The Taming of
the Shrew*, but the humour, the gaiety, the comic development
of the situation, and some of the most effective characters are
largely Wycherley's own. He makes his plot work for him, and
many of the best things in the play come from his exploitation
of the ironical possibilities in the situation, and from his
effective use of comic repetition. Don Diego, the Englishman
who has spent most of his life in Spain and has become in effect
a Spaniard, and the English Monsieur de Paris, who has spent
some months in France and now speaks his native tongue like
a Frenchman, are undoubtedly exaggerated to the point of
farce: Wycherley is often rather heavy-handed and emphatic.
But by 1672 the francophile Englishman was so well established
on the English stage that Wycherley could start where other
dramatists had left off, and count upon carrying an audience
with him. In any case, Monsieur de Paris is such a confident
and high-spirited fool that a good comic actor could easily
make him credible.

If Dryden admired Wycherley as the author of *The Plain-
Dealer*, the average playgoer probably liked him best for *The
Country Wife* (1675). Here the situation of a young rake just
returned from France who pretends to have lost his virility,
and makes the most of his supposed impotence, is so indelicate
that to give a bare outline of the plot is to convince all right-
minded people that the play is too indecent to discuss; but a
bare outline of *Hamlet* would hardly prepare the playgoer for
the tragedy that Shakespeare wrote. Starting from his one
lewd circumstance Wycherley created a comic fantasy as
brilliant and impudent as anything in Restoration comedy.
This is the best-constructed of all Wycherley's plays; indeed, it
is a masterpiece of easy, natural, and self-explanatory movement. The dialogue is penetrating and lively, and almost all
of it springs directly from the various situations in which the
characters find themselves. The humour is abundant, now
anticipating the epigrammatic technique of Wilde ('. . . though
I have known thee a great while, never go, if I do not love thee

as well as a new Acquaintance'), now reminding us of Shaw ('That's a good one! I hate a Man for loving you? . . . That he makes love to you, is a sign you are handsome . . .'). The naïve inexperience of the country wife Margery in this sophisticated society is perfectly displayed, culminating in her loyal defence of Horner's virility, and Horner's delightful aside to her, 'Peace, dear idiot!' Everywhere this play gives evidence of that 'incomparable vivacity' which John Dennis saw in his friend's work. But *The Country Wife* is not just a high-spirited and immoral romp; it offers a serious comment on contemporary marriage from several different angles. 'Women and fortune', Alithea tells her brother Pinchwife, 'are truest still to those that trust 'em.' The jealous Pinchwife does not trust his young wife, he has no real love for her and has only married her, as Horner suggests, to keep a whore to himself, and in consequence he dreads being made a cuckold. Jealousy in Restoration comedy is always a mark of ill breeding, but it is more than that; it is a sign that something has gone wrong with a marriage. Yet it is not enough *not* to be jealous. The one fixed point in Restoration comedy is the man of sense, the *honnête homme*, who has attained to his position of assured stability by a nice sense of self-control and an intelligent balancing of opposites. It is from his point of view—that of Harcourt in this comedy—that the other characters and their actions are invariably judged. In this question of sexual jealousy the right attitude lay somewhere between two extremes. The dilemma was nicely put by Merryman in Sedley's *Bellamira*: ''Tis a mad Age, a Man is Laught at for being a Cuckold, and wonder'd at if he take any Care to prevent it.' In *The Country Wife*, Sparkish, who is about to marry Alithea for the settlement that her brother will make her ('I must give Sparkish tomorrow five thousand pound to lye with my sister'), and for the sake of having a fine woman that he can parade as his possession, has no real love for Alithea. Wrapped up in his self-conceit he thrusts Alithea into the arms of Harcourt. 'You astonish me, sir,' says Alithea, 'by your want of jealousy.' The play is full of such ironies (Sir Jasper Fidget, with his chuckling jokes at Horner's expense, is the first of his victims); and the eagerness with which Lady Fidget, Mrs. Fidget, and Mrs. Squeamish grasp at opportunities while careful to preserve their 'honour' gives an added piquancy to Wycherley's satirical representation of the *beau monde*. To Macaulay *The Country Wife* was 'one of the most profligate and heartless of human compositions'. The world of the play is undoubtedly profligate and heartless, but Wycherley was well aware of that fact, and was saying so repeatedly within the limits of his dramatic form. That he was also carried away from time to time by the fun of the thing is equally true: on such occasions the artist takes over from the moralist, and Wycherley is developing an equivocal situation for all that it is comically worth. The chief stumbling-block for the modern reader is Horner, who is a very different person, as Macaulay had no difficulty in showing, from the honourable lover of Agnès in Molière's *L'École des Femmes*. The comparison is not indeed wholly relevant, for Wycherley was writing a very different sort of play; but in so far as we judge Horner as a man, he is a rake with only some of the qualities of the *honnête homme*. He is certainly not carrying out a clinical examination of the virtue of the various ladies who enter his china closet, but none the less his chief function in the play is to initiate the several actions and situations by which the victims of Wycherley's satire are exposed. As a character he is sacrificed to the plot, and is the dramatist's satiric instrument. Like the fictional authors of Swift's satirical pamphlets, as Paul Vernon has suggested, 'Horner has no consistent characterisation. He varies as the dramatist's satiric method varies.'

The Plain-Dealer (1676) is much the grimmest of Wycherley's four plays. The characters, with the exception of Fidelia, and, to a lesser extent, Eliza, are a collection of rogues, fools, and louts. When he printed his play Wycherley found a motto for it in Horace, but perhaps a better one would have been the words of the Clown in *All's Well that Ends Well*:

> Among nine bad, if one be good,
> There's yet one good in ten.

Fidelia, the one good, a Restoration descendant of Bellario in *Philaster*, seems, in her man's clothes and her chastity, much less real than anyone else in the play. In this play Wycherley is determined to think the worst, to suspect every motive. There are some scenes, such as that in which Novel, Oldfox, the Lawyer, and the Alderman successively take a precipitate leave of Manly when asked to do a good action, which have the primitive effectiveness of a morality play, or of a comparable scene

in *Timon of Athens*. Yet there are other scenes of admirable
comedy, as in that of the first meeting between Manly and
Widow Blackacre, where both try to talk about what is uppermost in their minds and ignore each other, or the conversation between Novel and Olivia, in which Olivia repeatedly
anticipates Novel and takes the words out of his mouth—both
good examples of the Bergsonian comic formula of 'anything
mechanical encrusted on the living'. It is conceivable that the
author of *The Plain-Dealer*, the creator of the snarling, brutal
Manly and the shameless Olivia, was not the hurt and bruised
Puritan that he sometimes thought to be, but rather the
professional satirist, an Oldham writing for the stage, determined to show the virility of his mind, as on other occasions he
had shown the virility of his body. There is at times an air of
protesting too much, of wearing too consciously the satirical
mask. 'Well, but railing is now so common,' Eliza tells Olivia,
'that 'tis no more Malice, but the fashion'; and Wycherley,
who in any case tends to underline every point he makes, may
have thought to set himself at the height of fashion in a censorious world. In his old age he used to tell Pope that Shadwell
'knew how to start a fool very well, but that he was never able
to run him down'; but Wycherley himself was in the habit of
running down his fools with a too Jonsonian thoroughness.
What is not in doubt is his firm and confident construction, his
clearly realized and boldly drawn characters, and the evidence
everywhere of a mind at work. Whatever else he was, Wycherley was no fool; his plays are free from the childish plotting that
marks the work of such writers as Mrs. Behn, and that is not
wholly absent from the plays of Congreve, and his comments
on the world around him are almost invariably shrewd and
vigorous.

It is one of the minor injustices of literary history that
Thomas Shadwell[1] should still live on uneasily in the ludicrous

---

[1] Thomas Shadwell (1642?–92), the son of a lawyer, was descended from an
old Staffordshire family. His life followed a common pattern among Restoration
dramatists: he was educated at Caius College, Cambridge, entered the Middle
Temple, read law for a time, and then abandoned it in favour of literature. He
began with a dramatic hit, *The Sullen Lovers* (1668), which owed some of its success
to the fact that two of the characters were satirical portraits of Sir Robert Howard
and his brother Edward. In all, he wrote fourteen comedies, two operas (he had
some skill in music), a tragicomedy, and a version of Shakespeare's *Timon of
Athens*. He had at one time been on friendly terms with Dryden, and what provoked the poet to lampoon him in *MacFlecknoe* is not certainly known: Shadwell,

image that Dryden created for him in *MacFlecknoe* and in the
second part of *Absalom and Achitophel*.

> The rest to some faint meaning make pretence,
> But Shadwell never deviates into sense.

That the author of *Limberham* should have succeeded in
persuading posterity that the author of *The Squire of Alsatia* is
unreadable is a remarkable tribute to the lasting power of great
satire. But that Dryden, conveniently forgetting the rant and
occasional nonsense of his own plays, should have libelled
Shadwell for want of sense was to attack his enemy where he
was strongest. Shadwell is nearly always sensible, refreshingly
so in an age of much adolescent farce and inane heroics. He was
a serious and intelligent student of contemporary human
character, who thought that an English comedy should consist of more than witty chatter and affairs of gallantry. His
master, as he is never tired of telling us in prologue and dedication, was Ben Jonson, and he inherited or assumed much of
Jonson's seriousness of purpose, his comprehensive awareness
of human folly, his downright utterance, and something (though
not always enough) of the maestro's ability to devise situations nicely calculated to expose his comic victims to the maximum of ridicule. Dryden's advice to Shadwell—'Do anything
but write'—was equally wide of the mark. By all normal
standards Shadwell *can* write, and only a critic with some
quite impossible Congreve in mind would wish to deny it. The
scene in *The Sullen Lovers* (Act III), in which Huffe insists on
describing the game of backgammon he has just played, although
based on a similar scene in Molière's *Les Fâcheux*, should
convince any reader not prepossessed by Dryden's criticism that
Shadwell is not only a brisk and lively writer, but that he has,
what is by no means common, a natural talent for reproducing
the ebb and flow of contemporary conversation. Again, the
opening scene in *The Squire of Alsatia*, where the Squire has his
first experience of the Whitechapel lingo, and that in *Bury
Fair* (II. ii), where the boisterous Oldwit peppers Lady Fantast
with his country wit, are the work of an intelligent dramatist
with a keen ear for the colloquial idiom. All the passages just

however, had the last laugh, for when Dryden lost the offices of Poet Laureate and
Historiographer Royal, Shadwell—a 'true blue Protestant'—succeeded to them
in 1689.

referred to have a cumulative effect, a sort of crescendo movement; the folly grows and spreads and multiplies as the scene
proceeds. There is perhaps nothing in Shadwell quite so good
as the best of Vanbrugh; but if Vanbrugh is to be praised
(and rightly) for his easy and natural dialogue, Shadwell
should come in for his snack of appreciation too.

Dryden's other brilliant fling at Shadwell—

> The Midwife laid her hand on his Thick Skull,
> With this Prophetick blessing—*Be thou dull*—

is not so easy to answer. Shadwell too often falls into the same
mistake as his master Jonson: he is apt to hold on to a joke too
long. Sir Positive in *The Sullen Lovers* ('a foolish knight'), Crazy
in *The Humourists* ('a fantastic coxcomb'), Sir Formal Trifle in
The Virtuoso ('a florid coxcomb'), all grow rather tedious before
we have done with them, although it is only fair to remember
that what tires the reader might continue to amuse the spectator a good deal longer. It is often so with Jonson, and (if we
were more often given a chance to put the matter to test) it
might well prove to be so with his Restoration son. Like
Jonson, Shadwell gains many of his comic effects by repetition;
we laugh because we are so well primed by what has gone before. In *The Squire of Alsatia*, for instance, he makes excellent
play with the Squire's pride in his newly acquired cant terms,
and the Squire's parting shot at the rogues who have just
cheated him is a delightful blend of his own natural idiom and
this other language of a few days' growth: 'Away with 'em.
Rogues! Rascals! *damned prigs!*' Here as elsewhere Shadwell
shows the true Jonsonian economy; his jokes are not so much
the 'natural sprouts' of his own brain as a sort of comic deposit
or distillation from situation and character. The joke was
already there, so to speak, waiting to be found, and Shadwell
had the sense to find it. This is perhaps to say that he excels in
humour rather than in wit; but if so, it is a humour that arises
from a keen awareness of the opportunities presented to him
by the turns and twists of his dramatic action. His best things
can rarely be removed from their context. In *Bury Fair*, for
example, the action turns upon the adventures of a supposed
French Count La Roche, who is in reality a barber and wig-
maker in disguise. For four acts we listen to La Roche's 'Vat is
dis?' and 'Me can no tell vat dey mean', and so too, with

admiration and delight, do Lady Fantast and her foolish daughter, Mrs. Fantast, who has fallen in love with the supposed count. When the inevitable exposure comes in Act V, their faith in the bogus count remains unshaken. 'Ha, ha, ha,' cries Mrs. Fantast, 'my Lady and I mistake Breeding and Quality, and take a Barber for a Nobleman! *Mon Dieu*, this is Malice, meer Envy of my Favours.' Proofs are offered, arguments are produced; but the ladies know better. At last Oldwit, Lady Fantast's husband, bursts in boisterously and taunts his wife and daughter with their vaunted good breeding: their fine Count is only a barber! Now comes Shadwell's final stroke. Mrs. Fantast is so enamoured that quite unconsciously she comes to adopt her count's broken English. '*Hélas!*' she cries, 'You be de very fine Judge indeed!' This may be fantastic enough, but the situation carries it off. Clearly Shadwell knew what would 'pit, box, and gallery it' in 1689. It is characteristic of his art, too, that Mrs. Fantast's lapse into broken English at this point is not *entirely* absurd; it has a sound basis in psychology. To such folly might a humour carry such a woman in an unguarded moment. Again this blending of the fantastic and the naturalistic is Jonsonian.

Indeed, almost everything in Shadwell reminds us of Jonson, as he meant it to do. (On 19 September 1668 Pepys found himself sitting next to Shadwell at a performance of *The Silent Woman*, and noted how the young dramatist was 'big with admiration of it'.) Much of his laughter springs from the baiting of fools, although on the whole Shadwell was kinder to his victims than Jonson was. The best parts of his comedies are usually concerned with the 'humour' characters, some at least of which are new; on the other hand, his young men and women of fashion are rarely in the slightest degree memorable. He has no Palamede and Rhodophil, no Dorimant, no Mirabell and Millamant; nor can he irradiate his plays with the easy wit of Etherege or the scintillating wit of Congreve. (In the Preface to his first comedy he sneers at those who believe that all the wit in plays consists in 'bringing two Persons upon the Stage to break Jests, and to bob one another, which they call Repartie'.) Like the author of *The Silent Woman*, Shadwell delights in practical jokes and horseplay of all kinds. In *The Virtuoso* old Snarl is baited by his nieces: 'Clarinda flings away his cane, Miranda breaks his pipe. . . . While he is stooping for

his pipe, one flings away his hat and periwig, the other thrusts
him down.' This is not the higher comedy; but such puerile
merriment is partly Shadwell's concession to his audience, and
partly the result of his lack of skill in plot-construction. Here
he parts company with Jonson.

What is most un-Jonsonian in Shadwell, and what—writing
when he did—he obviously felt bound to supply, was the sexual
intrigue which the contemporary audience expected. Shadwell
provides it in plenty, but it often seems to be uphill work with
him. How far he was prepared to go in this direction may be
seen in one of his most successful comedies, *Epsom Wells*
(1672). The moral tone of this play could hardly be lower. The
two young ladies 'of wit, beauty and fortune', Lucia and Carolina, are reckless but fundamentally decent; but Raines, Bevil,
and Woodly, the three 'men of wit and pleasure' with whom
they are involved, are unrepentant rakes. The two citizens,
Bisket a comfit-maker and Fribble a haberdasher, are repeatedly
cuckolded by their wives (Dorothy Fribble observing with
sardonic humour to Mrs. Bisket that her husband 'longs
mightily for a Child; and truly, Neighbour, I use all the means
I can, since he is so desirous of one'), and Justice Clodpate, a
country magistrate and an 'immoderate hater of London',
is cheated into marriage by Mrs. Jilt, 'a silly affected whore'
from London. Those last are in Shadwell's 'humours' vein and
provide some broadly effective character comedy, which
degenerates into farce when Clodpate is tied up in a white
sheet and mistaken for a ghost. If Shadwell still has his beloved Jonson in mind, *Epsom Wells* is his *Bartholomew Fair*, and
certainly this comedy has some of Jonson's abundance and robust
vitality. But Shadwell is here offering us an unpalatable mixture
of the modes. His strong hold on reality, his masculine coarseness, and his determination to leave nothing unsaid give to
this holiday comedy of sex adventure an earnestness and
seriousness, and therefore a viciousness, which the Ariel-like
Congreve for the most part avoids. Such a play as *Epsom Wells*
makes one realize how much the comedy of Etherege or
Congreve owes to its refinement of discourse and its fine
manners. Shadwell, at all events, is frequently gross. In *The
Humourists* one of the chief characters is poxed, and we are
frequently invited to join in the merriment that this affords to
the other characters. *The Virtuoso* is an even coarser play: in old

Snarl Shadwell has produced a study of sexual perversion, complete with a flagellation scene, and Lady Gimcrack's adventures with Bruce and Longaville are indecent even by Restoration standards.

In his prefaces and dedications Shadwell talks a good deal about his satirical intent, and about the need for poets 'to render their Figures of Vice and Folly so ugly and detestable, to make People hate and despise them, not only in others, but (if it be possible) in their dear selves'. He can, indeed, as in *A True Widow*, satirize the vicious; but more often, like most of his contemporaries, he seems to be critical of folly and affectation rather than of loose living and vice. The sexual irregularities of Raines and Bevil in *Epsom Wells* are not reprehended; they are acceptable lovers to Lucia and Carolina, although Lucia only accepts Raines 'upon trial' and Carolina is prepared to consider Bevil 'upon your good behaviour'. Woodly and his wife simply face facts and agree to separate. Lady Gimcrack in *The Virtuoso* is not 'punished' for her infidelities; Sir Nicholas Gimcrack is left to console himself with his whore. As for old Snarl, 'a great admirer of the last age, and a declaimer against the vices of this age, and privately very vicious himself', he marries *his* whore. When Bruce asks him sarcastically if gentlemen and men of honour were accustomed to do this 'in the last age', Snarl replies: 'In sadness, they have much ado to avoid it in this; if I have married one, she is my own; and I had better marry my own than another Man's, by the Mass; as 'tis fifty to one I shou'd, if I marry'd elsewhere, in Sadness.' This, then, is the true Shadwellian humour, sardonic and disenchanted. Shadwell takes a long, grim look at the world about him, and sets down his findings, leaving us, for the most part, to draw such conclusions as we may.

If John Crowne had fallen in the middle of the eighteenth century he would not have been quite a Goldsmith or a Sheridan, but he would probably have been a better Colman, and a figure of more importance than literary historians have allowed him to be. He sometimes writes nonsense, but he always knows when he is doing so; it is never the naïve nonsense of Mrs. Behn, but the forced farce of a playwright who is himself a man of sense and discrimination and is compelled to write down to the level of an audience which has little of either. Crowne could undoubtedly have written better plays if his audience had wished for better; he has a good eye for the natural fool as well as for the artificial fop.

What he can do comes out clearly in his first comedy, *The Country Wit* (1676). This play, based on Molière's *Le Sicilien, ou L'Amour peintre*, drags rather badly for the first two acts: Crowne's dialogue is not taut enough to hold the interest when nothing much is happening, or when his characters are only involved in the usual love intrigues. But with the entrance of the country squire, Sir Mannerly Shallow, towards the middle of Act III, the scene brightens. (This delayed entrance of the chief comic character was to be repeated by Crowne in *Sir Courtly Nice*.) The astonishment of his man Booby that Londoners can live in the same street without knowing each other, and his bewildered 'How do they do not to know each other? do they do it on purpose?' belongs rather to the old natural comedy of the Elizabethans than to the artificial comedy of the Restoration. Besides being the cause of much innocent laughter, Sir Mannerly is also made the vehicle of some amusing satire on the Heroic Drama: the Restoration dramatists lived off each other's nonsense, and such satire was in no danger of being unintelligible to the small theatre-going public who had all seen the same plays. For the next few years Crowne turned his attention to tragedy, and when his next comedy appeared in 1683 it was a political satire, *City Politiques*. As one of the Tory poets he felt bound to enter the political conflict that followed upon the Popish Plot, and his play must be judged as a piece of successful Tory propaganda. Much of the action is farcical, and the adulterous association of the Podesta's wife with Florio, and of the toothless old Bartoline's wife with Artall, not to mention Craffy's attempts upon his father's young wife, give *City Politiques* what was required to make a Restoration comedy.

But Crowne's heart was not in seduction, and he would almost certainly have written less indecently if contemporary taste had not insisted that a comedy without cuckolding was no comedy at all. Indeed, looking back in his old age on the plays he had written, he staked a claim for his decency: 'Many of my Plays have been very successful, and yet clean. Sir Courtly Nice is as nice and clean in his Conversation, as his Diet and Dress. And Surly, though he affects ill manners in every thing else, is not guilty of obscene talk.' What in fact is new in *Sir*

Courtly Nice (1685) is the extreme fastidiousness of Crowne's delightful fop, extending not only to his toilet and the food he eats, but to his delicate revulsion from unpleasant smells. Sir Courtly has even given his attention to the art of bed-making; his gentleman is an adept at it:

Sir Courtly. . . . He has a delicate hand at making a Bed, he was my Page, I bred him up to it. . . .

Leonora. And my Woman has a great Talent.

Sir Courtly. Is it possible? Ladies commonly employ ordinary Chamber Maids—with filthy Aprons on, made by sluttish Women that spit as they—spin—foh!

With considerable skill Crowne brings the coarse and down-right Surly into collision with Sir Courtly on several occasions, and the contrast of manners is highly effective. A further effective contrast is provided by Testimony, 'a canting hypocritical fanatic', and Hothead, 'a choleric zealot against fanatics', and those two clash comically whenever they meet. Along with Sir Courtly and Surly, they are the dramatist's own contemporary additions to his Spanish source, Moreto's *No puede ser.* In all his plays Crowne sometimes delights us with the originality and aptness of his expression; he took a natural pleasure in writing well, and we are always conscious of the poet behind the drama-tist. The brutal Surly, for instance, courts Violante in the usual libertine terms of men of his kind, and Farewel, who is present, offers ironically to excuse Surly's 'rank expressions', but Violante will have none of it:

Vio. No, no, they signifie his own filthy meaning, and the truth is, Love has no other sense in this corrupt Age. . . . This ruins all Conversation, Men are always driving their brutal Appetites to the Plays, the Court, the Church, like Drovers their Beasts to every Market; and there's no conversing with 'em, unless you take the Cattle off their hands.

On the grounds of good morality and good writing this is a notable retort.

In 1690, with the Protestant William now on the throne, Crowne returned to a rather ineffective mixture of comedy and satire in *The English Friar.* The comic scenes throw some light on what he obviously believed to be a general worsening in public manners. The town sparks here are a dull and brutal collection of drunken rowdies led by Young Ranter, who is rather surprisingly described as a man of quality. Crowne's last attempt at comedy, *The Married Beau: or, The Curious Impertinent* (1694), in which a vain husband is cuckolded after persuading his friend to tempt his wife's virtue, is less a comedy than a problem play. It is significant that the more serious passages are in blank verse, and Mrs. Lovely might almost have stepped out of a play by Thomas Heywood. Based on the story of the *curioso impertinente* in *Don Quixote*, which Southerne had used ten years earlier for *The Disappointment*, Crowne's play has at least some psychological interest—a claim which cannot readily be made for many Restoration comedies. The subsequent repentance of the wife is managed without heroics, and Crowne's handling of the situation is symptomatic of the sentimentalism that was now creeping into late seventeenth-century drama, and perhaps of that uncertainty of treatment which results from a change of taste.

Edward Ravenscroft[1] was a playwright in the same honourable sense as the man who can make a wheel is a wheelwright. He had nothing whatever to say to his age, but he could put together a comedy with professional skill. His method of working is well seen in his first play, *The Citizen turn'd Gentleman* (1672; reissued in 1675 as *Mamamouchi*), which had an immediate and prolonged success with both the Town and the Court. We learn from Downes the prompter that Nokes, who played the part of old Jordan, 'pleased the King and Court better than in any character, except Sir Martin Mar-all'. This farcical comedy of intrigue was constructed from Molière's *Le Bourgeois Gentilhomme* cleverly fused with his *Monsieur de Pourceaugnac*, for Ravenscroft had discovered, like most of his contemporaries, that there was not nearly enough action in one French comedy to fill out an English play. As Courtall put it in *She Wou'd if she Cou'd*, 'A single intrigue in Love is as dull as a single Plot in a play, and will tire a Lover worse than t'other does an Audience'. Whatever Ravenscroft touches he coarsens, and Molière's delicate wine is transformed into strong October

---

[1] Edward Ravenscroft (1644–1704), son of a barrister of the Inner Temple, was himself a member of the Inner, and later of the Middle, Temple. With the immediate success of his first comedy, *The Citizen turned Gentleman* (based on Molière's play) he abandoned the law for literature, and wrote in all twelve plays, mainly comedies and farces. His libertine comedy, *The London Cuckolds*, was regularly performed on Lord Mayor's day until Garrick dropped it in the 1750s.

ale. But he knew what he was doing; indeed, his success was due no less to his knowledge of what would please an English audience than to the hard work he put into his plots. It is a tribute to his craftsmanship that if Molière's plays had not survived we should never guess that *The Citizen turn'd Gentleman* was not a play of native English growth; for although Ravenscroft frequently sticks close to Molière, he gives a purely English turn to the characters and the dialogue. Sir Simon Softhead in this play (Molière's M. de Pourceaugnac) is a Suffolk knight born and bred at Bury St. Edmunds, where he used to romp with little Peggy, George Goodale's daughter at the Rose, a 'witty little baggage' that he would 'run after to kiss from one room to another'. There is no equivalent in Molière for this picture of an English squire in his amorous moments, but even when Ravenscroft is translating his author almost *verbatim* he remains astonishingly English.

In *The Careless Lovers* (1673) he again found part of his plot in *Monsieur de Pourceaugnac*, and for the passages between Careless and Hillaria he appears to have taken some hints from the Celadon–Florimel scenes in *Secret Love*. It is characteristic of Ravenscroft's grosser appeal that for the scene in which Dryden's Florimel dressed as a man encounters Celadon and the two naïve young women who have fallen in love with him, Ravenscroft gives us a scene in a tavern where Hillaria meets Careless with two bawds. This comedy is also remarkable for a 'proviso scene' between Careless and Hillaria in which both stake their claim for complete liberty after marriage: Careless is free to have his mistress and Hillaria her gallant. To Lovell and Jacinta, the conventional lovers, Careless explains the situation: 'You shall see our Marriage . . . go on more cheerfully than yours, made out of Stark Love and desperate Affection; we, like two Birds (though we roost together at Night) will have our freedom all Day, and flie Chirpping about. . . .' The libertine element in Restoration comedy reached its height in the 1670s.

Ravenscroft's third comedy, *The Wrangling Lovers*, followed in 1676, a play of the Spanish intrigue kind set in Toledo, and, like most plays of this type, comparatively decent. With his next venture, *Scaramouch A Philosopher . . . A Comedy after the Italian Manner* (1677), based on *Les Fourberies de Scapin* and *Le Mariage Forcé*, he broke new ground, and in the prologue claimed to be doing so. Tiberio Fiorilli and his troupe of Italian comedians had visited London in 1673; they returned in the following year, and were acting again at Court in the summer of 1675. It was this new craze for the Italian comedians that Ravenscroft now exploited; he introduced into his play the typical characters of the *commedia dell'arte*, as well as some scraps of Italian, and started a minor theatrical fashion. Harlequin and Scaramouch appear in the second part of Mrs. Behn's *The Rover* (1680), and in her pantomime-farce, *The Emperor of the Moon* (1687), and about 1686 William Mountfort's *The Life and Death of Doctor Faustus . . . With the Humours of Harlequin and Scaramouche* was running at the Dorset Garden theatre. The great days of Harlequin, however, did not arrive on the stage until the early years of the eighteenth century.

Ravenscroft's next comedy, *The English Lawyer* (1677), an adaptation of George Ruggle's Latin play *Ignoramus* (performed at Cambridge in 1615) is of no great account. But with *The London Cuckolds* he had another resounding success. Here again he got some help from Molière (this time from *L'École des Femmes*), but he also worked in bits and pieces from several other sources to make a droll and highly indecent comedy in which three London citizens are successfully cuckolded. This is the old pagan comedy of sex, the worship of Dionysus in seventeenth-century London. Ravenscroft's play got away to a good start, for it appeared on the stage in November 1681, when Shaftesbury's faction in the City was at its most violent, and when the cuckolding of citizens, in real life or in comedy, became almost a patriotic duty. Addressing the Whig citizens in the epilogue Ravenscroft promised to keep on railing at them,

> Till you, the Bullys of a Common-wealth,
> Leave breaking Windows for a loyal health.

This gay and impudent play remained popular long after the original epilogue had lost its relevance; it became a regular part of the saturnalia of Lord Mayor's day, and was repeated every November till Garrick removed it from the bills in 1751. By 1709, however, Steele could refer to it in a *Tatler* as 'that heap of vice and absurdity', and even Cibber, in his *Apology*, considered it to be 'the most rank play that ever succeeded'.

There is some evidence that *The London Cuckolds* shocked at least some of the contemporary audience, for Ravenscroft's

next play, *Dame Dobson: or, The Cunning Woman* (1683), a free
translation of Thomas Corneille's *La Devineresse,* was entirely
decent. Ravenscroft did not fail to point out this fact himself,
and ironically called it his 'recantation play'. Professor Nicoll
believes that *Dame Dobson* 'pays tribute to the growing force of
moral sentiment rising after 1682', and sees in it an example of
'the rapid change in the spirit of the age'; but this is perhaps
to take too hopeful a view of an isolated play. Chastity to
Ravenscroft was probably not much more than a new gimmick.
It is true that for some time before the appearance of Collier's
Short View there were signs, among some sections of the audience
at least, that the stage libertinism of the 1670s was becoming
less tolerable. But equally certainly there was no widespread
outbreak of decency between 1682 and 1700. The dramatists
had to cater for the audience as they found it, and important
though the ladies were, the men (at any rate for comedy) were
more important still. When the actor George Powell produced
The Cornish Comedy in 1696, there were some complaints about
its obscenity, which apparently surprised the author:

There is one Objection, made by Persons of that strange Antipathy to any thing that is obscene that the least tincture of it
strangely Disorders them, that is laid to its Charge, which, after the
Plays I have seen crowded and admired, did not a little surprize me;
for I was so far from being Conscious to my self of having intrenched
on Decency more than ordinary, that my greatest fear was, that it
would prove too Modest for this Age: But I hope this is only a
piece of Female Hypocrisie, and that which is condemned in
publick will be Matter of private Diversion.

As an actor Powell must have had a good idea of what would
please, and if *The Cornish Comedy* gave offence, it was probably
not on account of the fornication, but of the crude and vulgar way
in which it was handled. It is significant, too, that in a decade
in which it is often supposed that the theatre was becoming more
decorous, Powell gave his highly indecent epilogue to be spoken
by a little girl of seven.

Ravenscroft's last two comedies, *The Canterbury Guests* (1694)
and *The Anatomist: or, The Sham Doctor* (1696) add little or
nothing to his reputation, although, as a successful farce, the
latter kept the stage until the close of the eighteenth century.
Historically, however, he is of considerable significance: he did
perhaps more than any other dramatist to popularize farce in

the later years of the seventeenth century. Farce in one form or another had been appearing sporadically since the Restoration—in *The Wild Gallant*, in the tub scene of Etherege's first play, in Davenant's *The Man's the Master* (1668), in Orrery's farcical comedies, *Guzman* (1669) and *Mr. Anthony* (1672), and in many other places. As early as 1668, in the Preface to *An Evening's Love*, Dryden remarks contemptuously on 'those farces which are now the most frequent entertainments of the Stage', and he can foresee no end to them 'till we forbear the translation of French Plays'. But the popularity of Ravenscroft's plays in the early 1670s undoubtedly gave a fresh stimulus to his contemporaries to take an easy way to success; and although, in the prologue to *The Assignation* (1672), Dryden sneered at Mamamouchi and the audiences which took such a naïve delight in him, he was swimming against the stream. Farce appeared frequently in the plays of Shadwell, Mrs. Behn, and Durfey in the 1670s and later; Otway scored a hit with *The Cheats of Scapin* (1676), taken from Molière's play; and between 1674 and 1675 Thomas Duffet made a small satirical corner for himself with three farcical burlesques: *The Empress of Morocco*, *The Mock-Tempest* (a travesty of Davenant's and Dryden's opera), and *Psyche Debauch'd* (a similar travesty of Shadwell's *Psyche*). In 1684 Nahum Tate hit the taste of the Town with *A Duke and No Duke*, which survived as a popular afterpiece all through the eighteenth century, and he tried again with another farce, *Cuckolds-Haven*, the following summer. What is perhaps more significant, a number of actor-authors, who must have been thoroughly familiar with the tastes of the contemporary audience, chose to write farces or farcical comedies. Thomas Betterton, Cave Underhill, Thomas Jevon, William Mountfort, Thomas Doggett, and George Powell all produced plays of this type, and some of those— notably Doggett's *The Country Wake*—had a long acting life. As the century drew to a close, farce was firmly established in the theatres, and even the fastidious Congreve was driven to introduce some farcical business into his comedies to satisfy current expectations.

Some attempt has been made in recent years to suggest that Mrs. Behn[1] was not quite so black as she has been painted;

---

[1] Reliable facts about Aphra Behn (1640–89) are hard to come by, but she appears to have visited Surinam in 1663–4, to which, it is said, her father (who

indeed, there has always been a tendency (due perhaps to masculine gallantry) to treat her plays too kindly. That said, we may allow her what we may allow to Mrs. Centlivre in the next generation, the ability to keep a comedy moving with a kind of bustling vigour. She is most successful in her comedies of intrigue, such as *The Dutch Lover* (1673) and *The Rover* (1677). In the former she depends almost entirely upon comic business, but the plot is over-complicated and rests upon too many hackneyed conventions of the theatre. Her recipe for this kind of play is to take three or four pairs of lovers, involve them in misunderstandings, blunders, overheard conversations, jealousies, and quarrels, and add an amorous song or two for flavouring. Her young men are interested only in the prospect of making the young women their mistresses, but (as in the comedies of so many of her contemporaries) they must be brought in the end, protesting comically, to matrimony. In this way Alonzo of *The Dutch Lover* is compelled to marry Euphemia. This 'Flanders colonel' would have preferred to steal the apple by climbing the garden wall; instead, he has been manœuvred into a shop and forced tamely to buy it. To complicate her plot, Mrs. Behn has introduced another pair of lovers, Silvio and Cleonte, who believe themselves to be, but are not, brother and sister. She amuses herself by skating over thin ice, knowing all the time (although the audience is deceived) that the water beneath is only a few inches deep. When she has obtained all the excitement possible from this equivocal situation, old Ambrosio steps forward and explains that Silvio is not the brother of Cleonte at all. This sort of situation is, of course, a legacy from Jacobean drama, and it is only one of Mrs. Behn's several debts to the plays of 'the last age'.

The Rover is a better comedy; the plot is less fantastic. But the assumption that the whole duty of man is to have a successful intrigue with one or more young women is stronger than ever. In the long run Mrs. Behn defeats the ends of the comedy of intrigue by having too much of it. A detective story in which

died on his way there) had been appointed Lieutenant-Governor. She was certainly acting as a Royalist agent at Antwerp in 1666, in concert with William Scott, son of Thomas Scott the regicide. Nothing certain is known about Mr. Behn, who may have been a London merchant of Dutch extraction. From 1670 onwards Mrs. Behn wrote eighteen plays, mostly comedies, some of which (e.g. *The Rover*) were very successful, and she also wrote occasional poems. Her prose fiction belongs to her later years.

all the chief characters are murderers would soon forfeit our attention; murder only remains interesting when it is something out of the ordinary, and the same is true (if less absolutely) of the sexual intrigues on which Mrs. Behn depends for most of her comic effect. By constant repetition the suspense which such situations ought to generate fails to make much impression; the elastic has been stretched too often. A father may lock up his daughter, or a brother his sister, to keep her out of harm's way, but we know that the girl will get the key to the garden gate or climb over the wall, just as we know that a tom-cat will climb in through the pantry window. In any case, we soon cease to feel any interest in Mrs. Behn's crude young men, who are invariably actuated by one monotonous and obsessive motive. Still, there are distinctions to be made even here; and it can be said for Willmore in this comedy that he is less boring than some of his kind, and that in Hellena Mrs. Behn has drawn a young woman who is both lively and attractive, and in whose unashamed hedonism there is even a kind of innocence. Professor Nicoll is surely right in finding the influence of Celadon and Florimel on Mrs. Behn's young couple.

> *Will.* Marriage is as certain a Bane to Love, as lending Money is to Friendship: I'll neither ask nor give a Vow, tho I could be content to turn Gipsy, and become a Left-hand Bridegroom, to have the Pleasure of working that great Miracle of making a Maid a Mother, if you durst venture; 'tis upse Gipsy that, and if I miss, I'll lose my Labour.
>
> *Hell.* And if you do not lose, what shall I get? A Cradle full of Noise and Mischief, with a Pack of Repentance at my Back? Can you teach me to weave Incle to pass my time with? 'Tis upse Gipsy that too.
>
> *Will.* I can teach thee to weave a true Love's Knot better.
>
> *Hell.* So can my Dog.

There are no such redeeming strokes in *Sir Patient Fancy* (1678), indecent even for Mrs. Behn, in *The Roundheads* (1681), in which she rewrites Tatham's *The Rump*, or in *The City-Heiress* (1682), a coarsened version of Middleton's *A Mad World, My Masters*, where the scene between Sir Charles Meriwill and Lady Galliard in Act IV reaches a new depth of crudity. These last two were her anti-Whig contributions to the theatre at the time of the Popish Plot. That such a play as *The*

Roundheads could be performed in 1681, when some of the characters satirized were still alive, not only indicates the state of delirium to which the Shaftesbury faction had brought public opinion, but suggests the limits of Restoration taste: Mrs. Behn's sole purpose was to blacken the 'good old cause', and it is symptomatic of the poverty of motive that runs through Restoration comedy that she could find no better way of doing so than by resorting once again to the worn-out machinery of cuckoldry.

A modern critic has found a strain of 'moral seriousness' in her late comedy *The Lucky Chance* (1686), and, less plausibly, has suggested that 'mere cuckolding does not suffice for her lovers'. To this it can only be replied that if her lovers really do have such feelings they prefer at least to make sure of the cuckolding first: Gayman in this comedy is not apparently troubled by any moral scruples on that score. What gives *The Lucky Chance* some claim to moral seriousness is the fact that it illustrates, to a rather fuller extent than usual, 'the way of the world': the two cuckolds, Sir Feeble Fainwood and Sir Cautious Fulbank, are rich elderly citizens who have taken to themselves young and attractive wives. If that is not a moral justification for what follows, it does at least give it a solid ground of probability, and the point at issue is further driven home by the fact that Leticia, contracted to young Bellmour, has been tricked into marrying Sir Feeble by being told that her lover is dead. This comedy, although it is spoilt in places by some childish farce, shows how good a craftsman Mrs. Behn had become by the close of her career as a dramatist; the opening scene introduces us by means of lively action and natural dialogue to almost all the chief characters, and makes a complicated situation crystal clear. Her dialogue is not very polished, and only intermittently witty, but it is at times wonderfully realistic. The scene between Gayman and his landlady in the second Act is in its way a little masterpiece:

> *Gayman* . . . But here's old Nasty coming. I smell her up.—Hah, my dear Landlady. Quite out of breath—a Chair there for my Landlady.
>
> > *Enter* Rag *and* Landlady.
>
> *Rag.* Here's ne'er a one, Sir.
>
> *Land.* More of your Money and less of your Civility, good Mr. Wasteall.

Gay. Dear Landlady—

Land. Dear me no Dears, Sir, but let me have my Money—
   Eight Weeks Rent last Friday; besides Taverns, Ale-houses,
   Chandlers, Landresses' Scores, and ready Money out of my
   Purse; you know it, Sir.

Gay. Ay, but your Husband don't; speak softly.

The landladies of Restoration comedy, from *The Wild Gallant*
onwards, are among the most natural of the stock types; and
Mrs. Behn's Gammer Grime, with her feminine frailty for her
handsome young lodger and the extremities to which she is driven
to keep him in cash, is a fine piece of humorous observation.

It is perhaps significant that Mrs. Behn's first play was
called *The Forced Marriage* (1670), a tragi-comedy in which the
solution is obtained by a very artificial, not to say forced, contrivance, and that she returned to this theme of the folly of
parents who compel their children to marry against their
choice in *The Town-Fop* (1676), a rather grim comedy based
on George Wilkins's *The Miseries of Enforced Marriage,* and
again in *The False Count* (1682). In *Sir Patient Fancy* it is not a
parent but financial necessity that has driven a young woman
to marry an old husband, and in the end she is granted a separation without having to return the money he has given her. It is
difficult to decide whether Mrs. Behn is being romantic or
realistic in her handling of such situations. Certainly the happy
endings that she provides for her comedies by way of divorce
and separation take little account of reality. In real life divorce
was rare, expensive, and hard to obtain. Restoration comedy
from first to last was on the side of the young, but that hardly
distinguishes it from the comedy of other periods: what gives
it a good deal of its characteristic content is the extent to which
it was concerned with the problems occasioned by the contemporary marriage of convenience. In dealing so fully and frankly
with the situations to which loveless marriages arranged by
fortune-hunting parents gave rise, the dramatists were facing
the facts of the world they lived in. But in their need to make
a comedy end happily they were continually driven to fall back
on implausible tricks, on improbable reconciliations and
changes of heart, and in general on solutions which were
frankly escapist. The dance with which so many Restoration
comedies ended was often no more than a dance of puppets.

As a woman Mrs. Behn may have been more than usually interested in the problems which contemporary marriage practice created for her own sex, and to some extent she succeeds in stating them; but, writing as she was for a living, she could never allow herself to forget that 'the stage but echoes back the public voice', and any criticism she had to offer tended to become obscured by her compliance with those situations and attitudes which were then thought essential for a successful comedy.

Tom Durfey[1] (it is significant that no one ever thought of calling him Thomas) was another popular dramatist who firmly believed that 'the Drama's laws the Drama's patrons give'. Among the secondary writers of the period he has at least the importance of the playwright who gives the public what (allowing for one or two inevitable failures) it appears to have wanted. He began writing plays in his early twenties, when Charles II was in his late middle age, and he was still happily producing comedies and operas in the reign of Queen Anne. Durfey was not a thinker, and his moral standards were not high; but he took considerable pains over the construction of his plays, the plots of which were borrowed frequently from the earlier drama. He had, too, the ability to create comic character by a sort of natural mimicry of old age, rusticity, stupidity, and so on; and anything that he failed to write into the part Nokes and Leigh could supply. His first comedy, *Madam Fickle* (1676), is typical of his early work. Madam Fickle, deserted by her husband and determined to be revenged on the opposite sex, has three lovers whom she plays off against each other. The plot therefore turns largely upon her efforts to keep the three men apart, and when this is no longer possible, to convince each in turn that he is her real choice. The role of the husband disguised as a servant, who finally steps forward and reclaims his wife, is not satisfactorily motivated, but in this sort of farcical comedy we do not examine motives too closely. Much of the laughter comes from two comic brothers played

---

[1] Tom Durfey (or D'Urfey; 1653–1723) was a French Huguenot by descent who became *plus Anglais que les Anglais*. He was a prolific writer for the stage, turning out some thirty plays; and from the days when Charles II could be seen 'leaning on Tom Durfey's shoulder . . . and humming over a song with him' till the reign of Queen Anne he remained a popular public figure. In so far as he is still generally remembered it is by the several volumes of *Pills to Purge Melancholy*, a collection of his own songs and those of other popular writers of the time.

by Nokes and Leigh: Toby, a country bumpkin, and Zechiel, a student at the Temple with a thin veneer of town culture. *Madam Fickle* shows Durfey's talent for extricating his characters from difficult situations by their impudent improvisation, and though there is little wit (and there was never to be much in Durfey) there is abundant humour and high spirits.

His second comedy, *The Fool Turn'd Critic*, which was produced in the same month, is an even more elaborate tangle of plotting, counterplotting, and cross-purposes. The following year his third comedy of intrigue, *A Fond Husband*, so pleased Charles II that he was present at three of the first five nights. This play deals with a cuckolded husband, Peregrine Bubble, who is so completely credulous that his wife Emillia carries on an intrigue with her lover Rashley in front of his eyes. When his sister Maria and his friend Ranger try to make him realize what is going on and attempt to expose the two lovers, they continually escape detection by some ingenious contrivance. Again Durfey was indebted to Nokes and Leigh, the former taking the part of Bubble, and the latter playing 'Old Fumble, a superannuated alderman', almost blind and deaf—an effective study of decrepitude. In a theatre in which so many of the comedies are over-burdened with a complex plot *The Fond Husband* is relatively simple, and the way in which the successive crises are circumvented by impudence and stratagem, if sometimes farcical, is broadly effective.

Durfey, at the age of twenty-four, was now the author of three comedies and a tragedy, *The Siege of Memphis*. His comedies had obviously pleased the Town; but the opening lines of the prologue to *The Fond Husband* suggest that although he knew what he could do, he also knew that the critics expected something that he was not giving them:

> If Plot and Bus'ness Comical and New,
> Could please the Criticks that sit here to view,
> The Poet might have thought this Play would do.
> But in this Age Design no praise can get:
> You cry it Conversation wants, and Wit;
> As if the Obvious Rules of Comedy
> Were only dull Grimace and Repartée.
> Such, Sirs, have been your Darlings prov'd of late. . . .

Durfey, however, continued to supply the stage with comedies full of 'plot and business', the plot usually involving sexual intrigue and much of the business remaining farcical and improbable. In so far as he develops, it is in his ability to come closer to life as it is actually lived. *The Virtuous Wife* (1679) opens with a lively and natural scene between the rather jaded Beverley and his mistress Jenny Wheadle, and goes on to a very spirited quarrel between Beverley and his wife Olivia, who complains of his habit of snoring in bed:

> *Oliv.* . . . your Mouth open, as if you were swallowing the Jealous Aire, that was to be vented against me the next morning, and snoring in such a horrid Whistling Tone, such a Barbrous Untunable Key—that the poor Bellman has often stood frighted at the dore, with the apprehension of Ghosts and Murders.
>
> *Bever.* What's this? I snore? I tell thee, Thou most intollerable provoking Woman, No man in Christendom sleeps more silently than I, or with a clearer Conscience, I thank Providence.

At several points in this play Durfey verges on the sentimental, and he comes still closer to it in *Love for Money* (1691), where three of the chief characters, young Merriton, his father, and the orphan Mirtilla, are virtuous and triumphant. When (III. i) Mirtilla, believing herself to be a penniless orphan and not the heiress she turns out to be, refuses young Merriton, we are listening to the sort of dialogue that might have been written a century later by Richard Cumberland or Hugh Kelly:

> *Mirtilla.* What Comfort can there be in Love curb'd and confin'd by Poverty? . . .'Tis not for my own sake that I deny, but, Sir, for yours; if we were married, perhaps I should love ye, nay love ye dearly; perhaps have Children too, some half a dozen pretty smiling Blessings to cling around and help Life's tedious Journey with the dear nonsence of their pratling Stories. But should the freezing hand of Want afflict us, what should we do, but sit by our small fire, Tears in our Eyes and throbing Griefs at Heart, to see our little Flock of unfledg'd Cupids shivering with Cold as wanting necessaries, who looking wishly on us seemed to say, why should you marry thus to make us miserable? . . . Can I see him that lies within my Arms so full of cares he scarce has time for Love, rise early to provide for me and mine, and I not knit, or sow, or spin or something?

It is significant that although Mirtilla's speech is printed as prose, it is written in the plangent and flowing blank verse that is so often the vehicle for the more heart-rending passages

in the sentimental drama. Coming from Durfey, who always
tried to be in the fashion, the virtuous and unselfish Mirtilla is
indeed significant: by 1691 the tears that had flowed for Otway
in tragedy were becoming increasingly possible in comedy.
The world of Durfey's early plays was one in which every
difficulty could yield to ingenuity, and in which nothing essentially mattered because nothing was quite real; but here we
have a character facing facts, and while that lasts we are in
a different world altogether. Although *The Richmond Heiress*
(1693) has the usual cuckolding scenes, it may be looked upon
as a mild satire upon fortune-hunting: the rich young heiress
Fulvia ends by discarding all her suitors, since 'such a general
defect of honesty corrupts the Age'. Like almost all Durfey's
comedies, this one depends to an excessive degree on characters
who go about in disguise, and his slender hold on the probable
may be gauged from a scene in which not only the heroine
feigns madness, but a messenger from one of her lovers also pretends to be a madman so that he may deliver his message.

It would be wrong to suppose that Durfey's progress along the
path of virtue was now uninterrupted. He veered back rather
sharply into the lewd with the three parts of *The Comical History
of Don Quixote* (1694, 1696), although the humour of the country
wench Mary the Buxom, speaking in a broad west-country
dialect, is vulgarly effective. To an audience in the 1690s,
however, obscenity was one thing and natural vulgarity
another, and *Don Quixote* appears to have had a rather mixed
reception. Jeremy Collier attacked it in 1698 in the *Short View*
on his usual grounds of profanity, abuse of the clergy, and want
of modesty in regard to the audience. What he has to say on
the third count probably explains the exception taken to this
play: it was 'low'. He diverts the ladies, says Collier, 'with the
Charming Rhetorick of *Snotty-Nose, filthy Vermin in the Beard,
Nitty Jerkin, Louse-Snapper, and the Letter in the Chamber-pot.* . . .
This is rare stuff for Ladies, and Quality!' As for profanity
and abuse of the clergy, Collier was apt to find such things
where no one else would; but in fact Durfey was prosecuted for
profanity in 1698. By that year, when he wrote *The Campaigners*,
one might have expected to find in him some traces of the new
spirit of reformation. So to some extent one does. Colonel
Dorange, who has wronged the virtuous Angellica, repents
and marries her, but not before he has inadvertently cuckolded

his friend the Marquis for the price of a hundred pistoles, ignorant of the fact that the mercenary lady in whose chamber he appears 'unbuttoned' in the fifth act is in fact his friend's wife. When the circumstances are explained to him, the Marquis, who is a man of honour, forgives the Colonel with some dignity; indeed, the two men almost consolidate their friendship on the basis of their joint contempt for the unfaithful and rapacious Marquise, but whether this is a fine stroke of comedy or a serious claim for the virtue of male friendship it is hard to say. *The Campaigners*, at any rate, belongs to that late seventeenth-century type of comedy in which the rake repents in the fifth act. But Durfey, on whose shoulder Charles II had once leant while humming over a song with him, was not giving up much ground. The play is prefaced by an unrepentant prose reply to Collier's *Short View* and it contains a splendidly unregenerate and defiant song in Act IV, 'New Reformation begins through the Nation', in which Durfey stigmatizes 'stubborn Non-Jurors' who 'for want of employment now scourge the lewd times'. Durfey was doing his best to keep the dirty old flag flying. He was still writing plays and songs in the reign of Queen Anne, and was one of the best-known figures of his day; but no one was prepared to take him quite seriously. He sang in public, and anyone who does that in England is apt to be thought slightly absurd; he spoke with a stutter, he was convivial and amusing in company, and so he was referred to rather patronizingly by duller men than himself as 'honest Tom Durfey'. His comedies, it is true, were buoyed up more by good nature than by wit; but from first to last he was a highly efficient man of the theatre, and during four successive reigns one of the most successful entertainers of his age.

It has been customary to dismiss the three comedies of Otway with impatient contempt, and it is true that his fun is sometimes of the laboured sort that we might expect from a writer of tragedy. Left to himself, Otway would probably have chosen to write satirical comedy: what he did in fact write, having to please the players and the playgoers, was farcical comedy uneasily streaked with satire. *Friendship in Fashion* (1678) oscillates precariously between farce and a disturbing realism; and the bitterly sarcastic passage at the beginning of Act V between Goodvile and his wife shows what Otway might have done in a kind of realistic comedy which would have been the counterpart

of his domestic tragedy. How strong was Otway's grasp of
the actual may be seen if we set his Goodvile beside Wycherley's Horner. If Horner is not quite the amoral fairy that
Lamb made him out to be, he remains a sufficiently cool and
remote personality to move lightly in the world of intellectual
comedy; but Otway's Goodvile is the *homme sensuel*, mean,
lecherous, and greedy, a man who we should like to think never
existed, but whom we are compelled to accept as humiliatingly
true to life. In *The Soldier's Fortune* (1680), which Downes tells
us 'took extraordinary well', Otway again comes close to life in
such passages as that in which Courtine complains of the
treatment of the disbanded soldier. When the country is in
danger, it is 'Heavens bless you, Sir, the Laird go along with
you!' but when the danger is past—'Fogh, ye Lowsy Red-coat
rake hells! hout ye Caterpillars, ye Locusts of the Nation, you
are the Dogs that would enslave us all, plunder our Shops, and
ravish our Daughters, ye Scoundrels.' This seventeenth-century
version of Kipling's 'It's Tommy this, an' Tommy that . . .' has
the bitterness of personal experience behind it; the poetic
Lazarus is displaying his sores. It is perhaps only in this play
that Otway succeeds fully in combining his sense of the actual
with the cathartic gaiety of comedy: in Sir Jolly Jumble he has
created his one really memorable comic character, a shocking
old pervert into whom he has somehow managed to infuse an
infectious good humour. The stage success of this study in
senile perversion may have prompted him to repeat the formula (much less pleasingly) in the Antonio scenes of *Venice
Preserv'd*. Otway's interest in the sexual pervert has probably
little personal significance, and is rather an indication of the
taste of his audience; the age looked for refinements in lewdness
no less than in wit. His last comedy, *The Atheist: Or, The Second
Part of The Soldier's Fortune* (1683), has the same disconcerting
mixture of lewd comedy and satire, but this time 'it met with
many enemies'. The audience may have been alienated by the
dramatist's disenchanting exposure in Courtine of what a rake
is really like after he is married, and in Sylvia of the destructive
effect that such a man has on his unfortunate wife. For all its
persistent satire on married life, Restoration comedy usually
avoided looking too closely at the raw reality of a broken marriage; but Otway, the romantic lover of Elizabeth Barry, appears
to have been obsessed by the infidelities of husbands, and, to

the extent that he was so, he failed to play the accepted comedy game. The laughter in this play comes mainly from the scenes between Beaugard, who has inherited a fortune from his uncle, and his impoverished and reprobate father, who continually sponges on him and then promptly loses the money on gaming. This shameless old rogue was played by Leigh, who had also impersonated Sir Jolly Jumble in the earlier comedy. Those two droll parts were not merely written *for* Leigh: they were obviously inspired by him. Old Beaugard's final settlement with his son is a humorous variation on the conventional proviso scenes of Restoration comedy:

> Now, Jacky Boy; Jacky, you Rogue, shall not I have a little spill out of this Portion now, hah? . . . Three Bottles of Sack, Jack, *per diem*, without Deduction, or false Measure: Two Pound of Tobacco *per* Month; and that of the best too. . . . Buttock-Beef and March-Beer at Dinner, you Rogue: A young Wench of my own chusing, to wait on no body but me always: Money in my Pocket: An old Pacing Horse, and an Elbow-Chair.

Young Beaugard can well afford to be generous, and his good-natured acceptance of his graceless parent is a fair measure of the moral level of this comedy: 'Look you, Sir: Though you have been a very ungratious Father, upon condition that you'll promise to leave off Gaming, and stick to your Whoring and Drinking, I will treat with you.'

Nathaniel Lee was about as well suited for writing comedy as Durfey was for tragedy, and his one venture into the comic mode, *The Princess of Cleve* (1681?), was apparently written in a fit of pique at the prohibition of his Protestant play, *The Massacre of Paris*. He may or may not have been in an unusually sour temper when he wrote *The Princess of Cleve*, but he certainly produced a play which has nauseated most of the critics. Turning to it after reading his *Lucius Junius Brutus* was for Professor Nicoll like coming upon 'a rotting dung-heap'. Anyone who has read the play will probably agree that it smells of corruption, but it would be wrong to assume that Lee himself was unaware of it; indeed, he would have welcomed Professor Nicoll's reaction, for he had deliberately set about to provoke it. Basing his play on the Countess de La Fayette's romantic novel, *La Princesse de Clèves*, he leaves the Princess much as he found her, but he treats her lover Nemours as an insatiable rake.

For when they expected the most polish'd Hero in Nemours, I
gave 'em a Ruffian reeking from Whetsone's-Park. The fourth and
fifth Acts of the *Chances*, where Don John is pulling down; *Marriage
Alamode*, where they are bare to the Waste; the *Libertine* and *Epsom-
Wells*, are but Copies of his Villany.

The result is a play which, with the unrestrained wenching
of Nemours, the confession of the Princess to her husband and
his subsequent death, and the unseemly sub-plot involving two
husbands and their wives, can only be described in Lee's own
words as 'this Farce, Comedy, Tragedy, or meer Play'. What
possessed Lee to write it, and in so doing to bite the hand that
paid at the box-office? Was he already in revolt from the
theatrical convention which assumed, as Collier was to put it,
that 'a fine Gentleman is a fine Whoring, Swearing, Smutty,
Atheistical Man', and that 'Libertinism and Profaneness,
Dressing, Idleness, and Gallantry are the only valuable Qualities'? In the Duke of Nemours Lee seems to be saying to his
audience: 'This is the sort of character you admire. Well, take
a good look at him, and see what your precious Dorimants are
really like.' It is significant that when he wrote this play he
apparently had the recent death of Rochester very much in his
mind. 'I saw him [Rosidore] dust,' says one of his characters,

> I saw the mighty thing a nothing made,
> Huddled with Worms, and swept to the cold Den,
> Where Kings lye crumbled just like other Men.

There follows a notable tribute to Rochester's wit and abundant
genius. But later (III. i) Nemours exclaims significantly: 'Therefore the Fury of Wine and Fury of Women possess me waking
and sleeping; let me Dream of nothing but dimpl'd Cheeks,
and laughing Lips, and flowing Bowls, Venus be my Star, and
Whoring my House, and Death I defie thee. Thus sang Rosi-
dore [i.e. Rochester] in the Urn.' Like almost everyone else
Lee had been under the spell of Rochester's remarkable gifts,
but it may be that Rochester's early death and his deathbed
repentance, made famous by Bishop Burnet's account of it, had
shocked him into pondering on the moral bankruptcy of the
most celebrated fine gentleman of his day, and that Nemours is
another adumbration of Rochester, seen through the eyes of
Burnet rather than of Etherege.

It is significant that Southerne's most popular comedy, *Sir*

Anthony Love (*c.* 1690), was also his poorest; it was written for
Mrs. Mountfort, and its success was largely due (as Southerne
handsomely acknowledged) to her acting in the title role, and
also, no doubt, to the never-failing delight given to the simple-
minded by seeing an attractive woman masquerading in man's
clothes. The action is sometimes farcical, and the dialogue is
often spun out to a tedious length without being particularly
witty; but even here there are some signs of an unusually acute
observation of human behaviour and human motives. In *The
Wife's Excuse* (1691) these become much more frequent. Significantly, this intelligent play appears to have been a failure. In
some verses which Dryden wrote to Southerne it appears that
it had not 'pleased the Box and Pit', and that although it was
neither hissed nor damned it was 'with a kind Civility dismiss'd'.
In this play Southerne puts the whole business of cuckolding on
a psychological basis; he is more interested in accounting
for it than in demonstrating it for the delight of the pit and
boxes. His audience, on the other hand, did not want to have
their favourite comic theme subjected to such an analysis,
however penetrating; for this was to spoil their fun, to question
the very assumptions on which the comedy of sex rested.
Southerne's presentation of character, too, is at once subtler
and more complex than that attempted by most of his contemporaries. The behaviour of Mrs. Friendall when her cowardly
husband is insulted in public is a good example of Southerne's
close observation of the human mind; and so, too, are her
subsequent reflections: 'Whatever I think of him, I must not
let him fall into the Contempt of the Town. Every little Fellow,
I know, will be censoriously inquisitive and maliciously witty
upon another Man's Cowardise, out of the pleasure of finding
as great a Rascal as himself.' There is a cool detachment about
Southerne, a disenchanted vision which enables him to face
frankly the motives of a Mrs. Witwoud ('Undone her self, she
wou'd undo the Sex. . . . Bawds have some good Nature, and
procure Pleasure for Pay: Witwoud has baser Ends, a general
Ruin upon all her Friends'), or to comment on the vanity of
'these young girls', each of whom imagines that, however often
some profligate may have betrayed her friends, *she* 'has something particular in her Person, forsooth, to reclaim and engage
him to her self'. *The Maid's Last Prayer* (1693) is more farcical,
and has less of this telling exposure of human weakness; but in

such characters as Lord Malepert, Captain Drybubb, and Lady Susan (another part for Mrs. Mountfort) Southerne comes nearer to a purely comic effect. Comedy, however, was not really his *métier*; his characters are more apt to interest than to amuse us, and he is always attempting rather more in comedy than the genre will allow him to perform. His merits are fairly enough summed up by a contemporary critic:

There's a Spirit of Conversation in every thing he writes. I think very few exceed him in the Dialogue; his Gallantry is natural, and after the real manner of the Town; his acquaintance with the best Company entered him into the secrets of their Intrigues, and no Man knew better the Way and Disposition of Mankind.

When Mrs. Bracegirdle appeared before the Drury Lane audience on 16 January 1693 to speak the prologue to Congreve's first comedy, she made the conventional request for a kind reception to a young author. But never, perhaps, had the English theatre seen such a first play as *The Old Bachelor*: Congreve[1] did not try his wings with tentative flutterings; he flew straight up into the tree and started to sing. The opening dialogue between Bellmour and Vainlove has all the assurance of a practised hand, and as scene follows scene the feast of epigram and the flow of repartee never fail. The discriminating may have detected a new idiom, a new inflexion in the voice, a cooler and more consciously sophisticated affectation in the manner; the less discriminating must have felt that here

---

[1] William Congreve (1670–1729) was born at Bardsey, a few miles from Leeds, in 1670, but from the age of about 5 grew up in Ireland, where his father, an army officer, was posted at Youghal in County Cork. He was sent to an excellent school in Kilkenny (where Swift had also been a pupil), and he followed Swift to Trinity College, Dublin, in 1686. Two years later he was in England, and was admitted to the Middle Temple in March 1690, where he acquired some genuine knowledge of the law. In 1692 he published his novel *Incognita*. The following year his first comedy, *The Old Bachelor* (helped by some revision from Dryden), was performed with outstanding success. In the autumn of the same year the more satirical *Double Dealer* met with a cooler reception, but Congreve delighted the Town again with his *Love for Love* in 1695, and further consolidated his reputation with his solitary tragedy, *The Mourning Bride*, in 1697. He replied rather ineffectively to Collier's *Short View* in 1698. The unenthusiastic reception in 1700 of his finest play, *The Way of the World*, was obviously a disappointment to him, and the growing objection to profaneness and immorality on the stage may have still further discouraged him, for he wrote little else for the theatre. In middle age the sedentary Congreve suffered from gout and overweight, and was almost blind from cataracts in the eyes. From 1695 onwards he was given a number of minor government posts, and from 1714 until his death he held the lucrative Secretaryship of Jamaica, which he administered by a paid deputy.

was everything that they wanted from a comedy, better done than it had ever been done before. Yet viewed in the light of his later comedies *The Old Bachelor* shows some signs of immaturity. In his desire to hit the mark Congreve has shot at too many targets. He wavers between humours and manners, between farce and sophisticated comedy, between the real and the fantastic; he keeps five different actions going, and he throws in some singing and dancing for good measure. But the tone is comic throughout, and the play has the high spirits, characteristic of a young man's play, that can carry an audience along in spite of some rather laboured artifice in the plot, and some exaggeration in the characters. Captain Bluffe, with his 'By the immortal thunder of great guns!', comes straight out of Jonsonian comedy, but is clearly less of a contemporary type than Bobadill was to the Elizabethans. On the other hand, Heartwell, who owes something to Wycherley's plain-dealer, is a thoroughly Restoration humour-character: his comic despair—'What am I come to? a woman's toy at these years! ... That ever that noble passion, lust, should ebb to this degree!'— would have been barely intelligible in the age of Jonson, but is an embodiment of one of the basic assumptions on which Restoration comedy rested. Congreve may not have seen any further than the best of his contemporaries in comedy, but from the first he saw with devastating clearness. Even more significant of the new age is Vainlove, who repudiates Araminta because she has been won too easily ('Tis dull and unnatural to have a hare run full into the hounds' mouth . . . I would have overtaken, not have met, my game'). For an audience to be able to appreciate a Vainlove, or the fashionable affectation of Congreve's dialogue (seen at its best in the scene between Araminta and Belinda in St. James's Park), a degree of refined artificiality was required which Jonson's audience, and no doubt many of Congreve's, had not yet reached.

When *The Double Dealer* (1693) was published it contained some commendatory verses by Dryden in which the old dramatist generously recognized in the new one's work all the best that the age had produced, including 'Etherege his courtship' and 'the satire, wit, and strength of manly Wycherley'. Having demonstrated his command of fashionable courtship in his first comedy, Congreve was now trying his hand at the vigorous satire of *The Plain-Dealer*. (The motto from Horace which he prefixed

to the play, '*Interdum tamen, et vocem Comœdia tollit*', sufficiently
indicates his intention.) In *The Old Bachelor* Bellmour had met the
protestations of a lady's maid about her mistress's honour by the
bland assertion, 'Nay, nay; look you, Lucy, there are whores of
as good quality'; in his new play Congreve set out to demonstrate this in the person of Lady Touchwood, Lady Froth, and
Lady Plyant, each of whom cuckolds her husband. The two
last of these ladies carry on their intrigues within the accepted
conventions of Restoration comedy, but the scheming Lady
Touchwood, disappointed in her passion for the virtuous
Mellefont, would be more at home in a Victorian melodrama.
So, too, would the villain Maskwell, who pretends friendship
to Mellefont only to further his plot to have him disinherited
and to obtain his mistress. In spite of some excellent scenes, an
ingenious plot, and comic dialogue which flows naturally from
the characters and is not a matter of purely verbal wit, this is
hardly Congreve at his best; it is Congreve consciously writing
a strong play, and is for him a *tour de force*, a solitary venture
into a downright kind of satire for which his delicate and
fastidious temperament was not very well suited. In the Dedication of this comedy Congreve showed his disappointment
with its mixed reception in some sentences which he omitted
from all later editions. Recalling how the Town had lavished
praise on his first play, 'when I thought I had not Title to it',
he explained that he had now tried to write a less imperfect
play which they might praise with more justice. 'But I find
they are to be treated cheaply, and I have been at an unnecessary expence.' When *Love for Love* was produced about eighteen
months later he spared no expense in wit and humour, but he
took good care to provide the sort of entertainment that his
audience could be counted upon to enjoy. Since this comedy,
as he claimed in the prologue, had 'something that may please
each taste'—farce and high comedy, plot, amusing characters,
wit and humour and gaiety, but also, in the scenes in which
Angelica appears, a serious treatment of marriage—it repeated
the success of *The Old Bachelor*. The comic characters are more
varied than those in his first play, and many of them—Scandal,
Tattle, Miss Prue, Ben, Sir Sampson Legend, Foresight,
Valentine's man Jeremy—are more fully developed. All of
these characters are for different reasons comic in themselves,
and are made more comical by the situations in which Congreve

has involved them. The plot, too, is full of business without being confusing, and the whole play has a rollicking and spontaneous vigour quite distinct from the more laboured ingenuities of his earlier work. It marked the highest point of Congreve's popularity as a writer of comedies.

Five years later he produced his last comedy, *The Way of the World*, and it was a comparative failure. Not all of the play was above the heads of his audience: Sir Wilful in his cups and the 'boudoir Billingsgate' of Lady Wishfort were well within their range. But Congreve on this occasion had written to please himself and a few discriminating friends, and he knew, or says he knew, that this comedy was not suited to 'that general taste which seems now to be predominant in the palates of our audience'. His finer things were thrown away on the average playgoer: his subtle discrimination of a Witwoud from a Truewit; his gentle satire on the artificialities of polite society; his concern for intelligent behaviour, personal integrity, the golden mean; his fastidious choice of words and the delicate turn of his ideas. In such a scene as that in which Millamant discusses with her maid Mincing the superiority of verse over prose for pinning up her hair we have the very poetry of affectation; but this was perhaps one of those beauties which, as he said of the finer things in Terence, 'the greater part of his audience were incapable of tasting'. *The Way of the World* has some of the most brilliant conversation in our literature, and some of the most devastating wit. Congreve's special note of droll satire is heard perfectly in the scene between Lady Wishfort and her maid Foible (III. i), when she looks in the mirror and laments how badly her face compares with her picture:

> *Lady Wish.* Let me see the Glass—. . . . I look like an old peel'd Wall. Thou must repair me, Foible, before Sir Rowland comes, or I shall never keep up to my Picture.

> *Foib.* I warrant you, Madam; a little Art once made your Picture like you; and now a little of the same Art must make you like your Picture. Your Picture must sit for you, Madam.

No wonder if such wit, so calm, so precise, so exquisitely muted, met with an uncertain hearing in the pit and boxes, and never reached the gallery at all. Congreve had finished with the stage; it asked more than he was prepared to give, for, as

Mirabell puts it, 'to please a fool is some degree of folly'. He had given a good deal of thought to the problems of characterization in a play; his own characters in *The Way of the World* range from the broadly hilarious to the more nicely discriminated, and he has found a personal mode of speech for almost every one of them. Here, as in other respects, he is to be praised, not for any striking originality, but for bringing to perfection what other men had done before him.

What is new in *The Way of the World* is the glimpse that we have in Mirabell and Millamant of a world of genuine feeling and permanent relationships. As Professor Fujimura says, Congreve is obviously turning away in his last play 'from the naturalistic philosophy of wit comedy, and is making concessions to morality, good sense, and sensibility'. Less than a year after this play was produced the church bells rang in the eighteenth century, and all but rang out the old comedy of wit. To some extent Congreve may have anticipated what was coming, but he had no desire to take part in it; he looked back rather than forward. His main contributions to English comedy lie in his intelligent and subtle awareness of the modes and manners of artificial society brought into sharp contrast with the natural and the vulgar, in his own cool poise and detachment, and in his impeccable style, which sterilizes immorality and indecency, and touches with beauty whatever it shines upon. In the world of seventeenth-century London the mind of Congreve (as Coleridge once observed of Charles Lamb) 'looked upon the degraded men and things around him like moonshine on a dunghill which shines and takes no pollution'.

In this account of Restoration comedy little attempt has been made to discuss it in terms of rigid categories, partly because those categories are far from being rigid in practice, and the same play may be a blend of the comedy of humours, of intrigue, and of wit, and may also contain satirical, or sentimental, or purely farcical passages. All of those elements are to be found in varying degrees in *The Way of the World*, and make any such label as 'the comedy of wit' inadequate and misleading. Nor is it usually possible to discuss the work of any one dramatist in terms of one dominant type of comedy. While it is true, for instance, that Shadwell can be associated fairly enough with a Restoration variant of the Jonsonian comedy of humours, such a term fails to allow for the predominance of wit comedy in *Epsom Wells,* or of sentimental comedy in *The Squire of Alsatia.* As for *A True Widow,* Shadwell had no doubt that 'the Scene in the second Act, wherein Lady Busy would persuade Isabella to be kept, will live, when the Stuff of . . . Scribblers (more fit for Drolls than Plays) shall be consum'd in Grocery-ware, Tobacco, Band-boxes, and Hat-cases, and be rased out of the Memory of Men'. Whether posterity has endorsed this claim or not, there can be no doubt that the moral-satirical stand taken by Shadwell in this scene is uncharacteristic of Restoration comedy as a whole, and quite unlike that taken in his own *Epsom Wells.* So, too, at different times such playwrights as Crowne or Durfey write comedies of a very different kind, and in the transitional 1690s we can get a play like William Mountfort's *Greenwich Park* which is a mixture of all the modes.

We are on safer ground if we try to chart the larger changes of fashion within the whole period. Here we have noted an early phase in which some traces of platonic love still linger on, and the new plays are almost equally divided between those of humours and manners. A Fletcherian type of tragi-comedy, with little connection between the serious and the comic plots, remains popular (or at least continues to be written) for the first two decades. What has been called 'the gay couple'— sometimes, indeed, two or even three such couples—gradually begin to play an increasingly important part in the comic action, and for some time their activities are comparatively innocent, expressing little more than the reckless gaiety of youth and the witty and high-spirited duel of sex. By the 1670s, however, a more conscious libertinism has become apparent, and some measure of cuckoldry has become almost a *sine qua non* of a modern comedy. Before long this provokes among some dramatists a satirical reaction, either from sheer boredom with a monotonous theme, or from some degree of moral revulsion; but by other dramatists the waning effectiveness of sexual licence is met by giving us still more of it, as in *The London Cuckolds,* or (in a search for novelty) by the introduction of sexual perversions of one sort or another. In the late 1680s and the early 1690s, when the two companies were united, there is a general lowering of intellectual standards in the theatre, and a corresponding growth of farce and farcical

comedy; but in the more serious plays it becomes increasingly
clear that the rake-hero is giving way to the man of sense, and
that comedy, so long a male preserve, is now being influenced
by the female part of the audience. More and more the free-
ranging hero is tamed and brought to heel, the rake is reformed,
and the joys of virtuous marriage are proclaimed. Even
Congreve, whose first comedy is a brilliant variation of the old
sex revel, with little or no concession to the reformation of
manners, comes at last in *The Way of the World* to a consideration of life on terms a good deal more mature than those of the
carefree sixties. As John Harrington Smith put it:

> Not for Mirabell and Millamant is the spontaneous lightness of
> heart of Celadon and Florimel: they achieve perfection in the gay
> manner, but only through poise and courage. After all, they are
> almost the last lovers in a world which was dying and yet was the
> only possible one for them. And if they stand undaunted at the
> prospect, Congreve does not quite do so. There is no defiance in
> the play, but for all its greatness there is weariness.

In the new and damper atmosphere after 1700 the old squibs
of irreverent wit begin to sputter feebly, and for the most part
fail to go off; and the eighteenth-century drama moves mind-
lessly towards a naturalism in which ordinary citizens and their
wives and daughters say and do ordinary things for a middle-
class audience which wants to see its own life mirrored upon
the stage. If we may adapt the words of Bishop Hurd to a
different context, what we got by this revolution was a great
deal of good (but often dull and superficial) sense: what we
lost was a world of fantasy and fine phrasing, and a witty and
intelligent questioning of conventional standards.

About the true nature and value of Restoration comedy
critical opinion has been unusually divided in the present
century, and almost the only points of agreement are that
neither the crude moral test of Jeremy Collier and Lord
Macaulay nor the amoral acceptance of Charles Lamb will do.
In 1937 Professor L. C. Knights shifted the direction of attack
by finding that Restoration comedy was confined to 'a miserably
limited set of attitudes', and by asserting that the criticism its
defenders must answer is not that it is immoral, but that it is
'trivial, gross and dull'. Defenders have not been wanting in
recent years; and the comedy of Dryden, Etherege, Wycherley,
and Congreve (few modern critics seem to be familiar with any

other) is now seen as offering a serious and consistent criticism
of contemporary life, embodying an attitude of philosophical
libertinism, and submitting inadequate moral attitudes and
social customs to the ridicule or contempt of satire. So far has
this moral and intellectual rehabilitation proceeded that it has
now perhaps overshot the mark. No one today is likely to agree
with Lamb that the writers of Restoration comedy presented
'altogether a speculative scene of things, which has no reference
whatsoever to the world that is'; but if Lamb was trailing his
coat, at least he did full justice to that fantastic and antinomian
element in comedy which now seems to be in some danger of
disappearing altogether from modern critical thinking. It is
surely time to return to a position which Etherege or Congreve,
if they were not being driven to answer someone like Collier,
would have readily accepted: when a Restoration audience
went to Drury Lane or Dorset Garden to see a comedy it
expected to laugh, and it laughed at the conduct and conversation of a Dorimant or a Fainall or a Mirabell because they were
delightfully impudent, or slightly outrageous, or 'mannerly
obscene'. In so laughing it obtained that comic catharsis which
Lamb had in mind when he contemplated a life with 'no
meddling restrictions', in which for a couple of idle hours he
'respired the breath of an imaginary freedom'. What a contemporary audience met with in a Restoration comedy was not
an accurate representation of its own normal behaviour (for
that would hardly describe the action of *The Country Wife*,
and if it did, then why laugh?), but an idealized, although still
recognizable, and sometimes malicious projection of the life it
knew; in which, after a series of hair's-breadth escapes for the
gallants, there comes a happy ending for those who matter
and a dismissive ridicule of those who don't. For the audience
of a Restoration comedy, then as now, there was therefore an
element of wish-fulfilment, and that sort of gratification which
comes from being faintly but pleasantly shocked. Dryden,
Etherege, Sedley, Wycherley, Congreve, and the rest were
surely a good deal less seriously concerned than seems to be now
generally believed to attack the morality of their own day,
and much more concerned to make fun of it for their legitimate comic purposes.

IV

POETRY

(1)

WHATEVER value we may place upon the work of Dryden and his contemporaries, there can be no question that in the years following upon the Restoration the status of poetry was high. Verse of one sort or another was not only widely written; it was also subjected to constant criticism in coffee-houses, discussed in letters and pamphlets, expounded and defended in prefaces and dedications. For one professional there were a hundred amateurs, typified by such men as Sir Carr Scroope, endlessly venturing on a song or an epilogue or a lampoon, and occasionally in a lucky hour achieving memorable expression. If such writings got beyond circulating in manuscript, they might appear in one or more of the numerous songbooks or poetical miscellanies of the period, such as *The Academy of Compliments* or *Covent Garden Drollery*. For poets with a more serious purpose—moral, religious, philosophical, political—there were various forms of satire and panegyric, the heroic poem, the verse essay, and that unhappy legacy of Abraham Cowley to his fellow countrymen, the pindaric ode—fatally easy to write, almost impossible to write well. Among the longer poems of the period there are also a considerable number of translations of the Greek and Latin poets, from John Ogilby's *Iliad* in 1660 to Dryden's *Aeneid* in 1697.

The influence of Charles II on the verse writers of the period is not easy to assess, but he was certainly a connoisseur of wit and humour and raillery in verse and prose, and he was by no means insensitive to the prestige that his poets could confer upon the monarchy: so long as he was upon the throne they had someone to please who had both intelligence and discrimination—a situation which no longer existed for the poets of George I or George II. In his 'funeral-pindarique' on Charles II, Dryden celebrated the King as a great encourager of the arts; and although he could not resist remarking that he had given little financial help to his poets, who subsisted 'like Birds of Paradise, that liv'd on morning dew' (Dryden's own pension as Poet Laureate had been very irregularly paid out of the King's chronically impoverished treasury), yet he did at least acknowledge the King's genuine interest in the work of his poets:

> Oh never let their Lays his Name forget!
> The Pension of a Prince's praise is great.

The whole passage in which this exclamation occurs is so shot through with ambivalence that the second of those two lines might be taken as a sarcasm, but it is more likely that Dryden intended a sincere compliment.

The King appreciated his poets not merely because they wrote amusing comedies, witty prologues and epilogues, and pretty amorous songs: they also wrote (and in the case of Dryden and some others could be personally encouraged to write) political poems that would put the case attractively for the King and his Tory ministers, and ridicule and discomfit the Opposition. The Whig party naturally replied in kind through its own poetical pensioners, and political verse played a very considerable part in rousing and sustaining party feeling in times of crisis. Apart from such immediately practical considerations, poetry (and more especially heroic poetry) exalted the monarchy and gave dignity and importance to the national life. For many years Dryden toyed with the idea of writing an epic poem, and in dedicating *The Conquest of Granada* in 1672 to the Duke of York he seemed to suggest that the subject would be the House of Stuart, and more especially Charles II and his brother James. The return of Charles in 1660 had been celebrated by almost every living poet of note except Milton and Marvell, and by innumerable forgotten versifiers all striving to consolidate and give dignity to a great national occasion. The coronation of the following year brought forth further effusions of loyalty, as did victories over the Dutch, royal visits to the theatre, and much else. The unfortunate Richard Flecknoe, acting hopefully on unreliable information, produced a poem 'On the Queen's being with Child'; when the news proved to be false, he was so far from wishing to let the matter drop quietly that he wrote a second poem 'On her Miscarrying', and printed them both prominently in his volume

A Farrago of Several Pieces (1666). At the death of Charles II in 1685, and at that of Queen Mary ten years later, the poets were at work again, writing for the most part funeral-pindaric odes, but also pastoral elegies and straightforward panegyrics. Among those who mourned the death of Queen Mary were Tate, Walsh, Tutchin, Dennis, Motteux, Samuel Wesley, Edmund Arwaker, Stepney, Congreve, Robert Gould, and Samuel Cobb. So numerous were the tributes that someone found it worth while to write a poem called *The Mourning Poets*, and someone else wrote a bad-tempered poem, *Urania's Temple: Or, A Satyr upon the Silent Poets*, castigating those (including Dryden) who had failed to contribute to the national mourning. The death of Dryden himself in 1700 was the occasion of a volume called *Luctus Britannici*, containing about fifty poems in English and Latin 'by the most Eminent Hands in the two Famous Universities, and by several Others', and of another called *The Nine Muses*, written 'by Nine severall Ladies'. Great statesmen, the immediate supporters of the monarchy, were frequently celebrated in panegyrics, as in Dryden's New-Year's Day poem, *To my Lord Chancellor* (1662), or Settle's time-serving *Panegyric on the Loyal and Honourable Sir George Jefferies, Lord Chief Justice of England* (1683). So, too, dukes and duchesses and other members of the nobility were addressed, congratulated, commiserated, or mourned in elegies when they died. Little of all this verse makes tolerable reading today; but it served, like liveried servants and rich equipages and elaborate funeral monuments, to distinguish the great, to maintain the prestige of an aristocracy in the minds of common men, and in general to uphold what we should now call the 'establishment'. It was public poetry, intended to make a dignified impression, to gratify and magnify the recipient; the poet therefore composed his piece in the manner of a public orator, conscious not only of the distinguished person who was being addressed, but of the audience which was listening. It can hardly be supposed that Settle's panegyric on Jeffreys could have been read with much interest by anyone but the Lord Chief Justice himself; but if he 'lived in Settle's numbers one day more' and suitably rewarded his panegyrist, the poet had achieved most of what he set out to do.

Alongside this complimentary and public verse, however, there was a much more robust and popular kind that gave enormous satisfaction to a wide variety of less polite readers. It is to be found at the very beginning of the period in the writings of Robert Wild,[1] whose celebrated *Iter Boreale*, a poem on General Monck's march from Scotland to London, appeared in 1660. In his *Essay of Dramatic Poesy* Dryden gave reluctant testimony to the popularity of Wild's 'clownish kind of raillery' with the London citizens, who could be seen 'reading it in the midst of 'Change time; nay, so vehement they were at it, that they lost their bargain by the candles' ends'. *Iter Boreale* is full of puns and conceits and easily intelligible wit:

> Ringers, hands off: The Bells themselves will dance
> In memory of their deliverance.
> Had not George shew'd his Metal, and said Nay,
> Each Sectary had born the Bell away.

This is a sort of poor man's metaphysical poetry. In the same robust and often ribald tradition were Alexander Radcliffe, author of *The Ramble*, Tom Brown, Tom Durfey in some of his longer poems, and various writers of bacchanalian verse.

The great popular poet of the Restoration, however, was Samuel Butler,[2] whose *Hudibras* still remains as a sort of national monument to tell us what many Englishmen thought and believed three hundred years ago. Who now reads Butler? How many twentieth-century readers setting out hopefully on that

---

[1] Robert Wild (1609–79), son of a shoemaker of St. Ives, Huntingdonshire, became a Scholar of St. John's College, Cambridge, and obtained the living of Aynho, Northants, in 1646. As a loyal Presbyterian clergyman he welcomed the Restoration in 1660 with various poems, including the popular *Iter Boreale*, but was none the less ejected from his living in 1662 when the Act of Uniformity came into force.

[2] Samuel Butler (1612–80) was the son of a Worcestershire farmer, and was educated at the King's School, Worcester. He was for a time some sort of attendant to Elizabeth, Countess of Kent, at her seat in Bedfordshire, where he met John Selden. Biographical facts about Butler are meagre; but he appears to have served in the capacity of secretary or attendant to several country gentlemen, one of whom, Sir Samuel Luke, a Presbyterian Cromwellian general, is usually taken to be the original of Hudibras. For a short time in 1660 he was secretary to Richard Earl of Carbury, who was then Lord President of Wales. The publication of *Hudibras* (Pt. I, 1662; Pt. II, 1663) made Butler famous, and among his most devoted readers was Charles II. He accompanied the Duke of Buckingham on a diplomatic journey to France in 1670, served as his secretary from 1670 to 1674, and (according to tradition) helped him in the composition of *The Rehearsal*. The neglect of Butler became legendary, but it has been exaggerated: he received several grants from the King. He is said, however, to have died in penury. He was described by Anthony Wood as 'a boon and witty companion, especially among the company he knew well'.

jolting and rattling journey through *Hudibras* have ever got beyond the first canto? Any dictionary of quotations will demonstrate beyond all possible doubt that Butler was once highly popular; but if he still has his addicts today, most modern readers know the quotations from *Hudibras* because they are quoted, and not because they have met them in their context. Butler's reputation, indeed, has suffered an almost complete reversal: in his own day he was enjoyed by readers who were unlikely to read much else, but if he is read at all today it is probably by those who have read so much that they have also read *Hudibras*. Yet although it is chiefly the learned reader that Butler still attracts, this is the wrong sort of reader for *Hudibras*: the robust parsons and lawyers and country squires who welcomed the poem with bellows of happy laughter were the men who could really appreciate what Butler was doing. They had the immediate knowledge needed to understand his allusions, they responded sympathetically to his cavalier contempt for mechanics and tradesmen, and they were tough enough to enjoy his verbal singlestick, and to bump along happily on his unsprung couplets. What Butler has to say about Presbyterians, Independents, Anabaptists, or Quakers, predestination, the Covenant, the Directory, and much else, was once what large numbers of Englishmen wanted to have said; but today those matters have lost the burning relevance they once had, and the modern reader is likely not only to be unmoved, but also to be frequently puzzled. The poem that the Restoration reader and his sons and grandsons so enjoyed has almost completely evaporated.

Yet something remains; enough, perhaps, to preserve the peculiar essence of the poem. *Hudibras* is unmistakably English, in the same vigorous, bustling way as Skelton's *Elinour Rumming* or Jonson's *Bartholomew Fair*, or the cartoons of Rowlandson and Gillray. It has the virtues of the home-made; it is wholesome and sustaining, and it has a flavour all its own. Considered as a work of art it is clumsy and monotonous; but it survives because of the energy of the poet's mind and the vigour of his personality, and also because of the crude strength of its metrical structure—it is as if Butler had built his couplets of such durable material that they would be capable of taking twice the amount of strain that he ever puts upon them. The reader of *Hudibras* finds himself hurried along by the scamper-

ing fancy of the author; Butler takes charge of him, entertains
him with a buoyant confidence, never leaves him alone for a
moment's reflection. He is our greatest literary buffoon in verse,
amusing himself at the same time as he delights his reader
with his apparently extempore brilliance. In the composition
of his verses he combines the foreseen with the fortuitous, the
purposive with the spontaneous. He yields frequently to the
suggestions of rhyme—

> For Rhyme the Rudder is of Verses,
> With which like Ships they stear their courses—

and yet he seems always to say what he meant to say. Indeed,
the air of spontaneity is perhaps more apparent than real.
From the evidence of his notebooks it is clear that he had the
same habit as Pope of hitching his thoughts into rhyme, and
laying them aside to be worked up later and introduced at
some appropriate place in one of his poems. The notebooks,
too, show him fairly frequently altering a passage in octosyllabic couplets to the longer measure of the pentameter;
and there is ample evidence in the form of alternative readings
that Butler was not content to 'dash thro' thick and thin', but
laboured carefully at his verses.

The modern reader's neglect of *Hudibras* has led to a corresponding ignorance of Butler's minor satirical poems, which
deserve to be better known. With the exception of the mock-
heroic pindaric ode 'To the Memory of the most renowned
Du-Vall' (the highwayman), these remained in manuscript
until they were printed in the two volumes of *Genuine Remains*
(1759) by Robert Thyer. They include satires on the Royal
Society, French fashions, the licentiousness of Restoration
England, marriage, drunkenness, heroic drama, the abuse of
learning, and an ironical panegyric on the Hon. Edward Howard
whose abortive attempts at epic poetry (like those of Blackmore
in the next generation) were a source of mild fun to an essentially anti-heroic age. These minor pieces serve to show the
range of Butler's mind, as well as his wit and humour, but they
sometimes indicate, too, his isolated and ambiguous position
in the world of post-Restoration England; the disapproving
voice we hear might at times be that of Clarendon (who was
only four years Butler's senior), and at no time does Butler
appear to be other than a rather uneasy survivor in the London

of Charles II. What is constant with him is a rare combination of wit and good sense, in an age that was always ready to sacrifice sense to wit. With Butler wit and fancy are so abundant that they invariably provide an appropriate setting for his sense, and are never a mere substitute for it. In the next fifty years he had many imitators, but none of them—Samuel Colville, William Cleland, Archibald Pitcairne, William Meston, Durfey, or Ward—could wield the quarter-staff of Samuel Butler.

Hudibras contains burlesque elements, but is not itself a burlesque poem. In 1664 Charles Cotton[1] started an English fashion for burlesque in England by publishing his *Scarronides*, a travesty of the first book of the *Aeneid*, following it up a year later with a similar vulgarization of the fourth book. (Scarron's *Virgile travesti* had appeared in 1648.) In 1664 Homer was subjected to similar treatment in James Scudamore's *Homer à la Mode*; and the Dryden–Tonson edition of Ovid's Epistles (1680) provided the occasion for two burlesques: *The Wits Paraphrased* and Alexander Radcliffe's *Ovid Travestie*, which ran to three editions between 1680 and 1696. In 1669 Wycherley had contributed to the genre a burlesque *Hero and Leander*, and in 1675 Cotton turned his attention to Lucian, and published *Burlesque upon Burlesque; . . . Being some of Lucian's Dialogues Newly put into English Fustian*. The 'English fustian' was the Hudibrastic tetrameter, the metre normally employed for English burlesque; and although Scarron was the ultimate progenitor of the kind, the more immediate influence was undoubtedly Butler. The public for such crude, sniggering, schoolboy denigration of Virgil and Ovid had no doubt mixed motives for their enjoyment. Some of Cotton's readers had been

---

[1] Charles Cotton (1630–87) was the son of a country gentleman who possessed estates in Derbyshire and Staffordshire, and who was the friend of Donne, Jonson, Izaak Walton, Herrick, and other literary men of his day. The younger Cotton travelled in his early manhood in France and probably in Italy. He took to writing at an early age, and was one of those who contributed (along with Dryden) to the volume of memorial poems for Henry, Lord Hastings. In 1656 he married a sister of Colonel Hutchinson. His father died in 1658, leaving his estate embarrassed by lawsuits, and his son was compelled in 1665 to sell off part of the property to pay his debts. He published a number of translations from the French, including one of Montaigne's Essays, and he wrote a second part of Walton's *Compleat Angler* (1676). His burlesques of Virgil (1664) and of Lucian (1675) proved very popular, as did his long poem, *The Wonders of the Peak* (1681). There is little evidence that his best poetry, contained in the posthumous *Poems on Several Occasions* (1689), attracted much attention.

'lashed into Latin by the tingling rod' and were only too glad to guffaw as adults at what they had hated as schoolboys; others had no Latin and perhaps found their satisfaction in mocking at what they could not enjoy, and others again may have taken a perverse delight in destroying the thing they loved. Whatever motives may have been at work, Cotton's *Scarronides* had run through nine editions by 1700, and was clearly one of the most popular works in verse of the whole period. The vogue for travesty in the later seventeenth century is an aspect of English taste that has not been sufficiently considered; the popularity of such works as *Scarronides* suggests that Sir Wilfull Witwoud was much nearer the norm of Restoration culture than Mirabell and Millamant.

Verse was extensively employed in the political controversies of the later seventeenth century. Much of this political poetry was satirical, but some of it was panegyrical; and the two kinds (referred to by Marvell as 'panegyric and philippic') continued to be written in large quantities, and sometimes coalesced in the same poem. Since political poetry was intended to influence the largest possible public in the quickest possible way, it was often crude in both content and style, and had little of that 'fine raillery' that Dryden admired, and that he was to achieve so admirably in *Absalom and Achitophel*. A good deal of verse satire took the form of shapeless invective, but a series of satirical moulds was invented or rediscovered—advices to a painter, litanies, mock elegies, visions, dreams, allegories, beast fables, and the like—and such indirect methods give the various pieces some literary interest. 'Advices to a Painter' were popular in the late 1660s and 1670s, and may be regarded as typical examples of Restoration verse satire. They took their origin from Waller's *Instructions to a Painter, for the Drawing of the Posture and Progress of His Majesty's Forces at Sea* (1666), a panegyrical poem on the Duke of York's naval victory at Solebay over the Dutch, in which Waller praised the conduct of the Duke by telling an imaginary painter how to portray the victorious engagement. Waller's poem was an ingenious variation on straightforward panegyric, but it lent itself to satirical exploitation by anyone who found more to blame than to praise in contemporary England. A few months after the publication of Waller's verses some ingenious satirist produced *A Second Advice to a*

Painter, for Drawing the History of our Naval Business, in which the naval action celebrated by Waller was seen from a very different point of view. This was followed by a third, a fourth, and a fifth 'Advice', and all four were issued together in one volume without a publisher's imprint (1667), and ascribed, probably wrongly, to Sir John Denham. Before the end of the century some of those 'Advice' poems were to be attributed (foolishly) to Milton, and (more plausibly) to Marvell, who is almost certainly the author of *Last Instructions to a Painter*, first published in 1689, some years after his death. It is highly improbable that any one writer would have used the same satirical vehicle so many times, and it seems more reasonable to believe that after the satirical possibilities suggested by the *Second Advice* became apparent, several other satirists joined in the fun. The exploitation of the 'Advice' form is characteristic of Restoration satire: new vehicles were frequently invented and then used over and over again. The significance of the repetition is that once a satirical gambit has become familiar the reader knows at once where he stands, and is alert and ready to take the point; the danger is that if the gambit becomes too familiar it may fail to generate the small shock of surprise that is essential for the satirical effect.

At such times of crisis as the Dutch wars, the Popish Plot, or the bringing in of the Exclusion Bill, the normal stream of satirical verse became a flood. Most of this verse was anonymous, but some of it can be ascribed to such authors as Shadwell, Settle, and Durfey, and to such almost forgotten writers as Samuel Pordage, Richard Duke, and John Ayloffe. Anti-government verse was in general too dangerous to print, and circulated only in manuscript, but some of it appeared in anonymous broadsides or pamphlets with fictitious imprints. Even so, Sir Roger L'Estrange and the messengers of the press succeeded in hunting down a number of printers, who were duly prosecuted and punished; one of the most persistent, Francis ('Elephant') Smith, was in trouble in 1667 for publishing the second and third *Advices*. It was not until after the Revolution that most of the Whig and anti-Catholic poems became generally available in such collections as *The Muses Farewell to Popery and Slavery* and *Poems on Affairs of State*; but the identification of the authors, already uncertain in the reign of William and Mary, is in most cases now virtually impossible.

Among those uncertain authors was Andrew Marvell.[1] More attention might have been paid to his satirical verse if there had been less dubiety about the canon of his work; but even so, those who have ventured to discuss it have found little to praise. To turn from Marvell's lyrical and meditative poetry to such halting and hobbling verse as we find in 'Clarendon's House-warming' or 'The Statue in Stocks-Market' is to enter a world of coarse controversy and ribald abuse. Such topical name-calling, however, must be judged by its immediate effectiveness, and something must be allowed for the traditional roughness of satire, and for the fact that the public to which Marvell was appealing would respond most readily to downright and uninhibited statement, and to the sardonic humour that often went with it. Such readers, too, would enjoy his rough colloquial verse, which is in any case an excellent medium for conveying contempt. As Professor Legouis has suggested, the English satirist who most obviously influenced Marvell was John Cleveland. That influence is clearly seen in the comparatively early 'Character of Holland', which is enlivened by a good deal of metaphysical wit, and which generates power by dwelling steadily on the same theme. Marvell's more usual practice was to choose a topic, such as the statue of Charles II erected by Sir Thomas Viner in the Stocks-Market, and then to spread out from there in all directions. Occasionally, however, he found a satirical framework (as in *Last Instructions to a Painter*) which enabled him to achieve a comprehensive denunciation of the times without losing all sense of form. Yet even here he suffers from a plethora of material: too much had gone wrong too quickly in England since the Restoration to allow Marvell to concentrate his attack. He is perhaps seen at his best in 'The Dialogue between the two Horses' (if indeed this poem is not, as Professor George de F. Lord has suggested, the work of Ayloffe), where the humour of the situation is fully exploited, and the satirical vehicle is highly effective. As the two sculptured horses grumble and gossip in the absence of their riders

---

[1] During the reign of Charles II Andrew Marvell sat as M.P. for Hull, but rarely intervened in the debates. His verse after 1660 was almost entirely political and satirical; and he also published *The Rehearsal Transprosed*, 1672–3 (in reply to Samuel Parker's *Discourse of Ecclesiastical Polity*), and his *Account of the Growth of Popery and Arbitrary Government in England* (1677). From 1663 to 1665 he acted as secretary to the Earl of Carlisle in his embassy to Russia, Sweden, and Denmark. He died after a brief illness in 1678.

(Charles I has gone to see Archbishop Laud, and Charles II
to cuckold a scrivener) they symbolize the long-suffering English
people bearing on their backs the intolerable burden of the
Stuart dynasty. 'Canst thou divine', asks the first horse, 'when
things shall be mended?' To which the second horse replies:
'When the reign of the line of the Stuarts is ended.' The poem,
if it is Marvell's, must come out of his latest almost republican
phase, when he looks back nostalgically to the days of Cromwell:

> Tho' his Government did a Tyrant's resemble,
> Hee made England great and it's enemies tremble.

The early death of John Oldham[1] at a time when his poetic
powers were obviously increasing makes it difficult to assess him
on his actual achievement. In a generous and moving tribute to
the young poet Dryden asserted that Oldham's soul was 'cast
in the same poetic mould' as his own, and that 'one common
note on either lyre did strike'. But Dryden had many notes,
Oldham only one or two. To Dryden again, Oldham was the
young 'Marcellus of our tongue', and among his contemporaries
his early death was generally felt to be a serious loss to English
poetry. If Oldham was indeed an earlier John Keats, he was a
Keats of the Restoration; harsh, masculine, satirical, and
severely limited in his sensitiveness. In the anti-romantic
world of Oldham, Cleopatra is 'the Egyptian punk' and Homer
the poet who sang 'the Grecian bullies fighting for a whore'.
There is admittedly much vigour in his crabbed youth; he
moves with a kind of clumsy buoyancy, tumbling over his feet and
talking all the while as he goes. His thoughts, as he says himself,

> so throng to get abroad,
> They over-run each other in the crowd;

and in a characteristically unlovely metaphor he contrasts this
happy state of affairs with the slowness of most scribblers, whose
verses come only with much straining:

> They void 'em dribbling, and in pain they write.

---

[1] John Oldham (1653–83), the son of a Nonconformist minister who was
'silenced' in 1662, was educated at Tetbury Grammar School and St. Edmund
Hall, Oxford, graduating B.A. in 1674. He kept himself by teaching, first by
obtaining the post of usher in Whitgift's free school at Croydon, and later as tutor to
the sons of gentlemen. His *Satire against Virtue* (1679) and his *Satires upon the Jesuits*
. . . *and Some Other Pieces by the same Hand* (1681) made him well known to the
literary men of the day, including Dryden, before his early death from smallpox.
After his death his *Works* went through many editions in quick succession.

Oldham's contemporary reputation was built mainly upon
the four *Satires upon the Jesuits* (1679–81), and these are concerned
with issues which are hardly likely to arouse much interest
today. This young Juvenal, writing in the heat of the Popish Plot,
drowns the Jesuits in a flood of vituperation. In his first satire
the ghost of Henry Garnett (executed for being concerned in
the Gunpowder Plot) addresses a cabal of Jesuits immediately
after the murder of Sir Edmundberry Godfrey, and urges them
on to greater deeds. In the second Oldham employs the method
of direct vituperation. In the third Loyola is seen propped up
on his deathbed ('And from his mouth long strakes of drivel
flow'), giving his last instructions to his disciples on how to
carry on the nefarious work; and in the fourth he is made, like
Chaucer's pardoner, to give a cynical account of various holy
relics. The four satires are an exercise in sustained, and therefore monotonous, invective. The abuse is continuous and un-
qualified, the voice is loud, emphatic, and brazenly confident;
when we come to the last line of each satire we are conscious of
a sudden cessation of noise. Nothing very subtle has been said;
and the awkwardness of the verse and the uncouthness of the
rhymes, which Oldham's critics have so often pointed out, are
everywhere apparent. Since Oldham can write with colloquial
ease in his imitations of Horace, it may well be that the harshness and the rough-hewn strength of the *Satires upon the Jesuits*
are a result of a deliberate attempt to reproduce the powerful
invective of Juvenal. He packs his lines with nouns and verbs
('Pox, Ague, Dropsie, Palsie, Stone, and Gout'), and he never
allows the pace to slacken; it is perhaps just as well, for if the
reader were given a chance to pause he might start to think.
Occasionally an extravagant hyperbole reminds us of the rants
of heroic drama, as when Garnett, gloating over the Protestant
victims of Bloody Mary, reflects how much further the persecution could have been carried if *he* had been her counsellor:

> And when 'twas dark, in every Lane and Street
> Thick flaming Hereticks should serve to light,
> And save the needless Charge of Links by night.

If the modern reader gets less entertainment from the
Satires upon the Jesuits than their reputation might lead him to
expect, he is likely to get a good deal more than he anticipates
from some of Oldham's other poems. His pindarics are as

diffuse as most of their kind; but the long ode 'Upon the Works of Ben Jonson' is at least good sense; and in one interesting passage he takes his stand with those neo-classical critics who despise 'the meer fanaticks and enthusiasts in poetry', and claims for Jonson that his imagination, although 'brisk and mettled', was 'a managed rage'. There is something of Jonson's laboured fullness in Oldham's 'A Drunkard's Speech in a Mask', which ends in a highly effective burst of maudlin triumph. But the best of Oldham is to be found in such poems as 'A Satire addressed to a Friend', where he draws upon his own experience as an usher in a grammar school, and achieves an emotional integrity and a sense of control that are much less evident in his more flamboyant satires. Best of all are his imitations of Horace. His rendering of the ninth Satire of the first Book ('As I was walking in the Mall of late') is a little masterpiece, beautifully lively and colloquial; a Restoration poem that happened to be written by a Latin poet sixteen hundred years earlier. Oldham also produced imitations of the *Ars Poetica*, and of Juvenal's third and thirteenth satires. In all of those he gave his author a contemporary English setting, and it is in such adaptations of an ancient poet to the modern world that his chief claim to historical importance lies.

Among the various rough and raucous satirists of the period, Robert Gould wrote formal satires that occasionally strike an unconventional note. From an autobiographical poem 'To the Rev. Mr. Francis Carey' we learn that he had been in domestic service, and he has some bitter comments to offer on the attitude of the master and the mistress to those whom they employ. If Gould had developed this unfamiliar vein of social criticism a little further, he might be better known today; but he is usually content to write general and exaggerated invective, as in his *Satire against Women* (his most popular work), or *The Corruption of the Times by Money*, or his coarse satire on the stage, *The Play-House*. The editor of the collected edition of his poems (1709) thinks that (although he knew no Latin) he wrote with 'the solidity of Virgil, the sprightliness of Horace, and the tartness of Juvenal'. There is no sign of Virgil or Horace in Gould's comprehensive and unsparing denunciations, but much of Juvenal, who was no doubt known to him through his English imitators. Gould is, in fact, a minor Oldham, and in some verses he acknowledges his debt to that poet:

I had, my Oldham, not a Muse but Thee;
Ev'n Thou wert all the Mighty Nine to me!

To descend any further, and read the work of such a satirist as
Richard Ames, is to scrape the very bottom of a muddy barrel,
but his vigorous and often obscene doggerel satisfied the crude
taste of a masculine public.

If we look for refinement in the writings of the Court wits—
Dorset,[1] Sedley, Rochester, and the rest—we shall find it, but
only intermittently. As men of letters the Court wits were
collectively of considerable importance; individually, with the
exception of Rochester, their poetry is now best read in anthologies. In their own day, however, they had the additional
importance of being the arbiters of literary taste, and several
of them (Lord Dorset especially) were repaid by the uncritical
adulation of Dryden and many lesser men. Because of their
rank and their genuine talent the Court wits set the fashion in
poetry for some forty years, and made the writing of verse a
modish pursuit. Sir Courtly Nice in Crowne's comedy prided
himself on his ability to compose songs to his mistress, like a
gentleman 'soft and easy'; the knack of writing a song or a
prologue was part of his intellectual 'garniture', no less essential than his gloves or his lace ruffles.

The verses of the Court wits appeared in the numerous poetical
miscellanies, and in such larger collections as *Poems on Affairs of
State*. They wrote love songs and drinking songs, epigrams,
prologues and epilogues, lampoons, lyrics for other men's
plays or for their own; they translated or imitated Horace,
Martial, Boileau, and other poets; they satirized such over-
ambitious writers as the Hon. Edward Howard in the 1660s and
Sir Richard Blackmore in the 1690s; they libelled politicians,
kept-mistresses (notably the King's), and even the King himself; and they quarrelled with and attacked each other. Much of
this scabrous literature circulated in manuscript in a black
market run by such shady characters as Captain Robert
Julian, 'Secretary to the Muses'. Some of it has survived in

---

[1] Charles Sackville, sixth Earl of Dorset and first Earl of Middlesex (1638–
1706), led a dissipated life in his youth with such friends as Etherege and
Sedley, but volunteered in 1665 for service with the fleet (on which occasion he
wrote his celebrated song, 'To all you ladies now at land'), and took part in the
action against the Dutch off Lowestoft (3 June). In later life he became a generous
and amiable patron of poets and dramatists, the *arbiter elegantiae* of his day, and in
the reign of William and Mary a respected elder statesman.

manuscript collections and commonplace books, but much
more has irretrievably and unregrettably perished. Almost all
the verse of the Court wits was occasional, much of it was
highly personal, and some of it was accurately described by
Rochester as 'mannerly obscene'. Most of the extant songs of
Dorset and Sedley are mannerly enough, and it would be easy
to exaggerate the bawdiness of the Court wits. Yet their indecencies are sometimes startling. Rochester's devoted admirer
Robert Wolseley undertook, with a good deal of special pleading, a defence of his author's obscenity; his most convincing
argument is that Rochester's obscene pieces were never meant
for the cabinets of ladies or the closets of divines, 'or for any
publick or common Entertainment whatever, but for the private
Diversion of those happy Few whom he us'd to charm with his
Company and honour with his Friendship'. No doubt most of
the indecent verses of Dorset, Etherege, and Rochester were
private *jeux d'esprit* not intended for publication; and that some
of them survive in print is mainly due to the cupidity of seventeenth-century booksellers and the assiduity of twentieth-
century editors.

When Pope characterized 'the wits of either Charles's days'
as 'the mob of gentlemen who wrote with ease', he did not
intend to praise them. Many years earlier, in a letter to Henry
Cromwell, he had stated his opinion of those gentleman authors:

I take this poet [Crashaw] to have writ like a Gentleman, that is,
at leisure hours, and more to keep out idleness than to establish a
reputation: so that nothing regular or just can be expected from him.
All that regards Design, Form, Fable (which is the Soul of Poetry),
all that concerns exactness, or consent of parts (which is the Body)
will probably be wanting; only pretty conceptions, fine metaphors,
glitt'ring expressions, and something of a neat cast of Verse (which
are properly the dress, gems, or loose ornaments of Poetry) may
be found in these verses.

It is true that noblemen and gentlemen like Dorset, Mulgrave,
Sedley, and Etherege, and lesser wits like Sir Carr Scroope and
Fleetwood Shepherd, wrote for the most part only in their
leisure hours, and that their verses have most of the features
enumerated by Pope. Even so, those poets succeeded by their
own standards. Poetry to a man like the Earl of Dorset was
very much a matter of 'dress, gems, or loose ornaments'; he
wrote in the same way as he appeared and behaved in polite

society, with a sort of graceful negligence. But since he rarely ventured beyond short pieces (apart from 'To all you ladies now at land', the satirical song is his special contribution to English poetry), he could concentrate his attention on the 'turn' and on the shaping of an idea, as in 'Dorinda's sparkling wit and eyes'. Indeed, 'all that concerns exactness, or consent of parts' is so far from being absent that it is one of the undoubted achievements of the Court wits in their short lyrical poems. In Etherege's 'Cloris, it is not in our power', or in Sedley's 'Not, Celia, that I juster am', we meet with that kind of shaped argument that gives to the Restoration lyric its characteristic form: what is said, no matter how trivial or specious, is said with grace and control and finality. If those poets wrote in their leisure hours, they were clearly prepared to concentrate their mind on what they were doing, and the best of them had the ability 'to write with fury, but correct with phlegm'. It would be hard to distinguish the individual note in a song by Etherege or Sedley, and to attempt to do so would be to mistake the mode: it is characteristic of the gentleman that he shares with other gentlemen a patrician style and an upper-class point of view. Occasionally, it is true, we are surprised by something with a less modish and more haunting beauty—

> Love still has something of the Sea
> From whence his Mother rose—

but after that fine opening Sedley's song lapses into the commonplace. On the other hand, Mrs. Behn's 'Love in fantastic triumph sat' sustains the promise of its opening line, and achieves a kind of baroque beauty.

Occasionally the wits went beyond a song or a lampoon, but their longer pieces were apt to be disparate fragments loosely strung together. The physically and mentally unattractive John Sheffield, Earl of Mulgrave,[1] was the author of *An Essay on Satire* which is in effect a series of scurrilous lampoons on all those with whom he had quarrelled, with here and there a

---

[1] John Sheffield, third Earl of Mulgrave and first Duke of Buckingham and Normanby (1648–1721), saw active service both in the fleet and in the army, and in 1680 was in command of an expedition to relieve Tangier. He obtained various Court and State employments in the course of a long and varied life, and was a patron of Dryden and a friend of Pope. He had what Pope called 'the nobleman look', but seems to have been cordially disliked by some of his fellow peers for his pride and conceit.

good line or a telling couplet. His most celebrated piece was his *Essay on Poetry*, in which the noble author pontificated on the various kinds, rebuked Rochester for his ribald and nauseous songs, and uttered some critical commonplaces on dramatic writing. The Earl of Roscommon[1] was perhaps no better a poet than Mulgrave, but he was a much worthier man. Not only did he 'boast unspotted bays' (a negative achievement of some distinction in the reign of Charles II), but he interested himself and sought to interest others, including Dryden, in the un-English project of forming an academy that would 'refine and fix the standard of our language'. Among the fairly numerous Arts of Poetry, his *Essay on Translated Verse* (1684) is one of the most successful. To complain of its want of originality is beside the point; such originality as Roscommon attempts or attains lies not in his thoughts, but in his 'well-exprest' presentation of them. His allusions, images, similes, and occasional aphorisms were all useful, because, as Johnson once said of rhetorical ornament in general, 'they obtain an easier reception for truth'.

John Wilmot, Earl of Rochester,[2] was not in most respects different from his fellow poets, but he brought an intenser energy of mind and feeling to both his life and his poetry. What is perhaps equally important, he had a habit of retreating at

---

[1] Wentworth Dillon, fourth Earl of Roscommon (1633?–85), was educated at the Protestant University of Caen, travelled in Europe, and was a good deal more learned than most of his fellow peers. He projected a small literary academy in imitation of that at Caen, and Dryden, Halifax, Dorset, and a few others were associated with it, but it came to nothing.

[2] John Wilmot, second Earl of Rochester (1647–80), was at Wadham College from 1660 to 1661, but then continued his education on a tour of Europe. Like several of his dissolute contemporaries he fought bravely at sea in the Second Dutch War, notably in the engagement off Bergen. He was a favourite of Charles II, who always relished wit, but his profligate escapades and his outspoken comments frequently led him into trouble, and he was banished from the Court on several occasions. After trying unsuccessfully to abduct a rich heiress, Elizabeth Malet, he married her in 1667, but did not seriously reform his erratic and unpredictable behaviour. He was a patron of various poets and dramatists, but proved—at least with Dryden—an unreliable one. Rochester's health broke down in 1679, and in the autumn of that year he invited Gilbert Burnet to visit him and talk with him about religion and morality. Burnet's account of those discussions and of the Earl's genuine repentance in the last months of his life was published shortly after his death. Only a few of his poems had appeared in his own lifetime, although many circulated in manuscript. In 1680 a collection of his *Poems on Several Occasions* (many not by Rochester) was published with the fictitious imprint of 'Antwerp'. A more reliable edition was published by Jacob Tonson in 1691.

intervals from the Court and the life of the Town, either to recover his health or to escape from those embarrassments that the wild career of a rake brought upon him; and alone with himself in the country he had leisure for meditation, reading, and writing. With the possible exception of the Marquis of Halifax, he was certainly the most brilliant person at the Court of Charles II, and there is ample evidence that he made a deep impression on his contemporaries. Rochester had intelligence of a very high order; indeed, he was intelligent in everything except his life. 'He loved to talk and write of speculative matters', Burnet tells us; but he also loved to drink and whore, and his life was a long struggle between his intelligence and his appetites. What matters is that he did nothing by halves; in his cups or in his writing he had an incandescent energy (he is a sort of aristocratic Burns) that glowed with 'a hard gem-like flame'; and if, as Pater held, 'to maintain this ecstasy is success in life', Rochester succeeded abundantly.

When we turn to his writings, we find a handful of songs ('Absent from thee I languish still'; 'An age in her embraces past'; 'All my past life is mine no more') which are of finer quality than any written by his contemporaries, and spring from a deeper source of experience than the Restoration poet normally drew upon. In some other short pieces ('My dear mistress has a heart'; 'While on those lovely looks I gaze'; 'Vulcan, contrive me such a cup') Rochester writes at least as well as Dorset or Sedley at their best. It was his ambition to stamp his unique personality on every poem he wrote, so that the world might see 'it could have been produc'd by none but me'. While some of his songs are hardly to be distinguished from those written by his contemporaries, others are highly individual, and a few, such as the 'Song of a Young Lady to her Ancient Lover', are unique. The same is true of a number of his satirical poems, notably that ironical piece 'The Maimed Debauchee', which comes from the mood of amoral and amused contemplation that is one of Rochester's characteristic positions. In 'A Letter from Artemisa' and 'Tunbridge-Wells', where the fastidious aristocrat looks with polite disgust at the third-rate world of contemporary English society, with its fops, bullies, coxcombs, squires, citizens, cuckolding wives, and cuckolded husbands, we are in the realm of

Restoration comedy; and although Rochester professed to have no desire

> to make a Play-house ring
> With the unthinking Laughter, and poor praise
> Of Fops and Ladies,

he showed in the two satires just mentioned that he had the gift of comic observation and the ability to reproduce contemporary dialogue. A profounder and more disturbed Rochester is to be seen in his most famous poem, 'A Satire against Mankind', which owes something to Boileau's Eighth Satire, but perhaps more to Montaigne, and a good deal to Hobbes and La Rochefoucauld. This poem, with its distrust of rationalism and its emphasis on 'right reason'—

> That Reason which distinguishes by Sense,
> And gives us Rules of good and ill from thence—

that reason, in fact, which enables us to live in accordance with our natural impulses and obtain the maximum of satisfaction from them, is perhaps the clearest contemporary expression of that sceptical, hedonistic, 'libertine' philosophy which, for many of the cleverest young men of the day, 'called all in doubt' in religion and morality.

The other Court wits lived and wrote at a lower pressure. Wycherley, who had a comparable intellectual energy, appears to have lost his touch almost completely when he wrote verse. The verses he collected in *Miscellany Poems* (1704) may have been the work of his later years when his memory was impaired, but they are certainly cluttered and repetitious: Wycherley clearly achieved a far more effective concentration of his thoughts in prose than he could ever manage in verse. Many gentlemen who were outside the immediate circle of the Court wits were yet influenced by their style of writing. Among those was the soldier, John, Lord Cutts, who wrote a verse apology for 'such gentlemen as make poetry their diversion, not their business', and averred, 'My Muse shall be my Mistress, not my Wife'. Once at least he reached the limited perfection of which he was capable in a charming lyric:

> Only tell her that I love,
> Leave the rest to her and Fate. . . .

At the close of the century the thin talent of William Walsh[1] was still producing variations on the conventional themes. Pondering much about 'the fair sex', he went to his grave without finding one of them that he could marry: like the despairing lover of his best-known song, he no doubt reflected that 'a neck when once broken can never be set'. There is little in Walsh's well-turned verses to suggest that they were written in accordance with one of his critical precepts—to obtain the love of a mistress, and not for 'the getting of fame or admiration from the world'. It is true that he avoids forced conceits, and that he addresses himself to the task of describing the changing feelings of a lover; but he takes good care to maintain a dignified front, and wit and elegance successfully restrain the language of the heart. He probably comes nearest to revealing his amatory experience when he tells one of his ladies that he would be content to go without her favours provided that she also slighted all other men:

> I can endure my own Despair,
> But not another's Hope.

Love poetry unlike any other of the period is to be found in *Female Poems on Several Occasions* (1679) written by 'Ephelia', whose identity is unknown. What distinguishes Ephelia is a forthrightness of utterance and a quite unusual facing of facts, as in the poems describing her relationship with 'J.G.', which seem to be based on genuine experience. In such verses as 'Why do I love? Go, ask the glorious Sun' and 'You wrong me, Strephon, when you say' we meet with a candour and an honest self-analysis that are comparatively rare in Restoration poetry.

Another oddly isolated and under-valued poet is Charles Cotton, whose posthumous volume of *Poems on Several Occasions* (1689) appears to have aroused little contemporary interest, and who was probably little known by the time of Addison and Pope, except for his burlesque poems and *The Wonders of the Peak*. Yet there is more and better poetry in the 1689 volume than is to be found in any other minor poet of the Restoration: if this was not recognized at the time is must have been because

---

[1] William Walsh (1663–1708) was a Worcestershire gentleman with literary pretensions, for whose *Dialogue Concerning Women* (1691) Dryden wrote a short Preface. He wrote short poems in the fashionable idiom of the day. In later years he came to know the young Pope and undertook to set him right about poetry.

Cotton's natural vein was out of fashion. There was still a public for the natural that was at the same time low; but by 1689 the polite reader expected a good deal more sophistication and artificiality than Cotton usually gave him. He had to wait until the beginning of the nineteenth century for genuine recognition; and then Wordsworth, Coleridge, and Lamb testified freely to the pleasure his poetry gave them. It was Wordsworth's belief that in versatility of genius Cotton 'bore no obvious unresemblance' to Robert Burns; but this comparison may have been prompted by Wordsworth's uneasy awareness that the two poets shared the same convivial habits. Although there *is* some resemblance—the gaiety which will sometimes turn to melancholy, the unrepentant amorousness, the sincerity and directness of feeling and expression, the close familiarity with Nature—it might be nearer the mark to compare Cotton with Herrick. He comes nearest to Herrick's delight in simple, natural things in his four series of quatrains on Morning, Noon, Evening, Night:

> Now doors and windows are unbarr'd,
> Each-where are chearful voices heard;
> And round about Good-morrows fly,
> As if day taught Humanity.

Cotton has much, too, of the colloquial ease of the Cavalier song-writers, and he favours the conversationally abrupt opening ('Pish! 'tis an idle fond excuse'; 'Prithee, why so angry, sweet?'; 'Lord! how you take upon you still'). There are fewer traces of metaphysical poetry; but those occur occasionally, as in a simile in 'La Illustrissima' about Almanna's eyes, which can draw all hearts by their attraction 'as warm chaf'd jet licks up a trembling straw'. Here and there the conceits are more reminiscent of Sir Philip Sidney's generation than of the Restoration: in 'The Surprise' Cotton describes a fair nymph sitting by the side of a river, and reading nothing less than the *Arcadia*:

> The flouds straight dispossest their foam,
> Proud so her mirrour to become;
> And ran into a twirling maze,
> On her by that delay to gaze. . . .

This, indeed, is almost the *Arcadia* versified. No doubt some of his love songs are conventional exercises; yet the prevailing

impression made by them is that they spring from actual experience, and that his Celia and Phyllis are as real as bonny
Jean and Highland Mary. In his 'Invitation to Phyllis' it is
his own estate that he describes; in summer, when 'crystal
Dove runs murmuring still', and in winter when the trees

> their Naked bones
> Together knock like Skeletons.

There is a quiet reasonableness in Cotton's love-poetry that
gives it an authentic note; he is not going to hang himself for
love, and he is not prepared to sue *sine die*, but his feelings are
genuine. Those feelings, of whatever sort, he often expresses
with a touching simplicity ('Good God! how sweet are all
things here!') that can come only from those who live in willing
submission to 'the essential passions of the human heart'. No
wonder that Wordsworth admired this poet of Dovedale who
had lived much of his life in hourly communication 'with the
best objects from which the best part of language is originally
derived'. Wordsworth was right, too, in attributing to Cotton
fancy rather than imagination, even in his celebrated poem on
Winter. There was a fantastic streak in Cotton which turned
his thoughts to the odd and the extravagant, sometimes with
misplaced ingenuity as in the *Scarronides*, but with the happiest
results in his Rabelaisian verses on 'The Great Eater of Gray's
Inn', and, more daintily, in his whimsical poem on the Great
Frost.

In the reasons given by Thomas Flatman[1] for writing his
poetry we hear unmistakably the voice of the typical minor
poet; he wrote 'to give present ease to the pains of his mind', and
to pass the time innocently when he had nothing to do that he
liked better. We find what we should expect from such origins:
Flatman's poetry is cultured, often low-spirited, and not marked
by any great urgency of feeling or liveliness of fancy. He seems
to have a good share of what Thomas Gray was to call 'leuco-
choly', and to have been familiar with that condition in which,
as he put it himself, 'to live [is] only not to die'. In so far as
there can be a poetry of low spirits Flatman achieves it, but the
strings of his fiddle are often damp, and scarcely twang. It is no
accident that his best-known poem is the song entitled 'Death'

---

[1] Thomas Flatman (1637–88), educated at Winchester College and New College, Oxford, was a miniature painter of considerable ability. His *Poems and Songs*
(1674) reached a fourth edition in 1686.

('Oh the sad day'), for it is in the contemplation of mortality that he finds his surest inspiration. Accustomed to taking his pleasures sadly, Flatman secretes a self-pleasing melancholy when he contemplates 'death's dismal evening drawing on', or 'Nature's dark retiring room', or thinks of London in the time of the Great Plague as 'that illustrious Golgotha'. Although Rochester, less perceptively than usual, dismissed him as 'that slow drudge in swift Pindarick straines', Flatman's predilection for the pindaric ode (in which he mourns with dignity the deaths of the Earl of Ossory, the 'incomparable Orinda', and others) was justified by his unusually sensitive ear for rhythm, and by his ability to control elaborate rhythmical movements. Not much more than a sensitive ear distinguishes the poetry of the almost totally forgotten Philip Ayres, whose sonnets and emblems look back to an earlier generation, and who translated with a gentle persistence from Greek, Latin, Italian, Spanish, Portuguese, and French poetry. He is almost devoid of imagery; and in spite of the generous claims made for him by Saintsbury, he scarcely impinges upon the mind of the reader.

Among the numerous minor poets of the period the names of Richard Duke, George Stepney, and Charles Montague, Earl of Halifax, are preserved for posterity by their inclusion in the eighteenth-century collection for which Johnson wrote his *Lives*; others survive, like Edmund Arwaker, because their very scarcity has given them a posthumous value in the catalogues of second-hand booksellers. The 'Poems on Several Occasions' of such minor writers as Duke, Stepney, Edward Leigh, Jeremiah Wells, Matthew Stevenson, John Whitehall, Thomas Fletcher, Daniel Baker, and Lady Mary Chudleigh differ considerably in content; but, in addition to numerous occasional poems, they tend to include songs, elegies, epistles, translations, and pindaric odes. Of the many poets who set out to imitate the pindarics of Cowley, his friend Sprat[1] ('Pindaric

---

[1] Thomas Sprat, D.D. (1635–1713), Dean of Westminster from 1683 and Bishop of Rochester from 1684, was educated at Wadham College, Oxford, of which he was a Fellow from 1657 to 1670. After publishing some poems he acquired a considerable reputation by vindicating his fellow countrymen in his *Observations on Monsieur de Sorbier's Voyage into England* (1664), and still more by his *History of the Royal Society* (he was one of the early Fellows) in 1667. Politically, Sprat was something of a timeserver; he published an account of the Rye House plot in 1685, he sat on James II's Ecclesiastical Commission, and he had the King's Declaration of Liberty of Conscience read in Westminster Abbey, emptying the Abbey in the process. In 1692 he was the victim of a conspiracy to prove

Sprat') was one of the most successful. Sprat's conceits are often ingenious without being forced; wit and sense have reached a working agreement. Otway's pindaric, 'The Poet's Complaint of his Muse', is a curious hybrid which is partly autobiographical and charged with an unfashionable emotionalism, and partly a satirical account of the Shaftesbury faction, cast in an allegorical form that clearly shows the influence of Spenser.

There is little religious verse after 1660 (Milton, Traherne, and Henry Vaughan in his latest volume excepted) to compare with that written in the first half of the century: in an age in which poetry had come more and more to deal with public concerns, it had become less easy to express the inner and private life of the spirit. Bishop Ken wrote some hymns which are still remembered, and Nathaniel Wanley, a sensitive and devout soul whose verse has only recently come to light, was the author of a number of poems in which the influence of Vaughan is unmistakable. He never rose much above earnest meditation, however, and one likes the poet better than the poems. Samuel Wesley, the father of two more famous sons, published in 1693 *The Life of our Blessed Lord and Saviour Jesus Christ*, a heroic poem in ten books which was perhaps helped to reach several editions by its sixty copperplates and some 'necessary notes'. It does have, however, a long and interesting Preface on heroic poetry, written with that colloquial ease which the example of Dryden must have made both possible and popular. The Dissenters, too, had their poets and versifiers. Benjamin Keach's *War with the Devil* (1674) and John Mason's *Spiritual Songs* (1683) are only two examples of works which were reprinted over and over again, and were enjoyed by the same public as read *The Pilgrim's Progress*.

A better writer, with a more interesting mind, is John Norris of Bemerton,[1] another rather isolated figure among the poets of the 1680s. Most of his poetry was probably written while

that he was plotting the restoration of James II, but published a lively and successful vindication of his innocence. Sprat was an able preacher and an active Dean of Westminster, but contributed little to the study of divinity.

[1] John Norris (1657–1711) was educated at Winchester College and Exeter College, Oxford, became a Fellow of All Souls, and in 1692 was appointed Rector of Bemerton. As a supporter of Malebranche he published *An Essay towards the Theory of the Ideal and Intelligible World* (1701–4), and he was one of the early critics of Locke's *Essay concerning Human Understanding*. Norris also published miscellanies in verse and prose, and a number of devotional works.

he was a Fellow of All Souls College, and its moral and religious tone is very different from that of the fashionable verse of the day. What he thought of that verse was stated with his usual brevity and point in his Preface to *A Collection of Miscellanies* (1687). Poetry, he complained, 'is now for the most part dwindled down to light, frothy stuff, consisting either of mad extravagant Rants, or slight witticisms, and little amorous Conceits, fit only for a Tavern entertainment, and that too among Readers of a Dutch palate'. His own poetry is full of small felicities, sufficiently unusual to attract the attention, if not perhaps to detain it for long. It is a poetry of retirement, of contentment with little; and Norris continually voices the superiority of meditation and learning to riches and mundane glory, dwelling much on the contemplation of death and on a future state. All this would hardly make for liveliness, but the turns of thought and expression are individual, and at times odd and original. In 'My Estate', for example, he characteristically contrasts his own humble contentment with the cares of the rich landowner, in whose meadow the tranquil poet can sit beneath a tree, writing his poetry:

> What to you *care*, does to me *pleasure* bring,
> You own the Cage, I in it *sit* and *sing*.

As the shades of neo-classicism begin to lengthen over English poetry in the 1690s, the odd and the original become less frequent and correspondingly more precious. But we find both oddness and originality in 'The Old Man's Wish' of Walter Pope, one of the most charming poems of the whole period, and again in his *jeu d'esprit*, 'The Salisbury Ballad', which must be about the first poem in English to be accompanied by a mock-learned commentary. Among the other unclassifiable eccentrics was Thomas Heyrick, whose *Poems* (1691) included 'The Submarine Voyage', a pindaric-type poem in four parts. Heyrick was not a John Keats, but his underwater world reminds one at times of the third Book of *Endymion*, and must have seemed to the average poetry-reader of the day very queer stuff indeed.

(11)

With this literary background in mind it is now possible to see the poetry of John Dryden in perspective, and to realize how much he transcended his poetical contemporaries in almost every kind that he attempted. His earliest surviving poem, 'Upon the Death of Lord Hastings', appeared in a volume called *Lachrymae Musarum* in 1649, when the poet was still a Westminster schoolboy. As was customary on such occasions, the tears had quite as much of the salt of wit as of grief: Ptolemy is summoned to take 'this Hero's altitude', and the poet reflects that if Tycho Brahe were still alive he would use his astrolabe to find out 'what new star 'twas did gild our Hemisphere'. Such passages, and the notorious one on the smallpox of which Hastings died, show the young Dryden revelling in the conceits and the points of wit that he had learnt from Cowley, 'the darling of my youth'. Equally significant is the emphatic and colloquially uneven metre of this immature metaphysical poet. Listening to such a couplet as

> Is Death (Sin's wages) Grace's now? shall Art
> Make us more Learned, onely to depart?

we catch no hint of the mature poet. This might be Dryden's voice still cracked in the puberty of his poetry; it is, in fact, the voice of Cleveland, echoed by an apt schoolboy.

It seems probable that Dryden went on writing poetry after he left Westminster School; but if so, there is almost nothing to show for it in the next ten years. When in 1659 he emerges again with his *Heroic Stanzas* to the memory of Oliver Cromwell, he is in his twenty-eighth year, and he has caught very successfully the poetic manner of Davenant, and adopted the four-line stanza of *Gondibert*. He is now master of a controlled and balanced rhythm, and he has arrived at that precision of thought and expression, and that characteristic mode of definition by antithesis which is to distinguish his mature work—

> The quarrell lov'd, but did the cause abhorre,
> And did not strike to hurt but make a noise.

There are still some traces of the metaphysical poet and of wit-writing, but it is now becoming clear that Dryden has a good deal that he genuinely wants to say, and his way of saying it is no longer Cowley's. How far he is giving us his own thoughts, and not merely thoughts that might be thought about Cromwell, it is not easy to decide; but, like all his later poetry, this poem is intellectually exciting. We attend because Dryden makes it worth our while to read with attention.

Having buried the dead in the *Heroic Stanzas*, Dryden proceeded in the following year, along with almost all of his
poetic contemporaries, to welcome home the living Charles.
The King reached London at the end of May, and Dryden's
Astræa Redux was on sale by the middle of June. His couplets
have that firm, confident movement—strength with mobility,
measure with variety—which wins the willing assent of the
reader. He was writing here of what he knew from personal
experience; and although his vision of the crowds that choked
the beach at Dover, and 'made a wilder torrent on the shore',
is fine enough, it is not more interesting than his precise
description of the months immediately preceding the Restoration, when young men who had never known real gaiety
'envy'd gray hairs that once good days had seen', and of the
quiet way in which the 'blessed change' stole upon the nation.
Long frost is generally followed by violent floods:

> Our thaw was mild, the cold not chas'd away
> But lost in kindly heat of lengthned day.

Dryden might so easily have falsified the facts and suggested
a sudden and spontaneous revulsion from the old regime;
instead, he describes with complete integrity what had actually
happened—the gradually dawning consciousness of an impending change which accompanied the tentative and exploratory
negotiations with the exiled King. *Astræa Redux* belongs to that
large class of panegyrical poems written during the reign of
Charles II, and is therefore pitched on a heroical key, with
biblical and classical allusions and various kinds of rhetorical
heightening; but it is characteristic of Dryden that however
much he may embellish the facts he still sticks to them. To the
same year belong his verses to Sir Robert Howard 'On his
Excellent Poems'. Here we have the first clear indications of
Dryden the critic, and growing evidence of the fact that (as
Johnson suggested) 'the favourite exercise of his mind was ratio-
cination'. Equally remarkable is the free ranging of his mind,
which Dryden was to compare to 'a nimble spaniel' which 'beats
... through the field of memory, till it springs the quarry it hunted
after'. In complimenting Howard, for example, on his ability
to combine the useful with the delightful, Dryden remarks:

> We're both enrich'd and pleas'd, like them that woo
> At once a Beauty and a Fortune too.

To find a new turn for Horace's *qui miscuit utile dulci* is a small triumph of 'what oft was thought but ne'er so well exprest'. If there was ever anything in Shadwell's taunt that Dryden came up to London from Cambridge 'a raw young fellow of seven and twenty', he must have acquired very quickly the polish of the Town. In his panegyric verses on the King's coronation in the following year there is a new courtliness and less of a merely academic wit. Dryden recalls the Civil War in a characteristically heroic image of the Flood:

> In that wild Deluge where the World was drownd,
> When life and sin one common tombe had found,
> The first small prospect of a rising hill
> With various notes of Joy the Ark did fill—

where what might have been merely grandiose is given an odd authenticity by the awareness shown in the word 'various'. With how graceful a turn, too, Dryden celebrates one of the King's most attractive qualities, his clemency:

> Among our crimes oblivion may be set,
> But 'tis our King's perfection to forget.

In these coronation verses and in those 'To My Lord Chancellor' (1662) Dryden has shed the too-frequent similes of his earliest writing; the argument is more continuous, and he has begun to realize the advantages of the verse paragraph. By 1665, when he writes some complimentary verses to the Duchess of York on the Duke's victory over the Dutch fleet, he has acquired an easy command of the panegyric poem; and in his final comparison of the Duchess to the new-born phoenix adored by her feathered subjects—

> Each Poet of the air her glory sings,
> And round him the pleas'd Audience clap their wings—

he achieves a delicate and artificial beauty that he never bettered.

In complimenting his brother-in-law, Sir Robert Howard, Dryden had suggested that such poems as his could never have been formed by 'atoms casually together hurl'd', but were obviously due to 'the providence of wit'. In *Annus Mirabilis* (1667) we are perhaps all too conscious of the providence of wit: what is there has been sought for, and seems rarely to have presented itself spontaneously. Since Dryden had already a

well-stocked mind, his poem abounds in picturesque images, and
in overt or concealed allusions, echoes, and imitations. *Annus
Mirabilis* is indeed full of felicities of very different kinds: the
dignified, almost sublime, description of how the rival fleets
furled their sails for the coming engagement ('Their folded
sheets dismiss the useless air'); the lurid light of burning London on the River, carrying the poet's mind back to Virgil's
description of blazing Troy, only to focus a moment later on
the delicate improbability of 'And wond'ring fish in shining
waters gaze'; the attack on the Spice Fleet, when, in keeping
with this wonderful year,

> Some preciously by shatter'd Porc'lain fall,
> And some by Aromatick splinters die.

The nimble spaniel of Dryden's wit courses to and fro and never
rests; sometimes it springs the strangest game, but Dryden's
gun blazes away indiscriminately. The poet defines *Annus
Mirabilis* in his Preface as a historical poem; it is not epic
because it has not unity of action, and is in any case too short.
The action and actors, however, 'are as much heroick as any
poem can contain', and Dryden acknowledges his debt to
Virgil, who 'has been my master in this poem'. Yet it is primarily a piece of wit writing, with the varied imagery and
rapid transitions of metaphysical poetry; the heroic element
maintains a rather precarious existence in face of such period
comparisons as that of the winds to crafty courtesans who withhold the flames of the Great Fire from burning 'but to blow
them more'. *Annus Mirabilis* remains an interesting hybrid,
but (like the later *Hind and the Panther*) it leaves an impression
of the sum being less than the parts; it is 'everything by starts
and nothing long'. As Dryden was to observe in his more judicious old age, 'An author is not to write all he can, but only all
he ought'.

For almost fifteen years he did not publish another long
poem. During this extended interval he was almost wholly
engaged in writing for the stage. When at length he returned
to poetry in 1681 it was with a maturity that would be otherwise unaccountable if we were to forget the discipline and
facility which this dramatic writing had given to his thinking and his mode of expression. For all their fatuity of action and
emotional exaggeration, his heroic plays, and more recently

All for Love, had taught him how to argue in verse, to put an imaginary case, to juxtapose and develop conflicting ideas. When, therefore, in 1681 he wrote *Absalom and Achitophel*, he was not moving into entirely unfamiliar regions, but adapting for political satire a technique he had already mastered. Nor was the field of political poetry entirely new to him: his long poems of the 1660s were all partly political in content, and *Annus Mirabilis* in particular had been designed deliberately to counteract republican propaganda and to vindicate Charles II, whose kingly qualities were stressed in the poem, and who was shown as having been favoured by heaven when the further spread of the Great Fire was averted as the result of his prayers. Although Dryden (as he was to observe of himself in the Preface to *Religio Laici*) was 'naturally inclined to scepticism in philosophy', and although he had a very open mind on literary and artistic and many other matters, he was almost from the start much less uncommitted in his political beliefs, which from 1660 onwards were firmly royalist and conservative. In the long political crisis of 1679–82, when Shaftesbury and the Whigs made use of the Popish Plot to bring in a Bill to exclude the Catholic Duke of York from the succession, his natural conservatism was intensified; and although as Poet Laureate he would naturally be expected to support the Court interest, there is every reason to believe that he did so with complete conviction. In *Absalom and Achitophel* we have the necessary conditions for great satire: the writer really cares about the cause he is asserting, but is not so personally involved in the events as to have lost control of his temper. It was Dryden's belief that 'the nicest and most delicate touches of satire consist in fine raillery'; and he added, in words that fit perfectly his own poem, 'How easy is it to call rogue and villain, and that wittily! But how hard to make a man appear a fool, a blockhead, or a knave, without using any of those opprobrious terms!' In his willingness to give Shaftesbury a fair run for his money, Dryden's long dramatic training in allowing his heroic villains to state their case comes into play, and he is obviously influenced, too, by Milton's Satan and the debates of the fallen angels. As a man of letters Dryden had a quite unusual talent for controversy, with a penetrating eye for the weakness of his opponent's case and an unfailing tact in concealing the weak points of his own. Dryden taking sides, therefore, is still Dryden the imaginative writer, adopting more than one point of view and sustaining various roles, as he had done in *All for Love* with Antony, Ventidius, and Alexas, each of whom is an interested party with a case to be put by the dramatist. In his political poems Dryden is not, of course, impartial; but, as Keats was to say of the 'camelion poet', he takes 'as much delight in conceiving an Iago as an Imogen'. His task in *Absalom and Achitophel* was to denounce and ridicule the Whigs, while at the same time preserving the glory and importance of the King and his ministers; he had to combine the heroic with the ridiculous in a new kind of heroic satire, which would have, as he said of Boileau's *Lutrin*, 'the majesty of the heroic, finely mixed with the venom of the other'. *Absalom and Achitophel* is therefore by no means a purely satirical poem, but it is a landmark in English satire. To readers who had delighted in Butler's rumbustious tetrameters or in the rough and emphatic invective of Marvell, of Oldham, and of their many cruder contemporaries, the spectacle of Dryden skating along imperturbably and cutting his figures on the political ice must have come as a revelation of what polite literature could achieve. The age prided itself on its refinement, its modernity, its sophistication, but so far there had been little to justify such complacency. Here at last in the careless ease and assured control of Dryden we meet with the poetry of the polite world, the sort of poetry that could be appreciated by a Halifax or an Evelyn.

The satirical character sketches in *Absalom and Achitophel* vary in accordance with the person under attack: that of the chief conspirator Achitophel is in the heroic style, Zimri is subjected to delicate raillery, and Shimei and Corah, being 'low' characters, are given a rougher and more colloquial, but no less expert, drubbing. The biblical framework was already familiar to Dryden's readers: Charles II had often been compared to David, and the David–Absalom–Achitophel situation had recently been used by several contemporary writers. In Dryden's hands the biblical parallel gave his poem an added dimension; and, as Mr. Ian Jack has said, it helped to give it 'an air of objectivity more impressive than the direct exclamatoriness so common in political satire', besides enabling Dryden to establish and maintain the heroic tone that he desired for this poem on a grave political crisis. Exception has

sometimes been taken to the structure of the poem, more particularly to the way in which it ends. Johnson's complaint that
the reader feels cheated by too easy a solution has frequently
been repeated: 'Who can forbear to think of an enchanted
castle, with a wide moat and lofty battlements, walls of marble
and gates of brass, which vanishes at once into air when the
destined knight blows his horn before it?' But Johnson's
metaphor is perhaps hardly fair to Dryden's intention and
achievement; the speech of 'the godlike David' with which
the poem ends strikes the desired note of majestic omni-
competence. It would be fairer to ask, 'Who can forbear to think
of the sun breaking majestically through the dark clouds, and
with the brightness of his beams dispersing the threatening
storm?'

Whatever political effect Dryden's poem may have had on
the country at large, it failed to influence the carefully picked
London Grand Jury which, on 24 November, threw out the
bill of indictment against Shaftesbury. The Whigs were understandably jubilant, and a medal was struck to commemorate
the occasion. The idea for a satire on those new developments
may have come from the King himself, who is said to have given
the poet the subject of *The Medal* when walking with him one
day in the Mall. At all events, Dryden's poem was published
about four months after *Absalom and Achitophel*. So far as the
medal is concerned, Dryden has done with it after twenty-five
brilliantly contemptuous lines; the rest of the poem is devoted
to ridicule and straight invective of Shaftesbury and his party.
The opening sketch of the Whig statesman, who

> Groan'd, sigh'd, and pray'd, while Godliness was gain;
> The lowdest Bagpipe of the squeaking Train,

whose 'nimble wit outran the heavy pack', and who, even when
he gave apparently sincere advice to his royal master, 'had a
grudging still to be a knave', is a memorable study of hypocrisy,
equivocation, political timeserving, and unprincipled ambition.
Dryden's genuine fear that the popular appeal of Shaftesbury
and his faction was opening the way for anarchy gave to his
invective a new severity, and the poem ends with a gloomy
prophecy of the chaos that will come again if, as a result of
Shaftesbury's stirring up rebellion, the people rise against their
sovereign king. The harshness of the invective is reflected in the

language of the poem, which is less uniformly heroic than that of *Absalom and Achitophel*, and descends at times to the rough idiom of the market-place. The same tone of sincere indignation rings out in the prose Epistle to the Whigs prefixed to the poem: the author of *The Medal* was not just producing an exercise in Juvenalian satire; he was an angry, and almost certainly a frightened, Englishman.

Dryden was now thoroughly fleshed in political blood. For a second part of *Absalom and Achitophel*, written by Nahum Tate and published late in 1682, he contributed some two hundred lines of brilliant ridicule and abuse of various Whig agitators and pamphleteers, notably Elkanah Settle ('Doeg') and Thomas Shadwell ('Og'). In several prologues and epilogues written about this time he did not hesitate to comment again on the troubled political scene. In the spring of 1682 the Duke of York, who had been virtually banished to Scotland for two years, was allowed to return to London; and on 21 April he attended a special performance of Otway's *Venice Preserved*, a play in which Shaftesbury was ridiculed in the person of the lecherous old senator Antonio. For this royal night Dryden wrote a prologue, and some time later he wrote another for a similar visit of the Duchess. Dryden's sense of occasion was hardly ever at fault, and he opened the first of those two political prologues with some nicely timed denigration of Scotland and the Scots. The Duke was back in London, he had returned to civilization, he was sitting there in the royal box on a warm evening in spring. How good, Dryden wants the audience to feel, to have him back again in his rightful place! How different is this gay and friendly city from the barbarous country of dour Whigs and Presbyterians to which he had been banished for so long! And so Dryden proceeds to set the tone with that sort of confident exaggeration which a public theatre and a grand occasion can so easily support:

> In those cold Regions which no Summers chear,
> When brooding darkness covers half the year,
> To hollow Caves the shivering Natives go;
> Bears range abroad, and hunt in tracks of Snow:
> But when the tedious Twilight wears away,
> And Stars grow paler at th'approach of Day,
> The longing Crowds to frozen Mountains run,
> Happy who first can see the glimmering Sun! . . .

Dryden had never visited Scotland, but it is unlikely that he thought of it as being quite so arctic a land as he makes it appear. This is rather a case of that delightful heightening to which he often refers in his critical writings: ' 'Tis true, that to imitate well is a poet's work; but to affect the soul, and excite the passions, and, above all, to move admiration, . . . a bare imitation will not serve.' Dryden's audacities were not always happy, but he was rarely at his best unless he was taking some sort of risk. By 1682 he had a sure grasp of how far he could allow hyperbole to go; those 'Dalilahs of the theatre' which he had followed unthinkingly in the days of his rhymed heroic plays he now courted with a more experienced and more critical eye.

To 1682 (his own *annus mirabilis*) belongs *MacFlecknoe*, but it is now known that this highly developed lampoon on Shadwell was written some years earlier. In an age in which repartee and satirical wit were so much valued it is not surprising to find authors frequently exercising their critical ingenuity upon one another. They were competing, too, not only for the attention of a small and closely integrated reading and theatre-going public, but also for the approval and support of the little group of aristocratic patrons to whom they dedicated their works. The malicious gossip of coffee-house wits, the natural envy of the less successful, and the pure mischievousness of such intellectual mavericks as Rochester, did much to exacerbate the relations of literary men. The good-natured Dryden suffered with the rest, although the attacks upon him became numerous and scurrilous only after the appearance of his political poems in the early 1680s. He did not remain entirely silent under attack, but he was not easily provoked, and he never retaliated with a *Dunciad*. Why, therefore, he decided about 1678 to overwhelm Shadwell with ridicule in a sort of one-man *Dunciad*, or why, having written it, he allowed it to remain in manuscript (the first edition of the poem 'printed for D. Green, 1682' is thought to be a piracy) has never been adequately explained. In March 1678 he had contributed a prologue to Shadwell's *A True Widow*, and although this action does not necessarily show that the two men were on terms of friendship, it does at least indicate that they had not quarrelled permanently at that date. Lampoon was not Dryden's normal mode of attack. Writing in 1693, he characterized it as 'a dangerous sort of weapon', since 'we have no moral right on the reputation of other men'. He could see only two fair excuses for having recourse to lampoon: to revenge some notorious abuse, and to obliterate someone 'when he is become a public nuisance'. If the question had been put to Dryden, he would probably have offered the second of those two reasons as his justification for writing *MacFlecknoe*; and he might also have agreed with an anonymous defender of Pope's *Dunciad*: 'Gentlemen should consider that to some people Dulness is provoking; and that in such case, to call Gentlemen dull is no Abuse, though it may be Rudeness.' For all his genuine ability as a comic dramatist, there was undoubtedly a streak of dullness in Shadwell, a bias towards the obvious and the absurd, a tendency to labour a point in a fashion very unlike the casual and unemphatic mode of Restoration comedy. The good-humoured offhand way in which Dryden disposes of Shadwell is itself a demonstration of how effective that witty and ironical mode could be. The mock-heroic technique had never before been applied at such length to the ridicule of an English author, but Dryden showed his literary tact by not maintaining the heroic note for too long at a time. *MacFlecknoe* proceeds by a mingling of irony with direct abuse; the peculiar effect of the poem comes from a succession of abrupt and often concealed descents from the sublime to the vulgar or the ridiculous. The reader is continually falling through Dryden's trap-doors in the same way as Shadwell himself ('the yet declaiming Bard') disappears from view at the end of the poem.

Towards the close of 1682 appeared *Religio Laici*. It may seem odd to find Dryden, in the full production of his political satires, turning his mind to the writing of religious poetry, but *Religio Laici* is religious poetry in only a limited sense. It is true that the poem is in part a sincere confession of faith, and a discussion of the grounds for religious belief. Dryden had for long been interested in such questions, and a translation by his young friend Henry Dickinson of Father Simon's *Histoire critique du Vieux Testament* was only the immediate occasion for his focusing his attention on the reliability of the Scriptures on which Protestantism was based. But if the poem is a product of Dryden's genuinely sceptical and inquiring mind, it is also in part controversial, and to that extent political in an age in which religion and politics were almost inseparable. 'I

pretend not to make myself a judge of faith in others,' he wrote
in the Preface, 'but onely to make a confession of my own.' If
Dryden really thought that he was not attacking the faith of
others in this poem, the satirical habit must have become so
much second nature with him that he had grown unaware of
its operation. It has been suggested that *Religio Laici* may be in
part a reply to Martin Clifford's *Treatise of Human Reason*,
which, although on the surface a plea for toleration, managed,
as Professor Hooker pointed out, 'to assure nonconformists of
all types that they were the real champions of truth', and further
tried to convey the impression that 'dissent and divergencies
are in themselves ultimate values, regardless of what they
stand for or what they diverge from'. Although Dryden makes
some thrusts in *Religio Laici* at the Roman Catholic priests who
kept the people in intellectual ignorance and 'parcel'd out the
Bible by retail', his most scornful ridicule is reserved for the
Protestant Dissenters, who are as usual equated with the rabble.
When Protestantism put the Bible 'in every vulgar hand',

> The tender Page with horney Fists was gaul'd;
> And he was gifted most that loudest baul'd:
> The *Spirit* gave the *Doctoral Degree*:
> And every member of a *Company*
> Was of *his Trade*, and of the *Bible free*.

Dryden's solution in 1682 is to take the *via media* of the Church
of England, avoiding both extremes. If our reason still stickles
at belief, we can at least keep silent,

> For points obscure are of small use to learn:
> But Common quiet is Mankind's concern—

a political conclusion that would have been heartily endorsed
by the King and his ministers. *Religio Laici* belongs to that
'mixed way of writing', so characteristic of Dryden and of
his age, that led to tragi-comedy in drama, and in this sort
of ratiocinative poetry to a mixture of religious confession,
theological argument, and satirical commentary. Theoreti-
cally, the disparate elements ought to be at loggerheads, but in
practice they blend together in Dryden's poem into an impressive whole, because Dryden carries the reader along by the
unfailing energy of his mind and his writing. *Religio Laici* is in
the form of a Horatian epistle; and 'the expressions of a poem
design'd purely for instruction', he tells us, 'ought to be plain

and natural, and yet majestick'. The much-admired opening
lines—

> Dim, as the borrow'd beams of Moon and Stars
> To lonely, weary, wandring Travellers,
> Is Reason to the Soul . . .—

are in all three veins at once; and where the poet drops to a
more familiar style he has managed the transitions so easily
that the descent is almost imperceptible, and always acceptable.

Dryden's conversion to Roman Catholicism took place at
some time in the year 1685. That he had been growing more
deeply concerned about his own personal religion may be seen
from his pindaric 'Ode to the Pious Memory of . . . Mrs Anne
Killigrew', a young poetess who had died of smallpox in the
summer of that year. In this poem (which Johnson considered
to be 'undoubtedly the noblest ode that our language ever has
produced') Dryden interpolates at one point a penitent confession of his own contributions to the moral pollution of 'this
lubrique and adult'rate age', and more especially those which
had served to increase 'the steaming ordures of the Stage'. Few
would now agree with Macaulay that he was only climbing on
to the Roman Catholic bandwagon in the reign of James II
when he went over to the Church of Rome: in *Religio Laici* he
had already shown himself to be genuinely concerned about
the problem of authority in religion. 'When he finally confessed
to himself', as Professor Bredvold says, 'that the Anglican
Church had renounced the necessary principle of authority, he
went over to the Church which seemed to him still to possess it.'
There is no reason to suppose that he ever wavered again. He
had now been in turn a Protestant and a Roman Catholic;
but from first to last he seemed to get more satisfaction from
speculating and arguing about his religion than from quietly
practising it. As a Catholic he may well have attained to that
peace of mind which he had so long and so earnestly sought
for; but when, after an interval, he returned to the stage with
Amphitryon, it was to give the public another 'lubrique and
adult'rate' play, with no indications of a chastened spirit. And
if he no longer believed that 'priests of all religions are the same',
he never developed more than a very tepid enthusiasm for the
priestly vocation. He did, however, campaign actively for his
new faith, and it was in a mood of controversial confidence that

he now turned in 1686–7 to writing *The Hind and the Panther*.
This poem, the longest of his original works, is at once brilliant and exasperating; nowhere is the writing more assured
and sophisticated, and nowhere is the vehicle more unsophisticated and absurd. Apart from the unsuitability of the beast
fable for complex theological argument, Dryden constantly
breaks through the flimsy animal fiction and carries on the discussion in literal terms. 'Is it not as easie', asked the two
authors of *The Hind and the Panther Transversed*, 'to imagine two
Mice bilking Coachmen, and supping at the *Devil*, as to suppose a *Hind* entertaining the *Panther* at a *Hermits Cell*, discussing
the greatest Mysteries of Religion, and telling you her son
Rodriguez writ very good Spanish? . . . But this is his new way
of telling a story, and confounding the *Moral* and the *Fable* together.' In our own time Professor Earl Miner has put Dryden's
beast fable in its historical setting, and has offered the most sympathetic interpretation of the poem's structure yet attempted;
but (in a phrase used by Dryden and other dramatists of the late
seventeenth century) 'it wo' not be'. *The Hind and the Panther*
remains a monstrous aberration of genius: Dryden was always
capable of unhappy, no less than happy, audacities, and of
making elementary mistakes in literary decorum. In this
strange medley of religious confession, theological argument,
and personal satire, of allegory and the actual, of the heroic,
the plain, and the familiar styles, he is at his furthest point from
the canons of neo-classicism. We read the poem because it is a
pleasure to be with Dryden; it is the mind of Dryden that we
are in contact with, and the voice of Dryden that we hear
throughout. That alone gives the poem any unity it may have.

Dryden's ability to meet the sort of demands made upon
a Poet Laureate may be studied in *Threnodia Augustalis*, the
'funeral-pindaric' which he wrote on the death of Charles II,
and in *Britannia Rediviva* (1688), the long panegyrical poem in
heroic couplets with which he greeted the birth of a son to
James II. To these may be added *Eleonora* (1692), another
panegyrical poem which he wrote in memory of the Countess of
Abingdon, on the invitation of her sorrowing husband. In all
these poems, and especially in the two last, Dryden started
from 'one bare circumstance' and proceeded to elaborate upon
it. The only hard fact about the baby prince (afterwards the
Old Pretender) was that he had been born; and so far as the

Countess was concerned, Dryden had never met her, and was
forced to rely on such information as he could gather from her
friends or family. Those three poems have never had many
admirers, and yet they contain passages of noble rhetoric and
persuasive statement. All three are characteristic of Dryden's
poetic activity: he has a self-induced energy, he concentrates
his mind on a theme until confused ideas, as he once put it,
begin 'tumbling over one another in the dark', and 'the sleeping images of things' start moving towards the light. It is, as
Coleridge saw, the force and fervour of the poet that spirits up
the thoughts and images in such a poem as *Eleonora*. 'The wheels
take fire from the mere rapidity of their motion.'

This self-generating energy is to be seen at work again in the
brilliant prologues and epilogues that Dryden wrote for his
own and other men's plays. There are almost a hundred of
those short pieces written over a period of nearly forty years,
and together they form an important part of the poet's total
output. Many of them have little or no relevance to the play
to which they are attached, but most of them have a theme
which Dryden develops with casual wit and colloquial ease,
and (it must be added) with a good deal of *double entendre* and
some obscenity. Since he was on familiar terms with both
actors and audience, he could adapt a prologue to a speaker, to
the hearers, and to the circumstances; and he knew perfectly
how to exploit the intimate relationship that existed in the
small Restoration theatres between author and player on the
one side of the stage and audience on the other. He was a
master at once of the dignified compliment (for some royal
occasion or for an Oxford audience) and of the polite sneer; he
knew how to solicit the sympathy of an audience without being
subservient, and how to insult some sections of it without for-
feiting the favour of those who mattered. In his prologues and
epilogues, too, there is constant and lively allusion to the events
of the day and to the activities of men and women of fashion;
and his imagery catches and holds the attention by its relevance, its variety, its topicality, its frequent originality and
unexpectedness, and above all by its suitability for arousing in
an audience the desired reactions. In this field, as in so many
others, Dryden easily surpassed all his contemporaries; but the
writing of a witty prologue or epilogue was a challenge that
many lesser men successfully met. In an age of public poetry

this direct address to a listening audience was perhaps the most public of all kinds, and the consciousness of a special occasion stimulated the wits to give of their best.

The familiar and conversational manner which was natural to the prologue and epilogue spread outwards from the theatres into other forms of verse, until it became for many kinds of poetry the customary way of writing. It is to be found again (where, indeed, one would expect it) in Dryden's various verse epistles, from such early examples as those addressed to Sir Robert Howard and Dr. Walter Charleton to the later and perfectly controlled epistles 'To my Dear Friend Mr. Congreve' (1694), and, in the last year of the poet's life, 'To my Honoured Kinsman John Driden, of Chesterton'. Taken together, Dryden's epistles show him at his most urbane, commenting freshly and sagaciously upon the contemporary world, and moving easily from the familiar and colloquial to such heightened lines as those addressed to the young Congreve, with their biblical and classical overtones:

> Our Builders were, with want of Genius, curst;
> The second Temple was not like the first:
> Till You, the best Vitruvius, come at length;
> Our Beauties equal; but excel our strength.
> Firm Dorique Pillars found Your solid Base:
> The fair Corinthian Crowns the higher Space;
> Thus all below is Strength, and all above is Grace.

The last quarter of the seventeenth century was marked by a renewed interest in the classical poets and in turning their work into English verse. Besides Hobbes's Homer (1675–6) and the labours of the industrious Thomas Creech on Theocritus, Lucretius, Horace, and Manilius, there were various other translations from Anacreon, Musaeus, Catullus, Horace, Juvenal, Martial, Ovid, Persius, Propertius, Tibullus, and Virgil; and in prose, there were translations, in whole or in part, of Aesop, Lucian, Plutarch, Polybius, Xenophon, Cicero, Sallust, Seneca (L'Estrange's digest of Seneca's *Morals*, 1678, was one of the most widely read books of the period), Suetonius, and Tacitus. Even Mrs. Behn, who had no Latin, was not to be left out, and contributed a metrical 'Paraphrase on Oenone to Paris' for Tonson's volume of Ovid's *Epistles* (1680). To this same volume Dryden contributed three of the twenty-three pieces.

In his later years Dryden turned more and more to translation.

Between 1684 and 1693 Tonson published three volumes of *Miscellany Poems*; and to these Dryden contributed translations from Ovid, Theocritus, Virgil, Lucretius, Horace, and Homer. For Tonson's folio of *The Satires of Juvenal and Persius* (1692) he turned five of the sixteen satires of Juvenal into English verse and all six of Persius, besides writing the long dedicatory 'Discourse concerning the Original and Progress of Satire'. The crowning achievement of his classical translation, *The Works of Virgil*, was published in 1697, 'adorned with a hundred sculptures', containing a Life of Virgil and a Preface to the *Pastorals* by Knightly Chetwood, and a Preface to the *Georgics* by the young Joseph Addison. Another young friend, William Congreve, came to his help in a different way: this 'excellent young man' undertook to review Dryden's translation of the *Aeneid* and compare his version with the original. Three years later Dryden published his last volume, *Fables, Ancient and Modern*, consisting almost entirely of verse translations, including eight passages from the *Metamorphoses*, the first Book of the *Iliad*, three of Boccaccio's tales, Chaucer's 'The Knight's Tale', 'The Nun's Priest's Tale', 'The Wife of Bath's Tale', 'The Character of a Good Parson', and the non-Chaucerian 'The Flower and the Leaf'. After the poet's death, further versions made by him from Ovid appeared in 1704 and 1709. In all, his various translations amount to about two-thirds of his total poetical output.

Dryden had given as much thought to the problems of translation as to any of the other critical topics that he brought his mind to bear upon; and in discussing the difficulties of the translator and the varying challenge which different poets presented he came nearest to that close consideration of the text which we associate with twentieth-century criticism. In his own practice he tried to steer between the two extremes, of paraphrase (which was too licentious) and of literal translation (which failed to preserve the spirit of the original); but the difficulty of rendering into English a poet who wrote in Latin— 'a language wherein much may be comprehended in a little space'—frequently drove him to some form of paraphrase entailing slight omissions as well as additions to bring out the poet's sense. Dryden also faced the problem of finding an English equivalent for the classical poet's versification: some translators (he believed) completely blurred the distinction

between Virgil and Ovid 'by endeavouring only at the sweetness and harmony of numbers', instead of trying to reproduce
Virgil's sonorous and perpetually varied verse, and the smooth,
rapid, and much less varied or majestic verse of Ovid. At his
best Dryden succeeds in carrying his precepts into practice,
although the English heroic couplet tends to level the distinctions that he is endeavouring to observe. In the Dedication of *Examen Poeticum* he claimed that his translations from
Ovid seemed to him to be 'the best of all my endeavours in this
kind', either because Ovid was easier to translate than most
other poets, or because 'he was most according to my genius'.
Dryden had always an amiable way of believing that his most
recent work was his best, but his renderings of Ovid are often
felicitous, for Ovid's thought is basically antithetical, and his
elegiacs go naturally into heroic couplets. Dryden appreciated
Ovid's witty 'turns', he liked him because he was 'well-bred,
well-natured, amorous, and libertine', and because he was easy
and lucid. In his younger days, too, he had admired him for
his ability to show 'the various movements of a soul combat-
ing betwixt two different passions': of all the ancient poets he
considered Ovid to have had a 'genius most proper for the
stage' (Dryden was clearly thinking of the heroic play), although
in his later years he was to contrast the artificiality of Ovid with
the naturalness and good sense of Chaucer. He reproduced
brilliantly the artificial beauty of Ovid in the long lyrical
address of Polyphemus to Galatea—

> Oh lovely Galatea, whiter far
> Than falling Snows, and rising Lillies are—

and in a quite different vein he was completely successful in his
zestful and racy rendering of 'Baucis and Philemon', written
late in life and about the same time as his version ('The Cock
and the Fox') of Chaucer's 'Nun's Priest's Tale', when he was
himself returning more frequently to the pleasures of country
life. Elsewhere he plunges into a vigorous translation of Ovid's
fights and battles, handling them, as Professor Kinsley has
suggested, 'with the enthusiastic violence common to poets who
have not seen military service'. Dryden kept coming back to
Ovid; and he was remarkably successful in giving his versions
'a kind of cadence, and, as we call it, a run of verse, as like the
original as the English can come up to the Latin'.

Before his translations from Lucretius appeared in *Sylvae*, the whole of the *De Rerum Natura* had already been translated by Creech,[1] a young Oxford scholar. Creech's version had been hailed by John Evelyn, who had attempted the first book himself shortly before the Restoration, and praised not only by such poets as Otway, Tate, Duke, and even Mrs. Behn (who spoke of 'Divine Lucretius, and Diviner You'), but also by a number of scholars who were in a better position to appreciate the difficulties involved. Creech has some spirited passages, and he grapples conscientiously with the text, but his translation fails on the whole to reproduce those qualities that Dryden singled out in Lucretius: his magisterial confidence, and 'a certain kind of noble pride and positive assertion of his opinions', expressed everywhere in 'the loftiness of his expressions, and the perpetual torrent of his verse'. Faced with a poet whose confident dogmatism reminded him of 'our poet and philosopher of Malmesbury', Dryden conformed his genius to that of Lucretius, and 'laid by [his] natural diffidence and scepticism for a while'. In the long passage 'Against the Fear of Death' from Book III, the torrent of Dryden's own verse and the unremitting ardour with which he pursued the argument of his author produced one of the most masculine poems of this most masculine poet.

The tenderness and simplicity which he noted in Theocritus were qualities with which Dryden was much more slenderly endowed; and although he thought that the Doric dialect of Theocritus had 'an incomparable sweetness in its clownishness', he made no attempt to find an equivalent in English, frightened by the example of Spenser, and reminding himself that he was translating Theocritus for the benefit of ladies, 'who neither understand nor will take pleasure in such homely expressions'. Of his few versions of Horace, the best are the second epode on the joys of a country life, and, more notably, his rendering into pindaric verse of the twenty-ninth ode of Book III, which he said he had attempted to make his masterpiece in English. He

[1] Thomas Creech (1659–1700) was a scholar of Wadham College, and in 1683 became a Fellow of All Souls College. He gained a considerable reputation by his translation of Lucretius (1682), which was not increased by his subsequent translations of Horace, Theocritus, and other classical writers. For some time before his death his behaviour had become noticeably odd, owing (as it was afterwards asserted) to a frustrated love affair. He was found dead in an apothecary's garret in June 1700, having committed suicide in a rather bungling fashion.

was not mistaken: this ode, at once free and controlled, is one
of Dryden's firmest achievements. He knew that the secret of
the pindaric form lay in the poet's ability to make 'the cadency
of one line . . . a rule to that of the next':

> Be fair, or foul, or rain, or shine,
> The joys I have possest, in spight of fate, are mine.
> Not Heav'n it self upon the past has pow'r;
> But what has been, has been, and I have had my hour.

The same power to control large rhythmic units informs the
magnificent opening stanza of the *Song for St. Cecilia's Day* ('From
Harmony, from heavn'ly Harmony . . .'), and produces the
more obvious felicities of *Alexander's Feast*.

With Juvenal, Dryden was on the familiar ground of satire,
and he caught well some of the qualities in this poet that he
singled out for mention: his impetuosity, his vehement scorn,
his ability to drive his reader along with him and to press home
his attack ruthlessly. Dryden pursues Juvenal with unflagging
gusto; his translation has colloquial freedom and vigour, and all
the marks of something that it was a pleasure to do. What it
lacks is Juvenal's stateliness: Dr. Johnson, who had earned the
right to judge, thought that Dryden's versions had kept the wit,
but failed to preserve the dignity of the original.

When it came to Virgil, Dryden practically admitted that the
poet of the *Aeneid* was untranslatable. He considered Virgil to
be the 'closest' of the Latin poets, crowding his sense into the
narrowest possible compass; the sound in Virgil, too, was constantly an echo of the sense, and was therefore infinitely varied;
and he was endlessly figurative, leaving much to be imagined
by the reader. Again, that 'majesty in the midst of plainness' which
Virgil had at command did not come so easily to Dryden; and
the Latin poet's restrained and delicate turns were sometimes
coarsened by Dryden's robust rhetoric, or vulgarized by his
much less fastidious mind. For Virgil's imitative harmony he
tried hard to find equivalents in English, and in passages describing storms and fights and athletic contests he revelled in
sound effects, in the same *bravura* spirit as informs his *Song
for St. Cecilia's Day* and *Alexander's Feast*. He also gave much
thought, at times too much, to finding words which were
'significant and sounding'; epic poetry, he believed, required
ornament, and that was not to be had from 'our old Teuton

monosyllables'. He therefore went in search of polysyllabic words
of Latin origin; and in general, but more especially with Virgil's
epic, feeling that the language of ordinary discourse required
heightening, he was sometimes too concerned to avoid what he
called 'village words'. In the *Eclogues* he is usually simpler, and
has some delicate and moving passages. In the *Georgics*, although
he had once praised Virgil for the power he showed in that
poem of giving dignity and importance to matters which 'are
neither great in themselves, nor have any natural ornament
to bear them up', he is usually surprisingly free from verbal
heightening:

> For e're the rising Winds begin to roar,
> The working Seas advance to wash the Shoar:
> Soft whispers run along the leavy Woods,
> And Mountains whistle to the murm'ring Floods:
> Ev'n then the doubtful Billows scarce abstain
> From the toss'd Vessel on the troubled Main:
> When crying Cormorants forsake the Sea,
> And stretching to the Covert wing their way:
> When sportful Coots run skimming o're the Strand;
> When watchful Herons leave their watry Stand,
> And mounting upward, with erected flight,
> Gain on the Skyes, and soar above the sight. . . .

What buoys up Dryden's *Georgics* is less a matter of poetic diction than of the firm placing of words, and of his magisterially
confident rhymes and rhythm.

In the 'Dedication of the *Aeneis*' Dryden acknowledged the
help he had got from an unpublished version of the poem by
Richard, fourth Earl of Lauderdale; but recent scholarship has
shown that his debt to his predecessors was a good deal more
extensive. Besides Lauderdale, he frequently consulted the
despised Ogilby, Thomas May (for the *Georgics*), and the versions of various gentlemen translators who had turned individual
passages or episodes into English verse. He took pains over the
text, consulted the editors and commentators, and weighed up
one interpretation against another; he took a hint or sometimes
a whole line from a previous translation, or combined phrases
from two different translators to form his own line or couplet.
He was clearly aiming at the definitive English translation;
and if he kept quiet about most of his indebtedness, he could
hardly be expected to advertise it. That in spite of all this toil

and experiment his translation of Virgil moves (to use one of his own favourite phrases) on carpet-ground, is a remarkable tribute to the intellectual and rhythmical energy that fused the parts into a continually developing whole. To Pope, Dryden's Virgil was the most noble and spirited translation in any language; and for the next hundred years it continued to fertilize English poetry, and to give delight to the English common reader.

Dryden's poetical versions of Boccaccio's prose tales left him much freer to improvise, and indeed they can scarcely be called translations. All three are love stories; but it is love as it was understood and expressed in contemporary tragedy—a mixture of lust, heroic sentiment, horror, and violence. After his close and severe labours on Virgil, the versification of those tales of Boccaccio must have seemed almost a holiday task. The free and rapid flow of his narrative style has been rightly admired; but why Wordsworth should have considered those versions of Boccaccio to be 'the best, at least the most poetical of his poems' is incomprehensible, unless he is simply expressing his preference for the more open couplets in which they were written. Dryden's versions of Chaucer are again a special form of translation. After three hundred years of linguistic change, the reader of the late seventeenth century did not find Chaucer at all easy to read, and Dryden set out to rescue the old poet by modernizing his language. In the event, Dryden's 'Palamon and Arcite' is a medieval structure altered to suit a more modern taste; the story of Emily and the two knights is seen in the light of seventeenth-century heroic romance. When Chaucer's Queen wept,

> so dide Emelye,
> And alle the ladies in the companye;

but, in Dryden,

> when she began,
> Through the bright Quire th'infectious Vertue ran.

Clearly we are in a different world; and the change is not just one of tone, attitude, sentiment, and of the words which convey these, but, once again, of the ringing and dominant sound of Dryden's couplets, which constantly drown the gentle, unemphatic, and at times even tentative voice of Chaucer. If Dryden really had 'a natural diffidence and scepticism', that is about the last impression we are likely to get from the bounding confidence of his verse. Regularizing Chaucer's metre was not the least of the services that he thought he was performing for the old poet; for to readers in 1700 (who read him in Speght's edition) the need to pronounce Chaucer's weak final syllables seems to have been generally unknown. Believing, too, that Chaucer lived 'in the infancy of our poetry', Dryden did not think it necessary to tie himself to a close translation, but felt free to add or omit as he thought fit, and did so the more readily because he found that he had a soul congenial to Chaucer's. This congeniality is most apparent in 'The Cock and the Fox', where he enters fully into the fun of Chaucer's tale, and where his own occasional heightening suits well with its mock-seriousness. It will be recalled that in 1693 he had said that Ovid was 'most according to [his] genius'; and now in 1700 he had made an almost identical statement about Chaucer. However we are to reconcile those two claims (and he made similar statements about Homer and Horace), there can be no question that Dryden felt a genuine admiration for Chaucer; and in his memorable critical contrast of those two poets, in the Preface to the *Fables*, he made the surprising discovery, as W. P. Ker pointed out, that Ovid was less classical than Chaucer, who followed nature everywhere and was indeed 'a perpetual fountain of good sense'.

Dryden's progress as a poet seems to run contrary to normal experience. In his early years he often gives the impression of searching for thoughts and similes; if they will not come to him of their own accord, he is prepared to go and look for them. In his middle and later years, as he said himself, 'thoughts, such as they are, come crowding in so fast upon me, that my only difficulty is to choose or reject'. So far from there being any slackening, there is actually a quickening of the imagination; and with a greater pressure of thought, he has also learnt how to order it and keep it moving along. His poetical progress, too, has some resemblance to that of Pope, who, after wandering for some time 'in Fancy's maze', ultimately 'stoop'd to Truth'. For Dryden, 'Fancy's maze' is represented by a succession of fantastic heroic plays which can never have been much more than a kind of hopeful make-believe to him, and in which he had continually to strain and force his invention. When he turned in the 1680s to writing his political and religious poetry, he was on firmer ground: Shaftesbury and Buckingham, Protestantism and Roman Catholicism, Whigs and Tories— all these were *true*, as Almanzor and Montezuma and the Love-and-Honour debates were not; and Dryden's writing takes on a new zest and assurance and authority in consequence. From first to last, however, he never gave up what Neander (following Horace) called the poet's 'licence of *quidlibet audendi*'; in an age that was moving, largely under his own guidance, towards a literature of neo-classicism, he retained the right to launch beyond his depth and be indiscreet. He is, indeed, 'the very Janus of poets'.

V

PROSE FICTION

IN any assessment of English prose fiction in the last decades of the seventeenth century it is necessary to take into account the various types of reader for whom it was written, and the extent to which each individual piece was original work or some form of translation or adaptation. The native English strain is more likely to be found in such popular pieces as Richard Head's *The Life and Death of Mother Shipton*, which could be enjoyed by the barely literate, than in the few English examples of the heroic romance or in the numerous short novels describing love affairs in oriental courts. Yet it is not always easy to guess what sort of public a writer had in mind. A glance at *Bateman's Tragedy: Or, The Perjur'd Bride Justly Rewarded* would suggest that this tale of a rejected lover who hanged himself outside the bedroom door of the girl who had promised to marry him was a chapbook intended for apprentices and maidservants; but although the cuts are of the crudest and the climax is lurid, the style is distinctly literate. Much of the fiction of the period, however, was clearly addressed to the upper-class reader, who, when not reading a romance or a novel, might be watching a play at the theatre.

When Peter Anthony Motteux started *The Gentleman's Journal* in 1692 it contained sections on current news, history, philosophy, poetry, and music, but also, significantly, a certain amount of prose fiction. In spite of its title Motteux's miscellany was designed to appeal to ladies as well as gentlemen, and it was primarily for the fair sex, as he explained, that he usually inserted a short novel in each number. The readers of romances and novels at this time appear to have been predominantly feminine, and much of their reading matter came to them from across the Channel, either in the original or in translation. By 1660 most of the work of Gomberville, La Calprenède, and the Scudérys had been translated into English by John Davies of Kidwelly and others. After the Restoration Milton's nephew, John Phillips, produced versions of La Calprenède's *Pharamond* and Mlle de Scudéry's *Almahide*. The Countess de La Fayette's *La Princesse de Clèves* was translated in 1678, the year after its publication in Paris. Most of the French heroic romances, usually published in folio, had gone through a considerable number of editions by 1700, but were gradually losing ground before the end of the century. To some extent their place was being taken by the *nouvelles* and secret histories of such writers as Marie Desjardins, Gabriel Brémond, Mlle de la Roche-Guilhem, Sieur de Préchac, and the Countess D'Aulnoy, many of which had been 'done out of French' by Ferrand Spence, Peter Bellon, and others. The popularity of the *Lettres Portugaises* in L'Estrange's English version of *Five Love-Letters from a Nun to a Cavalier* (1678), together with the various additions and replies, is a clear indication of the contemporary taste for stories of amorous intrigue. Spain, too, contributed a little to this rising tide of foreign fiction. In 1694 Walter Pope, less concerned to render his author word for word than to 'make him speak English', put out a translation of *Select Novels*, the first six by Cervantes and the last by Petrarch.

The anti-romances of Paul Scarron and Furetière were even more popular, at least with male readers. Translations of Scarron by John Davies and John Phillips were followed by *The Whole Comical Works* at the hands of Tom Brown and others, and this version ran through a succession of editions. In 1667 L'Estrange had published a lively translation of *The Visions of Quevedo*, which was frequently reprinted in the next thirty years, and *The Novels* 'faithfully Englished' appeared in 1671. An attempt was made by the industrious Phillips to supersede Thomas Shelton's translation of Cervantes by a *Don Quixote* 'made English according to the Humours of our modern Language'. The contemporary taste for anti-romantic and satirical fiction is also reflected in Ferrand Spence's loose version (from the French) of Lucian's *Works* (1684–5), and in the better translation by Tom Brown and others which was undertaken towards the close of the century. In 1694, too, there appeared a translation of Petronius by William Burnaby.

The English reader, therefore, was both able and willing to read in his own language the prose fiction of other nations. He was less well served by the writers of his own country. There was, it is true, Roger Boyle, Earl of Orrery, whose *Parthenissa* (1654–76) still remains, like an extinct volcano, to be examined by the curious. Orrery follows the elaborate plan of his French contemporaries and predecessors, and the story of Artabanes and Parthenissa is interrupted by a series of secondary episodes as new strangers appear and proceed to tell their own tale. The reader is therefore involved in a circular movement, which carries him slowly along but never seems to get him much further. This is fiction by the leisurely for the leisured; and the movement of Orrery's prose, though less elaborate than that of Sidney's *Arcadia*, has the unhurried elegance of a writer with all the time in the world. Time is indeed required to develop this kind of romance; for, in addition to the vicissitudes of fortune, the lovers are consumed by doubt and despair, and tortured by hesitations and misgivings. 'Your scruples are much greater than their cause', Parthenissa tells Artabanes on one occasion, and her remark has the widest possible application in this world of anxious lovers whose wretchedness is largely self-induced. Time is needed, too, to define those nice distinctions which constantly intrude themselves on the minds of the lovers: the right attitude has to be struck, the precise balance has to be achieved between conflicting ideas and emotions, and these become at times so fine-drawn as to be almost inapprehensible to the vulgar reader. On the other hand, Orrery was not incapable of describing action, whether historical or imaginary (*Parthenissa* is a blend of history and fiction), and in his well-informed battle scenes we are reminded that he had seen a good deal of active service, and was the author of an authoritative *Treatise of the Art of War* (1677). After his own fashion, too, he had mastered the style required for the heroic romance. In a Preface to one of his many translations Ferrand Spence remarks on 'that delicate turn of thought and expression' which is expected in works of prose fiction, and Bishop Huet, in his *Lettre sur l'origine des romans* (translated into English as *A Treatise of Romances*, 1672), commends romances not only because they give young women invaluable moral guidance about the nature of love, but also because they refine and polish wit. The patrician prose of Orrery is perhaps more remarkable for its stateliness than for its wit, but he is by no means without his delicate turns, and when Artabanes, wounded in a tournament in which he had appeared as Parthenissa's champion, writes to her, 'I must beg her to believe that the wounds I have received from her Beauty are far more dangerous than those I have received for it', we can see the sort of thing that high-born maidens 'longen after' in the mid seventeenth century. At all events, so good a judge as Dorothy Osborne was impressed by *Parthenissa*. ''Tis handsome language,' she wrote, 'you would know it to be writ by a person of good quality, though you were not told it.'

Boyle was probably in his early thirties when he began to write *Parthenissa*. Sir George Mackenzie's[1] *Aretina; or, The Serious Romance* appeared in 1660 when its author was twenty-three, and John Crowne, who published *Pandion and Amphigenia* in 1665, was, on his own confession, 'scarce twenty years of age when [he] fancyed it'. In 1664 Pepys tore up the manuscript of a romance he had written at Cambridge when he was about twenty; and about the same age Temple was sending to Dorothy Osborne his translations and adaptations of a number of short French romances. Youth was no handicap for this sort of fiction, for the world to be portrayed was rather what the author would like it to be than what it really was. Mackenzie's *Aretina* begins picturesquely enough with the rescue of two ladies, loaded with shackles and stripped to the waist, who are being lashed by a pair of cruel ruffians. The ten armed men who are in charge of them are killed or driven off by two brave knights; the elder lady then proceeds to tell her story, the elder of the two knights tells his, and Philarites, the younger knight, who has fallen in love with Aretina, is so overcome by her beauty that he swoons away. From this point Mackenzie's romance, which was never completed, traces the Aretina–Philarites love story to within sight of a happy conclusion, but there are many vicissitudes, including a love-letter forged by a jealous rival and designed to kindle jealousy in the heart of Aretina; a war between the Egyptians and the Persians (in which Philarites 'did by his sword subscribe two hundred passports for eternity' and 'the greenest pile of grasse was scarleted

---

[1] Sir George Mackenzie (1636–91) was called to the Edinburgh bar in 1659, and at first distinguished himself by his opposition to the Earl of Lauderdale, but later became his subservient supporter. He was made Lord Advocate for Scotland in 1677, and earned a grim reputation by his persecution of the Covenanters. His literary interests first found expression in his 'serious romance' *Aretina* (1661), and from that date until his death this 'noble wit of Scotland', as Dryden called him, published numerous legal, political, and historical works, and a number of moral essays and discourses. He was virtually the founder of the Advocates' Library in Edinburgh. His interesting *Memoirs of the Affairs of Scotland* did not appear until 1822.

by the Persian blood'); and a civil war among the Egyptians
(in which a young man who suffers from cancer, finding that
he cannot by art prolong his life, is 'resolved to do it by fame',
and undertakes to blow up a strategic bridge and so bring
about the total destruction of the enemy). Mackenzie's fertile
imagination is still busily at work when his story comes to an
abrupt end; but he is as much concerned with the telling as
with the tale, and with the opportunities it provides him to
introduce short discourses, to argue moral paradoxes, and to
exercise his skill in oratory and letter-writing. As he explains in
his prefatory 'Apologie for Romances', it was 'to form to my
self a style that I undertook this piece', and in his ingenious
narrative and artificial prose he travels hopefully and beautifully if he never quite arrives. The problem of Crowne's
Pandion and Amphigenia is not why he should have written it, but
why he published it. Both the dedication and the address to the
reader are apologetic and self-depreciatory, as of one who has
outgrown the follies of his youth. What Crowne feels entitled to
claim for his romance is originality—'all is Genuine, nothing
stole'. This may possibly be true of the various episodes, but in
style and mode of expression he is heavily indebted to Sidney's
Arcadia, with his 'winged choristers', his lovers 'wrapped in
Sleep's care-charming mantle', his similes and his pathetic
fallacy. As the story slowly unwinds, the action becomes more
and more fantastic: Pandion conceals his name and calls himself Dampion, but later disguises himself as a woman, and the
action is further confused by the obscure emergence of a false
Pandion. In due course even Crowne himself has had enough
of this folly, and almost yawns in the face of the reader. Near
the end he admits that he has not brought all his lovers out of
the labyrinth in which he has placed them, but the reader is
advised that he can do that for himself by following 'the vulgar
Rule of Romances . . . that the Knight must kill the Gyant and
get the Lady'. It would be reassuring to believe that Crowne
had set out with the intention to satirize the romances, but he
makes it quite clear that his story has disintegrated because his
own interest in it has totally collapsed. 'And those that are not
pleased with this Conclusion, let them throw away as many
idle hours as I have done, and they may compleat that Story
which hath now quite jaded and dull'd my Pen.'

There is little need to explore this *cul de sac* of English fiction any further. It is enough to mention John Bulteel's *Berinthia* (1664), 'a romance accommodated to history' which was set in the reign of King Cyrus, and the still less readable allegorical-religious romance, *Bentivolio and Urania* of Nathaniel Ingelo, which plumbs the depths of boredom, but which ran through four editions between 1660 and 1682. Writing of the fourth edition, in which Ingelo had explained that 'the obscure words throughout the book are interpreted in the margin', Sir Walter Raleigh permitted himself a characteristic protest: 'Its unillumined profundity swarms with low forms of life; polysyllabic abstractions crowd its pages, and deposit their explanatory spawn upon its margin; "the very deep did rot".' The fiction of the later seventeenth century was often, indeed, formidable. In 1671 Edward Pococke the younger published a Latin translation of Ibn al Tufail's philosophical romance *Hai Ebn Yokdan*, and this was twice translated into English, by George Keith the Quaker in 1674, and by George Ashwell in 1686. Among its readers was George Barclay, who got from it a proof of his doctrine of the Inner Light. Another philosophical romance which found a translator was Baltasar Gracián's *The Critic*, turned into English in 1681 by Sir Paul Rycaut. Something of a curiosity is Captain Edward Panton's *Speculum Juventutis* (1671), the story of a young nobleman Sisaras, whose rash and misguided conduct is the result of a faulty education. In his dedication to Charles II Panton explains that he has written his romance for the instruction of 'unruly youth', believing that it will have a better chance of doing good than

> more sowr and severe pieces of Morality, especially written by Divines, against whom they have a picque as designers on their Liberty; like wild Asses in the Mountains kicking with the heel their drivers, telling them they get good Livings by Preaching good life; arming themselves with the whole Armour of Ungodliness against them, even out of the holy Magazine of Scriptures, . . . making those Sacred Oracles, like those of Delphos, echo their fancies. . . .

Panton's young hero disobeys his parents, elopes with a young woman they disapprove of, and later, in spite of much good advice that reaches him from various mouthpieces of the author, falls in love with the wife of a friend. Panton's intentions were of the best, but it seems unlikely that such an overtly didactic work did much to check the errors of unruly youth. On the other hand, the Hon. Robert Boyle's religious romance, *The*

Martyrdom of Theodora, written in his early youth but not published till 1687, is less obviously didactic and achieves more. Boyle, who had set himself to enlarge upon a brief account of his heroine which he had come across when turning over the pages of a martyrology, succeeded better than one might expect in penetrating to the feelings and motives of his two chief characters, however remote in time and alien in circumstance.

A more usual form for religious fiction was allegory. Bunyan's outstanding contributions to this genre are considered elsewhere, and they are indeed far more remarkable than anything else of the kind. Simon Patrick's popular book, *The Parable of the Pilgrim* (1665), which has been thought to be a possible source for *The Pilgrim's Progress*, employs the fictional framework of a journey through life, but in a rather perfunctory and discontinuous way. The writer who comes nearest to Bunyan in his allegorical zest is another Baptist preacher, Benjamin Keach (1640–1704), whose *Travels of True Godliness* was in great demand among the religious-minded. Keach has a good deal of Bunyan's ability to drive home the realities of human behaviour in terms of allegorical figures and their arguments, and he has something of Bunyan's plain idiomatic style. When Riches falls sick and is inclined to listen to True Godliness, Dr. Self-Love advises him not to give way: 'Divert yourself among the brave Heroes you used to keep Company with, get to the Tavern, or to some Play-House, but be sure at no time you read any Book besides your Books of Accompts, and Romances, or such like. . . .' When at last True Godliness speaks his mind, Riches raises the rabble on him— Pride, Ignorance, Wilful, Hate-good, Tosspot, Outsides, Riot, and the rest. In a companion piece, *The Progress of Sin; Or The Travels of Ungodliness*, Keach has a long and interesting section on the arraignment, trial, and sentence of Sin. These 'apt and pleasant allegories', as they are called on the title-page, have nowhere quite the intensity of Bunyan, but they are thoroughly workmanlike, and in their dialogue they are colloquial and true to human nature. Although allegory was chiefly used in devotional literature, it sometimes reared its abstract head in political writings. It appears in *An Historical Romance of the Wars* (1694), an obscure secret history involving William of Orange (Nasonius) who usurped the throne of

Utopia when he drove out Eugenius (James II), but also introducing such implausible personifications as Fictitiosa (the Spirit of Lying) and Diabolica (the Spirit of Ingratitude).

Secret histories, which form one of the largest divisions of fiction at this period, are sometimes a good deal more interesting than this. In 1661 there appeared, in two parts, *Don Juan Lamberto: Or, A Comical History of the Late Times*, attributed by Anthony Wood to Thomas Flatman. Written in the archaic language of the old romances and printed in black letter, this is an amusingly satirical account of the intrigues of Lambert, Fleetwood, Vane, Desborough, and other Commonwealth leaders in the time of Richard Cromwell, 'sirnamed for his great valour the Meek Knight'. But we also meet with such minor characters as Yllil the Necromancer (William Lily, the astrologer), and we even get a glimpse of Westminster School in the days of Dr. Busby's predecessor, Lambert Osbolston:

> Now it so came to passe that at that time there lived there a Gyant who was a very cruell and imperious Dominator over the buttocks of youth, one that spared none but very greivously and sorely lashed all alike: he was hight Sir O beston, whose Schoole was like Kalybs Rock, where you heard nothing all day long but the screekes and rufull groanes of children and boyes elaborately corrected.

Flatman can afford to be good-humoured, for he is pursuing a discredited and beaten party; but some later secret histories, written when events were still in the balance, are more malicious. *The Perplex'd Prince* (1682) is a secret history designed to show that the Duke of Monmouth (Hiclacious) is the legitimate son of the King of Otenia, who, while an exile, had married Lucilious (Lucy Walters), a beautiful girl of humble birth. The villain of this piece is the Prince of Purdino (James, Duke of York). The following year saw the publication of *The Fugitive Statesman*, 'in requital for *The Perplex'd Prince*', a fictional demonstration of Monmouth's illegitimacy and an attack on the Earl of Shaftesbury. The abdication of James II encouraged the writing of a number of secret histories, such as *The Amours of Messalina Late Queen of Albion* and *The Royal Wanton* (both of which may have originated in France), and an oriental tale in two parts by Peter Bellon, *The Court Secret*. This last is a characteristic mixture of fact and fiction: the love affair between Ibrahim and Roxana, who is drugged and raped in mistake for the sister of Respet (Father Petre), is brought in so that Roxana may bear a son who can be introduced as the child of the childless Queen. In 1690 appeared *The Pagan Prince*, a 'comical history' attacking James II and the Roman Catholics. About the same time a *Secret History of the Dutchess of Portland*, enlivened by a good deal of dialogue, presented the reading public with 'an Account of the Intreagues of the Court during her Ministry'. *Woman's Malice, A Novel* (1699) is said to be 'a True History of the Amours of an Eminent Person of Quality', who may perhaps be identified with Louis Duras, Earl of Feversham. All of these are in varying degrees scandalous; but *The Secret History of the Most Renowned Queen Elizabeth and the Earl of Essex* (on which John Banks based his tragedy, *The Unhappy Favourite*) is free from indecency, and has the added interest of being told for the most part in the words of the characters themselves. On the other hand, *The Secret History of the Duke of Alençon and Queen Elizabeth*, which introduces a Princess Marianna who turns out to be a daughter of Henry VIII's first wife Catherine, gives a venomous account of Elizabeth. Marianna is accepted by her sister Queen Mary, but Elizabeth does all that she can to discredit her legitimacy, and finally succeeds in putting an end to her life by means of a pair of poisoned gloves. This ugly and libellous travesty of history was clearly a piece of Catholic propaganda, and may not have been the work of an English writer. As literature, those secret histories have little beyond ingenuity to recommend them, but as political documents they are of considerable interest, and they point to that growing interest about what was happening behind the scenes which was also affecting the work of the legitimate historians. This genre was still flourishing in the hands of Mrs. Manley and others in the early eighteenth century. Closely related to the secret history is a story such as *The Player's Tragedy* (1693), which recounts in fictional form the passion of young Lord Mohun (here called the Count de la Lune) for Mrs. Bracegirdle (Bracilla), and its fatal outcome in the murder of Mountfort the player (Monfredo).

For a rather different kind of reader there were lives of rogues and criminals, now appearing in considerable number. Here again it is not easy to tell where fact ends and fiction begins. The chief English contribution to the literature of roguery is, by international standards, third-rate: *The English*

Rogue described in the Life of Meriton Latroon is a derivative work, with little of the satirical observation of manners that enlivens the Spanish examples of this kind, and with an undue concentration on erotic adventures. The first and best part appeared in 1665, and was the work of Richard Head (d. 1686?). It must have found numerous readers, for in 1668 Francis Kirkman the bookseller (b. 1632) thought it worth his while to put together an unauthorized second part, and this was followed by a third and a fourth part in 1671 which were presented to the public as the work of both men. What responsibility Head had for the two last parts is not certain. 'We have club'd so equally,' Kirkman claimed, 'and intermixt our stories so joyntly, that it is some difficulty for any at first sight to distinguish what we particularly writ.' But in his *Proteus Redivivus* (1675) Head denies this claim: he had meant to add a second part, 'but the Cudgels were snatched out of my hands before I had fairly laid them down'. He claims for himself the first part only, and adds that 'the Continuator hath allready added three Parts to the former, and never (as far as I can see) will make an end of pestering the World with more Volumes, and large Editions'. Whatever may be the truth here, the first part of *The English Rogue* is undoubtedly the most interesting, not merely because such amoral and inconsequential narratives become progressively tedious, but because Head appears to be drawing upon personal experience for at least some of his material. In his *Proteus Redivivus* he actually complains that he has been thought to be not merely the author of the book, but the actor too, and Kirkman informs us that it was this vulgar mistake that caused Head 'to desist from prosecuting his story'. Some at least of Meriton Latroon's early misfortunes in Ireland and the account of his schooldays read like autobiography; but there can be no question that most of *The English Rogue* is no more than a lively compilation based on material taken from *Lazarillo de Tormes*, Quevedo, the *Decameron*, the jest books, and many other printed sources, although Head makes a point of denying this. Yet, however derivative the adventures may be, they are told in a happy-go-lucky and colloquial fashion. Head claims, fairly enough, that he has written in a style that is 'plain and familiar, rejecting bombast Expressions, thinking them most happy when most easily to be understood'. Latroon's account of how he ran away from school and lived for some time on nuts and blackberries might almost come, *mutatis mutandis,* from the early pages of *Colonel Jack.* Head presented the events of his hero's life in a more or less unbroken sequence; in his continuation Kirkman followed the more erratic course of a series of separate narratives told by different characters who happen to cross the path of Latroon, and those narratives in turn are apt to hive off into separate stories-within-stories. The method is chaotic, but as the interest of those ramshackle adventures lies almost wholly in separate incidents, and not in the relationship or development of characters, it makes little difference whether the story progresses or not. Since Kirkman had been apprenticed to a scrivener, and had later set up as a bookseller, we may perhaps assume that at least some of the rogueries connected with those two professions fell within his own personal experience, but elsewhere he is obviously pilfering from books and pamphlets, or simply drawing upon his own scatological imagination.

It is clear, however, that the literature of roguery would not have flourished as it did in the later seventeenth century without a plentiful supply of ingenious criminals—thieves, cheats, gamesters, sharpers, wheedles, town-shifts, forgers, highwaymen, and the rest. The careers of Mary Carleton, Claude Du Val, Major Clancie, William Morrell, and many others provided a biographical basis which allowed for the addition, in varying degrees, of fictitious elements. The documentation for Mary Carleton was already considerable, including *An Historical Narrative of the German Princess* said to be written by herself, before Francis Kirkman published his account of her life and adventures, *The Counterfeit Lady Unveiled* (1673). Kirkman took over much of the existing material, but was at pains to inform the reader that he had obtained his facts not only from the books written about her, but also from herself, from her husband, and from 'those who were considerably concerned with her'. As he proceeds, however, he weaves in other material derived from the general literature of roguery, but goes out of his way on such occasions to vouch for its authenticity. After telling us some traditional anecdotes about the cheating of a weaver and a tailor, he adds: 'And now, Reader, let me tell you and assure you, that those three last Adventures . . . are certainly true, for they [the weaver and the tailor] are both my Relations, and lately gave me this Account of their misfortunes.' We might be listening to Defoe. Kirkman's public was, in fact, roughly the same as that of Defoe a generation or so later, but Elkanah Settle, who also wrote rogue histories, was addressing himself to a rather more sophisticated reader. His amusing account of the celebrated confidence trickster William Morrell, *The Notorious Impostor* (1692), is told in a satirical style, with a good deal of ironical understatement and some facetious asides. When Morrell, who keeps deserting his various brides as soon as he has got their money, poses as a Norfolk gentleman in order to gain the hand of a Bath innkeeper's daughter, Settle explains that he has first to make sure 'what Portion the Damsel had, for without a spill of yellow Boys, naked White and Red had but indifferent Charms with him'. Satisfied that she is worth the trouble, he 'plies her home with all the Rhetorick that Love can afford', and his man gossips among the servants about 'what a Worthy Gentleman his Master is, being a Rich Norfolk Gentleman (a pretty large stride from Bathe) of 500 a year'. Something of this facetious delight in the deception of the innocent remains in the rogue histories that Defoe was to write in the 1720s; but because Moll Flanders and Roxana tell their own stories, we come much closer to their real feelings and to the circumstances that shape the life of a criminal.

The close links between biography and fiction at this time may be seen in the persistent claims made by Aphra Behn that her romantic and sometimes improbable stories are actually true. In the dedication to *The Fair Jilt* (1688) she says that she is well aware that all she writes must pass for fiction, and she therefore desires 'to have it understood that this is Reality and Matter of Fact, and acted in this our latter Age'; she had herself often seen the hero of this novel, and part of his story she had 'from the Mouth of this unhappy great Man, and was an Eye-witness to the rest'. Later, in telling his story, she mentions his arrival at Antwerp 'about the time of my being sent thither by King Charles'. In her Dedication to *The Lucky Mistake* (1689) she makes the rather less absolute claim that this story 'has more of reality than fiction; if I have not made it fuller of in-treague, 'twas because I had a mind to keep close to the Truth'. As for *Oronooko*, the hero is not a feigned character 'whose Life and Fortunes Fancy may manage at the Poet's Pleasure. . . . I was myself an Eye-witness to a great Part of what you will find here set down; and what I could not be Witness of, I receiv'd from the Mouth of the chief Actor in this History, the *Hero* himself, who gave us the whole Transactions of his Youth.' It was in Surinam that Mrs. Behn claims to have met him, and she makes a point of describing that country, its fauna and flora, and the magnificent feathers with which the natives made clothes and wreaths for their heads, necks, arms, and legs. 'I had a Set of these presented to me, and I gave 'em to the King's Theatre; it was the Dress of the Indian Queen, infinitely admir'd by Persons of Quality. . . .' Such apparently authentic documentation has led many readers to accept Mrs. Behn's claims at their face value, and to believe (as may be true) that at least some of her stories were based on actual people and events. She did, in fact, visit Surinam in 1663–4, and a few years later she was acting as a secret-service agent in the Low Countries. Yet she may only have used her familiarity with those different countries to substantiate her claims to have met and conversed with the chief characters in her stories. At all events, at a time when rogue biographies and secret histories were much in fashion, the real or supposed authenticity of a story was an asset to the writer of fiction. It certainly helped to ensure the popularity of *Love Letters between a Nobleman and his Sister* (in three parts, 1683–7), which is generally attributed to Mrs. Behn. The nobleman in question was Forde, Lord Grey of Werk, who fell in love with his sister-in-law, Lady Henrietta Berkeley, and eloped with her in 1682. Their story is unfolded in an exchange of passionate letters, together with those of various other correspondents, and the use made of the epistolary mode of narration anticipates the technique of Richardson in a number of interesting ways.

A collection of Mrs. Behn's *Histories and Novels* was published in 1696, and had run through four editions by 1700. They answer perfectly to Johnson's definition of the word 'novel' as 'a small tale generally of love'. What chiefly accounts for the popularity of these stories is indeed the author's apotheosis of love (virtuous love in *Oronooko* and *The Lucky Mistake*, selfish and unmitigated lust in *The Fair Jilt*), and the unexpected changes of fortune which the ungovernable passion of her lovers brings about. She has been praised for her feminism, but she seems more concerned to establish the power than the virtue of her own sex. In *The Nun, Or the Perjured Beauty*, the

heroine Ardelia carries her inconstancy to an extreme, leaving
Don Antonio for Don Henriques, Henriques for a nunnery,
and the nunnery for Don Sebastian, with the result that all the
chief characters have met with a violent death by the end of
the story. Given a fickle woman like Ardelia, anything and
everything may happen; she has only to change her mind for a
new crisis to develop. But this sort of story says nothing, does
nothing: Mrs. Behn is merely moving the pieces around on the
board. The heroine of *The Fair Jilt* is again amorous, incon-
stant, and utterly unprincipled, slandering a handsome young
priest whom she has failed to seduce, hiring a love-struck page
to poison her sister, and, when that fails, persuading her
noble but doting husband to shoot the girl. All these grim
happenings are designed to show the power of love, the irresistible attraction of a *femme fatale*. We may regret for Mrs. Behn's
sake, if not for our own, that she lived before the days of the
cinema. Her *Agnes de Castro*, which is at once more natural and
more civilized, is said by her twentieth-century editor to be
'founded upon' a novel by Mlle de Brillac, but is in fact no
more than a translation. Mrs. Behn's reputation as a writer of
prose fiction rests most securely on *Oronooko*, not only because of
its dramatic interest, but because of her presentation of a
heroic character without any of the usual heroics of the period.
As a noble savage Oronooko has some historical importance,
and in her contrast of his nobility with the brutality of the white
settlers Mrs. Behn sees to it that the immorality and irreligion
of the Christians are fully exposed. In most of her work she
appears to have a divided aim, or no aim at all except to
provide sensation: in *Oronooko* she has for once a moving story
to tell and allows herself to be penetrated by its situations.

A collection of *Modern Novels*, published in 1692 in twelve
volumes, points to the popularity of those tales of love, intrigue,
and gallantry, but also emphasizes the poverty of the English
contribution to this genre. Of the forty-six stories which make up
the collection, all but a few are translations from the French. One
of Mrs. Behn's only English rivals was Richard Blackbourne,
whose novel of intrigue, *Clitie*, was introduced to the world
by Nahum Tate in 1688, shortly after the author's 'untimely
death'. This tale of two star-crossed lovers, whose happiness
is frustrated by a scheming maid and her brother, but who
eventually overcome all their dangers and misunderstandings,

is not set in England, but appears to be an original work. More characteristic of the native English taste for fiction is a collection of *Delightful Novels Exemplifyed in Eight Choice and Elegant Histories* (fourth impression, 1686). Some of the stories in this volume come a good deal closer to ordinary life than is usual in the novel at this period. In one of them an uncle attempts to murder his rich young niece and so get possession of her estate, but Cratander, a young man to whom she had given hospitality when he was benighted, and who is sleeping in the house when the uncle and his accomplices arrive, rushes to the door and in the darkness shoots the uncle dead and wounds one of the accomplices. What follows is a sort of primitive detective story. On the day of the uncle's funeral the corpse is not on view, his wife explaining that he died of an apoplexy and that 'being a Corpulent Fat Man the Coffin was nail'd up early in the Morning for fear the Body, which began already to Corrupt, should be offensive to the Company'. It now occurs to Cratander that the man he wounded must have had his wounds dressed by a local surgeon, and if he can find the surgeon he may get a clue to what happened. In due course he traces the surgeon and finds out the name of the wounded man, who confesses under examination. Cratander, of course, marries the rich young lady. Several of the short novels in this collection are mystery stories of one kind or another, and are told with some skill. The opening words of Novel 7, for example, make an immediate bid for the reader's attention:

> The vast Number of Candles that in the Winter Quarter are hung out every Night, and serve as an Ornament to the Streets of London, began to light those who walk late without Torches, when one of the most Famous Surgeons of that populous City was sent for in great hast, and his Assistance desir'd at a House not far distant from his own, where he was immediately conducted, and there found a very Handsom Young Gentleman (whom the Company called Leander) very desperately wounded, and upon search found he had received two dangerous pricks from a Sword. He heard those about him whispering that he had given himself those Wounds. . . .

If this is not quite Conan Doyle, it is a fair seventeenth-century anticipation of him. Most of the stories in *Delightful Novels* deal with middle-class characters, and as the century draws to a close this sort of fiction begins to appear rather more frequently. *A Sunday's Adventure, Or, A Walk to Hackney* (an example of epistolary fiction) recounts the progress of an inconclusive intrigue with a girl in a boarding-house. *The Compleat Mendicant*, a story about a virtuous young man who drifts from one occupation to another, is intended to show that the picaresque tale need not be a succession of immoral adventures. A more lively offshoot of the picaresque is to be found in various short pieces by Ned Ward, as, for example, *A Trip to Jamaica*, *A Step to Stir-Bitch-Fair*, *A Frolic to Horn-Fair*, and, of course, *The London Spy*. These are all written in Ward's racy prose, but others, like *A Walk to Islington*, are in verse. It should be remembered that a good deal of the fiction of the period was, like Dryden's *Fables*, in verse form. One curious and interesting piece by an unknown author, *Gallantry-à-la-Mode* (1674), narrates three separate stories in octosyllabic couplets. The most interesting is the second, in which a gallant recounts the progress of an intrigue with a girl called Phyllis. This is, in fact, a novel in verse, in which the writer pays considerable attention to the thoughts and feelings of his characters, and what they really think as well as what they say they think. In some of his luxuriant descriptive passages, too, he comes near to being a Restoration Keats.

On the border-line of fiction there are a number of minor genres that contributed something to the development of the novel, by way of character study, the telling of a story, and the creation of a realistic environment for the display of characters. In *CCXI Sociable Letters* the Duchess of Newcastle attempted with some success to express 'under the cover of letters . . . the Humours of Mankind and the actions of man's life, by the correspondence of two ladies living at some short distance'. She even out-did Samuel Richardson by writing about a gentleman who married his kitchen-maid, but here as elsewhere the idea is better than its development. Various collections of real or fictitious love-letters proved popular after the Restoration, and provided the reader with a story that was self-explanatory. Equally popular were the political-social-satirical *Letters of a Turkish Spy* of Giovanni Paolo Marana, which began their long life in an English translation in 1687. The numerous Theophrastan characters which were published in the seventeenth century contributed a good deal to the analysis of types, and in such pieces as 'The Character of a Town-Gallant' and 'The Character of a Town-Miss' (1675) we get lively pictures of the contemporary social scene, as we do also in the various satirical descriptions of the fashionable world written in the manner of Lucian or Petronius. The vogue for Æsop was reflected not only in the several translations of the *Fables*, but also in a number of imitations. Fiction of a very different sort is to be found in *The Description of a new Blazing World* (1666), a fantastic example of science fiction by the indefatigable Duchess of Newcastle. The *voyage imaginaire* is also represented by Henry Neville's *The Isle of Pines* (1668), Richard Head's *O-Brazile: Or, The Inchanted Island* (1675), and Joshua Barnes's *Gerania* (1675). Neville and Head both write in a level narrative style that is well suited to their strange subject-matter; but Barnes, who takes us to the land of the Pigmies 'on the utmost Borders of India', has little to tell us when we get there, and writes in the pedantic style of a seventeenth-century Cambridge don. If *Gerania*, as has been suggested, gave Swift some hints for his 'Voyage to Lilliput', he has completely transmuted Barnes's baser metal.

The various works so far mentioned in this chapter have been considered because they form part of the history of English prose fiction; but their intrinsic value is such that no well-read man need reproach himself if he never turns their pages. For the most part they are deficient in one element which we have come to regard as essential to the novelist: curiosity about the thoughts and feelings of their fellow men was singularly inactive among the storytellers of this period. We get plenty of action, and we are assured that the characters are moved by passionate feeling, but there is little psychological insight. Most of the best writers of the day wrote for the theatre, and there seems to be no good reason why the same intellectual detachment and delicately precise writing that went into the best comedies should not have found their way into the novel. Yet there is little of either. One year before the Restoration, however, Walter Charleton (1619–1707) produced a small masterpiece in *The Ephesian Matron*, a sophisticated re-telling of the Petronius story of the widow who fell in love with the handsome soldier while she was inconsolably mourning her dead husband in his tomb. The charm of Charleton's narrative lies in his poise, his amused good-breeding, and his understatement. When the soldier has brought the sorrowing lady round to a state of tranquillity by the use of wine and food, Charleton breaks off, in the manner of Sterne, to give us a discourse of several pages on the nature of the soul. Is it, as Epicurus said, 'a certain composition or contexture of subtle Atoms'? But then he comes back to the widow:

Returning to our Matron, I find my self surprised with more of wonder and amazement than the Soldier was when he first beheld her. . . . What therefore should I think? To imagine that she . . . whose tears are yet scarcely dry, still sitting in a damp and horrid Charnel-house, at the dead time of the night, and upon the Coffin of her *Dearest All*: To imagine (I say) that this Woman should be so soon ingulphed in the delightful transports of *a new Love*, and that with a Fellow so much a Stranger, so much her Inferiour: This certainly is not only highly improbable, but unpardonably scandalous. . . .

No other English writer of fiction achieved this easy self-possession or struck so perfect an attitude until, in 1692, at the age of 22, Congreve published *Incognita: Or, Love and Duty Reconcil'd*. In this dramatically constructed novel Congreve is in complete control of his story and of his reader, commenting easily on the events and the characters, promising certain developments and then subjecting the reader to deliberate delays, keeping him always in good humour with a delicate raillery. The tone is perfectly caught in the first account of the fair Incognita: 'I should by right now describe her Dress, which was extreamly agreeable and rich, but 'tis possible I might err in some material Pin or other, in the sticking of which may be the whole grace of the Drapery depended.' Congreve does not ridicule his characters; their artificiality and romanticism may provoke a smile, but lovely women are still lovely, and handsome and accomplished young men are still to be admired. Novels, he believed, are of a more familiar nature than romances, 'come near us, and represent to us Intrigues in practice, . . . such which not being so distant from our Belief bring also the pleasure nearer us'. So we are allowed to go on believing in the characters and the story, but not too much. The world in which they move is formalized by the writer's amused detachment; it has the delicate, immutable, and ornamental quality of a scene in a glass paper-weight. Congreve's ironical causerie with his reader has been compared to that of Fielding with his; but the voice we hear in *Incognita* is like nothing so much as that of the author of *Zuleika Dobson*.

VI

ESSAYS, LETTERS, AND JOURNALS

I. THE ESSAY

(1)

THE development of the familiar essay in England was slower than might have been expected. So long as the potential essayist was isolated in a country rectory or meditating his past life in a rural retirement, he tended to write sententiously on moral and religious subjects, and with little real awareness of a reader to be addressed. But after the Restoration, with the rapid development of a well-organized literary community in London, the author–reader relationship was correspondingly transformed, and the writer was able to direct his observations to a body of readers whom he could easily visualize, and with whom he might almost be said to converse. Even so, it was some time before these new conditions led to any considerable growth in essay writing. The easy and familiar tone of Dryden in the various prefaces that he wrote for his plays was partly due to many of those pieces being addressed to individuals in the form of dedications, but also to his awareness of the fact that most of his readers had already seen his plays, and that to this extent an acquaintanceship already existed. Long before he had reached old age, however, Dryden's conversational manner had become habitual with him, and in this, as in so many other directions, his influence on the age must have been considerable. That the average writer of the period was feeling his way towards a more familiar mode of expression may be seen from the large number of political or economic pamphlets that were written in the form of 'A Letter to a Friend in the Country'. Much of L'Estrange's writing was in the form of dialogue, and even more perhaps than Dryden, he was responsible for the colloquial and personal turn that so much of the writing took after the Restoration. None the less, some of the essayists remained oddly aloof and uninfluenced by this new familiarity. The breakthrough did not come until the early years of the next century, when the periodical essay paper, with a regular body of subscribers and therefore of constant readers, was firmly established.

Some of the essays published between 1660 and 1700 were the work of elderly men living in retirement and looking back on the vanities of their youth. Sir William Killigrew's *Midnight and Daily Thoughts*, published when he was about ninety, belong rather to the sphere of pious ejaculations and sermons than to the essay, as do the *Contemplations, Moral and Divine* of Sir Matthew Hale, and the *Occasional Meditations* of Mary Rich, Countess of Warwick. The essays written in his old age by the Earl of Clarendon are on such Baconian topics as 'Pride', 'Anger', 'Envy', or on such more contemporary and even personal themes as 'Impudent Delight in Wickedness' and 'The Want of Respect due to Age'. The moral essays of Sir George Mackenzie, distinguished by Dryden as 'that noble wit of Scotland', include one preferring Solitude to Public Employment, which evoked a reply by John Evelyn. Mackenzie, whose interest in morality was more speculative than practical, pronounces on such subjects as Fame, Bigotry, and Virtue more Pleasant than Vice, in a transitional style that is at once magisterial and personal. Much the same may be said of Sir Thomas Pope Blount, another of those authors who proclaimed his love of retirement, and whose *Essays on Several Subjects* (1692) show a pleasantly sceptical mind at work, but working at no great pressure. The *Essayes or Moral Discourses* of Sir Thomas Culpeper are the diversions of a man who appears to have the reading of a gentleman, and who believes that an essay should be familiar and should treat of men and manners with 'a pertinent ingenuity', but he has little to say and his prose is loose and shapeless. On the other hand, the *Discourses and Essays* of Francis, Viscount Shannon (a member of the remarkable Boyle family) are at once moral, lively, and well written. In his Dedication to the Countess of Northumberland he offers an engaging explanation of why he has written these essays 'useful for the Vain Modish Ladies and their Gallants'. He is making amends, he tells her, for the slips of his own youth. 'My design here is, that because I did in my Youth perswade some young Wives to do what they ought not, I would now in my old age perswade all young Wives and Women to do what they ought.' Anxious, too, to avoid the well-worn topics of essay-writers and to deal with 'virgin-themes', he writes against 'keeping misses', marrying for 'meer love', old men marrying young women, excessive drinking, long dull sermons, and much else. It is true that he is not quite an Addison; but in his concern for the fair sex and in his good-humoured, urbane, and occasionally witty discussion of social problems he shows Addison's willingness to improve, while never forgetting to please.

The essay as the conscious product of retirement from the world is seen at its best in two much more celebrated writers, Abraham Cowley and Sir William Temple. Cowley[1] had been one of the many expectant Englishmen whose hopes of preferment were disappointed after the Restoration. Retirement (to a small estate at Chertsey in Surrey) was therefore thrust upon him. There, although he complained to his friend Sprat that his tenants would not pay their rent, and that his meadows were 'eaten up every night by cattle put in by neighbours', he tried to make a virtue of necessity and wrote his charming essays on such subjects as Liberty, Solitude, Obscurity, Greatness, The Garden, and one 'Of Myself'. The manner is often that of Montaigne, to whom indeed he occasionally alludes. Cowley does not hesitate to indulge in mild introspection, to express his own personal peculiarities and preferences; he tells us about the copy of Spenser that used to lie in his mother's parlour when he was a boy; how he was 'infinitely delighted with the stories of the Knights, and Giants, and Monsters' and with 'the tinckling of the Rhyme and Dance of the Numbers', and how he 'was thus made a Poet as immediately as a Child is made an Eunuch'. So far as his celebration of retirement is concerned, Cowley's position is that of Horace on his Sabine farm, free from the noise and polluted air of the Court, enjoying his books and his wine and the temperate delights of rural life, and praising the virtue of the golden mean. If there is something of *faute de mieux* in all this, Cowley plays the part of the rural philosopher with sufficient conviction to prevent us from doubting his integrity. After all, he has no thought of overdoing the simple life; he is thinking in terms of £500 a year, with a few good servants and horses, well-cooked meals, clothes not rich but

---

[1] After the Restoration Cowley published a volume of *Verses lately written upon Several Occasions* (1663). His essays, first published in the *Works* (1668), were almost certainly written during his post-Restoration retirement at Chertsey in Surrey.

warm and comely, a convenient brick house and a fruit and flower garden, where the water will be 'every whit as clear and wholesome as if it darted from the breasts of a marble Nymph, or the Urn of a River-God'. Ultimately, however, it is the confessional note, the voice of the essayist who is taking the reader into his confidence, that remains the dominant impression:

I confess, I love Littleness almost in all things. A little convenient Estate, a little chearful House, a little Company, and a very little Feast; and, if I were to fall in love again (which is a great Passion, and therefore, I hope, I have done with it) it would be, I think, with Prettiness, rather than with Majestical Beauty.

Here and there he allows himself some gentle mockery. When he laughs at those ladies of quality who wear such high shoes that they need someone to lead them, 'and a Gown as long again as their Body, so that they cannot stir to the next Room without a Page or two to hold it up', we may think for a moment that we are listening to the voice of Addison; but this sort of social criticism is quite incidental in Cowley, who is less concerned to reform the world than to show how happily he has detached himself from it. Only once, perhaps, in 'The Dangers of an Honest Man in much Company', when he finds that the inhabitants of Chertsey are not, as he had hoped, like those in Sidney's *Arcadia*, does Cowley's philosophy of mild disengagement deepen into something nearer to misanthropy. For the most part his thought is as tranquil as his prose style, which Johnson found to be 'easy without feebleness, and familiar without grossness', and which delighted Lamb by its 'graceful rambling'.

The reputation of Sir William Temple[1] has never fully

---

[1] Sir William Temple (1628–99) was the son of Sir John Temple, Master of the Rolls in Ireland. In 1648 he met Dorothy, daughter of Sir Peter Osborne, and fell in love with her. After a long courtship, during which she wrote her well-known letters to him, they were married in 1655. Temple was employed in various diplomatic missions, and successfully negotiated the Triple Alliance in 1668 between England, Holland, and Sweden, only to see it sabotaged later by Charles II's secret understanding with Louis XIV. In retirement he consoled himself by writing his *Essay upon the Original and Nature of Government* and other works. He was sent to The Hague in 1674, and brought about the marriage between William of Orange and Princess Mary. Later, refusing several offers of high office, he was again relegated to comparative obscurity. After the Revolution he lived in retirement at Sheen and later at Moor Park, and as an elder statesman was consulted from time to time by the new King. In the spring of 1689 Jonathan Swift entered his household, served him as a secretary, and ultimately became the editor of his works.

recovered from the vigorous denigration of Macaulay. There was undoubtedly a good deal of the epicurean and the dilettante in Temple, but his withdrawal from the political scene was due much less to pusillanimity than to his honesty of intention, and to his justifiable disgust with the unprincipled policies of Charles II and his ministers, and their betrayal of his work as a negotiator. 'I have had in twenty years experience', he wrote, 'enough of the uncertainty of princes, the caprices of fortune, the corruption of ministers, the violence of factions, the unsteadiness of counsels, and the infidelity of friends.' He was not just striking a virtuous attitude; he had given politics a fair trial, and for a man of his fastidious temperament it had been more than enough. It is therefore fairer to Temple to think of him, not as a politician who dabbled in literature, but as a man of letters who had burnt his fingers in politics, and who withdrew from public affairs to the care of his family and the cultivation of his garden when he realized that he could do little good elsewhere. His youthful essays and romances show unmistakably that he was a born writer, and it is not a sin to like writing, even when a man has comparatively little to say. What Temple liked best was setting down, in his easy and cultivated prose and after the fashion of Montaigne, his own personal opinions. For a man who had a good deal of gentlemanly reserve in his dealings with other people, he is surprisingly free with his confidences when he comes to write essays. But this is in the English tradition: what is said with difficulty in private is told without inhibition to the whole world. In this, and in his composed but natural prose, he was a model for Addison, who had also a good deal of Temple's cool and fastidious temperament. Even in such a work as his *Observations upon the United Provinces of the Netherlands*, which has been called 'the first serious and intelligent attempt to interpret the people and polity of one country sympathetically to another', Temple dawdles pleasantly at the entrance to tell us that he has written for his own entertainment, since he is now 'wholly useless to the publique' and has none of those thoughts of increasing his wealth 'which busie the World'. He finds himself bored with the pleasures of younger and livelier men, and cannot do as much reading as he would like 'from the care of my eyes (since an illness contracted by many unnecessary diligences in my Employments abroad)'. So he takes to writing.

We are obviously meant to be impressed, and Temple's tendency to strike attitudes in public becomes at times too insistent, but this is the mode of the familiar essayist. At its best his literary conversation has the same quality as his sister found in his table talk, which she admits she ought to have recorded, and which 'would have bin very entertaining to those that should read it, as it was to soe many that heard it; but the frequency of it discouraged me from soe great a taske'.

Temple's special contribution, and the quality that makes him, far more than Cowley, the father of the eighteenth-century essay, is his willingness to pronounce confidently on any topic that happens to come up. He clearly assumed, as Addison did after him, that a gentleman of intelligence and adequate reading, with the leisure to think things out, could venture his opinions, not only on literature and morality, but on religion, science, scholarship, government, history, and many other subjects which today most of us have abandoned to the specialist. When, for example, he is discussing the Dutch as a trading nation he pauses to speculate on the likelihood that trade may make a nation unfit for warfare. But then another thought strikes him; differences of climate and diet may have a good deal to do with natural courage, which springs from 'the heat or strength of spirits about the heart'. Here Temple is on fairly safe ground; he is not laying himself open to the sneers of the specialist, for medical knowledge in his day had hardly reached the stage where one man's opinion was better than another's. In other fields, however, where knowledge was further advanced and more fully organized, Temple's amateur status exposed him to some criticism, and finally, in his disastrous remarks on the Epistles of Phalaris, to ridicule. On this, as on other occasions, he had only been passing a few remarks, keeping the conversational ball rolling, and he must have been surprised to find himself involved in a heated controversy with scholars like Bentley and Wotton. The gentleman-amateur was being challenged by the professionals. In this battle between the Ancients and Moderns Temple might equally well on some other occasion have championed the opposite side; he was not a man of strong convictions, and he had the open and discursive mind of the essayist. What prompted him to take up the cause of the Ancients was probably a half-conscious feeling that the Moderns were upstarts and the Ancients belonged to an old family; he must have felt later that the exposure of the Epistles of Phalaris by Bentley, a scholar whose business it was to keep up the stock of the Ancients, was almost a stab in the back. Five or six years later, when he was verging on seventy, he began to draft a reply, but he never completed it. He had nothing useful to say on the authenticity of the Epistles, but he composed a long satirical passage attacking modern scholarship in a fashion that anticipates Pope's satire, and another passage on modern science that might have been written by Swift. The day of the amateur was far from over: Bentley and Wotton had won a battle, but not a war. The common reader could still enjoy the writings of Sir William Temple, as he was soon to enjoy and admire those of Addison; but although Addison was prepared, like Temple, to discourse easily in almost any field of knowledge, he had taken rather more trouble to inform himself, and to keep in touch with the best thought of his own day.

Jeremy Collier,[1] who deserves more praise as a writer than he has usually received, wrote some fifty essays on such topics as Pride, Clothes, Duelling, Old Age, and the Entertainment of Books. Those are, no doubt, the essays of a clergyman, and Collier is not quite so disinterested as Addison and Steele; yet his expressed aim differs hardly at all from that of the authors of the *Tatler* and the *Spectator*. The design of his essays is 'to disingage us from Prejudice and false Reasoning. To Proportion our Hopes and our Fears. To keep us from drawing our Pretensions too Big, and our Faults too Little. 'Tis to expose the Weakness of Atheism, and to Unmask the Deformities of Vanity and ill Nature. In short, 'tis to direct the Offices of Life, and reach into Business and Conversation.' If this were all, it would at least establish Collier's claim to be a worthy man; but fortunately he was also a well-read and lively writer, who kept his mind in training and who was fully aware of what was going on around him. Some of his ideas he borrows from such writers as Cicero, Montaigne, Bacon, and Pascal, but he has no

---

[1] Jeremy Collier (1650–1726) refused to take the oaths to William and Mary after the Revolution, and became one of the leaders of the non-juring clergymen. He was outlawed in 1696 for publicly absolving on the scaffold two of the men found guilty of plotting to assassinate William III; but (according to Colley Cibber) the King, who was no lover of the theatre, was so pleased with Collier's *Short View of the Immorality and Profaneness of the English Stage* (1698) that he issued a *nolle prosequi*. Collier, who was a man of genuine learning, published an *Ecclesiastical History of Great Britain* in two volumes (1708, 1714).

difficulty in striking out sparks of his own. Although he has not quite so allusive a mind as Addison, he is always alert and discursive and he bestirs himself to be entertaining to the reader. Authors, he tells us, are like women in one respect: they commonly Dress when they make a Visit. Respect to themselves makes them polish their Thoughts, and exert the Force of their Understanding more than they would, or can do, in ordinary Conversation: So that the Reader has as it were *Spirit* and *Essence* in a narrow Compass; which was drawn off from a much larger Proportion of Time, Labour, and Expence.

Collier writes like a gentleman, at times even a little modishly. Whatever faults of excessive zeal he may have shown in his *Short View*, he cannot be accused in his essays of 'coming to battle like a dictator from the plough', nor of losing his good manners and civility. Yet he nowhere shows a well-bred indifference about any of the topics he discusses; there is always a serious edge to his argument, and something at times of the sarcasm of Robert South.

Another clergyman, John Norris of Bemerton, who has been described as 'the last offshoot from the school of Cambridge Platonists', wrote essays on such themes as Seriousness, the Advantages of Thinking, and the Care and Improvement of Time. Norris had an easily metaphorical style and a well-stocked mind (he was one of the small group who helped to answer the questions sent in by correspondents to John Dunton's *Athenian Mercury*), but he tended to write short discourses rather than essays. 'Were Angels to write,' he observes, 'I fancy we should have but few Folios'; and his moral seriousness and preference for brevity probably inhibited a natural allusiveness. Only perhaps in Cowley and Temple does the familiar essay—personal, idiosyncratic, rambling, reminiscent—reach in this period a full and uninhibited development.

The word 'essay' was used at this time to describe discussions and arguments of many kinds, ranging from pamphlets of a few pages to Mary Astell's *Essay in Defence of the Female Sex* (1696) and Locke's *Essay concerning Human Understanding*. Similarly, works with such titles as 'Reflections', 'Remarks', 'Discourses', 'Some Considerations', 'Some Thoughts', are often cast into the form of an essay. Among those with a critical or literary interest are Thomas Baker's *Reflections upon Learning* (1699), where there is some discussion of English prose style and of pulpit oratory, and *An Essay concerning Critical and Curious Learning* (1698), whose author, T. R. (who is almost certainly not Thomas Rymer), gives his views on the battle between the Ancients and the Moderns. Whoever he may be, T. R. indulges in some complacent sitting on the fence: he professes to admire scholarship, but finds much of it to be pedantry; and he praises 'experimental philosophy', but ridicules those who 'carry on their Experiments to the Land of the Moon', and who 'instead of improveing useful Navigation, will propose Methods for Ships sailing under Water, and such like Contradictions of Nature'. In short, he has the attitude and the prejudices of Swift without his wit. The critical essay is better represented in Charles Gildon's collection of *Miscellaneous Letters and Essays* (by 'several Gentlemen and Ladies', 1694), which includes discussions of *Paradise Lost* and of Rymer's *Short View*, besides 'An Essay at a Vindication of Love in Tragedies' and 'An Apology for Poetry'; and in James Wright's *Country Conversations* (clearly influenced by Bouhours's *Entretiens*), with its civilized consideration of such topics as modern comedies, translated verse, and painters and painting. The public for such informal and good-tempered literary and artistic discussion was clearly growing.

The men of science occasionally published their discoveries and speculations in the form of essays, as did Robert Boyle in *Certain Physiological Essays* (1661). Much closer to the literary essay are his *Occasional Reflections upon Several Subjects* (1665), the work which Swift parodied in his 'Meditation upon a Broom-Stick'. Somewhere between the essay and the 'character' comes Walter Charleton's *Brief Discourse concerning the Different Wits of Men* (1669), which has some psychological interest and is enlivened by a good deal of satirical comment. The 'ranging wit', Charleton tells us, is one who 'discourseth copiously rather than closely', and when such wits reach the end of their fine harangues, 'if their auditors shew any signs of Complacency and good Humour, . . . the same ariseth rather from Joy that they are at length delivered from the importunity of them'. Here and elsewhere Charleton analyses those wits and would-be wits that the dramatists were soon to make familiar in their comedies. Some of the same ground is covered rather more seriously, and with a touch of originality, by David Abercromby in *A Discourse of Wit* (1686). The author (like Charleton, a physician) writes what amounts to a series of essays on such topics as 'The Character of a Pretender to Wit' and 'The Art of Writing Wittily', reserving his highest praise for men of science like Boyle; indeed, his chief reason for writing his treatise was 'to furnish the Virtuosi with matters fit for in- genious Conversations'.

(II)

Between the essay and the 'character' in this period there is often very little difference. The Theophrastan type-character was still being written, and is quite favourably represented by Richard Flecknoe, whose sixty-eight *Enigmatical Characters* were published in 1658, and reprinted several times, with a few additions, in the next twenty years. Flecknoe's prose, which also includes a number of essays on such subjects as Wit, History, Music and Poetry, Language, is a good deal more interesting than his verse, and is by no means the 'nonsense absolute' of Dryden's dismissive phrase. The appearance in 1699 of a translation of forty-four Characters by Theophrastus and La Bruyère might seem to indicate that the taste for the Theo- phrastan character was still active, but in fact its great days were past. That this was so is perhaps indicated by the failure of Samuel Butler to publish his remarkable series of characters, which remained in manuscript until the middle of the eight- eenth century. On any count Butler's characters (of which there are almost two hundred) form one of the outstanding contributions to Restoration literature. The man who wrote them was a sort of later Ben Jonson, a wit among scholars and a scholar among wits, with the intellectual confidence of wide and unselective reading, and that contempt for pedantry which comes most easily to the non-academic writer. Milton could have appreciated his learning, but probably felt him to be lacking in seriousness; the King and the Court could certainly enjoy his wit, but were no doubt daunted by his learning. Butler himself repudiated 'the modern False Doctrine of the Court, that Men's Naturall Parts are rather impared than improv'd by Study and Learning'; but he also knew that 'no men are so indefatigable Drudges in all manner of Sciences as those to whom Nature has allow'd the weakest abilities to attaine to any perfection in them: for Dunces are commonly observ'd to be the hardest Students'. Holding such views, Butler was inevitably self-isolated from most of his contemporaries in the new post-Restoration England; but from his position of critical detachment he looked with a penetrating and disenchanted eye at 'A Modern Politician', 'A Duke of Bucks', 'A Lawyer', 'A Small Poet', 'A Time-server', and the rest, and the satirical force of his unsparing analysis is often increased by its close relevance to the times in which he lived:

The easiest Way to purchase a Reputation of Wisdom and Knowledge is to slight and under-value it; as the readiest Way to buy cheap is to bring down the Price: for the World will be apt to believe a Man well provided with any necessary or useful Commodity which he sets a small Value upon.

. . . Flattery is but a kind of civil Idolatry that makes Images it self of Virtue, Worth, and Honour in some Person that is utterly void of all, and then falls down and worships them. And the more dull and absurd these Applications are, the better they are always received: for Men delight more to be presented with those Things they want, than such as they have no need nor use of.

Wherever we read in the characters we find Butler making the shrewdest judgements of his fellow men, and pushing his analysis of human behaviour further than almost any of his contemporaries. There is enough satirical observation and worldly wisdom in Butler's characters to set up half a dozen Wycherleys and Congreves for life with all the character material they could possibly need. It is hard not to feel a sense of waste: so much wisdom embodied in a form that was already becoming old-fashioned, and so concentrated a mode of expression that it would require the dilution of drama or prose fiction to make it easily palatable to the common reader. It was such a dilution that the old closely packed character was to get at the hands of Addison and Steele. The finest achievements of the period lay, however, not in the Theophrastan character, but in the remarkable portraits of actual historical figures scattered through such works as Clarendon's or Burnet's histories, or in Halifax's character of Charles II.

II. LETTER-WRITING

Among the fashionable accomplishments of the wit was letter-writing, which, in certain of its aspects, was looked upon as an extension of polite conversation, but which on occasion came close to the familiar essay. The popularity of the epistolary style may be gauged from the numerous collections of letters made in the 1690s by Charles Gildon, John Dennis, Tom Brown, and others; and their range may be seen from such titles as 'Letters of Love and Gallantry', 'Familiar and Courtly Letters', 'Letters of Wit, Politics and Morality'. In this way some of the correspondence of Dryden, Rochester, Etherege, the Duke of Buckingham, Wycherley, Otway, Mrs. Behn, Congreve, and other lesser wits appeared in their own lifetime, or shortly after their death. In this literary field the French were acknowledged masters; and among the writers especially admired (and translated) were Jean-Louis Guez de Balsac, Scarron, Fontenelle, and, more especially towards the end of the century, Voiture, who had been much commended by Bouhours, and was praised by Dennis for being so 'easie and unconstrained, and natural when he is most exalted', although his style was 'too little diversify'd'. The interest in letter-writing also led Tom Brown to translate some of the Epistles of Pliny the Younger and of Cicero; and there were a number of volumes, such as *The Academy of Compliments*, intended to provide instruction in letter-writing and models to imitate.

The end product of all this epistolary activity is of very mixed quality. Much of the correspondence appearing in contemporary printed collections shows a self-conscious straining after wit, or disintegrates into exercises in elaborate compliment or tedious and artificial gallantry: the writer seems to be rehearsing a speech in front of his mirror. Most of the love-letters, too (those of Otway to Mrs. Barry are an exception), have the air of being written with an eye to publication. Among the liveliest examples of the fictitious letter are those in Charles Gildon's *The Post-boy robbed of his Mail* (1692).

In view of the vogue for letter-writing after the Restoration it is disappointing that so little genuine correspondence has survived. Much of what has come down to us is related to specific fields of activity: political, as with Marvell's letters to the Mayor and Aldermen of Kingston upon Hull; scientific, as with Hooke, Newton, Locke, and their contemporaries; antiquarian, as with Anthony Wood and his friends. A more familiar correspondence is that between Sir William Petty and Sir Robert Southwell, entirely natural, friendly, and ranging over many fields of interest. One of the liveliest and most un-affected correspondents of the Restoration period was Henry Savile, whose letters to Rochester, together with Rochester's replies, give a lively picture of the world of fashion, and whose correspondence with his elder brother, the Marquis of Halifax, does honour to the characters of both men, and to their qualities of both mind and heart. An easy and affectionate raillery per-meates this correspondence. To Halifax, who has been saying how much he longs to visit 'poor old Rufford' (his country seat) Henry Savile replies: 'Your philosophical contemplation of not seeing Rufford makes my worship smile. When a lover is absent of his own choice it is a sign of a very moderate pas-sion, and such has yours always been for Nottinghamshire. . . .' In much the same vein Halifax writes to his younger brother, who has been having an affair with Anne, Countess Dowager of Manchester: 'I don't know how far your passion for a fair lady may make your return at this time uneasy to you, but I am such a clown as to think there are two reasons to make a man at least content to leave a mistress, for anger if she is not kind, and to cure a surfeit if she is, but this is such unmanly doctrine that I will not provoke you with any more of it.'

Of Dryden's letters and of Congreve's surprisingly few sur-vive; and not many of those are as interesting as we should expect a letter from Dryden or Congreve to be. Of Etherege's entertaining letters there are even fewer, and those dating mostly from his later years, when, as James II's Resident Minister at Ratisbon, he wrote home nostalgically to his old friends in London. At Ratisbon he remained true to what Leslie Stephen stigmatized as 'his habits of squalid debauchery', which Etherege himself probably described more accurately when he told a friend how he preferred 'to jolt about in poor hackney coaches to find out the harmless lust of the town than to spend the time in a room of state in whispers to discover the ambitious designs of princes'. The letters (to Dryden, to the Earl of Middlesex and others) of this reluctant and negligent ambassador are among the most delightful of the whole period, and they have the comic detachment that we associate with the author of *The Man of Mode*. Writing from Ratisbon, he tells Sir William Trumbull, a future secretary of state: 'I was going about making of legs and muttering compliments and had wished a merry Christmas to half the Ministers here when I was

stopped by a small fever. . . .' Bored by it all, Etherege remains
the traditional English amateur, carrying out his duties just
seriously enough not to be recalled, and taking his fun where he
can find it; but, so far as letter-writing is concerned, he had a
genius that was denied to Wycherley and Congreve and many
other men who equalled him in wit.

Such was the appeal of the epistolary style in the age of
Dryden that it was employed in one form or another for many
different kinds of writing. By Dryden himself and his fellow
writers it was used, in a slightly exalted idiom, for dedicating
their works to noblemen and gentlemen; it was adopted by
Congreve, Dennis, and others for literary theory and criticism;
by others for recounting their travels and adventures, or for
writing fiction; by others again for discussing religious, scientific, economic, and, above all, political topics. As Major
Oldfox put it in *The Plain-Dealer*, 'A Letter to a Friend in the
Countrey . . . is now the way of all such sober, solid persons as
my self, when they have a mind to publish their disgust to the
Times; tho' perhaps, between you and I, they have no Friend
in the Countrey'. In one way or another the Restoration
writer sought to get on familiar terms with his readers; and the
letter, with its immediate and easy approach of writer to reader,
was perhaps the simplest and most natural way of achieving that
relationship.

III. THE PERIODICAL

Much of the journalistic writing of the period appeared in
the form of pamphlets; but by the close of the century important developments had taken place in the newspaper and in
other kinds of periodical publications. During the Civil War
and the interregnum a considerable number of Royalist and
Parliamentary mercuries, diurnals, and intelligencers supplied
English readers with foreign and domestic news. In the later
years of the Protectorate Cromwell virtually suppressed all
unofficial newsbooks, and left Marchamont Needham in control
of the field with his two sixteen-page weeklies, *The Publick
Intelligencer* (Mondays) and *Mercurius Politicus* (Thursdays). With
the death of Cromwell, Needham lost his monopoly; a number
of suppressed periodicals resumed publication, and some new
ones were started, including two weeklies written by Henry

Muddiman, *The Parliamentary Intelligencer* (later *The Kingdom's Intelligencer*) and *Mercurius Publicus*. These were the only two to survive the Restoration, and they lasted until 1663. The new regime was not in favour of a free press, and was particularly hostile to a free dissemination of news. In June 1662 an Act was passed (usually referred to as the Licensing Act) 'for preventing abuses in printing seditious, treasonable, and unlicensed books and pamphlets'. This Act made it necessary for every publisher to obtain the approval of an official licenser, it reduced drastically the number of printers and printing presses, and it laid down heavy penalties for any breach of the regulations. The following year Roger L'Estrange[1] became Surveyor of the Press, and by virtue of this office was given the monopoly of publishing news. On Monday, 31 August 1663, he issued the first number of his newsbook *The Intelligencer*, and followed it on Thursday, 3 September with *The News*. From the point of view of Charles II and his ministers L'Estrange was an excellent choice; he had no desire to see any newspapers published at all, and said so in the first number of *The Intelligencer*: 'A publick Mercury should never have my vote, because I think it makes the Multitude too familiar with the Actions and Counsels of their superiors, too pragmatical and censorious, and gives them not only an itch, but a kind of colourable right and License to be meddling with the Government.' Still, he had been given a monopoly to publish the news, and he would do it. 'Once a week', he thought, 'may do the business'; but he condescended so far as to let the public have the news twice a week. L'Estrange was, in fact, a brilliant journalist, and was soon to show himself to be one of the ablest of the political pamphleteers, but his heart was never in the business of supplying his fellow countrymen with unadulterated news. On 16 November

---

[1] Sir Roger L'Estrange (1616–1704) took an active, but not very glorious, part in the Civil War, was imprisoned for some time by the Parliament, and after an abortive Royalist rising in Kent escaped prudently to the Continent in 1648. He showed more vigour and determination in 1659–60 in helping to bring about the restoration of the monarchy, and in 1663 was rewarded with the post of Surveyor of the Imprimery. Besides publishing for several years his own two newspapers, *The News* and *The Intelligencer*, and numerous pro-government pamphlets, he kept a close watch on the press, and hunted down unlicensed printers and anti-government publications. After the changed days following the Revolution he was several times in trouble, and supported himself and his extravagant wife mainly by a series of lively translations, including *The Fables of Aesop and other Eminent Mythologists* (1692).

1665, when the Court was at Oxford to escape the Plague, Henry Muddiman re-entered the field by bringing out the first number of *The Oxford Gazette* (soon to be re-named *The London Gazette*), a folio half-sheet in double columns, and some weeks later L'Estrange abandoned his two newsbooks. For the next thirteen years *The London Gazette* (published with authority) remained the only English newspaper. It marks the break from the old newsbook format to that of the modern newspaper, with its columns of news and advertisements. Until 1679 the Government had a stranglehold on the press, and so far as the development of the newspaper is concerned the period from 1660 to 1679 is one of almost complete stagnation. It would undoubtedly have remained so if the King had had his way.

In January 1679 Charles abruptly dissolved Parliament. In the turmoil occasioned by the Popish Plot and the Exclusion Bill three short-lived parliaments followed in quick succession, the last (March 1681) being dissolved almost as soon as it had opened. One of the casualties of this prolonged crisis was the Licensing Act, which was due for renewal in May 1679, but was not in fact renewed; instead, a royal proclamation ordered the seizure of all libels against the Government and the arrest of the authors and printers concerned. Some months before the Act had expired Henry Care started publishing his anti-Catholic *Weekly Pacquet, Or Advice from Rome*, and succeeded in carrying it on, with some interruption in 1680, until 1683. A more important name in the history of English journalism, however, is that of the ardent Whig Benjamin Harris.[1] On 7 July 1679 (and the date has an obvious relevance to the fact that the Licensing Act was no longer in force) Harris brought out the first number of his half-sheet folio newspaper, *The Domestic Intelligence; Or, News both from City and Country*, which, with several changes of title and one serious interruption, ran until April 1681. Early in 1680 he was arrested for publishing

---

[1] Benjamin Harris came into prominence in the later years of Charles II's reign, but England was no place for this anti-Catholic journalist in the reign of James II, and he fled (or simply emigrated) to New England, where he started in Boston the first American newspaper, *Public Occurrences, Both Foreign and Domestic*, on 25 September 1690. It appears to have been quickly suppressed, but Harris became 'Printer to His Excellency the Governor, Sir William Phips . . . and Council'. In 1695 he was back in England, publishing a succession of newspapers, and, in the reign of Queen Anne, almanacs.

An Appeal from the Country to the City, fined £500, and sentenced to stand in the pillory. Since he could not pay the fine he remained in prison till December, but even so managed to keep his paper running until the middle of May, and resumed it on his release in December. *The Domestic Intelligence*, which came out on Tuesdays and Fridays, for the convenience of the country posts, settled the format of the English newspaper for the rest of the century; its two pages carried the foreign and domestic news in double columns, and included some advertisements on the back page. It is clear that Harris had correspondents in different parts of the country, and from the first his paper was well supplied with home news, even if it did not always prove to be accurate. On 9 September 1679 he printed a paragraph about Samuel Pepys's having gone to Windsor to kiss the King's hand, but having been refused admission because he stood charged with treason. Pepys must have made him withdraw this calumny, for on 19 September Harris inserted a complete denial of the story:

These are to give Notice, That all and every part of the Relation Published in the *Domestick Intelligence* the 9th of this Instant September, touching *Samuel Pepys*, Esq; is as to the matter, and every particular Circumstance therein mentioned, altogether False and Scandalous; there having no such passage happened, nor any thing that might give Occasion for that Report.

This obviously dictated retraction was repeated in the next issue. Harris was continually in trouble of one sort or another, and finally emigrated to America, where he started up again in Boston and published the first (and only) number of the first American newspaper.

If the Whig Harris is one of the heroes of Restoration journalism, the Tory Nathaniel Thompson is another. Thompson broke into newspaper journalism in a characteristically impudent fashion on Friday, 29 August 1679. On that day he started publishing a new *Domestic Intelligence* almost identical in appearance with Harris's paper, and in order to deceive the public into believing that they were in fact buying Harris's paper, called it No. 16, which was the number of Harris's issue for that day. Harris promptly drew attention to the fraud, and informed his readers that the spurious paper was supposed to be the work 'of a base and scandalous Person who has been in Prison for printing Popish books and catechisms'. Thompson made an ingenious come-back by asserting that it was really Harris's *Domestic Intelligence* that was the spurious publication:

There hath lately dropt into the World an Abortive Birth (some fifteen days before the Legitimate Issue) by a Factious, Infamous and Perjur'd Anti-Christian, a senseless lying Pamphlet by the name of the City and Country News. . . . This Pamphlet-Napper and Press-Pyrat hath cruised abroad since he put up for himself; to make prize of other mens Copies, to stuff his own Cargo with ill gotten profit, making his business Cheating and Usurpation to Defraud all men. . . . Now I leave your selves and all Honest men to be judges whether of the two be the best Intelligence. . . .

From now on, Harris and Thompson, like their predecessors of interregnum journalism, were to carry on a cat-and-dog fight in their two newspapers, and as other journals were started, they too joined in the fray. The washing of each other's dirty linen in public became a regular custom of English newspapers, and in a political age was no doubt one of their most attractive features. Like Harris, Thompson was in constant trouble with the law. He kept his paper going until 14 May 1680, in spite of the fact that he was in prison for part of that time; in March 1681 he revived it with a new title, *The Loyal Protestant and True Domestic Intelligence*, and carried it on twice a week until November 1682. He made one last attempt to revive his newspaper in February 1683, but in March he was again sent to prison for publishing false news, and this time he gave up the struggle.

In 1679–80 Harris and Thompson had the field pretty much to themselves, although several short-lived Intelligences, Mercuries, and Courants were started by publishers willing to make capital out of the political crisis. In May 1680 a new situation developed. Since the King could not renew the Licensing Act except by means of Parliament, he consulted the judges to find out whether he had the power to suppress all newspapers by the exercise of the royal prerogative. The judges unanimously decided that he had that power. *The London Gazette* for 17–20 May 1680 thereupon carried a royal proclamation prohibiting the printing and publishing of any newsbooks and pamphlets that had not been licensed by His Majesty's authority. This proclamation put a sudden stop to the unlicensed newspapers, and left *The London Gazette* once more alone in the field. But the effect was only temporary: one by one, like birds that have been scared from the corn, they came hopping back and started up again. On 28 December (the same day as Harris resumed his paper) Langley Curtis started a *True Protestant Mercury*, which was to run for nearly two years. Early in 1681 Francis ('Elephant') Smith brought out a *Protestant Intelligence*, John Smith revived his *Currant Intelligence*, and Nathaniel Thompson his *Loyal Protestant*. In April Richard Janeway came out with the first number of his *Impartial Protestant Mercury*, and Thomas Benskin produced a new *Domestic Intelligence . . . impartially related*, both of which survived for over two years. So much for the royal authority. By the spring of 1681, indeed, the situation was worse, from the Government's point of view, than it had been before the proclamation, which had complained of 'the idle and malicious reports' which were being circulated by the press. Almost all the new papers claimed on the front page that they were publishing the news 'to prevent false reports', and some of them added the words 'impartial' or 'impartially related' to their title. Some of them were, in fact, more or less impartial or independent, but the majority were Whig and therefore anti-Government. Against this constant barrage of Whig criticism the Government had little to throw until in February 1681 Edward Rawlins started his dialogue paper, *Heraclitus Ridens*, and in April L'Estrange began writing his *Observator*. The only way to discourage the Whig journalists was to prosecute them relentlessly, and this the Government did, relying on a compliant judicature to see that they were found guilty and stiffly sentenced. No doubt the Whig journalists and publishers took chances from motives that were not necessarily of the highest or most disinterested kind; but they showed great pluck and endurance, and the stand they made in those years of political crisis was an important factor in developing the liberty of the English press, and indeed the liberty of the subject. What finally put almost all of them out of business by the close of 1682 was the tactical defeat of the Whig party, and the assertion of the royal power that followed. Of the two periodicals which had the Government's blessing, *Heraclitus Ridens* came to an end on 22 August 1682, the author explaining that he was giving up because he had now no opponents left to answer. L'Estrange, however, carried on with *The Observator* until March 1687.

Between 1683 and 1688 the newspaper was practically dead, except, once more, for *The London Gazette*, which continued to sail along on an even keel. From February to October 1688 it was joined by a weekly paper called *Public Occurrences Truly Stated*, published 'with allowance'. This was written by two turncoats, Henry Care, the old baiter of the Roman Catholics, and, on Care's death, by Elkanah Settle, whose anti-Catholic *Character of a Popish Successor* had appeared in 1681. Among the public occurrences which Care had to chronicle was the famous trial of the Seven Bishops, and he played it down as much as possible. With the Revolution of 1688 several publishers obviously felt that the time had come to take a chance again, and a number of short-lived papers began to appear. The author of one of those, *The London Courant*, gives us an interesting glimpse of the prevailing uncertainty about what was really happening in the winter of 1688. Writing in his opening number, 12 December 1688, he remarks:

It having been observed, that the greater the itch of curiosity after News hath been here of late, the less has the humour been gratified: Insomuch, that a modest enquiry where his Majesty, or his Royal Highness the Prince of Orange was, or what they were doing, could scarce be resolved till the news had been exported and imported in a Foreign News-Letter. . . . What more acceptable service could be done than to rescue Truth, the Daughter of Time, from the Pretensions of Supposition and Fiction?

None of the earliest of these papers appears to have been licensed, but in January *The Orange Gazette* and *The London Intelligence* both carried, rightly or wrongly, the words 'with allowance'.

This brief efflorescence was all over in a few months, and again the development of the newspaper suffered a check. In 1695, however, when the question of renewing the Licensing Act came up in Parliament, arguments (based on a reasoned statement drawn up by John Locke) were brought forward to show that the Act had not really fulfilled the purpose for which it was designed, and that nothing which it did could not be done equally well by the ordinary processes of the law. The Act was therefore allowed to lapse, and although printers and publishers could still be prosecuted for circulating false news, the English newspaper was at last able to develop in comparative freedom. Three notable papers, which survived well into the eighteenth century, first appeared in the spring of 1695: the Tory *Postman* and *Post-Boy*, and the Whig *Flying Post*, all published three times a week. By the end of the century they had been joined by a number of other shorter-lived journals; and on 11 March 1702 came the first number of the first English daily paper, *The Daily Courant*. There had been a number of weekly papers before 1700, but none of them lasted long; the weeklies did not become firmly established until the reign of George I.

In addition to the newspapers, a considerable number of periodicals of a miscellaneous kind, many of them short-lived, were published between 1660 and 1700, and in one way or another these anticipated, however crudely, many of the main developments of modern journalism. Of the more literary sort some were jocose or satirical, such as *Hippocrates Ridens* (1686), which set out to ridicule 'the Impudence and Mischief of Quacks and Illiterate Pretenders to Physick', and Tom Brown's *The Infallible Astrologer* (1700), which satirized the same John Partridge that Swift was to finish off eight years later. The victim of the short-lived *Advice from Parnassus* (1680) and of *News from the Land of Chivalry* (1681) was Sir Roger L'Estrange—'Il Signior Ruggiero del Estraneis' in the first of those, and 'Don Rugero de Strangemento, Kt. of the Squeaking Fiddle-Stick' in the second. Significantly, both periodicals are in the form of fiction, the latter written in what appears to be a compound of Cervantes and Rabelais. Fiction of various kinds was the subject-matter of a fair number of periodicals, which apparently escaped the wrath of the licenser even in the most difficult times. A series of 'Poor Robin' miscellanies provided the Restoration reader with bawdy anecdotes and picaresque narratives, and exposed the lower reaches of London life. They begin with *Poor Robin's Intelligence* (1676–7), a sort of late seventeenth-century offspring of the old jest books, and this elicited a well-written *Poor Gillian* (1677), addressed (but not very modestly) to the female sex. *Poor Robin's Memoirs*, which followed in the same year, is a facetious rogue-history dealing with the adventures of 'S. Mendacio'. Several other 'Poor Robins' were published at intervals, the latest, *Poor Robin's Intelligence, Or News from City and Country*, appearing in 1691; it is a salacious record of goings-on about town, and the publisher appeals to 'All Gentlemen, Ladies and others that have any Ingenious Comical Relations worth our Communicating to the world (provided they be exactly true)' to send them to his office, and 'they shall have them inserted with the Auxilliary help of *Poor Robin*'s Varnish'. If we may judge by the character of the anecdotes actually printed, most of them must have been submitted by 'others'. Further examples of satirical and picaresque narratives are to be found in *Mercurius Infernus: Or, News from the other World* (1680: a little too early to be the work of Tom Brown), and *The English Guzman* (1683). At the close of the century the monthly *London Spy* of Ned Ward took the reader on an extended trip through the various strata of London life.

Many of the most vigorous periodicals were devoted to political or religious comment. The dialogue form used in *Heraclitus Ridens* and *The Observator* proved to be highly popular and was adopted by other journalists as a racy and colloquial means of discussing the affairs of the day. Any writer who employed this technique could see to it that his Whig, or Tory, or anti-Catholic protagonist got the best of it. Long before Rawlins and L'Estrange discovered the effectiveness of the dialogue debate, it had been used, surprisingly enough, in a trade paper, *The City and Country Mercury* (1667), where the latest prices of sugar, raisins, brandy, fish, and other commodities were set forth in a conversation between Citizen and Countryman. A special feature of *Heraclitus Ridens* was the mock-advertisement, but this too had appeared some years earlier in the original *Poor Robin's Intelligence*. The most important of the anti-Catholic periodicals was Henry Care's *The Weekly Packet, Or Advice from Rome* (there were several changes of title), which first appeared on 3 December 1678, some months before the lapse of the Licensing Act, and continued until the summer of 1683. *The Catholic Intelligence* ('published for the Edification of Protestants') carried in 1680 a series of blasphemous and obscene news items and stories, and *The Conventicle Courant* (1682) conducted a more sober campaign against the Dissenters.

An interesting development of the 1690s was the quiz paper, one of John Dunton's[1] numerous projects. In March 1690,

---

[1] John Dunton (1659–1733) was the son of a clergyman, and began his career as a publisher in 1682. He visited New England in 1685, returning in the autumn of 1686. According to his own statement, he published six hundred books. In later years he took to writing political pamphlets on the side of the Whigs, by which time his natural eccentricity was progressing into some form of mental derangement. The chief authority for his early career is his own *Life and Errors of John Dunton* (1705).

with the assistance of Richard Sault and Samuel Wesley, he launched *The Athenian Mercury*, in which every week a series of questions—scientific, literary, philosophical, and miscellaneous—which had been sent in by readers, were given serious answers, enlivened by some light relief. So accurately had Dunton gauged the interests of a new middle-class reading public that he was able to keep his periodical running for over seven years. His success led to a rival question-and-answer paper in which Tom Brown had a hand, *The Lacedemonian Mercury* (1692), but this survived for only a few months. *The Ladies Mercury* in the following year, which lasted for only four numbers, may have set its sights too low; it announced that learning, the arts, and the sciences were all to be avoided, and instead of those intellectual topics the paper would provide 'for Martha's humbler part a little homely Cookery, the dishing up a small Treat of Love, etc.'. The ladies, however, were already getting from Dunton the sort of thing that they really wanted; and indeed it was part of the objection of the rival *Lacedemonian Mercury* that Dunton's highly successful periodical was full of 'impertinent Questions of Apprentices and Chamber-maids . . . instead of enquiring into the Solution of Witty and Judicious Points relating to History and Philosophy'. With *The Athenian Mercury* we come near to the sort of intelligent but not too erudite family reading that was to be provided for the next generation by Addison and Steele: politics and controversy were avoided, but an honest attempt was made to satisfy the curiosity and arouse the rational wonder of a semi-educated public. That such readers now existed in sufficient numbers may be seen from the publication in 1678 of Nathaniel Wanley's engaging compilation, *The Wonders of the Little World*, and from the rather similar collections of Nathaniel Crouch, such as *Admirable Curiosities, Rarities and Wonders in England, Scotland and Ireland* (1682) and *The Surprising Miracles of Nature and Art* (1683). Dunton himself reached much the same public again in 1694 with *The Ladies Dictionary*, a fat little book of 528 pages stuffed with miscellaneous information designed to interest all the female sex 'from the Lady at the Court to the Cook-maid in the Country'.

Periodicals of a different kind catered for the reader who sought specialized knowledge. *The City and Country Mercury* already mentioned was followed by other trade and advertising papers. There was one outstanding journal of trade and technology, John Houghton's *A Collection of Letters for the Improvement of Husbandry and Trade* (1681–3), which he revived in 1692 and brought out at intervals till 1703. With the encouragement of some of the Fellows of the Royal Society, Houghton published much highly useful information on agriculture (including agricultural machines and instruments), mining, forestry, and fishery, and on such trades as brewing, tanning, dyeing, pottery, and glass-making. From time to time, finding that 'the Generality are desirous of News', he inserted a few scraps of it, such as his account of a dead whale washed ashore at Wisbech, whose 'belly lay in huge wallops, and was very soft'. Less well known today than the *Philosophical Transactions* of the Royal Society, which began to appear in 1665, Houghton's *Collection* is important for the publicity it gave to those new technological inventions and improvements which before long helped to make England the leading industrial nation in Europe.

Some indication of the steady growth of the reading public is afforded by the increasing number of periodicals which published catalogues of new books, beginning with *Mercurius Librarius* in 1668, and by those, such as *Weekly Memorials for the Ingenious* (1682–3) and *The History of the Works of the Learned* (1699–1712), which gave an account of current literature published in Europe. Across the Channel similar compilations were being published by Jean Le Clerc, by Pierre Bayle, and by J. Basnage de Beauval in his *Histoire des Ouvrages des Sçavans*. Here again Dunton, whose books are always a good index to contemporary taste, entered the same field with a folio volume of nearly 500 pages, *The Young Student's Library* (1692), containing extracts and abridgements of 'the Most Valuable Books Printed in England, and in the Foreign Journals, from the year Sixty Five to this Time'. A few reviews of books were now beginning to appear occasionally, even in the regular newspapers. On 31 October 1679, for example, Nathaniel Thompson included reviews of Evelyn's *Sylva* and of several other books in his *Domestic Intelligence*; but such insertions are probably to be attributed to a dearth of real news.

Finally, the 1690s saw the birth of what may be described as the first English literary magazine. In January 1692 Peter

Anthony Motteux[1] published the first number of *The Gentleman's Journal*, and succeeded, not without difficulty and frequent earnest appeals for contributions, in keeping it going for almost three years. Its advertised contents were news, history, philosophy, poetry, and music, and some of all these duly appeared, but a notable feature was the inclusion of short 'novels', and the number for May 1692 carried a long notice of Dryden's tragedy *Cleomenes*. The opening number ran to 64 pages, but thereafter Motteux was content with only half that size, for he seems to have been faced with writing most of the magazine himself. What contributions he did receive tended (as other editors have found) to be mainly in verse; and in February 1693 he was driven in despair to set some subjects for essays. Two readers responded with answers to his first question, 'Which is the most useful of all the arts?', and he was able to print their contributions in his next number. But running a literary magazine in the 1690s was uphill work, and in November 1694 Motteux gave up the struggle. From this time on, however, the development of periodical journalism was rapid and permanent; and Defoe, Addison, Steele, and their contemporaries only extended and improved upon what their seventeenth-century predecessors had already begun.

[1] Peter Anthony Motteux (1660–1718) was born in Rouen, and came to England after the Revocation of the Edict of Nantes. Besides editing (and writing most of) *The Gentleman's Journal*, he wrote a number of plays and operas, translated *Don Quixote*, and was part-translator of Rabelais. He came to an unfortunate end in a brothel.

VII

BIOGRAPHY; HISTORY; TRAVEL LITERATURE

I. BIOGRAPHY

(I)

BIOGRAPHY was slow to develop as a literary kind, and such critical pronouncements as are made about it tend to repeat a few commonplaces: biography is a form of history, treating the life of one person; it deals, as Bacon had said, with 'worthy personages' and with both their public and private actions, but it should avoid the trivial and concentrate on those deeds and on those aspects of character which will best serve as a pattern for lesser men. Although, as Bishop Sprat noted in his Life of Cowley, most readers still seemed to prefer the pompous histories of great men, there was a growing awareness of the fact that 'it is from the practice of men equal to our selves that we are more naturally taught how to command our Passions, to direct our Knowledge, and to govern our Actions'. Biography, then, could profitably stoop to an Abraham Cowley, but in practice the larger lives still dealt mainly with kings and statesmen, bishops and generals. Even so, they might have been a good deal more interesting than they usually were if another of Sprat's principles had been less generally accepted: to print the life of a private man was to make it public, and much that would have interest and significance for a man's private friends would 'lose all manner of taste' if it were read by 'those that are indifferent'. Accordingly, after telling us what an excellent letter-writer Cowley was, and how many of his intimate letters he had in his own possession, Sprat fails to give us a single example of them. The writer whose views on biography come nearest to those usually held in the present century is Dryden. In his Life of Plutarch (1683) he commended biography for the intimate picture it gives of a man's life. The biographer can profitably descend into

minute circumstances and trivial passages of life. . . . You are led into the private Lodgings of the Heroe: you see him in his undress,

and are made Familiar with his most private actions and conversations. You may behold a Scipio and a Lelius gathering Cockle-
shells on the shore, Augustus playing at bounding-stones with Boyes;
and Agesilaus riding on a Hobby-horse among his Children. The
Pageantry of Life is taken away; you see the poor reasonable Animal,
as naked as ever nature made him; are made acquainted with his
passions and his follies, and find the *Demy-God*, a *Man*.

If Dryden had ever carried those ideas into practice he would
have been, for better or worse, a seventeenth-century Lytton
Strachey. Unfortunately he never wrote the life of anyone he
knew personally, and his short Lives of Plutarch and Lucian,
prefixed to translations of their works, do not give him the
chance to enter into minute circumstances, since his materials
for both writers were of the scantiest—scarcely sufficient, as he
said of Lucian, to fill a page, from his birth to his death. What
Dryden did with those two authors is an exercise in graceful
amplification; his biographical method is roughly that which
was to be followed by Johnson in his *Lives of the English
Poets*.

However he may have been influenced by theory, the late
seventeenth-century biographer could hardly help being
affected, consciously or unconsciously, by contemporary practices in the literary world. The growing fashion among publishers of supplying a prefatory life with the collected works of
an author led to the production of many biographies, such as
the Lives of Milton by Edward Phillips and John Toland, and
Abraham Hill's Life of Isaac Barrow prefixed to the first
volume of his *Works* (1683); and since brevity was of some
importance in this context, the biographer was led to shape his
material and to aim at being concise. Funeral sermons, which
were published in large numbers throughout the period, often
contained a good deal of biographical information, and included an estimate of the character of the deceased. A funeral,
it is true, is hardly an occasion for the unvarnished truth, and
eulogy and moral instruction were usually uppermost; but
when the dead man was both good and great and the preacher
was an intimate friend, the content of a funeral sermon might
be of considerable interest. In this way Burnet preached
admirably at the funeral of the Hon. Robert Boyle (1692) and
at that of Archbishop Tillotson (1694). Given the right circumstances, a funeral sermon might become famous, such as

that composed by Robert Parsons for the Earl of Rochester, describing his deathbed repentance.

The influence on biography of the character writers, who were still active after the Restoration, is difficult to gauge. Since the Theophrastan character is the description of a type (although many such types were no doubt based on actual examples), it is an abstraction rather than the assessment of an individual person. But it must have encouraged psychological discrimination, the orderly presentation of ideas, and that satirical turn of thought and phrase which was so widespread at the time. For character sketches of actual men and women there was ample precedent in Plutarch, and in the ancient and modern European historians. Tacitus and Suetonius were favourite authors in seventeenth-century England, and among the continental historians of a later day Thuanus, Davila, Bentivoglio, and Strada, who frequently introduce portraits of historical personages, were widely read, as were the seventeenth-century French writers of *mémoires* and *portraits*.

Many of the Lives written in this period were undertaken with a didactic end in view. Samuel Clarke, a compiler of ecclesiastical biographies, whose *Collection of the Lives of Ten Eminent Divines* (1662) is characteristic of his pious and industrious work, made no secret of his godly intentions. If there is any weakness in the good men whose lives he is recording it must be passed over in silence. 'We must eye them, as we look into Glasses, to dress and adorn ourselves thereby. We must eye them for imitation: We must look upon the best, and the best in the best.' The result is usually biography which has been drained of almost all human interest, but the contemporary reader can hardly have found it so, for many of Clarke's books went through several editions. Indeed, the market for such collections of short Lives was considerable: on the level of mere hack work we have Clement Barksdale's *Memorials of Worthy Persons* (1661) and his *Remembrancer of Excellent Men* (1670), as well as a number of volumes by that indefatigable compiler Nathaniel Crouch, whose *Unfortunate Court-Favourites of England* (1695) anticipates the work of Elizabeth and Agnes Strickland in the nineteenth century.

The political appeal of biography may be seen in the various martyrologies which were compiled after the Restoration, such as Winstanley's *The Loyall Martyrology* (1661), James Heath's

New Book of Loyal English Martyrs and Confessors (1663), and David Lloyd's *Memoires of the Lives, Actions, Sufferings, and Deaths . . . in our own late Intestine Wars* (1668), all setting forth the lives of those who suffered in the Royalist cause during the Civil War. Similarly, *The Western Martyrology* recounted the sufferings of those who were sentenced by Jeffreys during the Bloody Assizes of 1685. Some biographies, such as James Heath's *Flagellum* (1663), a virulent attack on Cromwell, frequently reprinted, were violently partisan; others, like Sir Robert Howard's *History of the Reigns of Edward and Richard II*, while ostensibly lives of historical persons, were in reality making use of political parallels to reflect upon contemporary seventeenth-century problems. In this way Richard Perrinchiefe's *The Life of Agathocles* (1676) is in reality a sustained attack on 'the Monster of our Times', Oliver Cromwell, 'the disagreements being but few'. Not all of the biographical collections of the period had a moral or political aim. By the close of the century the English reader was becoming accustomed, in such compilations as Edward Phillips's *Theatrum Poetarum* (1674) and, above all, in Wood's *Athenae Oxonienses* (1691–2), to being given the facts, however briefly, and whether they were exemplary or not. At the other end of the moral spectrum from Samuel Clarke, he could read numerous Lives of rogues and criminals, sensational in content, but in general plainly enough written. *The Cheating Solliciter Cheated* (1665) recounts the life and death of Richard Farr, who ended his career at Tyburn. Farr, who began as a link-boy, was able to rise to higher things with the help of his natural wit and his manner of speech, 'which being slow and drawling, but smooth and oylie, did give him a more easie admittance into the acquaintance and familiarity of those he had Design upon'. He ended his career, which was unredeemed by a single spark of humanity, as a sort of Jonathan Wild, a receiver of stolen goods, but owed most of his fortune to false actions at law supported by the perjured evidence of his accomplices. More characteristic of the rogue history is Elkanah Settle's *The Life and Death of Major Clancie* (1680), which contains some ingenious deceptions, and may draw for some of its material on the semi-fictitious literature of roguery.

Such brief Lives as those just mentioned hardly offered the biographer much scope for shaping his material; and the

predominantly antiquarian spirit of men like Anthony Wood
and John Aubrey encouraged the collection rather than the
digestion and orderly presentation of their biographical data.
But when we turn to the larger and more formal Lives the
achievement is for the most part disappointing. Many of the
biographies which appeared after the Restoration were written
by or about bishops, and were formidable in their length and
in their treatment. In such works as Peter Heylyn's Life of
Archbishop Laud, *Cyprianus Anglicus* (1668), or John Hacket's
Life of Archbishop Williams, *Scrinia Reserata* (1693), the man
is buried beneath the rubble of political and ecclesiastical
history, and the same is true of John Strype's series of massive
and shapeless biographies of churchmen which begins with his
Memorials of Thomas Cranmer (1694). Richard Parr's *Life of
Ussher* (1686), another great folio, is an early example of the
'life and letters' biography. In contrast to such agglomerations,
Dr. John Fell's *Life of Dr. H. Hammond* (1661) had shown how
an ecclesiastical biography should be written. The course of
Hammond's comparatively uneventful life is presented to us in
an orderly way, and his piety, his charity, and his influence
on the young are illustrated by relevant anecdotes. Fell writes
with some distinction of style, but what chiefly gives this biography its value is its unfailing relevance; the biographer stays
with Dr. Hammond and keeps on writing about him and not
about the historical background. We end by having a perfectly
clear and lively impression of a good man.

Among the longer non-ecclesiastical biographies, *The Life
of General Monck* (1671), written by Thomas Gumble, one of his
chaplains, has at least the virtue of being well informed. From
1656 onwards Gumble has been 'an Eye and Ear-Witness of
all Negotiations'; for the earlier years he received help from
Monck's friends, and was able to use the journal of a high-
ranking flag-officer to describe Monck's actions at sea. Gumble
was therefore well provided with authentic material, and he
gives a particularly full account of the events leading up to the
Restoration. His attitude to Monck is on the whole reverential,
but his narrative is enlivened by some sarcastic comments.
Although he has 'set his brightest side to the world', Gumble
has 'stood too near him to assert that he was all Gold', and he
mentions one fault in particular—he 'esteemed riches a little
too much'. Gumble, it is true, goes on to extenuate this

weakness by observing that, like Henry VII, the General had experienced 'the straitness of fortune in his younger years'; but such frankness is rare in the biography of the period.

For the most part, the more interesting biographies are the shorter ones. Burnet,[1] who had observed that short Lives had the advantage of 'inviting many readers', was himself the author of two that reached a wide public. In writing *The Life and Death of Sir Matthew Hale* (1681) from material supplied by Hale's friends, he naturally thought of this good Christian and incorruptible judge as a splendid pattern of virtue for the reader, and was convinced that 'such plain and familiar instances . . . do both direct him better and perswade him more' than the lives of kings and princes, which are at once more remote and almost certainly less edifying. But in the course of illustrating Hale's firm but gentle character he introduces a number of anecdotes, telling us how his kindness extended to his superannuated horses and to an old blind dog, and how 'he was scarce ever seen more Angry than with one of his servants for neglecting a Bird that he kept, so that it Died for want of Food'. *Some Passages of the Life and Death of John Earl of Rochester* (1680) is a very different sort of Life. In the autumn of 1679, when the dissolute young Earl 'was slowly recovering out of a great Disease', he invited Burnet to come and see him. The two men met frequently at Rochester's London house until he

---

[1] Gilbert Burnet (1643–1715) came from an old Aberdeenshire family. A moderate episcopalian, he was greatly influenced as a young man by the saintly Bishop Leighton. He accepted the living of Saltoun near Edinburgh, but left it in 1669 to become for some years Professor of Divinity at Glasgow University. Meanwhile he had travelled in Europe and made more than one visit to the Court in London, where he was apparently on terms of some familiarity with the King (who made him one of his chaplains) and with the Duke of York. So far he had supported the Earl of Lauderdale, but he now criticized his handling of Scottish affairs, and lost his favour and that of the King. Burnet then came south and was appointed chaplain of the Rolls Chapel; he became a well-known preacher. The first volume of his *History of the Reformation* was published in 1679, and a second volume two years later. By September 1683 he had become increasingly distasteful to the King and his brother, and crossed over to France, staying there for about a year, mostly in Paris. On the accession of James II his position became precarious; he left England again in 1685, and in 1686 was invited by William of Orange to stay at The Hague, where he became his close adviser on English affairs. He accompanied William to England in 1688, and the following year was made Bishop of Salisbury. Burnet continued to play a considerable part as a Whig bishop until his death. His *History of my own Time* came out posthumously in two volumes (1723, 1734).

returned to the country in April, and there, in July, they saw each other again a few days before he died, apparently a sincere penitent. What Burnet has given us is a fascinating, and at times moving, account of Rochester's conversion. As Johnson put it to Boswell, we have a good *death*, but not much *life*; yet Burnet did provide a brief résumé of Rochester's early life sufficient for his purpose, and then concentrated on the long series of theological discussions that they had together. These have the interest of a contest between two utterly diverse gladiators; yet in this prolonged debate neither man was talking for easy victory. At an early stage the Earl told Burnet that he was open to conviction, and that he would conceal nothing from him, 'but lay his thoughts open without any Disguise; nor would do it to maintain Debate, or shew his Wit, but plainly to tell me what stuck with him'. On his part Burnet listened to Rochester's questions and criticisms and occasional jibes with patience and forbearance, and met them with shrewd, earnest, and intelligent arguments. As the story unfolds, both men grow in stature, and both become more likeable. Apart from its obvious authenticity, what gives Burnet's narrative its distinction is the intellectual integrity of both men—on no other basis would either of them have consented to carry on the discussion—and the unbroken concentration of the narrator on the matter in hand. Burnet had no talent for self-suppression; and yet it is the dying Rochester of whom we are most conscious throughout. After this intimate and revealing work, Burnet's long biographical *Essay on the Memory of the Late Queen* (1695) is inevitably a formal tribute; but it is well constructed and, for Burnet, carefully, and even elegantly, written.

Among the more intimate biographies of the period is Richard Baxter's *A Breviate of the Life of Margaret Baxter* (1681), written soon after her death 'under the power of melting Grief'. Moving though this tribute is, it is no mere panegyric; Baxter had a mind formed by a lifetime of disciplined and subtle thinking, and in displaying the character of this good woman with whom he had lived for nineteen years 'in constant Love, and Peace, and Concord', he also dwells with psychological discrimination on the way in which her very virtues sometimes betrayed her into little faults. If Baxter's motive for writing this biography was to obtain relief from an oppressing sorrow, his main reason for publishing it was his belief that it would be useful to other people. John Evelyn, writing his *Life of Mrs. Godolphin* under a similar cloud of grief, never intended it for publication, and it was not printed until the nineteenth century. Margaret Blagge, one of the Queen's maids of honour, a beautiful, charming, and virtuous girl in a singularly unvirtuous Court, married Sidney Godolphin and died shortly after the birth of her first child in 1678. When her friendship with Evelyn began in 1672 she was twenty, and he over fifty. 'My very Soule was united to hers', Evelyn wrote after her death, '. . . for never was there a more virtuous and inviolable friendship.' Whatever we are to think of this strange relationship (and it would not be difficult to see in Evelyn an example of that perverted puritanism that Restoration satirists were never tired of exposing), his religious friendship with Margaret Blagge was clearly the one great emotional experience of his life. Equally clearly, when he wrote his account of her some years after her death, it took its origin from 'emotion recollected in tranquillity', which, as he contemplated it, renewed the sharp sense of bereavement that he had originally felt. As the father–lover relives in memory those blissful hours, his prose rises to a note of ecstasy that is quite unusual in a man of his class, education, and religion. One's only doubt is whether Evelyn fully understood the nature of the emotion he felt so powerfully.

In 1667 the uninhibited and scatter-brained Margaret, Duchess of Newcastle,[1] published a biography of her husband. On this occasion she was on her best literary behaviour, even somewhat over-awed by the occasion, and digested her material into four books. Yet much as she tried to be discreet and impartial and to invest her biography with the dignity that became a great public figure who was still alive, she managed in the third book to introduce many details which at that time were considered to be too personal and familiar. 'He is neat and cleanly,' she writes, 'which makes him to be somewhat long in dressing, though not so long as many effeminate persons are. He shifts ordinarily once a day, and every time when he uses Exercise, or his temper is more hot than ordinary.' It must

---

[1] Margaret Lucas (1623–74), Duchess of Newcastle, was a maid of honour to Queen Henrietta Maria, and was married in 1645 to William Cavendish, Marquis (afterwards Duke) of Newcastle. On their return to England after the Restoration the eccentric Duchess was something of a figure of fun to the King's fashionable courtiers. She wrote copiously—poems, plays (unacted), and a good deal of miscellaneous prose.

have been this sort of information that prompted Pepys to call her biography ridiculous, and her husband 'an asse to suffer her to write what she writes to him, and of him'.

Another uninhibited eccentric, but a much better writer, is Walter Pope,[1] one of those amiable amateurs who lighten for a few moments the burden of the literary historian by strolling casually on to the field of literature, and discoursing easily and facetiously upon this and that. His first known publication is the satirical *Memoires of Du Vall* (1670), which, according to Anthony Wood, took well and sold about 10,000 copies. Claude Du Vall, a good-looking young highwayman of French origin, had been captured and sentenced to death; while he was in the condemned cell many ladies are said to have interceded for his life, and after he had been hanged large crowds went to view his body where it lay in state in a London tavern. This early example of a popular personality inducing mass hysteria gave Dr. Pope his satirical motif; his pamphlet was intended, as the title-page explains, to be 'a severe reflection on the too great fondness of English ladies for French footmen', but it also ridiculed the romantic glorification of a successful criminal. Pope's small triumph in the ironical, written with delicacy and humour, looks forward to Fielding's treatment of Jonathan Wild. In 1679, when he was over seventy, Pope published a Life of his friend Seth Ward, but the pleasing garrulity of this biography is not so much the result of old age as the natural expression of Pope's lively and communicative character. Not only does he digress, but he even digresses from his digressions; and in this and in his habit of taking the reader into his confidence he sometimes anticipates the author of *Tristram Shandy*. Since he was intimate with Bishop Ward for many years he has much of interest to tell us, and he has none of Sprat's disapproval of recounting *trivia*. He makes it clear, for example, that Ward was something of a valetudinarian, and 'delighted much in Fysic Books, which wrought the Effect upon him which they usually do upon Hypocondriacal Persons, that is, made him fancy that he had those Diseases which he there found describ'd, and accordingly take Remedies for them'. In our gratitude for

---

[1] Walter Pope (d. 1714) was educated at Westminster School, Trinity College, Cambridge, and Wadham College, Oxford, becoming a Fellow of Wadham in 1651 and a Doctor of Medicine in 1661. From 1661 to 1687 he was Professor of Astronomy at Gresham College in succession to Christopher Wren, and he was one of the early Fellows of the Royal Society.

such human disclosures we are apt to overlook the fact that Pope touches much too briefly on Ward's mathematical studies, and skates very lightly over his willingness to change sides before and after the Restoration. Yet in his preference for dwelling on the unimportant, Pope is in a very English, if not, indeed, the main English, tradition.

Those two great collectors of biographical facts, Anthony Wood[1] and John Aubrey, were friends for many years, and shared an enthusiasm for antiquarian studies; in temperament and natural ability, however, they differed greatly. Wood was industrious, plodding, and methodical, and performed what he set out to do. While he was preparing his work on the history and antiquities of Oxford University, Dr. John Fell urged him to include short biographical notices of those writers and bishops who were alumni. Out of this suggestion came ultimately Wood's *Athenae Oxonienses*, which appeared towards the end of his life in two folio volumes (1691–2). Wood had taken great pains, searching in archives, newspapers, books, and pamphlets, and maintaining a large correspondence with fellow antiquarians (notably Aubrey, who sent him his 'collections'), and with the owners of books and manuscripts. Amongst the large mass of miscellaneous and often valuable information that he had accumulated in this way over a long period there were inevitably some errors, and since Wood's most noticeable literary quality was asperity, there were many harsh judgements when he came to write up his material. Few today would read the *Athenae Oxonienses* for, or with, pleasure, but as

---

[1] Anthony Wood was born in 1632 in an old house opposite the gate of Merton College, Oxford, and died there in 1695. He was educated at Merton (B.A. 1652), but was disappointed in his hopes of obtaining a fellowship, probably on account of a peevish streak in his temperament which grew more pronounced with age. He never adopted any profession, but in 1656 his desultory studies were given a new direction by his reading Dugdale's *Antiquities of Warwickshire*, and he determined to compile a similar volume for Oxfordshire. He travelled extensively in Oxfordshire, collecting inscriptions, etc., but the projected work was never completed. With the encouragement of Dr. John Fell, however, he compiled his *History and Antiquities of the University of Oxford*, which was published in a Latin translation with the University imprint in 1674. Wood rewrote and extended his original version in English, and this was edited by John Gutch and published in 1792–6. His other great work was his biographical dictionary of Oxford men, *Athenae Oxonienses*. A prosecution instigated by the second Earl of Clarendon for a libel on his father in this work led to Wood's being expelled from the University, and still further embittered his last years. Wood corresponded with a considerable number of his fellow antiquaries, such as Ralph Sheldon, William Fulman, and John Aubrey, but ultimately quarrelled with most of them.

a biographical dictionary it marks an advance on anything of the kind that had preceded it.

John Aubrey[1] had a genuine passion for antiquarian studies, but it was mixed up with so many other interests, all struggling to assert themselves, that he never quite succeeded in completing any task that he set himself. Wood, who had good reason to be grateful for his help, dismissed him in a characteristically bad-tempered outburst as 'a pretender to antiquities . . . a shiftless person, roving and magotie-headed, and sometimes little better than crased', who, 'being exceedingly credulous, would stuff his many letters sent to A. W. with fooleries, and misinformations, which sometimes would guid him into the paths of errour'. All this could have been more generously put, but Wood's estimate of Aubrey contains a good deal of truth. He had endless curiosity and enthusiasm, but little judgement; his mind was a piece of fly-paper that trapped whatever happened to be floating by at the time. Facts, half-facts, traditions, gossip, anecdotes, folklore, and pure fiction all claimed his ready attention, and settled together in his brain in a state of absolute equality. The only work that he succeeded in publishing (the year before his death) was his *Miscellanies* (1696), described as 'a Collection of Hermetic Philosophy' and dealing with occult phenomena. But he also left in manuscript a large collection on the natural history and antiquities of Surrey (called by him 'A Perambulation of . . . Surrey'), which was edited and published in 1719, and similar collections for Wiltshire, full of curious and interesting information which he had acquired by patient and prolonged visits and inquiries. Aubrey may have been unmethodical and undisciplined, but he knew what he was doing. Many curiosities, he once reflected, would be quite forgotten 'did not such idle fellows as me putt them

[1] John Aubrey (1626–97) inherited a considerable estate from his father, a country gentleman, but by 1670 it was almost all dissipated by lawsuits. Aubrey's antiquarian interests went back at least to the time when he was an undergraduate at Trinity College, Oxford, and he made extensive collections relating to the natural history and antiquities of Surrey and Wiltshire, not published until the eighteenth and nineteenth centuries respectively. The only book published by Aubrey himself was his *Miscellanies* (1696), dealing with omens, dreams, apparitions, and other occult phenomena. He had many friends, including Hobbes, whose life he wrote, and he passed on this and his many other biographical jottings to Anthony Wood, who made use of them for his *Athenae Oxonienses*. It was a note of Aubrey's on the Earl of Clarendon that led to Wood's prosecution and expulsion from the University.

downe'. Writing to Wood in 1680 about the biographical notes he was compiling for him, Aubrey remarked: ' 'Tis pitty that such minutes had not been taken 100 yeares since or more: for want thereof many worthy men's names and notions are swallowd-up in oblivion; as much of these also would, had it not been through your Instigation: and perhaps this is one of the usefullest pieces that I have scribbeld.' Since Aubrey was well connected and highly sociable he was able to draw upon a wide circle of friends for much of the biographical information that he sent to Wood, most of which would never otherwise have come the way of the Oxford recluse. Aubrey would talk to anyone—to sextons and schoolmasters, farmers and book-sellers and country parsons, to 'the parish clerk's wife' and 'old Hughes the gunsmith'. With something expected of him, and a definite focus given to his instinct for collecting, Aubrey was now in high spirits. 'I doe it playingly', he told Wood. He wrote in short and lively bursts, tumbling down his factual bric-à-brac as he got it, and leaving Wood to sort it out. Since Edmund Malone first wrestled with them in 1792 Aubrey's biographical manuscripts have presented a tough and almost insoluble problem to his editors. The longest and best organized of his Lives is that of Hobbes, whom he knew well, and whose life he had planned to write before he met Wood. Without Aubrey much indeed would have been swallowed up in oblivion; and since he wrote a lively and spontaneous prose, setting things down, as he put it, 'tumultuously', every page carries the indelible mark of his eager and gentle personality.

(11)

So far as the revelation of personality is concerned, the most remarkable writing of the period is almost all in the form of autobiography, and more especially in the accounts of their inward experience written by members of various religious sects. The greatest of those, *Grace Abounding*, is noticed elsewhere, but many other devout men and women left narratives of their spiritual travails. One of the strangest (but something more than a curiosity) is Lodowicke Muggleton's[1] *The Acts of the*

---

[1] Lodowicke Muggleton (1609–98), a tailor, began to have inward revelations in 1652, and was soon convinced that he and his cousin John Reeve were prophets of a new dispensation. They attracted some followers, but in 1653 were charged with blasphemy and sentenced to six months' imprisonment. On the

Witnesses of the Spirit, published in 1699, the year after his death. In 1651 he and his cousin John Reeve (by a process that is never made clear) proclaimed themselves to be the two last prophets to appear on earth before the Day of Judgement. It was revealed to Reeve that God had put into their mouths the two-edged sword of his Spirit, and that those whom they pronounced blessed were blessed to all eternity, and those whom they pronounced cursed were damned for evermore. This spiritual weapon they proceeded to employ freely, using especially the objurgatory edge and damning to eternity all scoffers and unbelievers and false prophets. Reeve died in 1658, and Muggleton carried on alone. Scoffed at, pelted, and molested, but always retaliating like an angry scorpion with the sting of his terrible curses, he was finally arrested on a charge of blasphemous writing, fined, and sentenced to stand three times in the pillory. Much of this follows a familiar seventeenth-century pattern, but Muggleton emerges from the ruck of sectarians because, like Bunyan, he had an unexpected gift of writing. Some time after he was released from prison in 1677 he wrote his autobiography, a sort of modern Acts of the Apostles, which was clearly intended as a justification of his own life, but which may also have been undertaken to reassure and fortify his spirit after the traumatic experience of his trial, conviction, and punishment. The measured rhythms and much of the language are, inevitably, those of the English Bible; but Muggleton's intense self-awareness, his essential honesty, and his power-loving and authoritarian character are present on every page. An immeasurable gulf separates the writing of this seventeenth-century tailor and of Bunyan and George Fox from that of their more educated contemporaries. We may not care for the mind that is revealed in Muggleton's *Acts of the Witnesses*, but a mind is there, in all its depths and frustrations and strange aberrations and exaltations, as it rarely is in the polite literature of the period. In the last part of his book, in a passage that might have come from *The Holy War*, Muggleton describes his trial and his subsequent sufferings when he was

death of Reeve in 1658 Muggleton continued to travel about the country making converts; his trial in 1677 for blasphemous writing, when he was fined £500 and sentenced to stand three times in the pillory, was the culminating point of a troubled career. His later years were comparatively peaceful. His remarkable autobiographical work, *The Acts of the Witnesses of the Spirit*, was published the year after his death.

exposed, 'as a Mark for everyone to throw a Stone at me', in the pillory:

> My Books were offered up in three burnt Offerings unto the Unknown God, as three Sacrifices before my Face, the smoke of them ascended into my Nostrils, which caused me to cry to Heaven for Vengeance upon those great Men of the Earth that were the Cause of those burned Offerings unto Devils.
>
> And I myself was offered up as a Sacrifice three Times to the rude Multitude: For the People came from the four Winds, or from the four Quarters of the City, and Suburbs round about; they were a Multitude without Number. . . .

This culminating persecution in the life of the prophet demands and gets impressive treatment: Muggleton sees himself as the last in a long line of martyrs, and is writing his testament to sustain his faithful followers until the Day of Judgement shall come. But such writing could only flow from a supreme sense of conviction, which may originally have been self-induced, but which had long since become a settled habit of the mind.

An unshakeable conviction is again the most immediately obvious quality in the *Journal* of George Fox.[1] With very little education to blur the impressions made upon a strong and questioning mind, he saw whatever he saw in a moment of revelation which blinded him to everything else. An idea once obtained in this way could never be modified; it became for Fox the absolute truth, and he was prepared to live with it and to let it govern his thoughts and actions, whatever the consequences might be. In this way, as he was walking in a field one morning, the Lord 'opened' to him that 'being bred at Oxford or Cambridge was not enough to qualify men to be ministers of Christ'. He wondered at this revelation at the time because he

---

[1] George Fox, the founder of the Society of Friends, was born in 1624, the son of a Leicestershire weaver. In his early twenties he wandered about the country seeking religious guidance and enjoying several mystical experiences, and at length, in 1647, he first 'declared truth' to the people of a Cheshire village. He now became an itinerant preacher, requently undergoing arrest and suffering physical violence for preaching in 'steeple houses' and elsewhere. His followers soon numbered several thousands, and with the help of Margaret Fell, who later became his wife, the Society of Friends was firmly and permanently organized. Fox's missionary journeys took him to Scotland, Ireland, North America, the West Indies, and Holland. He died in 1691. His famous *Journal*, revised by a committee under the superintendence of William Penn, was published in 1694.

knew that most people took the opposite view. 'But I saw it
clearly as the Lord opened it to me, and was satisfied, and
admired the goodness of the Lord who had opened this thing
unto me that morning.' The inner light revealed deeper truths
to Fox than this, but the mode of revelation is characteristic.
He was not perhaps in the full sense a mystic, and yet there are
passages in his *Journal*, particularly for the early years, where he
seems to be recapturing a mystical experience. In 1648 (he was
then twenty-four) he had many successful encounters in steeple-
houses and courts of law, his sense of vocation was strong, and
the number of Friends was steadily growing. Looking back on
those happy days he recalls a feeling of exaltation: 'All things
were new; and all the creation gave another smell unto me
than before, beyond what words can utter. . . . I knew nothing
but pureness, and innocency and righteousness. . . .' Fox's
Journal is literature in a rather special sense; it was dictated
to various amanuenses, and bears many traces of its colloquial
origin.

As the Friends increased in numbers, the teaching of George
Fox attracted men of very different kinds and education.
Thomas Ellwood, the son of an Oxfordshire squire, unworldly
and yet business-like, devout and yet without marked spiritual
exaltations, suffering with patience but stubborn in his convictions, gives an account of his early life with the gentle
dignity of a peaceable man called upon to face danger and
endure imprisonment. Similarly, Isaac Penington, in *A Brief
Account of my Soul's Travels towards the Holy Land*, narrates his
spiritual history in a flowing and singularly winning prose.
This literature of inward experience is comparatively uncom-
mon in men and women of the Anglican communion, but
springs without inhibition from the various sectarians. Vavasor
Powell, a piercing independent preacher whose intransigence
makes it difficult to define his religious affiliations, left a fragmentary autobiography which has many of the characteristic
marks of the genre. His conversion began when, suffering from
'a very sore and great pain of the Tooth-ach', he happened to
read in a godly book that 'if the pains of one little bone, or
tooth, be so grievous for a few days, what then will the pains of
the whole body and soul be in hell for evermore?' In its record
of temptations, visions, and providential escapes this autobiography is typical of many written at this time.

None of those so far mentioned has much resemblance to the autobiography of Richard Baxter,[1] published in 1698, some years after his death, with the title *Reliquiae Baxterianae*. Baxter, who might with almost equal justice be placed among the Church of England divines or among the Nonconformists (he favoured a modified form of episcopacy, but declined Charles II's offer of a bishopric), was an intellectual who came ultimately to believe that the best kind of study is that 'which maketh men better and tendeth to make them happy'. In an age of bitter religious strife he laboured unceasingly, but for the most part in vain, to reconcile men of different opinions and persuasions, and to heal the division among Christians. At times, it is true (as at the Savoy Conference in 1661), he stickled for non-essentials, and he was never an easy man to shift from any logical position he had taken up; but, in a remarkable passage of self-analysis in the *Reliquiae*, he shows how age had mellowed him, and how increasingly he had become 'more inclinable to reconciling principles'. By temperament a Puritan, he had none the less a natural preference for the order and discipline of a national church, and a corresponding distaste for sectarianism, fanaticism, and the spiritual egoism inseparable from those whose religion was largely an affair of personal revelations. When in his old age he came to write an account of his life, he had almost none of those spiritual disclosures to make that form the staple of *Grace Abounding*. 'It is Soul-Experiments', he tells us, 'which those that urge me to

---

[1] Richard Baxter (1615–91) was, in his own words, the son 'of a mean freeholder, called a gentleman for his ancestors' sake'. He obtained some education for three years at the free school at Wroxeter, but was in fact largely self-educated. In 1633 he was ordained by the Bishop of Worcester, and began to preach at Dudley, and later at Bridgnorth. In 1641 he received a call to Kidderminster, where his preaching became famous, and where his personal scruples about episcopacy and other matters inclined him towards presbyterianism. He sided with the Parliament during the Civil War, and became an army chaplain, but he took a personal line in the national divisions, always obeying the dictates of his conscience. In 1651 he published *The Saint's Everlasting Rest*, almost the first, and, along with *A Call to the Unconverted* (1658), the most popular of his devotional works. After the Restoration he was appointed a royal chaplain, and he took an active part in the Savoy Conference, but refused an offer of the bishopric of Hereford. The hardening attitude to the Nonconformists after 1662 finally drove Baxter into their ranks, and he suffered the usual petty persecutions, culminating in his imprisonment (1685–6), after being vilified at his trial by Jeffreys. His wife Margaret had died in 1681. His last years in the reign of William and Mary were more peaceful, and were partly employed in writing his autobiographical *Reliquiae Baxterianae*, published in 1696.

this kind of Writing do expect that I should especially communicate to others'; but he intends only to show how his mind and heart have changed since the days of his youth and immaturity. 'And for any more particular Account of Heart-Occurrences, and God's Operations on me, I think it somewhat unsavory to recite them; seeing God's Dealings are much what the same with all his Servants in the main, and the Points wherein he varieth are usually so small, that I think not such fit to be repeated.' Baxter had read too many of those confident accounts of God's dealing with his servants to wish to add another to them, and his finely reasonable nature probably recoiled from what he must have felt to be the spirit of delusion in many of those spiritual autobiographies. 'Whatever the soul of man doth entertain', he had written in *The Saint's Everlasting Rest*, 'must make its first entrance at the understanding; which must be satisfied first of its truth, and secondly of its goodness, before it find further admittance. If this porter be negligent, it will admit of anything that bears but the face of truth and goodness....' With many of the religious-minded of the period that porter had certainly been negligent or not on duty at all; and one of the most moving qualities in Baxter is his intellectual integrity, his willingness to examine his own motives and to admit his past errors. But if his Christianity is reasonable, he is still a good seventeenth-century man fully alive to the power of feeling, and very far from thinking Christianity not mysterious. In an age of intolerance his moderation and his wide and catholic sympathy are remarkable, and they flow not from an easy indifference, but from a mind that was great enough to take the largest view, and from a heart that was filled with love for his fellow men.

All the autobiographies so far dealt with were either published during the author's lifetime, or intended for publication. There are others, however, which were meant to be read only by the writer's children or by other close relatives and friends, and were in consequence not published until long afterwards. Lucy Hutchinson's *Memoirs of the Life of Colonel Hutchinson*, written to preserve his memory for her children, but also to console herself for her own loss, have the unique importance of portraying the life of an influential Puritan family during the Civil War, and have also, like so many other Puritan writings, a considerable psychological interest. Colonel

Hutchinson, a contemplative civilian who suddenly found himself thrust into a post of danger, where he was called upon not only to organize and lead fighting men but to cope with a frustrating and disloyal committee, was clearly a difficult man, quick-tempered and stubborn, and little suited for working along with others. He acted independently, always on principle, and with an almost Godwinian concern for the repercussions of any action on everyone who could possibly be concerned; if he was ever in doubt about the right course of action he prayed for guidance and invariably got it. As one of the regicides, he was in grave danger after the Restoration of being excepted from the Act of Indemnity. He would almost certainly have suffered the fate of some other regicides if his wife had not written, unknown to him, a long penitent letter, forged his signature to it, and sent it to the Speaker of the House of Commons. Yet Hutchinson was far from happy about his deliverance; he had clearly been bracing himself for martyrdom, and he felt a sense of guilt at not suffering with his brother judges on the gallows. There is a certain nobility in this lonely, conscientious, uncomfortable, upright personality; the Colonel is a sort of Puritan Quixote, living in a dream world of moral perfection while a stream of historical events and characters flows past him and leaves him standing where he always was, striking impressive attitudes. Lucy Hutchinson herself is still more interesting. She needed to believe in her husband, and although she professes to be writing 'a naked and undressed narrative' and 'speaking the simple truth of him', she often comes close to panegyric, perhaps to hide from herself his weak points. She herself was a woman of strong character, a Lady Macbeth who sometimes acted while her husband hesitated or sought guidance, but very much of a woman still. Even in her late middle age she had not forgotten what she looked like as a girl and the first impression she must have made upon her future husband. 'She was not ugly in a careless riding-habit', she tells us; 'she had a melancholy negligence both of herself and others, as if she neither affected to please others, nor took notice of anything before her. . . .' Her comments on those she dislikes (and they appear to include almost all the Cavalier party and most of the Parliamentarians) can be acid, as when she expresses scorn that one Gilbert Milligan, 'a man of sixty, professing religion, and having but lately buried a religious matronly gentlewoman, should go to an alehouse to take a flirtish girl of sixteen'. The *Memoirs* are full of such asperities: Lucy Hutchinson's world is one of Puritan men and women, not as they would have liked to be thought to be, but as they often errantly and inadequately were.

Anne, Lady Fanshawe (1625–80), widow of Sir Richard Fanshawe, the translator of Guarini's *Pastor Fido*, was another woman determined to let her son know what an excellent man his father was. Her *Memoirs* are for the most part anecdotal and objective; but since she had lived an adventurous life and her marriage was an unusually happy one, the story that she has to tell remains fresh and interesting. Still more interesting, however, is the autobiography of Anne, Lady Halkett (1622–99). Much of it concerns her three love affairs: with the son of Lord Howard of Escrick when she was twenty-one; with the Royalist (and later Commonwealth) agent Colonel Joseph Bampfield, who, when he asked her to marry him, either did not know or omitted to tell her that his wife was still alive; and finally with a worthy Scottish widower, Sir James Halkett, whom she married in her thirty-fifth year. Her fragmentary autobiography was in print in the early eighteenth century, and it might have provided Samuel Richardson with all the material he could possibly need for another novel; for Lady Halkett, intelligent, lively, resourceful, far from indifferent to moral and religious scruples, and yet placed in an equivocal position by her love for an adventurer, was the sort of heroine that Richardson could not have failed to appreciate. To her own friends Colonel Bampfield may never have appeared to be anything better than a Lovelace, but she herself continued to believe in his integrity until she was compelled at length to face the facts and break off all further relations with him. A good deal of her material is of historical interest (she helped Bampfield to contrive the escape of the young Duke of York); and as an account of a young woman living on her own resources in seventeenth-century England and Scotland this autobiography is a document of considerable human value.

Among autobiographies which were published during the author's lifetime, and may therefore be thought to have had some influence on the development of this genre, two deserve mention for their confident oddity. Both are exceedingly rare books which have never been reprinted, and are consequently little known. In 1673 Francis Kirkman the bookseller published an account of his life which he called *The Unlucky Citizen*. Although he was mainly concerned with relating his misfortunes, he also gave some account of his boyhood love of reading romances, his apprenticeship to a scrivener, and finally his setting up as a bookseller. At this point he was blissfully happy. 'I was free from all Commands, I could go to bed when I would, and rise when I would, I could Eat and Drink when I pleased, Write and Read, walk abroad, or stay at home when I had a mind to it: So great a content and satisfaction is there in being at one's own dispose.' But now followed a series of lawsuits and arrests, and his misfortunes had begun. All this Kirkman relates in an easy gossipy narrative, calculated, as he explains, 'for the Meridian of this City, chiefly for City Readers'. Unfortunately he keeps breaking off to introduce 'comical stories' which have nothing to do with his own life, and what might have been a unique biography, written in a style approximating to that of Defoe, ends by being a fictional farrago. Equally digressive is *A Voyage round the World*, published serially in 1691, in which John Dunton relates the story of his early life. 'I came peeping into the world', he tells us with characteristic freedom, 'as brisk as a little Minew leaps up at a fly in a summer's evening; and soon fell a tugging my nurse's brown breasts, as hard as the country fellows do the bell-ropes on a Holy-day.' We are told of his misadventures as a child (he was nearly drowned in a river, he once swallowed a lead bullet, he was almost choked when an ear of barley stuck in his throat), of his apprenticeship to a bookseller, and later of his various rambles abroad. Dunton writes rather in the manner of Walter Pope, on the friendliest of terms with his readers. People 'don't know what to make on't', he confides to them in the second number. 'They can neither find beginning nor ending, head nor tail, nor can't for their lives tell what the author would be at, what he drives at or intends in part or whole.' Dunton himself, however, is clearly pleased with his own eccentricity, and is confident that his book must be both pleasant and diverting 'to those who do but understand the whim on't'.

However significant they may be of the growing tendency to gossip with the reader, such 'maggoty-headed' autobiographies as Dunton's are still exceptional. More conventional are *The Memoirs of Sir John Reresby*, a Yorkshire baronet and member of Parliament. Since he knew both Danby and Halifax and had some inkling of what was going on behind the scenes, his memoirs have considerable value for the historian; but perhaps their chief value lies in the extent to which they bring out the predicament of an average place-seeking politician trying to adjust himself to the veering policies of the last two Stuart kings. Reresby's troubles came to a head in 1688, when, as the Governor of York, he had to decide whether to remain loyal to a discredited king or join most of his influential friends on the bandwagon of William of Orange. Reresby's *Memoirs* were not published till the eighteenth century, but those of Sir William Temple covering the years 1672 to 1679 appeared in the author's lifetime. Temple's *Memoirs*, another blend of history and autobiography, which ran through four editions between 1692 and 1700, and which even Macaulay found 'very agreeable', imparted to the contemporary reader a good deal of secret history when the turn of events had made such revelations possible.

After the Revolution, secret histories of the reigns of Charles II and James II, varying in authenticity and sometimes in the disguise of fiction, became popular reading. The one outstanding book of this kind is *The Memoirs of the Count Grammont*. Written in French by Anthony Hamilton (1646?–1720), the *Memoirs* were poorly translated into English in 1714 by Abel Boyer, and are now generally read in the improved version published by Sir Walter Scott. Hamilton, who was the Chevalier Grammont's brother-in-law, claimed only to 'hold the pen', but if he got most of his information from Grammont he deserves the highest praise for the disengaged and ironical mode of his narrative style. As one of his French editors puts it, 'Si nous voulions offrir à un Anglois le modèle de la plaisanterie françoise, ce seroient les Mémoires de Grammont'. For the English reader the most interesting parts of Hamilton's book are those that deal with the years immediately after the Restoration, when Grammont was an exile at the Court of Charles II. No doubt some fiction is mixed with the facts, but much of what we are told can be corroborated. How deftly Hamilton can treat his material may be seen from his droll account of the Earl of Northesk returning unexpectedly from Scotland to learn that the Duke of York is upstairs with his wife, and his being forced to endure the pleasantries of the Duke's gentleman, who does not know that he is talking to the lady's husband. Such situations are indeed the raw material of Restoration comedy.

If the period is rich in memoirs and autobiographies, it is also remarkable for the number of interesting diaries that have survived: those of Evelyn and Pepys, for very different reasons, are perhaps as well known today as anything written in their time. The public and private virtues of John Evelyn[1] were outstanding; and if they did not render him unique at the Court of Charles II they made him a rather isolated figure. He worked hard and efficiently on various commissions, he was incorruptible, he behaved admirably during the Plague and on many other occasions, he was not self-seeking. Yet he is a man more easy to praise than to love. What his character lacked was any real warmth; he habitually did his duty because it was his duty to do it. Mr. Esmond de Beer, whose estimate of Evelyn is as judicious as it is well informed and sympathetic, sums up his character admirably: Evelyn had the courage of endurance, but not an active courage. 'Had martyrdom been thrust upon him he would have accepted it cheerfully, but if any proper alternative had been open to him, he would have leaped at it.' He had an active and inquiring mind; he was a connoisseur of such things as architecture, painting, music, coins, sermons, and natural scenery; he was well informed on horticulture and arboriculture, and he took an intelligent interest in most of the scientific activities of the Royal Society. From time to time he put together his thoughts on some topic that interested him: *Fumifugium* (1661) suggests ways of turning London into a smokeless zone; *Tyrannus, or the Mode* (1661) castigates the English subservience to French fashions of dress; *Numismata* (1697) is 'a discourse of medals, antient and modern', and *Acetaria* (1699) 'a discourse of sallets'. *Sylva*, his *magnum opus*, a lengthy work on forest trees, is noticed elsewhere. Evelyn was indeed a serious virtuoso, with a practical bent to his mind.

[1] John Evelyn (1620–1706), the son of a Surrey country gentleman, spent the years between 1643 and 1647 in extensive travel in France and Italy, and he was abroad again for a good part of the years 1649–52. In 1652 he settled at Sayes Court near Greenwich, and (literally) cultivated his garden, which became famous. He was one of the original Fellows of the Royal Society, and was its secretary for a year in 1672–3. Evelyn held a number of minor government offices, but kept more or less aloof from political controversy. He published his *Sylva: or a Discourse of Forest Trees* . . . in 1664, and a number of minor works both before and after that date. His *Diary*, with a selection of his letters, was first made public in 1818–19.

Unfortunately he was a pompous and often pedantic writer. *Fumifugium* is written with a stately air of mild facetiousness, and Evelyn drags in needless citations from Vitruvius, Hippocrates, Aulus Gellius, and other ancient writers to support statements which are usually self-evident.

His *Diary*, which begins with an account of his early life and travels in Europe and continues almost to the day of his death in 1706, is not quite what at first sight it seems to be. Early in life he had acquired the habit of jotting down memoranda on the blank pages of almanacs. Later in life (Mr. de Beer thinks not earlier than 1660) be began to copy those memoranda into a volume which is headed 'Kalendarium', at the same time introducing additional comments and some material from printed sources. From about 1684 the entries in the 'Kalendarium' appear to be more or less contemporary with the events recorded, and in the later years of his life Evelyn drew some of his material from contemporary newspapers and occasionally from pamphlets. While his *Diary* will always remain a valuable source for English history in the later seventeenth century, it tells us little about Evelyn himself. We are in no doubt that his heart bleeds for his country and that he detests immorality and irreligion; we can sense everywhere his lively curiosity and his liking for order and method; but he keeps us at a distance. We never once see him as Pepys saw him at a supper party in 'such a spirit of mirth' that he 'did make us all die almost with laughing'.

The *Diary* of Samuel Pepys[1] is a very different thing. His interests were fairly evenly divided between a contemplation of the world outside himself and an awareness of his own reactions to it. No doubt the objective facts that make up so much of the *Diary* are the main attractions for many of his readers:

[1] Samuel Pepys (1633–1703), the son of a London tailor, was educated at St. Paul's School and Magdalene College, Cambridge. He married the young daughter of a Huguenot who had settled in England in the reign of Charles I. Through the influence of his father's first cousin, Sir Edward Montagu, afterwards Earl of Sandwich, Pepys obtained a post in the Navy Office and by his own competence and industry rose rapidly, until he became Secretary of the Navy. He was deprived of this office in 1679 owing to a trumped-up charge against him, but was reinstated by James II in 1686, only to be dismissed again when the King abdicated. Elected a Fellow of the Royal Society in 1665, he was President from 1684 to 1686, and in his years of retirement at Clapham he kept up a correspondence with many of his old scientific friends. Pepys was a notable collector of broadside ballads, and these, with his books, pamphlets, and diary in cipher, are now in Magdalene College, Cambridge.

the barrel of oysters bought from the old woman in Gracious Street, the half-crown he gave to Mrs. Knipp's maid for bringing him a message ('and had a kiss or two—*elle* being mighty *jolie*'), the execution of Colonel James Turner at St. Mary Axe, when Pepys 'got for a shilling to stand upon the wheel of a cart, in great pain, above an hour before the execution was done'. Such factual pieces of bric-à-brac are fascinating: we read on in the same spirit as we wander through an antique shop, never knowing what our next find will be. But what really sets the *Diary* apart is the revelations it offers of a man's behaviour and character. On 13 May 1665 he goes, after office hours, to get his watch back from his watch-maker: 'But Lord, to see how much of my old folly and childishnesse hangs upon me still, that I cannot forbear carrying my watch in my hand in the coach all this afternoon, and seeing what o'clock it is one hundred times, and am apt to think with myself how could I be so long without one. . . .' The extrovert who hears and records and the introvert who muses on his experience come together again in his account of the death and burial of his brother Tom. During his brother's illness Pepys was genuinely distressed, but now that Tom is dead and the usual arrangements have to be made he bustles characteristically into action. He takes charge of the funeral, down to the smallest details of the burnt claret and the six biscuits apiece for the mourners, and arranges for his brother to be buried in St. Bride's Church, near the grave of their mother. Here, on the morning of the funeral, he finds himself talking with an almost Shakespearian gravedigger, who assures him in return for a present of sixpence that he will do the corpse 'all the civility' he can. 'I will justle them together,' he tells Pepys, 'but I will make room for him.' Down it all goes in the *Diary*, with the reflection that the gravedigger's manner of speaking was 'very remarkable; as of a thing that was now in his power to do a man a courtesy or not'. The funeral service follows in due course. 'And so I saw my poor brother laid into the grave.' But now it is the turn of the living:

And so all broke up; and I and my wife, and Madame Turner and her family, to her brother's, and by and by fell to a barrell of oysters, cake, and cheese of Mr. Honiwood's, with him, in his chamber and below, being too merry for so late a sad work. But, Lord! to see how the world makes nothing of the memory of a man an hour after he is dead! And, indeed, I must blame myself; for though at the sight of him dead and dying, I had real grief for a while, while he was in my sight, yet presently after, and ever since, I have had very little grief indeed for him.

Even when a man is only committing his thoughts to a private diary, such honesty as Pepys shows here is far from common. His habit of impartial self-analysis is quite exceptional. Everywhere in the *Diary*, too, we meet with a man who is obviously getting more out of life than most of his fellows. Pepys had a lively curiosity and a range of interests stretching from the trivial to the philosophical, but he had also an unusual capacity for enjoyment and for many kinds of experience; he was, as Wordsworth said of the Poet, 'a man pleased with his own passions and volitions, and who rejoices more than other men in the spirit of life that is in him'. When a man is writing a diary in cipher he does not have to pretend or put on airs, and since he has no other reader than himself he need have no reticences. But if he is habitually formal or inhibited in the presence of other people, he will almost certainly find it difficult, as John Evelyn did, to be anything else when he is writing his diary. The perpetual freshness and naturalness and the engaging intimacy of Pepys's diary are there because he was that sort of man.

It is not always remembered that Pepys was a young man, not yet twenty-seven, when he began keeping his diary, and only thirty-six when he laid it down. If he gives the impression of being very much of a married man, that is to be accounted for by the fact that he married when he was twenty-two and his wife Elizabeth a girl of fifteen. His youth will help to explain his extra-marital irregularities, but it also helps to account for one of the most engaging features of the *Diary*—his startled realization of the way in which his betters lived, and his fascinated sense of being let into the secrets of a world for which his social background (his father was a London tailor) had given him little preparation. In the years immediately following the Restoration we are able to watch him, like so many of his fellow countrymen, ridding himself of his Puritan inhibitions, becoming a constant playgoer, and indulging in most of the pleasures of the Town. Yet he remained a regular churchgoer, and in spite of periodical lapses (of which he was always heartily ashamed) he retained his capacity to be shocked by dissolute company and lewd talk. But however loose that company might be, it was also, he reflected, 'full of wit, and worth a man's being in for once, to know the nature of it and their manner of talk and lives'. It was all experience: Pepys walked with an inquiring innocence in the most unsavoury places, a sort of seventeenth-century mass-observer, storing away facts as a squirrel stores nuts. The *Diary* is probably more often read in than read through; but to follow Pepys from the first entry on 1 January 1660 to the last on 31 May 1669 is to read a story of growing achievement as the young civil servant mastered his work. Such later glimpses of him as we get in the Tangier diary reveal a man with the same close attention to business; and in his correspondence in later life with his literary and scientific friends we meet with the same inquiring mind, now exercised for the most part on worthier objects. What is missing in later years is the delighted vision of the young man for whom every common London sight had all 'the freshness of a dream'. The *Diary* remains unique, a glorious accident of authorship that no one else could have written.

If we may judge from the number of them that have survived, the keeping of diaries—from motives of self-examination and self-regulation or merely from the diarist's unashamed interest in himself and in the world about him—must have been fairly common. Men who 'used the sea', such as Henry Teonge the naval chaplain (1621–90) or James Yonge the naval surgeon (1646–1721), took naturally to keeping a personal log. Teonge, a cheerful, warm-hearted man, who had the amiable habit of composing songs when the weather was calm, quickens his narrative with many human touches, not least his account of the captain's little son, 'whoe though so younge, yet with his mayd to leade him by his dading sleeves, would he goe from gun to gun, and put his finger to the britch of the gun, and cry Booe'. Bachelors like Robert Hooke or Anthony Wood may have kept a journal as a form of companionship, or simply from a life-long habit of making notes. Both men, at least, had much of interest to record (which is more than can be said of Elias Ashmole, who filled his diary with gruesome accounts of his boils and toothache); and the diary of Wood has the additional value of revealing vividly the austere, studious, uncomfortable life and the discontented personality of a sardonic Oxford scholar. Much of that life was spent in his lonely attic opposite the gate of Merton College, which had failed to make him a Fellow, and there in the bitter winter of 1684 his ink froze for several nights running in its bottle by the fireside. There, too, he grumbled about a new Warden whose wife had made the College spend about £10 on a large looking-glass 'for her to see her ugly face, and body to the middle, and perhaps lower', and another £40 on a bedstead, because the existing one was too short, 'so perhaps when a short warden comes, a short bed must be bought'. One of our last glimpses of Wood is on Magdalen Bridge, shaking his cudgel at an undergraduate who kept telling him that he had abused his grandfather in the *Athenae Oxonienses*, 'and followed me muttering till I came to Magdalen College corner'. Wood's diary is an amalgam of personal jottings and notes made from various printed sources. That of Narcissus Luttrell, on the other hand, stretching from 1678 to 1714, was compiled largely from contemporary news-papers by a recluse who took little part in contemporary life, but found a vicarious satisfaction in chronicling the activities of other people. With Luttrell we pass from the diarist proper to the annalist, from the autobiographical to the historical.

II. HISTORY

Between 1660 and 1700 a good deal of historical writing was going on, but much of it was not published until the following century. After a civil war it was natural that many writers should be concerned with the immediate past of their country, but what a man might write he was not necessarily free to publish, unless it was favourable to the new regime. James Heath's *Brief Chronicle of the late Intestine War* (1663) is typical of the one-sided and biased accounts which found favour im-mediately after the Restoration. Even as late as 1676 Burnet's first historical work, *Memoirs of the Dukes of Hamilton*, was held up for some time until the King and the Duke of Lauderdale were satisfied that nothing in it was unfit to be published, and Burnet was almost certainly compelled to omit or modify certain pas-sages. After 1688 some works were licensed for the press that would certainly not have been allowed to appear in the two previous reigns, notably Edmund Ludlow's *Memoirs* (1698–9). So long as some of those who had played a part in recent events were still alive publication might be dangerous. 'A piece of this nature,' Clarendon wrote of his *History of the Rebellion*, 'wherein the infirmities of some, and the malice of others, must be boldly look'd upon and mention'd, is not likely to be published in the age in which it is writ. . . .' Whether his *History* could have appeared safely in the seventeenth century is problematical; it was published in 1702–4, and even then it aroused considerable excitement. Again, it was never Burnet's intention to publish his *History of my own Time* while he was still alive; the first volume, with some judicious suppressions, appeared in 1723, about eight years after his death, but a good deal too soon for some of his contemporaries who lived long enough to read it.

In surveying the historians of this period it is not always easy to decide where history ends and autobiography begins. Some of the most important historical writing after the Restoration takes the form of memoirs, and if the writer played, or believed that he had played, an important part in contemporary affairs his memoirs are likely to be as much autobiographical and partisan as historical. The struggle between the King and Parliament in the 1640s, which had forced most Englishmen to take sides, continued in an altered form after the return of Charles II, and further political and religious divisions produced a series of crises that intensified the already conflicting loyalties. In the circumstances it is impossible to expect complete impartiality in a Clarendon or a Burnet when they are writing about their own times; and even when a historian is exploring the remoter past or dealing with such apparently innocuous subjects as English county history, his religious and political prejudices are apt to keep breaking in. Historical writers in the later seventeenth century constantly thought of the past in relation to the present. The opening sentence of Clarendon's *History* clearly states his intention in tracing the course of the Rebellion: he wishes posterity to understand that 'nothing less than a general Combination, and universal Apostacy in the whole Nation from their Religion, and Allegiance' could have brought about such a total disaster in so short a time. Similarly, Gilbert Burnet saw the Reformation of the sixteenth century as a great spiritual process that had not yet reached its culmination, and expressed his belief that 'the present age' was called upon 'to complete and adorn that work, which was managed by men subject to infirmities, who neither could see every thing, nor were able to accomplish all that they had projected and saw fit to be done'. Clarendon honestly believed that he was setting down the facts of history 'with all faithfulness and ingenuity; with an equal observation of the faults and infirmities of both sides', and the honesty of Burnet's intentions may be seen in the fullness with which he documented his history of the Reformation. Yet impartiality was not in the air that men breathed in the seventeenth century.

In such an atmosphere it was dangerous to publish even the bare facts of history. John Rushworth (1612?–90), the perfect secretary, who had been taking minutes, reporting speeches, and collecting State documents, newspapers, and pamphlets since about 1640, brought out the first volume of his *Historical Collections* in 1659, and followed it with two more volumes (covering the years 1629–40) in 1680. He was at once accused of partiality, inaccuracy, and concealment of the truth by Royalist writers, notably by John Nalson (1638?–86), who published, with the approval of Charles II, two rival volumes in 1682, *An Impartial Collection of the Great Affairs of State*, covering the years 1638–42. In the same year another industrious compiler, Bulstrode Whitelocke (1605–75), brought out his *Memorials of the English Affairs*. Whitelocke had held various posts of some importance during the Protectorate, and was therefore a suspect character; it was no doubt for this reason that the Earl of Anglesey, who wrote a Preface for the volume, tried to forestall criticism. Good historians, he observed, do not take sides, nor do they stir up political passions:

> The Reader comes not to engage or list himself in a Party, but expects with an honest Neutrality to make Profit and a laudable Spoil from the Quarrels and Miscarriages of others; and without declaring either for a Guelph or Gibellin, comes to reap the true Fruit of all the Toil and Dangers that both have undergone. . . .

The ideal reader, no doubt; but few in the 1680s could have achieved such detachment. Still, the publication of historical material on this large scale must have accustomed the contemporary reader to expecting historical documentation, and this had in due course a considerable influence on the professional historians.

Edward Hyde,[1] created Earl of Clarendon in 1661, had the

---

[1] Edward Hyde, Earl of Clarendon, (1609–74) the son of a country gentleman, was educated at Magdalen Hall, Oxford, and later studied law. He entered Parliament in 1640 and at first sided with the popular party; but his convinced

highest qualifications for writing a history of the Civil War in England. He was almost an exact contemporary of John Milton, and in his moral seriousness and adherence to principle he was in no way his inferior. He was, as he claimed himself, 'not . . . altogether an incompetent Person' to undertake such a work, 'having been present as a Member of Parliament in those Councils before, and till the breaking out of the Rebellion, and having since had the Honour to be near two great Kings in some Trust'. In this mild assertion we may recognize the English habit of understatement carried to an extreme: Edward Hyde had been the trusted, indispensable, and endlessly judicious adviser of Charles I and his son. He had known most of the chief actors on both sides, and had been in a unique position to observe what was going on and to understand how and why historical events developed as they did. The England that he watched disintegrating in the 1640s was perhaps a merry England of his own imagining, but he never wavered in his admiration for the 'genius and constitution of the Kingdom', and for 'the old foundation of the established government, and the good known laws'. In a portrait of himself which he inserted into his autobiography he enunciates clearly the principles on which he had always acted. After stating that he was devoted to the person of Charles I and believed him to be 'the most and the best Christian in the world', he says of himself, in words that might have been written by Edmund Burke:

He had a most zealous Esteem and Reverence for the Constitution of the Government; and believed it so equally poised, that if the least Branch of the Prerogative was torn off, or parted with, the Subject suffered by it, and that his Right was impaired: And he was as much troubled when the Crown exceeded its just Limits, and thought its Prerogative hurt by it. . . . He did really believe the Church of England the most exactly formed and framed for the

episcopalism, together with other motives, led him before long to side with the King, and even before the outbreak of the Civil War he had become one of his most trusted advisers. He followed Prince Charles into exile, and it was at this time (1646) that he began to write his *History*. At the Restoration he returned as Lord Chancellor, and on the occasion of the King's coronation in 1661 was made Earl of Clarendon. He played a dominant part in the post-Restoration settlement in Church and State, but the unsatisfactory progress of the Dutch War and his growing unpopularity at Court led ultimately to his impeachment in November 1667, and he fled to France. There he spent his last years in exile, completing and revising his *History*, and writing his autobiography.

Encouragement and Advancement of Learning and Piety, and for the Preservation of Peace, of any Church in the World: that the taking away any of its Revenue, and applying it to secular Uses, was Robbery, and notorious Sacrilege; and that the diminishing the Lustre it had, and had always had in the Government, by removing the Bishops out of the House of Peers was a Violation of Justice; the removing of a Land-mark; and the shaking the very Foundation of Government.

When Clarendon's earthly paradise was regained in 1660 and Milton's was lost, the ideal failed once again to correspond with the reality, but it remained always before Clarendon's eyes, and guided his political thinking.

Clarendon wrote his *History*, it has been said, 'because he had nothing else to do'. With the final defeat of the Royalists in the early spring of 1646, Prince Charles withdrew to the Isles of Scilly, and Edward Hyde accompanied him. There, on 18 March, he began to write his narrative of the Rebellion and of the events that had led to it. After some weeks the Prince went for greater safety to Jersey, and there Hyde continued to write his *History*. In Jersey he had little or no access to documents or printed papers (he says himself that he was writing 'without any other help than a few diurnals'), but he managed to bring the narrative down to the opening of the campaign of 1644. In the summer of 1648 he was forced to break off and rejoin Prince Charles in Paris, and he appears not to have returned to his *History* until 1671, when he was in exile in France. There he had already written his autobiography, and almost his last work was to revise and complete his *History*. He could claim, in a much fuller sense than Burnet, to be writing 'a history of my own time'. He was able to record not only what had happened, but what people felt about it at the time. When, for example, he comes to deal with one of the chief grievances of the pre-war period, the levying of ship money, he tells us that what really incensed people was not so much the demand for money as the enforcement of that demand by the Star Chamber after the judges had found that the tax was lawful. At that point many who had concurred in 'doing something for the King's service, as a testimony of their affection, which they were not bound to do', and who had told themselves that if the tax became a burden 'they might resort to the law for relief and find it', now began to have second thoughts:

But when they heard this demanded in a Court of Law, as a Right, and found it, by sworn Judges of the Law adjudged so, upon such grounds and reasons as every Stander by was able to swear was not Law, and so had lost the pleasure and delight of being Kind, and Dutiful to the King; and, instead of Giving, were required to Pay, and by a Logick, that left no man any thing which he might call his Own; they no more look'd upon it as the Case of One man, but the Case of the Kingdom, nor as an Imposition laid upon them by the King, but by the Judges; which they thought themselves bound in Conscience to the publick Justice not to Submit to.

In a modern historian such a passage would be looked upon as the result of brilliant insight; but with Clarendon, who was *there* at the time, it is less a question of insight than of the thing observed, understood, and recorded. It is perhaps this contemporaneousness as much as anything else that gives to his *History* its authenticity and freshness; but it is this too that accounts for the inclusion of some trivial episodes and anecdotes that rather detract from the majestic sweep of the narrative. *The History of the Rebellion* falls somewhere between formal history and memoir writing.

One of the most remarkable features of the *History* is Clarendon's ability to keep together under a steady and unhurried review a detailed complex of events, circumstances, policies, and personalities. His examination of the causes that led to the outbreak of war is patient and objective, and, so far as it goes, remarkably fair. He has no easy explanation of the drift towards rebellion, but looks for it in errors of policy and tactics, in royal sins of omission and commission, in accident, in the luxuriousness and greed and ambition and factiousness of individuals and classes in the community. Here the qualities of statesman, judge, and civil servant combine to produce a penetrating report on the state of the nation. Of some of the larger movements of history he seems to be unaware, and there his conservatism may have misled him. He has been blamed for over-emphasizing the personal factor in his interpretation of events, and from time to time his feelings come to the surface and find expressions in a sharp scorn for the King's enemies which gives an edge to the narrative. At the same time his willingness to admit, within the bounds of his loyalty to the King, that grave mistakes had been made both before and during the war, goes far to impress us with his impartiality. Clarendon came from a family that had produced several notable judges, and his judicial manner is not a mere stylistic device, but a genuine expression of the man himself. It is true that a man may be judicial without being right, but Clarendon was rarely wrong. Charles I was a fatal compound of rigidity and opportunism, of stubbornness and rashness, and he listened to many advisers, not least his Queen. Clarendon was no opportunist; he took the long-term view that compromise and expediency would only lead to worse trouble in the end. While the war lasted he was in favour of the King's trying to reach a peaceful settlement (which would admittedly have entailed some compromise); but with the final defeat of the royal armies he appears to have felt that the restoration of the monarchy must be left to time and a change of heart in the English people, and in this, as in so many other matters, he has history on his side. The final impression made by Clarendon is the quite exceptional wisdom of the man. This appears nowhere better than in the celebrated character sketches scattered through his *History*. They show, of course, remarkable shrewdness in balancing the good against the ill in men's characters and careers; but what we have to keep reminding ourselves about those judicial assessments is that Clarendon was writing about his contemporaries, and as often as not was the first to write about them: he is summing up for posterity. About four-fifths of his autobiography deals with the events following the Restoration; his account of what happened in England from 1660 until his banishment in 1668 is of absorbing interest. Since it was written for the information of his children only, it often deals with the secret history of the time; and although even here the habits of a lifetime prompt him to discretion about such matters as the King's mistresses, he reveals fully the intrigues of the Court and is sometimes ruthless in his judgements of the King's favourites. Yet of the King himself he writes more in sorrow than in anger. Bounty and generosity, he felt compelled to admit, were 'a flower that did never grow naturally' in the hearts of the Stuarts; and—coming nearer to his own case—they 'did not love the conversation of men of many more years than themselves, and thought age not only troublesome but impertinent'. Yet both the father and the son whom he had served so faithfully had more of good than of evil in them:

The Truth is: It was the unhappy Fate and Constitution of that Family, that They trusted naturally the Judgments of those who were as much inferiour to them in Understanding as They were in Quality before their own, which was very good; and suffered even their Natures, which disposed them to Virtue and Justice, to be prevailed upon and altered and corrupted by those who knew how to make Use of some one Infirmity that They discovered in them.

This patient and incorruptible servant had deserved to work for better masters.

No one could possibly describe Edmund Ludlow[1] as impartial, nor would he have wished to be thought so. But if bias and stubbornness and one-sidedness are likely to make a man's testimony suspect, they also help him to maintain a consistent point of view, and, with Ludlow, they give to his *Memoirs* an acrid quality that is highly individual. Those memoirs cover the whole period of the Civil War, with the trial and execution of the King (Ludlow was one of his judges), the Protectorate, the uncertain months when Monck was preparing the way for the Restoration, Ludlow's flight to Geneva, and his life as an exile at Vevey. In his account of the Civil War he gives us a keener impression of the day-to-day fighting, with its small skirmishes, scuffles in the streets of country towns, and attacks on fortified houses, than we usually get from the professional historians, who inevitably concentrate most of their attention on the important battles. Again, his narrative of the tense weeks before the return of Charles II and the first three months following his Restoration brings us very close indeed to a memorable crisis in English history and to the anxieties of a hunted man. Writing in exile long after the events he describes, Ludlow sometimes gets his facts wrong, and when he recounts the disagreements between himself and the other Parliamentary leaders in shaping a new regime, his limitations as a politician,

[1] Edmund Ludlow (1617?–92), the son of Sir Henry Ludlow, and M.P. for Wiltshire, was educated at Trinity College, Oxford, and joined the Parliamentary forces at the outbreak of the Civil War. He fought at the Battle of Edgehill, and took part in many subsequent engagements, becoming in due course one of Cromwell's lieutenant-generals. As one of Charles I's judges, he signed the death warrant in 1649. After the proclamation of Cromwell as Protector he refused to acknowledge his authority, feeling that Cromwell was betraying what he and others had fought for, viz. 'that the nation might be governed by its own consent'. As one of the surviving regicides he was in mortal danger after the Restoration. In August 1660 he fled the country and ultimately settled at Vevey, where, apart from one brief visit to England after the Revolution, he spent the rest of his life.

his rigidity, and his unawareness of the changing circumstances of the day become painfully obvious. What distinguishes him is his unwavering republicanism, which brought him into sharp and fearless collision with Cromwell the Protector and with all those who put political expediency before abstract principle. For Ludlow the Civil War had been fought to determine 'whether the King should govern as a god by his will and the nation be governed by force like beasts; or whether the people should be governed by laws made by themselves, and live under a government derived from their own consent'. It is true that for Ludlow 'the people' were only the people he approved of, and no doubt he deserved the epithet 'wooden-headed' that Carlyle so frequently applies to him. But as he recounts how he saw all that he had fought for being betrayed, first by Cromwell and later by Monck, he takes on a kind of lonely and obstinate dignity. Although his motive in writing his *Memoirs* was partly one of self-justification, he also believed, like most of his contemporaries, in the didactic value of history, and held that 'the memory of those men whose lives have been remarkable for great and generous actions ought to be translated to posterity with the praises they have deserved, that others may be excited to an imitation of their virtues. . . .'. Accordingly he held up to admiration Bradshaw, Ireton, Vane, Overton, and those of his fellow regicides who suffered for their beliefs and actions after the Restoration by being hanged, drawn, and quartered. Being Ludlow, however, he also believed that ' 'tis as just that the names of those who have render'd themselves detestable by the baseness of their crimes should be recorded, that men may be deterr'd from treading in their steps, lest they draw upon themselves the same infamy'. The march of events and Ludlow's confidence in his own rightness presented him with many such objects of infamy, from Cromwell and Monck and the future Earl of Shaftesbury down to the many lesser men who swerved from that narrow path of virtue which was so obvious to Ludlow, and along which he himself tramped with austere and precisian confidence. But although he is narrow and rigid he has also the intensity of the Puritan; and his *Memoirs*, in spite of their self-righteous tone, recount the personal tragedy of a man who has devoted his life to a lost cause in which he has never for one moment ceased to believe. It is as if one of the fallen angels had written his own version of *Paradise Lost*.

Two men who had been on opposite sides in the Civil War, Thomas, Lord Fairfax (1612–71) and Sir Philip Warwick (1609–83) left behind them brief historical memoirs. The *Short Memorials* of Fairfax were written for his own satisfaction and 'in Gratitude to God for his many Mercies and Deliverances' while the author fought for the Parliamentary cause in the North, and also, after he became Commander-in-Chief in 1645, to justify 'those Actions which seem'd to the World most questionable'. This spare and soldierly narrative, brief, home-spun, not 'set down . . . in that methodical and polish'd Manner as might have been done', is a sort of English *De Bello Gallico*. Warwick calls his *Memoirs of the Reign of King Charles I*, written in his old age, an 'immethodical story', and it is so. Its chief value lies in its character sketches of Laud, Strafford, Charles I, and Cromwell, and in the personal details and anecdotes that he occasionally introduces. For those 'little stories' and trivia he excuses himself by recalling that Plutarch brought in the private conversation of Alexander the Great and Julius Caesar when writing his *Lives*. Warwick was a loyal servant to Charles I, and he looked forward—'when I part from the dunghill of this world'—to meeting the King again 'and all those faithful spirits who had virtue enough to be true to him, the church, and the laws to the last'.

Gilbert Burnet's first historical work, *The Memoirs of the Lives of . . . James and William Dukes of Hamilton*, is as clumsily constructed as its title, but it gives a clear indication of what he thought the historian should do. Burnet had been given access to the Hamilton papers, and this mass of correspondence and other documents revealed in great detail the dealings of Charles I and Charles II with Scotland. Although he believed that men who have been engaged in state affairs are 'the fittest to write History, as knowing best how matters were designed and carried on', he could lay no claim to that sort of knowledge on this occasion, for most of the events with which he had to deal happened when he was a small boy. But if he could not be a Philip de Commines or a Thuanus, he was still in a privileged position for a historian, since next to those who have actively participated in the events they describe, 'those that have had the perusal of the Cabinets of great Ministers, and of Publick Records, are the best qualified for giving the World a true Information of Affairs'. The historian, then, had to get behind the scenes, and to record 'the secret Causes and Counsels of the greatest Transactions'. Burnet's natural inquisitiveness would have prompted him to ferret out the secret history of any period in which he was interested, but the accident which placed the Hamilton papers in his hands while he was still in his early thirties probably determined his future development as a historian. His original intention was to make use of his documents to construct a consecutive narrative of events (and if he had stuck to that method he would probably have produced a more readable volume); but he was persuaded by Sir Robert Moray to alter his plan and insert most of the papers at full length. Burnet's own justification of this method shows how tastes were changing: the Restoration reader, he claimed, no longer enjoyed fictitious speeches put into the mouths of generals and statesmen, but 'people desire to see Papers, Records, and Letters published at their full length'. He notes, too, how the publication of French *mémoires* had stimulated an interest in the secret history of great men and of public transactions.

In 1676 a French translation of Nicholas Sanders's *De Origine ac Progressu Schismatis Anglicani*, first published in 1585, prompted Burnet to undertake a comprehensive reply to this Roman Catholic account of the Reformation. In 1679, when the feelings aroused by the Popish Plot were at their height, he brought out the first volume of *The History of the Reformation*, and followed it in 1681 with a second volume which took the narrative down to the reign of Queen Elizabeth. For the first volume he received the thanks of both Houses of Parliament, and the whole work superseded anything of the kind that had been written before, and established his reputation as an English author. Of the ecclesiastical historians who immediately preceded him Burnet mentions two: Fuller and Heylyn. Fuller, he objected, affected 'an odd way of writing', and what was inexcusable in Heylyn was his failure to document his statements, 'which is not to be forgiven any who write of Transactions beyond their own time, and deliver new things not known before'. Burnet made no such mistake. As in his previous historical work, he quoted some documents in full and gave the substance of others; but so extensive was his manuscript material that he decided to print all the more important documents complete at the end of the work. Burnet, however, was not the first or the last scholar to keep the public waiting for what he had promised them: the documentary evidence did not appear until 1714, when it was published in a third volume, which also incorporated a considerable number of corrections made by the author himself, or sent to him by friendly, and sometimes unfriendly, readers. Few writers have shown Burnet's willingness to acknowledge, and even call attention to, their own mistakes and shortcomings. When he found himself unable to read a manuscript, he said so frankly: he had struggled hard to decipher a papal bull, but 'could not read three words together in any place of it', and although he showed it to others 'that were good at reading all hands, yet they could not do it'. Burnet had taken pains to obtain his facts. He had examined all the public records he could come by; he had searched for manuscripts, and had been allowed to examine many in the Cottonian Library, and some belonging to Edward Stillingfleet and other friends and well-wishers; he had read widely in the controversial literature of the sixteenth century. But he had worked at speed, and often in the face of difficulty and obstruction; he had therefore made some mistakes in transcription, and some in translation, and occasionally he had misinterpreted the evidence. All those errors were seized upon by his political and ecclesiastical enemies, and made the most of; but his essential honesty of intention and general accuracy cannot be questioned. Burnet had made a genuine effort to explain the origins of the Reformation, and to write history, not mere polemics. For several generations of English Protestants *The History of the Reformation* was a sort of justification of their faith. It was also, as Sir George Clark has claimed, 'the first English book which told the story of a great historical change as a coherent whole and in the light of the great issues which it decided, while at the same time presenting a great body of documentary evidence'.

Yet it is for his *History of my own Time* that Burnet is usually read today, a work that is a blend of history, autobiography, anecdote, and gossip, mixed with shrewd and well-informed, but also at times ill-informed, comments on the world of his own day. When in 1683 he began to set down 'a relation of all that I had known to that time', he seems to have been thinking of writing nothing more than memoirs; but in the course of the years he revised his manuscript more than once, and by the time that it had reached its final form the memoirs had come nearer to being history. Even so, they remain for the most part a personal account of events and characters. 'Where I was in the dark,' he explains, 'I past over all, and only opened those transactions that I had particular occasions to know, . . . leaving publick transactions to Gazetts and the publick historians of the times.' As he proceeded with his narrative, however, he felt from time to time the need to bridge the gaps in his own personal knowledge by making use of secondary sources, and on such occasions he can be oddly naïve. 'All this I thought fit to lay together,' he observes on one occasion, 'and to fill as it were an empty place in my history.' His more usual practice was to pass rapidly over any lacuna in his knowledge, and concentrate on those matters about which he was better informed. When he is apparently drawing upon ample information, we have still to ask how reliable it is. His intentions were certainly honourable, but he was apt to accept statements that a less credulous writer would have rejected, or at least questioned. Burnet was the victim of his own sociable and buoyant temperament. This ebullient Scot was something of a busybody, with a Boswellian fondness for thrusting himself into all companies, and engaging all and sundry in conversation. In such circumstances there was always the chance that one of his victims might protect, or amuse, himself by giving his questioner false information, and yet where it is possible to check Burnet's facts against documents they are in the main right. What we get from him is often not quite history, but something that is of real value to the historian: he frequently tells us what people were thinking or talking about at the time. Because he concealed nothing in his *History* that he thought fit to be known, he made many enemies, who had a vested interest in denying his veracity, and who did their best to discredit him. He appears to have been a man whom it was almost impossible to frighten, and he was always forthright and outspoken. He remonstrated with Charles II about his immoral way of life, he demonstrated to the Duke of York the errors of the Roman Catholic religion, he explained to Lauderdale how he was mishandling Scottish affairs, and he spoke to William of Orange about the need 'to change his cold way'. Burnet must have exasperated and infuriated men in all ranks and stations, but he could not be ignored. He is a bigger man, and perhaps a better historian, than he has usually been allowed to be.

It amused the Tory Swift to mark his own copy of the *History*, not only with such jibes as 'Dunce', 'Puppy', and 'Scotch dog', but also with fairly frequent censures of Burnet's English, and the cry has been taken up by critics of boring rectitude whose own prose never approaches the vigour and liveliness of Burnet's. Scots may seek to defend his Scotticisms, but there can be no excuse for his occasional awkwardness and even obscurity of expression. Yet the prose of Burnet must be judged on the same terms as we judge that of Defoe; it is the prose of a man whose mind is teeming with ideas, and who sets them down on paper in the same confident and immediate way as he talks. He certainly revised his first drafts more than there is any reason to suppose that Defoe ever revised his; but his style remains natural, unpretentious, colloquial, and, like the author himself, busy, bold, and abundantly alive. That he was capable of writing with dignity and in a more formal style may be seen from the concluding pages of his *History*, or from the singularly moving 'Meditation on my Voyage to England', a paper written in 1688 when he was on the point of accompanying the Prince of Orange on his invasion of England, and had good grounds for thinking that he might well be going to his death. Again, when he writes one of those character sketches which are among the especial achievements of his *History*, the fact that he is constantly weighing up the evidence and balancing the pros against the cons, gives his sentences rather more shape than usual, although even here they frequently overflow in parentheses and subordinate clauses. Burnet is at least a writer of irrepressible energy; if it is sometimes the energy of the bluebottle bumping against the window pane, it gives to everything he writes an exuberance and forthrightness that make him highly readable.

Towards the end of the century a notable advance in Old English studies was made by a number of dedicated scholars at Oxford and Cambridge. In the 1690s the chief centre of research was at The Queen's College, Oxford, where Edward Thwaites (1667–1711), who had himself come under the influence of George Hickes, inspired and trained a group of young Anglo-Saxon scholars, including Christopher Rawlinson, William Nicolson, and Edmund Gibson. A necessary preliminary to such studies was the publication, one year before the Restoration, of William Somner's *Dictionarium Saxonico-Latino-Anglicum*. In due course a number of editions of chronicles and other Old English texts were produced by both Oxford and Cambridge scholars, and this antiquarian activity reached a climax in 1703 with the appearance of the first volume of the *Linguarum Veterum Septentrionalium Thesaurus* of George Hickes. Among the Oxford scholars one of the more isolated and neglected men was the industrious William Fulman, whose folio volume of English historical writings, *Rerum Anglicarum Scriptores Veteres*, was published in 1684. Two similar volumes were produced by Thomas Gale of Cambridge.

Sir William Dugdale (1605–86) belongs to an earlier generation, but two volumes of his *Monasticon* came out after the Restoration; his historical work on the English legal system, *Origines Juridiciales*, appeared in 1666, and *The Baronage of England* in 1675–6. His son-in-law, Elias Ashmole (1617–92), brought out his own *magnum opus* in 1672, *The Institution, Laws and Ceremonies of the Order of the Garter*, the fruit of prolonged and industrious research. Dugdale's *Antiquities of Warwickshire* (1656) had provided a noble pattern for English county historians, and undoubtedly stimulated this type of historical and antiquarian research. Among his numerous successors one of the ablest was Robert Thoroton, whose *Antiquities of Nottinghamshire* appeared in 1677. Dr. Robert Plot's *Natural History of Oxfordshire* (1676), followed by a similar volume on Staffordshire ten years later, belongs to a different order of history, in which 'philosophical' investigation into such matters as soil, minerals, animals, plants, and climate takes precedence over antiquarian inquiries. From county history it was only a step to parochial history. One of the earliest works of White Kennett (1660–1728), another Oxford man who had come under the influence of Hickes, was his *Parochial Antiquities* (1695), in which he dealt with the early history of Ambrosden 'and other adjacent parts in the counties of Oxford and Bucks'. In a dedicatory Epistle he affirmed that he was 'under no concern to vindicate it from the slights and ridicules that may be cast upon it by idle witty People, who think all History to be Scraps, and all Antiquity to be Rust and Rubbish'. The new studies, it is clear, were making their way against considerable opposition. In his Preface, however, Kennett struck a more confident note: 'I cannot but congratulate the present Age, that a genius to our National Antiquities seems now to invigorate a great many Lovers of their Country. . . .' Antiquarianism had undoubtedly become endemical in learned circles, and the utter devotion with which it was often pursued sometimes suggests that seventeenth-century fanaticism was emerging again in a new and more benign form. The natural enemies of the antiquarian were not confined to 'idle witty people': Bishop Burnet, for instance, reacted with uncharacteristic bad temper when Henry Wharton, author of *Anglia Sacra*, criticized his medieval scholarship in *A Specimen of some Errors and Defects in the History of the Reformation*. Burnet had little use for monkish chronicles, considering them full of fabulous stuff, and written in a barbarous style by men of little or no judgement. 'If any one that has more Patience than I', he wrote, 'can think it worth the while to search into that Rubbish, let him write volumes of Anglia Sacra and have the Glory of it for his Pains.' Burnet's attitude to men like Wharton was roughly the same as that of Pope in the next generation to Thomas Hearne and Lewis Theobald; and a similar contempt was often expressed for the virtuosi who collected, not historical facts, but specimens of natural history or ancient art. Scholarly research was slowly gaining recognition, but the scholar was (and is) an object of easy satire.

Henry Wharton, who died in 1695 at the age of thirty, was a remarkably erudite young man. When, at the age of twenty-seven, he published his *Anglia Sacra* (1691) in two large folio volumes containing edited texts of chronicles, of the lives of bishops, and of other documents relating to their sees, he made available an invaluable collection of materials for future historians of the Early Church in England. Wharton was sustained in those vast labours by his passion for antiquarian research, but also, as Professor Douglas has said, by 'the desire to discover in the past a justification of the ecclesiastical system that he served'. Similar motives lay behind the learned and well-argued *Origines Britannicae* (1685) of Edward Stillingfleet, which brought the early history of the Church down to the fifth century. Stillingfleet was also giving support to William Lloyd's *Historical Account of Church Government* of the previous year, which in its turn had been written in opposition to 'the arguments that have been used of late times against episcopal government'.

In the course of his own argument Lloyd had found it necessary to question the authenticity of some forty of the early Kings of Scotland, and this rash venture provoked a reply from the King's Advocate in Edinburgh, Sir George Mackenzie. Known among his fellow countrymen as 'bloody Mackenzie' for the ruthlessness with which he prosecuted the Covenanters, he now defended the antiquity of the royal line of Scotland in two treatises which showed the same uncompromising determination. In such various ways the writing of history and antiquarian research became involved in modern controversy; the past was continually throwing its admonitory shadow across the troubled present.

In his old age Sir William Temple turned his attention to the early history of his country, and published in 1695 *An Introduction to the History of England*, which carried the story down to the reign of William the Conqueror. Even in the existing state of Anglo-Norman studies Temple could have been a good deal better informed, but he was not the man to waste his time on 'all such reading as was never read'. Yet he brought the wisdom and experience of a statesman to bear on the Norman Conquest, and his interpretation of events was independent and at times surprisingly similar to that of twentieth-century scholars. In his Preface Temple, whose attitude to monkish chroniclers was much the same as Burnet's, remarked upon the undeveloped state of historical writing in England: those who had so far attempted it had too often been wretched writers, unable to judge what should be left out and what included. It was sad to reflect that 'so ancient and noble a Nation as ours . . . should not yet have produced one good or approved general History of England'. Temple's contemporaries were still reading Sir Richard Baker's *Chronicle of the Kings of England* (1643), a substantial folio which was reprinted no less than seven times between 1660 and 1700. Yet before the century was out two attempts were made to write that general history which Temple desired to see. Robert Brady (d. 1700), a royal physician who had been appointed Keeper of the Records in the Tower and had made good use of his opportunities for research, brought out the first volume of his *Compleat History of England* in 1685, and followed it with a second volume in 1700. Brady, who was a high Tory, was certainly not unbiased, but he had gone to the sources and had made use of the recent researches of other men.

His royalist interpretation of English history brought into the field the Whig James Tyrrell (1642–1718), a country gentleman and a friend of John Locke, who had written a reply to Filmer's *Patriarcha*. In 1696 he published the first volume of *A General History of England* which was intended to expose the errors of Dr. Brady. A second volume followed in 1700, and the third and last, bringing the work down to the reign of Richard II, in 1704. So far as scholarship was concerned, the histories of both Tyrrell and Brady reflected the new interest in scholarly research, but they were still far from meeting Temple's demand for a well-ordered and well-written account of English history.

III. THE LITERATURE OF TRAVEL

The traveller who writes down his experiences is often a special sort of autobiographer, and what he has to tell us will vary with his interests and with the purpose of his travels. So far as European travel is concerned, the purpose was usually educational and cultural. As the editor of Sir Andrew Balfour's *Letters . . . to a Friend* put it in 1700, 'Indeed, the World is a Theater, in which we may see not only the different productions of Nature, but also all the Arts and Mysteries of Government, and all the wayes of improving Nature by Art; and every Climate affords new Scenes for improving Geography, Natural and Civil Historie, Medicine, Commerce, and all the Mechanick Arts'. When the young John Evelyn travelled in the Netherlands, France, and Italy in the 1640s, he was mainly interested in viewing such things as antiquities, curiosities of nature and art, painting and architecture, gardens and landscape in general, and had comparatively few observations to make on the manners and customs of the people inhabiting the countries he visited. John Ray, travelling through various European countries from 1663 to 1666 with Francis Willughby, was primarily concerned with collecting plants, although, realizing 'the paucity of those who delight in studies and enquiries of this nature', he compiled a narrative of the whole journey with more general observations. On the whole, his account is less entertaining to the general reader than Willughby's brief *Relation of a Voyage made through a great part of Spain*, in which the Spaniards are subjected to some unsparing criticism.

A number of the accounts published were clearly intended as guide-books for travellers. Balfour (1630–94), who had been the travelling tutor of Lord Rochester, actually addressed his letters to one such young man, giving him directions about the day's journey and where to stop for the night, and advising him about the gardens, the monuments and sepulchral inscriptions, the cabinets of the curious, and so on, that he ought to see. The Baedeker of the period was undoubtedly Richard Lassels (1603?–68), author of *The Voyage of Italy* (1670). Lassels, a Roman Catholic priest who had been a travelling tutor, and who knew his way well about France and Italy, has a lively style, and occasionally indulges a taste for the facetious. In Venice he notes the wide hoops worn by the ladies: 'Two of these Ladies meeting one another in these narrow streets, make as great an embarras as two carts of hay do upon London-bridge: and I have seen their Ladyships strangely puzzled how to juggle themselves into a narrow Sedan or Litter: indeed half of my Lady hangs out. . . .' *The Voyage of Italy* appeared simultaneously in Paris and London, a number of unobtrusive changes being made for the London edition to remove some comments on heretics that would have been offensive to Protestant readers. In an age of religious intolerance continental travel was bound to raise such issues. Much of the appeal of Burnet's *Some Letters. Containing an Account of what seemed most Remarkable in Switzerland, Italy, etc.* (1686), which ran through six editions in two years, consisted in the reactions of the author of *The History of the Reformation* to the various religious communities among whom he sojourned. Burnet was at least an inquiring, and often a remarkably tolerant, traveller; but Theophilus Dorrington, who published in 1699 his *Observations concerning the Present State of Religion in the Romish Church . . . Made in a Journey through some Provinces of Germany*, was mainly interested in warning his fellow countrymen (and more especially young travellers) against 'the Popish superstition and corruption' they would meet with in foreign lands. This he faithfully performs in many passages, but when he allows himself to describe Antwerp, Louvain, Cologne, and other cities, he can be intelligent and perceptive.

A traveller with no particular axe to grind, and with interests that were both wide and miscellaneous, was Dr. Edward Browne (1644–1708), the son of a more famous father, Sir

Thomas Browne. In his younger days he was a frequent traveller, and he went into eastern Europe, which few Englishmen
had visited. Dr. Johnson, who had probably skimmed rapidly
through Browne's books, thought that his scientific cast of mind
had led him 'to enquire most after those things by which the
greatest part of mankind is little affected'; but although Browne
was greatly interested in mines and museums and physic
gardens, he was also an intelligent observer of manners and
customs, and of almost everything that was 'naturally, artificially, historically and topographically remarkable'. Another
young traveller who went further afield than most was Sir
George Wheler (1650–1723), who in 1675 visited Greece
(eleven years before the Parthenon was partially destroyed by
the Venetian bombardment), in company with Jacob Spon.
Both men published accounts of their journey, Spon in 1678,
and Wheler four years later in a folio volume, *A Journey to
Greece*. Wheler's account owed a good deal to that of Spon, and
his own original contribution was mainly in the form of botanical observations, but for most of his fellow countrymen it was
to be the standard English book on modern Greece for many
years to come.

Diplomatic missions were the occasion for a few published
accounts of foreign countries. In 1663, when the Earl of Carlisle, Ambassador Extraordinary to Russia, Sweden, and Denmark, visited those countries, he had with him Andrew Marvell
as secretary to the mission, and as under-secretary Guy Miege,
who published in 1669 *The Relation of the Three Embassies*. In 1676
Robert South went as chaplain to Laurence Hyde, Earl of
Rochester, on a mission to Poland. In a long letter to Edward
Pococke, published by Edmund Curll in a volume of *Posthumous Works*, South gave an account of the chief cities of Poland,
described the elaborate ceremonies at a Court wedding he had
attended, the pomp of Polish funerals, the inconveniences of
travelling in that country, and much else. But the outstanding
work of this kind is Sir William Temple's *Observations upon the
United Provinces*, one of the most popular books of the whole
period. Temple was able to write with the detached observation of a stranger, and the sympathy of one who was a true
friend to the Dutch people and who had lived long enough
among them to know them well. Another book which was
probably in every gentleman's library was Sir Paul Rycaut's

The Present State of the Ottoman Empire (1668), a large work which was frequently reprinted. Rycaut (1628–1700), who was secretary to the English ambassador and had lived in Turkey for five years, was not (as he pointed out himself) one of those 'hasty travellers . . . who are forced to content themselves with a superficial knowledge', but was able to discuss the Turkish government, religion, and military forces at length, and to give a good description of the people and their way of life.

The literature of travel had, like biography, its eccentrics. One of these was Dr. Martin Lister (1638?–1712), who in 1698 published *A Journey to Paris*. His book, which quickly ran through three editions, must have interested many contemporary readers; but Lister's tendency to record trivialities and to ramble from one topic to another invited the ridicule of Dr. William King in his satirical piece, *A Journey to London*, which he facetiously fathered on the egregious M. de Sorbière. In a Montaigne-like passage Lister had remarked: 'I took more pleasure to see Monsieur Breman in his white Wastcoat digging in the Royal Physick Garden, and sowing his Couches, than Monsieur de Saintot making room for an Ambassador'; and King, with such a passage in mind, tells his readers: 'I saw a Boy that had harness'd two Dogs, which draw a small Voiture with a Burden in it, and I saw a little Master in a little *Vinegretté*, drawn along by two Boys, much bigger than himself, and push'd behind by a Maid.' For Dr. King, and for others of his mind, literature had not yet become safe for impertinency.

Touring in England, Wales, and Scotland was still in its infancy; but in 1675 the industrious John Ogilby (1600–76), who had produced a number of volumes dealing with India, China, Japan, Africa, and other remote places, turned his attention nearer home and published the first and only volume of his *Britannia*, illustrated by 100 copperplates. This *de luxe* roadbook was followed by a number of more modest compilations, such as *An Historical Account of Mr. Rogers's Three Years Travel over England and Wales* (1694), a humble forerunner of Defoe's *Tour*. By the last decade of the century Celia Fiennes had begun her horseback journeys across England. Much incidental description of the English scene is, of course, to be found in such sources as George Fox's *Journal*, in private correspondence, and in the facetious 'Trips' and 'Journeys' of Ned Ward, Mrs. Manley, and others.

Scotland was at this time almost a foreign country, and was certainly little visited by Englishmen. For that reason, but also for its intrinsic interest, Martin Martin's *A Late Voyage to St. Kilda* (1698) is a book of some importance. Martin (d. 1719) quite consciously presented the 180 inhabitants of the remote Hebridean island as living in a sort of golden age, 'so little inclined to Impose upon Mankind, that perhaps no place in the World at this day knows such Instances of true primitive Honour and Simplicity', and, like More's Utopians, setting no value upon gold and silver. In a later work, *A Description of the Western Islands of Scotland* (1703), we can see how the new scientific wind is blowing when Martin tells us that 'Natural and Experimental Philosophy has been much improv'd' in modern days, 'and therefore Descriptions of Countries without the Natural History of 'em are now justly reckon'd to be defective'. He accordingly gives us full accounts of the fauna and flora of the Western Isles, but he also deals with ancient forts and stone circles, witchcraft and superstition, pagan survivals, and various local practices and customs. Dr. Johnson read Martin's book when he was a child, and he carried a copy of it with him on his tour with Boswell in 1773.

To the late seventeenth-century reader, however, travel normally connoted voyages or journeys to remote countries, and the remoter the better. Exquemelin's *Buccaniers of America* was translated in 1684, and with its tales of pirates, such as the Welshman Sir Henry Morgan, it proved to be very popular reading. More respectable voyages of exploration and discovery, however, found many serious readers, and added considerably to the Englishman's knowledge of the world. In 1666 the Royal Society issued 'Directions for Seamen bound for far Voyages', asking them to keep careful records of what they observed. In the same year Robert Boyle drew up a list of instructions to indicate the sort of information that would be welcomed by the Fellows of the Society, and this included a description of the inhabitants of distant countries, their physical features, diet, customs, diseases, the fruitfulness or barrenness of the women, and so on. By 1703, when John Churchill published his four-volume *Collection of Voyages and Travels*, the desired information was extended to include such matters as climate, government, religion, soil, languages, plants, animals, and natural or artificial rarities. Thus encouraged, a number of travellers published genuinely factual accounts of their often remarkable adventures, such as Lionel Wafer's *New Voyage and Description of the Isthmus of America* (1699), with its detailed account of trees and plants, and full description of the appearance, manners, customs, and even language of the native Indians. In *New England's Rarities Discovered* (1672) John Josselyn had given a careful account of the birds, beasts, serpents, fishes, and plants that he had seen in North America; and in *An Account of Two Voyages to New England* (1674), dedicated to the President and Fellows of the Royal Society, he provided further information about this still largely unknown territory. Josselyn has an engaging style, and he writes with emphatic contempt for those landlubbers who, 'sitting in the Chair of the scornful over their whiffs and draughts of intoxication will desperately censure the relations of the greatest Travellers'. Occasionally, however, the Fellows of the Royal Society must have raised an eyebrow when they read of Josselyn sailing, on 1 June 1638, past 'an inchanted island in very foggy weather'; or when they came on the account given him by 'one Mr. Mittin' of 'a Triton or Mereman which he saw in Cascobay. . . who laying his hands upon the side of the Canow, had one of them chopt off with a Hatchet by Mr. Mittin, which was in all respects like the hand of a Man, the Triton presently sunk, dying the water with his purple blood, and was no more seen'.

A more important work is Robert Knox's *Historical Relation of the Island of Ceylon*, published in 1681 with a Preface by Robert Hooke. Knox,[1] who was made a prisoner in 1659, when his father's ship was forced to run for shelter off the coast of Ceylon, remained in open captivity for more than nineteen years, and became thoroughly familiar with the country, its chief towns, its inhabitants and their way of life. On his eventual escape and return to England, he was with some difficulty persuaded by Hooke and others to write an account of the island and of his adventures, and this he did with intelligence and accuracy, introducing the English reader to a largely unknown but already advanced civilization.

The most famous seaman of the period, however, was

---

[1] Robert Knox (1641?–1720) was the son of a commander in the East India Company's service. In November 1659 the ship in which he was sailing was forced to put into Cottiar Bay, Ceylon, and he and his father and fourteen others were captured. He remained under open arrest for nineteen and a half years, escaping at length to Colombo and making his way home to England in 1680.

William Dampier,[1] whose *New Voyage round the World* (1697) ran rapidly through four editions before the close of the century, and was followed in 1698 by a volume of *Voyages and Descriptions*, giving in detail some of his experiences and observations not fully described in the earlier volume. In 1703 he published *A Voyage to New Holland* (i.e. Australia), the outcome of an expedition sponsored by the Admiralty, which was made difficult by a mutinous crew, and which ended in disaster with the loss of his leaky vessel and most of his papers. Dampier's books became extraordinarily popular, and must have been largely responsible for the boom in voyage literature in the early eighteenth century. As a buccaneer (from 1679 to 1688) he was able to record numerous adventures both on land and on the high seas; and as a scientific observer (the *New Voyage* was dedicated to the current President of the Royal Society) he was able to present accurate descriptions of whatever he saw. In the Preface to *A Voyage to New Holland* he apologized for both his matter and his manner of writing: it had been objected that his accounts and descriptions 'are dry and jejune, not filled with variety of pleasant Matter, to divert and gratify the curious Reader'. His answer is that he had another sort of reader in mind:

> But if I have been exactly and strictly careful to give only True Relations and Descriptions (as I am sure I have); and if my Descriptions be such as may be of use . . . to such Readers at home as are more desirous of a Plain and Just Account of the true Nature and State of Things Described than of a Polite and Rhetorical Narrative, I hope all the Defects in my Stile will meet with an easy and ready Pardon.

Dampier need not have worried: he writes in a natural, simple, and unimpeded fashion, and he finds the right words to make his readers see what he is describing. In his account of seals ('creatures pretty well known, yet it may not be amiss to describe them'), he tells us how they have long thick fins which

---

[1] William Dampier (1652–1715), the son of a tenant-farmer at East Coker, near Yeovil, went to sea in 1668. In 1673 he was in a naval engagement against the Dutch, and some years later he joined a party of buccaneers and took part in plundering Spanish possessions in South America. In 1698 he was given command of a vessel by the Admiralty, but proved to be an unsuccessful leader of men. In 1708 he signed on as a pilot with Captain Woodes Rogers in a voyage round the world, and it was during this cruise that Alexander Selkirk was rescued from the lonely island of Juan Fernandez. Dampier early formed the habit of keeping accurate records, and proved himself an excellent observer and navigator.

serve . . . instead of Legs to them when on the Land for raising their
Bodies up on end, by the help of these Fins or Stumps; and so
having their Tail-parts drawn close under them, they rebound,
as it were, and throw their Bodies forward, drawing their hinder-
parts after them; and then again rising up, and springing forward
with their fore-parts alternately, they lie tumbling thus up and
down all the while they are moving on Land.

Only the un-selfconscious author can write like this. 'Mr.
Addison', Pope once remarked, 'could not give out a common
order in writing from his always endeavouring to word it too
finely': Dampier, on the other hand, is the plain blunt man
who only speaks right on, and his honest and unpretentious
prose is adequate to every call upon it.

Those various accounts of unknown lands and their inhabitants made a considerable impact on the contemporary imagination; and a little later the voyage to far countries was to
have literary repercussions in the work of Defoe, Swift, and
many lesser men. Evidence drawn from the habits and beliefs
of primitive peoples was sometimes used by such writers as
Locke and Bentley to support their arguments about the origins of society or the nature of religion. The Deists welcomed
reports about the existence of natural religion among the
Indians and other tribes, and cited them in support of their contention that religion was invariably corrupted by priestcraft.
Some good Christians like the Revd. Lancelot Addison (the
father of the essayist), who had lived for many years among
nations of a different faith, were apt to feel that the English,
like the ancient Greeks, were too prone to think all nations
barbarous but their own. In the Preface to his *West Barbary*
(1671), dealing with the Moors of Fez and Morocco, Addison
admitted that his main purpose in writing his book was to make
apparent 'the Justice and Religiousness of a People esteemed
Barbarous, Rude, and Savage', and to make Christians examine
their credentials to be 'the only Illuminati of both'. Addison was
especially impressed by Moorish legal practice; the judges were
easy of access, and cases were tried fairly and without delay:
'Here's no Intreaguing the Plea with Resolutions, Cases, Presi-
dents, Reports, Moth-eaten Statutes, etc. But every thing is
determin'd according to the fresh Circumstances of the Fact,
and the Proof of what is alleg'd.' We might be listening to the
voice of Lemuel Gulliver.

In one way or another the armchair travel which the books of Lancelot Addison, Robert Knox, William Dampier, and others were now making possible, and the growing realization that civilizations of an advanced kind existed in many countries outside Europe, must have done a good deal to broaden the Englishman's mind; and an increasing awareness that religions are unexpectedly diverse, that morality is not absolute, and that social customs vary with race and climate and tradition, may have done something to make him a little less intolerant.

VIII

RELIGIOUS LITERATURE

(1)

NEXT to the Restoration of the monarchy, the most urgent task to be tackled in 1660 was the restoration, in some form or other, of th eChurch of England. If the general direction of the Restoration settlement was to be a return to the *status quo*, no department of the national life was in greater need of attention than the Church Establishment. The whole fabric of the Anglican Church lay in ruins, a reminder of the long years of Puritan rebellion, and a source of danger for the new order. What gave the settlement of the Church an especial urgency was the fact that the storm which had finally swept Charles I from his throne was partly of religious origin, and as the Civil War dragged on it was mainly the religious die-hards on both sides who kept up the national division, and ultimately made all compromise impossible. Events had proved to Charles II that his grandfather's 'No bishop, no king' was only too shrewd a forecast; and if the new King showed himself willing enough at first to reach an agreement with, at least, the Presbyterians, events drove Clarendon and others before long to oppose anything less than the complete restoration of the national Church, and the firm re-establishment of its episcopate and its authority.

The wave of popularity on which Charles came back to his throne in 1660 was due mainly to the fact that a majority of the nation ardently desired a return to constitutional government. The rule of a despot, the rule of the army, the rule of the saints, all these now seemed to most Englishmen intolerable; and to many it appeared that most of the nation's troubles had started from the determination of the individual to be a law to himself, and, more especially, to act in accordance with the guidance of his own conscience, and as the spirit moved him. Anglican divines spent a good deal of their time after the Restoration in preaching against the inner light, for they rightly recognized it as the greatest threat to a disciplined national Church. 'Let a man but persuade himself', said South,

that the *Spirit* dwells *personally* in him, and speaks upon all occasions to him; how easily and readily may he plead that the *Spirit* tells him he may kill his enemy, plunder his neighbour, cast off all obedience to his governors. . . . Thus the late rebel army having conquer'd and imprison'd their conscience as well as their prince, *completed* all by bringing *the Spirit* to their lure, and reducing Enthusiasm to an act; still governing all their transactions with their abused Sovereign by this invincible principle which enabled them with so much ease to charge through the obligation of all law, oaths, and promises whatsoever.

There is, indeed, no answer to those who see this inner light; and any government that has to control such subjects can effect little by argument or persuasion:

> For as of Vagabonds we say,
> That they are ne're beside their way:
> What'ere men speak by this *new Light*,
> Still they are sure to be i' th' right.
> 'Tis a *dark-Lanthorn* of the Spirit
> Which none see by but those that bear it.

In assessing the strength of the reaction against Puritanism in the years immediately following the Restoration, we cannot afford to forget the popularity of Butler's *Hudibras*, which put in an idiomatic and colloquial jingle what so many Englishmen had come to think and feel about the religious sectarians.

The danger to the Establishment was all the greater because the majority of the sectarians were, understandably enough, to be found among the poor and uneducated. Many of their preachers (not excepting Bunyan) gloried in their humble origin, and firmly believed that it gave them a better hope of salvation than the worldly goods of their richer neighbours, and that their lack of education saved them from the spiritual pride and corruption of the sophisticated. George Fox the Quaker had an 'opening from the Lord that to be at Oxford or Cambridge was not sufficient to fit a man to be a minister of Christ', and thereafter he 'regarded the priests less, and looked more after the dissenting people'. It was inevitable that the opponents of the sectarians should equate 'enthusiasm' and 'inspiration' with ignorance, and suggest that the inner light shone only for those who took the easy way, and who, either from intellectual incapacity or from laziness, preferred to base their religion on personal revelation. 'Some call it Gifts', Butler wrote,

and some *New Light*;
A Liberal Art, that costs no pains
Of Study, Industry, or Brains.

When Butler proceeded to draw a picture of the reformers at the outbreak of the Civil War, it was the tinkers, the sow-gelders, and the hucksters who were his bawling protagonists:

The *Oyster-women* lock'd their Fish up,
And trudg'd away to cry, *No Bishop*.
The *Mousetrap-men* laid *Save-alls* by,
And 'gainst *Ev'l Counsellors* did cry.
Botchers left old cloaths in the lurch,
And fell to turn and patch the *Church*. . . .

There was nothing High Church about John Locke; but he too, in a long psychological analysis of 'enthusiasm' in his *Essay concerning Human Understanding*, animadverted against those who preferred the easier way of revelation to 'the tedious and not always successful labour of strict reasoning'; and who believed that 'whatever groundless Opinion comes to settle itself strongly upon their Fancies, is an Illumination from the Spirit of God, and presently of divine Authority'. So, too, 'whatsoever odd Action they find in themselves a strong Inclination to do, that Impulse is concluded to be a Call or Direction from Heaven, and must be obeyed'.

In opposition to such ignorant opinionativeness the Anglican divines preached a reasonable Christianity, and laid much emphasis on sound moral conduct. In Simon Patrick's *Friendly Debate betwixt . . . a Conformist and a Non-Conformist* (1669), the Nonconformist objects to the sermons of Anglican divines on the ground that they are 'but rational discourses'. 'The Doctrine of *Good works*', he also complains, 'is always sounding from your Pulpits.' To this the Conformist retorts that 'rational' is not, as the Nonconformist appears to believe, the opposite of 'spiritual': it is the opposite of 'irrational' or 'absurd'. His quarrel with the Nonconformists is precisely that 'they taught men first to despise sober and plain Doctrine, which teaches them their Duty toward

God and their Neighbour, entertaining them with finer Speculations of pretended Gospel-Mysteries and Manifestations. . . .
Our Ministers teach men their Duty, and yours do not.' To the
essentially patrician Robert South, the spiritual democracy of
the sectarians was anarchy; the 'common rout' were like 'a
Drove of Sheep, or an Herd of Oxen', which may be 'managed
by any Noise, or Cry, which their Drivers shall accustom them
to'. All the more need, then, for their spiritual guides to be
educated men, since the knowledge of good and evil is 'a thing
too large to be compassed, and too hard to be mastered, without Brains and Study, Parts, and Contemplation; which Providence never thought fit to make much the greatest Part of
Mankind Possessors of'. It was the new and dangerous independence of the ignorant multitude that the Church set its face
against, in its own interest first of all, but ultimately in the
interest of the State. It was something new and undesirable,
and quite unknown 'till the late age', that any man who had
served his apprenticeship to a smith or a tailor should feel
himself entitled to 'commence Doctor or Divine, from the
Shop-board or the Anvil; or from whistling a Team, come to
preach to a Congregation'.

One of the clearest statements of the Anglican attitude to the
Dissenters is to be found in a continuation of Bacon's *New Atlantis* by Joseph Glanvill (1676).[1] There, in the fictitious setting
of Bacon's imaginary island, we meet with the unmistakable
equivalents of the English sectarians, in a country where

every Man vented his *Conceits* for *Articles of Faith*, and told his
Dreams for *Revelations*, and then pretended he was extraordinarily
enlightned, and strove to make Proselites, and quarrel'd with all
that did not embrace his Fancies, and *separated* from the *Communion* of the Church, and endeavour'd to involve the World in
Hurries and Distractions; and all *this*, for the sake of a few *pittiful,
needless, senseless Trifles*.

Faced with this situation, the anti-fanatical divines (all imbued
with the new scientific spirit)

[1] Joseph Glanvill (1636–80) was educated at Exeter College, and later at
Lincoln College, Oxford. In his early book, *The Vanity of Dogmatising*, he criticized the scholastic philosophy still dominant at Oxford. He became a Fellow of
the Royal Society in 1664, and continued to write treatises in favour of the new
science, but he also published a number of religious works. From 1666 until his
death he was Rector of the Abbey Church at Bath, where he lies buried.

took notice of the loud Out-cries and Declamations that were among all the Sects against *Reason*; and observ'd, how by *that means* all Vanities and *Phanatick* Devices were brought into Religion: They saw, There was no likelyhood any stop should be put to those Extravagancies of Fansie that were impudently obtruding themselves upon the World but by *vindicating* and *asserting* the use of *Reason* in *Religion*; and therefore their *private* Discourses and publick *Exercises* ran much *this* way; to maintain the sober use of our Faculties, and to expose all vain Enthusiasms.

Furthermore,

because Morality was despised by those elevated Fantasticks that talk'd so much of *Imputed Righteousness*, in the false sense, and accounted by them as a *dull* and *low* thing; therefore those Divines labour'd in the asserting and vindicating of this: teaching the *necessity* of Moral Vertues; that Christianity is the *highest improvement* of them; That the meer *first-table* Religion is nothing without the works of the *second*; that *Zeal* and *Devoutness*, and delight in *hearing Prayer*, and other externals of Worship, may be in very evil men. . . .

Glanvill was a latitudinarian; and in what follows—an assertion that most of the disputed points that separate Protestants are not fundamental at all, and that a little more charity and broad-mindedness would prevent most of the schisms and separations in the Church—he would no doubt have been repudiated by High-Church divines; but in his emphasis on reason and on morality and good works he was stating what was in fact orthodox Anglican doctrine.

Glanvill himself was a temperate man, but many of his fellow clergymen were not. Yet many devout Churchmen had worthy enough reasons for their dislike of the Dissenters: they loved the dignified worship of their Church, its liturgy, its rites and ceremonies. Good Anglicans, too, saw the Church of England as the *via media* between Roman Catholicism and Protestant dissent. To Simon Patrick, writing in 1662, it seemed only proper to praise 'that vertuous mediocrity which our Church observes between the meretricious gaudiness of the Church of Rome and the squalid sluttery of Fanatick conventicles'. The Papists, he continues (anticipating the basic metaphor of *A Tale of a Tub*), have overclothed their Church with a multitude of garments, while some modern reformers, to make amends, 'have stripped her starke naked, till she is become in a manner cold and dead'. In place of the dignified and traditional service of the Church of England, the sectarian preachers had substituted extempore prayers, and their congregations were at the mercy of some '*holderforth*' whose chief concern was, in the sarcastic phrase of South, 'to vaunt his spiritual clack'.

If this kind of thing was bad enough in England, it became insupportable when one crossed the Border, and got all the canting and snuffling piety of the Kirk expressed in an uncouth dialect. In 1692 a popular compilation called *The Scotch Presbyterian Eloquence* provided the English reader with choice extracts from extempore prayers ejaculated before Scots congregations. Thus Mr. John Dickson praying for grace is alleged to have cried: 'Lord, dibble thou the kail-seed of thy Grace in our hearts, and if we grow not up to good kail, Lord make us good Sprouts at least!' In a similarly familiar vein the incumbent of Pitsligo exclaimed in another prayer: 'O Lord, thou'rt like a Mousie peeping out at a hole of a Wall, for thou seest us but we see not thee!' Such reported utterances are probably authentic, or nearly so, and they betray a confident and democratic familiarity with the Almighty which could only appear to the good Anglican as the very height of irreverence. In the same volume we are also given some extracts from typical sermons preached in Scottish kirks, with much emphasis on the broken and smothered locution, the whining delivery, and the drivelling at mouth and eyes. 'All they do', we are told, 'is to affect the Passions, and not the Judgment.' It is the old familiar criticism of the unorthodox or evangelical preacher.[1] It was bad enough to have this sort of thing going on at all; it was still worse when those who frequented conventicles and encouraged this travesty of religious worship sneered at the decent and orderly services of the Established Church, 'scoffing at our Liturgy, and the Users of it', as South complained, 'and thereby alienating the Minds of the People from it, to such a degree, that many Thousands are drawn by them into a fatal Schism'. In the polemics of Anglican divines we can often hear the voice of the elder brother of the Prodigal Son: *he* has not indulged in spiritual orgies, *his* religion has remained decent

---

[1] On 14 May 1669 Pepys dined with Archbishop Sheldon at Lambeth, and after dinner the company were entertained by Cornet Bolton, 'a very gentleman-like man', that 'behind a chair did pray and preach like a Presbyter Scot, with all the possible imitation in grimaces and voice . . . till it made us all burst'.

and undramatic. The Anglican divine scorned to compete with the Nonconformist in his appeal to the passions; he would not stoop to turn his services into a puppet play, acting his part from the pulpit 'with a beggar's tone' or a 'lamentable look'. Such effects might appeal to the vulgar and unthinking, but to the educated man they were contemptible. And not merely contemptible; they were also dangerous. We may smile at Samuel Parker's suggestion (in *A Discourse of Ecclesiastical Politie*, 1670) that 'the most effectual cure of all our present distempers' would be an Act of Parliament 'to abridge Preachers the use of fulsome and lushious Metaphors'. But if the zeal of the Church of England had almost eaten him up, Parker knew what he was talking about: 'For were Men obliged to speak Sense as well as Truth, all the swelling *Mysteries of Fanaticism* would immediately sink into flat and empty Nonsense. . . .'

Many, no doubt, who were by no means ardent members of the Church found the idiom of the Dissenters offensive as a mere matter of taste. Such phrases as being 'Godded with God' and 'Christed with Christ', such 'unsavoury, clownish and undecent expressions' as repentance being a 'purgative' or 'pill', such morbid ideas as 'lying so long a-soke in the blood of Jesus', grated upon the ears of a Halifax or a Congreve no less than on those of a South or a Stillingfleet. They belonged to a jargon hideous in itself, and doubly unwelcome from its associations with the Commonwealth period. Class differences undoubtedly played a large part here. 'The better sort of Hearers', wrote Simon Patrick in 1669, 'are now out of love with these things.' Much of the preaching and the hortatory writing of the Nonconformists, in fact, has the characteristic marks of popular Sunday journalism, from which 'the better sort' of every generation can be counted upon to recoil. The Anglican distaste for the vocabulary and idiom of Nonconformist pastors and writers is one expression of the aristocratic spirit of the age.

To some extent, again, it is possible to see the division between Anglicans and Nonconformists as another aspect of the battle between the Ancients and the Moderns. The Anglican priest naturally felt himself to be the trustee of a venerable ecclesiastical tradition, performing the unvarying offices of the Church and celebrating its time-hallowed ritual. When he prayed, his prayers were not the spontaneous overflow of the thoughts that momentarily entered his mind as he faced his congregation, but the traditional and beautifully phrased exercises appointed for that particular day. When he preached, it is true that he was able to rely, like Swift's bee, on his own flights and his own language, but for the most part he used his freedom with a measure of restraint. The Nonconformist, on the other hand, seemed to him to take a mistaken delight in his ability to preach and pray extempore; and most Anglicans would probably have been willing to apply to him Johnson's remark on Macpherson's *Ossian*, that anyone might utter such stuff 'if he would *abandon* his mind to it'. Like Swift's spider, the Nonconformist boasted 'of being obliged to no other creature, but of drawing and spinning out all from [him]self'. The resemblance between religious and literary inspiration, and the implied inadequacy of both kinds as a basis for either religion or literature, was suggested by Dryden in some sarcastic observations on Elkanah Settle:

Mr. Settle having never studied any sort of learning but poetry, and that but slenderly, as you may find by his writings, and having besides no other advantages, must make very lame work on't; he himself declares, he neither reads nor cares for conversation; so that he would persuade us he is a kind of fanatic in poetry, and has a light within him, and writes by an inspiration. . . .

If we were to substitute Bunyan for Settle, and rewrite this passage to read: 'Mr. Bunyan having never studied any sort of learning but the Bible, and having besides no other advantages, must make very lame work on't', those words would express the view of most orthodox Anglican divines of the period. 'Inspiration' was a dangerous delusion, leading to every kind of eccentricity, individualism, and fanaticism, and ultimately making an orderly and law-abiding community impossible.

(11)

In view of the eminence of so many Anglican preachers after the Restoration, it may seem odd that some good Churchmen looked with disfavour on the keen contemporary interest in sermons. To men like South the craze for listening to sermons was an infallible mark of the sectarian, and therefore another legacy of the rebellion. In one of his own sermons he brings in a Puritan who claims that he is a great hearer and lover of sermons, which are the main business of his life, 'and tho' indeed, according to the good old Puritan custom, I use to walk and talk out the Prayers before the Church-door, or without the Choir, yet I am sure to be always in *at Sermon*'. Writing in 1673 the author of *The Ladies Calling* remarks: 'This last age has brought in such a partiality for preaching, that prayer seems comparatively despicable in their eyes.' No doubt there was some danger of the sermon's occupying a place of disproportionate importance among the Nonconformists, but before long this tendency was almost equally marked among the Anglicans. Preaching before the King, before the Lord Mayor, at the Temple, at Oxford and Cambridge, a Barrow or a South or a Tillotson all tended to rise to the occasion and put forth a set piece, and the habit of preaching elaborate sermons spread downwards to the lesser clergy. Towards the close of the century, in his *Discourse of the Pastoral Care* (1692), Burnet notes that preaching 'has now gained so much Esteem in the World, that a Clergyman cannot maintain his Credit, nor bring his People to a constant Attendance on the Worship of God, unless he is happy in these Performances'.

The keen contemporary interest in sermons is borne out not only by the comments of such a connoisseur as John Evelyn, but by the considerable number of discourses on the art of preaching published during the period. In the Anglican sermon there was a steady movement—perhaps more noticeable in theory than in practice—towards simplicity. In London and the two university towns a preacher might be addressing an educated and even learned audience; but in country towns and villages his fine phrases, nice distinctions, and learned allusions would mean little to the congregation. Critics of contemporary preaching such as Eachard, Glanvill, and James Arderne were thinking mostly of the rural parson; they were rightly concerned about the hungry sheep all over the country who looked up and were not fed, and who were therefore in some danger of being lost to the Church and won over to Nonconformity. There is some evidence, however, that a certain smattering of Latin and Greek in a sermon continued to impress simple folk, in the same way as the learning of Goldsmith's schoolmaster aroused the admiration of his pupils. The story is told of the famous oriental scholar Edward Pococke, who deliberately preached in as simple a style as possible to his parishioners at Childrey in Berkshire, but apparently disappointed them by doing so. 'Our parson is one Mr. Pococke,' a friend of his was told, 'a plain honest man,

but master, he is no Latiner.' One of the writers who undertook
to answer Eachard's criticism of clergymen who paraded their
learning in their sermons thought that it might be a good
thing 'for the minister to quote out of the learned Greek and
Latin, though nobody understands it, to distinguish him from
such who preach in English altogether at conventicles'. But
the modern practice was increasingly that recommended by
Glanvill in 1678, when he warned the young clergyman against
'an affected use of Scraps of Greek and Latin, things of no Service
to the vulgar, by whom they are not understood; and by the
wise they are now generally despised'. No less objectionable, it
was now thought, was the preacher who attempted to show his
ingenuity by choosing barren or difficult texts.

Equally out of fashion by the close of the century were those
stylistic devices which Glanvill summed up as 'a bastard kind
of eloquence . . . which consists in affectations of wit and
finery, flourishes, metaphors, and cadencies'. A plea for a
plain and simple style of preaching had been made as early as
1646 by John Wilkins in his *Ecclesiastes*, but the first notable
attack on pulpit eloquence after the Restoration came from
Robert South, in a sermon preached at Oxford in 1668. This
was all the more remarkable as it came from a man who was
at that time Public Orator to the University. Perspicuity,
plainness, and simplicity were the qualities that South advocated in preaching, and he condemned 'difficult Nothings,
Rabbinical Whimsies, and remote Allusions', together with
'highflown Metaphors and Allegories, attended and set off
with Scraps of Greek and Latin'. Although South was an im-
placable critic of the Nonconformists, it is clear that in his
strictures on rhetorical extravagance he was not thinking of
the dissenting preachers exclusively. In a well-known passage
where he is commending the preaching of St. Paul he glances
obviously at Jeremy Taylor: 'Nothing here of *the Fringes of the
Northstar* . . . nothing of *the Down of Angels Wings*, or *the beautiful
Locks of Cherubims*: no starched Similitudes, introduced with a
"*Thus I have seen a Cloud rolling in its airy Mansion*", and the like.'
In general, however, it is against the emotional style of the
sectarians that South directs his satire, and in this he is
followed by Simon Patrick, Samuel Parker, and others. As
for his own preaching style, South was a law to himself; so far
as plainness is concerned, he would often have had to admit,

video meliora, proboque; deteriora sequor. He was only as plain as his brilliant and mordant wit would allow him to be: it was men like Tillotson and Stillingfleet who established the cool and reasonable and lucid style that eventually came to be characteristic of Anglican preaching.

Where so much depends on fashions of taste, and where we have to reckon not only with brilliant individualists like South, but also with minority differences due to class or education, it is vain to look for unanimity in the theory and practice of preaching. If the general drift of Anglican sermons was towards sobriety and simplicity, there were 'pathetic' preachers like Anthony Horneck attracting large congregations, or the Scottish Bishop Robert Leighton, venerated by such different men as his fellow countryman Burnet in his own day, and the poet Coleridge in the nineteenth century. The sermons and other writings of this gentle and humble Christian have all the beauty of holiness, and Burnet's testimony to his power in the pulpit— 'I never once saw a wandering Eye where he preached; and have seen whole Assemblies often *melt in Tears* before him'— is not hard to credit. Among the Nonconformists there were plain and sober preachers such as Richard Baxter. The difficulty of pleasing different tastes was noted by Baxter in *A Call to the Unconverted*: 'If Ministers deal plainly with you, you say they rail. If they speak gently or coldly, you either sleep under them or are little more affected than the seats you sit upon.' In 1678, after advocating the plain style of preaching for many years, Glanvill appears to have had second thoughts about the effectiveness of the purely rational discourse. He does not intend, he now says, to reprehend all wit whatever in preaching:

For true Wit is a perfection in our faculties, chiefly in the understanding and imagination; Wit in the understanding is a sagacity to find out the nature, relations, and consequences of things: Wit in the imagination is a quickness in the phancy to give things proper Images; now the more of these in sermons, the more of judgment and spirit, and life: and without Wit of these kinds, Preaching is dull and unedifying.

It has been suggested that when he took this stand Glanvill had come under the influence of French criticism, such as that of Rapin, whose *Réflexions sur l'usage de l'éloquence de ce temps* had appeared in 1672, and was translated into English in the same year; but it is perhaps more probable that his partial recantation in favour of a warmer and more imaginative style was due to his own practical experience as a preacher. Although he was still convinced that 'the best and most lasting affections are such as are raised by the understanding and the knowledge of our duties and our interest', he had found that the plain rational sermon (Baxter's speaking 'gently and coldly') had little effect on the common people, whose 'affections are raised by figures and earnestness and passionate representations, . . . so that however little you may think these, they must be heeded, and suited to the capacity and genius of your hearers'. In theory, therefore, as well as in practice, we must expect to find a considerable variety of approach in the sermon, depending on the occasion and on the nature of the audience.

Finally, on the questions of whether sermons should be written out and read to the congregation, Anglicans and Non-conformists were divided, though again the lines of division are rather blurred. In the years immediately following the Restoration, extempore preaching seemed to most orthodox Anglican divines to be the mark of sectarian 'holders-forth', who ranted and wept and poured forth their unthinking and spontaneous verbiage about 'indwellings' and 'outgoings', 'free grace', 'motions of the spirit', 'closing with Christ', 'getting into Christ', and so on. This was indeed the 'mechanical operation of the spirit'. At the opposite extreme from this were the closely reasoned and carefully written sermons of men like Barrow and Stillingfleet. In fact, however, the Nonconformist sermon was often composed with great care; it might be read, but more often, perhaps, it was memorized. Here again Baxter expresses the difficulty of pleasing everybody: 'One will not hear a Minister because he readeth his Sermons, and another will not hear him because he doth not read 'em.' Unexpectedly enough, Charles II's taste in preaching must have had some influence on the practice of Anglican divines. The King had to sit through a large number of sermons in the course of a year, and he had a decided preference for the extempore address. In 1674 the practice of reading sermons was censured in 'the King's name' at both Oxford and Cambridge. At all events, the custom of preaching from notes appears to have become the usual practice in the Anglican service before the end of the century. Evelyn, who heard Sprat preach a fine sermon on 23 November 1679, remarked that 'Dr. Sprat's talent was a greate memorie, never making use of notes'; but such virtuosity was probably always unusual, and behind it, of course, lay the most careful preparation. 'I know indeed some that preach *without writing*,' Glanvill observes, 'but their preaching is not therefore *Extempore*; *Extempore* is *unthought*, not *unwritten*.' The normal practice, no doubt, lay somewhere between the two extremes of reading and of preaching without recourse to a manuscript; and this seems to be what Burnet has in mind in a passage dealing with preaching in his *Discourse of Pastoral Care*. Burnet is in favour of extempore preaching, provided a man has 'a Life and Flame in his Thoughts': if he has, 'he will often feel that *while he is musing, a Fire is kindled within him*, and then he will *speak with Authority*, and without Constraint'. He may even be carried 'as it were, out of himself', but yet (Burnet hastens to add) 'without anything that is frantick or enthusiastical'.

In general, the Anglican sermons of the later seventeenth century make better reading than those of the Nonconformists, if only because they are comparatively free from religious jargon, and because they suffer much less from an emotionalism that may have been moving when the sermon was delivered, but is either ineffective or even distasteful on the printed page. At their best they have the intellectual beauty of a well-sustained and illuminating argument.

This is nowhere better seen than in the sermons of Isaac Barrow.[1] If tobacco, as Barrow claimed, 'tended to compose and regulate his thoughts', it can rarely have been employed to better purpose. His sermons and theological writings are the product of a mind perpetually alert, but always equable. Barrow encourages his hearer or reader to think, but makes thinking easy and pleasant because each stage in the argument has been so well prepared for him, and is so lucidly expressed.

[1] Isaac Barrow, the son of a linen-draper, was born in 1630, educated at the Charterhouse and Felstead School, and then (during the Civil War) at Trinity College, Cambridge. In spite of his Royalist leanings he was elected a Fellow of Trinity in 1649. Out of sympathy with the England of Cromwell, he travelled in France, Italy, and the Near East from 1655 to 1659, and on his return took orders in the Church of England. After the Restoration he became in turn Professor of Greek at Cambridge, Professor of Geometry at Gresham College, and finally the first Lucasian Professor of Mathematics at Cambridge, resigning this chair to Isaac Newton in 1669 to pursue his theological studies. Charles II made him a royal chaplain, a D.D. by royal mandate in 1670, and in 1673 Master of Trinity College. He died at the age of 47, 'the best scholar in England', having published little; but his theological works (including his sermons and *A Treatise of the Pope's Supremacy*) were edited by Tillotson in four volumes (1683–7).

When Charles II made him (Barrow was one of his chaplains) Master of Trinity College, Cambridge, he observed that he was giving the appointment to 'the best scholar in England', and he was probably right. The width of Barrow's reading is perhaps most apparent in his *Treatise of the Pope's Supremacy*, where his controversial purpose necessitates frequent quotation from the early Christian Fathers and the later Catholic apologists. In his sermons, where he seems almost anxious to conceal his learning, he nevertheless marshals his argument with the relentless thoroughness of the scholar. Barrow wins us, not by any sudden flashes of insight or by any notable liveliness in his imagery, but by his complete mastery of his theme, and by a manly sincerity and simple goodness of heart. 'The proper work of Man,' he tells us, 'the grand drift of humane life, is to follow Reason, . . . not to sooth fancy, that brutish, shallow, and giddy power, able to perform nothing worthy much regard. . . . It is simple Reason (as dull and dry as it seemeth) which expediteth all the grand affairs, which accomplisheth all the mighty works that we see done in the world.' Barrow holds fast to reason, and indeed seeks to reason men into virtue. Yet it is not so much his rational faculty as his essential gentleness of heart that leads him, in one sermon after another, to exhort his hearers to love one another, and to refrain from uncharitableness, satirical jesting, and other unsociable acts. Much of his humane wisdom is that of the Cambridge Fellow accustomed to living in an academic society, and aware that men must bear with one another.

Barrow composed his sermons with care and deliberation, and in writing them he seems to have drawn freely on a copious and precise vocabulary. The most remarkable feature of his style is its occasional colloquialism, which mitigates his habitual seriousness with an air of pleasant negligence. Whether this style was natural to him, or caught by him from the prevailing idiom of the Court, or consciously adopted by him to lighten his discourse in an age 'wherein', as he complained, 'plain reason is deemed a dull and heavy thing', it is impossible to determine; but it is a feature of preaching that had become less common by the end of the century.

Robert South[1] is the kind of prelate that one would expect

---

[1] Robert South (1634–1716), the son of a London merchant, was educated at Westminster School (where Dryden was one of his contemporaries) and at Christ

to meet with in Restoration London. In an age that valued men of wit highly he could hold his own with the best of them; his drolleries and sarcasms invariably have a sharp edge, and are indeed the sudden thrusts of an intellectual aristocrat, exposing human weakness and pretence as relentlessly as the satire of Swift. Yet Dryden's favourite tag '*Nunc non erat his locus*' must apply in some measure to South's pulpit sallies. Swift kept his wit out of his sermons and saved it for his satirical pieces; if only South had written a few such pieces too he would have gained a securer place in the history of English literature. But although South's wit was sometimes indecorous in the pulpit, it was the natural expression of an acute and lively mind, and we have certainly no right to attribute it to any lack of serious intention. Indeed, no preacher ever pressed harder on the conscience of his congregation, and South could claim to possess abundantly one of the virtues that he remarked in the good clergyman, that of 'daring to look Vice in the face, though never so potent and illustrious'. With another of the clergyman's virtues—'to be Gentle, Courteous, and Compassionate to all'—he was more sparingly endowed. Towards the dissenting sects—the 'pert, empty, conceited Holder-forth' and his 'ignorant, whining, factious followers'—he showed no sort of mercy, and he pursued them in one sermon after another with the lash of his patrician and High-Church invective. But he showed the same forthright scorn for the Presbyterians with their 'post-dated Loyalty' who 'do but cover their Prevarication with a Fig-leaf', and for his own Anglican contemporary Sherlock, with whom he became involved in a controversy about the Trinity. In general he belongs to that type of divine who preaches for regular churchgoers, and is more concerned to strengthen the bonds that bind them to the Church than to reach the ungodly and the Nonconformist.

In the history of pulpit eloquence South is notable for his

Church, Oxford. He was ordained by the deprived Bishop Sydserf in 1658, and became in 1660 chaplain to the Earl of Clarendon, who procured for him the degrees of B.D. and D.D. three years later. From 1660 to 1667 he was Public Orator to the University of Oxford, and was soon well known for his witty and vigorous sermons, in which the Dissenters in particular were held up to scorn and ridicule. Charles II, who enjoyed his preaching, had some thoughts of making South a bishop, but forgot to do so. Late in life (1713) he was offered, but declined, the see of Rochester. In 1676 he went to Poland as chaplain to the English ambassador, and wrote a long and interesting account of that country in a letter to Edward Pococke.

ability to make his ideas immediately intelligible and memorable to the average churchgoer. He had, in a remarkable degree, what he called 'that Power or Ability of the Mind which suggests apposite and pertinent Expressions, and handsome Ways of cloathing and setting off those Truths which the Judgment has rationally pitched upon'. He had a natural gift for illustration and comparison, occasionally over-ingenious and sometimes calculated to disturb the equanimity of the more conventional worshipper, but never failing to arrest the attention. It is unlikely that any congregation ever slept at one of South's sermons, for the mind of the preacher was perpetually alert. 'Piety', as he once observed, 'engages no Man to be dull.' South's phraseology is close to the conversation of the polite gentleman, although at times, with its 'God is not to be flammed off with Lies' or 'that old formal Hocus who denied the Beggar a Farthing', it may verge (coming from where it does) on the over-colloquial. Perhaps his most remarkable gift as a preacher is an untiring energy of mind which advances the argument with an apparently effortless buoyancy. In one of his early sermons, 'The Scribe Instructed', he observed that a discourse 'which is carried on with a continued, unflagging Vigor of Expression can never be thought tedious, nor consequently long'. His own sermons certainly bear this out. Most of them were preached to learned or fashionable congregations, and his quick, logical, and allusive mind would have been unsuited to the intellectual small change of a country parish. But in his own field he was one of the great English masters of preaching; and it is only a decline of interest in sermons that has allowed the modern reader to remain for the most part ignorant of the remarkable vigour of South's mind, the brilliant relevance of his phrasing, and his penetrating knowledge of human nature.

More characteristic of the later-seventeenth-century divine is John Tillotson,[1] whose sober and reasonable sermons helped

---

[1] John Tillotson (1630–94), the son of a prosperous cloth-worker, was born at Sowerby, Yorkshire. He entered Clare College, Cambridge, at the time when Dr. Ralph Cudworth was Master, but he was never attracted by the school of Cambridge Platonists. He had for some time been moving away from his early Calvinism, and shortly after the Restoration he was ordained by Bishop Sydserf. He played some part at the Savoy Conference on the side of the Presbyterians, but soon conformed to the Church of England and quickly became a popular preacher, doing as much as any of his contemporaries to establish a plain style of pulpit oratory. He was appointed a chaplain to Charles II, Dean of Canterbury in 1672, Dean of St. Paul's in 1689, and, on the suspension of Sancroft in 1691, Archbishop

to establish the accepted style of preaching for several generations. Tillotson, who had been a Dissenter in his youth, may have gone out of his way to avoid the slightest trace of what good Anglicans would have called 'fanaticism'; but in any event he would have agreed with Swift that it is not the business of the preacher to 'move the passions', but 'only to work upon faith and reason'. Tillotson's intellectual position was accurately stated by himself in a sermon on 'The Hazard of being Saved in the Church of Rome', when he declared: 'I do in my Conscience believe the Church of England to be the best constituted Church this day in the world; . . . securing men on the one hand from the wild freaks of *Enthusiasm*; and on the other, from the gross follies of *Superstition*.' But whereas South had preached with almost greater fervour against the 'enthusiasm' of the Dissenters than against the 'superstition' of the Roman Catholics, Tillotson reserved his severest condemnation for the Church of Rome; indeed, this was about the only theme that could ruffle his quiet temperament. Normally, he preferred to avoid disputatious topics, devoting himself 'by the best arguments I could think of, to gain men over to a *firm belief* and serious *practice* of the main things of Religion'. Burnet, who knew him well, remarked on his 'clear head' and 'sweet temper', and the secret of Tillotson's success in an age torn by controversy probably lay in his emotional and intellectual equilibrium. One can respect Tillotson without finding his Addisonian equability very interesting. The quiet voice argues persuasively; the tone is eminently reasonable, and the exposition is so lucid that it must have prevailed with the humblest worshipper. But this even tenor and this engaging simplicity are apt in time to defeat their purpose: 'we cannot blame indeed, but we may sleep'. Tillotson is perhaps the preacher's preacher; but for the unrighteous or even the moderately good he is insufficiently stimulating. If he does risk a metaphor, it is usually a conventional one, such as 'healing divisions' or 'quenching flames'. But so far as his contemporaries were concerned, this was all in his favour; and we have it on Burnet's authority that he had 'the most correct style of all our divines, and was esteemed the best preacher of the age'. Decorum and drowsiness were setting

---

of Canterbury. Tillotson, a friend of Richard Baxter, tried hard to obtain some measure of comprehension for Protestant Dissenters, but remained inflexible towards Roman Catholicism.

in: the church was now a place for seemly worship, and the sermon was on the way to becoming a religious essay. The change may be gauged in part by the frequency with which Tillotson uses the first personal pronoun in his sermons (almost in the manner of Mr. Spectator), and by his tendency to put himself on the same level as his congregation, who are as often 'we' as 'you'. When he died in 1694, Burnet preached his funeral sermon and praised him for keeping a sort of golden mean in his sermons: 'Neither did his Thoughts sink, nor his Stile swell. . . . He said what was just necessary to give clear Ideas of things, and no more: He laid aside all long and affected Periods: His Sentences were short and clear; and the whole Thread was of a piece, plain and distinct.' That was how they wanted it in 1694; but it is hard to see why such homely virtues aroused such undoubted enthusiasm.

The same qualities are to be found in the sermons of Burnet himself, in those of Stillingfleet, of Sherlock, and of other eminent divines, and in such popular religious works as Sherlock's *Practical Discourse concerning Death* (1689), which had run through ten editions before 1700, and continued to console and sustain readers like Mrs. Veal and Mrs. Bargrave in the next century. What Pope called 'tomes of casuistry'—books arguing coolly and dispassionately cases of conscience—also found many readers: Jeremy Taylor's *Ductor Dubitantium*, published in two folio volumes in 1660 with a Dedication to Charles II, had reached a fourth edition by 1696. But alongside, and in constant conflict with, this reasonable Anglican tradition, were the much more evangelical, individualistic, and frequently eccentric doctrines and activities of the dissenting sects, who between them produced a vast body of religious literature, and one writer greater and more imaginative than any that the Church of England could show.

(III)

'Words are too awful an instrument of good and evil to be trifled with; they hold above all other external powers a dominion over thoughts. If words be not . . . an incarnation of the thought, but only a clothing for it, then surely will they prove an ill gift.' This pronouncement (it occurs in an essay of

Wordsworth's) might have been made by John Bunyan.[1]
Words, it is true, meant a great deal to him. How strong a
dominion they exercised over his thoughts may be seen, again
and again, from the way in which some phrase or sentence from
the English Bible suddenly speaks to him in an hour of crisis.
On such occasions it is, no doubt, the *thought* that comforts or
terrifies him, but the thought as it is incarnated in the familiar
words of the Authorized Version. Yet Bunyan would have
understood and accepted Wordsworth's almost puritanical
attitude to words: they were an instrument of good, a means
put into his hands by God for the reformation of sinners, but
they were also a constant temptation to the man whom God
had so endowed. When he was preaching well, he tells us, he
had often been 'tempted to pride and liftings up of heart', and
he had come to realize that the great gifts he possessed 'were
dangerous, not in themselves, but because of those evils that
attend them that have them, to wit, pride, desire of vain glory,
self-conceit, etc., all which were easily blown up at the applause
and commendation of every unadvised Christian'. The reader
of Bunyan is not especially concerned with whether he occasionally looked upon his work with complacent approval and found
that it was good. What is important is rather that his whole
endeavour was to use words so that they did God's work. He
was utterly sincere in this; and when he tells us that he would
have been happy to be hanged before the eyes of his congregation if that would be 'a means to awaken them, and confirm
them in the truth', we can take his statement quite literally.
That he should appear, and bulk large, in a history of English
literature is therefore at first sight a sign that he has failed in his

---

[1] John Bunyan, son of a Bedfordshire tinsmith or 'tinker', was born in 1628 in
the little village of Elstow, near Bedford, and received an education in reading and
writing at the village school. In 1646 he was drafted into the Parliamentary army,
and saw some service in and around Newport Pagnell which he may have turned to
account in *The Holy War*. His own early religious experiences are set forth in *Grace
Abounding*. In 1653 he joined a religious society at Bedford, and some time later
began to preach, while still practising his father's trade. His earliest writings (1656)
were directed against the Quakers. In November 1660 he was arrested as an
unlicensed preacher, and from January 1661, with a gap of a few weeks in 1666,
he was confined to Bedford Gaol until he was set free by the Declaration of Indulgence in 1672. During his imprisonment he supported his family by making
tagged laces, but he also found time to write *Grace Abounding* and various tracts.
His period of greatest literary activity came in his early fifties, with the publication of the first part of *The Pilgrim's Progress*, *The Life and Death of Mr. Badman*,
and *The Holy War*. He died on 31 August 1688, and was buried in Bunhill Fields.

mission, and that his readers are enjoying the tinkling of the cymbal instead of paying attention to the tune. But this, in fact, is what never happens with Bunyan. It is possible, of course, to discuss his prose style, his command of narrative, his keen sense of character, his skill in reproducing colloquial speech, and much else; but his reader is always and primarily aware of what is being said, of what *The Pilgrim's Progress* is *about*. Bunyan, in fact, has not failed in his intention: the perfection of his prose style is to be found in the extent to which his words are the incarnation of his thoughts; and its tremendous impact on the reader is largely due to his utter devotion to the spiritual business in hand. 'I could . . . have stepped into a style much higher than this in which I have here discoursed,' he tells us in the Preface to *Grace Abounding*, 'and could have adorned all things more than here I have seemed to do: but I dare not. God did not play in convincing of me; the Devil did not play in tempting of me; neither did I play when I sunk as into a bottomless pit, when *the pangs of hell caught hold upon me*: wherefore I may not play in my relating of them, but be plain and simple, and lay down the thing as it was.' Such lean and muscular prose as Bunyan's is comparatively rare in any literature; it is the prose of a spiritual athlete who has kept himself in perfect training for the race he has to run, the deadly serious writing of a man 'who looked not behind him, but fled towards the middle of the Plain'. Nothing more powerful is to be found in the whole literature of the Restoration; and only the most insensitive reader could fail to be moved by the controlled intensity of Bunyan's feeling.

But the reader of *Grace Abounding* and *The Pilgrim's Progress* has also to come to terms with Bunyan's mind, with his whole outlook on life. Here again there is never any question of Bunyan's power, for he is capable of raising emotions in the mind of his reader that range from delighted acquiescence to a kind of fascinated horror. Bunyan's conviction is so complete that he drives his reader relentlessly before him. Every issue is as clear as day to him; he thinks in terms of right and wrong, good and evil, true and false, salvation and damnation. To refine upon such distinctions would be to equivocate, to become a Mr. Worldly Wiseman or a Mr. Facing-both-ways. His complete conviction springs, of course, from his spiritual

experience, and from the habits of mind of the religious brotherhood and the social class to which he belonged. Some men are
saved, others are not; the man who is saved has obtained grace,
and unless he has been 'called' he is damned eternally. Bunyan
himself has suffered great agony of mind, 'fearing I was not
called, for, thought I, if I be not called, what then can do me
good?' The converted sinner felt the grace of God in his soul, as
Bunyan himself has described in *Grace Abounding*, though in
the sect to which he belonged it was customary to subject each
individual to a more objective test, and to call upon him 'to
give an account of the work of grace in his soul', and to accept
him as one of the brethren, or defer acceptance, or reject him,
on the testimony that he was able to offer. The contemplation of such a rigid religious community as Bunyan's brotherhood at Bedford is repellent to many people: the little soviet
of the saved sitting in judgement on 'Sister Cooper' or 'Friend
Allen' and deciding whether they were yet fit to join the congregation has all the marks of self-righteousness and spiritual
exclusiveness. But even to most Christians the absolute necessity of conversion, the existence of a clear dividing line between
the elect and the damned, is unacceptable doctrine. Yet it is
on this doctrine that all Bunyan's writings rest. For the modern
reader, in fact, he raises in its sharpest form a problem to which
twentieth-century literary criticism has given much attention:
the problem of belief. What Bunyan is hammering at so in-
sistently in book after book is something that means little to
many readers, and is indignantly rejected by others. Bunyan
is moved by a complete and unshakeable conviction that God's
will has been revealed to him. How, then, will his writings be
judged if he fails to convince his readers that his belief is justified or, worse still, if they look upon him as only a misguided
enthusiast?

When, in the winter of 1660–1, Bunyan was imprisoned in
Bedford Gaol, he was examined by the justices, who kept telling
him that he was possessed by the spirit of delusion. Some weeks
later Paul Cobb, Clerk of the Peace, was sent by the justices to
admonish him and to persuade him to submit himself to the
discipline of the Church of England. Bunyan told Cobb, however, that he must continue to preach God's word, for if a man
'hath received a gift of edification, it is his sin if he doth not lay
it out in a way of exhortation and counsel, according to the

proportion of his gift'. To which Cobb made the reasonable enough reply: 'But how shall we know that you have received a gift?'

> *Bunyan*. Said I, Let any man hear and search, and prove the doctrine by the Bible.
>
> *Cobb*. But will you be willing, said he, that two indifferent persons shall determine the case, and will you stand by their judgment?
>
> *Bunyan*. I said, Are they infallible?
>
> *Cobb*. He said, No.
>
> *Bunyan*. Then, said I, it is possible my judgment may be as good as theirs. . . .

But Bunyan knew that it was better than theirs; and he knew because he knew. When he preached or when he wrote he was not just commenting upon the Scriptures, or offering religious guidance or consolation: he was the instrument by which God spoke to the hearts of men and women. While he remained alive he was a problem to those in authority, and his claim to a divine calling and to 'gifts of edification' was one that could not possibly be ignored. Bunyan (and men like him) challenged the authority of the Church of England; he refused to worship in his parish church, and he claimed the right to preach not only to his own particular brotherhood at Bedford, but up and down the length of England. Outraged authority could and did lock up Bunyan for long periods, until death finally took him off their hands, and he ceased to be a political problem. But even today we cannot quite get the full significance of what Bunyan wrote if we ignore the man, and his claims to divine inspiration and guidance: he remains at least a pyschological problem. We must either accept those claims, or agree with the Bedford justices that he was in some degree subject to delusion and hallucination. Those who take the second view can point to the fairly frequent occasions on which he hears a voice speaking to him, and calling him so strongly that 'I turned my head over my shoulder, thinking verily that some man had, behind me, called to me'; or to his consciousness of the Devil's being so close to him that he thought he had 'felt him, behind me, pull my clothes'. But if much of Bunyan's experience is abnormal, it has often no more than the normal abnormality of the devout. The individual human creature, one of many millions placed on a certain spot of earth at a certain point in the long centuries

of human history, feels himself to be the particular concern of
an omnipotent and eternal God, who speaks to him, rebukes
him, envelops him with loving kindness, and is unceasingly
aware of and concerned about his inmost thoughts and his
every action. When, for example, Bunyan heard a loud voice
crying, 'Simon, Simon, behold, Satan hath desired to have you',
he did 'both see and feel' that it 'was sent from heaven as an
alarm, to awaken me to provide for what was coming'. To the
devout among his readers, or, at least, to the devout of his own
kind, Bunyan speaks a language that they can understand, for
they have had the same or similar experiences. For the rest of
his readers he must always be a man who walks apart, who
arouses curiosity as well as admiration; his sincerity is apparent,
his appalling sense of sin and his longing to be saved are deeply
impressive, but his spiritual struggles are agonies to be imaginatively apprehended rather than personally shared.

Bunyan the man remains a fascinating personality. There is
often an intellectual arrogance in the learned, a pride that
comes from book learning; but there is not infrequently, too,
an arrogance in the unlearned, a confidence attributable to the
pains and endeavours of self-education, and Bunyan was not
without a streak of this in his intellectual character. When a
man has done everything for himself he sets a value on his own
thoughts, and he is apt to regard with suspicion or contempt
the ideas that other men acquire from books or universities, or
from the easy commerce of an educated society. Bunyan has
the plain man's distrust of that academic learning which
leads other men to value ideas because they are interesting or
complicated rather than because they are true, and which encourages them to believe that the truth itself is not simple and
obvious, and that the distinction between right and wrong is
not clearly defined and immediately perceptible to any man
whose mind and heart are not corrupt. He is not ashamed of,
he even glories in, his humble origin and his lack of formal
education; for he knows that many things are hidden from the
wise and prudent that are revealed to the simple and humble.
In the prefatory Epistle to Bunyan's first book, *Some Gospel
Truths Opened*, John Burton asserts that 'this man is not chosen
out of an earthly, but out of the heavenly university, the Church
of Christ. . . . He hath through grace taken these three heavenly
degrees, to wit, union with Christ, the anointing of the spirit,

and experience of the temptations of Satan, which do more to fit a man for the mighty work of preaching the Gospel than all the university learning and degrees that can be had.' Bunyan, at any rate, was not conscious of any insufficiency in his intellectual equipment that could prevent him from disputing successfully with the Scribes and Pharisees of Restoration England, and in his encounters with Lord Chief Justice Kelyng and the other 'doctors and priests of the country' he more than held his own. He fought such argumentative skirmishes on ground that was entirely favourable to him: he was talking about what he knew; and what he knew—with all the intimacy of a seventeenth-century Nonconformist—was the English Bible from Genesis to Revelation, and his own pilgrim's-progress from a state of sin to salvation. On such ground Bunyan was the expert, and Sir John Kelyng the ignoramus. (Bunyan reports Kelyng as having remarked at one point: 'We know the Common Prayer Book hath been ever since the Apostles' time. . . .') Relying upon the Word of God, and cutting a straight path through the thicket of theological refinements and sophistications, Bunyan had an immediate answer for every argument, and could beat down his opponents with the full force of an undivided mind. What he knew he had 'proved upon his pulses'; he spoke from his heart on matters that were to him of the deepest concern. Everything that he writes, therefore, has the stamp of his own personal experience. 'I never endeavoured, nor durst, make use of other men's lines', he says, referring us none the less to the fifteenth chapter of Romans, where St. Paul claims that in preaching the gospel he has not built upon another man's foundation, and to the first chapter of Galatians, where the apostle says again that he has not received his gospel 'of man, . . . but by the revelation of Jesus Christ'.

If the secret of Bunyan's strength lies in his simple, forthright dealing with the problems of conduct and character, and in a strength of conviction which concentrated all his mental energy at one point, it would be a mistake to make too much of his lack of education, or to suggest that he did everything by a kind of inspiration. It is true that we know comparatively little about his reading, but it was not confined to the Bible and to those two godly best-sellers, *The Plain Man's Pathway to Heaven* and *The Practice of Piety*, which his first wife brought with her, and which first awakened in him 'some desires to religion'. We know, because he tells us, that some time later he had read Luther's *Commentary upon* . . . *Galatians*, which he preferred, 'excepting the Holy Bible, before all the books that ever I have seen, as most fit for a wounded conscience'. We may reasonably assume that the long years spent as a prisoner in Bedford Gaol were not entirely devoted to reading his Bible, to prayer and meditation, and to making tags for boot-laces to support his wife and family. At the very least he had read some of the books written by Quakers and by men of other religious sects, for he several times engaged in controversy with those men. What he read we can be sure that he read closely, but it is unlikely that his reading was ever extensive, either in range or in amount.

Yet as one reads Bunyan's own work one sees that in all those matters that concerned him he was far from being an un-educated amateur. His profession was saving souls; and on the whole question of spiritual health and sickness he had medi-tated long and deeply, and had indeed a specialized knowledge. We need go no further for evidence of his knowledge of reli-gious psychology than the ruthless self-examination of *Grace Abounding*, with its sharp analysis of the various stages on the road to conversion. When he had become a reformed character— as great a change, in its way, 'as for Tom of Bethlem to become a sober man'—his neighbours began to commend him to his face:

But, Oh! when I understood that these were their words and opinions of me, it pleased me mighty well: For though, as yet, I was nothing but a poor painted Hypocrite, yet I loved to be talked of as one that was truly Godly. I was proud of my Godliness; and I did all I did, either to be seen of, or to be well spoken of, by men: well, this I say, continued for about a twelve-month or more.

So, too, with his dancing, in which he had taken much delight. It was a hard struggle to give that up, but at last he succeeded, and then, as he says, 'I thought no man in England could please God better than I'. When Bunyan became a preacher the knowledge that he had gained of his own mind and motives in his long and painful struggle towards salvation was naturally at hand to help him diagnose the spiritual condition of other men and women, and by the time that he came to write *The Pilgrim's Progress* there was little that he did not know about the diseases, both acute and chronic, of the human soul. To the technique of preaching he brought the same searching and informed scrutiny. He had no illusions about easy success with his listeners: the thing was not just to interest his audience, but to win souls for God. 'It pleased me nothing', he tells us, 'to see people drink in Opinions if they seemed ignorant of Jesus Christ, and the worth of their own Salvation. . . .' The ignorant tinker remained to the end unread in almost all of the world's great literature, but in his own field he spoke and wrote with the authority of the expert. He kept steadily on his way, turning neither to the right hand nor to the left, ignoring everything that might distract his attention from the goal towards which he was travelling; his mind had an intensity that has never, perhaps, been equalled among English writers.

Whether Bunyan had become a Christian or not—and, if he had not, it is unlikely that he would ever have written a line—he would always, it seems, have lived at high pressure. His religious experiences intensified his feelings, but the feelings were there from the first. As a child he had been troubled by vivid dreams of devils and wicked spirits. At the age of nine or ten he sometimes felt such distress of mind, and such 'despair of Life and Heaven', that he often wished 'either that there had been no Hell, or that I had been a Devil; supposing they were onely tormentors'. When he tells us that up to the time of his marriage he had been 'the very ringleader of all the Youth that kept me company, into all manner of vice and ungodliness', those who are familiar with English village life may form the gloomiest conclusions about his behaviour; but Bunyan's standards were severe, and he may have been reproaching himself with nothing much worse than robbing orchards and henhouses, and with normal hooliganism. Of drunkenness and whoring (the latter he specifically denies) there is no evidence. What he charges himself with particularly is cursing, swearing, lying, and blaspheming the name of God, in which from childhood, he says, 'I had but few equals, especially considering my years'. Here again we may find the explanation in a nervous and excitable temperament. Bunyan did nothing by halves, he pushed everything to extremes; and if in his youth he swore and blasphemed, there is every reason to believe that he would do it more forcibly and more imaginatively than his neighbours, and that he would 'snatch a fearful joy' in the process. When he became religious, and entered upon that long period of spiritual crisis that preceded his conversion, he seems often to have been living in a state bordering on hysteria. Hearing some talk of what constituted the sin against the Holy Ghost he was horribly tempted to commit that very sin. 'If it were to be committed by speaking of such a word', he says,

then I have been as if my mouth would have spoken that word whether I would or no; and in so strong a measure was this temptation upon me, that often I have been ready to clap my hand under my chin, to hold my mouth from opening; and to that end also I have had thoughts at other times, to leap with my head downward, into some Muckhil-hole or other, to keep my mouth from speaking.

There is much of this suppressed violence in *Grace Abounding*, a constant effort to control the promptings of an impulsive nature. We are frequently told by Bunyan of how he is afflicted by a great trembling, how his body as well as his mind shakes and totters under the stress of his emotions. 'I felt such a clogging and heat at my stomach by reason of this my terrour, that I was, especially at some times, as if my breast-bone would have split in sunder.' In the metaphorical language (traditional in Puritan spiritual autobiography) in which he seeks to express his religious experiences, we meet most often with tempests, floods, and darkness, pits and quaking bogs, thunder and lightning, the characteristic imagery of fear, varied only very rarely with images of calm or delight.

Grace Abounding is one of the many accounts set down in writing in the seventeenth century of God's dealings with a human soul. Such accounts inevitably fall into some sort of pattern, a progress from the first conviction of sin, through doubt and anxiety and, at times, despair, to a state of grace. What sets Bunyan's spiritual autobiography apart from all others is, above all, as already suggested, the greater intensity of his feeling. There was no comfortable fat about Bunyan's soul to absorb the shocks of experience; he reacted to everything at once and with the whole man. He never learnt to compromise, to trim, to aim at an easier mark, to reassure himself by reflecting on his good intentions or recalling his past victories. All was to be fought for again every new day, and every fresh fight was as hard as the last. He is not, therefore, an easy author to live with, but if we open one of his books we cannot choose but hear. With the sustained intensity of his spiritual experience, too, there goes a power far above the ordinary to find those images which will best convey it to his reader. If he is the greatest of all our writers of allegory, he is still a memorable writer when, as in *Grace Abounding*, he is attempting nothing more than a straightforward narrative of what has happened to him. But that narrative has, from its very nature and substance, many of the elements of drama. What Bunyan has to describe is the most absorbing of all dramas, a struggle between the forces of good and evil for a man's soul; the issue is attended by doubts and uncertainties, by defeats and victories, advances and lapses, good days followed by bad ones. The tension is never relaxed; every fresh position won has to be held against an enemy who is always watching for his opportunity, and who has innumerable stratagems for recovering any ground he may have lost. That Bunyan seems often to be helping the adversary by his needless anxieties and self-reproaches, and that his agony of mind sometimes amounts to self-torture, only adds to the absorbing interest of the struggle. We are watching a sick man endeavouring to throw off a long and dangerous disease; if he makes it worse by his imaginary apprehensions, we know that those are part of the disease. Over *Grace Abounding* lie the shadows of fear, the terror of everlasting damnation, the despairing loneliness of one who fears that he is not 'called', and in those shadows all the issues take on a kind of nightmare horror. '*But how if the day of grace should be past and gone?*' he cries, in a renewed agony of doubt. 'How if you have overstood the time of mercy? . . . And to aggravate my trouble, the Tempter presented to my mind those good people of Bedford, and suggested thus unto me, That these being converted already, they were all that God would save in those parts: and that I came too late, for these had got the blessing before I came.' As we read his 'Brief Relation of the Exceeding Mercy of God in Christ, to his poor Servant, John Bunyan', we become more and more conscious of the author himself as a tragic hero, a man with more than the normal capacity for suffering, constantly thrown to the ground and yet struggling to his feet again, frequently on the point of utter despair, but never giving up, because to lose this fight would be to lose everything.

'I did labour so to speak the Word', Bunyan tells us, 'as that thereby (if it were possible) the sin and the person guilty might be particularized by it.' His power of particularizing, of making us sharply aware of the matter at issue, is one of the main ways by which he keeps a hold of his readers. The authenticity of his own spiritual experiences is often confirmed by some remembered detail, and made vivid for us by the homeliness of the setting or the imagery. Once, when a realization of the love of God came flooding in upon his torturing doubts and gave him a new hope, he was so elated by his discovery that, as he records, 'I remember I could not tell how to contain till I got home; I thought I could have spoken of his Love, and of his mercy to me, even to the very Crows that sat upon the plow'd lands before me. . . .' Such passages convince one of Bunyan's veracity. In that hour of spiritual ecstasy the crows *were there* upon the ploughed land; if they had been hens or seagulls Bunyan would have said so, for, like Wordsworth, he clung tenaciously to his past experience, and reproduced it with absolute fidelity. Time after time he introduces some strange episode in his spiritual life with such phrases as 'One day as I was standing at a neighbour's shop-window', or 'At another time, as I sat by the fire in my house', and we know that such authentication is not fictitious, but as actual as that of Wordsworth in 'We are Seven' or 'The Leechgatherer'. The ordinariness of the setting, too, not only vouches for the extraordinariness of the experience, but reinforces it by the sharpness of the contrast.

That Bunyan realized how apt the religious-minded are to exaggerate and even to prevaricate about their experiences may be deduced from an earnest assurance he gives us on one occasion that he is speaking the literal truth. After setting forth in some detail the wicked desires of his heart, he adds unexpectedly: 'I protest before God, I lye not, neither do I feign this sort of speech.' The very oddness of some of his experiences is the best guarantee of their authenticity. In his unregenerate days he had taken much pleasure in bell-ringing, but his conscience 'beginning to be tender', he left off what he now thought to be a vain and idle practice. Yet still he hankered after the old delightful pursuit, and he could not resist going along to the church to watch the other bell-ringers pulling at the ropes. But then his conscience smote him again, and he began to ask himself, 'How if one of the Bells should fall?' That would be the end of John Bunyan, his brains knocked out by the hand of God:

Then I chose to stand under a main Beam that lay over thwart the Steeple from side to side, thinking there I might stand sure: But then I should think again, Should the Bell fall with a swing, it might first hit the Wall, and then rebounding upon me, might kill me for all this Beam; this made me stand in the Steeple door; and now, thought I, I am safe enough; for, if a Bell should then fall, I can slip out behind these thick Walls, and so be preserved notwithstanding.

But not even at the steeple door could Bunyan feel safe, for it now entered his head that the steeple itself might fall; and so, after wrestling with his apprehensions, he was finally forced to fly, for fear the steeple should fall upon his head. There are several such passages in *Grace Abounding* where we are brought very close to the odd vagaries of the human mind and the psychological eccentricities of individual experience. Indeed, there is as much knowledge of the human heart and the human mind in Bunyan as we meet with in the whole body of Restoration drama. From a fearless analysis of his own thought and behaviour, he proceeded to the same close observation of his fellow men and women. His awareness of the strangeness of human behaviour, and his penetration into human motives, are at times quite startling.

In 1676, while suffering a third term of imprisonment, Bunyan was at work on a treatise called 'The Strait Gate: or the Great Difficulty of Going to Heaven'. He had been dwelling on the difficulty of attaining salvation, particularly for those who were mere 'professors', or Christians only in outward appearance, but also for those who genuinely sought to be saved. 'The world hateth thee if thou be a Christian; the men of the world hate thee; the things of the world are snares for thee, even thy bed and table, thy wife and husband, yea, thy most lawful enjoyments have that in them that will certainly sink thy soul to hell, if thou dost not strive against the snares that are in them.' Bunyan had been saying this sort of thing ever since he began preaching and writing. Now he was to say it again in a new way that would never be forgotten. Instead of straightforward exhortation or confession he was to present the vision of a man running from his own door, putting his fingers to his ears as he fled 'towards the middle of the Plain', and crying out 'Life! Life! Eternal Life!' What had happened was that as he pondered earnestly on the 'strait gate', with its implications of the Christian's journeying to Heaven, he had become more and more fully aware of the Christian life as a pilgrimage beset with dangers and temptations. The first glimmerings of *The Pilgrim's Progress* had come to him. To Bunyan it all seemed to happen without warning. As he tells us in 'The Author's Apology for his Book', he 'fell suddenly into an allegory', and his ideas multiplied so rapidly that he realized he could not possibly use them in the treatise he was then writing, but must give them a whole book to themselves. He wrote this book for his own pleasure, but when the work was finished he showed it to some of his religious brethren:

> Some said, John, print it; others said, Not so:
> Some said, It might do good; others said, No.

In those hesitations of the godly we get a glimpse of the stern and obdurate soil out of which this beautiful flower of the imagination so unexpectedly bloomed. That some of his neighbours should account *The Pilgrim's Progress* a piece of vanity, and that Bunyan should feel himself compelled to justify the work to them, is a measure of the narrowness and intellectual rigidity of the religious community in which he had been nurtured. Plain exposition and exhortation they knew and understood; but this new book by their brother was 'dark', indirect, 'feigned', fictitious—*not true*. They complained, too, that it lacked solidity, and they exhorted him to 'speak his mind', to say what he had to say without disguise. Allegory has a way of appearing in literature when the thing that it represents is already moribund: *The Faerie Queene* belongs to an age in which the old world of chivalry was no more than a memory, and *The Pilgrim's Progress* was written for a generation that was already losing the religious fervour of the old Puritan days in which Bunyan had spent his youth. But to all complaints about his use of allegory Bunyan could reply that there was ample precedent in Holy Writ for his allegorical fiction. His strongest argument, however, was the practical one: the allegorical method might prevail with some sinners who could not be reached in any other way. The fisherman must use every possible device to catch his fish; and there are some that cannot be taken with hook and line, but 'must be grop'd for and be tickled too'.

The modern reader, for whom most of the religious writing of the seventeenth century is tedious beyond belief, if not actively repellent, may well suppose that in matters of religion the seventeenth-century fish were hungry feeders, and that astonishingly little was needed to bait the hook. Even allowing for the allurement of controversy, for the emotional atmosphere engendered by the sharp fear of personal damnation to all eternity, and for the quickened apprehensions of a generation disciplined by listening to elaborate sermons that went on for two hours or more, it is still hard to see how the numerous religious writings of the period not only found readers, but went into numerous editions. Of Bunyan's own religious writings composed in the orthodox forms of the day, *The Barren Fig-tree* (1673) had reached five editions before the close of the century, and *A Few Sighs from Hell* (1658) and *Come and Welcome to Jesus Christ* (1678) had both gone to ten editions—only four fewer than the first part of *The Pilgrim's Progress*. The sale of religious books is never, perhaps, an entirely reliable guide to their real circulation, for so many copies are given away by the well-meaning to the ungodly; but it is impossible to deny the wide and intense appeal of devotional literature in the second half of the seventeenth century: it is one of the inescapable facts of the age. The public for such works was drawn from all classes, but predominantly, it would appear, from the middle class and the literate poor. When a large class of readers considers that fiction is false, and playgoing a sin, and that in any case all reading that does not tend directly to edification is frivolous or worse, there is little chance that other and more imaginative forms of literature will arouse their interest. Yet the overwhelming and continuing success of *The Pilgrim's Progress* seems to indicate that even in this middle- and lower-class public there were thousands of readers ready to welcome some kind of imaginative literature, provided that it was decent, and so long as it reflected what they would consider to be the good life. Imaginative literature, however, was almost wholly in the hands of the literary sons of Belial, and it mirrored an attitude to life with which such readers had no sympathy, and which indeed most of them utterly rejected. In the Restoration period, in fact, the literature of the upper class usually treats matters of little import with grace and charm, while the literature beloved by the middle and lower classes deals with the gravest concerns of human life, but usually fails to achieve more than earnestness and a sort of honest zeal. That Bunyan was able to write *The Pilgrim's Progress*

> in such a dialect
> As may the minds of listless men affect,

that he could give such literary grace to godliness and yet sacrifice nothing of the religious intensity to the fiction, sets the book by itself in the religious literature of the age. Only a religion such as Bunyan's could have given to his book its characteristic note of urgency, but that same religion (as some of his brethren so evidently felt) made it highly remarkable that a book in such a movingly fictitious form should ever be written.

Of Bunyan's originality there can be little doubt. 'Manner and matter', he claims, 'was all mine own'; and he tells us, too, that his story came from his heart to his head, and from thence 'trickled into his fingers'. The central idea of *The Pilgrim's Progress*—the life of the Christian on earth as a long and difficult journey or pilgrimage—was an ancient theme of devotional writers, and Bunyan owed something to his memories of chapbook versions of old romances, and to the emblem books of the sixteenth and seventeenth centuries. But Bunyan's allegory has all the marks of having come easily to the author, and of having been penned with that delight which he himself mentions; his characters and the incidents in which they are involved seem rarely to have been sought for, but to have presented themselves to his mind. What Bunyan had to say was not new; it was only his method of saying it that was unfamiliar. *The Pilgrim's Progress* covers much the same ground as *Grace Abounding*, but instead of setting down a narrative of his own conversion he now dramatizes the life of a Christian struggling with difficulties and temptations, and coming at last to his reward in heaven. Even the method was not entirely new for Bunyan. Already in *Grace Abounding* there is evidence of the visualizing quality of his mind in his vision of the sunny side of the high mountain, where the good people sat 'refreshing themselves with the pleasant beams of the sun', and in his description of his own frantic efforts to struggle through the narrow gap in the wall that encompassed the mountain, even until he was 'well-nigh quite beat out, by striving to get in'. Such a passage has the large simplicity and the same

memorable quality as his later descriptions of the Slough of
Despond or Doubting Castle, and it is significant, too, that the
conception of a kind of nightmare struggle is already present.

If *The Pilgrim's Progress* is an allegory of the Christian life in
general, it still retains traces of the author's personal experience.
It is characteristic of Bunyan, for example, that the dangers and
temptations which Christian, Faithful, and Hopeful have to
face are rarely those of the flesh. In Vanity Fair the pilgrims
have no difficulty in turning their eyes from the glittering
merchandise that is for sale there—'as Houses, Lands, Trades,
Places, Honours, Preferments, Titles, . . . Lusts, Pleasures, and
Delights of all sorts, as Whores, Bauds, Wives, . . . Silver, Gold,
Pearls, Precious Stones, and what not'. Their keenest temptations come from doubt, despondency, and from the pressure of
public opinion: from the difficulty of adhering to the high
standards of the Christian life when nearly all one's neighbours are ready to mock and jeer at godliness. Faithful, for
instance, had a hard time with Shame, who told him 'it was
a pitiful, low, sneaking business for a man to mind Religion',
and that 'a tender conscience was an unmanly thing, and that
for a man to watch over his words and ways, so as to tye up
himself from that hectoring liberty that the brave spirits of the
times accustom themselves unto, would make him the Ridicule
of the times'. Significantly, too, Shame told Faithful that few of
the mighty, rich, or wise were ever of his opinion, that most
of his fellow travellers were of base estate and condition, and
that they lacked education (they suffered from ignorance of the
times, 'and want of understanding in all natural Science'). In
such passages *The Pilgrim's Progress* becomes a little less than
universal, but only a little less, and rather more an expression
of seventeenth-century puritanism.

Although the power of Bunyan's allegory over our minds
is generated in the first place by the deep seriousness of
his Puritan view of life, it is also to be attributed to the
strong but controlled imagination of the artist. Bunyan's
language has often the sublimity characteristic of Hebrew
poetry:

So the one took the way which is called Danger, which led him
into a great Wood; and the other took directly up the way to
Destruction, which led him into a wide field, full of dark Mountains, where he stumbled and fell, and rose no more.

Such passages are haunted by the language and rhythm of the English Bible; and equally biblical are the huge and unde-fined landscapes, and the sense of doom and finality. The pre-vailing note of *The Pilgrim's Progress*, however, is one of simple, earnest, and *continuous* narrative. Bunyan's story marches on, up hill and down dale, like his pilgrims. It is told in a style that is often pleasantly colloquial, with its two men who came 'tumbling over the wall', and Apollyon who 'strodled quite over the whole breadth of the way', and the lock in Doubting Castle that 'went damnable hard'. This is the lan-guage of the working class of the seventeenth century, direct, unsophisticated, idiomatic, and proverbial, concerned always with getting the thing said, and never with making an impres-sion on the reader. With this natural style at his command, Bunyan can write beautifully idiomatic dialogue. Here he is following an old practice of preachers and religious writers, but going far beyond almost everything that had been done in this kind. As Pliable struggles in the Slough of Despond he shouts to Christian: 'May I get out again with my life, you shall possess the brave country alone for me!' And Mrs. Inconsi-derate, hearing that Christiana is planning to take the same journey as her husband, cries contemptuously:

Away with such Fantastical Fools from the Town! a good rid-dance, for my part I say, of her. Should she stay where she dwels, and retain this her mind, who could live quietly by her? for she will either be dumpish or unneighbourly, or talk of such matters as no wise body can abide; Wherefore, for my part, I shall never be sorry for her departure; let her go, and let better come in her room: 'twas never a good World since these whimsical Fools dwelt in it.

In such passages, too, one has reason to admire not merely Bunyan's ear for the turns of common speech, but his knowledge of the ways of the world.

If has often been remarked of Bunyan's allegorical personages that, beginning as mere abstractions, they quickly turn into human beings. In their desire to praise him, critics have said some things about Bunyan that would not have pleased him, and this is probably one of them. Bunyan took his abstrac-tions seriously, and intended them to strike upon the mind with the full force of a general application, and this they surely do, however lively and memorable his embodiment of them may be. What gives his allegorical personages their plausibility and

our keen sense of their individuality is chiefly their characteristic mode of behaviour and utterance. Atheist, hearing that the
pilgrims are on their way to Mount Sion, roars with laughter.
'Why, man?' says Christian, 'Do you think we shall not be received?'—'Received!' cries Atheist. 'There is no such place as
you Dream of, in all this World.' So, too, with Talkative, By-
Ends, Mr. Worldly Wiseman, and the rest: they not only represent an idea, but they act it and talk it, as Bunyan, the
shrewd observer of human nature, knows they would. But we
are never in any danger of forgetting what his allegorical
characters represent. It is by means of these lively and clearly
visualized personifications that he drags every issue into the
light, making us conscious of a situation and its significance
by presenting it in its simplest and most essential terms. No
doubt Bunyan's uncompromising mind, with its tendency to
simplify all human conduct into a choice between the mani-
festly good and the obviously evil, made it easier for him to
draw his allegorical figures with such a bold hand; but we
can still admire the workmanship and the result. Of his allegorical scheme in general it may be said that it is so completely fitted to convey the progress of a human soul through
life that it is hard to imagine any other taking its place. The idea
of a journey is entirely familiar, and beautifully simple; it leads
naturally to a succession of episodes, and it moves towards a
foreseen conclusion. In this it has an advantage over the more
desultory and casual adventures of Spenser's knights, who are
without any well-defined destination, and for whose progress,
therefore, we never develop much anxiety. Almost everything,
too, is happening in *The Pilgrim's Progress* to one man, or to
one man and his companion: the emphasis is where Bunyan
wanted it to be—on the lonely soul in desperate danger.

    In 1682 one Thomas Sherman published an unauthorized
continuation of *The Pilgrim's Progress* which prompted Bunyan
to write a Second Part (1684) to his own story. The account
of Christiana and her children has usually been found a good
deal less interesting than that of her husband; their pilgrimage
is certainly less dramatic, and is at times more reminiscent of
a pleasant family excursion into the country than of a journey beset with dangers and darkened with terror. With Mr.
Greatheart playing the part of a medieval knight, the role of
the pilgrims becomes almost passive, and we are in no fears

for their safety. There is, too, more of exposition and of catechism (as in the family's protracted stay in the House of the
Interpreter), and in general the tone is equable, and has little
of that note of urgency that characterized the vicissitudes of
Christian. The allegory dwindles at times to mere ingenuity.
When Christiana's little boy has eaten the fruit of Beelzebub's
orchard, he is given a purge 'made *ex carne & sanguine Christi*',
to be taken fasting 'in half a quarter of a pint of the Tears of
Repentance'. If we had met with this passage in a Restoration comedy satirizing the Puritans we should probably have
thought it a rather obvious piece of satire. In the first part of
The Pilgrim's Progress Bunyan had, in the main, been finding
symbols for his own spiritual struggle, and the autobiographical
basis of the book gave it an intensity that the more fictitious
vicissitudes of Christiana, Mercy, and the children could not
arouse. But it may be, too, that the conversion of women and
children seemed to Bunyan to require a different treatment,
and that he therefore laid more emphasis on instruction and
example than on the inner conflict which he had expressed in
the perils and trials of Christian, Faithful, and Hopeful. It is at
least some measure of Bunyan's greatness as a writer that he
does not repeat his effects, and that the atmosphere of the second
part is quite different from that of the first, consistently gentler,
more domestic, more sociable, and, with its many touches of
human nature and humorous observation, nearer to the work
of the disengaged writer of fiction. At the close of the book,
however—and most notably in the passing of Mr. Valiant-for-
Truth—Bunyan seems to recapture that intensity of feeling
and that bare splendour of style that had almost everywhere
marked the first part.

Between *The Pilgrim's Progress* of 1678 and its sequel in 1684
come the other two books of Bunyan's that are still read today.
In 1680 he published *The Life and Death of Mr. Badman*, in
which he undertook to show the plain man's pathway to Hell.
This book, in a dialogue between Mr. Wiseman and Mr.
Attentive (a form often used by religious writers before and
after Bunyan), narrates the life story of Mr. Badman from his
first childish transgressions of lying, swearing, and robbing of
orchards, to his later drinking, whoring, blaspheming, and cheating, and so to his death. He dies like Falstaff—'like a lamb,
or, as they call it, like a chrisom-child'; but Bunyan leaves us in

no doubt that he has gone to everlasting damnation. There is never anything sentimental about Bunyan, and he will have no truck with those comfortable hopes that prompt men to believe that things are not so bad after all: the notion that a quiet and easy death is the sign that a man has made his peace with God is for him a vulgar error, and he says so firmly. Like all Bunyan's writings *Mr. Badman* springs from the deepest convictions of the author; he means every word that he says. But he is dealing on this occasion with the ordinary lusts of the flesh, and with the petty contrivances and worldly deceits of a small tradesman who is without dignity or nobility of any kind. Bunyan is not out of his depth here; he knows the type well enough from long and repeated observation of his fellow citizens in Bedford and the neighbouring towns and villages. But in this book he is in the position of a magistrate reviewing the evidence, or of a doctor examining the symptoms, rather than (as in *The Pilgrim's Progress*) of the fellow sinner acutely conscious of the temptations to be overcome. He looks on at Mr. Badman's spiritual and physical degeneration, missing nothing of what actually occurs on such occasions, and stating the unwelcome facts with unflinching honesty; but he is so far from seeing anything attractive in the world of Mr. Badman and his cronies that he hardly feels their temptations as being temptations at all. A man who dislikes the taste of alcohol is not likely to become a drunkard; on the other hand, he is hardly likely to understand those who do. Even if he had fully understood, however, Bunyan would probably have avoided painting Mr. Badman's career in any but the most sordid colours; for, however little pleasure he may have taken himself in the lusts of the flesh, he knew only too well, as a pastor at Bedford, how attractive they were to many men and women. Mr. Badman, therefore, is conceived in almost purely animal terms—the dog returning to his vomit, the hog wallowing in his trough— but with those added streaks of meanness and grossness and vulgarity to which only humanity can descend. We miss the dignity of spiritual distress which transfigures Bunyan's pilgrims, and makes them walk in garments of shining light even before they reach the Celestial City. We feel that we are in low company, as Bunyan intended us to feel. We are also, unfortunately, in the rather prosy company of Mr. Wiseman and Mr. Attentive, and the narrative is carried forward with much repetition, and with a meticulous reference to Scriptural texts that inhibits attention and freezes response. Mr. Attentive has all the inquiring ignorance of the First or Second Gentleman in an Elizabethan play, and his neighbour Wiseman divides his time between recounting the career of Mr. Badman and digressing into long moral commentaries or citing cautionary tales from Samuel Clarke's *Looking-Glass for Saints and Sinners*.

With these reservations, however, *The Life and Death of Mr. Badman* is a powerful book. It is perhaps an exaggeration to call it 'the first modern English novel', but it gives us a brilliant transfer of English middle-class life in the seventeenth century, executed, after the fashion of transfers, in hard bright colours. The dialogue has at times a coarse vitality that it would be hard to parallel elsewhere. When Mr. Attentive inquires if Mr. Badman married again quickly after the death of his first wife, Mr. Wiseman's answer brings Mr. Badman before us in all his vulgar wheezing actuality: 'No, not a good while after: and when he was asked the reason he would make this slighty answer, Who would keep a cow of their own that can have a quart of milk for a penny?' A little later Wiseman sums up Mr. Badman's second marriage with idiomatic and proverbial brevity:

> *Atten.* And how long, I pray, did they live thus together?
> *Wise.* Some fourteen or sixteen years, even until, though she
>   brought something with her, they had sinned all away, and
>   parted as poor as howlets. And, in reason, how could it be other-
>   wise? he would have his way, and she would have hers; he
>   among his companions, and she among hers; he with his
>   whores, and she with her rogues; and so they brought their
>   noble to ninepence.

Equally close to the life Bunyan knew are the accounts of Mr. Badman's hypocritical wooing of his godly first wife, with his presents of 'a good book or two, pretending how much good he had got by them himself', and of his 'often speaking well of godly ministers, especially of those that he perceived she liked, and loved most', and the unsparing description of Mr. Badman's dishonest dealings as a tradesman, with his petty frauds and bogus bankruptcies. In such passages Bunyan has all the observation and the hard-headed awareness of Defoe.

In *The Holy War* (1682) Bunyan's remarkable gift of myth-making finds its most elaborate expression. His story of the conquest of the fair city of Mansoul by Diabolus, its redemption by Emmanuel, its subsequent fall from grace at the instigation of Carnal Security, the renewed rising of the Diabolonians, and the final return and victory of Emmanuel, enables Bunyan to deal once again with his favourite theme of Conversion. But this time he ranges in epic amplitude from the Fall of Man to the millennium, and succeeds incidentally in working a good deal of contemporary history into his narrative. Diabolus, for instance, occasionally acts like Charles II. In 1681, while Bunyan was at work on *The Holy War*, Charles was attempting to obtain control of the city corporations by replacing members on whom he could not rely by others who could be trusted to vote in accordance with his interests. The corporations controlled the election of burgesses, and the burgesses elected their members of parliament. In the spring of 1681 the two chamberlains of Bedford were dismissed on the grounds that they had not taken the sacrament at church within twelve months of their election. Some months later, the Deputy-Recorder, Robert Audley, was accused of being 'a great countenancer of conventicles and phanaticks in the town of Bedford', and it was moved in Council that he and other disaffected aldermen should be dismissed from office. Audley, however, who was a man of courage, went up to London, and in the presence of the King indignantly denied all the charges. He added that though he had never been to a conventicle in his life, he might start attending one if, as he heard, the preachers who addressed them were so much superior to those he had recently heard when he went to church. Those and other developments at Bedford are reflected in the reconstruction of the Mansoul corporation by Diabolus, the replacement of Mr. Conscience, the outspoken old Recorder, by Mr. Forget-Good, and the granting of a new charter to Mansoul. God the Father (Shaddai), the Son (Emmanuel), and Diabolus play their parts in Bunyan's dramatic narrative along with Lord Wilbewill, Alderman Atheism, Mr. Zeal-for-Good, the Lord Fornication, Mr. Hate-Bad, and scores of other shadowy figures. The personifications are sometimes crudely perfunctory, sometimes extremely elaborate; e.g. '. . . the children of Prudent-Thrifty, who dwelt with Mr. Mind (for Thrift left children with Mr. Mind, . . . and their names were Gripe and Rake-All; these he begat of Mr. Mind's bastard daughter, whose name was Mrs. Hold-fast-Bad'). It is difficult to grasp Mr. Mind's family relationships, and still harder to take any interest in them. But Bunyan himself has a simple zest for such fancies that sometimes leads him to minor triumphs of ingenuity. When Mr. Tell-Truth is giving evidence against Forget-Good he mentions some of his evil sayings:

> *Clerk.* Where did you hear him say such grievous words?
> *Tell.* Where? In a great many places, particularly in Nauseous Street, in the house of one Shameless, and in Filth Lane, at the Sign of the Reprobate, next door to the *Descent into the Pit.*

With such sophisticated embroideries Bunyan the artist decorates his theme. He is in fact more of the conscious artist in *The Holy War* than in any other of his works, and one is sometimes in danger of admiring the technical skill and neglecting the substance—a rare experience with Bunyan, who usually keeps art firmly in its place. At all events *The Holy War* is often highly readable, and such a passage as the trial of the Diabolonians—Mr. Lustings, Mr. Forget-Good, Alderman Atheism, and the rest—is effective both as drama and as allegory. For a generation accustomed to reading the shorthand reports of State trials it must have had a heightened relevance. If, in spite of such felicities, *The Holy War* must be reckoned, for Bunyan, a comparative failure, it is partly because he was trying to do too much, but chiefly because he had moved on from where his real strength lay—the drama of the individual soul—to a more elaborate and objective narrative of events and theological ideas.

(iv)

If Bunyan was unique as a writer among the Protestant Dissenters, he was only one of many who suffered for their faith, and who also wrote, and wrote voluminously. His fellow Baptist, Benjamin Keach, is noticed elsewhere in this volume, as are Richard Baxter, George Fox, and Lodowicke Muggleton. In sheer quantity of writing the Quakers probably outdid all the other sects; but most of that writing belongs rather to the history, or sub-history, of religion than to that of literature.

William Penn[1] was one of the most remarkable men of the age, and nothing can take from him the honour due to him as a good Christian and a brave man. He was a fearless and stubborn upholder of the rights of Englishmen under the law; a man of gentle and sweet temper who advocated toleration in an age of intolerance, and practised what he preached; a good friend to the oppressed and the unfortunate; and an idealist of tireless, if not always well-directed, energy. Some of that energy spilled over into his numerous homiletic and devotional writings; but as an author he is apt to be diffuse, and he has none of George Fox's mysticism, nor has he Fox's (or Bunyan's) power to express the inner religious life in terms of everyday experience. *No Cross, no Crown* (1668), written while he was a prisoner in the Tower at the age of twenty-four, has all the piercing conviction of a devout Christian; and yet, as he was to say himself of a later work, it is 'miscellaneous in the matter of it, and by no means artificial in the composure'. As a writer he is seen at his best in another very popular work, *Some Fruits of Solitude* (1693), where, in a series of 'reflections and maxims', he achieves a spareness and discipline of expression, and shows a knowledge of human nature that is not always apparent in his other writings, or in his conduct of affairs.

The one outstanding writer among the Friends was Robert Barclay (1648–90), whom Coleridge once called 'the St. Paul of Quakerism'. Barclay, who had enjoyed a more formal education than most of the Friends, brought a mind already trained in theology and ecclesiastical history to the writing of his famous *Apology for the True Christian Divinity* (1678). His calm and orderly mind is everywhere in firm control of his argument; and he has, to a high degree, that 'prospectiveness' which Coleridge saw as the mark of an educated writer, 'that surview

[1] William Penn, the son of one of Cromwell's admirals, was born in 1644, and disappointed his father by joining the Society of Friends in 1667. For publishing *The Sandy Foundation Shaken* in 1668 he was committed to the Tower of London (the first of several imprisonments), and it was while a prisoner there that he wrote his famous devotional work, *No Cross, no Crown*. On the death of his father he inherited an estate of £1,500 a year; and a large debt owed by the Crown to the Admiral was discharged in 1681 by the grant to his son of a tract of land in North America, which he named Pennsylvania, and for which, with the help of Algernon Sidney, he drew up a constitution and a code of laws. Penn, who had always been on friendly terms with the Duke of York, was favourably treated during the Duke's short reign as James II, but fell under suspicion for some time in the reign of William and Mary. His last years were embarrassed by financial difficulties and embittered by troubles in his young colony. He died in 1718.

which enables a man to foresee the whole of what he is to convey, appertaining to any one point; and by this means so to subordinate and arrange the different parts according to their relative importance as to convey it at once, and as an organised whole'. The unassailable certainty and precision of Barclay's thought gives to his prose an austere beauty. There are not many writers to whom the phrase 'sweetness and light' is so completely applicable.

It can hardly be applied at all to most of his contemporaries, whether Anglican or Nonconformist. If we venture into the dense undergrowth of religious controversy in the late seventeenth century, we find much bitterness, and the light is at best murky. What is constant in the disputants is an unshakeable conviction of their own spiritual or intellectual rectitude, and a corresponding assumption that the beliefs of other men are completely misguided—that, indeed, the whole battalion is out of step 'except our John'. The dissenting sects presented no sort of united front against the Church of England, but frequently warred with each other, and the Quakers came under fire from almost every quarter. Of all the resulting controversial, admonitory, and polemical writing, at once godly and uncharitable, little is remembered today, or worth remembering; but some of it can still be read by the tough-minded for the intellectual ardour with which the argument is pursued.

In the Anglican communion Edward Stillingfleet[1] was perhaps the most prominent and best-informed defender of the faith for some forty years; and on different occasions he was called upon to confute atheists, deists, Roman Catholics, and Protestant Dissenters. Towards the end of his life he became involved in a controversy with Locke, whose views on the Trinity he considered unorthodox, and was generally thought to have had the worst of it. Stillingfleet was a man of remarkable erudition, and Burnet's recommendation of him to William

---

[1] Edward Stillingfleet (1635–99) was educated at St. John's College, Cambridge, graduating B.A. in 1653 and becoming a Fellow of the College. He was ordained by the deprived Bishop of Exeter, but found plenty of time for study and writing. In his first book, *Irenicum*, he attempted to reconcile the differences between the Anglicans and the Presbyterians. His second book, *Origines Sacrae* (1662), a learned defence of the divine origin of the Scriptures, so impressed senior Churchmen that he became their leading apologist and controversialist. He was also a much admired preacher. Stillingfleet became Dean of St. Paul's in 1678, and Bishop of Worcester in 1689. His extensive collection of manuscripts was bought by Robert Harley; his books, purchased by Narcissus Marsh, are now in Dublin.

III as 'the learnedst man of the age in all respects' was nearer
the truth than some of Burnet's other judgements. Stillingfleet
began peaceably enough with his *Irenicum* (1659), a work intended to reconcile the Church of England and the Presbyterians by arguing that forms of Church government are not of
divine institution, and therefore offer no ground for separation. From this latitudinarian standpoint he moved in later
years towards a more authoritarian position. Richard Baxter
suspected that he grew more 'hot for prelacy' as he advanced
in the ecclesiastical hierarchy, but here again Burnet was
probably right in believing that in his desire to avoid the
imputations which his *Irenicum* brought upon him 'he went
into the humours of that high sort of people beyond what became him, perhaps beyond his own sense of things'. While still
only twenty-seven he published *Origines Sacrae*, a quarto volume
of over 600 pages, and a work of prodigious learning for so
young a man, in which he sought to arrest the spread of atheism
and scepticism by establishing the divine authority of the
Scriptures on historical grounds. Three years later he clashed
with the Roman Catholic apologists in *A Rational Account of the
Grounds of the Protestant Religion*, and again in 1671 in *A Discourse concerning the Idolatry practised in the Church of Rome*. When,
in the winter of 1685, James II made public two papers in his
brother's handwriting which showed that Charles II had
become reconciled to Roman Catholicism before his death,
and a third paper written by the Duchess of York describing
her conversion to the Church of Rome, it was inevitably
Stillingfleet who was called upon to answer them. This he did
by casting doubt on the authenticity of the first two papers,
and doing all he could to discredit the third. (Some months
later there appeared *A Defence of the Papers*: the defence of that
written by the Duchess was by Dryden, who may possibly
have had a hand in all three parts.) Stillingfleet's attitude to
the Dissenters was rather more tolerant, but in *The Mischief of
Separation*, which, like his *Origines Sacrae*, ran through several
editions, he left no doubt about his attitude to those who were
outside the communion of the Church of England. He was a
clear and methodical writer, and a much admired preacher:
Pepys, who first heard 'the famous young Stillingfleet' in 1665,
noted that in the opinion of Archbishop Sheldon and some
others, he was 'the ablest young man to preach the Gospel of

any since the Apostles'. But Stillingfleet's real strength lay in his remarkable powers of application, in his ability (as Burnet saw) 'to make himself quickly the master of any argument which he undertook', and in his severe scholarship. In commending his *Origines Britannicae*, Richard Bentley, who had been his chaplain, rightly praised him for 'perusing multitudes of Authors, whether printed or in MSS.', but also for his 'great Knowledge and profound Judgment, in separating the Chaff from the Wheat, discarding what is Spurious, correcting what is Erroneous, and retaining and Establishing what is genuine, authentick, and well-grounded'.

A controversialist of a much less sober kind, but a livelier writer, was Samuel Parker (1640–88), whose *Discourse of Ecclesiastical Polity* (1670) launched a severe attack on the Dissenters, and, after occasioning some ineffectual rejoinders, finally provoked Marvell to write *The Rehearsal Transprosed* in 1672. Parker, a lapsed Puritan who had become what was then known as a 'high-flier', was perturbed by the increasing tendency, after the fall of Clarendon, to grant toleration to the Dissenters. From Hobbes he took the idea that what a man thought was his own business, so long as he kept his thoughts to himself, but that what he said and did were the concern of the State. He therefore argued that 'there is not the least possibility of settling a Nation but by Uniformity in Religious Worship; that Religion may, and must be governed by the same Rules as all other Affairs and Transactions of Humane Life; and that nothing can do it but severe Laws, nor they neither, unless severely executed.' Parker, a classic example of the man whose religion is motivated by a hatred of that of other men, had a satirical wit and an undoubted ability to say with a trenchant finality what he thought. In Marvell he met an adversary who was a master of banter and deflation, and who took him quietly to pieces without really answering his arguments. *The Rehearsal Transprosed* is rambling, shapeless, and often trivial and irrelevant; but, in the words of Bishop Burnet, Marvell was 'the liveliest droll of the age', and there was no age in which lively drolls were better appreciated. Parker replied, and other High-Church pamphleteers came to his aid; but Marvell finally demolished Parker in *The Rehearsal Transprosed: The Second Part*, and 'from the King down to the tradesman his book was read with great pleasure'.

It was banter again that accounted for the success of John Eachard[1] in *The Grounds and Occasions of the Contempt of the Clergy* (1670), a work which provoked several replies. Concern about the status of the clergy, their emoluments, their education, and the effectiveness of their preaching had already been expressed by various Churchmen before Eachard turned his attention to those questions; but Eachard was a much livelier writer than most Restoration divines, and he addressed himself not merely to the religious, but to the polite reader of the day. He was by no means indifferent to the sufferings and shortcomings of the poorer clergy, but he wrote about them with a certain detachment. A Rochester or a Sedley could therefore read his *Grounds and Occasions* with pleasure, and so with some chance of profit, when they would have rejected or ignored the more earnest and pressing arguments of the conventional divine. At times, indeed, they might even feel that they were enjoying a snatch of dialogue from a Restoration comedy:

> And what a pleasant sight is it, to see the Man of God fetching up his single Melancholy Cow from a small rib of Land that is scarce to be found without a Guide! Or to be seated upon a soft and well grinded pouch of Meal! or to be planted upon a Pannier, with a pair of Geese or Turkies bobbing out their heads from under his Canonical Coat! . . . Or to find him raving about the Yards, or keeping his Chamber close, because the Duck lately miscarried of an Egg, or that the never-failing Hen has unhappily forsaken her wonted Nest!

Such delightful drollery might have come from the lips of Millamant rejecting an invitation to visit her country cousins. It was perhaps inevitable that Eachard's sincerity should be questioned, and that many of his readers should suspect that he showed some of that contempt for the clergy which he sought to explain; but although his satire has none of the deadly seriousness of Swift, and has a good deal of the unconcern of comedy, there are no real grounds, and few occasions, for doubting his honesty of purpose. The success of his book, which had reached about a dozen editions before the century closed, was due no doubt to its humour and liveliness, but also to its

---

[1] John Eachard (1636?–97) spent most of his life at Catharine Hall, Cambridge, which he entered in 1653, and of which he became a Fellow in 1658 and Master in 1675. During his later years he devoted himself to raising money for the rebuilding of the College, but died with the work uncompleted.

civility and to its admirably unemphatic tone. In *Speculum Crape-Gownorum* (1682) John Phillips, the facetious nephew of Milton, carried on Eachard's criticism of the clergy, borrowing a good deal from *The Grounds and Occasions* in the process, but producing some satirical felicities of his own.

Eachard also took part in one of the few controversies that united almost all religious men of every denomination. Ever since the publication of *Leviathan* in 1651 Hobbes had been under constant attack, for he appeared to undermine both religion and morality. The great guns of Cudworth, Henry More, and Bishop Bramhall were trained against his materialism and determinism; Glanvill attacked him in *Sadducismus Triumphatus* for not believing in witches; Bishop Richard Cumberland in *De Legibus Naturae* (1672) upheld against him the doctrine that man is naturally good; and in *Mr. Hobbs's State of Nature Considered* (1672) Eachard brought his bantering technique to bear on that libertine attitude to life which Hobbes was generally thought to have endorsed and encouraged. If Hobbes was sometimes 'the cause that wit is in other men', and often the target of such abuse as that of Bishop Vesey, who called him 'a pandor to bestiality', and deplored 'the atheism he has spued out of his mouth', he was normally answered in more considered language. As Dr. Samuel Mintz has shown, Hobbes forced his critics to debate with him on his own terms, and not by simply citing Scripture or falling back on traditional authority. 'The critics were satisfied that they had cut Hobbes down to size; in fact they had yielded, slowly and imperceptibly but also very surely, to the force of his rationalist method.'

As the century entered upon its last decade, the religious temper became increasingly affected by that rationalism—or, to use Locke's term, reasonableness—that was spreading into many different areas of thought and action. In part the process, in both religion and politics, was an inevitable dying down of the fires of enthusiasm that had blazed so fiercely in the earlier decades. Controversy, sectarianism, intolerance, and persecution had by no means disappeared, but compromise and toleration were spreading, and to some extent at least the toleration was due to a growth of scepticism. Deism (the word dates from the 1680s in English) took various forms, and unbelief was sufficiently widespread to induce the Hon. Robert Boyle to provide in his will for the endowment of an annual series of lectures in defence of natural and revealed religion, 'to prove the truth of the Christian religion against infidels'. Richard Bentley, who gave the first series of those lectures or sermons in 1692, held forth powerfully against 'the folly and unreasonableness of atheism', but several of his successors directed their attention to a defence of revelation. The writings of the late-seventeenth-century deists, as represented by men like Charles Blount (1654–93), a disciple of Lord Herbert of Cherbury, whittle away some of the main doctrines of Christianity and argue for the sufficiency of natural religion; but it was still dangerous in the 1690s to come right out into the open.

Much more influential were those Christians who, while not denying revelation, tended with John Locke[1] (in the *Essay concerning Human Understanding*) to argue that 'God has furnished Men with Faculties sufficient to direct them in the Way they should take, if they will but seriously employ them that Way, when their ordinary Vocations allow them the Leisure'. (A similar position had been taken up by Martin Clifford (d. 1677) in *A Treatise of Human Reason*, which touched off a considerable controversy in 1672.) It was no doubt this 'do it yourself' religion of Locke's that accounted for some of the wrath of Stillingfleet and those other incensed divines who attacked him in the 1690s. So far as Christianity was concerned, Locke had tried to make his mind a *tabula rasa*. Before writing *The Reasonableness of Christianity* (1695) this gifted amateur theologian had resolved to study the New Testament as if he were reading it for the first time, forgetting all that the commentators had written, and interpreting the Gospels by the light of his own reason. In pursuing this course he managed to persuade himself that Christianity was a religion suited to the meanest capacity, and that all that was needed could be found

[1] John Locke (1632–1704) was educated at Westminster School and at Christ Church, Oxford, and remained at Oxford for some years teaching various subjects. In 1667 he settled in the house of the first Earl of Shaftesbury as his physician, and supervised the education of his son, and of his much more important grandson, the third Earl of Shaftesbury. He was given several minor government appointments, but retained his connection with Oxford until he was expelled in 1684 for his supposed complicity in Shaftesbury's plots. Locke now went to live in Holland, but returned to England early in 1689 with the future Queen Mary. The *Essay concerning Human Understanding* was published in 1690, and from this time until his death Locke continued to write his various works on government, toleration, religion, and trade. He advised William III's ministers on the coinage problem, and became a member of the newly founded Council of Trade in 1696, resigning on account of ill health in 1700.

in the Holy Scriptures: the difficulties had been largely super-
imposed upon it by the divines.

The Writers and Wranglers in Religion fill it with niceties, and
dress it up with notions; which they make necessary and fundamental parts of it; As if there were no way into the Church but
through the Academy or Lyceum. The bulk of Mankind have
no leisure for Learning and Logick, and superfine distinctions of the
Schools. Where the hand is used to the Plough and the Spade, the
head is seldom elevated to sublime Notions, or exercised in mysterious reasonings. 'Tis well if Men of that rank (to say nothing of the
other Sex) can comprehend plain propositions, and a short reasoning about things familiar to their Minds, and nearly allied to their
daily experience. Go beyond this, and you amaze the greatest part
of Mankind.

Locke was making a protest within Protestantism; he was recalling Protestantism to its origins, and trying to scrape off the
theological accretions that had collected upon it. It is true that
he himself brought a trained mind to bear on the subject, but
this did not make him any less objectionable to the clergy: so
far as divinity was concerned, he was an unregistered practi-
tioner. Yet Locke's position was difficult to turn. Like Chillingworth, whom he greatly admired, he devoutly believed in
both reason and the Bible, and saw no possibility of any conflict between the two. God had given reason to every man, and
reason, as he argued in the *Essay*, 'is natural Revelation,
whereby the eternal Father of Light and Fountain of all
Knowledge communicates to Mankind that Portion of Truth
which he has laid within the Reach of their natural Faculties'.
His opponents could hardly wish to be driven into contending
for the unreasonableness of Christianity, although they might
well question Locke's contention that 'nothing that is contrary
to, and inconsistent with, the clear and self-evident Dictates of
Reason has a Right to be urged, or assented to, as a Matter of
Faith'. In the clear light of reason what was left of the Christian
mysteries? And if the truths of religion were revealed to every
Christian who read his Bible carefully, what place was there
for the clergy and the Church? In *The Reasonableness of Christianity*, as Leslie Stephen suggested, Locke saw himself sweeping
away the rubbish of theologians, as in the *Essay* he had set
himself to remove the accumulated rubbish of metaphysicians.
In his gently reasonable (and therefore to some men provoking)

fashion he was attempting a drastic simplification by a return to what he believed to be the few essentials of religion and a religious life. Among the things that he considered inessential were the various rites and ceremonies and controversial doctrines that separated the different denominations from one another; and in his *Letters on Toleration* he called, like Chillingworth, for an end to claims of infallibility, and to the persecution of men (English in England, Scots in Scotland, and so on) for not accepting doctrines and practices that were repugnant to their reason. More clearly, perhaps, than any of his contemporaries, Locke saw that dissent only thrived on persecution, that 'there is one thing only which gathers people into seditious communion, and that is oppression'. Here, as elsewhere, his common sense and the rarefying effect of his logic helped to bring on the calmer days of the next century.

Locke was a devout, but in some ways an unorthodox, Christian. By a number of his antagonists he was accused of Socinianism, or what would now be called Unitarianism; and although he denied this, some of his pronouncements laid him open to the charge. What is not in doubt is the encouragement he gave (however unintentionally) to the spread of deism. When in 1696 John Toland (1670?–1722) published his *Christianity not Mysterious*, in which he sought to show that 'there is nothing in the Gospel Contrary to Reason, nor Above it; and that no Christian Doctrine can be properly call'd A Mystery', the work provoked an immediate outcry in England, and in the following year the Irish House of Commons ordered it to be burnt by the common hangman. Where Locke had been characteristically cautious and naturally devout, his embarrassing disciple—a lapsed Catholic, an unorthodox Protestant, and a very confident young man—had been deliberately provocative. The later gibe of Pope that Toland was 'prompt at priests to jeer' is not unjust. There was, Toland insisted, a sacerdotal conspiracy to veil the clear truths of Christianity in mystery: you can make new discoveries in Law or Medicine or in the other arts and sciences, and be encouraged and rewarded for your endeavours; but not in religion, which is 'maintain'd to be obscure, and very industriously made so!' In taking what at that time was a brave stand on reason, Toland made use of some of Locke's arguments and distinctions, and in general followed (a good deal more jauntily) in Locke's footsteps. But because he had a cruder mind than Locke, and went further in discounting revelation, it is perhaps easier to see in Toland's writing the wider significance of deism as an aspect of the new scientific movement. When Toland says that he is not one of those 'who first imagine or receive an opinion, and then study proofs to establish it', or when he complains that 'the holy Scripture is put to the Torture to countenance the Scholastick Jargon, and all the metaphysical Chimeras of its Authors', we can see that he is fighting a religious Battle of the Ancients and Moderns, with the Fathers and later theologians replacing Aristotle and the scholastic philosophers as the obscurantist voices of authority. In their examination of the Christian religion both Locke and Toland were approaching the evidence in the spirit of the Royal Society's motto— *nullius in verba*. Toland's *Christianity not Mysterious* may be a forgotten work today, but what it gives us is something of real significance, the growing pains of Protestantism.

IX

PHILOSOPHY; POLITICS; ECONOMICS

I. PHILOSOPHY

OF the various seventeenth-century philosophers dealt with in the previous volume, several of the Cambridge Platonists (notably Henry More and Ralph Cudworth) lived on and continued to write after the Restoration. It was not until 1678 that Cudworth finally published the vast work on which he had toiled for many years, *The True Intellectual System of the Universe*—a year that also saw the publication of *The Pilgrim's Progress*, the Sermons of Isaac Barrow, and Robert Barclay's *Apology for the True Christian Divinity*. Among the lesser-known philosophers of the next generation who wrote within our period, the most distinguished are Richard Burthogge (d. 1694?) and John Norris of Bemerton, both of whom were critics of Locke. Burthogge, a medical man and an admirer of Locke, whom he saluted as 'one of the greatest masters of reason', nevertheless produced his own *Essay upon Reason and the Nature of Spirits* (1694), in which he disagreed with Locke's doctrine of primary qualities, and asserted the relativity of *all* knowledge. Norris, an Oxford man, may be looked upon as the last of the Cambridge Platonists. His chief philosophical work, *An Essay towards the Theory of the Ideal or Intelligible World* (1701–4), which falls just outside our period, shows him to have been an English follower of Malebranche, holding with the French philosopher the idealist position that we 'see all things in God'. By the close of the century the Cambridge Platonists were on the decline; and by the time that Pope wrote the fourth Book of *The Dunciad* he was able to scoff at those 'who reason downward, till we doubt of God', or, in Warburton's gloss, 'who, instead of reasoning from a *visible World* to an *invisible God*, took the other road; and from an *invisible God* . . . reasoned *downwards* to a *visible World* in theory . . .'. After 1690 the immediate future of philosophy lay unmistakably with John Locke.

The attitude of modern philosophers, and more especially of English philosophers, to Locke is curiously ambiguous. They point out inconsistencies in his use of philosophical terms, such as 'idea' and 'perception'. They show that some of his fundamental distinctions, like that between primary and secondary qualities, are outmoded and untenable. They find his philosophical system to be piecemeal and unsystematic, and accuse him of not being fully aware of his presuppositions, or of those scholastic and Cartesian elements in his thinking which are at variance with his own empiricism. It is true that all philosophical systems become to some extent outmoded by the passage of time, and philosophers are aware that the history of philosophy is 'the progressive clarification of difficult and elusive ideas'. Yet most philosophers, when looking back at the past, tend to reserve their professional admiration for those shapely theoretical structures of thought which are to be found in thinkers like Descartes, Spinoza, and Leibniz. Nothing could be less like the philosophy of Locke, who says himself, in the Epistle to the Reader, that his *Essay concerning Human Understanding* was begun by chance, when 'five or six Friends meeting at my Chamber, and discoursing on a Subject very remote from this, found themselves quickly at a stand, by the Difficulties that rose on every side'. Locke realized that before they went any further with their discussion 'it was necessary to examine our own abilities, and see what objects our understandings were, or were not, fitted to deal with'. Accordingly he drew up some 'hasty and undigested thoughts' for their next meeting, 'which having been thus begun by Chance, was continued by Intreaty; written by incoherent parcels; and, after long intervals of neglect, resum'd again, as my Humour or Occasions permitted; and at last, in a retirement, where an Attendance on my Health gave me leisure, it was brought into that order thou now seest it'. So far was Locke from admiring metaphysical speculation that he was in general contemptuous of it; and in the *Essay*, where his intention was to inquire into the origin, certainty, and extent of human knowledge, he was as much concerned to state what the mind of man cannot hope to know as what it can. Indeed, one of the advantages that he foresaw from such an inquiry was that it might be 'of use to prevail with the busie Mind of Man, to be more cautious in meddling with things exceeding its Comprehension; to stop, when it is at the utmost Extent of its Tether; and to sit down in a quiet Ignorance of those Things, which, upon Examination, are found to be beyond the range of our Capacities'. This 'wise passiveness' is hardly likely to commend a philosopher to his fellow philosophers; and Locke's determination not to perplex himself and others 'with disputes about things to which our understandings are not suited' must seem to the metaphysician almost an abdication of his philosophical function.

Yet in spite of his shortcomings and inconsistencies and timidities, respect for Locke and his philosophical achievement continues to be felt and proclaimed today by almost every philosopher who has occasion to mention him. In the changing intellectual climate of the twentieth century Locke stands like last week's snowman on the green lawn, his reputation essentially unmelted in the general thaw. One explanation of his continuing influence is offered by Professor D. J. O'Connor, who points out that when we read philosophy, 'we are not going to an authority for information but to the product of a lively mind which will stimulate us to philosophize for ourselves. There is no necessary connection between the philosophical fertility and suggestiveness of a writer and the consistency of his system or the logical rigour of his demonstrations.' Locke continues to stimulate the mind of later generations because he gives us the results of his own hard thinking. He owed something to Hobbes and Descartes; but when he was at work on the *Essay* he was mainly concerned with contemplating the workings of his own mind, and most of what he has to say is the product of that concentrated reflection. The *Essay* is full of such phrases as 'I appeal to every man's own thoughts' or 'If any one will examine himself', indicating at once the introspective method by which Locke himself proceeded, and his constant appeal to experience. Locke's whole theory of knowledge is, of course, based on experience; and although Hobbes had anticipated him by asserting that 'the original of all the Thoughts of men is that which we call Sense, for there is no Conception in a man's mind which hath not at first, totally or by parts, been begotten upon the organs of Sense', it is Locke who is usually thought of as the founder of philosophical empiricism. Making use of a metaphor which was already current among the Stoics, he compares the mind of the infant to 'white paper, void of all characters', and proceeds to ask:

'Whence has it all the materials of Reason and Knowledge? To this I answer, in one word, From *Experience*: in that, all our Knowledge is founded; and from that it ultimately derives it self.' The doctrine of innate ideas which Locke spent so much time in demolishing is so little regarded today that we are apt not to give him sufficient credit as an innovator. He was not tilting at windmills. A belief in innate ideas was still held in part by Descartes and Leibniz; and in England it had informed the philosophical thinking of such men as Lord Herbert of Cherbury and Dr. Ralph Cudworth, and was still orthodoxy at the universities. In basing human knowledge on sensation Locke was carrying out his professed aim of 'clearing the Ground a little, and removing some of the Rubbish that lies in the way to Knowledge'. But while the main purpose of the *Essay* was to examine the nature and the limits of knowledge, Locke was also an innovator (although here again he was anticipated by Hobbes and others) in the light he frequently threw on the working of the human mind. In his discussion of the way in which ideas come to be associated, and in his casual references to child psychology or to the mind of the savage, he was opening up new areas of inquiry which not only enlarged the outlook of contemporary readers, but also influenced poets and novelists for several generations.

The influence of Locke was indeed profound, and it was exerted in many different directions. To some extent it was due to the character of the man himself. Modest, patient, undogmatic, he set himself to examine the evidence for man's intellectual processes in the same humble and inquiring spirit as that of Robert Boyle experimenting with his retorts and limbecks in his 'elaboratory'. Locke had been a Fellow of the Royal Society since 1666, and in his investigation of the human mind he employed the Baconian method of induction. He felt his way along cautiously and slowly, putting forward his findings with a disarming mildness, and with a reasonableness based on ample (at time almost too ample) evidence. As Bertrand Russell has said, 'This temper of mind is obviously connected with religious toleration, with the success of parliamentary democracy, with *laissez-faire*, and with the whole system of liberal maxims'. Locke was slightly ahead of his time: even in the reign of Queen Anne the political and religious temperature was still running high, but he did more than anyone else to reduce it to the level it eventually reached under the Hanoverian kings. What Wordsworth said of the poets may be said with equal truth of Locke: 'Every author, as far as he is great and at the same time *original*, has had the task of *creating* the taste by which he is to be enjoyed.' When Locke's *Essay* was first published it met with considerable opposition; but by the second quarter of the eighteenth century it had become part of the intellectual heritage of the educated Englishman, and its influence, with the help of Voltaire, spread to France and to almost the whole of Europe.

In seeking to account for the influence of the *Essay concerning Human Understanding*, the deliberately simple style in which Locke expressed his ideas must not be forgotten. He hated the pride of the scholar and his 'learned gibberish'; he had nothing but contempt for 'the disputing and wrangling philosophers' who covered their ignorance 'with a curious and inexplicable web of perplexed words'. In an uncharacteristically metaphorical passage he suggested that

there is no such way to gain admittance, or give defence to strange and absurd Doctrines, as to guard them round about with Legions of obscure, doubtful and undefined Words. Which yet make these Retreats more like the Dens of Robbers, or Holes of Foxes, than the Fortresses of fair Warriours: which, if it be hard to get them out of, it is not for the strength that is in them, but the Briars and Thorns, and the Obscurity and the Thickets they are beset with. For Untruth being unacceptable to the Mind of Man, there is no other defence left for Absurdity, but Obscurity.

Locke can write here in this rhetorical way because this is a passage of persuasion; he is exposing a sham, and wishes the reader to share his own feelings about it. But when the matter in hand is exposition he is normally bare and simple. In his Epistle to the Reader he claims, with a modesty that for once must surely verge on the ironical, that he does not address himself to his betters. If any such choose to read his book, he warns them beforehand

not to expect anything here, but what being spun out of my own course Thoughts, is fitted to Men of my own size, to whom, perhaps, it will not be unacceptable, that I have taken some Pains to make plain and familiar to their Thoughts some Truths which established Prejudice, or the Abstractedness of the Ideas themselves, might render difficult. . . . I think it necessary to make what I have to say as easie and intelligible to all sorts of Readers as I can. And I had much rather the speculative and quick-sighted should complain of my being in some parts tedious, than that any one, not accustomed to abstract Speculations, or prepossessed with different Notions, should mistake, or not comprehend my meaning.

In all this Locke was being a good Royal Society man, carrying out its stylistic programme for 'a close, naked, natural way of speaking, . . . bringing all things as near the mathematical plainness as they can', more completely and successfully than most of the Fellows were able to do. At all events, he kept the common reader in mind from beginning to end, making intelligibility and precision the standard for his writing. It was Addison's professed aim in the *Spectator* essays to bring philosophy 'out of closets and libraries, schools and colleges, to dwell in clubs and assemblies, at tea-tables and in coffee-houses'; but this translation had already been accomplished by Locke. The prose style of the *Essay* has been variously characterized as 'homely', 'wooden', and 'bleak', and most non-philosophic readers have probably wished from time to time (as Johnson apparently did with Swift) that the author would occasionally 'hazard a figure'. Such light-and-shade as Locke provides usually comes not from figures of speech, but from his examples, illustrations, and appeals to our experience. We read on, but more for profit than for pleasure; and we do not have to be numbered among 'the speculative and quick-sighted' to find the *Essay* at times tedious and repetitive.

The third book of the *Essay* is concerned with Words; with the way in which they are misused, and with the extent to which 'their uncertain and mistaken significations' are responsible for 'a great many of the controversies that make such a noise in the world'. Many of the words used by the various sects in philosophy and religion do not convey any clear idea to the mind, and (Locke suggests) are not intended to; but worse still is the deliberate abuse of language by those who are arguing only for victory. How much better it would be for mankind, 'whose concernment it is to know things as they are, and to do what they ought', if words were always used with their plain and direct meaning, and not employed to 'raise mists' in men's minds. When at last Locke comes to consider 'figurative speech' he finds that also to be an abuse of language; wit and fancy are always more welcome to the average reader

than 'dry truth and real knowledge'. And yet, 'if we would
speak of Things as they are, we must allow, that all the Art of
Rhetorick, besides Order and Clearness, all the artificial and
figurative applications of Words Eloquence hath invented,
are for nothing else but to insinuate wrong Ideas, move the
Passions, and thereby mislead the Judgment; and so indeed
are perfect cheat'. As with Hobbes, *wit* ('the assemblage of
ideas, and putting those together with quickness and variety')
is contrasted with *judgement* ('separating carefully, one from
another, ideas wherein can be found the least difference'), and
in Locke the contrast is very much to the disadvantage of the
former. Wit, in fact, is of use only for decorative purposes; and
without the amplifications of wit 'many of the . . . poets' works
might be contained in a nut shell'. And a good thing, too,
Locke obviously thinks. In *Some Thoughts concerning Education*
he warns the parent against allowing his son to waste his time in
writing verses, although elsewhere he admits that poetry may
be read for diversion and delight. The whole weight of Locke's
great influence was cast on the side of 'truth and good reason';
he was calling for sound judgement, unadulterated and un-
adorned fact, and clear, logical statement. For imaginative
literature the losses can be set against the gains. From now on,
as Bishop Hurd pointed out, the imagination was forced 'to
ally herself with strict truth, if she would gain admittance to
reasonable company. . . . What we have gotten by this revolution, you will say, is a great deal of good sense. What we have
lost, is a world of fine fabling.'

II. POLITICS

During the later decades of the seventeenth century, as at
other periods, most political writing was inevitably aligned
to the course of events, and at times of political crisis the flow
of political pamphlets reached flood level. The strict control of
the press exercised by Sir Roger L'Estrange kept anti-Government writing within bounds in the first half of Charles II's
reign, but with the lapse of the Licensing Act in 1679 and the
development of the Popish Plot in the autumn of 1680 the
press teemed with pamphlets. A few years earlier, distrust of
the King's increasing tendency to absolutism, and the rising
excitement over the question of the succession, had led to a

good deal of anti-Stuart and anti-Catholic writing, in both verse and prose. Late in 1677 Marvell's *Account of the Growth of Popery, and of Arbitrary Government in England* set the tone for much subsequent pamphleteering. It was so effective a statement of Whig views that the Government offered a reward of £100 to discover the author, and the Tory L'Estrange significantly condemned it on the ground that it was written 'to insinuate that the King is in some cases Accomptable to his People'. One of the most effective of the many attacks on the Government, Charles Blount's *An Appeal from the Country to the City* (1679), voiced the Whigs' grievance at the King's failure to summon his Parliament; and among the many attacks on the Catholic Duke of York fostered by the Earl of Shaftesbury were the damaging *Character of a Popish Successor* (1681) by Elkanah Settle, and *Julian the Apostate* (1682) by the intrepid and hard-hitting clergyman Samuel Johnson (1649–1703).

On the Government side the great specialist in rebuttal was L'Estrange himself, who not only published answers to the first three of the pieces just mentioned, but also answered and attacked such widely different opponents as Richard Baxter and Lord Halifax, and continually harried the Whig journalists and publishers with the process of the law. In *An Account of the Growth of Knavery* (his reply to Marvell's *Account of the Growth of Popery*—L'Estrange was a good hand at titles), he remarked that 'a man may see with half an eye' how Marvell '*aggravates*, or *extenuates*, *disparages*, or *commends*, *reflects* upon, or *passes* over, as well *Actions*, as *Men*, according to the various Aspects of *Affections*, or *Parties*; and without any regard to the Pulse or Truth of Publick Proceedings'. These words could easily be thrown back upon L'Estrange himself, for his skilful defence of the policies of Charles II and James II was successfully conducted for nearly thirty years on just such party lines, and he was well accustomed to argue for victory rather than for truth. As a political journalist he is the forerunner of Defoe and Cobbett. His historical importance in helping to establish that conversational type of prose which became widespread during the Restoration period can hardly be overestimated; he is always and immediately intelligible, and his idiom is that of the tavern and the market-place mixed with the fashionable slang of the day, appealing not to gentlemen and scholars but to men of affairs, to shopkeepers and artisans. His prose abounds

with homely words and phrases—'one egg is not liker another';
'This is only crying Whore first'; 'to turn up trump'; 'to go
thorough-stich'; ''tis early days yet', and so on. He is an adept
at putting a situation in a vigorous metaphor: when Halifax
in his *Letter to a Dissenter* suggested that James II's Declaration
of Indulgence must be viewed with suspicion, the loyal
L'Estrange leapt to the King's defence with 'A Man helps his
friend up the Ladder; and has his Teeth Dash'd out for his
Pains'. He continually addresses his reader-listener with a 'Well!',
or 'You cannot but take notice...', or '"But what", ye'll say...';
and he puts him at his ease with a frequent use of colloquial
contractions such as 'on't', 'to't', 'e'en', etc. He breaks off
from time to time to tell a story, and that gives him the chance
to introduce a snatch of racy dialogue. In all this L'Estrange,
the gentleman born, is adopting a dramatic personality: he is
the plain, blunt Englishman, the honest and indignant lover
of his King and country who sees them both being threatened
by a parcel of knaves and fanatics actuated by the principles of
1641. His self-made image is that of Shakespeare's Antony:

> I only speak right on;
> I tell you that which you yourselves do know.

He had taken up this position in 1663 when he started the
Intelligencer and the *News*, and he maintained it all through
his years of political propaganda: 'Nor shall I give my self
much pain about the *style*, but let it e'en prove as it hits and
lye as it falls (saving only a constant reverence to authority and
truth).' He was perhaps at his best when he employed his
favourite dialogue form, as in the *Observator*, where the credulous and misinformed victim of Whig propaganda could be
set right by reason and common sense, or in *Citt and Bumpkin*,
where L'Estrange works more by a method of self-exposure.
But everywhere in his political writing we find the same sense
of urgency, the same air of righteous indignation, and the colloquial syntax that goes with it. 'For a Party that calls it self
Protestant', he writes in *The Reformed Catholic*,

a Party in full Cry upon the scent of Popery; a Popish Plot upon
Oath too at the same time upon the Life of the King, upon the
Life of our King, upon our Religion and Government; and that
Plot, at that instant, under a strict Examination; the same Party
at the same time also pressing for Justice upon the Conspirators,

nay, and complaining of the remissness of the Prosecution, notwithstanding the most exemplary Rigor in the Case that ever was known in this Nation: For this Party (I say) under these Circumstances to flie in the Face of the Government, let the World judge if ever there was a more Consummate piece of Wickedness. . . .

It would be easy to mistake such writing for Defoe's, with its apparently extempore movement towards a climax, its 'nay' and 'let the world judge', and especially its 'I say' to pull the sentence together when it seems to be on the point of disintegrating. Defoe cannot have approved of L'Estrange's political principles, but he may well have learnt from him how to express his own.

Most of the political writing of the Whig and Tory journalists took the form of in-fighting; punch and counter punch, hitting above, around, and below the belt. But out of all this uninhibited pamphleteering certain dominant issues emerged, and in one or two works those issues were debated on a less polemical and more philosophical level. The main political problem during the reigns of Charles II and James II concerned the status and (to use Milton's term) the tenure of kings, and the proper distribution of power between king and parliament. Republicanism as an alternative to monarchy hardly entered into the reckoning of most Englishmen: in the words of Lord Halifax (a reliable witness), there was 'a general dislike to it'. Yet some men still looked back with admiration to the classical republicanism of Greece and Rome, and more recently to the modern example of Venice; and the great names of Plato, Aristotle, Cicero, and the Machiavelli of the *Discorsi* gave authority to a kind of state, and a form of government, very different from the monarchical absolutism that Charles II and his ministers were trying to establish and to justify in the closing years of his reign. In such a political milieu open and avowed republicanism had become extremely dangerous, but it was still reasonably safe to object to the divine right of kings and to argue in favour of a limited monarchy.

In 1680 Henry Neville (1620–94), an old republican and a friend of Harrington, published his long political dialogue, *Plato Redivivus*, in which he put forward the view that owing to the wider distribution of property in modern days the traditional basis of government in England was out of date, and that the economic power which was now actually in the hands of the people must inevitably lead to changes in the political system, more especially in the relative importance of the sovereign and the legislature. Neville was careful to carry on his discussion (between an English gentleman, a physician, and a Venetian nobleman) within the framework of monarchy; but his king was to be something like the Venetian Doge, and most of the power actually exercised by Charles II, over foreign affairs, the public revenue, the army and navy, and the filling of civil and ecclesiastical offices, was to be handed over to four great councils, appointed by parliament for three years. Those suggestions, and a further proposal to replace the House of Lords by an elected senate, after the fashion of Venice, clearly show the influence of Machiavelli (whose *Discorsi* Neville had translated), and his general agreement with the views of Harrington. *Plato Redivivus* caused a stir, and evoked a considerable number of replies. Neville was accused of trying to 'cully' the King out of his rights, and even of wishing to set up a republic. He was probably still a republican at heart, but in this work at least he was prepared to accept a severely limited monarchy as the only practical solution in the existing political atmosphere.

Of the other old republicans who survived from pre-Restoration days the most convinced was the unfortunate Algernon Sidney,[1] who died on the scaffold in 1683 for his real or supposed complicity in the Rye House plot. Part of the evidence against him consisted of his unpublished papers, which were finally given to the world in 1698 as *Discourses concerning Government*. The case against Sidney, and the extent to which he was one of the martyrs for English liberties, may be gauged from the exclamation of Lord Chief Justice Jeffreys before passing sentence of death: 'When men are riveted in opinion that kings may be deposed, that they are accountable to their

---

[1] Algernon Sidney (1622–83), a son of the second Earl of Leicester, and a brother of Waller's 'Sacharissa', took up arms against Charles I, and was severely wounded at Marston Moor. In 1649 he was appointed one of the commissioners for the trial of the King, but took no part in the proceedings, and did not sign the death warrant. Later he came to regard Cromwell as a tyrant. Although he was not excepted from the Act of Indemnity in 1660, he chose to live abroad until 1677. On his return he made no secret of his republican principles, but is not known to have taken any steps to put them into practice. In 1683, however, he was tried before Jeffreys on the charge of being involved in the Rye House plot, and condemned to death on insufficient evidence.

people . . ., 'tis high time, upon my word, to call them to account.' In his own able defence of himself at his trial it was one of Sidney's contentions that the papers found in his study were 'all old ink, . . . writ perhaps these twenty years'. Yet at the same time he asserted (what was true) that they appeared to have been drawn up as an answer to Sir Robert Filmer's *Patriarcha* (1680). It seems probable that although Filmer's book, laying down the doctrine of the divine right of kings and the absolute necessity for passive obedience on the part of subjects, was the immediate occasion for Sidney's *Discourses*, some of the material embodied in them had been incorporated from his earlier writings on political theory. This, and the fact that he never revised or apparently intended his papers for publication, would help to account for the long-winded and repetitive nature of Sidney's argument. Yet that argument is clear enough, and much of it is drawn from Milton's reply to Salmasius in the *Pro Populo Anglicano Defensio*, supplemented by Sidney's own wide reading in biblical, classical, and later literature, and by his familiarity with European political history. On the surface the *Discourses* might be read as presenting a case for limited monarchy. 'There never was a good government in the world', Sidney had written, 'which did not consist of the three simple species of monarchy, aristocracy, and democracy.' To Sidney, however, the monarchical rule was best vested, not in a hereditary monarchy, but in elected rulers such as the Roman consuls or the Doge of Venice, and the whole bias of his mind was towards a sort of aristocratic republicanism. He might well have said to Charles II what Andrew Melville said to his grandfather, that he was 'but God's silly vassal'. As it was, he made very clear his dislike of kings, their servile ministers, their parasites and pimps and mistresses, and the political corruption that went with them. Men, he thought, had only to ask themselves

whether Bawds, Whores, Thieves, Buffoons, Parasites and such vile wretches as are naturally mercenary, have not more Power at Whitehall, Versailles, the Vatican, and the Escurial, than in Venice, Amsterdam, and Switzerland: whether Hyde, Arlington, Danby, their Graces of Cleveland and Portsmouth, Sunderland, Jenkins, or Chiffinch, could probably have attained such Power as they have had amongst us, if it had bin disposed by the Suffrages of the Parliament and People.

Sidney was, in the words of Burnet, 'a man of most extraordinary courage, a steady man, even to obstinacy', and one 'who had set up Marcus Brutus for his pattern'. He had, indeed, much of the firmness and lonely idealism of Brutus, and such influence as he had came rather from the firmness with which he stood by his republican beliefs than from anything new in his statement of them. Yet there is a Roman dignity in Sidney's prose style, and among those who responded to it in later years was Coleridge. 'Read Algernon Sidney,' he said; 'his style reminds you as little of books as of blackguards. What a gentleman he was!'

In 1672 Sir William Temple wrote a characteristically judicious 'Essay upon the Original and Nature of Government'. Although it is unlikely that he could have known Filmer's still unpublished *Patriarcha*, he must have been familiar with his *Observations concerning the Original of Government* (1652), and therefore with his theory that the State is the macrocosm of the family. Temple kept an open mind on the origins of government, but he was sceptical about the explanations given by 'the great writers concerning politics and laws', who held that men in a state of nature were either sociable or in a state of war with one another, and that in either case they entered into a contract to give up their individual freedom for the sake of securing their lives and property under some king or magistrate. To Temple it seemed easier to suppose that a family becomes a little kingdom, and that a kingdom is only a great family. But to the Whig political theorists the patriarchal explanation of monarchy was something that had to be resisted at all costs, for it led in the hands of Filmer to the justification of absolute government.

Among the earliest and ablest replies to Filmer was the *Patriarcha non Monarcha* of James Tyrell, the friend of John Locke. But Locke himself, who published his *Two Treatises of Government* anonymously in 1690, also devoted the first treatise to that sort of tedious, paragraph-by-paragraph reply to Filmer of which the seventeenth-century reader could never apparently have too much. As Mr. Peter Laslett has convincingly argued, most of the *Two Treatises* was almost certainly written between 1679 and 1681, when Locke was working closely with Shaftesbury; and occasional references to events of 1688–9 are due to subsequent revision of the manuscript before publication. If this is so, Locke's work was originally intended as a statement of the Whig case against the drift towards absolute government in the last years of Charles II's reign, and not as a justification of the Revolution of 1688. But of course it is that too; and in the second treatise, shaking himself free from the inhibiting presence of Filmer, Locke writes 'An Essay concerning the True Original, Extent, and End of Civil Government', which carries the discussion out of the seventeenth century and into the modern world. So far as the 'original' is concerned, Locke substituted one political fiction for another in his attempt to base government on the old notion of a historical contract in which the 'people' consented at some point of time to give up their natural liberty in order 'to unite for the mutual Preservation of their Lives, Liberties and Estates, which I call by the general name, Property'. It was not enough for Locke to found his political system on what men wanted now; he still had to find a historical and philosophical justification for what the majority of Englishmen showed in 1688 that they were determined to have. He was answering the upholders of the divine right of kings, and so he had to make out a case for the inalienable right of the people. But what was important for the future was his firm insistence that kings are accountable to their subjects, and that the people, who have given their consent, can also withdraw it, if the ruler exceeds his powers. One of the notable provisions of the Act of Settlement of 1701 was to be that judges could not be removed from office *quamdiu se bene gesserint*: Locke, it might be said, had enunciated the principle that the King *could* be removed from office if he misbehaved himself. He himself was in favour of a limited hereditary monarchy; but at the philosophical level on which he was writing he made it clear that there were other possible choices. A 'politic society' comes into being when a number of individuals freely join together to make one society, and those individuals, 'when they are thus incorporated, might set up what form of Government they thought fit'. Government of whatever kind, however, must be for the good of the people, and the legislature must be widely representative of the people. For Locke, as for most of his contemporaries, the 'people' was, on the whole, the propertied classes, but at least it can be said of him that he never compromised about their sovereignty, and that, like Cromwell, 'he gart kings ken that they had a lith in their neck'.

Locke's political theory was not always based on reliable premisses and it led him into some serious inconsistencies; but his influence on liberal thought in the century that followed, in England, France, and America, was immense. To his own contemporaries he offered a philosophical justification of the Whig revolution; and his influence lay not only in what he said, but in the way he said it. Locke can be tedious by reason of his very exhaustiveness, his determination to stop every loophole of possible objection; the habit of answering an opponent has become so ingrained that when he has no opponent to answer he imagines one, and puts objections into his mouth. But all this made for that calm reasonableness and common sense which were his chief legacy to the next age. As a century of violent political warfare and controversy drew to a close, the tolerant voice of Locke could be heard patiently arguing in level tones, reducing problems to their simplest terms, putting cases, answering objections, dealing with the inflammatory issues of the day in a context of abstract theory, and in a slow, pondered and unemotional prose. If it cannot quite be claimed that 'he brought philosophy down from heaven, to inhabit among men', and if his political philosophy was by no means disinterested, he at least showed his fellow countrymen the possibility of discussing the burning issues of the day calmly, impersonally, and unrhetorically.

In the closing years of the century the voice of Whig political theory continued to be heard in such pamphlets as *An Argument showing that a Standing Army is inconsistent with a free Government* (1697) by John Trenchard and Walter Moyle, and in some of the writings of John Toland, who edited Milton's prose works and the *Oceana* of Harrington. The popularity of Robert Molesworth's *An Account of Denmark* (1694) was due less to its virtues as a travel book (although these are considerable) than to his ruthless exposure of how the Danes had recently thrown away their liberties when they voluntarily changed their kingdom from an elective monarchy to 'as absolute a Monarchy as any is at present in the World'. This Danish betrayal of liberty was all part of that slavery which in the past two hundred years had 'crept upon Europe', and Molesworth emphasized the fact that it had occurred in a Protestant kingdom, and had been aided and abetted by the Lutheran clergy. Molesworth's anti-clericalism is apparent, but it leads him to insist that there is no reason to suppose that tyranny can be established only in a Popish kingdom: Protestant England, in fact, had been drifting towards an absolute government in the 1680s, and Molesworth makes the shrewd suggestion that 'the late King James's Attempts to bring in Popery was the principal Thing which rescued our Liberties from being entirely swallowed up'. As for the Danish people, they have now found that 'the little Finger of an absolute Prince can be heavier than the Loins of many Nobles', but at least they have the consolation of seeing their former oppressors, the nobility, 'in almost as miserable a Condition as themselves'.

Those two last observations are ironical enough to have come from the pen of George Savile, Marquis of Halifax,[1] who brought to bear on the contemporary political scene a judgement remarkable for both its penetration and its serenity. Halifax was at once committed and detached. He was intimately involved in English politics for thirty-five years, and on more than one occasion his resolute intervention determined the course of events; on the other hand, he was no believer in parties and factions, and his independence of mind and an aristocratic fastidiousness kept him from becoming emotionally involved or stampeding with the political herd. It was inevitable that such a man should be misrepresented by the very extremists from whom he held aloof, and Halifax was assailed as a timeserver by those whose policies or prejudices he happened at any hour of crisis to oppose. Yet he gloried in the name of 'trimmer'. Why, he asked, should men who 'have played the Fool with throwing *Whig* and *Tory* at one another, as Boys do Snow-Balls' grow so angry at the new word *trimmer*, 'which by its true signification might do as much to put us into our Wits, as the other hath done to put us out of them? . . . This

[1] George Savile, Marquis of Halifax (1633–95), the son of a Yorkshire baronet, entered Parliament in 1660, and almost from the first took an independent line in political affairs. He was created Viscount Halifax in 1668 (Earl in 1679, Marquis in 1682). In the heated debates over the Exclusion Bill he finally swayed the House of Lords against Shaftesbury and his supporters, and he remained a powerful influence at Court until the death of Charles II. In the short reign of James II he dropped out of favour, for he had never made any secret of his anti-Catholic convictions. In December 1688 it fell to him, as chairman of a committee of peers, to ask William of Orange to undertake the provisional government of the country, and in February 1689 to request William and Mary to accept the crown. Halifax became Lord Privy Seal, but resigned in February 1690, although he still spoke in the debates of the House of Lords. In his last years he wrote a number of political pamphlets.

innocent word *Trimmer* signifieth no more than this, That if
Men are together in a Boat, and one part of the Company would
weigh it down on one side, another would make it lean as much
to the contrary; it happeneth there is a third Opinion of those
who conceive it would do as well if the Boat went even, without
endangering the Passengers. . . .'

It is easy to think of the trimmer as a man who is so cautious
that he avoids taking any decisions, and hesitates to identify
himself with any cause or any positive course of action. But
this was not the view of Halifax, whose trimmer was committed
to taking decisions all the time, because he had adopted a
position that called for the exercise of his judgement as the
political situation developed, and in which unthinking loyalty
to a party had no place. As he put it in *A Rough Draft of a New
Model at Sea*,' . . . there is hardly a single Proposition to be made
which is not deceitful, and the tying our Reason too close to it
may in many Cases be destructive. Circumstances must come
in, and are to be made a part of the Matter of which we are to
judge; positive Decisions are always dangerous, more especially
in Politicks.' Such an attitude could admittedly lead to pure
opportunism; but Halifax was saved from that by his steady
adherence to certain fundamental principles that were ultimately based on his understanding of the English people, and
his own unshakeable patriotism. The most famous expression of
his love of England is to be found in *The Character of a Trimmer*:

Our Trimmer is far from Idolatry in other things, in one thing
only he cometh near it, his Country is in some degree his Idol; he
doth not Worship the Sun, because 'tis not peculiar to us, it rambles
about the World, and is less kind to us than others; but for the
Earth of England, tho perhaps inferior to that of many places
abroad, to him there is Divinity in it, and he would rather dye than
see a Spire of English Grass trampled down by a Foreign Trespasser:
He thinketh there are a great many of his mind, for all plants are
apt to taste of the Soyl in which they grow, and we that grow here
have a Root that produceth in us a Stalk of English Juice, which is
not to be changed by grafting or foreign infusion. . . .

If this passage is not quite typical, in so far as it is charged with
a feeling that breaks through the habitual restraint and ironical
detachment of the writer, it has his easily colloquial style; and
the metaphors drawn from nature are characteristic of the man
who cultivated with deep satisfaction his estate at Rufford, and,

in later years, his garden at Acton. A notable consequence of his love of England was his deep distrust of France, and his conviction that the French desire to dominate in Europe was the main threat to English liberties.

How far his dislike of the Roman Catholic religion played a major part in determining the attitude of Halifax to the French nation it would be hard to say, if only because it is difficult to tell what his own religious beliefs really were. In his *Advice to a Daughter* he begins by stressing the importance of religion, and goes so far as to say that 'in a strict sense it is the only thing necessary'. In adding that it should be free from superstition, and that true religion is a cheerful thing, 'though the Spiritual Cooks have done their best to give an ill Relish to it', he appears to be glancing alternately at the Catholics and the Dissenters; and in assuring his daughter that 'Religion is exalted Reason' and that it is 'Morality improv'd and rais'd to its height', he probably had in mind the Anglican communion. Yet his own religious attitude is perhaps most accurately expressed in an observation to be found among his *Political Thoughts and Reflections*: 'Most Men's Anger about Religion is as if two Men should quarrel for a Lady they neither of them care for.' His antipathy to Roman Catholicism comes out most clearly in *The Character of a Trimmer*, where he writes of 'the old Lady of Rome' who 'sitteth in her Shop, and selleth at dear Rates her Rattles and her Hobby-Horses, whilst the deluded World still continueth to furnish her with Customers'. But he also objects to the 'too busy diligence' of the dissenting clergy; and in a striking passage he warns the clergy of the Church of England that they had better realize they are living in the modern world, and that the old unquestioning obedience to their authority is a thing of the past:

Our Trimmer . . . thinketh that the Liberty of the late times gave men so much Light, and diffused it so universally among the people, that they are not now to be dealt with as they might have been in Ages of less enquiry; and therefore tho in some well chosen and dearly beloved Auditories, good resolute Non-sense back'd with Authority may prevail, yet generally Men are become so good Judges of what they hear, that the Clergy ought to be very wary how they go about to impose upon their Understandings, which are grown less humble than they were in former times. . . . Now the World is grown sawcy, and expecteth

Reasons, and good ones too, before they give up their own Opinions to other Mens Dictates, tho never so Magisterially deliver'd to them.

What lies behind this passage is partly Halifax's dislike of those High-Church divines who arrogated to themselves the right to lay down the law on political matters, partly his determination to resist any encroachment on the Englishman's liberty, but above all his own political awareness of the way in which Englishmen were thinking and feeling *then*. As a statesman it was his business to keep up to date, to sense the changing attitudes of his fellow countrymen, and to find out what lay behind those attitudes. Although in the *Rough Draft* he decided that Englishmen were as averse to a despotic government as to a republic, and that a 'mixed government' was the only kind that would last long, he also knew that 'it is hard at any time to determine what will be the Shape of the next Revolution'. Even with a mixed government the constitution of its several parts was subject to alteration, for better or for worse, 'according as Circumstances shall arise to induce a *Change*, and as Passion and Interest shall have more or less Influence upon the Publick Councils'.

Halifax, then, is never the political philosopher in his study evolving schemes of government in a vacuum, but the practical statesman addressing himself to the changing problems of the day. He appears to have written little until the last decade of his life, and then most of what he wrote had an immediate relevance to the political situation. This is obviously true of his *Letter to a Dissenter* (on James II's Declaration of Indulgence), *The Anatomy of an Equivalent* (on James II's offer of some 'equivalent' security for the repeal of the Test and Penal laws), and of his *Cautions offered to the Consideration of those who are to chuse Members to serve for the Ensuing Parliament* (of 1695). But it is also true of *The Character of a Trimmer*, which, as Miss Foxcroft showed, was written in 1684, and sent anonymously to the King to justify a policy of moderation and prudence, in opposition to the extreme course of action advocated by the High Tories.

Why Halifax, who wrote so well, wrote so little, is hard to explain. However carefully pondered his views invariably were, he appears to have written fluently and without inhibition; indeed, he expressed himself with an informal elegance which marks the culminating point of Restoration prose. He had at his command a flow of apt and lively metaphor. The opinions of men, he tells us, are too apt to be formed by partiality and common prejudices, with the inevitable result that they change their minds at every new crisis: 'This is a pearching upon the Twigs of things, and not going to the root.' His fondness for metaphors drawn from growing things appears to come from his deepest nature, and may perhaps be related to his conception of the State as a living organism. Equally characteristic is his habit of antithesis, which is the natural expression of a mind poised between two extremes. In this, it may be claimed, he is representative of what is most permanent in the character of his fellow countrymen. Englishmen are not free from anger and prejudice and extremism; but in their best moments they come round to that attitude of practical tolerance which was habitual with the finest and most civilized statesman at the Court of Charles II.

III. ECONOMICS

The history of economic theory in England is usually seen as a slow and uncertain movement towards the light that finally broke upon the minds of men with the publication of Adam Smith's *The Wealth of Nations* in 1776. *Enfin Malherbe vint.* It is certainly impossible to claim for any writer earlier than Adam Smith a consistent economic theory that aimed at taking account of all the facts, and expounded them in a coherent system. Such writing on trade as we find in the later seventeenth century was often the work of merchants who were addressing themselves to a particular situation, and whose economic proposals were by no means disinterested. Of these men one of the best known is Sir Josiah Child (1630–99), a director of the East India Company, who published his *Brief Observations concerning Trade* in 1668, and brought out an enlarged version of the same work, *A Discourse about Trade*, in 1690. Child has been claimed as an early advocate of free trade, but it seems truer to say that he was a mercantilist who was willing to see those restrictions removed that conflicted with his own interests, while retaining others that were favourable to them. In general, men like Child, or Nicholas Barbon, the author of *A Discourse of Trade* (1690), were capable of particular insights, but were much less able to see 'how parts relate to parts, or they to whole'. Child at least must be given credit for insisting on the importance of the commercial and industrial classes in the community. It was, he claimed, the merchants, artificers, farmers, and those who worked for them that brought wealth to a nation from abroad; whereas the nobility, gentry, lawyers, physicians, scholars, and shopkeepers 'do only hand it about from one to another at home'.

What Adam Smith called 'the mercantile system' was still economic orthodoxy in the late seventeenth century. Wealth consisted in money or in bullion; and a nation was wealthy when it held large stocks of gold and silver, and when it exported more goods (and especially manufactured goods) than it imported, and so had a favourable trade balance. In the reign of Charles II England had a highly managed economy, with numerous import tariffs and export reliefs, and with prohibitions and regulations of many kinds. In the first year of the Restoration a Council for Foreign Plantations and a Council for Trade were established. In 1672 Shaftesbury persuaded the King to set up a new Council of Trade and Plantations, of which in the following year John Locke became the secretary. The new Council was dissolved in the spring of 1675; but when, in 1696, William III agreed to the establishment of a Board of Trade, Locke was named as one of the commissioners. Those various bodies were mainly fact-finding and advisory, and were perhaps more concerned with day-to-day problems than with laying down economic principles. Occasionally, however, as with the problems arising in the 1690s from the deterioration of the coinage, or with lowering or raising the rate of interest, matters of theory and principle were inevitably raised. On the first of those problems Nicholas Barbon (d. 1698) favoured a devaluationary policy and supported it with some lively, but at times irrelevant, writing; while Locke, true to his belief in natural law, advocated reminting the coinage at the old standard. Locke's arguments carried the day, and the recoinage of silver was carried out in 1696 under the direction of Sir Isaac Newton, who had been appointed Warden of the Mint, and later became Master. Locke was credited by Macaulay with having thought out for himself a theory of political economy substantially the same as that which Adam Smith afterwards expounded, and one that was in some respects 'more complete and symmetrical'. He certainly realized that economic affairs are governed by natural laws, and that the market value of goods, for example, depends upon the relationship of what we now call supply and demand, and he therefore deserves all the credit he can get for helping to raise economic theory to the status of a science. But his faith in those natural laws was far from being unlimited, and he appears to have thought of them as working only in restricted areas. His repeated insistence in *Some Considerations of the Consequences of the Lowering of Interest and Raising the Value of Money* that the Government must take steps to assure a proper balance of trade, not to mention his proposal to suppress the woollen manufacture of Ireland and replace it with linen, suggests, as Dr. Letwin has said, that 'he was very much an advocate of government intervention in economic affairs'.

One remarkable little work, however, published anonymously in 1691, anticipated most of the later arguments for free trade. Sir Dudley North's[1] *Discourses upon Trade* is not much more than a pamphlet; but never, perhaps, has so much economic good sense been packed into so small a space in such plain and simple language. 'Trade', North explains, 'is nothing else but a Commutation of Superfluities: for instance, I give of mine what I can spare, for somewhat of yours which I want, and you can spare.' From this definition he goes on to explain that silver and gold are only standards of value useful for exchange, and that, like everything else that men buy and sell, the price of these precious metals fluctuates with alterations in supply and demand. Rent, which is the price paid for using someone else's land, and interest, which is the price paid for borrowing someone else's money, are similarly governed by the law of supply and demand, and therefore both rent and interest must be left to find their own level. ('It will be found best for the Nation to leave the Borrowers and the Lender to make their own Bargains.') The notion that a country grows rich by hoarding all the gold and silver which trade brings in 'hath been a Remora, whereby the growing Wealth of many Countries has been obstructed', and is exposed for the error it is by supposing the same principle being put into practice in domestic

---

[1] Sir Dudley North (1641–91), son of the fourth Baron North, and a brother of Lord Chancellor (Francis) North and of Roger North the biographer, became a wealthy merchant in the Turkey Company.

trade between one town or county and the rest of the country. These are a few of North's maxims, and the case for free trade and the absence of government regulations is reiterated in the final words of a Postscript: 'Thus we may labour to hedge in the Cuckow, but in vain: for no People ever yet grew rich by Policies; but it is Peace, Industry, and Freedom that brings Trade and Wealth, and nothing else.' What distinguishes North's *Discourses* is the use he makes of a few general principles which enable him, in the words of a modern scholar of economic theory, 'to provide a mechanistic explanation of an economic process, and to reach policy conclusions that are deducible strictly from the premisses'. At the same time, he never thinks of men as machines, and indeed draws some of his principles from the differences in human nature and human behaviour. North's reputation dates from the rediscovery of his work about a hundred years after his death. According to his brother Roger North, writing in the early eighteenth century, the *Discourses* were then 'utterly sunk, and a copy not to be had for money'. But if they were neglected by Sir Dudley North's contemporaries, their value has been amply recognized in modern times; and in the judgement of Dr. Letwin 'they contain a theoretical structure of power unequalled in their time, the peak of economic thought during the seventeenth century'.

There remains one striking and very different figure, Sir William Petty,[1] in many ways typical of the new, modern men who were coming into prominence after the Restoration. Physically large and ebullient, good-natured but involved in endless quarrels, a mathematician who became an Oxford Professor of Anatomy and a Gresham Professor of Music, the inventor of a mode of 'double writing', of a double-bottom ship, and of a light-weight chariot to cope with the rocks and bogs of Kerry, a cartographer who made a notable survey of Ireland, one of the original Fellows of the Royal Society and one of the founders (1684) and the first President of the Dublin

[1] Sir William Petty (1623–87), the son of a clothier, obtained a good education, by his own efforts, in France and Holland. In 1649 he took a degree in medicine at Oxford, and two years later became Professor of Anatomy there, and was one of the group of Oxford scientists who met in the rooms of Robert Boyle or of the Warden of Wadham (John Wilkins). Some time before the Restoration he undertook a survey of Ireland for the Government, showing a remarkable aptitude for statistical work. Petty was one of the original Fellows of the Royal Society, and was especially interested in technological developments and inventions, as well as in economic and demographic problems.

Philosophical Society, Petty was something of a character, whose original and inventive mind left its mark in many different fields of activity. His ideas, it is true, were often much better than his execution of them; but he brought to bear on political economy the observational methods of the Royal Society, collecting facts and figures, and then proceeding to interpret them. He had helped John Graunt with his *Natural and Political Observations upon the Bills of Mortality* (1662), a landmark in the history of statistical science; and in his own *Political Arithmetic* (he appears to have invented the term) he aimed at expressing himself 'in Terms of *Number, Weight,* or *Measure*; to use only Arguments of Sense, and to consider only such Causes as have visible Foundations in Nature; leaving those that depend upon the mutable Minds, Opinions, Appetites, and Passions of particular Men, to the Consideration of others . . .'. *Political Arithmetic* deals with the real and potential wealth of England, which is contrasted favourably with that of France, and makes use of such vital and trade statistics as Petty could lay his hands on. As he put it himself, in his rather amateur fashion, 'the Observations or Positions . . . upon which I bottom the ensuing Discourses are either true, or not apparently false, . . . and if they are false, not so false as to destroy the Argument they are brought for; but at worst are sufficient as Suppositions to shew the way to that Knowledge I aim at'. Petty can indeed claim to have shown the way; but his facts and figures are nearly always inexact, and are often based on optimistic averaging or ingenious guesswork. In general, he was much too willing to arrive at conclusions before adequate statistics had become available. He is seen at his best in an early work, *A Treatise of Taxes and Contributions* (1662), which, with its 'several intersperst Discourses and Digressions', ranges much more widely than the title might suggest. So far as economic theory is concerned, he shows a clear understanding that those taxes are to be avoided that reduce output, and he is before his time in his treatment of rent and several other economic matters. With all his other gifts he is also a lively writer, and the originality and gaiety of his mind frequently come through in his prose. In dealing with the question of lotteries, for example, he takes his usual independent line:

Now in the way of Lottery men do tax themselves in the general, though out of hopes of Advantage in particular: A Lottery therefore is properly a Tax upon unfortunate self-conceited Fools; men that have a good opinion of their own luckiness. . . . Now because the world abounds with this kinde of fools, it is not fit that every man that will may cheat every man that would be cheated; but it is rather ordained, that the Sovereign should have the Guardianship of these fools, . . . even as in the case of Lunaticks and Idiots.

No doubt Petty did too much to do anything supremely well; but a man who relaxed by translating Psalm 104 into excellent Latin verse, whose conversation delighted Charles II, and who wrote with equal facility on trade, coinage, population, mathematics, medicine, music, shipbuilding, the art of dyeing, clothmaking, and much else, would be unusual in any age. Pepys, who recorded some details of his conversation, summed him up as 'the most rational man that ever I heard speak with a tongue'; and Evelyn, who had met most of the great men of the day, had 'never known such a genius'. Perhaps a better word to describe him would be 'polymath'; but among the many inquiring minds who met and conversed in the early years of the Royal Society, Sir William Petty was certainly one of the most remarkable.

X

SCIENCE

IN the prefatory Epistle addressed to the reader of his *Essay concerning Human Understanding*, Locke surveyed the scientific progress made in his own day. 'The commonwealth of learning', he affirmed, 'is not at this time without master-builders whose mighty designs, in advancing the sciences, will leave lasting monuments to the admiration of posterity.' Everyone could not hope to be a Boyle or a Sydenham, but even in an age which had produced such masters as Huygens and 'the incomparable Mr. Newton' there was still plenty of scope for lesser men who could act as under-labourers

in clearing the Ground a little, and removing some of the Rubbish that lies in the way to Knowledge; which certainly had been very much more advanced in the World, if the Endeavours of ingenious and industrious Men had not been much cumbred with the learned but frivolous use of uncouth, affected, or unintelligible Terms, introduced into the Sciences, and there made an Art of to that Degree, that Philosophy, which is nothing but the true Knowledge of Things, was thought unfit or uncapable to be brought into well-bred Company, and polite Conversation. Vague and insignificant Forms of Speech, and Abuse of Language, have so long passed for Mysteries of Science, and hard or misapply'd Words, with little or no meaning, have, by Prescription, such a Right to be mistaken for deep Learning and heighth of Speculation, that it will not be easie to persuade either those who speak, or those who hear them, that they are but the Covers of Ignorance, and hindrance of true Knowledge.

In those words Locke not only adumbrated his own endeavours in the famous *Essay*, but pointed to the main area of dispute between the new science and the traditional learning of the schools. Hobbes had already jeered at the obscurantist jargon of the Aristotelians, with their 'intentional species' and their 'sympathies and antipathies, names of excuses rather than of causes'; but even in 1690, although the old learning was every-where in retreat, Locke still felt that the process of rubbish disposal was still far from complete. What had to be changed was a whole way of thinking; the disputative method of the schoolmen was becoming more and more discredited as a mode of intellectual procedure, and the emphasis now fell on observation and experiment carried on as a great co-operative venture. Disputation might keep men's wits sharp and enable them to defend traditional intellectual positions against those who had neither their training nor their vocabulary, but it was not likely to increase the boundaries of knowledge. As Sprat put it in one of the many apt metaphors in his *History of the Royal Society*:

> For running, walking, wrestling, shooting, and other such active sports will keep men in health, and breath, and a vigorous temper: but it must be a supply of new food that must make them grow: . . . it must be a continued addition of observations which must nourish, and increase, and give new Blood, and flesh, to the Arts themselves.

The remarkable development of science in seventeenth-century England was no doubt due in part to the fortunate birth of one or two men of genius; but the same generation produced a remarkable number of less gifted scientists, and more still of Locke's 'under-labourers', who, if they had been born fifty years earlier, would almost certainly have achieved far less than they actually did. It was one of the arguments offered in support of the new science that, whereas the old 'dogmatical philosophy' was the exclusive preserve of the privileged in the two universities, observation and experiment were within the powers of all intelligent men. While Sprat made considerable play with the fact that the Fellows of the Royal Society were mainly noblemen or gentlemen, he was not unaware that the pursuit of 'the true knowledge of things' is also a democratic concern, in which artisans, merchants, and even mechanics have their part to perform. Some account of the origins of the Royal Society has been given in the previous volume; and from the time of the granting of the royal charter on 15 July 1662 its influence grew steadily, through its meetings, its foreign correspondence, its experiments, and the publication of its *Transactions* and of such an epoch-making volume as Newton's *Principia* (1687). Its royal founder, it is true, gave it little but an amiable acquiescence, and sometimes not even that. On 1 February 1664 Pepys stood by at Whitehall while the King ridiculed Sir William Petty's new double-bottomed boat, and laughed at the members of the Royal Society 'for spending time only in weighing of ayre and doing nothing else since they sat'. In this, as in other things, the King gave a dubious lead to his subjects, and baiting the virtuosi became a recognized field of activity for the wit; but the Society proceeded serenely on its way, stimulating discussion and providing a clearing-house for new inventions, observations, and discoveries. The contrast between the scientists and the men of letters in the Restoration period is striking: while the literary world was split by controversy and personal quarrels, the scientists pooled their resources, and if they were drawn into controversy it was usually (though not invariably) to make common cause against the declared enemies and denigrators of the new philosophy. No doubt the air of ingenuous inquiry and well-mannered argument that permeates the early exchanges of the Royal Society owed something to the presence in its deliberations of a considerable number of gentlemen-virtuosi, such as Pepys and Evelyn, who had not much scientific reputation at stake. But good-tempered discussion was one of the aims of the Society. When the original members met together at Oxford shortly after the Civil War, their first purpose (as Sprat tells us) was 'onely the satisfaction of breathing a freer air, and of conversing in quiet with one another, without being ingag'd in the passions and madness of that dismal Age'; and this spirit of uncontroversial inquiry became a tradition that was usually honoured by the Fellows. In his Preface to *The Sceptical Chemist* Boyle explained that he had taken pains to carry on his argument in an amiable fashion, in the hope that some of his readers might discover that 'a man may be a champion to truth without being an enemy to civility, and may confute an opinion without railing at them that hold it'. In a century which had so far been rent by religious and political conflict, the growth of a spirit of free and unpartisan inquiry was of the greatest value. Anything that could release the mind of men from the intolerance of party or sect and that mid-century spirit of 'enthusiasm' which most Englishmen now deplored was in tune with the spirit of the new age.

The harmony which Boyle and others were so anxious to preserve became troubled in due course by some inevitable discord. The two great influences on English science after the Restoration were Bacon and Descartes, and to some extent they were responsible for a difference of emphasis in scientific studies. From Bacon the new philosophy derived its insistence on observation and experiment; from Descartes it learnt the importance of the mathematical approach to scientific problems. Ideally there was no occasion for conflict: the mathematical calculations of a Newton depended for their data on previous observation, and the observations and experiments of a Boyle could ultimately be formulated in a scientific law. The whole tendency of Boyle, however, and of the Royal Society in its earliest years, was to concentrate on the collection of evidence and to withhold judgement. Hypotheses were in order, but at this early stage they must be put forward very tentatively. Boyle was criticized by Huygens for having reached so few general conclusions from all his numerous experiments. He might have defended himself as Sprat defended the Royal Society:

To this fault of *Sceptical doubting* the Royal Society may perhaps be suspected to be a little too much inclin'd: because they always professed to be so backward from *setling* of *Principles*, or fixing upon *Doctrines*. . . . It is their study, that the way to attain a *solid speculation* should every day be more and more persued: which is to be done by a long forbearing of *speculation* at first, till the matters be ripe for it; and not by madly rushing upon it in the very beginning.

So, too, in publishing his *Micrographia* (1665), Robert Hooke ventured to suggest that his book might help to show that what was needed for a reformation in natural philosophy was not so much 'any strength of imagination, or exactness of method, or depth of contemplation . . . as a sincere hand, and a faithful eye, to examine and to record the things themselves as they appear'. The science of nature had been for too long 'only a work of the brain and the fancy'.

But this halcyon period of the retort and the microscope, of the hand and the eye, was not to last unchallenged for long. Although Sprat was able to praise the Royal Society for its freedom from animosities and faction, personal disagreements began to make themselves felt, disputes over priority in discovery and invention, and failures of understanding and sympathy due to a divergence of approach among the different branches of science. Even Sprat allowed himself some tempered criticism of Descartes, who was to be admired for freeing his mind from outworn ideas, but who made the mistake of believing that he could fill the resulting vacuum with an intellectual structure built upon solitary thinking, the cogitations of his own mind unaided by any form of external observation. Descartes came under criticism, too, because his theory of vortices was thought to support a merely mechanical conception of physical law, and to leave no scope for the divine will to operate. None the less, the desire to be 'setling of principles or fixing upon doctrines', and to do so by means of those mathematical calculations in which Newton was supreme, could not be suppressed; it led inevitably to a new distribution of emphasis, and, among the general body of scientists, to some division of interest. If we are to believe Pope, Newton 'could hardly avoid showing his contempt for your virtuoso collecters and antiquarians'. No doubt, as science became a fashionable pursuit, it attracted many brainless people, and collecting has always been one of the pleasanter substitutes for thought. The virtuoso, at any rate, was one of the main targets for satirical attack for several generations. As late as 1742 Pope thought him well worth his ridicule:

> Yet by some object ev'ry brain is stirr'd;
> The dull may waken to a Humming-bird; . . .
> The mind, in Metaphysics at a loss,
> May wander in a wilderness of Moss.

To the last line Pope added the note: 'Of which the Naturalists count above three hundred species'; the assumption being that they were wasting their time in a quite ridiculous way. It was just this attitude that Boyle was at pains to combat: nothing in nature was too low or too trivial to be investigated. He had been experimenting (he once told his readers) on the nature and use of dungs: 'And although my condition does (God be praised) enable me to make experiments by others' hands, yet I have not been so nice as to decline dissecting dogs, wolves, fishes and even rats and mice, with my own hands.' In the satire of the period, such as Shadwell's *The Virtuoso*, it is almost always the collector and the experimenter who are ridiculed: there is not much attempt to laugh at the work of men like Newton, which, however little it may have been understood by the average man, was of the kind that he had been taught to respect. When Boyle's Themistius, in *The*

Sceptical Chemist, the expounder of the traditional peripatetic philosophy, claims that 'it is much more high and philosophical to discover things *a priori* than *a posteriori*', he was stating no more than most men still believed.

The building up of what would now be called the public image of the Royal Society was considerably helped by two men who became Fellows, but who were not so much scientists themselves as interested and persuasive propagandists. In 1661, with the publication of *The Vanity of Dogmatizing*, Joseph Glanvill opened his long campaign against the scholastic philosophy and in favour of the experimental approach to natural phenomena. Glanvill, whose book glows with the enthusiasm of a young convert, was casting off the burden of the stale and unprofitable learning which he had acquired at Oxford, and stepping out lightly and confidently into a newly discovered world. It is his enthusiasm for the new philosophy that gives his writing its buoyancy, but it is his ability to marshal his ideas into an orderly argument (perhaps the traditional Oxford education had done more for him than he would admit) that makes his first book so effective a statement. From a series of examples of what men do not yet know, he proceeds to consider the various reasons for men's 'backwardness to acknowledge their own ignorance and errour', devotes several chapters to what was soon to be a familiar criticism of the peripatetic philosophy, and concludes with an eloquent apology for the new methods of scientific inquiry. He has, too, the gift of illustrating his points with apt metaphors and examples, the most celebrated of these, the story of the Scholar Gypsy, being introduced to demonstrate the occurrence of telepathic communication. As a pioneer work designed to break down opposition to new ideas and open men's minds to possibilities they had dismissed, or never even considered, *The Vanity of Dogmatizing*, if we allow for some ignorance and some over-emphasis, could hardly be bettered. In 1665 Glanvill republished it, with some slight revisions and a long dedicatory Epistle to the Royal Society, as *Scepsis Scientifica*. What may be called the third edition appeared in a completely revised and much shorter form in his *Essays on Several Important Subjects* (1676). The original work had been written in a decidedly ornate prose with unmistakable echoes of Sir Thomas Browne; in the final revision this bravery of language has largely disappeared, and Glanvill shows everywhere his respect for the stylistic ideals of the Royal Society, rejecting those 'amplifications, digressions and swellings of style' that had come so naturally and pleasantly to him as a young man. In the revision of 1676 'praterlapsed ages' become 'past ages', 'preponderate much greater magnitudes' is changed to 'out-weigh much heavier bodies', and 'we think it so piaculous' to 'we think it such presumption'.

What Glanvill had to say to his own generation was mainly said in his first book, but he continued to write copiously for the rest of his comparatively short life. In *Plus Ultra* (1668) he discoursed on the improvements to useful knowledge made by 'the illustrious Mr. Boyle' and other modern experimental scientists. Here again we have an elaboration of the Baconian strictures on the scholastic philosophers, whose subtle disputation never 'brought the world so much practical, beneficial knowledge as would help towards the cure of a cut finger'. The emphasis so frequently placed on useful knowledge by the apologists of the Royal Society was natural and proper; but it enabled their opponents in the ensuing controversy to benefit from that prestige which, in academic circles at least, always attaches to useless knowledge. In 1666 Glanvill, who had taken holy orders and who was always interested in the occult, published a treatise on witches and witchcraft, best known by the title given to it in a later edition, *Sadducismus Triumphatus*. It may seem odd to find this prophet of enlightenment arguing in favour of the existence of witches, but Glanvill had not really changed his ground: he was still fighting dogmatism, the dogmatism of these modern days which held that the continuing belief in witchcraft was a mere superstition. Yet if his argument is not inconsistent with his normal attitude of sceptical inquiry, he cannot claim to be wholly disinterested, and towards the end he almost admits as much: 'We live in an age wherein Atheism is begun in Sadducism: and those that dare not bluntly say, *There is no God*, content themselves, for a fair step and introduction, to deny there are spirits or witches.' No witches, no God: it is this conviction that is really responsible for Glanvill's treatise. *Sadducismus Triumphatus* remains a curious reminder of the uncertainty all through this period of what are now called the 'climates' of opinion.

The other, and more official, champion of the virtuosi was

Thomas Sprat, like several of the early scientists a Wadham man, whose *History of the Royal Society* (delayed by the Plague and the Great Fire) appeared in 1667. Sprat's book, with a prefatory Ode to the Royal Society by Cowley, is in three parts; it opens with a review of learning up to his own day, passes on to an account of the origin and development of the Society, and ends with a reasoned defence of its activities, in which Sprat sets out to prove that

the increase of Experiments will be so far from hurting, that it will be many waies advantageous, above other Studies, to the wonted Courses of Education; to the Principles and instruction of the minds of Men in general; to the Christian Religion, to the Church of England; to all Manual Trades; to Physic; to the Nobility and Gentry; and the Universal Interest of the whole Kingdom.

In his desire to convince the universities and the Church that their vested interests are not in danger, Sprat is a good deal more tactful and conciliatory than Glanvill; he writes like a public relations officer, conscious that he has a good case but not seeking to press it too far. As for religion, 'the present Inquiring Temper of this Age' is similar to that which brought about the Reformation and the Protestant religion; and if we may look forward in the future to more of those changes 'to which Religion has bin always subject', we may be fairly sure that they will be neither 'to the advantage of implicit Faith [the Church of Rome], nor of Enthusiasm, but of Reason'. Although the religious opinions of the individual Fellows of the Royal Society were no doubt sufficiently varied, the latitudinarian position of Sprat himself, who claimed that 'the universal Disposition of this Age is bent upon a rational Religion', probably represented the views of the majority. At this stage Sprat and most of his contemporaries saw only the advantages of a reasonable religion, and believed that the more they were able to reveal the wonderful working of secondary causes the more men would be drawn to worship of the great First Cause. The shadow of deism was creeping slowly forward, but had not yet darkened the bright and innocent scene. For Sprat, at all events, the man who really set himself to examine and understand 'the wonderful Contrivance of the Creation' would find it natural 'to apply and direct his praises aright: which no doubt, when they are offer'd up to Heven from the mouth of one who has well studied what he commands, will be more sutable to the Divine Nature than the blind applauses of the ignorant'. Sprat's argument throughout is calm, methodical, confident, and reassuring, and he writes with a balanced ease and a resounding reasonableness which still impressed Dr. Johnson a hundred years later—as well it might, for Sprat's prose is often remarkably Johnsonian.

Sprat spends so much of his time in thinking up and answering possible objections, that we may easily be led to overestimate the extent of the opposition which the Royal Society encountered in its early years. There was, however, some expressed criticism, and no doubt an undercurrent of silent distrust and misgiving. We learn from Evelyn that in the summer of 1669 Robert South delivered a speech at the opening of the Sheldonian Theatre in Oxford which was 'not without some malicious and undecent reflections on the Royal Society as underminers of the University', and here and there in his sermons we meet with indirect but sarcastic observations on the new philosophy. Dr. Fell at Oxford and Dr. Gunning at Cambridge were clearly unsympathetic, and stood by the traditional learning of the universities. The most formidable critic of the virtuosi was the Warwick physician Henry Stubbe (1632–76), who was thought by Anthony Wood to have been encouraged by Fell to reply to Glanvill and Sprat, those two Oxford graduates who had bitten the hand that fed them. Stubbe was either a very angry man, or was highly successful in giving that impression. He is seen at his best, and his worst, in *Plus Ultra reduced to a Non Plus* (1670), a long rambling attack on Glanvill, in which he expressed the opinion that there was every day 'a greater necessitie of securing our Eares with black wooll or Wax against the Buz and Noise of these Prattleboxes', and claimed that he was writing in defence of 'the ancient Education of this Kingdom, the two universities, and the Protestant Church'. Stubbe, who seems to have been particularly incensed by Glanvill's scornful reference to the cure of a cut finger, was far from being uninformed in at least some fields of science; but for the purposes of abuse he used any argument that came to hand: telescopes are not really reliable; much of what Glanvill mistakenly calls new was known to Aristotle; if we should find that the planets are inhabited, it wouldn't make a pennyworth of difference to anyone—'we shall not finde out any gainful commerce with them; nor need we dread that they will piss out our Eyes as we look up'. (This last was a palpable hit, for both Sprat and Glanvill had emphasized the utilitarian value of the new scientific discoveries.) Here and there Stubbe touches upon one of the real issues that divided the traditionalists from the new men. He had once known a brilliant young scholar 'who died before that Ignorance and the Virtuosi grew prevalent', and from him he had learnt that

for a man to desert those Studies which qualifie him for a sociable life, and were of importance to the preservation of the Government and Countrey he lived in, this was a kinde of salvagenesse, had more of the Anchorete then of Civil Prudence, and was to be encouraged in a Cloyster, or in the deserts of Thebais, then to be made a practice among wise Statesmen.

For this young man, as for Johnson in the next century, the knowledge of external nature was clearly not 'the great or the frequent business of the human mind', and Stubbe, too, would have agreed that 'we are perpetually moralists, but we are geometricians only by chance'.

In some admonitory words addressed to the Wits near the end of his *History* Sprat had suggested that they ridiculed the new philosophy because it was new, and because they themselves were unwilling to take any pains about it. This was a shrewd enough diagnosis so far as it went; but, to the Restoration wit, the virtuoso was a figure of fun because he was thought to be completely detached from the normal concerns of men and women, because he was hopelessly unbalanced and one-sided, and because the fleas and vinegar eels and cockles that absorbed his attention were naturally contemptible. All this made him a fit person to be laughed at or to be cozened and cuckolded in a modern comedy. Even the King, as we have seen, could laugh at the notion of weighing air; and Samuel Butler in 'The Elephant in the Moon' thought of at least some of the virtuosi as men

who greedily pursue
Things wonderful, instead of true,

and in another satirical piece jeered at their endeavours

To find the North-west passage out,
Although the furthest Way about.

When we turn to the published work of the scientists, we find that some of them, like Newton, gave their discoveries to the world in Latin, and that of those who wrote in English the best scientists were sometimes the worst writers, and the best writers the most dubious scientists. The Honourable Robert Boyle[1] was the embodiment of all that was best and most characteristic of the Royal Society in its earliest years, admirable as a man and indefatigable as an experimenter. In his first, and in some ways his best, scientific work, *New Experiments . . . touching the Spring of the Air* (1660) he published the results of his experiments on the problems of combustion and respiration as affected by the air of the atmosphere; and in *The Sceptical Chemist* one year later he subjected the traditional chemical theories to a destructive criticism, and offered a definition of the element which marks the starting-point of modern chemistry. He prosecuted his inquiries on the widest possible front, touching on optics, physiological medicine, thermodynamics, hydrostatics, luminescence, magnetism and electricity, and much else. Left to himself he would have been content to work in his laboratory and gather evidence, believing that natural philosophy would have advanced much more rapidly if men had not been 'so forward to write systems of it'. But he had to publish his results, and when he left his laboratory, where he was at home and happy, and went to his writing-desk, where he was neither, he was like Coleridge's swan crushing the reeds on the river bank. On his own showing, the loose papers on which he habitually wrote piecemeal were almost invariably in a state of chronic muddle, scattered, mislaid, imperfect, blotted and erased, and (as he says of one manuscript) 'written at somewhat distant times and places, and hastily tacked together, so that when the latter sheets were penning the former were often not at hand'. The prose resulting from those chaotic circumstances was loose, prolix, and wandering. The structure of Boyle's sentences was dictated by the need to make detailed and comprehensive statements that would leave nothing out,

[1] Robert Boyle (1627–91), a son of Richard Boyle, first Earl of Cork, settled at Oxford in 1654, and erected a laboratory there, with Robert Hooke as his chemical assistant. He was one of the founders of the Royal Society, and took an active part in its early proceedings, publishing voluminously his own experiments in chemistry and physics. Boyle, who was a deeply religious man, also wrote several moral and religious essays, and founded the Boyle Lectures for the defence of Christianity against unbelievers.

and that would stop every avenue to misunderstanding; but the frequent introduction of modifications, amplifications, and second thoughts leaves the reader with little or no sense of direction:

I will not here debate whether there may not be a multitude of these corpuscles, which by reason of their being primary and simple, might be called elementary, if several sorts of them should convene to compose any body, which are as yet free, and neither as yet contexed and entangled with primary corpuscles of other kinds, but remains liable to be subdued and fashioned by seminal principles, or the like powerful and transmuting agent, by whom they may be so connected among themselves, or with the parts of one of the bodies, as to make the compound bodies, whose ingredients they are, resoluble into more, or other elements than those that chymists have hitherto taken notice of.

The weight of such sentences is so evenly distributed over subordinate clauses and alternatives that everything appears to be equally important, and the reader is left to sort things out for himself. When he is rather less under the pressure of scientific fact and is justifying the work of the virtuosi, as in *The Usefulness of Experimental Philosophy* (1664), Boyle can sometimes write more clearly and consecutively, but composition always came hard to him. If, as Sprat claimed, the Royal Society wished to promote 'not the Artifice of words, but a bare knowledge of things', Robert Boyle was undoubtedly their man.

In one of his happier phrases Boyle once expressed his admiration for minute objects by observing: 'I must confess my wonder dwells not so much on Nature's clocks (if I may so speak) as on her watches.' In assessing the impact of the new science on the imagination of the later seventeenth century we should give full value to the work of the microscopists. Malpighi in Italy, Leeuwenhoek in Holland, Nehemiah Grew and Robert Hooke in England all revealed to their contemporaries the complex and hitherto unsuspected structure of minute living things. The wisdom of God was manifested as never before when the microscope made clear the delicate loveliness of a fly's wing or the more alarming beauty of a flea. Nehemiah Grew (1641–1712) directed his attention to the anatomy and physiology of vegetables, and in *The Anatomy of Plants* (1682) gathered together the results of some twenty years' research. Among the other discoveries with which he may be credited is the true existence of sex in plants. Towards the end of his life he contributed a large folio volume to the growing field of physico-theological literature, *Cosmologia Sacra, or a Discourse of the Universe, as it is the Creature and Kingdom of God* (1701). As a writer he has little distinction, but as a patient and intelligent investigator he has an honourable place in the history of botany.

Robert Hooke[1] was a very different sort of man. He had a natural flair for speculation, and he roamed happily over the whole field of science. He had, too, a remarkable mechanical skill, and it was this that first brought him into contact with the leading men of science a few years before the Restoration. There followed a fruitful period when he worked as Boyle's paid assistant: an ideal combination of the patient experimenter never hasty to reach general conclusions, and the agile theorist who was also expert and ingenious in finding practical ways and means of extending knowledge. To Hooke must go the credit of improving Guericke's air-pump, which led to Boyle's discoveries about the elasticity, compressibility, and weight of air. In his spare time he had been making microscopical observations, and in 1665 he published, with the imprimatur of the Royal Society, an elegant folio, *Micrographia*, illustrated with thirty-eight plates of his own beautifully executed drawings. Hooke proceeded, very sensibly, from man-made objects (needles, razors, lawn, taffeta) to such natural objects as cork, leaves, seeds, the sting of a bee, and the teeth of a snail, taking occasion to remark in passing that the finest that man can do is rough and inept compared to the work of God. All his ambition, he professed, was to serve the great philosophers of this age 'as the makers and the grinders of my Glasses did to me; that I may prepare and furnish them with some Materials which they may afterwards order and manage with better skill, and to far greater advantage'. When we turn to the text of his book,

[1] Robert Hooke (1635–1703) was educated at Westminster School (under Dr. Busby) and at Christ Church, Oxford. His mechanical skill attracted the attention of the group of scientific men then at Oxford, and he became assistant to the Hon. Robert Boyle, helping him materially in the construction of his air-pump. In 1662 he became Curator of Experiments to the Royal Society, a Fellow in the following year, and Secretary from 1677 to 1682. He was appointed Professor of Geometry at Gresham College in 1665. After the Fire of London he became City Surveyor, and himself designed a number of important buildings.

however, we find that he has given us a good deal more than he has promised; the observations are there, but so too is a good deal of ingenious theory. In this respect he was irrepressible; he continued to speculate ingeniously on a wide variety of scientific problems, and either made, or anticipated, some of the most important discoveries of the age. He seems at times to have had an imaginative awareness of scientific laws without being able to demonstrate them; he claimed, indeed, to have anticipated Newton's law of universal gravitation, but he lacked the mathematics necessary for working it out. Hooke was a lively and lucid writer, with the gift of exposition that Boyle so notably lacked. He is an odd combination of the man of science and the artist, the technologist and the theoretician, the humble collector of data and the buoyant and cheerful essayist. How little he allowed the collective gravity of the Royal Society to inhibit his natural liveliness may be seen from his opening observations on the louse, 'a Creature so officious, that 'twill be known to every one at one time or other, so busie, and so impudent, that it will be intruding it self in every one's company, and so proud and aspiring withall, that it fears not to trample on the best, and affects nothing so much as a Crown; feeds and lives very high . . .', and so on. Having got all this said (and Boyle can hardly have approved of this disquisition on the part of his protégé), Hooke returns to his usual clear, idiomatic, and evocative description of the object under observation. He was a natural writer, without either pedantry or ostentation, coming nearer perhaps than any of his scientific contemporaries to the style of writing that the Royal Society had made its ideal.

John Evelyn had a lifelong interest in the rarities of nature and of art. When he was a young man making the tour of Europe his interest was equally divided between the master-pieces of painting and architecture, the first elephant he had ever seen (at Rotterdam), which he observed to be 'flexible and nimble in its joynts, contrary to vulgar tradition', and a woman at Amsterdam 'who had ben Widow to 25 Husbands, as they told us'. In later life he became a genuine expert in several fields, and his *Sylva, or a Discourse of Forest-Trees* (1664) was for long the chief source of information on the cultivation of trees and the uses to which the various kinds of timber could be put. One of the two appendices, *Kalendarium Hortense: or the*

Gardener's Almanac ran through many separate editions before the close of the century. Evelyn, who was addressing himself mainly to gentlemen and persons of quality who were land-owners, and not to 'our ordinary Rusticks (meer Foresters and Wood-men'), writes in the grand manner; and indeed a certain undemocratic pomposity was never wholly absent from his mode of expressing himself. (He had once intended to write a History of Trade, but gave up the idea because, as he told Boyle, it involved 'many subjections, which I cannot support, of conversing with mechanical capricious persons'.) In *Sylva*, at any rate, we meet with a sort of mid-eighteenth-century poetic diction, by means of which vulgar and mechanical activities are made more acceptable to the polite. Thus trees, which provide 'hortular ornament' and a home for 'canorous birds', are not planted but 'interred' (after sufficient 'stercoration'), and 'extravagant' branches have to be lopped to allow for the penetration of 'that . . . chearful vehicle, light, which the gloomy and torpent north is so many months depriv'd of'. Nothing could be further from the style of discourse recommended by the Royal Society. As chemistry, physics, botany, and the other sciences progressed, a specialized terminology, unintelligible to the common reader, was inevitably being evolved; but Evelyn's terms are often more erudite than scientific.

The humility and goodness of Robert Boyle reappear in John Ray,[1] an inquiring spirit of rare quality, methodical, persistent, wide-ranging, and singularly alive to the significance of what he saw and recorded. His observation was more particularly exercised on botanical, zoological, and geological matters, but he also published a glossary of dialect words (1674). It is mainly as a botanist that he earns his place in the history of science. His *Historia Plantarum*, in three folio volumes, 1686–1704, has had a permanent influence on the classification of

---

[1] John Ray (1627–1705), the son of an Essex blacksmith, was educated at Cambridge University, and subsequently lectured there successively in Greek, mathematics, and Latin. In 1658 he made the first of his series of botanical tours, in the Midlands and North Wales, and two years later he published the first of his catalogues of plants. In that year he took holy orders. His *Historia Plantarum* appeared between 1686 and 1704. Although primarily a botanist, he was also well-informed in zoology, and he interested himself too in philological matters, publishing *A Collection of English Proverbs* in 1670. His physico-theological work, *The Wisdom of God manifested in the Works of the Creation* (1691), went through many editions.

plants; but as this and similar works of his were written in
Latin they fall rather outside our scope. As a writer in English
he is now chiefly remembered for his work of popular science,
or physico-theology, *The Wisdom of God manifested in the Works
of the Creation*. Here, indeed, Ray was a good deal less of an
innovator than in his botanical and zoological studies: Henry
More, Cudworth, Wilkins, Boyle, Stillingfleet, and others had
already illustrated the wisdom of God from the natural world,
and Ray occasionally borrowed some of his examples from them.
The Wisdom of God, however, reached the serious-minded reader
of every degree of education; it is well planned, and simply, if
not very elegantly, written, it abounds with more information
about animals and plants than any of his predecessors had
given, and it is irradiated by the enthusiasm of a genuinely
simple and devout man. It must also have performed, like the
Tatler and *Spectator* in the next generation, a useful service
in providing topics for conversation and encouraging mild
speculation. How is it, for instance, that birds 'tho' they bring
but one morsel of Meat at a time, and have not fewer (it
may be) than seven or eight Young in the Nest together, which
at the return of their Dams, do all at once with equal greediness
hold up their Heads and gape'—how is it that the parent birds
should yet manage not to 'omit or forget one of them, but
feed them all?' Ray does not know the answer (he is unwilling
to believe that birds can count), nor did his readers; but such
problems are of the widest possible interest, for they are within
every reader's field of reference, and they are puzzles to be
solved. The appeal of Ray's book was not unlike that of
Nathaniel Wanley's *The Wonders of the Little World* or Dunton's
question-and-answer periodical, *The Athenian Mercury*. In the
development of his theme, Ray occasionally borders on *naïveté*,
as when he demonstrates that insects (which we should be glad
to be without) are useful to mankind 'if not immediately, yet
mediately', since they are food for the birds from which we get
the feathers to stuff our beds and pillows and the quills with
which we write. In short, whatever is in Nature is right. In
1676, after the death of his friend Francis Willughby the
naturalist (1635–72), Ray published his *Ornithologiae tres libri*,
and followed it up with an enlarged and elaborately illustrated
English version, *The Ornithology of Francis Willughby* (1678).
In 1686 he brought out Willughby's *De Historia Piscium*.

Willughby, like Ray, has some importance in the history of the classification of natural species.

Since the scientists who are of importance here are those who may be considered in relation to English literature, it is not possible to do more than mention such distinguished mathematicians and astronomers as Isaac Barrow, John Wallis, Lawrence Rooke, Seth Ward, and above all Sir Christopher Wren, who seemed to Robert Hooke to be the very Archimedes of his age, since 'scarce ever met in one man in so great a perfection such a mechanical hand and so philosophical a mind'. When Sprat decided to illustrate the work of the Royal Society by the multifarious activities of a single Fellow it was Wren that he chose as his example. Among the distinguished medical men were Thomas Sydenham, Francis Glisson, Thomas Willis, and Jonathan Goddard. Sydenham (1624–89), the friend of Boyle and also of John Locke, who was himself a physician, showed some lack of sympathy with the work of his contemporaries, and he was never a member of the Royal Society; but his claim to have written nothing that was not the product of faithful observation indicates the modern temper of his mind.

Observation played only a minimal part in Thomas Burnet's[1] *Telluris Theoria Sacra* (1681), the English version of which was published three years later. The earth, he believed, was originally as smooth as an egg, and the Deluge was caused by the crust caving in: great fragments fell down into the abyss, and the subterranean waters rushed upwards and covered the globe, and then slowly retreated again to fill the chasms that had been caused. Burnet, who associated the terrestrial disorder with the Fall of Man and the ensuing curse on the earth, constructed his theory from what he found in the Bible, and then filled in the gaps by plausible conjecture. Moses had imputed the Deluge to a disruption of the abyss, and St. Peter had accounted for it by the fact that the earth was obnoxious to absorption in water. 'But it was below the dignity of those

---

[1] Thomas Burnet (1635?–1715) was educated at Cambridge University, where he came under the influence of Ralph Cudworth and John Tillotson, and was elected a Fellow of Christ's College in 1657. He was appointed Master of the Charterhouse in 1685, and is said to have been thought of at one time as a possible successor to Tillotson as Archbishop of Canterbury, but to have been passed over because of suspicions about his orthodoxy. Such suspicions, based on his *Sacred Theory of the Earth*, were no doubt increased by the publication of his *Archaeologiae Philosophicae* (1692), where he gave a non-literal interpretation of the first book of Genesis.

sacred pen-men', Burnet explained, '. . . to shew us the causes of this disruption: this is left to the enquiries of men.' It was in fact part of the divine plan that men should use their reason, and by giving us merely the bare facts God intended 'to excite our curiosity and inquisitiveness after the methods by which such things are brought to pass'. Thus encouraged, Burnet let his fancy roam, and arrived at what, in 1681, was perhaps as good a guess as anyone else's. But already his traditional assumption that mountains and seas were the marks of disorder after the Fall was becoming old-fashioned. In 1627 George Hakewill had argued that the physical features of the earth represented the order of divine law, and not the disorder of original sin; and Bishop Wilkins had claimed in 1638 that mountains were so far from being a deformity that 'if well considered, they will be found as much to conduce to the Beauty and Conveniency of the Universe as any of the other Parts'. The argument from utility was developed by Henry More (who called mountains 'Nature's stillatories'), by John Ray, and by several other Fellows of the Royal Society. One way or another, Burnet's book provoked a considerable controversy, and called forth some ingenious theories, such as that of Edmund Halley (elaborated by William Whiston) that the Flood was caused by the earth passing through the tail of a comet.

But if Burnet could be· confuted as a man of science, he stood head and shoulders above his critics as a writer. *The Sacred Theory* shows how far a confident and rhythmical prose may go in making a reader accept statements that are very slenderly supported by evidence. So convinced was Burnet himself that it is sometimes hard to remember that what he describes so vividly never actually occurred. In some passages we might be listening to an eye-witness account:

The pressure of a great mass of earth falling into the abyss . . . could not but impel the water with so much strength, as would carry it up to a great height in the air, and to the top of any thing that lay in its way, any eminency, high fragment, or new mountain. And then rolling back again, it would sweep down with whatsoever it rush'd upon, woods, buildings, living creatures, and carry them all headlong into the great gulph. Sometimes a mass of water would be quite struck off and separate from the rest, and tossed through the air like a flying river; but the common motion of the waves was to climb up the hills or inclin'd fragments; and then return into the valleys and deeps again, with a perpetual fluctuation going and coming, ascending and descending, 'till the violence of them being spent by degrees, they settled at last in the places allotted for them....

It will be observed how Burnet passes from 'could' and 'would' to the simple assertion of 'was' and 'were'; but the reader 'stands secure amidst a falling world' because Burnet pursues his great argument with a Miltonic grandeur and reverence that give to his wildest descriptions an air of authenticity. His prose is very far from the norm of the period; but it is significant that in an age which was becoming less imaginative in both poetry and prose, some of the most sustained flights of the imagination were achieved by writers who, under the influence of the Old Testament or the Book of Revelation, contemplated such cataclysmic events as the Flood, or dwelt pindarically with Pomfret and others on the Last Day and the General Conflagration and ensuing Judgement.

The influence of the Royal Society on English prose style has been emphasized so much in recent years that it is now perhaps in some danger of being exaggerated. In a well-known passage in his *History of the Royal Society* Sprat emphasized the importance placed by the Fellows on a clear and unaffected style, avoiding 'the luxury and redundancy of speech' and 'this trick of Metaphors, this volubility of Tongue' which still (in 1667) 'makes so great a noise in the World'. The ideal to be aimed at by the Fellows was 'a close, naked, natural way of speaking; positive expressions; clear senses; a native easiness; bringing all things as near the Mathematical plainness as they can; and preferring the language of Artizans, Countrymen, and Merchants, before that of Wits, or Scholars'. While the influence of at least some of the scientists on English prose was on the side of simplicity, it must be remembered that the written work of most of them did not reach anything like general circulation, and it should not be forgotten that while Robert Hooke came very near to realizing the ideal of 'so many things almost in an equal number of words', Boyle and Evelyn were very far from achieving it.

Yet there can be no question that the scientific, medical, and technological writings of the seventeenth century exercised a very real and permanent influence on the vocabulary of English prose, encouraging and familiarizing the use of abstract and general terms, making possible the growth of metaphors from physical science and that magniloquent expression which is to be found in one of the main streams of eighteenth-century prose, and also affected—often happily, but sometimes less fortunately—the diction of poetry. The extent to which the discoveries of the scientists fired the imagination of the poets and gave them the themes for their poetry varied from one poet to another. To Sprat in 1667 it seemed evident that 'the Wit of the Fables and Religions of the Ancient World is well nigh consum'd', and poets could find 'in the Works of Nature an inexhaustible Treasure of Fancy and Invention, which will be reveal'd proportionably to the increas of their Knowledge'. But he was also well aware that poets were apt to be conservative and ill informed about the new philosophy because they were 'unwilling to take pains about it'; and to a considerable extent (although there were to be some notable exceptions) he proved to be right. A hundred years later the poets were still ringing their changes on the old classical mythology, and there must have been many readers who agreed with Dr. Johnson that 'the machinery of the Pagans is uninteresting to us', and that 'the attention naturally retires from a new tale of Venus, Diana, and Minerva'.

XI

CRITICISM

CRITICISM became an increasingly prominent activity in the literary world of the late seventeenth century. If it sometimes seemed to Dryden that contemporary English criticism was little better than 'hangman's work', and that 'we are fallen into an age of illiterate, censorious, and detracting people, who, thus qualified, set up for critics', he usually preferred to think of criticism as 'a standard of judging well', with particular emphasis on 'those excellencies which should delight a reasonable reader'. That there was a serious interest in critical principles (as distinct from critical personalities) may be seen from the fact that much of the work of Boileau, Le Bossu, Rapin, Saint-Évremond, and other French critics was quickly made available for the English reader in translation. Native English criticism had been rather slow to develop, but was rapidly making up the lost ground. Not only did many of the poets and dramatists set forth their critical ideas in prefaces and dedications, but the last few decades of the century saw the emergence of such men as Rymer and Dennis, who were primarily critics rather than creative writers. Critical dictionaries and miscellanies were now beginning to appear, and may be seen as supplying literary information and critical opinion for a public that now felt the need for such reading. In this way Edward Phillips's *Theatrum Poetarum* (in the Preface to which some have seen the hand of his uncle, John Milton) and Gerard Langbaine's *Account of the English Dramatic Poets* (1691) provided a mixture of biographical and critical reading matter; and Sir Thomas Pope Blount's compilation *De re poetica* (1694), although the author rarely ventures on a judgement of his own, has at least the merit of presenting a representative selection from contemporary critical opinion, not only on authors, but on literary kinds and on some of the chief literary topics of the day.

In 1690, in the second volume of his *Miscellanea*, Sir William Temple published 'An Essay upon the Ancient and

Modern Learning', and by so doing brought to a sharp focus in England a critical controversy that had been developing for several decades. In France a few years earlier Charles Perrault had put forward the claims of the Moderns to have surpassed the Ancients, and in 1688 Fontenelle had supported those claims in his *Digression sur les anciens et les modernes*. No considered reply had been made to either Perrault or Fontenelle by their fellow countrymen when Temple wrote his essay, and he made it clear that his immediate reason for writing was to protest against Fontenelle's denigration of the Ancients, but also to answer an extravagant panegyric of modern learning that he had come across at the end of Thomas Burnet's *Sacred Theory of the Earth*. Temple was too shrewd to put forward a blanket defence of the Ancients, and for the most part contented himself with arguing against the superiority of the Moderns. But he was clearly trailing his coat at times, and his obvious willingness not to accept the Moderns at their own valuation invited a reply. When the reply came, it was temperate, comprehensive, and well informed: William Wotton (1666–1726), in his *Reflections upon Ancient and Modern Learning* (1694), admitted the pre-eminence of the Ancients in poetry and the arts, but firmly asserted the superiority of the Moderns in learning and sciences. Temple's unlucky decision to illustrate the virtues of ancient literature by claiming that 'the oldest books we have are still in their kind the best', and to cite in proof the *Epistles* of Phalaris and the *Fables* of Æsop, provoked a devastating rejoinder from Richard Bentley, who demonstrated in an appendix to the second edition of Wotton's book that the *Epistles* were a forgery of the early Christian period and that the *Fables* belonged to a later date than had been supposed. Subsequent developments involving the Christ Church wits and scholars and culminating in Swift's *The Battle of the Books* are well known. Amateurs of the curious will note that in this contest the case for the Ancients was put by a man who was no great scholar and whose outlook was essentially modern and sceptical, and that of the two Moderns Wotton was a learned classical scholar and Bentley the greatest scholar of the day. Yet Wotton (who had been an F.R.S. since 1687) drew many of his arguments from Glanvill's *Plus Ultra* and the *Philosophical Transactions*, and Bentley, although not a Fellow, was greatly interested in the work of the Society, as he showed clearly when he gave the first series of Boyle Lectures in 1692.

In calling the quarrel over the Ancients and the Moderns 'a most idle and contemptible controversy' Macaulay mistook its real significance in England, where the debate turned much less on the comparative merits of ancient and modern poets and dramatists than on the notable advances made in learning and science since the beginning of the seventeenth century. In its wider aspects the controversy was therefore one between the traditional learning of the schools and the new learning of the men of science, between the authority of the Aristotelians and the spirit of free inquiry and scepticism associated with the inductive approach of men like Bacon, Boyle, and Newton. The mind of Sir William Temple was easily sceptical, but he chose to bring his scepticism to bear on scientific discoveries which he had either failed to examine or whose significance he had failed to grasp, and he even questioned the utility, if not the validity, of the Copernican system and of Harvey's discoveries on the circulation of the blood. Wotton exposed such sophistries mercilessly when he remarked that while ancient or modern superiority in the arts was open to argument, the case was quite different with the mathematical and physical sciences, since those were dependent upon 'induction of particulars' and demonstration. The various sciences

are Things which have no Dependence upon the Opinions of Men for their Truth; they will admit of fixed and undisputed Mediums of Comparison and Judgment: So that . . . a fair Comparison between the Inventions, Observations, Experiments and Collections of the contending Parties must certainly put an end to the Dispute, and give a more full satisfaction to all sides.

Yet if the battle in England was fought on a wider front than that of *belles lettres*, it still affected very considerably the views of the literary critics. On the whole, this was a period of rather uneasy neo-classicism, a neo-classicism that was constantly subjected to modification, and that was sometimes attenuated to the point of almost total disappearance. The rules were tolerable provided they were interpreted after the fashion of Rapin as having been drawn by Aristotle from the practice of the Greek poets: if well considered, they would be found to 'reduce Nature into method' and to be based upon 'good sense and sound reason rather than on authority and example'. The poets should, of course, study nature, and not just follow her interpreters, Aristotle and Horace. 'But then', as Dryden observed, 'this also undeniably follows, that those things which delight all Ages must have been an imitation of Nature. . . . Therefore is Rhetorick made an Art: therefore the Names of so many Tropes and Figures were invented; because it was observ'd they had such and such effect upon the Audience.' There were other occasions, however, when the sceptical side of Dryden's mind was uppermost, and when he felt strongly that the remarkable modern developments in science could and would be matched by a corresponding progress in literature. In *An Essay of Dramatic Poesy*, in which Dryden's whole discourse was sceptical like 'the modest inquisitions of the Royal Society', Eugenius argued that if natural causes were now better known, because they were more intensely studied than in the time of Aristotle, it followed that with the same pains poetry and the other arts could arrive nearer to perfection. Some years later, speaking directly for himself, Dryden expressed the hope that in pointing out faults in the dramatists of 'the last age' he would not be thought arrogant: 'For we live in an Age so Sceptical, that as it determines little, so it takes nothing from Antiquity on trust; and I profess to have no other ambition in this Essay, than that Poetry may not go backward when all other Arts and Sciences are advancing.' Dryden was so open-minded, and he fluctuated so often in his critical attitude, that only a chronological treatment would give an adequate account of his changing critical positions. But his chronic hesitation between a deep respect for the Ancients and an awareness that the modern world was very different from that of ancient Athens and Rome was shared in varying degrees by most of his contemporaries. Many English writers tried to subscribe to neo-classical doctrine because they believed, or were being frequently told, that only by doing so could they achieve the reasonable and the credible and the universally and permanently valid in life and literature; others, perhaps, paid lip service to the rules because the Rymers were ready to pounce if they ignored them. But there were also many who had serious reservations about the rules, and who tried in their critical pronouncements to prevent them from being too stringently applied. The total situation, it has been suggested, is analogous to that in religion, where the latitudinarians were in favour of either comprehension or toleration, and were prepared to assert that if men agreed upon essentials the actual form of worship or of Church discipline need not be absolutely uniform. If everyone who published his views on literature in this period had been as rigid and dogmatic as Thomas Rymer,[1] it would be easier to chart the critical currents; but much of the criticism produced took the form of a defensive attempt to rationalize contemporary creative practice. It can at least be said, however, that in the late 1670s and the early 1680s, when the work of Rapin, Boileau, and Le Bossu became better known, and when Rymer set himself up as their English salesman, Dryden came over—for some time at least—to the neo-classical point of view, and the same is true in varying degrees of many of his contemporaries. Rapin's *Réflections sur la poétique d'Aristote* (1674), Boileau's *L'Art poétique* (1674), and Le Bossu's *Traité du poème épique* (1675) could not possibly be ignored, and for some time diverted English criticism from its normal easy-going course, but by the 1690s the English spirit of independence and compromise was reasserting itself.

The fact that the dominant literary form in Restoration England was drama made it almost inevitable that a rigid neo-classicism should prove unacceptable. An audience is more quickly bored, and more prone to express its boredom, than a reader; and English audiences had little or no interest in the unities, were not sensitive to questions of decorum, were allergic to long declamatory speeches, delighted in action, and saw nothing improper in mingling tragedy and comedy. Much of the dramatic criticism of the period, mainly in the form of prefaces, dedications, prologues, and epilogues, was the work of the dramatists themselves, and in the circumstances most of it was intended to justify the sort of plays they had written to please an English audience. On the lowest rung of

---

[1] Thomas Rymer (1641–1713), the son of a Yorkshire squire, was educated at Sidney Sussex College, Cambridge, proceeded to Gray's Inn, and was called to the bar in 1673. He became interested in the earlier drama, and himself published a 'regular' play, *Edgar*, in 1678, and in the same year his critical attack on the Elizabethan drama, *The Tragedies of the Last Age Considered*. His neo-classical views were repeated and extended in *A Short View of Tragedy* (1692). In that year he was made Historiographer Royal in succession to Shadwell, and soon began to work on his *magnum opus*, a collection of treaties between England and foreign powers from the year 1101 onwards, of which, with the title of *Foedera*, fifteen volumes had appeared before his death.

the critical ladder Mrs. Behn took the stand that there were no other rules for plays 'besides the making them pleasant'; but this was an extreme position that was not often adopted. In the Preface to his first comedy Shadwell took some pride in having ('as near as I could') preserved the three unities and kept the scenes unbroken, but those virtues, he complained, were lost upon the audience, who objected that his play lacked action. 'Men of Quality, that write for their Pleasure,' Shadwell observed, 'will not trouble themselves with Exactness in their Plays; and those that write for Profit would find too little Encouragement for so much Pains as a correct Play would require.' Why, indeed, should Shadwell bother, when, as he observed in the Preface to *The Humourists*, the greater part of an audience 'are more pleas'd with Jack-Pudding's being soundly kick'd, or having a Custard handsomely thrown in his Face, than with all the Wit in Plays'? Although Dryden never forgot that 'we are bound to please those whom we pretend to entertain', he allowed himself frequent jibes at the low taste prevailing in the London theatre. So far as writing a regular neo-classical play was concerned, he showed in *All for Love* that he could come near to doing it, but he set no great store by the achievement, and considered that he had observed the unities 'more exactly . . . than perhaps the English theatre requires'. That theatre was just a hundred years old when Dryden wrote those words, but it had produced a body of drama more remarkable than that of any other European country, and the plays of Shakespeare, Beaumont and Fletcher, and Jonson were among the favourite entertainments of the English stage. If Rymer was prepared to call *Othello* 'none other than a Bloody Farce, without salt or savour', few of his fellow countrymen could agree with him. The English—dramatists as well as their audiences—had too deep an emotional investment in Shakespeare to put up for long with any criticism that did not come to terms with him. As Addison was to put it, 'Our inimitable Shakespear is a Stumbling-block to the whole Tribe of . . . rigid Criticks. Who would not rather read one of his Plays, where there is not a single Rule of the Stage observed, than any Production of a modern Critick, where there is not one of them violated?' The usual critical compromise was to say that if Shakespeare and his fellows had lived and written after the Restoration they 'had doubtless written more correctly', since, as Dryden put it, poetry in their day was 'if not in its infancy among us, at least not arriv'd to its vigor and maturity'. But to say that they would have written more correctly was only to say that their plays would have been even better than they are.

In defending their own modern plays Dryden and his contemporaries were concerned to make out a case for a specifically national drama, one that not only differed from the ancient classical drama and from the neo-classical plays of modern France, but started with certain advantages which it was generally held the Elizabethans did not have. In constructing that case they relied partly on historical arguments: time does not stand still; manners and customs, religious beliefs, social observances, and much else change from one age to another. In his Preface to *Four New Plays* (1665) Sir Robert Howard undertook to show how 'the manner of Stage-Entertainments have differ'd in all Ages', and Samuel Butler ('Upon Critics who judge of Modern Plays Precisely by the Rules of the Antients') took exception to critics like Rymer who seek to

> Reduce all Tragedy by Rules of Art
> Back to its Antique Theater, a Cart . . .
> As if the Antique Laws of Tragedy
> Did with our own Municipall agree. . . .

On the other hand, Rymer answered those who used the argument that 'Athens and London have not the same Meridian' by asserting that '*Nature* is the same, and *Man* is the same: he *loves, grieves, hates, envies,* has the same *affections* and *passions*, in both places, and the same springs that give them motion. What mov'd *pity* there will *here* also produce the same effect.' Most English dramatists, however, were convinced that—for comedy especially, but also for tragedy—ancient Athens and seventeenth-century London were two very different places. In his Preface to *Oedipus* Dryden was prepared to admit that the ancient method of writing tragedy might be best and most natural, as it was certainly the easiest for the dramatist. But the Athenian drama with its Chorus, its single scene for each Act, and its simple plot 'had a perfection differing from ours. . . . Custom likewise has obtain'd, that we must form an underplot of second Persons, which must be depending on the first; and their by-walks must be like those in a Labyrinth, which

all of 'em lead into the great Parterre; or like so many several
lodging Chambers, which have their out-lets into the same
Gallery.' Again, in the *Essay of Dramatic Poesy*, Eugenius made
a legitimate historical point when he observed that in Roman
comedy the women play a comparatively insignificant part,
and the heroine has 'the breeding of the Old Elizabeth way,
for Maids to be seen and not to be heard'. As for the Elizabethans, they were nearer in time to Dryden and his contemporaries, but to the men of the Restoration, highly conscious
of their modernity, they were yet in many ways remote, and
even primitive. In his epilogue to the Second Part of *The
Conquest of Granada* Dryden ran over some of the points that
separated them from the men and women of his own day.
The Elizabethan dramatists, he says, were highly successful in
their own day because they 'conform'd their Genius to their
Age'; but that was a dull age with little notion of Love and
Honour which are now so important, and little of that witty
conversation which is the particular grace of modern drama:

> Wit's now arriv'd to a more high degree;
> Our native Language more refin'd and free.
> Our Ladies and our men now speak more wit
> In conversation, than those Poets writ.

In his prose *Defence of the Epilogue* Dryden elaborates on those
distinctions and on the new refinement in wit, language, and
gallantry, and stresses the importance to the dramatist of having easy access to the best and most fashionable society, and of
having an educated audience able to judge and criticize his
work. No doubt Dryden underestimates the culture of the
Elizabethans and overestimates the refinement of his own age;
but he makes out his case that a different kind of drama—
urban, modish, and thoroughly up-to-date—is required to suit
the taste of a different sort of audience.

The English and the French were rivals in drama as in
much else. The main English objection to French plays was
that they had insufficient action. In adapting a French or
Spanish comedy for the London stage dramatists like Shadwell
and Ravenscroft almost invariably drew their material from
more than one play or added something of their own. It required no ordinary skill, Crowne said of his comedy *Sir Courtly
Nice*, 'to build a little Shallop [Moreto's *No puede ser*], fit only

for the Spanish South Seas, into an English Ship Royal'. In the same way Dryden had found that classical models were 'too little for English tragedy, which requires to be built in a larger compass'. Dryden's most sustained discussion of French drama occurs in the *Essay of Dramatic Poesy*, where Neander dwells on the French fondness for long speeches ('which tire us with their length') and the English preference for action. He notes, too, the French love of regularity, resulting in a 'dearth of plot and narrowness of imagination', but he is prepared to admit that if the French have too little action in their plays the English can be blamed for having too much. In general, the need to justify English practice, combined with a nationalistic desire to score off the polite and punctilious but too servile French, provoked most Englishmen into sharp disagreement with anything approaching a strict neo-classicism in the theatre. It became a critical cliché of the period to assert that if the French had all the correctness the English had the energy and genius. In the Preface to *All for Love* Dryden had already anticipated, and probably inspired, Pope's 'We cannot *blame* indeed—but we may *sleep*'. As late as 1697 he breaks out characteristically: 'Let the French and Italians value themselves on their Regularity; Strength and Elevation are our Standard.' Some twenty years earlier he had objected to 'our *Chedreux* critics' who formed their judgements on the practice of the French dramatists, and he had asserted his own independence: 'But for my part, I desire to be try'd by the Laws of my own Country; for it seems unjust to me, that the French should prescribe here, till they have conquer'd.'

A good deal of the critical endeavour of the period was devoted to a not very successful attempt to frame such laws. One of the principles most frequently cited (and this had often a particular reference to the limitations imposed by the unities) was the pleasure to be derived from variety. Even John Dennis, who was normally a staunch upholder of the rules, found himself faced in his comedy *A Plot and no Plot* with the problem of how 'to reconcile variety to unity', and was forced to violate the unity of place. 'But regularity in a Comedy', he assured his readers, 'signifies little without Diversion.' Near the end of the century the anonymous author (Elkanah Settle?) of *A Farther Defence of Dramatick Poetry* (1698) sums up and seeks to justify the English practice of sacrificing regularity to variety:

> If the French can content themselves with the sweets of a single Rose-bed, and nothing less than the whole Garden and the Field round it will satisfie the English; every Man as he likes: Corneille may reign Master of his own Revels, but he is neither a Rule-maker nor a Play-maker for our Stage. And the Reason is plain: for as Delight is the great End of Playing, and those narrow Stage-restrictions of Corneille destroy that Delight by curtailing that Variety that should give it us, every such Rule therefore is Nonsense and Contradiction in its very Foundation.

The argument from variety was of course particularly useful for the defence of 'mixed' plays in which comedy was mingled with tragedy. The neo-classical objection to such a practice was that it constituted a breach of decorum. In his *Observations on Monsieur de Sorbier's Voyage into England* Sprat advanced the argument that it was not indecent to 'thrust in men of mean condition amongst the actions of Princes', because in real life kings came into contact with all sorts of men: why, then, should that 'misbecome the Stage which is always found to be acted in the True Theatre of the World'? No doubt the argument had a peculiar relevance to the *demi monde* that frequented the Court of Charles II, but it rests on the assumption that art and life are identical. Rymer and Dennis at least condemned tragi-comedy outright. Not all the dramatists by any means were in favour of it; but of those who condemned it in theory some complied with the taste of the age and apologetically provided it. If he had been left a free choice Dryden might have avoided mixing comedy with tragedy, and in the Preface to *Troilus and Cressida* he actually condemned the practice on the grounds that two independent actions 'distract the attention and concernment of the audience'. He pointed to his own *Marriage-à-la-Mode* as a play which has two actions not depending on one another, and which therefore (to his present neo-classical way of thinking) could not be excused. Two years later, however, he announced in his Dedication of *The Spanish Friar* that he had chosen to satisfy his own humour, 'which was to tack two plays together, and to break a rule for the pleasure of variety'. Earlier, Neander had defended 'under-plots or by-concernments', provided that they were 'carried on with the motion of the main Plot; just as they say the Orb of the fix'd

Stars, and those of the Planets, though they have motions of their own, are whirl'd about by the motion of the *primum mobile*, in which they are contain'd'. He returned to this argument (and to the astronomical simile) in his *Discourse concerning . . . Satire* (1693); but in his final pronouncement on tragicomedy in *A Parallel of Poetry and Painting* (1695) he dismissed it as 'wholly Gothic' and 'an unnatural mingle'. The usual objection, voiced by Sir Robert Howard and others, was that it divided the attention of the audience, 'who may not so suddenly recollect themselves as to start into an enjoyment of the Mirth or into a concern for the Sadness'. To this plausible contention Neander replied by an appeal to experience: if the eye can pass rapidly from an unpleasant object to a pleasant, why should we think that the soul of man is heavier than his senses? In any case, 'contraries, when placed near, set off each other. . . . A Scene of mirth mix'd with Tragedy has the same effect upon us which our musick has betwixt the Acts.' To make out his case Dryden would have had to take it a good deal further than he did, but he was almost alone in the period in seeking to defend tragi-comedy on psychological grounds.

A different sort of defence for the irregular English play was put forward by Shadwell in his Preface to *The Sullen Lovers*. Exception had been taken to the 'want of design' in this comedy. To this Shadwell replied, rather dubiously, that no one should expect 'such Intrigues in the little Actions of Comedy as are requir'd in Plays of a higher Nature'. He went on, however, to offer a more convincing argument:

But in Plays of Humour, where there are so many Characters as there are in this, there is yet less Design to be expected: For, if after I had form'd three or four prating Fops in the Play I made it full of Plot and Business, at the latter End, where the Turns ought to be many and suddenly following one another, I must have let fall the Humour, which I thought wou'd be pleasanter than Intrigues could have been without it. . . .

This case, too, requires more development than Shadwell gives it, and Dennis was to claim (quite as plausibly) that humour was more proper for comedy than wit, because 'it gives a necessary occasion for action, which wit does not'. But in seeking freedom to develop his beloved humours Shadwell is in the English tradition, which has almost always favoured the

uninhibited growth of any character or situation that has come
to life in the mind of the writer. If something has to give place
on such occasions it is regularity, or decorum, or both. Dryden
had no special wish to develop the humours, partly because,
as Dennis pointed out, humours were 'more to be found in low
Characters than among Persons of a higher Rank'; but he
certainly wanted freedom for that play of witty conversation
and repartee which he considered to be one of the graces
of modern comedy, and which abounds in the comedies of
Etherege, Wycherley, and Congreve, and in some of his own.
Eugenius again, in *An Essay of Dramatic Poesy*, had called
attention to 'that soft passion' love, which had been almost
ignored by the Ancients but which was all-important in modern
drama, and had argued that for the natural development of a
love-affair the dramatist required more scope than the regular
play allowed him. There are 'a thousand . . . concernments of
Lovers, as jealousies, complaints, contrivances and the like,
where not to open their minds at large to each other, were to
be wanting to their own love, and to the expectation of the
Audience, who watch the movements of their minds, as much
as the changes of their fortunes'. Again the case is being put for
a greater amplitude and liberty to permit that psychological
development which the rich character-study of English drama
required.

Among the other topics on which the English critics rang
their changes was that of poetic justice. The phrase is Rymer's,
but the doctrine that a dramatist must see to it that his wicked
characters are punished and the virtuous ones rewarded was a
commonplace of Renaissance criticism, however little many of
the dramatists allowed it to deflect the course of their action.
As Rymer puts it, Sophocles and Euripides

finding in History the same *end* happen to the *righteous* and to the
unjust, vertue often opprest, and *wickedness* on the Throne, they saw
these particular *yesterday-truths* were imperfect and unproper to
illustrate the *universal* and *eternal* truths by them intended. Finding
also that this *unequal* distribution of rewards and punishments did
perplex the *wisest,* and by the *Atheist* was made a scandal to the
Divine Providence, They concluded that a *Poet* must of necessity see
justice exactly administered, if he intended to please.

The future Historiographer Royal went so far as to say that
History 'grossly taken' is 'neither proper to *instruct* nor apt to

please', and the dramatist who makes use of historical facts must therefore contrive something more accurate and philosophical than history. So far as tragedy was concerned, few cared to quarrel with Rymer and the solid front of the French neo-classical critics; and the willingness of the English writers of tragedy to administer poetic justice was no doubt made easier by the remoteness and unreality of the tragic plays most of them wrote. When pity became the dominant note in drama-tists like Banks and Otway, the innocent were shown as suffer-ing, but little or no critical theory accompanied the practice. A clear indication of public taste is to be seen in the fact that when Shakespeare's tragedies were altered for the Restoration stage by Tate and others they were supplied with the poetic justice that Shakespeare had failed to provide. As late as 1699, in his *Ancient and Modern Stages Survey'd*, Dr. James Drake took Dryden to task for failing to observe poetic justice in his *Cleomenes*, where virtue is 'everywhere depressed, and calami-tous, and falls at last unavenged'. Congreve was more conven-tional, and in his *Amendments of Mr. Collier's . . . Citations* he was able to enumerate in detail the various ways in which he had distributed awards and punishments in *The Mourning Bride*.

If the doctrine of poetic justice could be extracted from the *Poetics* it was not easy to square with Aristotle's clear pronounce-ment that tragedy evoked pity and fear. As Dr. Sarup Singh has pointed out, most of the Restoration dramatists who consciously aimed at arousing those emotions believed that they had achieved it by bringing a wicked character to his merited doom (so striking terror into the hearts of the audience) and making an innocent character suffer. It was left to the maligned Rymer, in *The Tragedies of the Last Age*, to attempt a critical reconciliation of pity and fear with the principle of poetic justice. Returning to the *Poetics*, he insisted that pity and fear were to be aroused by the same character, the hero of the play, and that to achieve this end his misfortunes should not be wholly merited or entirely unmerited. Dryden, who in his period of heroic drama had followed Corneille in proclaiming that 'admiration and concernment' were the emotions evoked by serious plays, came rather slowly round to Rymer's inter-pretation of tragic pleasure, but was never more than half-hearted in his acquiescence. Although in his 'Heads of an

Answer to Rymer' he agrees that pity and fear are among the
proper means to encourage virtue and discourage vice, which
he regards as the true ends of tragedy, he will not admit that
they are the only ones:

> For all the passions, in their turns, are to be set in a ferment;
> as joy, anger, love, fear, are to be used as the poet's common-
> places, and a general concernment for the principal actors is to be
> raised, by making them appear such in their characters, their words,
> and actions, as will interest the audience in their fortunes.

Among the passions that Dryden has particularly in mind is
that of love. In that passion, he asserts, how far the Ancients
fall short of—Fletcher!

In writing their comedies the English dramatists paid little
attention to poetic justice. Had they done so, Jeremy Collier
would have had less reason to denounce the immorality of the
English stage. In theory, however, from Flecknoe at one end
of the period to Collier at the other, it was widely agreed that
comedy should expose vice and folly, and so act as a deterrent.
After the appearance of Collier's *Short View* in 1698 the comic
dramatists were almost unanimous in claiming that they had
always tried to do what Collier demanded—'to recommend
Virtue and discountenance Vice, . . . to expose the Singulari-
ties of Pride and Fancy, to make Folly and Falsehood contemptible, and to bring every Thing that is Ill under Infamy,
and Neglect'. Shadwell was among the more consistent advocates of a satirical kind of comedy, which had as its objective
'the Cheats, Villanies and troublesome Follies in the common
Conversation of the World', and 'the affected Vanities and
artificial Fopperies of Men, which . . . they take Pains to acquire'.
By rendering fops and knaves ridiculous 'we make them live to
be dispised and laugh'd at, which certainly makes more impression upon Men than even Death can do'. In his Preface to *The
Royal Shepherdess* he claimed to have observed the rules of
morality and good manners by exalting virtue and depressing
vice; and he added, in what looks like a thrust at Dryden, that
his play might have had a better reception if he had done the
exact opposite:

> For I find it pleases most to see Vice encourag'd, by bringing the
> Characters of debauch'd people upon the Stage, and making them
> pass for fine Gentlemen, who openly profess Swearing, Drinking,

Whoring, breaking Windows, beating Constables, etc. and that is
esteem'd among us a gentile Gaiety of Humour, which is contrary
to the Customs and Laws of all civilized Nations.

This is one of the rare moments of truth in Restoration criticism: Shadwell was letting the side down. Although Dryden
had praised Jonson for punishing vice and rewarding virtue in
Volpone, he asserted in the Preface to *An Evening's Love* (1671)
that the chief end of comedy is 'divertisement and delight',
and had no difficulty in showing that Plautus, Terence, and
Jonson did not invariably punish vice. His ingenious explanation that his own young rakes were only sowing their wild oats,
and were reclaimed—not rewarded—by marriage has already
been noted; and in this same Preface he also offered an intelligent comment on the delayed action of comedy, which works
directly on the ill nature of an audience, and, by first inducing
them to laugh, later persuades them to despise, and so to submit
themselves to self-examination and amendment. In taking a
stand against overt correction Dryden was not quite alone, but
in general poetic justice was accepted as a necessary part of
the theory of comedy, however little it was honoured in practice.

Among the advances which Dryden was quite sure his own
age could claim was that made in the language which poets now
used. He spent a good deal of time in condemning, with very
little historical sense, real or supposed solecisms in the Elizabethan drama, its frequent improprieties of expression, and
the uncouthness and lack of euphony in the dialogue. It became
a critical commonplace that the English language was now
more correct and refined, and for that very reason better suited
for poetry. For the wit-comedy of polished and sophisticated
society that Dryden himself admired this might be so; the
natural vulgarities of Jonson's Cob and Tib were not in much
demand, for 'Gentlemen will now be entertain'd with the
follies of each other; . . . and surely, their conversation can be
no jest to them on the Theatre, when they would avoid it in the
street'. The second half of this statement may seem to us a
non sequitur; and Dorimant's banter with the orange-woman,
to say nothing of the brisk vulgarity of some of Shadwell's
characters in his popular *Epsom Wells* (which had three command performances in 1672, and a fourth the following winter),
would indicate that Dryden was here pushing refinement
further than most of his contemporaries. Yet his belief that

Suckling, Waller, and Denham had immeasurably improved
the language and the style of poetry was shared by most of his
contemporaries; and Roscommon's warning against anything
pedantic in the language of the poet—

> For none have been with Admiration read,
> But who, beside their Learning, were Well-bred—

was characteristic of the wits who dominated the polite literature of the time. The improvement, or change, was concerned
not only with refinement but also with simplicity; it involved
the substitution of the 'turn' for the conceit, of general for
technical terms, of the literal for the metaphorical (Dryden
found Shakespeare's style 'pestered' with figurative expressions),
of the easy and conventional metaphor for the more difficult
and unusual, and, in both poetry and prose, of a smooth for an
irregular cadence. Yet Dryden had some reservations about
the suitability of this correct but attenuated style for epic and
tragedy. In the Preface to his version of *Troilus and Cressida* he
makes the curious admission that although he has in general
refined Shakespeare's language he has at other times 'conformed' his own to Shakespeare's, with the result that 'the
language is not altogether so pure as it is significant'. When
Dryden uses the word 'significant' in this sense he usually means
'poetical'. In the Preface to *Don Sebastian*, after remarking on
'the lustre and masculine vigour' of the style, he draws attention to the fact that, like Milton in *Paradise Lost*, he has made
use of some old words 'for their significance and sound'.

An important influence contributing to simplicity was the
simultaneous condemnation in France and England of florid
pulpit oratory, which had been rejected as early as 1646 by
John Wilkins in his *Ecclesiastes*, and was to be further repudiated
or derided by such men as Barrow, South, Eachard, James
Arderne, Glanvill, John Phillips, and Bishop Burnet. Since a
widespread movement towards simplicity followed, or coin-
cided with, this critical drive, and since frequent listening to
sermons was almost unavoidable and to many people pleasur-
able at this period, the contribution made by the preachers to
the new trend towards simplicity must have been considerable.
The parallel influence exercised by the Royal Society is not
today likely to be underestimated.

Among the critical discussions which stemmed directly from

the problems of the creative writer was that concerned with translation. Here again the question of language became important (Dryden, for instance, noting the prevalence in English of monosyllables clogged with consonants 'which are the dead weight of our mother-tongue'); and, as we might expect, the most detailed and perceptive examination of the problems involved came from the greatest poetical craftsman of the period. In the Preface to his translation of Ovid's *Epistles* (1680) and that to *Sylvae* (1685), in his Dedication for *Examen Poeticum* (1693) and for his translation of the *Aeneid* (1697), and finally in his Preface to the *Fables* (1700), Dryden faced the difficulties of the translator, who must be thoroughly familiar not only with Greek and Latin, but also with 'the properties and delicacies' of his mother tongue. Each writer sets a different problem, for the translator must try to reproduce that particular character of an author 'which distinguishes him from all others'. He will not succeed by metaphrase (turning an author word by word), and he will not even make the attempt if he aims only at imitation ('taking only some general hints from the original, to run division on the ground work as he pleases'). For Dryden the best method was paraphrase, where the author's words may not be strictly followed, but where the translator aims at being faithful to his sense. Almost no one at this time was in favour of metaphrase, and imitation (influenced by the successful practice of Denham and Cowley) was most popular in the earlier half of the period. 'There are certain Garbs and Modes of speaking', Denham had explained in 1667, 'which vary with the times . . . and therefore if Virgil must needs speak English, it were fit he should speak not only as a man of this Nation, but as a man of this Age.' Dryden's preference for paraphrase was shared by most of the translators, but in both theory and practice the general tendency was towards a closer translation than Dryden usually attempted. In his claim to have made Virgil 'speak such English as he would himself have spoken, if he had been born in England and in this present age', Dryden is at least half way to the practice of imitation. In general, Restoration critics accepted the fact—more frankly and realistically than those in some other periods—that translations must bear the stamp of the age in which they are made. If Spingarn exaggerates a little when he says that the seventeenth century had no conception of the historical or scientific functions of translation, he is

surely justified in claiming that the translators thought primarily of producing a new work of art which could be enjoyed
without constant reference to, or awareness of, the original. It is
in this context that Roscommon can write of the translator
'*improving* what was writ before', by the exercise not of his
invention, but of his judgement.

Criticism of the epic during the Restoration period is necessarily rather more academic than that of the drama, since the
only epic practitioners were Edward Howard and Sir Richard
Blackmore. Dryden, however, had given serious thought to
writing an epic poem, and his interest in the form is reflected
in various prefaces, notably in the long and rambling Discourse
prefixed to his translation of Juvenal. Contemporary English
critics could look back to *The Faerie Queene* and *Paradise Lost*,
to Davenant's *Gondibert* and Cowley's *Davideis*; and in his
elaborate examination of Blackmore's *Prince Arthur* (1696)
Dennis produced one of the first set pieces of literary criticism
in English. Le Bossu's definition of the epic was generally
accepted: 'L'ÉPOPÉE est un discours inventé avec art, pour
former les mœurs par des instructions déguisées sous les
allégories d'une action importante, qui est racontée en Vers
d'une manière vrai-semblable, divertissante et merveilleuse.'
Some of the more interesting English discussion centred on the
relative importance of the probable and the marvellous. The
insistence of Rymer (following Rapin) that poetry 'has no life,
nor can have any operation without probability', and Boileau's
'Rien n'est beau que le vrai: le vrai seul est aimable', comman-
ded a good deal of respect and were not seriously challenged
by many English critics. But in the matter of *vraisemblance*
Dryden made a distinction between what could be done in
epic and what in tragedy when he argued that many things
which 'are real beauties in the reading would appear absurd
upon the stage'. In his *Apology for Heroic Poetry* he protested
against the ridiculous praise of the natural, when 'all that is
dull, insipid, languishing, and without sinews in a poem' is
called an imitation of nature. The epic poet can go beyond
nature, if (as Aristotle said) his imaginary beings are founded
on popular belief; poetry does not call for literal belief on the
part of the reader, who is 'pleas'd with the Image, without
being cozen'd by the Fiction'. As for those readers who think
that the flights of heroic poetry are 'bombast, unnatural and

meer madness', they are setting up their limited reason against that of Homer, Virgil, Tasso, Milton, and all those who have admired them through the ages. 'You must prove why that ought not to have pleas'd, which has pleas'd the most Learned, and the most Judicious; and to be thought knowing, you must first put the fool upon all Mankind.' The verdict of posterity was frequently cited to bend the arguments of the more rigid and doctrinaire critics. John Dennis, a great admirer of Milton, was thinking, in his *Remarks on Prince Arthur*, along the same lines as Dryden, when he wrote of 'extraordinary hints' that come to the writer of genius, and of the 'furious joy, pride, or astonishment' that accompany them. Here, as elsewhere in Restoration criticism, we have to remember the context in which such remarks were made: Dryden and Dennis would both have held that those flights which were suitable for heroic poetry were not appropriate for most other kinds. The consciousness of the 'kinds'—heroic, tragic, comic, elegiac, pastoral, etc.—and what style and treatment were correct for each, runs through the criticism of the whole period.

Among the more special issues that divided the critics of heroic poetry was that of the right machinery in a modern epic poem. Rapin and Boileau had come out firmly against any mixture of paganism and Christianity in the same poem, and Boileau was against the use of Christian machinery at all. Here again the English had a stake in Milton, but the critics were by no means unanimous. Temple was against, and Blackmore for, Christian machinery, and Dennis wavered. Dryden offered his own compromise when he suggested that the proper machinery for a Christian epic was that of guardian angels, although wicked spirits (working with the divine permission) were also acceptable. With such momentous speculations Dryden employed his enforced leisure in the reign of William and Mary.

In this short survey it has seemed best to consider criticism rather than critics, and to dwell on the greatest common measure of critical agreement rather than to emphasize the views of individual critics. Of these critics Dryden is by far the most important, not only for the range and flexibility of his critical writing, but for the example he gave to his contemporaries. He fertilized the whole field of polite letters in his own day by constantly turning over the soil, and he established a habit of urbane and unpedantic writing about books and authors which, with certain notorious exceptions, has continued to be in the main English tradition. Of his critical predecessors the one who comes nearest to Dryden in humanity, good temper, and colloquial liveliness is Sir Philip Sidney. Dryden mentions *The Defence of Poesy* as early as 1664 in his dedicatory Epistle to *The Rival Ladies*, and it seems possible that the civilized and discursive tone of his own criticism owes something to the gentle Sidney. All Dryden's critical writings are addressed to the polite; sometimes to an Orrery, a Dorset, or a Mulgrave, always to the well-informed and cultured reader, never to scholars and specialists. Good manners, therefore, control his criticism, and to some extent limit its penetration and thoroughness. He will break off in the middle of a discussion with 'I fear I have been tedious' or 'I am still speaking to you, my Lord, though in all probability you are already out of hearing': such expressions show Dryden's constant awareness of the polite reader who must not be bored, and his own desire to be easily readable. To be unwilling to bore one's readers is the mark of an amiable writer; but it sometimes leads Dryden to abandon the pursuit of truth too soon, or to evade a critical issue with a shrug of the shoulders. 'I will not say,' he observes of Jeremy Collier, '*The Zeal of God's House has eaten him up*; but I am sure it has devour'd some Part of his Good Manners and Civility.' This is a splendidly effective retort, but it is scarcely an answer. The undogmatic nature of his criticism is due in part to the sceptical turn of his mind, but also to his ability to enjoy writers of very different kinds: Virgil and Shakespeare, Ovid and Chaucer, Milton and Samuel Butler, Sophocles and William Wycherley. Although his only critical symposium was *An Essay of Dramatic Poesy*, almost all his prefaces put a case, or express an opinion, rather than deliver an *ex cathedra* judgement. Since Dryden, like other writers, sometimes sought to erect his preferences into laws, we must expect a certain amount of inconsistency in his critical pronouncements: what he says depends on what he is enjoying at the moment. He had the same catholic enjoyment of good literature that Hazlitt was to show in the nineteenth century; but he made a more determined effort than Hazlitt ever did to express that enjoyment in terms of literary principles.

Consistency, on the other hand, is just what we do find in Thomas Rymer; a consistency maintained at the cost of undeniable rigidity. Aristotle, as Dryden once observed, was that rare sort of universal genius who could 'penetrate into all arts and sciences, without the practice of them'; but in default of another Aristotle's appearing Dryden would continue to believe that 'the judgment of an artificer in his own art should be preferable to the opinion of another man'. Although Dryden had an uneasy respect for Rymer's learning, it seems unlikely that he ever thought of him as the English Aristotle. With his insistence on the French neo-classical principles of probability, reasonableness, and decorum, Rymer is the doctrinaire and judicial critic *par excellence*, more concerned (one sometimes feels) to uphold the majesty of the law than to inquire into the particular circumstances of the case that has come before him. His impact on his own age is not easy to assess; he was praised by some and condemned by others—he was never ignored. His most influential follower, as Professor Zimansky has pointed out, was that other writer of a *Short View*, Jeremy Collier, who took over some of Rymer's arguments and much of his critical manner. It was the manner as much as the matter that made an impression, and the manner was dictated by the spirit of a witty age. Rymer was a scholar and Collier was a parson, but both men intended to be widely read, and both accordingly were at pains to affect a colloquial ease, and to avoid any imputation of pedantry. Cracking in 1678 his rather laboured and derisory jokes to show that he was every bit as much of a wit and man of the world as that Fleetwood Shepherd, Esq., to whom, in the form of a letter, his *Tragedies of the Last Age Considered and Examined* was addressed, Thomas Rymer, of Gray's-Inn, Esquire, never really achieved the modish style of the Restoration wit. But it is highly significant that he tried.

It is indeed the witty man of the world who dominates the literary scene in the later seventeenth century. Almost all the drama, most of the poetry, and much of the occasional prose are the work of intelligent persons of quality or of middle-class men of letters who lived in or about the fashionable world, shared its attitudes, and spoke its language. The voice of the wit is sometimes heard even in the pulpit, in the sermons of

South, and it gives a keener edge to the political discourses of
Halifax and to Eachard's discussion of the status of the clergy.

It is true that there was another more popular tradition of
writing to be found in the prose of Bunyan, in the dialogue
discussions of L'Estrange, in the news paragraphs of Benjamin
Harris and his fellow journalists, and in the colloquial memoirs
of Bishop Burnet. There are other writers, too, who stand apart
from their contemporaries, either because, like Clarendon, they
belong to an earlier generation, or because they are university
men rarely looking beyond the walls of their college and so
preserving an old-fashioned academic tradition, or simply
because, like the author of *The Sacred Theory of the Earth*, they
are eccentrics. The scientists wrote, or tried to write, a prose
of their own, and Anglican clergymen usually spoke and wrote
in a style that was recognizably ecclesiastical. It has, indeed,
been one of the aims of this volume to show that a considerable
variety exists in the period, and that some of its finest writing is
in a very different tradition from that of Dryden, Halifax, and
Temple.

Yet in the long run it was the tradition of the gentleman
writer that prevailed. It is characteristic of the gentleman that
he lives in a polite society and subscribes to its usages: he can
express himself in his own individual fashion (and being
English will almost certainly do so), but he will take care that
he does not push his individuality so far that it becomes a
source of annoyance or embarrassment to other people. Like a
good host he will consider the convenience and pleasure of
those he is entertaining: he will maintain a natural poise; he will
not ride his own ideas too hard, but will offer them to the company equally, amiably, and unpedantically, and, if he can
manage it, with a witty turn of thought and phrase. Translated
into terms of writing, this means that the Restoration gentleman was always conscious of his readers, that he aimed to
please them, and that his writing was controlled by the demands
of easy and unimpeded communication rather than those of
emphatic and idiosyncratic self-expression. The prose that resulted from these conditions was disciplined and yet comparatively informal; colloquial, but at the same time premeditated
and delicately phrased. The same virtues are to be found in
much of the verse of the period, not merely in prologues and
epilogues, but in such poems as Rochester's *Satire against*

Mankind and Dryden's *Religio Laici*. An age of discussion had set in, of persuasion rather than exhortation, of reason rather than rapture; and it produced a prose which the English, who tend to measure their literary greatness in terms of poetry, have never sufficiently admired.

CHRONOLOGICAL TABLES

Date	Public Events	Literary History	Verse
1660	General Monck and Edward Montagu (later Earl of Sandwich) bring about the Restoration with the help of Edward Hyde (Earl of Clarendon, 1661). Convention Parliament, 25 Apr.–29 Dec. Charles II lands at Dover, 25 May. Act of Indemnity. Duke of York m. Anne Hyde. Duke of Gloucester d. Ten of the regicides executed (Oct.). Hyde Lord Chancellor (from 1658).	Pepys begins his Diary, 1 Jan. Patents to erect two playhouses and form two companies of players granted to Thomas Killigrew and Sir William Davenant. Foundation of Royal Society. (Charter granted 15 July 1662.) Bunyan arrested as an unlicensed preacher. Defoe b. Southerne b.	R. Wild, *Iter Boreale*. Dryden, *Astraea Redux*. Sir R. Howard, *Poems*. A. Brome, *Songs and Poems*.
1661	Rising of Fifth Monarchy Men led by Thomas Venner. Coronation. Cavalier Parliament (8 May–Jan. 1679). Savoy Conference. Execution of the Earl of Argyll. Corporation Act.	Bunyan sentenced to three months' imprisonment, but refusing to give an undertaking not to preach, he remains a prisoner in Bedford Gaol (with one small break) until 1672. La Calprenède, *Pharamond*. Fuller d.	Dryden, *To His Sacred Majesty*. Waller, *A Poem on St. James's Park*.
1662	Act of Uniformity. Charles m. Catherine of Braganza. Henry Bennet (later Earl of Arlington) becomes Secretary of State. On 24 Aug. Baxter, Calamy, and some 1,200 other nonconforming clergymen lose their livings. Declaration of Indulgence.	*The Book of Common Prayer* (with a few minor revisions) restored to use. Licensing Act (drastically reducing the number of printers and printing presses). Pascal d. R. Bentley b. Molière, *L'École des femmes*.	Dryden, *To My Lord Chancellor*. Butler, *Hudibras*, Pt. i.
1663	Attempt made by the Earl of Bristol to impeach Clarendon. Gilbert Sheldon	L'Estrange made 'Surveyor of the Imprimery' and one of the licensers of the	Butler, *Hudibras*, Pt. ii. Cowley, *Verses upon Several Occasions*.

Date	Prose	Drama (date of acting)
1660	Boyle, *New Experiments ... Touching the Spring of the Air.* Harrington, *Political Discourses.* J. Taylor, *Ductor Dubitantium.* Winstanley, *England's Worthies.*	Tatham, *The Rump.*
1661	Boyle, *The Sceptical Chemist.* Boyle, *Some Considerations touching the Style of the Holy Scriptures.* Glanvill, *The Vanity of Dogmatizing.* J. Graunt, *Natural and Political Observations on the Bills of Mortality.* P. Heylyn, *The History of the Reformation.* Sir G. Mackenzie, *Aretina.* Cowley, *A Proposition for the Advancement of Experimental Philosophy.*	Cowley, *Cutter of Coleman Street.*
1662	Hooker (d. 1600), *Works.* Fuller (d. 1661), *Worthies of England.* Stillingfleet, *Origines Sacrae.* Sir W. Petty, *A Treatise of Taxes and Contributions.*	Sir R. Howard, *The Committee.*
1663	Boyle, *Some Considerations touching the Usefulness of Natural Philosophy.*	Dryden, *The Wild Gallant.* J. Wilson, *The Cheats.* Sir S. Tuke, *The Adventures of Five Hours.*

Date	Public Events	Literary History	Verse
	succeeds William Juxon as Archbishop of Canterbury.	press. He issues his two newspapers, *The News* and *The Intelligencer* (until Jan. 1666). Shakespeare, Third Folio.	
1664	Conventicle Act	S. de Sorbière's *Relation d'un Voyage en Angleterre*. John Twyn hanged for printing 'a seditious, poisonous and scandalous' book. Vanbrugh b. Prior b. Katherine Philips d.	Cotton, *Scarronides*.
1665	War declared against the Dutch (the Second Dutch War). Naval victory off Lowestoft (June). Defeat at Bergen (Aug.) The Plague. Court leaves London in July, and goes to Oxford in Sept. Parliament meets there in Oct. Dissenters further harassed by the Five Mile Act.	The Royal Society begins publication of *Philosophical Transactions*. Henry Muddiman starts the official *Oxford Gazette* (renamed *The London Gazette*, Feb. 1666). La Rochefoucauld, *Maximes*.	Marvell, *Character of Holland*.
1666	French join the Dutch in the War against England. Court returns to London (Feb.). The Four Days' Battle at sea, 1–4 June. English naval victory off North Foreland (25 July). The Fire of London, 2–6 Sept.	Parliament censures Hobbes's works. Shirley d. Boileau, *Satires*. Molière, *Le Misanthrope* and *Le Médecin malgré lui*.	Waller, *Instructions to a Painter* (followed by various satirical 'Advices', 1666–7). A. Brome *et al.*, trans. *The Poems of Horace*.
1667	Dutch burn ships in the Medway. Peace with France and the United	Cowley d. Taylor d. Swift b. Racine, *Andromaque*.	Milton, *Paradise Lost*. Dryden, *Annus Mirabilis*. Marvell, *Clarendon's*

Date	Prose	Drama (date of acting)
		Sir R. Stapylton, *The Slighted Maid*.

Date	Prose	Drama (date of acting)
1664	Evelyn, *Sylva*. Tillotson, 'The Wisdom of being Religious'. Stillingfleet, *A Rational Account of the Grounds of the Protestant Religion*.	Dryden and Howard, *The Indian Queen*. Etherege, *The Comical Revenge*. Dryden, *The Rival Ladies*. Orrery, *Henry V*. J. Lacy, *The Old Troop*.
1665	Crowne, *Pandion and Amphigenia*. Head, *The English Rogue*, Pt. i. D. Lloyd, *The Statesmen and Favourites of England*. Sprat, *Observations on Monsieur de Sorbier's Voyage into England*. Walton, *Life of Richard Hooker*. Hooke, *Micrographia*. Casaubon, *A Treatise concerning Enthusiasm*.	Dryden, *The Indian Emperor*. Orrery, *Mustapha*. Theatres closed 5 June, by proclamation, on account of the Plague.
1666	Bunyan, *Grace Abounding*. Glanvill, *Philosophical Considerations concerning Witches and Witchcraft*. Tillotson, *The Rule of Faith*. Orrery, *Parthenissa* (the last part).	Theatres re-open, 29 Nov.
1667	Sprat, *The History of the Royal Society*. H. More, *Enchiridion Ethicum*. Duchess of Newcastle, *Life* of her husband.	Dryden, *Secret Love*. Dryden and the Duke of Newcastle, *Sir Martin Mar-all*. Dryden and Davenant, *The*

Date	Public Events	Literary History	Verse
	Provinces signed at Breda, 21 July. Clarendon dismissed and impeached. He withdraws to France, 29 Nov.	Molière, *Tartuffe*.	*House-Warming* and *Last Instructions to a Painter*.
1668	Triple Alliance negotiated by Sir W. Temple between England, Holland, and Sweden (Jan.).	Davenant d. Dryden becomes Poet Laureate. Penn committed to the Tower.	Cowley, *Works*, ed. Sprat (including the first publication of the Essays, and Sprat's Life of Cowley).
	Treaty of Aix-la-Chapelle (Apr.).	*Mercurius Librarius; Or, A Catalogue of Books* (the Term Catalogues) begins. La Fontaine, *Fables*. Molière, *Amphitryon*.	Denham, *Poems and Translations* (i.e. collected works).
1669	The King asks Parliament for money to pay his debts. Parliament responds by inquiring into the conduct of public expenditure, and is prorogued. The Queen Mother, Henrietta Maria, d.	Denham d. Racine, *Britannicus*. Molière, *Monsieur de Pourceaugnac*.	*The New Academy of Compliments*.
1670	The Cabal is formed. Duke of Albemarle (General Monck) d. Secret Treaty of Dover. Louise de Kerouaille (later Duchess of Portsmouth) comes to England. Charles II's sister, the Duchess of Orleans, d.	Congreve b. Pascal, *Pensées*. Molière, *Le Bourgeois gentilhomme*. Racine, *Bérénice*.	
1671	Duchess of York d. Temple recalled from Holland. Louise de Kerouaille openly recognized as the King's mistress.	Molière, *Les Fourberies de Scapin*.	Milton, *Paradise Regained* and *Samson Agonistes*. *Westminster Drollery*. *Oxford Drollery*.
1672	Stop of the Exchequer (Jan.), suspending interest on	Bunyan freed by Declaration of Indulgence and resumes	J. Phillips, *Maronides*. *Covent Garden Drollery*.

Date	Prose	Drama (date of acting)
	Sir P. Rycaut, *The Present State of the Ottoman Empire.*	*Tempest.* Orrery, *The Black Prince.*
1668	Dryden, *An Essay of Dramatic Poesy.* Heylyn, *Cyprianus Anglicus* (Life of Laud). Glanvill, *Plus Ultra.* Penn, *The Sandy Foundation Shaken.* Wilkins, *Essay towards a Real Character and Philosophical Language.* Sir Josiah Child, *A New Discourse of Trade.*	Etherege, *She Wou'd if she Cou'd.* Sir R. Howard, *The Great Favourite.* Shadwell, *The Sullen Lovers.* Sedley, *The Mulberry Garden.* Dryden, *An Evening's Love.*
1669	Penn, *No Cross, No Crown.* W. Charleton, *A Brief Discourse concerning the different Wits of Men.*	Dryden, *Tyrannic Love.*
1670	Baxter, *The Life of Faith.* Milton, *The History of Britain.* Parker, *A Discourse of Ecclesiastical Polity.* Walton, *Life of George Herbert*, and the collected *Lives* of Donne, Wotton, Hooker, and Herbert. Eachard, *The Grounds and Occasions of the Contempt of the Clergy.*	Mrs. Behn, *The Forced Marriage.* Dryden, *The Conquest of Granada,* Pt. i. Shadwell, *The Humourists.*
1671		Dryden, *The Conquest of Granada,* Pt. ii. Wycherley's first play, *Love in a Wood.* Settle, *Cambyses* (?). Buckingham *et al.*, *The Rehearsal.*
1672	Ashmole, *Institution, Laws, Ceremonies of the Order of the Garter.* Marvell, *The Rehearsal Transprosed.*	Wycherley, *The Gentleman Dancing-Master.* Dryden, *Marriage-à-la-Mode.*

Date	Public Events	Literary History	Verse
	loans. Declaration of Indulgence. War declared on the States General (the Third Dutch War). Indecisive Battle of Southwold Bay. The Earl of Sandwich lost in the action. Assassination of the De Witt brothers. William of Orange becomes Stadholder. Shaftesbury Lord Chancellor.	preaching, but is again imprisoned for a short period. Addison b. Steele b. Racine, *Bajazet*. Molière, *Les Femmes savantes*.	
1673	Declaration of Indulgence revoked. The Test Act. Sir Thomas Osborne (later Earl of Danby) succeeds Clifford as Lord High Treasurer. Duke of York m. Mary of Modena. Shaftesbury dismissed from the Chancellorship and ordered to leave London. He now goes into Opposition.	The Marvell–Parker controversy. Molière, *Le Malade imaginaire*. Molière d.	Davenant, *Works*.
1674	Peace treaty with Dutch. Collapse of Cabal. Shaftesbury dismissed from Privy Council. Buckingham dismissed, and joins the opposition.	Milton d. Herrick d. Traherne d. Racine, *Iphigénie*. Boileau, *Le Lutrin* and *L'Art Poétique*. Clarendon d. at Rouen, and is buried in Westminster Abbey, 4 Jan. 1675.	Flatman, *Poems and Songs*.
1675	Royal proclamation for enforcing the laws against Nonconformists. The King, heavily in debt, asks Parliament for a supply, but is granted only money for the navy. Work begins on Wren's St. Paul's Cathedral.	Ogilby, *Britannia*. Saint-Simon b. Order for the suppression of coffeehouses (for political reasons): almost immediately afterwards withdrawn.	Cotton, *Burlesque upon Burlesque*. Marvell(?), *A Dialogue between the Two Horses*.

Date	Prose	Drama (date of acting)
	Temple, *Observations upon the . . . Netherlands.* J. Josselyn, *New England's Rarities Discovered.* Cumberland, *De Legibus Naturae.* Eachard, *Mr. Hobbes's State of Nature Considered.*	Ravenscroft, *The Citizen turned Gentleman.* Dryden, *The Assignation.* Shadwell, *Epsom Wells.*
1673	Obadiah Walker, *Of Education, especially of Young Gentlemen.* W. Cave, *Primitive Christianity.* R. Leigh, *The Censure of the Rota.*	Mrs. Behn, *The Dutch Lover.* Ravenscroft, *The Careless Lovers.* Dryden, *Amboyna.* Settle, *The Empress of Morocco.* Pordage, *Herod and Mariamne.*
1674	J. Josselyn, *Two Voyages to New England.* Rymer, trans. of Rapin's *Réflexions sur la Poétique d'Aristote* (with critical Preface). Dryden *et al.*, *Notes and Observations on the Empress of Morocco.* M. Clifford, *A Treatise of Human Reason.*	Operatic version of *The Tempest.* Duffet, *The Mock Tempest.* Lee's first play, *Nero.*
1675	E. Phillips, *Theatrum Poetarum.* Shaftesbury, *A Letter from a Person of Quality to his Friend in the Country.* J. Barnes, *Gerania.*	Wycherley, *The Country Wife.* Crowne, *Calisto* (at Court). Shadwell, *Psyche.* Otway's first play, *Alcibiades.* Dryden, *Aureng-Zebe.* Crowne, *The Country Wit.*

Date	Public Events	Literary History	Verse
1676	The King concludes another secret treaty with Louis XIV, and becomes his pensioner (£100,000 per annum).		
1677	Buckingham, Shaftesbury, Salisbury, and Wharton committed to the Tower. William and Mary m.	Harrington d. Barrow d. La Calprenède's *Pharamond* and Scudéry's *Almahide* trans. by J. Phillips. Racine, *Phèdre*.	Tate, *Poems*.
1678	Treaty of Nijmegen. Titus Oates and Israel Tonge give evidence on oath to Sir Edmundberry Godfrey (28 Sept.) of a Popish plot. Mysterious death of Godfrey (Oct.). Five Catholic lords sent to the Tower. Edward Coleman executed. Danby impeached by Commons.	Popish Plot pamphlets, 1678–81. H. Care, *A Pacquet of Advice from Rome* (3 Dec. 1678–13 July 1683). Marvell d. Farquhar b. Narcissus Luttrell begins his *Brief Historical Relation* (ending Apr. 1714). Mme. de La Fayette, *La Princesse de Clèves*.	H. Vaughan, *Thalia Rediviva*. Butler, *Hudibras*, Pt. iii.
1679	Dissolution of Cavalier Parliament. New and predominantly Whig House of Commons meets on 6 Mar. Duke of York sent abroad. Danby committed to the Tower (where he remains for five years). Habeas Corpus Act. Exclusion Bill, 21 May. The King dissolves Parliament, 12 July. Monmouth defeats Covenanters at Bothwell Brig. Further executions of Catholics.	Beaumont and Fletcher, Second Folio. Spenser, *Works*. Hobbes d. Orrery d. Licensing Act not renewed owing to the hasty dissolution of Parliament. Benjamin Harris starts *The Domestic Intelligence* in July. Many other newspapers spring up in this and the two following years. Royal proclamation (31 Oct.) ordering the seizure of all libels against the Government, and the apprehension of	Oldham, *Garnet's Ghost*. 'Ephelia', *Female Poems*.

Date	Prose	Drama (date of acting)
1676	Cotton, *The Compleat Angler*, Pt. ii. Glanvill, *Essays on Several Important Subjects*.	Settle, *Ibrahim.* Etherege, *The Man of Mode.* Shadwell, *The Virtuoso.* Otway, *Don Carlos.* Mrs. Behn, *The Town-Fop.* Durfey, *Madam Fickle* and *The Fool turned Critic.* Wycherley, *The Plain-Dealer.*
1677	Marvell, *An Account of the Growth of Popery.* R. Plot, *Natural History of Oxfordshire.* Burnet, *Memoirs of the . . . Dukes of Hamilton.*	Crowne, *The Destruction of Jerusalem.* Lee, *The Rival Queens.* Mrs. Behn, *The Rover.* Durfey, *A Fond Husband.* Dryden, *All for Love.* Dryden, *The State of Innocence* (published, not acted).
1678	Bunyan, *The Pilgrim's Progress*, Pt. i. Barclay, *An Apology for the True Christian Divinity.* Barrow, *Sermons preached on Various Occasions.* Cudworth, *The True Intellectual System of the Universe.* Calderwood (d. 1650), *The True History of the Church of Scotland.* Rymer, *Tragedies of the Last Age Considered.* Walton, *The Life of Dr. Sanderson.* L'Estrange, *An Account of the Growth of Knavery.* L'Estrange, trans. *Five Love Letters from a Nun to a Cavalier.*	Shadwell, *Timon of Athens.* Mrs. Behn, *Sir Patient Fancy.* Lee, *Mithridates.* Dryden, *The Kind Keeper.* Shadwell, *A True Widow* (perhaps 1679). Otway, *Friendship in Fashion.* Dryden and Lee, *Oedipus.*
1679	South, *Sermons* (followed by five further volumes). Burnet, *History of the Reformation*, Vol. i. (Vol. ii in 1681; Vol. iii in 1714). *An Appeal from the Country to the City.* L'Estrange, *The Reformed Catholic.*	Mrs. Behn, *The Feigned Courtezans.* Dryden, *Troilus and Cressida.* Lee, *Caesar Borgia.* Durfey, *The Virtuous Wife.*

Date	Public Events	Literary History	Verse
	Illness of Charles II. The Duke is sent for, and made High Commissioner in Scotland. New Parliament meets (Oct.), and is at once prorogued. Shaftesbury dismissed from the Council.	their authors and printers.	
1680	The Duke of York returns from Scotland in Feb., but is obliged to go back in Oct. Shaftesbury and other Opposition leaders indict the Duke of York and the Duchess of Portsmouth as Popish recusants. Monmouth makes quasi-royal progress through the Westcountry (Aug.–Sept.). Second Exclusion Bill rejected by the Lords on a second reading, largely through the efforts of Halifax (Nov.). Viscount Stafford executed.	Langbaine, *An Exact Catalogue of all the Comedies* (etc.) S. Butler d. Rochester d. La Rochefoucauld d.	Roscommon, trans. of Horace's *Art of Poetry*. Dryden *et al.*, trans. of Ovid's *Epistles*. Otway, *The Poet's Complaint of his Muse*. A. Radcliffe, *Ovid Travestie*. Rochester, *Poems by the E— of R—* ('Antwerp' edition).
1681	Parliament dissolved, 18 Jan. New Parliament (again predominantly Whig) summoned to Oxford (Mar.). Shaftesbury proposes that the Protestant succession should be secured by naming the Duke of Monmouth heir to the throne. New Exclusion Bill brought in. The King	John Houghton's periodical, *A Collection of Letters for the Improvement of Husbandry and Trade* (8 Sept. 1681–16 June 1683). Pro-government periodicals, *Heraclitus Ridens* and L'Estrange's *Observator*. Calderon d.	Cotton, *The Wonders of the Peak*. Oldham, *Satires upon the Jesuits*; *Satire against Virtue*; *Horace's Art of Poetry Imitated*. Dryden, *Absalom and Achitophel* (17 Nov.). Marvell, *Miscellaneous Poems* (the first collected edition of his verse).

Date	Prose	Drama (date of acting)
1680	Filmer (d. 1653), *Patriarcha*. Barrow, *A Treatise of the Pope's Supremacy*. Bunyan, *The Life and Death of Mr. Badman*. Burnet, *Passages of the Life and Death of the Earl of Rochester*. L'Estrange, *Citt and Bumpkin*. L'Estrange, trans. of *Select Colloquies of Erasmus*. Temple, *Miscellanea*, Pt. i. H. Neville, *Plato Redivivus*.	Otway, *The Orphan*. Settle, *The Female Prelate*. Otway, *The Soldier's Fortune*. Lee, *The Princess of Cleve* (perhaps later). Lee, *Theodosius*. Dryden, *The Spanish Friar*. Lee, *Lucius Junius Brutus*.
1681	Hobbes, *Behemoth* (unauthorized ed. in 1679). Dryden, *His Majesty's Declaration Defended*. Baxter, *A Breviat of the Life of Margaret . . . Charlton*. Settle, *The Character of a Popish Successor*. R. Knox, *An Historical Relation of the Island of Ceylon*.	Mrs. Behn, *The Rover*, Pt. ii. Tate's version of *King Lear*. Banks, *The Unhappy Favourite*. Shadwell, *The Lancashire Witches*. Mrs. Behn, *The False Count*. Ravenscroft, *The London Cuckolds*. Mrs. Behn, *The Roundheads*.

Date	Public Events	Literary History	Verse
	promptly dissolves Parliament, and rules without another until his death. Reaction in the country against the Whigs. Oates forbidden the Court. Shaftesbury committed to the Tower on a charge of high treason (July). The Bill of Indictment thrown out by a London Grand Jury (24 Nov.). A medal struck to commemorate this Whig triumph.		
1682	Chelsea Hospital founded. Duke of York returns from Scotland (Mar.), and resumes residence in London (June). Shaftesbury takes some steps towards raising a rebellion, but flees to Holland in Nov. Monmouth makes a second progress in the West, and is arrested in Stafford.	Whig attacks on *Absalom and Achitophel* and *The Medal* (*The Medal of John Bayes*; *The Tory Poets*; etc.). Sir T. Browne d. *Weekly Memorials for the Ingenious; Or, An Account of Books . . .* (1682–3).	Dryden, *The Medal*. Mulgrave, *An Essay upon Poetry*. Dryden, *MacFlecknoe* (publication unauthorized). H. Playford, Wit and Mirth: *An Antidote against Melancholy* (3rd edn.). Radcliffe, *The Ramble*. Dryden and Tate, *Absalom and Achitophel*, Pt. ii. Dryden, *Religio Laici*. Creech, trans. of *Lucretius*.
1683	Shaftesbury dies in Holland. The Charter of the City of London declared forfeited after *Quo Warranto* proceedings. The Rye House Plot. Lords Essex and Russell and Algernon Sidney committed to the Tower. Russell and Sidney executed. Monmouth goes to Holland.	Oldham d. Walton d. T. Killigrew d. J. Chalkhill (*fl.* 1600), *Thealma and Clearchus*. Fontenelle, *Dialogues des morts*.	P. Ayres, *Emblems of Love*. Oldham, *Poems and Translations*. T. Shipman, *Carolina*. J. Mason, *Songs of Praise*.

Date	Prose	Drama (date of acting)

1682 | Bunyan, *The Holy War.*
Burnet, *The Life and Death of Sir Matthew Hale.*
Petty, *Essay concerning the Multiplication of Mankind.*
Whitelock, *Memorials of English Affairs.*
N. Grew, *The Anatomy of Plants.*
Ray, *Methodus Plantarum Nova.* | Southerne's first play, *The Loyal Brother.*
Banks, *Virtue Betrayed.*
Mrs. Behn, *The City Heiress.*
Otway, *Venice Preserved.*
Dryden and Lee, *The Duke of Guise.*
The two companies united. |

1683 | Barrow, *Works,* ed. Tillotson.
Dryden *et. al.,* trans. of Plutarch's *Lives* (1683–6).
Dryden, *Vindication of The Duke of Guise.*
Settle, *A Narrative of the Popish Plot.*
Keach, *The Travels of True Godliness.* | Crowne, *City Politics.*
Otway, *The Atheist.*
Lee, *Constantine the Great.* |

Date	Public Events	Literary History	Verse
	Increased severity in treatment of Dissenters.		
1684	Monmouth in Holland. Danby released (Feb.). Duke of York back at the Admiralty (May).	Corneille d.	Creech, trans. of Horace and Theocritus. Roscommon, *Essay on Translated Verse.* Tonson, *Miscellany Poems.* (Further volumes appeared in 1685—*Sylvae*; 1693—*Examen Poeticum*; 1694 —*The Annual Miscellany*).
1685	Charles II d. 6 Feb. James II (aged 52) becomes King. Halifax is President of the Council: Rochester, Sunderland, and Godolphin are the real advisers. Coronation, 23 Apr. Scottish rising led by the Earl of Argyll in favour of Monmouth is suppressed, and Argyll executed at Edinburgh (June). Monmouth lands at Lyme Regis (June), is defeated at Sedgemoor, and executed, 15 July. The Bloody Assizes. Halifax dismissed (Oct.), leaving Sunderland as the chief minister. Revocation of the Edict of Nantes (Oct.).	Baxter imprisoned. Shakespeare, Fourth Folio. New Licensing Act. Otway d. Roscommon d.	Dryden, *Threnodia Augustalis.* Waller, *Divine Poems.* S. Wesley, *Maggots.* *Poems by Several Hands*, ed. Tate. *Miscellany, being A Collection of Poems*, ed. Mrs. Behn.
1686	The King begins to appoint Catholic peers as Privy Councillors, and to staff the army with Catholic officers. He keeps a large body of troops in camp at Hounslow. Penn induces the	Sir T. Browne (d. 1682), *Works.* Sir W. Dugdale d. Fontenelle, *Entretiens sur la pluralité des mondes.*	Bunyan, *A Book* [of verse] *for Boys and Girls.* Anne Killigrew, *Poems* (contains Dryden's Ode to her memory).

Date	Prose	Drama (date of acting)
1684	Bunyan, *The Pilgrim's Progress*, Pt. ii. T. Burnet, *The Theory of the Earth* (original Latin version, 1681). Dryden, trans. of Maimbourg, *The History of the League*.	Rochester, *Valentinian* (at Court; published 1685, with R. Wolseley's Preface). Southerne, *The Disappointment*. Tate, *A Duke and no Duke*.
1685	Stillingfleet, *Origines Britannicae*. Cotton, trans. of Montaigne's *Essays*.	Crowne, *Sir Courtly Nice*. Dryden, *Albion and Albanius*.
1686	R. Parr, *Life of James Ussher*. Burnet, *Some Letters containing an Account . . . of Switzerland, Italy, etc.*	Mrs. Behn, *The Lucky Chance*.

Date	Public Events	Literary History	Verse
	King to issue a proclamation of pardon (Mar.) to all those in prison for conscience' sake: 1,200 Quakers released. The King sets up an Ecclesiastical Commission.		
1687	Rochester dismissed. Magdalen College resists the attempt of the King to impose on it a Catholic President. Many Fellows deprived in consequence.	Duke of Buckingham d. Waller d. Sir W. Petty d. Winstanley, *Lives of the English Poets*. Speght's *Chaucer* reprinted. Newton, *Principia*. M. Clifford, *Notes upon Mr. Dryden's Poems*.	Ayres, *Lyric Poems*. Dryden, *Song for St. Cecilia's Day*. Dryden, *The Hind and the Panther*. Prior and Montagu, *The Hind and the Panther Transversed*. Norris, *Miscellanies* (verse and prose). Gould, *The Laureate*.
1688	James II's Declaration of Indulgence (Apr.). Birth of his son (the Old Pretender) in June. The Trial of the Seven Bishops (29–30 June). James recalls troops from Ireland and Scotland. Sunderland dismissed. William of Orange lands at Torbay, 5 Nov., and advances towards London. Danby supports William in Yorkshire. Flight of James from Whitehall on 11 Dec. He is captured and returns to London, but finally reaches France on 25 Dec.	Bunyan d. Cudworth d. A. Pope b. Shadwell becomes Poet Laureate. La Bruyère, *Caractères*. Perrault, *Parallèles des anciens et modernes*.	Dryden, *Britannia Rediviva*.
1689	Convention Parliament, 22 Jan. Crown offered to William and Mary.	Selden (d. 1654), *Table Talk*. Mrs. Behn d. S. Richardson b.	Cotton, *Poems on Several Occasions*. *The Muses Farewell to Popery and Slavery*.

Date	*Prose*	*Drama (date of acting)*
1687	Halifax, *A Letter to a Dissenter.* J. Phillips, trans. of *Don Quixote.*	Mrs. Behn, *The Emperor of the Moon.* Sedley, *Bellamira.*
1688	Halifax, *The Character of a Trimmer.* Halifax, *Advice to a Daughter.* Joshua Barnes, *Life of Edward III.*	Shadwell, *The Squire of Alsatia.*
1689	Locke, *A Letter concerning Toleration.* Sherlock, *A Practical Discourse concerning Death.*	Shadwell, *Bury Fair.* Dryden, *Don Sebastian.*

Date	Public Events	Literary History	Verse
	Burnet Bishop of Salisbury. Coronation, 11 April. The Toleration Act. War declared on the French (May). Viscount Dundee killed at the Battle of Killiecrankie. The Grand Alliance. The Bill of Rights, 16 Dec.	Racine, *Esther*.	Gould, *Poems*.
1690	James lands in Ireland (Mar.). William crosses to Ireland (June), and defeats James at the Battle of the Boyne. Anglo-Dutch naval defeat off Beachy Head (June–July).	R. Barclay d. Dunton starts *The Athenian Gazette*, 17 Mar. (continued as *The Athenian Mercury* to June 1697).	Waller, *Poems*, Pt. ii (with Preface attributed to Atterbury).
1691	William goes to Holland. Tillotson succeeds Sancroft as Archbishop of Canterbury.	Etherege d. Fox d. Baxter d. Hon. Robert Boyle d. Boyle Lectures founded. Racine, *Athalie*.	Rochester, *Poems on Several Occasions* (Tonson edition).
1692	Marlborough dismissed. Somers Attorney General. Massacre of Glencoe. Defeat of French fleet at La Hogue. Battle of Steenkirk.	St. Évremond's *Miscellaneous Essays* trans. (with a Character by Dryden). Jonson, Second Folio. Motteux, *The Gentleman's Journal* (Jan. 1692–Nov. 1694). Shadwell d. Tate becomes Poet Laureate. Lee d.	Dryden, *Eleonora*. Walsh, *Letters and Poems, Amorous and Gallant*. Dennis, *Poems in Burlesque*.
1693	Loss of the Smyrna convoy to the French under Tourville. Battle of Landen (Neerwinden).	Mme. de La Fayette d.	*Examen Poeticum*. Dryden *et al.*, trans. of *Juvenal* and (by Dryden) *Persius*.

Date	Prose	Drama (date of acting)
1690	Locke, *An Essay concerning Human Understanding*. Locke, *Two Treatises of Government*. Locke, *Second Letter concerning Toleration*. Petty (d. 1687), *Political Arithmetic*. Temple, *Miscellanea*, Pt. ii (containing, *inter alia*, 'An Essay upon the Ancient and Modern Learning'). Pepys, *Memoirs of the Navy*.	Crowne, *The English Friar*. Southerne, *Sir Anthony Love*. Dryden, *Amphitryon*.
1691	Congreve, *Incognita*. Wood, *Athenae Oxonienses*. Ray, *The Wisdom of God Manifested in the Works of the Creation*. H. Wharton, *Anglia Sacra*. Sir Dudley North, *Discourses upon Trade*.	Durfey, *Love for Money*. W. Mountfort, *Greenwich Park*. Dryden, *King Arthur*. Southerne, *The Wife's Excuse* (Dec.?).
1692	Bunyan, *Works*, Vol. i (no more issued). Bentley, *A Confutation of Atheism* (the first series of Boyle Lectures, 1692–3). Locke, *A Third Letter for Toleration*. Burnet, *A Discourse of Pastoral Care*. L'Estrange, *Fables of Aesop and Other Mythologists*. Sir T. Pope Blount, *Essays on Several Subjects*. Gildon, *The Post-Boy Robbed of his Mail*.	Durfey, *The Marriage-Hater Matched*. Dryden, *Cleomenes*. Settle and Purcell, *The Fairy Queen*. Shadwell, *The Volunteers*.
1693	Rymer, *A Short View of Tragedy*. Locke, *Thoughts concerning Education*. Dennis, *The Impartial Critic*. Penn, *Some Fruits of Solitude*.	Congreve's first play, *The Old Bachelor* (Mar.). Durfey, *The Richmond Heiress*. Congreve, *The Double Dealer* (Oct.).

Date	Public Events	Literary History	Verse
1694	Bank of England founded. Triennial Act. Queen Mary d.	Tillotson d. Voltaire b. Philip Dormer Stanhope, fourth Earl of Chesterfield b.	*The Annual Miscellany.* Addison, 'An Account of the Greatest English Poets' (included in the above).
1695	Beginning of the Whig Junto and of party government. Capture of Namur. Currency problems.	H. Vaughan d. Halifax d. Wood d. Dorothy Osborne d. Licensing Act not renewed. Rapid growth of newspapers: *The Post Boy, The Postman, The Flying Post,* etc.	Blackmore, *Prince Arthur.* Memorial poems to Queen Mary collected in *The Mourning Poets.*
1696	A recoinage agreed to by Parliament, the expense to be met by a window tax. Jacobite plot to assassinate the King at Turnham Green.	Mme. de Sévigné d. Bayle, *Dictionnaire historique et critique.*	Metrical version of the Psalms by Tate and Brady. Oldmixon, *Poems on Several Occasions.*
1697	Execution of Sir John Fenwick. Treaty of Ryswick. Parliament calls for a rapid demobilization of the armed forces. Clamour against a standing army.	Hogarth b. Pamphlet literature for and against standing armies in time of peace.	Dryden, *Alexander's Feast.* W. Pope, *The Wish.* Dryden, trans. of *Virgil.* Blackmore, *King Arthur.* *Poems on Affairs of State,* Pts. i and ii.

Date	Prose	Drama (date of acting)
1694	Fox, *Journal* (ed. T. Ellwood). J. Wright, *Country Conversations.* Wotton, *Reflections upon Ancient and Modern Learning.* Sir T. Urquhart's trans. of *Rabelais* (1653) completed by Motteux. R. Molesworth, *An Account of Denmark.* Halifax, *A Rough Draft of a New Model at Sea.* R. Burthogge, *An Essay upon Reason, and the Nature of Spirits.*	Dryden's last play, *Love Triumphant.* Southerne, *The Fatal Marriage.* Crowne, *The Married Beau.* Durfey, *The Comical History of Don Quixote.*
1695	C. Blount, *Miscellaneous Works.* Burnet, *An Essay on the Memory of the Late Queen.* Locke, *The Reasonableness of Christianity.* Temple, *Introduction to the History of England.* Tillotson (d. 1694), *Works.* Dryden, trans. of Du Fresnoy's *De arte graphica* (with the prefatory 'Parallel of Poetry and Painting'). T. Tanner, *Notitia Monastica.*	Congreve, *Love for Love.* Gould, *The Rival Sisters.* Southerne, *Oronooko.* Granville, *The She Gallants* (c. Dec. 1695/Jan. 1696). Betterton forms a new company, with Elizabeth Barry, Anne Bracegirdle, and other dissatisfied players.
1696	Aubrey, *Miscellanies.* Baxter (d. 1691), *Reliquiae Baxterianae* (ed. M. Sylvester). Toland, *Christianity not Mysterious.* Whiston, *A New Theory of the Earth.* Dennis, ed., *Letters upon Several Occasions* (by Dennis, Dryden, Congreve, Wycherley, with select letters of Voiture). C. Leslie, *The Snake in the Grass.* Anon., *An Essay in Defence of the Female Sex.*	Cibber's first play, *Love's Last Shift.* Dogget, *The Country Wake.* Motteux, *Love's a Jest.* Ravenscroft, *The Anatomist.* Vanbrugh, *The Relapse.*
1697	Bentley, 'Dissertation upon the Epistles of Phalaris' (in the second edition of Wotton's *Reflections*). Collier, *Essays.* Rochester, *Familiar Letters . . .* Dampier, *A New Voyage round the World.* Defoe, *An Essay upon Projects.* Norris, *An Account of Reason and Faith . . .* W. Pope, *The Life of Seth Lord Bishop of Salisbury.*	Congreve, *The Mourning Bride.* Vanbrugh, *The Provoked Wife.* Dennis, *A Plot and no Plot.* Settle, *The World in the Moon.*

Date	Public Events	Literary History	Verse
1698	The Darien Scheme. First Partition Treaty.	Ward, *The London Spy* (monthly to Apr. 1700). Milton, *Prose Works*, ed. Toland. The Collier controversy begins. Boyle, Atterbury, and others reply to Bentley's *Dissertation upon . . . Phalaris*.	
1699	Whig Junto breaks up.	Stillingfleet d. Temple d. *The History of the Works of the Learned* (to 1712).	Garth, *The Dispensary*. T. Brown, *A Collection of Miscellany Poems*.
1700	Death of the Duke of Gloucester. Second Partition Treaty.	Death of John Dryden (1 May). *Luctus Britannici* and *The Nine Muses* (volumes of memorial poems to Dryden).	Blackmore, *A Satire against Wit*. J. Pomfret, *The Choice*. Dryden, *Fables Ancient and Modern*. T. Brown et al., *Commendatory Verses on the Author of the two Arthurs*. S. Cobb, *Poetae Britannici*. S. Wesley, *An Epistle to a Friend concerning Poetry*. J. Tutchin, *The Foreigners*. Defoe, *The Pacificator*.

Date	Prose	Drama (date of acting)
1698	Mrs. Behn, *The Histories and Novels.* Collier, *A Short View of the Immorality and Profaneness of the English Stage.* Ludlow, *Memoirs.* A. Sidney, *Discourses concerning Government.* Andrew Fletcher of Saltoun, *A Discourse of Government relating to Militias.* Martin, *A Late Voyage to St. Kilda.* Defoe, *The Poor Man's Plea.*	Granville, *Heroic Love.* Crowne, *Caligula.* Motteux, *Beauty in Distress.* Durfey, *The Campaigners.* Farquhar's first play, *Love and a Bottle.*
1699	Lord Fairfax, *Memorials.* Toland, *Amyntor.* W. King, *Dialogues of the Dead.* Dampier, *Voyages and Descriptions.* Muggleton, *The Acts of the Witnesses.*	Farquhar, *The Constant Couple.*
1700	Halifax, *Miscellanies* (i.e. collected writings). Harrington (d. 1677), *Works.* Brown, *Amusements Serious and Comical.* Motteux, trans. of *Don Quixote,* vol. i.	Burnaby, *The Reformed Wife.* Congreve, *The Way of the World.* Vanbrugh's alteration of Fletcher's *The Pilgrim,* with Dryden's *Secular Masque.*

BIBLIOGRAPHY

This bibliography is arranged in six sections:

I. General Bibliographies and Works of Reference.
II. General Collections and Anthologies.
III. General Literary History and Criticism (general history and criticism; rhetorical theory and prose style; history and criticism of poetry; history and criticism of drama; history of ideas).
IV. Special Literary Studies and Literary Forms (language; journalism; fiction; essays, characters, and letters; historical and biographical literature; classical and foreign relations; contemporary criticism; printing and bookselling).
V. The Background of Literature (political history and political thought; religion and religious thought; science and scientific thought; travel; social life; education and culture; the arts).
VI. Individual Authors.

Since this volume covers the period immediately following upon Douglas Bush's *English Literature in the Earlier Seventeenth Century*, many of the titles listed by him in the general sections of his bibliography are applicable here too. When I have to repeat his entries I have not usually sought for elegant variation, but have often quoted him verbatim. I have been rather less ample, however, in one or two of my sections, and have occasionally referred the reader to his volume for a fuller treatment.

The following abbreviations are used in the citing of some works of reference and current periodicals:

ABBREVIATIONS:

Anderson	R. Anderson, *The Works of the British Poets* (13 vols., 1792–5)
ARS	*Augustan Reprint Society*
BNYPL	*Bulletin of the New York Public Library*
Bush	Douglas Bush, *English Literature in the Earlier Seventeenth Century* (2nd. ed., rev., 1962)

CBEL	*Cambridge Bibliography of English Literature*
Chalmers	A. Chalmers, *The Works of the English Poets* (21 vols., 1810)
DNB	*Dictionary of National Biography*
EC	*Essays in Criticism*
ELH	*A Journal of English Literary History*
ESEA	*Essays and Studies by Members of the English Association*
HLB	*Huntington Library Bulletin*
HLQ	*Huntington Library Quarterly*
JEGP	*Journal of English and Germanic Philology*
JHI	*Journal of the History of Ideas*
Johnson	*The Works of the English Poets* (68 vols., 1779–81)
Macdonald	Hugh Macdonald, *John Dryden: A Bibliography of Early Editions and of Drydeniana* (1939)
MLN	*Modern Language Notes*
MLQ	*Modern Language Quarterly*
MLR	*Modern Language Review*
MP	*Modern Philology*
NQ	*Notes and Queries*
OBS	*Oxford Bibliographical Society Proceedings & Papers*
PBSA	*Papers of the Bibliographical Society of America*
PMLA	*Publications of the Modern Language Association of America*
PQ	*Philological Quarterly*
RES	*Review of English Studies*
Saintsbury	*Minor Poets of the Caroline Period*, ed. George Saintsbury (3 vols., 1905–21)
Spingarn	*Critical Essays of the Seventeenth Century*, ed. J. E. Spingarn (3 vols., 1908–9; repr., Indiana University, 1957)
SEL	*Studies in English Literature, 1500–1900*
SP	*Studies in Philology*
UTQ	*University of Toronto Quarterly*
Wing	*Short-Title Catalogue . . . 1641–1700*, ed. D. Wing (3 vols., Columbia, 1945–51)

I. GENERAL BIBLIOGRAPHIES AND WORKS OF REFERENCE

Among the older bibliographical aids R. Watt's *Bibliotheca Britannica* (4 vols., 1824) keeps its place on library shelves, and W. T. Lowndes, *Bibliographer's Manual of English Literature* (rev. ed. by H. G. Bohn, 6 vols., 1869) is still a useful and surprisingly comprehensive guidebook. For almost complete coverage there is the *British Museum General Catalogue of Printed Books* (now effective to 1965). *The Term Catalogues 1668–1709*, ed. E. Arber (3 vols., 1903–6), and *A Transcript of the Registers of the Worshipful Company of Stationers; from 1640–1708 A.D.*, ed. G. E. B. Eyre *et al.* (3 vols., Roxburghe Club, 1913–14; repr., New York, 1950) are especially useful for our period. The chief bibliographical aid for the late seventeenth century is Donald Wing, *Short-Title Catalogue of Books Printed in England, Scotland . . . 1641–1700* (3 vols., Columbia, 1945–51). There are supplements to this by M. I. Fry and G. Davies (*HLQ* xvi, 1953), J. E. Tucker (*PBSA* xlix, 1955), W. G. Hiscock (1956), J. Alden (University of Virginia, 1958), E. Wolf (Philadelphia, 1959). P. G. Morison has compiled *An Index of Printers, Publishers and Booksellers in the Wing Bibliography* (University of Virginia, 1955); and Wing has published *A Gallery of Ghosts. Books Published between 1641–1700 Not Found in the Short-Title Catalogue* (New York, 1967). A *Catalogue of the Petyt Library* (1964) is of special interest, since it lists a collection formed mainly in the late seventeenth century and not subsequently augmented.

CBEL, ed. F. W. Bateson (4 vols., 1940), has a *Supplement*, ed. G. Watson (1957), covering 1935–55, and the whole work is in process of being revised and brought up to date under Watson's editorship. There is an abridgement, *The Concise Cambridge Bibliography of English Literature*, ed. Watson (1958), but its usefulness for scholars is limited by its concision. Two smaller bibliographies, with critical comment, are V. de S. Pinto's *The English Renaissance 1510–1688* (1938; rev. 1951), and H. V. D. Dyson and J. E. Butt, *Augustans and Romantics 1689–1800* (1940; rev. 1961). A. G. Kennedy and D. B. Sands, *A Concise Bibliography for Students of English* (4th ed., Stanford, 1960) is compact and useful, although necessarily highly selective for any one period. R. G. Stamm's *Englische Literatur* (Berne, 1957) gives a critical review of modern scholarship on English literature, 1500–1900. Since 1961 *Studies in English Literature* has carried a critical account of 'Recent Studies in the Restoration and Eighteenth Century'.

For the late seventeenth century the essential bibliography of scholarly work is that published since 1926 by the *Philological Quarterly*, covering the years 1660–1800, with critical notices of some of the more important publications. The bibliographies from 1926 to 1950 have been republished in 2 vols., ed. L. A. Landa and A. Friedman (Princeton, 1950–2), and those from 1951 to 1960 have been similarly edited by G. J. Kolb and C. A. Zimansky (2 vols., 1962). The *PQ* bibliographies may be supplemented by *The Year's Work in English Studies* (English Association, since 1919–20), which has a descriptive commentary; *Annual Bibliography of English Language and Literature* (Modern Humanities Research Association, since 1920); the Annual Bibliography included in *PMLA* since 1956; *Dissertation Abstracts: Abstracts of Dissertations and Monographs in Microfilm* (University Microfilms, Ann Arbor, since 1938); *Abstracts of English Studies* (University of Colorado, since 1958). The *Johnsonian News Letter* has been listing and commenting on new books and articles in our period since 1940.

Some miscellaneous works of reference are: F. Madan, *Oxford Books; a Bibliography of Printed Works*, vol. iii, 1651–80 (1912; repr., 1931); S. Halkett and J. Laing, *Dictionary of Anonymous and Pseudonymous English Literature*, rev. by J. Kennedy et al. (8 vols., 1926–56); *Annals of English Literature*, ed. W. Davin and R. W. Chapman (2nd ed., rev., 1962); Sir Paul Harvey, *Oxford Companion to English Literature* (4th ed., rev., 1967); A. Brett-James, *The Triple Stream: Four Centuries of English, French and German Literature 1531–1930* (1954), which has parallel chronological tables; C. L. Barnhart, *New Century Handbook of English Literature* (New York, 1956); D. C. Browning, *Everyman's Dictionary of Literary Biography* (1958).

Biographies of most of the authors mentioned in the text will be found in *Biographia Britannica*, ed. A. Kippis (6 vols., 1778–93), and in *DNB*; and accounts of some of them in the writings of their contemporaries, such as John Aubrey, Anthony Wood, William Winstanley, and Gerard Langbaine (*infra*, VI), and in S. Johnson, *Lives of the English Poets* (4 vols., 1781), and D. E. Baker, *Biographia Dramatica*, ed. I. Reed (2 vols., 1782).

II. GENERAL COLLECTIONS AND ANTHOLOGIES

1. Prose

General collections and anthologies of prose include the following: H. Craik, *English Prose* (5 vols., 1893–6; vol. iii);

R. P. T. Coffin and A. M. Witherspoon, *A Book of Seventeenth-Century Prose* (New York, 1929); C. A. Moore, *Restoration Literature: Poetry and Prose 1660–1700* (New York, 1934; repr., 1962); R. F. Brinkley, *English Prose of the Seventeenth Century* (New York, 1951); J. H. Hanford, *A Restoration Reader* (Indianapolis, 1954); M. A. Shaaber, *Seventeenth-Century English Prose* (New York, 1957); D. Novarr, *Seventeenth-Century English Prose* (New York, 1967); A. D. Ferry, *Religious Prose of Seventeenth-Century England* (New York, 1967). Shorter extracts will be found in W. Peacock's *English Prose*, vols. i–ii (1921; repr., 1931), and P. Ure's *Seventeenth-Century Prose* (Pelican, 1956).

Some contemporary pamphlets were reprinted in *The Harleian Miscellany* (1744–6; ed. T. Park, 10 vols., 1808–13), and in *Somers Tracts* (1748–52; enlarged ed. by Sir Walter Scott, 13 vols., 1809–15). A few pieces will be found in Sir C. H. Firth, *Stuart Tracts, 1603–1693* (1903), and W. H. Dunham and S. Pargellis, *Complaint and Reform in England 1436–1714* (New York, 1938). D. Nichol Smith's *Characters from the Histories and Memoirs of the Seventeenth Century* (1918) gives a comprehensive selection from Clarendon, Burnet, and other writers of the period.

2. VERSE

A. E. Case's *Bibliography of English Poetical Miscellanies 1521–1750* (1935), supplemented by N. Ault's list in *CBEL*, is almost exhaustive. W. J. Cameron has compiled a *Bibliography of English Poetical Miscellanies 1660–1700 in the Alexander Turnbull Library* (Wellington, N.Z., 1939). For song-books there are C. L. Day and E. B. Murrie, *English Song-Books 1651–1700: A Bibliography* (1940), and their 'English Song-Books 1650–1702, and their Publishers' (*Library* xvi, 1936). M. T. Osborne's *Advice-to-a-Painter Poems, 1635–1856. An Annotated Finding List* (University of Texas, 1949) supplies a bibliographical account of an important minor genre; and J. Alden's *The Muses Mourn* (University of Virginia, 1958) provides a checklist of verse occasioned by the death of Charles II. There are bibliographies for the Court Poets in J. H. Wilson and in V. de S. Pinto (*infra*, III. 3). H. Macdonald's bibliography of John Dryden (*infra*, Dryden, VI) takes in much of the minor poetical writing of the period.

The number of verse miscellanies published between 1660 and 1700 is extensive. Many of them were political; e.g. *The Rump* (1660; 1662), chiefly made up of derisory political songs; *The Muses Farewel to Popery and Slavery* (1689), and the various volumes of *Poems on Affairs of State*, beginning with four parts in 1689. A modern collection of *Poems on Affairs of State: Augustan Satirical Verse 1660–1714* (distinct from the above) is now under way, and three volumes have so far appeared: vol. i, ed. G. de F. Lord; vol. ii, ed. E. F. Mengel; vol. iii, ed. H. H. Schless (Yale, 1963–8), fully annotated and preceded by critical introductions. A number of contemporary 'Drolleries' collect some of the best verse of the period. The most important of these, *Covent Garden Drollery* (1672), has been ed. M. Summers (1927) and ed. G. Thorn-Drury (1928). Other collections, e.g. *Westminster Drolleries* (1671–2), have been edited, not very satisfactorily, by J. W. Ebsworth (1875), who also edited *The Bagford Ballads* (2 vols., 1878). The best collection of ballads for our period is *The Pepys Ballads*, ed. H. E. Rollins (8 vols., 1929–32). Earlier modern collections include *Political Ballads of the Seventeenth and Eighteenth Centuries*, ed. W. W. Wilkins (2 vols., 1860), and *Roxburghe Ballads*, ed. W. Chappell and J. W. Ebsworth (9 vols., 1871–97). Among later collections of ballads and songs are: *Loving Mad Tom. Bedlamite Verses of the XVI and XVII Centuries*, ed. J. Lindsay (1927); *Broadside Ballads of the Restoration Period* (the Osterley Park ballads), ed. F. B. Fawcett (1930); *The Common Muse: An Anthology of Popular British Ballad Poetry XVth–XXth Centuries* (1957; repr. 1965); *Wayside Poems of the Seventeenth Century*, ed. E. Blunden and B. Mellor (Hong Kong University, 1963). Some other titles will be found in Bush, IV. 2.

Among special collections are: J. S. Farmer's *Musa Pedestris. Three Centuries of Canting Songs* (1896), and *National Ballad and Song. Merry Songs and Ballads prior to the Year A.D. 1800* (5 vols., 1897); J. W. Draper's *A Century of Broadside Elegies* (1928), and R. A. Aubin's *London in Flames, London in Glory: Poems on the Fire and Rebuilding of London, 1666–1709* (Rutgers University, 1943).

Some of the Restoration poets are collected in S. Johnson's *The Works of the English Poets* (68 vols., 1779–81), and in the collection of A. Chalmers with the same title (21 vols., 1810), and in R. Anderson's *The Works of the British Poets* (13 vols., 1792–5). A few are available in *The Works of the Most Celebrated*

Minor Poets (2 vols., 1749), and in *The Works of Celebrated Authors* (2 vols., 1750). Some Restoration poetry will be found in *The Oxford Book of Seventeenth-Century Verse*, ed. Sir H. J. C. Grierson and G. Bullough (1934). Annotated anthologies for students include: *A Collection of English Poems 1660–1800*, ed. R. S. Crane (New York, 1932); *English Poetry of the Seventeenth Century*, ed. R. F. Brinkley (New York, 1936; repr., 1951), and *Seventeenth-Century Poetry*, ed. R. C. Bald (New York, 1958). A few Restoration poets appear in G. Saintsbury's *Minor Poets of the Caroline Period* (3 vols., 1905–21).

Among anthologies mainly or wholly lyrical are the following: *Musa Protera: Love Poems of the Restoration*, ed. A. H. Bullen (1889); *Cavalier and Courtier Lyrists*, ed. W. H. Dircks (1891); A *Book of Seventeenth-Century Lyrics*, ed. F. E. Schelling (Boston, 1899); *The Lyrists of the Restoration*, ed. John and Constance Masefield (1905); *A Treasury of Seventeenth-Century Poetry*, ed. H. J. Massingham (1919); *A Little Ark*, ed. G. Thorn-Drury (1921); *Seventeenth-Century Lyrics*, ed. N. Ault (1928), and *A Treasury of Unfamiliar Lyrics* (1938); *Restoration Verse, 1660–1715*, ed. W. Kerr (1930); *Aspects of Seventeenth-Century Verse*, ed. P. Quennell (1933); *Songs from the Restoration Theatre*, ed. W. Thorp (Princeton, 1934); *Songs of the Restoration Theatre*, ed. P. J. Stead (1948); *Rare Poems of the Seventeenth Century*, ed. L. B. Marshall (1936); *A Collection of Poems by Several Hands Never Before Published*, ed. F. A. Needham (1934); *Sir Richard Blackmore and the Wits* (University of Michigan, 1949), which prints the commendatory and discommendatory verses; *Restoration Carnival: Five Courtier Poets*, ed. V. de S. Pinto (1954).

3. DRAMA

Bibliographies of English drama may be said to begin with Gerard Langbaine's *New Catalogue of English Plays* (1688), which is itself an expansion of several earlier catalogues (1661, 1671, 1680). John Mottley compiled 'A Compleat List of all the Dramatic Poets', appended to T. Whincop's *Scanderbeg* (1747). D. E. Baker's *The Companion to the Play-House* (2 vols., 1764), revised by I. Reed as *Biographia Dramatica* (2 vols., 1782), and again by S. Jones (4 vols., 1812), provided earlier generations with a useful bibliographical tool. In the present century there have been: M. Summers, *A Bibliography of the Restoration*

Drama (1935); A. Harbage, *Annals of the English Drama 975–1700* (University of Pennsylvania, 1940; rev. S. Schoenbaum, 1964); G. L. Woodward and J. G. McManaway, *A Check List of English Plays 1641–1700* (University of Chicago, 1945; *Supplement* by Fredson Bowers, University of Virginia, 1949). A. Nicoll, *A History of Restoration Drama* (1923) has an appendix listing Restoration plays, together with their early performances and editions. In his revised *History of English Drama 1660–1900* (6 vols., 1952–9), vol. vi is 'A short-title Alphabetical Catalogue of English Plays . . . 1660–1900'. All the plays performed during the Restoration will now be found in *The London Stage, 1660–1800: A Calendar of Plays, Entertainments and Afterpieces*, ed. W. van Lennep *et al.* (Southern Illinois University, 1960–5), of which the first volume, ed. W. van Lennep (1965), covers our period. The second and third volumes of Sir Walter Greg's *Bibliography of the English Printed Drama to the Restoration* (1951–7) take in some plays as late as 1689, and include Latin plays and lost plays. For the drama immediately preceding the Restoration, G. E. Bentley's *The Jacobean and Caroline Stage* (5 vols., 1941–56), should be consulted. C. J. Stratman has compiled a *Bibliography of English Printed Tragedy 1565–1900* (Southern Illinois University, 1966).

A few of our plays are reprinted in the last two volumes of R. Dodsley's *Select Collection of Plays*, ed. W. C. Hazlitt (15 vols., 1874–6). Among other collections are *Bell's British Theatre* (36 vols., 1791–1802); *The British Theatre* (with biographical and critical remarks by Mrs. Inchbald, 25 vols., 1808); *The British Drama* (with critical remarks by Richard Cumberland, 14 vols., 1817). The plays of Orrery, Etherege, Wycherley, Shadwell, Sedley, Mrs. Behn, Otway, Lee, and Congreve are all available in modern collected editions; and there are editions of some of the minor dramatists in J. H. Maidment and W. H. Logan, *Dramatists of the Restoration* (14 vols., 1872–9). A few plays are available in M. Summers, *Restoration Comedies* (1921); D. H. Stevens, *Types of English Drama 1660–1780* (Boston, 1923); B. Dobrée, *Five Restoration Tragedies* (World's Classics, 1928) and *Five Heroic Plays* (World's Classics, 1960); D. MacMillan and H. M. Jones, *Plays of the Restoration and Eighteenth Century* (New York, 1931); C. A. Moore, *Twelve Famous Plays of the Restoration and Eighteenth Century* (New York, 1933); A. E. Morgan, *English Plays 1660–1820* (New York, 1935); C. M.

Gayley and A. Thaler, *Representative English Comedies*, vol. iv (New York, 1936); G. H. Nettleton and A. E. Case, *British Dramatists from Dryden to Sheridan* (New York, 1939); J. H. Wilson, *Six Restoration Plays* (Boston, 1959); G. Falle, *Three Restoration Plays* (New York, 1964); C. Spencer, *Five Restoration Adaptations of Shakespeare* (University of Illinois, 1965).

There are various eighteenth-century collections of prologues and epilogues; e.g. *A Collection and Selection of English Prologues and Epilogues* (4 vols., 1779). A modern selection, focused on the Restoration, is A. N. Wiley's *Rare Prologues and Epilogues 1642–1700* (1940).

For contemporary dramatic criticism, see III. 4 and IV. 7, *infra*.

III. GENERAL LITERARY HISTORY AND CRITICISM

This section comprises: (1) General literary history and criticism; (2) Rhetorical theory and prose style; (3) General and special history and criticism of poetry; (4) General and special history and criticism of drama; (5) The history of ideas.

1. GENERAL LITERARY HISTORY AND CRITICISM

The literature of the late seventeenth century is dealt with in *CHEL*, vol. viii, and in some chapters of vols. vii and ix. Shorter histories of English literature are those of E. Legouis and L. Cazamian (Paris, 1924; trs. 1926–7; last rev. ed. 1957); W. F. Schirmer, *Geschichte der englischen Literatur* (Halle, 1937; rev. ed., 2 vols., 1954); G. Sampson, *Concise Cambridge History of English Literature* (1941); A. C. Baugh *et al.*, *A Literary History of England* (New York, 1948), the Restoration period by G. Sherburn; H. Craig *et al.*, *History of English Literature* (New York, 1950), the Restoration period by L. I. Bredvold; D. Daiches, *A Critical History of English Literature* (2 vols., 1960). More exclusively focused on our period are: R. Garnett, *The Age of Dryden* (1897); O. Elton, *The Augustan Ages* (1899), which takes a European view of the literature; B. Wendell, *The Temper of the Seventeenth Century in English Literature* (New York, 1904); F. R. Gallaway, *Reason, Rule, and Revolt in English*

Classicism (New York, 1940); A. D. McKillop, *English Literature from Dryden to Burns* (New York, 1948); J. Butt, *The Augustan
Age* (1950, rev. 1965); K. M. P. Burton, *Restoration Literature*
(1958); C. V. Wedgwood, *Seventeenth-Century English Literature*
(1950; repr. 1961), and *Poetry and Politics under the Stuarts* (1960;
repr. University of Michigan, 1964); *From Dryden to Johnson*, ed.
B. Ford (Pelican Guide to English Literature, vol. iv, 1957);
D. J. Milburn, *The Age of Wit* (New York, 1966). J. H. Wilson's
The Court Wits of the Restoration (Princeton, 1948) gives a lively
account of the writers with whom he deals. There are three
chapters on the Restoration in Sir Edmund Gosse's *History of
Eighteenth Century Literature, 1660–1780* (1889), and A. Beljame's
Le Public et les hommes de lettres en Angleterre . . . 1660–1744 (Paris,
1881; trs., with an introduction by B. Dobrée, 1948) deals
with the Restoration in a pained, and at times indignant,
manner.

Studies and volumes of collected papers relevant to the period
include the following: E. Dowden, *Puritan and Anglican* (1900);
Myra Reynolds, *The Learned Lady in England* (Boston, 1920);
Sir Walter Raleigh, *Some Authors* (1923); H. Walker, *English
Satire and Satirists* (1925; repr. New York, 1965: see also III. 3
for further works on satire); Sir H. J. C. Grierson, *Cross Cur-
rents in English Literature of the XVIIth Century* (1929; repr. New
York, 1958); G. Kitchin, *A Survey of Burlesque and Parody in
English* (1931); *Seventeenth Century Studies*, ed. R. Shafer (Univer-
sity of Cincinnati: 1st ser. 1933; 2nd ser. 1937); B. Willey, *The
Seventeenth Century Background* (1934), and 'The Turn of the
Century' (Grierson *Festschrift, infra*); Sir Charles Firth,
Essays Historical and Literary (1938); C. A. Moore, *Backgrounds
of English Literature, 1700–1760* (University of Minnesota, 1953);
W. P. Ker, *On Modern Literature*, ed. T. Spencer and J. Suther-
land (1955); *Coleridge on the Seventeenth Century*, ed. R. F. Brinkley
(Duke University, 1955); George Williamson's collected studies:
Seventeenth Century Contexts (1960; University of Chicago, 1961),
The Proper Wit of Poetry (1961), *Milton and Others* (1965);
D. F. Foxon, 'Libertine Literature in England 1660–1745' (*The
Book Collector* xii, 1963).

Among papers which increase understanding of the period
are the following: P. S. Wood, 'Native Elements in English
Neo-Classicism' (*MP* xxiv, 1936) and 'The Opposition to Neo-
Classicism in England, 1660–1700' (*PMLA* xliii, 1928); L. I.

Bredvold, 'The Rise of English Classicism: a Study in Methodology' (*Comparative Literature* ii, 1950); D. F. Bond, 'Distrust of Imagination in English Neo-Classicism' (*PQ* xiv, 1935) and 'The Neo-Classical Psychology of Imagination' (*ELH* iv, 1937); B. H. Bronson, 'When was Neo-Classicism?' (S. H. Monk *Festschrift, infra*); R. M. Krapp, 'Class Analysis of a Literary Controversy: Wit and Sense in Seventeenth-century English Literature' (*Science and Society* x, 1946); H. W. Smith, 'Reason and the Restoration Ethos' (*Scrutiny* xviii, 1951–2) and 'Nature, Correctness and Decorum' (ibid.); J. Sutherland, 'The Impact of Charles II on Restoration Literature' (A. D. McKillop *Festschrift, infra*).

The following *Festschriften* contain papers referred to in various sections: *Seventeenth Century Studies Presented to Sir Herbert Grierson* (1938); *Essays Critical and Historical Dedicated to Lily B. Campbell* (University of California, 1950); *The Seventeenth Century: Studies in the History of English Thought and Literature, from Bacon to Pope, by Richard Foster Jones and Others* (Stanford, 1951); *Studies in the Literature of the Augustan Age: Essays Collected in Honor of Arthur Ellicott Case*, ed. R. C. Boys (University of Michigan, 1952); *Studies in Honor of John Wilcox*, ed. A. D. Wallace *et al.* (Wayne State University, 1958); *Essays in Literary History Presented to J. Milton French*, ed. R. Kirk *et al.* (Rutgers University, 1960); *Restoration and Eighteenth-Century Literature: Essays in Honor of Alan Dugald McKillop*, ed. C. Camden (University of Chicago, 1963); *Of Books and Humankind. Essays . . . to Bonamy Dobrée*, ed. J. Butt (1964); *Essays in English Literature of the Classical Period presented to Dugald MacMillan*, ed. D. W. Patterson *et al.* (University of North Carolina, 1967); *Studies in Criticism and Aesthetics 1660–1800. Essays in Honor of Samuel Holt Monk*, ed. H. Anderson *et al.* (University of Minnesota, 1967); *Renaissance and Modern Essays: Presented to Vivian de Sola Pinto*, ed. G. Hibbard (1966).

There is little Scottish poetry in our period. Histories of the literature include: Hugh Walker, *Three Centuries of Scottish Literature* (2 vols., 1893); J. H. Millar, *Literary History of Scotland* (1903) and *Scottish Prose of the Seventeenth and Eighteenth Centuries* (1912); G. Gregory Smith, *Scottish Literature* (1919); Agnes Mure Mackenzie, *Historical Survey of Scottish Literature to 1714* (1933).

For Welsh literature there are J. C. Morrice, *Wales in the*

Seventeenth Century: Its Literature and Men of Letters and Action (1918), and W. J. Hughes, *Wales and the Welsh in English Literature from Shakespeare to Scott* (1924).

2. RHETORICAL THEORY AND PROSE STYLE

Among studies of rhetorical theory and practice the most useful for our period are W. P. Sandford, *English Theories of Public Address, 1530–1828* (Columbus, Ohio, 1931), and W. S. Howell, *Logic and Rhetoric in England, 1500–1700* (Princeton, 1956). Some studies of Ramist logic (whose influence was not yet dead) will be found in Bush.

For prose style, various articles by M. W. Croll deal in general with an earlier period, but are none the less relevant to later developments; they have now been collected as *Style, Rhetoric and Rhythm*, ed. J. M. Patrick *et al.* (Princeton, 1966). With rather more of a focus on the late seventeenth century is G. Williamson's *The Senecan Amble: A Study in Prose Form from Bacon to Collier* (1951; repr. University of Chicago, 1966), and his 'Restoration Revolt Against Enthusiasm' (*SP* xxx, 1933). Three wide-ranging surveys which take in our period are: F. P. Wilson, *Seventeenth Century Prose* (University of California, 1960); J. Sutherland, *On English Prose* (University of Toronto, 1957); and I. A. Gordon, *The Movement of English Prose* (1966). K. G. Hamilton's *The Two Harmonies: Poetry and Prose in the Seventeenth Century* (1963), although the emphasis falls on poetry, is relevant here.

The most important contemporary pronouncement on prose style was that of Sprat in his *History of the Royal Society* (1667). For the influence of science on late seventeenth-century writing, the modern authority is R. F. Jones, whose various papers on this and other aspects of prose style are available in the Jones *Festschrift* (*supra*, III. 1). To those must be added a later paper, 'The Rhetoric of Science in England of the Mid-Seventeenth Century' (A. D. McKillop *Festschrift, supra*, III. 1), and *The Triumph of the English Language* (*infra*, IV. 1). Two papers with a bearing on the influence of science on prose style are those of F. Christensen (*MLQ* vii, 1946), and A. C. Howell (*ELH* xiii, 1946).

There is a paper by J. Sutherland, 'Restoration Prose' (William Andrews Clark Memorial Library, 1956). (On this, see L. T. Milic, 'Against the Typology of Styles', *Essays on the*

Languages of Literature, ed. S. Chatman *et al.*, Boston, 1967.)
Various aspects of seventeenth-century prose are discussed
by J. Bennett (*RES* xvii, 1941); H. Macdonald (*RES* xix, 1943,
and 'Banter in English Controversial Prose after the Restoration', *ESEA* xxxii, 1947); J. I. Cope, 'Seventeenth Century
Quaker Style' (*PMLA* lxii, 1956). The use of the prose dialogue during the period is examined by B. V. Crawford (*PMLA*
xxxiv, 1919) and E. R. Purpus (*ELH* xvii, 1950). An interesting dead-end in Restoration prose is illustrated in *Two Seventeenth-Century Prefaces*, ed. A. K. Croston (1949), who prints
the preface to N. Fairfax's *A Treatise of the Bulk and Selvedge of
the World* (1674). M. Williamson writes on 'The Colloquial
Language of the Commonwealth and Restoration' (English
Association Pamphlet, 1929). Among studies which fall between language and prose style are C. D. Cecil's paper on 'The
Idealized Speech of Restoration Comedy '(*Études anglaises* xix,
1966), and a chapter on 'The Conventions of Speech' in R. C.
Sharma's *Themes and Conventions in the Comedy of Manners* (New
York, 1965).

L. T. Milic has compiled *Style and Stylistics; an Analytical
Bibliography* (New York, 1967).

3. HISTORY AND CRITICISM OF POETRY

W. J. Courthope's *History of English Poetry* (1903–5; repr. 1911)
deals with the late seventeenth century in vols. iii–v. Among
more recent books with a wide range are: F. W. Bateson,
English Poetry and the English Language (1934) and *English
Poetry: A Critical Introduction* (1950); F. R. Leavis, *Revaluation:
Tradition and Development in English Poetry* (1936); Sir H. J. C.
Grierson and J. C. Smith, *A Critical History of English Poetry*
(1944; rev. 1947); Josephine Miles, *Eras and Modes in English
Poetry* (University of California, 1957).

Four books in which the transition to late seventeenth-
century poetry is traced are: G. Williamson, *The Donne Tradition: A Study in English Poetry from Donne to the Death of Cowley*
(Harvard, 1930); R. L. Sharp, *From Donne to Dryden* (University of North Carolina, 1940); P. Cruttwell, *The Shakespearean
Moment* (1954); G. Walton, *Metaphysical to Augustan: Studies in
Tone and Sensibility in the Seventeenth Century* (1955).

Studies concerned with a particular aspect or genre of poetry include the following: W. McN. Dixon, *English Epic and Heroic Poetry* (1912; repr. New York, 1964); R. D. Havens, *The Influence of Milton on English Poetry* (Harvard, 1922) and 'Changing Taste in the Eighteenth Century: a Study of Dryden's and Dodsley's Miscellanies' (*PMLA* xliv, 1929); R. Freeman, *English Emblem Books* (1948); C. W. Previté-Orton, *Political Satire in English Poetry* (1910; repr. 1968); A. Bevan, 'Poetry and Politics in Restoration England' (*Dalhousie Review* xxxix, 1959); I. Jack, *Augustan Satire: Intention and Idiom in English Poetry 1660–1750* (1952; repr. 1966); Rachel Trickett, *The Honest Muse, A Study in Augustan Verse* (1967); E. D. Leyburn, *Satirical Allegory: Mirror of Man* (Yale, 1956); W. O. S. Sutherland, *The Art of the Satirist* (University of Texas, 1965); A. B. Kernan, *The Plot of Satire* (Yale, 1965); Ruth Nevo, *The Dial of Virtue: A Study of Poems on Affairs of State in the Seventeenth Century* (Princeton, 1963); W. A. Chernaik, 'The Heroic Occasional Poem: Panegyric and Satire in the Restoration' (*MLQ* xxvi, 1965); J. A. Levine, 'The Status of the Verse Epistle before Pope' (*SP* lix, 1962): C. W. Peltz, 'The Neo-Classic Lyric' (*ELH* xi, 1944); H. M. Richmond, *The School of Love: The Evolution of the Stuart Love Lyric* (Princeton, 1964); H. F. Brooks, 'The "Imitation" in English Poetry, especially in formal satire, before the age of Pope' (*RES* xxv, 1949); M.-S. Røstvig, *The Happy Man: Studies in the Metamorphoses of a Classical Ideal 1600–1700* (Oslo, 1954); C. M. Simpson, *The British Broadside Ballad and its Music* (Rutgers University Press, 1966); C. C. Smith, 'The Seventeenth-Century Drolleries' (*Harvard Library Bulletin* vi, 1952). Among studies of the relationship of poetry with the other arts are: J. G. Hagstrum, *The Sister Arts: The Tradition of Literary Pictorialism from Dryden to Gray* (University of Chicago, 1958); H. V. S. Ogden (*JHI* x, 1949); J. Hollander, *The Untuning of the Sky: Ideas of Music in English Poetry* (Princeton, 1961).

For the Court poets there are J. H. Wilson (*supra*, III. 1); C. Whibley, *Literary Studies* (1919); and V. de S. Pinto, *The Restoration Court Poets* (British Council pamphlet, 1965). D. M. Vieth's *Attribution in Restoration Poetry* (Yale, 1963) offers much evidence on questions of authorship. The underground way in which Restoration verse was sometimes circulated forms the subject of two studies of 'Captain Robert Julian', by Brice Harris (*ELH* x, 1943), and by M. C. Randolph (*NQ* clxxxiv,

1943). P. A. Shelley has an account of William Hickes, a compiler of drolleries (*Harvard Studies and Notes in Philology and Literature* xx, 1938). The poets laureate of the period are discussed in E. K. Broadus, *The Laureateship. A Study of the Office of Poet Laureate in England* (1921), and K. Hopkins, *The Poets Laureate* (1954). For neo-Latin poetry there is L. Bradner's *Musae Anglicanae: A History of Anglo-Latin Poetry, 1500–1925* (1940).

Among more technical discussions are: Ruth Wallerstein, 'The Development of the Rhetoric and Metre of the Heroic Couplet, especially in 1625–45' (*PMLA* l, 1935); G. Williamson, 'The Rhetorical Pattern of Neo-Classical Wit' (*MP* xxxiii, 1935–6); M. C. Randolph, 'The Structural Design of the Formal Verse Satire' (*PQ* xxi, 1942); H. D. Weinbrot, 'The Pattern of the Formal Verse Satire in the Restoration and Eighteenth Century' (*PMLA* lxxx, 1965). J. Arthos, *The Language of Natural Description in Eighteenth Century Poetry* (University of Michigan, 1949), has its roots in our period; and K. G. Hamilton's *The Two Harmonies* (*supra*, III. 2) is mainly concerned with the last decades of the century. A. W. Allison's *Toward an Augustan Poetic. Edmund Waller's 'Reform' of English Poetry* (University of Kentucky, 1962) has much that is relevant to Restoration poetry. A number of studies of Restoration poets are reprinted in W. R. Keast's *Seventeenth-Century English Poetry. Modern Essays in Criticism* (New York, 1962).

4. History and Criticism of Drama

Early histories of the drama (usually containing discussions of the theatres, actors, acting, etc.) include a considerable number of lively, but often inaccurate, works dating from the early eighteenth century. Among these are J. Downes, *Roscius Anglicanus, or, An Historical Review of the Stage . . . from 1660–1706* (1708; ed. M. Summers, 1928). Cibber's *Apology for the Life of Mr. Colley Cibber Comedian* (1740; ed. R. W. Lowe, 2 vols., 1889, who prints as appendices J. Wright's *Historia Histrionica*, 1699, and Tony Aston's *Brief Supplement*, 1748) is invaluable for the light it throws on early acting and theatrical history. Compilations such as *A History of the English Stage* (1741) and W. R. Chetwood's *The British Theatre* (1750) must be used with caution. Among the more accurate early accounts are T. Davies,

Dramatic Miscellanies (3 vols., 1783–4), which has much interesting information. The standard eighteenth-century handbook to the drama was D. E. Baker, *The Companion to the Playhouse* (2 vols., 1764; rev. I. Reed as *Biographia Dramatica*, 2 vols., 1782). Many minor pieces of theatrical literature are listed in R. W. Lowe, *A Bibliographical Account of English Theatrical Literature from the Earliest Times to the Present Day* (1888).

The standard collection of annals of the English stage was for long that of J. Genest, *Some Account of the English Stage, from the Restoration in 1660 to 1830* (10 vols., 1832). This has now been superseded by *The London Stage, 1660–1800: A Calendar of Plays* (*supra*, II. 3), of which the first volume, ed. W. van Lennep, covers our period. Among a number of nineteenth-century histories of the stage are '*Their Majesties Servants*': *Annals of the English Stage from Betterton to Kean* (2 vols., 1864; rev. R. W. Lowe, 3 vols., 1888); P. Fitzgerald, *A New History of the English Stage* (2 vols., 1882); and H. B. Baker, *The London Stage from 1576 to 1888* (2 vols., 1889). There is much relevant material in *The Oxford Companion to the Theatre*, ed. P. Hartnoll (1951; rev. 1957). Two scholarly works concentrated on theatrical and stage conditions in our period are L. Hotson's *The Commonwealth and Restoration Stage* (Harvard, 1928), and E. Boswell's *The Restoration Court Stage* (Harvard, 1932). M. Summers, *The Restoration Theatre* (1932), contains much out-of-the-way information chaotically tumbled together. Several sections of W. J. Lawrence, *The Elizabethan Stage and Other Studies* (1912; repr. New York, 1963), deal with the Restoration theatre. There is a good Life of Thomas Betterton, the famous Restoration actor, by R. W. Lowe (1891), and the actresses are dealt with in J. H. Wilson's *All the King's Ladies* (University of Chicago, 1958). Wilson has also written on *Nell Gwyn* (1952), *Mr. Goodman the Player* (University of Pittsburgh, 1964), and on acting techniques in 'Rant, Cant and Tone on the Restoration Stage' (*SP* lii, 1955), as has H. Hunt in *Restoration Theatre* (*infra*). Another well-known player, Samuel Sandford, is discussed by R. H. Ross, Jr. (*PMLA* lxxvi, 1961). Discussions of stage production include R. Southern's *Changeable Scenery. Its Origin and Development in the British Theatre* (1952). For production and other questions relating to the stage the various volumes of *Theatre Notebook* (since 1945) and *Restoration and Eighteenth-Century Theatre Research* (since 1962) should be consulted.

Among works on the Irish stage are R. Hitchcock, *An Historical View of the Irish Stage* (2 vols., 1788–94), and W. S. Clark, *The Early Irish Stage: The Beginnings to 1720* (1955). For the Scottish stage there are J. Jackson, *The History of the Scottish Stage* (1793); J. C. Dibdin, *The Annals of the Scottish Stage* (1888); and R. Lawson, *The Story of the Scottish Stage* (1917). Provincial performances are discussed by S. Rosenfeld, *Strolling Players and Drama in the Provinces, 1660–1765* (1939). The same author has also written on 'The Players at Oxford, 1661–1713' (*RES* xix, 1943), and on *Foreign Theatrical Companies in Great Britain in the Seventeenth and Eighteenth Centuries* (1955). W. J. Lawrence (*supra*) discussed the early French players in London, and I. K. Fletcher the visits of Italian comedians (*Theatre Notebook* viii, 1954). E. L. Avery examined the composition of the Restoration audience (*PQ* xlv, 1966). The Restoration theatre features in such general studies as those of A. Thaler, *Shakespeare to Sheridan* (Harvard, 1922); A. Nicoll, *The English Theatre. A Short History* (1936); R. Stamm, *Geschichte des englischen Theaters* (Berne, 1951).

Some documents important for the late seventeenth-century theatre are printed by A. Nicoll (*infra*) and by L. Hotson (*supra*). Among other sources of theatrical information are: *The Dramatic Records of Sir Henry Herbert*, ed. J. Q. Adams (Harvard, 1922); A. F. White, 'The Office of Revels and Dramatic Censorship during the Restoration Period' (*Western Reserve Bulletin*, new ser. xxxiv, 1931); E. A. Langhans, 'New Restoration Theatre Accounts 1682–1692' (*Theatre Notebook* xvii, 1963), and 'Wren's Restoration Playhouse' (ibid. xviii, 1964); J. Freehafer, 'The Formation of the London Patent Companies in 1660' (ibid. xx, 1965); and on the same theme, G. Sorelius (*Studia Neophilologica* xxxvii, 1965).

Criticism of the drama may be said to begin with Samuel Pepys, whose fluctuating judgements are conveniently assembled by H. MacAfee in *Pepys on the Restoration Stage* (Yale, 1916; repr. New York, 1967). Critical statements about Restoration dramatists (often mixed up with biographical and other facts) may be found in G. Langbaine's *Account of the English Dramatick Poets* (1691) and in the revised version of C. Gildon, *The Lives and Characters of the English Dramatic Poets* (1699); *A Comparison between the Two Stages* (1702; ed. S. B. Wells, Princeton, 1942); G. Jacob, *The Poetical Register: or, The Lives and Characters of the Dramatick Poets* (1719), which has some biographical value, since some of the dramatists contributed accounts of themselves; T. Cibber, *The Lives of the Poets of Great Britain* (4 vols., 1753). Criticism is scattered through many of the nineteenth-century volumes mentioned earlier and later in this section, especially those listed under Comedy. A. W. Ward's *History of English Dramatic Literature to the Death of Queen Anne*, vol. iii (rev. ed. 1899) deals with Restoration drama, as do vol. viii of *CBEL* (F. E. Schelling, C. Whibley, and A. T. Bartholomew), and vols. iii–v of W. J. Courthope's *History of English Poetry* (1903–5; repr. 1911). Among other early twentieth-century accounts is that of G. H. Nettleton, *English Drama of the Restoration and Eighteenth Century, 1642–1780* (New York, 1914). The standard critical history is now that of A. Nicoll, *A History of Restoration Drama, 1660–1700* (1923; rev. 1952), which not only deals fully with the plays, but also discusses such matters as audience, actors and acting, and theatrical history, and supplies a checklist of plays, with dates of performance and publication. Shorter accounts are M. Elwin's *The Playgoer's Handbook to Restoration Drama* (1928), and J. H. Wilson's *Preface to Restoration Drama* (Boston, 1965). M. Summers's *The Playhouse of Pepys* (1935) is one of the few books attempting to give an extended treatment of the minor dramatists. A modern approach to Restoration drama will be found in *Restoration Theatre*, ed. J. R. Brown and B. Harris (1965). Two useful collections of critical papers are *Restoration Drama: Modern Essays in Criticism*, ed. J. Loftis (New York, 1966), and *Restoration Dramatists. A Collection of Critical Essays*, ed. E. Miner (Englewood Cliffs, N. J., 1966). Some other titles will be found below, listed under Comedy, Tragedy, and Opera. For the period immediately preceding the Restoration A. Harbage's *Cavalier Drama* (New York, 1936) gives an excellent critical survey, and takes in one or two of our dramatists.

The best critical view of the tragic drama of the period is B. Dobrée's *Restoration Tragedy 1660–1720* (1929). There is a critical study by E. Rothstein, *Restoration Tragedy* (University of Wisconsin, 1967). Other discussions will be found in M. E. Prior, *The Language of Tragedy* (Columbia, 1947); C. Leech (*Durham University Journal* xlii, 1950); M. T. Herrick, *Tragicomedy: Its Origin and Development in Italy, France and England* (University of Illinois, 1955; repr. 1962); E. Rothstein, 'English

Tragic Theory in the Late Seventeenth Century' (*ELH* xxix, 1962); G. Wilson Knight, *The Golden Labyrinth* (1962); and *Restoration Theatre* (*supra*). R. G. Noyes writes on 'Conventions of Song in Restoration Tragedy' (*PMLA* liii, 1938).

Among studies of the heroic drama are: L. N. Chase, *The English Heroic Play* (New York, 1903); B. J. Pendlebury, *Dryden's Heroic Plays. A Study of the Origins* (1923); C. V. Deane, *Dramatic Theory and the Rhymed Heroic Play* (1931). Among articles dealing with various aspects are those which are concerned with origins: C. G. Child (*MLN* xix, 1904); J. W. Tupper (*PMLA* xx, 1905: in relation to the plays of Beaumont and Fletcher); M. L. Poston (*MLR* xvi, 1921); W. S. Clark (*RES* iv, 1928, and the Introduction to his edition of Orrery, *infra*, VI). K. M. Lynch writes on 'Conventions of Platonic Drama in the Heroic plays of Orrery and Dryden' (*PMLA* xliv, 1929), and W. S. Clark on the definition of the heroic play (*RES* viii, 1932). Other titles will be found listed under Dryden, *infra*, VI. A. E. Parsons deals with 'The English Heroic Play' (*MLR* xxxiii, 1938), and A. Righter with 'Heroic Tragedy' in *Restoration Theatre* (*supra*).

Criticism of Restoration comedy begins effectively with Jeremy Collier's *Short View of the Immorality and Profaneness of the English Stage* (1698). There is a good bibliography of the Collier controversy in *CBEL*, and a fuller account in Sister Rose Anthony, *The Jeremy Collier Controversy 1698–1726* (Marquette University, 1937). Among discussions of the issues involved is that of J. W. Krutch, *Comedy and Conscience after the Restoration* (New York, 1924; repr. 1949). The early nineteenth-century criticism of Hazlitt (*English Comic Writers*, 1819) and of Lamb ('The Artificial Comedy of the Last Century'; repr. in *Essays of Elia*, 1821) was favourable to the Restoration dramatists; but Leigh Hunt's edition of Wycherley, Congreve, Vanbrugh, and Farquhar (1840) was dealt a heavy blow by Macaulay in *The Edinburgh Review* (lxii, 1841; repr. in editions of Macaulay's *Essays*). Later in the century Meredith's *Essay on Comedy* (1877) did something to neutralize the influence of Macaulay. Since the publication of J. Palmer's *The Comedy of Manners* (1913) and B. Dobrée's *Restoration Comedy* (1921) the reputation of the comic writers has risen, although the reasons given for enjoying them have varied considerably from one critic to another. There is a useful survey of the attitude to Restoration comedy in English and foreign criticism up to 1923 by W. Heldt (*Neophilologus* viii, 1923). Among subsequent studies are those of H. Ten Eyck Perry, *The Comic Spirit in Restoration Drama* (Yale, 1925), and K. Lynch, *The Social Mode of Restoration Comedy* (New York, 1926). The rising prestige of the comic drama was challenged by L. C. Knights in 'Restoration Comedy: the Reality and the Myth' (*Scrutiny* vi, 1937; repr. in *Explorations*, 1946); but he found little support, and was later answered by F. W. Bateson, John Wain, and others (*EC* vi, 1956; vii, 1957). More particular aspects were discussed by G. S. Alleman, *Matrimonial Law and the Materials of Restoration Comedy* (Wallingford, Pa., 1942); E. Mignon, *Crabbed Age and Youth: the Old Men and Women in the Restoration Comedy of Manners* (Duke University, 1946); J. H. Smith, *The Gay Couple in Restoration Comedy* (Harvard, 1948); D. R. M. Wilkinson, *The Comedy of Habit: An Essay in the Use of Courtesy Literature* . . . (Leiden, 1964). In some recent studies the scope has widened again: T. H. Fujimura, *The Restoration Comedy of Wit* (Princeton, 1952); Dale Underwood (*infra*, VI, Etherege); N. N. Holland, *The First Modern Comedies* (Harvard, 1959; repr. University of Indiana, 1967); J. Loftis, *Comedy and Society from Congreve to Fielding* (Stanford, 1959); C. Hoy, 'The Effect of the Restoration on Drama' (*Studies in Literature*, University of Tennessee, 1961); R. C. Sharma, *Themes and Conventions in the Comedy of Manners* (New York, 1965).

Among the numerous articles on Restoration comedy are some by E. E. Stoll in *Shakespeare Studies* (New York, 1927) and in *From Shakespeare to Joyce* (New York, 1944); B. V. Crawford (*PQ* viii, 1929); G. Montgomery (*California University Essays in Criticism*, 1929); C. Leech (*EC* i, 1959); D. S. Berkeley, 'The Art of "Whining" Love' (*SP* lii, 1955) and 'Préciosité and the Restoration Comedy of Manners' (*HLQ* xviii, 1955); M. Murdick in *English Stage Comedy*, ed. W. K. Wimsatt (Columbia, 1955); C. D. Cecil, 'Libertine and Précieux Elements in Restoration Comedy' (*EC* ix, 1959); P. Vernon, 'Marriage of Convenience and the Mode of Restoration Comedy' (*EC* xii, 1962); C. O. McDonald, 'Restoration Comedy as Drama of Satire' (*SP* lxi, 1964); J. Traugott, 'The Rake's Progress from Court to Comedy' (*SEL* vi, 1966). I. Simon reviews some recent criticism in 'Restoration Comedy and the Critics' (*Revue des langues vivantes* xxix, 1963).

For farce there is L. Hughes, *A Century of English Farce: A Study of Farce and Low Comedy* (Princeton, 1956) and 'Attitudes of Some Restoration Dramatists towards Farce' (*PQ* xix, 1940). For burlesque and parody: V. C. Clinton-Baddely, *The Burlesque Tradition in the English Theatre after 1660* (1952), and D. F. Smith, *Plays about the Theatre in England* . . . (New York, 1936).

For opera there are excellent accounts by E. J. Dent, *The Foundations of English Opera* (1928), and E. W. White, *The Rise of English Opera* (1951). A number of books on Henry Purcell (*infra*, V. 7.) are useful here.

The relationship of the drama of 'the last age' to that of the Restoration is the subject of a number of studies. For Shakespeare: H. Spencer, *Shakespeare Improved* (Harvard, 1927); L. Hook (*Shakespeare Quarterly* iv, 1953); W. M. Merchant (in *Restoration Theatre, supra*); G. E. Bentley, *Shakespeare and Jonson: their Reputation in the Seventeenth Century Compared* (2 vols., University of Chicago, 1945). For Beaumont and Fletcher: A. C. Sprague, *Beaumont and Fletcher on the Restoration Stage* (Harvard, 1926); J. H. Wilson, *The Influence of Beaumont and Fletcher on Restoration Drama* (Ohio State University, 1928). For Jonson: R. G. Noyes, *Ben Jonson on the English Stage 1660–1776* (Harvard, 1935); E. Tiedje, *Die Tradition Ben Jonsons in der Restaurationskomödie* (Hamburg, 1963). For Massinger: J. G. McManaway, 'Philip Massinger and the Restoration Drama' (*ELH* i, 1934).

The relationship of the earlier drama in general to that of the Restoration is the subject of G. Sorelius, *The Giant Race before the Flood: Pre-Restoration Drama on the Stage and in the Criticism of the Restoration* (Uppsala, 1966), and it is also treated by M. Ellenhauge (*infra*). Some of the more special studies cited above (e.g. those on the origins of heroic drama) are relevant here.

The influence of French and Spanish drama (mainly on the plays of Dryden) is dealt with by W. Harvey-Jellie, *Le Théâtre classique en Angleterre dans l'âge de John Dryden* (Montreal, 1933), and the French influence by M. Ellenhauge, *English Restoration Drama. Its Relation to past English and past and contemporary French Drama* (Copenhagen, 1933). The impact of Molière is the theme of D. H. Miles, *The Influence of Molière on Restoration Comedy* (New York, 1910); of a better book by J. Wilcox, *The*

Relation of Molière to Restoration Comedy (Columbia, 1938); and of a chapter by N. Suckling in *Restoration Theatre (supra)*. Within a rather more limited period there is A. de Mandach, *Molière et la comédie de mœurs en Angleterre 1660–1668* (Neuchâtel, 1946). D. F. Canfield writes on *Corneille and Racine in England* (New York, 1904); F. Y. Eccles on *Racine in England* (1922); and A. Lefèvre on 'Racine en Angleterre' (*Revue de la littérature comparée* xxxiv, 1960: with reference to Otway). There are short studies of Italian opera in England by A. Nicoll (*Anglia* xlvi, 1922), and of foreign opera by D. H. Walmsley (*Anglia* lii, 1928).

Special aspects of the Restoration drama and theatre are treated in the following books and articles: A. Nicoll, 'Political Plays of the Restoration' (*MLR* xvi, 1921); G. W. Whiting, 'Political Satire in London Stage Plays, 1680–83' (*MP* xxviii, 1930) and 'The Condition of the London Theatres, 1679–83' (*MP* xxv, 1927); L. Teeter, 'The Dramatic Use of Hobbes's Political Ideas' (*ELH* iii, 1936); Sheila Williams, 'The Pope-Burning Processions of 1679, 1680, and 1681' (*Journal of the Warburg and Courtauld Institutes* xxi, 1958); O. W. Furley, 'The Pope-Burning Processions of the late Seventeenth Century' (*History* xliv, 1959); D. F. Smith, *The Critics in the Audience of the London Theatres from Buckingham to Sheridan . . . 1671–1779* (University of New Mexico, 1953); A. N. Wiley, 'The English Vogue of Prologues and Epilogues' (*MLN* xlvii, 1932) and 'Female Prologues and Epilogues in English Plays' (*PMLA* xlviii, 1932); J. Sutherland 'Prologues, Epilogues and Audience in the Restoration Theatre' (B. Dobrée *Festschrift, supra*, III. 1); E. L. Avery, 'Rhetorical Patterns in Restoration Prologues and Epilogues' (*Essays . . . Presented to Bruce Robert McElderry*, ed. M. F. Schulz *et al.* (Ohio State University, 1968); J. O. Bartley, *Teague, Shenkin and Sawney, Being an Historical Study of the Earliest Irish, Welsh, and Scottish Characters in English Plays* (1954); J. E. Gagen, *The New Woman: Her Emergence in English Drama, 1600–1730* (1954).

5. THE HISTORY OF IDEAS

Some influential works are: Sir Leslie Stephen, *History of English Thought in the Eighteenth Century* (2 vols., 1876; repr. New York, 2 vols., 1962–3), of which some of the early sections deal with our period; Preserved Smith, *A History of Modern Culture*

(2 vols., 1930–4; repr. New York, 1962); A. O. Lovejoy, *The Great Chain of Being* (Harvard, 1936; repr. New York, 1960) and *Essays in the History of Ideas* (Johns Hopkins, 1948); P. Hazard, *La Crise de la conscience européenne 1680–1715* (Paris, 1935; trs. J. L. May, *The European Mind*, 1953); B. Willey, *The Seventeenth Century Background* (1934) and *The Eighteenth Century Background* (1940); Sir Ernest Barker *et al.*, *The European Inheritance*, vol. ii (1954).

Among books dealing with some of the seminal ideas of the period are: J. B. Bury, *The Idea of Progress* (1920); R. F. Jones, *Ancients and Moderns* (Washington University, 1936; 2nd ed. 1961); V. Harris, *All Coherence Gone* (University of Chicago, 1949); E. L. Tuveson, *Millennium and Utopia: A Study in the Background of the Idea of Progress* (University of California, 1949); H. Meyer, *The Age of the World* (Allentown, Pa., 1951); H. Macklem, *The Anatomy of the World: Relations between Natural and Moral Law from Donne to Pope* (University of Minnesota, 1958); M. L. Wiley, *The Subtle Knot: Creative Scepticism in Seventeenth-Century England* (Harvard, 1952); S. Kliger, *The Goths in England* (Harvard, 1952); Marjorie H. Nicolson, *Science and Imagination* (Cornell, 1956) and *Mountain Gloom and Mountain Glory: The Development of the Aesthetics of the Infinite* (Cornell, 1959); *Reason and the Imagination: Studies in the History of Ideas 1600–1800*, ed. J. A. Mazzeo (1962); H. G. van Leeuwen, *The Problem of Certainty in English Thought 1630–1690* (The Hague, 1963). Among papers that may be mentioned here are I. Simon, 'Pride of Reason in the Restoration' (*Revue des langues vivantes* xxv, 1959), and E. Miner, 'Dryden and the Issue of Human Progress' (*PQ* xl, 1961).

Other books and papers which would be relevant here are cited under V. 1, 2, 3; and many of the articles in *JHI* deal with issues and problems that were important to the late seventeenth century.

Among histories of philosophy are: W. R. Sorley, *A History of English Philosophy to 1900* (1920; repr. as *A History of British Philosophy*, 1965); Bertrand Russell, *The History of Western Philosophy* (1945; repr. New York, 1961); B. A. G. Fuller, *A History of Modern Philosophy* (New York, 1938; rev. 1945); F. C. Copleston, *A History of Philosophy*, vols. iv–v (rev. ed. 1958–9).

IV. SPECIAL LITERARY STUDIES AND LITERARY FORMS

This section comprises: (1) Language; (2) Journalism; (3) Fiction; (4) Essays, characters, and letters; (5) Historical and biographical literature; (6) Classical and foreign relations; (7) Contemporary criticism; (8) Printing and bookselling.

1. THE LANGUAGE

General histories giving some attention to this period include: H. C. Wyld, *History of Modern Colloquial English* (3rd ed., rev., 1953); G. H. McKnight, *Modern English in the Making* (New York, 1928); A. C. Baugh, *History of the English Language* (2nd ed., New York, 1957); C. L. Wrenn, *The English Language* (1949). A. G. Kennedy's *Bibliography of Writings on the English Language* (Harvard, 1927; repr. New York, 1961) is in process of being superseded by R. C. Alston's *Bibliography of the English Language from the Invention of Printing to the Year 1800* (Leeds and Bradford, 1965–   ; to appear in 20 vols.). Alston also edits the Scolar Press series of facsimile texts in which all significant linguistic works from 1500 to 1800 are to be reprinted. Several grammars of our period have been edited in the series *Neudrucke frühneuenglischer Grammatiken* (Halle, 1905–11), and C. Cooper's *English Teacher* (1687) by B. Sundby (Lund, 1953). The development of grammatical theory is studied by E. Vorlat, *Progress in English Grammar 1585–1735* (4 vols., Louvain, 1963).

Some advances in lexicography were made immediately before and during the Restoration period: T. Blount, *Glossographia* (1656); E. Phillips, *A New World of English Words* (1658); E. Coles, *An English Dictionary* (1676); *Cocker's English Dictionary* (1704). Etymological works are S. Skinner, *Etymologicon Linguæ Anglicanæ* (1671), and the *Gazophylacium Anglicanum* (1689). The standard survey is D. T. Starnes and G. E. Noyes, *The English Dictionary from Cawdrey to Johnson, 1604–1755* (University of North Carolina, 1946), which includes an appendix by G. E. Noyes, 'The Development of Cant Lexicography in England 1566–1785' (repr. from *SP* xxxviii, 1941). An earlier study is M. M. Matthews, *A Survey of English Dictionaries* (1933).

For proverbs there are *The Oxford Dictionary of English Proverbs* (1935; 2nd ed., rev., 1948; new and completely revised ed.

forthcoming); M. P. Tilley, *Dictionary of the Proverbs in England in the Sixteenth and Seventeenth Centuries* (University of Michigan, 1950). Two late seventeenth-century collections are *Pappity Stampoy. A Collection of Scottish Proverbs* (1663; ed. A. Taylor, *ARS*, 1955) and John Ray, *A Collection of English Proverbs* (1670).

Two important books with a bearing on the late seventeenth century are: R. F. Jones, *The Triumph of the English Language: A Survey of Opinions Concerning the Vernacular from the Introduction of Printing to the Restoration* (Stanford, 1953); E. J. Dobson, *English Pronunciation 1500–1700* (2 vols., 1957; rev. 1968). Among relevant papers are W. Matthews, 'Tarpaulin Arabick in the Days of Pepys' (L. B. Campbell *Festschrift, supra,* III. 1); M. Williamson (*supra*, III. 2); D. E. Givner, 'Scientific Preconceptions in Locke's Philosophy of Language' (*JHI* xxiii, 1962); I. Simon, 'Saxonism and the Hard-Words Dictionaries' (*Revue des langues vivantes* xxvi, 1960), 'Saxonism Old and New' (*Revue belge de phlologie et d'histoire* xxxix, 1961), and 'Critical Terms in Restoration Translations from the French' (ibid. xliii, 1965).

For the attempts to achieve a universal language, see Bush, IV. 1.

2. JOURNALISM

For newspapers and other periodicals the fullest bibliography is that of Graham Pollard in *CBEL* ii. Earlier lists include: [J. G. Muddiman] *Tercentenary Handlist of English and Welsh Newspapers, Magazines and Reviews* (1920); R. S. Crane and F. B. Kaye, 'Census of British Newspapers and Periodicals 1620–1800' (*SP* xxiv, 1927, and separately, University of North Carolina; useful for American readers since it lists American holdings up to the date of publication); A. J. Gabler, 'Checklist of English Newspapers and Periodicals before 1801 in the Huntington Library' (*HLB*, 1931); R. J. Mitford and D. M. Sutherland, 'A Catalogue of English Newspapers and Periodicals in the Bodleian Library 1622–1800' (*OBS* iv, pt. 2, 1935, and separately, 1936); P. Stewart, *British Newspapers and Periodicals, 1632–1800: A Descriptive Catalogue of a Collection in the University of Texas* (University of Texas, 1950); *Handlist of English Seventeenth Century Newspapers in the Guildhall Library* (1954); *British Union Catalogue of Periodicals . . . in British Libraries*, ed. J. D. Stewart, *et al.* (4 vols., 1955–8).

The older histories of the newspaper, such as A. A. Andrews' *History of British Journalism* (2 vols., 1859), and H. R. Fox Bourne's *English Newspapers* (2 vols., 1887; repr. New York, 1965) are marked by varying degrees of unreliability. S. Morison's descriptive account, *The English Newspaper* (1932), is accurate, and fully illustrated. J. Frank's *The Beginnings of the English Newspaper, 1620–1660* (Harvard, 1961), although stopping just short of our period, provides a useful introduction to the post-Restoration newspaper. R. M. Wiles, *Freshest Advices: Early Provincial Newspapers in England* (1965), has something on the late seventeenth century. The later pages of J. B. Williams [i.e. J. G. Muddiman], *The History of English Journalism to the Foundation of the Gazette* (1908), throw light on the early years of the Restoration newspaper, as does his book on Henry Muddiman, *The King's Journalist, 1659–1689* (1923). L. Hanson's *The Government and the Press 1695–1763* (1936) is useful, *inter alia*, for its account of the Licensing Act and its lapse. F. S. Siebert's *Freedom of the Press in England, 1476–1776* (University of Illinois, 1952) discusses government restrictions over three centuries, and J. Walker examines censorship of the press during the reign of Charles II (*History*, new ser. xxxv, 1950). P. Fraser deals with an important early source of news in *The Intelligence of the Secretaries of State and their Monopoly of Licensed News 1660–1688* (1956). A special type of journalism is treated by J. B. Williams, 'The Newsbooks and Letters of News of the Restoration' (*English Historical Review* xxiv, 1908). E. S. de Beer has written on 'The English Newspapers from 1695 to 1702' (*William III and Louis XIV. Essays 1680–1720 by and for Mark A. Thomson*, ed. R. Hatton and J. S. Bromley, 1968).

Early scientific journalism is discussed by R. P. McCutcheon (*SP* xxi, 1924); S. B. Barnes (*Scientific Monthly* xxxviii, 1934); D. McKie (*Philosophical Magazine*, 1948); and D. A. Kronick, *A History of Scientific and Technical Periodicals* (New York, 1962), which has a bibliography. S. B. Barnes has written on 'The Editing of Early Learned Journals' (*Osiris* i, 1936). For literary journals the standard accounts are W. Graham's *The Beginnings of English Literary Periodicals* (New York, 1926) and *English Literary Periodicals* (New York, 1930). (See also Motteux, *infra*, VI.) Early book reviewing is discussed by R. P. McCutcheon (*PMLA* xxxvii, 1922).

Among books and papers dealing with individual periodicals

and journalists are the following: P. M. Handover, *A History of the London Gazette, 1665–1965* (1965), and J. G. Muddiman (*supra*); G. Kitchin, *Sir Roger L'Estrange* (1913; for *The Newes* and *The Intelligencer*); P. Stewart, 'The Loyal London Mercuries' (*University of Texas Studies in English* xxviii, 1949); T. F. M. Newton (*Harvard Studies and Notes in Philology and Literature* xvi, 1934; for *Heraclitus Ridens*); B.-M. Stearns (*MP* xxviii, 1930; for *The Athenian Mercury*); D. Foster (*PMLA* xxxii, 1917; for *The Gentleman's Journal*; cf. also Motteux, *infra*, VI). J. G. Muddiman writes on Francis 'Elephant' Smith (*NQ* clxiii, 1932) and on Benjamin Harris (ibid.; see also *The King's Journalist, supra*); L. Rostenberg on Nathaniel Thompson (*Library*, 5th ser. x, 1955) and on 'Robert Stephens, Messenger of the Press' (*PBSA* xlix, 1955); S. Morison on *Ichabod Dawks and his News-Letter* (1931); C. Blagden on 'An Early Literary Periodical' (*Times Literary Supplement*, 3 December 1954: on *The History of the Works of the Learned*). L. Rostenberg's *Literary, Political, Scientific, Religious and Legal Publishing . . . 1551–1700* (New York, 1965) brings together much valuable information.

For Scottish periodicals there is W. J. Couper, *The Edinburgh Periodical Press* (2 vols., 1908). For the Irish press there are R. R. Madden, *The History of Irish Periodical Literature from the End of the Seventeenth Century . . .* (2 vols., 1867), and R. L. Munter, *The History of the Irish Newspaper 1685–1760* (1967), and the same author's *Handlist of Irish Newspapers 1685–1750* (Cambridge Bibliographical Society, 1960).

There is a bibliography of 'Studies of British Newspapers and Periodicals from the Beginning to 1800', by K. K. Weed and R. P. Bond (*SP*, extra ser. No. 2, 1946).

3. Prose Fiction

A few pieces have been reprinted in *Shorter Novels: Jacobean and Restoration*, ed. P. Henderson (Everyman, 1930); '*The Counterfeit Lady Unveiled*' *and other Criminal Fiction of Seventeenth-Century England*, ed. S. Peterson (New York, 1961); *Seventeenth Century Tales of the Supernatural*, ed. I. M. Westcott (*ARS*, 1958). Reprints of Mrs. Behn, R. Head, Settle, and Congreve will be found listed under those authors (VI, *infra*). The prefaces to Boyle's *Parthenissa* and Mackenzie's *Aretina* are included by

C. Davies in *Prefaces to Four Seventeenth-Century Romances* (*ARS*, 1953).

CBEL ii has a useful list of prose fiction, but the best bibliography for the period is C. C. Mish's *English Prose Fiction 1660–1700: A Chronological Checklist* (University of Virginia, 1952). Further information may be had from A. Esdaile's *List of English Tales and Prose Romances Printed before 1740* (1912), and F. P. Rolfe (*PMLA* xlix, 1934).

The fullest history is that of E. A. Baker, *The History of the English Novel*, vol. iii (1929; repr. New York, 1957). There are some lively passages in Sir Walter Raleigh's *The English Novel* (1894; rev. 1929), and a chapter on the seventeenth century in R. M. Lovett and H. S. Hughes, *The History of the Novel in England* (Boston, 1932). More special studies (sometimes with little to say about our period) are: C. E. Morgan, *The Rise of the Novel of Manners, 1600–1740* (Columbia, 1911); H. S. Hughes, 'English Epistolary Fiction before *Pamela*' (*Manly Anniversary Studies*, Chicago, 1923); G. F. Singer, *The Epistolary Novel* (University of Pennsylvania, 1933); C. E. Kany, *The Beginnings of the Epistolary Novel in France, Italy and Spain* (University of California, 1937); R. A. Day, *Told in Letters. Epistolary Fiction before Richardson* (University of Michigan, 1966), which supersedes earlier accounts, and has a useful bibliography; T. P. Haviland, *The Roman de Longue Haleine on English Soil* (University of Pennsylvania, 1931); B. J. Randall, *The Golden Tapestry. A Critical Survey of Non-Chivalric Spanish Fiction in English Translation, 1543–1657* (Duke University, 1963); F. W. Chandler, *The Literature of Roguery* (2 vols., Boston, 1907); A. J. Tieje, *The Theory of Characterization in English Prose Fiction prior to 1740* (University of Minnesota, 1916); Joyce M. Horner, *The English Women Novelists and their Connection with the Feminist Movement 1688–1797* (Smith College Studies in Modern Languages xi, 1929–30); B. G. MacCarthy, *Women Writers: Their Contribution to the English Novel 1621–1744* (1946); N. Würzbach, *Die Struktur des Briefromans und seine Entstehung in England* (Munich, 1964).

Discussions of particular works include E. Bernbaum, *The Mary Carleton Narratives* (Harvard, 1914); C. F. Main, 'The German Princess; or Mary Carleton in Fact and Fiction' (*Harvard Library Bulletin* x, 1956); J. E. Tucker, '*The Turkish Spy* and its French Background' (*Revue de la littérature comparée* xxxii, 1958) and 'On the Authorship of *The Turkish Spy: An État*

Présent (*PBSA* lii, 1958); W. H. McBurney, 'The Authorship of *The Turkish Spy*' (*PMLA* lxxii, 1957); F. C. Green, 'Who was the Author of the *Lettres Portugaises?*' (*MLR* xxi, 1926); S. Peterson, 'William Morrell and Late Seventeenth-Century Fiction' (*PQ* xlii, 1963). B. Boyce has written on 'The Effect of the Restoration on Prose Fiction' (*Studies in Literature* vi, University of Tennessee, 1961), and on 'News from Hell' letters (*infra*, IV. 4).

E. Bernbaum wrote annually for some years on 'Recent Works on Prose Fiction before 1800' (*MLN* xlii, 1927, etc.).

4. Essays, Characters, and Letters

Some essays are usually included in general anthologies (*supra*, II. 1), and in editions and selections of Cowley and Temple. Characters, more important for the earlier seventeenth century, are normally represented in our period by those of Samuel Butler. Collections of characters include R. Aldington, *A Book of Characters* (1924); G. Murphy, *A Cabinet of Characters* (1925); W. H. D. Rouse, *A Book of Characters* (1933); H. Osborne, *A Mirror of Charactery* (1933); R. Withington, *Essays and Characters: Montaigne to Goldsmith* (New York, 1933). For the non-Theophrastan character there are D. Nichol Smith's *Characters from the Histories & Memoirs of the Seventeenth Century* (1918), and V. de S. Pinto's *English Biography in the Seventeenth Century* (1951), which is focused on our period. H. Macdonald's *Portraits in Prose* (1946) covers a wider period, but includes some good examples from the late seventeenth century.

For the essay, critical comment will be found in W. L. Mac-Donald's *Beginnings of the English Essay* (University of Toronto, 1914); H. Walker's *The English Essay and Essayists* (1915); and E. N. S. Thompson's *The Seventeenth-Century English Essay* (University of Iowa, 1926).

For characters there are two comprehensive bibliographies: G. Murphy, *Bibliography of English Character-Books 1608–1700* (1925), and C. N. Greenough and J. M. French, *Bibliography of the Theophrastan Character in English* (Harvard, 1947). Henry Gally's 'Critical Essay on Characteristic Writings', prefixed to his translation of *The Moral Characters* of Theophrastus, 1723, has been ed. A. H. Chorney (*ARS*, 1952). There is a section in E. N. S. Thompson's *Literary Bypaths of the Renaissance* (Yale,

1924), and A. J. de Armond writes fully on 'Some Aspects of Character-Writing in the Period of the Restoration' (*Delaware Notes*, 16th ser., 1943). The fullest discussion of the influence of Theophrastus will be found in K. Lichtenberg, *Der Einfluß des Theophrast* . . . (Berlin, 1921). D. Nichol Smith (*supra*) provides an excellent historical introduction to the non-Theophrastan character. Two studies by B. Boyce, although based on pre-Restoration material, are relevant here: *The Theophrastan Character in England to 1642* (Harvard, 1947), and *The Polemic Character 1640–1661* (University of Nebraska, 1955).

Among comprehensive collections of letters are the following: Sir Henry Ellis, *Original Letters, Illustrative of English History* (11 vols., 1824–46) and *Original Letters of Eminent Literary Men of the Sixteenth, Seventeenth and Eighteenth Centuries* (Camden Society, 1843); J. O. Halliwell-Phillipps, *A Collection of Letters Illustrative of the Progress of Science in England from the Reign of Queen Elizabeth to that of Charles the Second* (1841); S. J. Rigaud, *Correspondence of Scientific Men of the Seventeenth Century* (2 vols., 1841). Collections with special relevance to our period include: *Charles II and Madame*, ed. C. H. Hartmann (1934); *Conway Letters*, ed. M. H. Nicolson (Yale, 1930); Lady F. P. and M. M. Verney, *Memoirs of the Verney Family* (4 vols., 1892–9); the *Letters* of Philip Stanhope, Earl of Chesterfield (1829); H. Savile, *Correspondence*, ed. W. D. Cooper (Camden Society, 1858) and the *Rochester–Savile Letters* (*infra*, VI, Rochester); Henry Sidney, Earl of Romney, *Diary and Times of Charles II* (with correspondence; ed. R. W. Blencowe, 2 vols., 1843). Lady Rachel Russell, *Letters, 1670–1723*, ed. Lord John Russell (2 vols., 1853); The *Petty–Southwell Correspondence 1676–1687*, ed. Marquis of Lansdowne (1928). Among contemporary collections are: *Letters upon Several Occasions*, ed. John Dennis (1696); *Familiar Letters Written by the Earl of Rochester* [and others], ed. Tom Brown (2 vols. 1697); *Letters of Wit, Politicks and Morality* (1701). Sir A. Bryant's *Postman's Horn. An Anthology of the Letters of Later Seventeenth Century England* (1936) gives a wide and varied view of the period.

W. H. Irving's critical survey, *The Providence of Wit in the English Letter Writers* (Duke University, 1955), has something to say on our period, and is useful on the continental background; and there are shorter accounts by E. N. S. Thompson, *Literary Bypaths* (*supra*), and R. W. Ramsey (*Essays by Divers*

Hands xiv, 1935). K. G. Hornbeak's *Complete Letter-Writer in English 1568–1800* (Smith College, 1934) and Jean Robertson's *Art of Letter Writing* (1942) are studies of epistolary theory and formal practice. For an interesting aspect of the literary extension of the letter, see B. Boyce, 'News from Hell: satiric communications with the nether world in English writing of the seventeenth and eighteenth centuries' (*PMLA* lviii, 1942).

5. HISTORICAL AND BIOGRAPHICAL LITERATURE

This section comprises historical writing, biography, autobiographies, and diaries.

Historiographical works include: H. E. Barnes, *History of Historical Writing* (University of Oklahoma, 1937); J. W. Thompson, *History of Historical Writing*, vol. i (New York, 1942); H. Butterfield, *Man on his Past: The Study of the History of Historical Scholarship* (1954; repr. Boston, 1960) and *The Englishman and his History* (1944). Works more closely related to our period are: E. N. Adams, *Old English Scholarship in England from 1566–1800* (Yale, 1917); D. C. Douglas, *English Scholars 1660–1730* (1939; rev. 1951); J. Butt, 'Facilities for Antiquarian Study in the Seventeenth Century' (*ESEA* xxiv, 1939); *English Historical Scholarship in the Sixteenth and Seventeenth Centuries*, ed. Levi Fox (1956); H. Davis, 'The Augustan Conception of History' (*Reason and the Imagination*, ed. J. A. Mazzeo, *supra*, III. 5); J. G. A. Pocock, *The Ancient Constitution and the Feudal Law: A Study of English Historical Thought in the Seventeenth Century* (1957); and studies of Burnet, Clarendon, Temple (*infra*, VI). W. Nicolson's *English, Scotch, and Irish Historical Libraries* (3rd ed., 1736) deals briefly with some of our historians.

Biographical collections include V. de S. Pinto's *English Biography in the Seventeenth Century* (1951), and D. Nichol Smith (*supra*, IV. 4). The standard critical work is D. A. Stauffer's *English Biography before 1700* (Harvard, 1930). There is briefer mention of some of our biographers in W. H. Dunn's *English Biography* (1916); H. Nicolson, *The Development of English Biography* (1928); Edgar Johnson, *One Mighty Torrent* (New York, 1937); F. P. Wilson, *Seventeenth Century Prose* (*supra*, III. 2); R. D. Altick, *Lives and Letters: A History of Literary Biography in England and America* (New York, 1965). One or two writers of the late seventeenth century are represented in J. L. Clifford's *Biography as an Art. Selected Criticism, 1560–1960* (1962).

For diaries and autobiographies there are bibliographies by W. Matthews: *British Diaries* and *British Autobiographies* (University of California, 1950, 1955). Some extracts are given in Sir A. Ponsonby's *English Diaries* (1923), *More English Diaries* (1927), and *Scottish and Irish Diaries* (1927), and in J. G. Fyfe's *Scottish Diaries and Memoirs 1550–1746* (1928). See also Bunyan, Aubrey, Pepys, Evelyn (*infra*, VI). Among critical discussions are: J. C. Major, *The Role of Personal Memoirs in English Biography and Novel* (University of Pennsylvania, 1935); M. Bottrall, *Every Man a Phoenix: Studies in Seventeenth-Century Autobiography* (1958); L. D. Lerner, 'Puritanism and the Spiritual Autobiography' (*Hibbert Journal* lv, 1957). W. Shumaker, *English Autobiography: Its Emergence, Materials, and Form* (University of California, 1954), is mostly concerned with post-Restoration developments, but J. N. Morris, *Version of Self. Studies in English Autobiography* (New York, 1966), deals with Bunyan, Fox, *et al.* Two books in which Puritan autobiography is fully discussed are: G. A. Starr, *Defoe and Spiritual Autobiography* (Princeton, 1965), and J. P. Hunter, *The Reluctant Pilgrim: Defoe's Emblematic Method and Quest of Form* (Johns Hopkins, 1966).

6. CLASSICAL AND FOREIGN RELATIONS

Bibliographies include F. Baldensperger and W. P. Friedrich, *Bibliography of Comparative Literature* (University of North Carolina, 1950), and Friedrich's *Yearbook of Comparative and General Literature* (ibid., 1952 ff.). There are extensive sections in *CBEL* ii, on 'Literary Relations with the Continent' and on 'Translations from the French'. The latter is supplemented by J. E. Tucker (*PQ* xxi, 1942), who similarly supplements the French translations entered in Wing (*PBSA* xlix, 1955). *CBEL* has also a useful list of translations of French fiction, 1660–1700, and lists of translations from other European literatures. For Spain there is a bibliography by R. U. Pane, *English Translations from the Spanish, 1484–1943* (Rutgers University, 1944).

For classical literature there are: H. Brown, 'The Classical Tradition in English Literature' (*Harvard Studies and Notes in Philology and Literature* xviii, 1935); F. M. K. Foster, *English Translations from the Greek: a Bibliographical Survey* (Columbia,

1918); F. Seymour Smith, *The Classics in Translation* (1930). There is an an extensive bibliography of translations from the Greek and Latin in *CBEL*.

For classical scholarship Sir J. E. Sandys's *History of Classical Scholarship*, vol. ii (1908), is the standard work. General surveys of the influence of the classics on English literature are inevitably brief on the forty years of our period. They include: G. S. Gordon *et al.*, *English Literature and the Classics* (1912); G. Murray, *The Classical Tradition in English Poetry* (1927); J. A. K. Thomson, *The Classical Background of English Literature* (1948), *Classical Influences on English Poetry* (1951), and *Classical Influences on English Prose* (1956); G. Highet, *The Classical Tradition: Greek and Roman Influences on Western Literature* (1949); D. Bush, *Mythology and the Renaissance Tradition in English Poetry* (University of Minnesota, 1932; repr. New York, 1957).

More specialized studies with a bearing on our period include: J. Conington, 'English Translations of Vergil' (*Quarterly Review* cx, 1861); J. S. Phillimore, *Some Remarks on Translations and Translators* (1919); E. Nitchie, *Vergil and the English Poets* (Columbia, 1919); H. Craig, 'Dryden's Lucian' (*Classical Philology* xvi, 1921). For discussions of Dryden's translation of Virgil, see Dryden, *infra*, VI, and his own dedicatory preface to that work. For his views on Ovid and the problem of translating him, see W. P. Ker's *Essays of John Dryden, passim*. Among other studies are: M. E. Smith, 'Aesop, a Decayed Celebrity. Changing Conceptions as to Aesop's Personality in English Writers before Gay' (*PMLA* xlvi, 1931); T. F. Mayo, *Epicurus in England 1650–1725* (Dallas, Texas, 1934); C. T. Harrison, 'The Ancient Atomists and English Literature of the Seventeenth Century' (*Harvard Studies in Classical Philology* xlv, 1934); G. D. Hadzits, *Lucretius and his Influence* (New York, 1935); W. B. Fleischmann, *Lucretius in English Literature 1680–1740* (Paris, 1964); E. S. Duckett, *Catullus in English Poetry* (Smith College, 1925); J. A. S. McPeek, *Catullus in Strange and Distant Britain* (Harvard, 1939); S. R. Ashby, 'The Treatment of the Themes of Classic Tragedy in English Tragedy between 1660 and 1738' (*Harvard Summaries of Theses*, 1927).

Neo-Latin writing is treated by F. A. Wright and T. A. Sinclair, *A History of Later Latin Literature* (1931), and by L. Bradner, *Musae Anglicanae: A History of Anglo-Latin Poetry, 1500–1925* (New York, 1940).

The influence of Hebrew literature is discussed by H. Fisch, *The Hebraic Element in Seventeenth Century Literature* (New York, 1964). For France there are several studies: L. Charlanne, *L'Influence française en Angleterre au XVIIe siècle* (Paris, 1906); A. W. H. West, *L'Influence française dans la poésie burlesque en Angleterre entre 1660 et 1700* (Paris, 1931); S. E. Leavitt, 'Paul Scarron and English Travesty' (*SP* xvi, 1919); H. Brown, *Rabelais in English Literature* (Harvard, 1933); C. Dédéyan, *Montaigne chez ses amis anglo-saxons* (2 vols., Paris, 1946); K. E. Wheatley, *Racine and English Classicism* (University of Texas, 1956). There is an account, with a bibliography, of John Davies of Kidwelly and his numerous translations, by J. E. Tucker (*PBSA* xliv, 1950). For other European countries there are: J. R. Murray, *The Influence of Italian upon English Literature during the Sixteenth and Seventeenth Centuries* (1886); H. G. Wright, *Boccaccio in England: From Chaucer to Tennyson* (1957); M. Hume, *Spanish Influence on English Literature* (1905); E. G. Matthews, *Studies in Anglo-Spanish Cultural and Literary Relations 1598–1700* (*Harvard Summaries of Theses*, 1938); Ethel Seaton, *Literary Relations of England and Scandinavia in the Seventeenth Century* (1935); G. Waterhouse, *The Literary Relations of England and Germany in the Seventeenth Century* (1914); T. de Vries, *Holland's Influence on English Language and Literature* (Chicago, 1916); H. J. Reesnik, *L'Angleterre et la littérature anglaise dans les trois plus anciens périodiques français de Hollande 1684 à 1709* (Paris, 1931). For China there is W. W. Appleton, *A Cycle of Cathay: the Chinese Vogue in England during the Seventeenth and Eighteenth Centuries* (Columbia, 1951). For a distinguished Arabist, see P. M. Holt, 'Edward Pococke 1604–1691: An English Orientalist' (*History Today* vii, 1957).

7. CONTEMPORARY CRITICISM

The standard collection is J. E. Spingarn, *Critical Essays of the Seventeenth Century* (3 vols., 1908–9; repr. Indiana University, 1957). A few pieces of the late seventeenth century are available in W. H. Durham, *Critical Essays of the Eighteenth Century* (Yale, 1915; repr. New York, 1961); A. H. Gilbert, *Literary Criticism: Plato to Dryden* (New York, 1940); S. Hynes, *English Literary Criticism: Restoration and Eighteenth Century* (New York, 1963); G. W. Chapman, *Literary Criticism in England, 1660–1800* (New York, 1966); E. W. Tayler, *Literary Criticism of*

17th Century England (New York, 1967). A number of minor critical pieces have been made available by the Augustan Reprint Society. For drama, the early pages of H. H. Adams and B. Hathaway, *Dramatic Essays of the Neoclassical Age* (Columbia, 1950; repr. New York, 1965) contain relevant material. See also Dryden, Sir Robert Howard, and Rymer in VI, *infra*, and *The Critical Works of John Dennis*, ed. E. N. Hooker (2 vols., Johns Hopkins, 1939–43). Sir Thomas Pope Blount's *De re poetica* (1694) gives what may be regarded as a conventional contemporary evaluation of poets and poetry, as (to a lesser extent) does Edward Phillips's *Theatrum Poetarum* (1675). Among a number of short treatises on preaching, J. Arderne's *Directions concerning the Matter and Style of Sermons* (1671) has been edited for the Luttrell Society by J. Mackay (1952).

For the French critics F. Vial and L. Denise, *Idées et doctrines littéraires du XVIIᵉ siècle* (Paris, 1922; 10th ed. 1937), offer a compendious selection of brief extracts arranged under critical topics. There is a useful and comprehensive selection by S. Elledge and D. Schier, *The Continental Model. Selected French Critical Essays of the Seventeenth Century, in English Translation* (University of Minnesota, 1960).

Some general surveys are: P. Hamelius, *Die Kritik in der englischen Literatur des 17. und 18. Jahrhunderts* (Leipzig, 1897); G. Saintsbury, *History of Criticism and Literary Taste in Europe* ii (3 vols., 1900–4) and *History of English Criticism* (1911); the introductions to Spingarn and to Hooker's *Dennis* (*supra*); W. K. Wimsatt and C. Brooks, *Literary Criticism: A Short History* (New York, 1957); G. Watson, *The Literary Critics* (1962). More strictly related to our period are J. W. H. Atkins, *English Literary Criticism: 17th and 18th Centuries* (1951), and A. Maurocordato, *La Critique classique en Angleterre de la Restauration à la mort de Joseph Addison* (Paris, 1964), which has an extensive bibliography.

Among more specialized studies are: A. F. B. Clark, *Boileau and the French Classical Critics in England, 1660–1830* (Paris, 1920); M. T. Herrick, *The Poetics of Aristotle in England* (Yale, 1930); T. R. Henn, *Longinus and English Criticism* (1934); S. H. Monk, *The Sublime: A Study of Critical Theories in XVIIIth-Century England* (New York, 1935; repr. University of Michigan, 1960), which reaches back into our period; J. E. Congleton, *Theories of Pastoral Poetry in England, 1684–1798* (University of

Florida, 1952); H. T. Swedenberg, Jr., *The Theory of the Epic in England 1650–1800* (University of California, 1950); two papers by R. S. Crane on neo-classical criticism (*UTQ* xxii, 1953; and *Critics and Criticism*, ed. R. S. Crane *et al.*, University of Chicago, 1952); C. A. Zimansky's introduction to *The Critical Works of Thomas Rymer* (*infra*, Rymer, VI); E. R. Marks, *Relativist and Absolutist: The Early Neo-Classical Debate in England* (Rutgers University, 1955); C. C. Green, *The Neo-Classic Theory of Tragedy in England during the Eighteenth Century* (Harvard, 1934; repr. New York, 1966); Sister Rose Anthony, *The Jeremy Collier Stage Controversy* (Marquette University, 1937; repr. New York, 1966); S. Singh, *The Theory of Drama in the Restoration Period* (Calcutta, 1963); T. A. Hanzo, *Latitude and Restoration Criticism* (*Anglistica* ser., Copenhagen, 1961); F. R. Amos, *Early Theories of Translation* (New York, 1920).

Among various special studies are those of Bredvold, Bond, Wood, Williamson, and Bronson (*supra*, III. 1); E. Nitchie, 'Longinus and the Theory of Poetic Imitation in... England' (*SP* xxxii, 1935); M. Kallich, 'The Association of Ideas in Critical Theory: Hobbes, Locke and Addison' (*ELH* xii, 1945); I. Simon, 'Critical Terms in Restoration Translations from the French' (*Revue belge de philologie et d'histoire* xliii, 1965); G. M. Miller, 'The Historical Point of View in English Criticism from 1550 to 1770' (*Anglistische Forschungen* xxv, Heidelberg, 1913); P. Legouis, 'Corneille and Dryden as Dramatic Critics' (Grierson *Festschrift*, *supra*, III. 1); Q. M. Hope, *Saint-Évremond: the Honnête Homme as Critic* (Indiana University, 1962); E. E. Williams, 'Dr. James Drake and the Restoration Theory of Comedy' (*RES* xv, 1939). The Ancients and Moderns controversy has occasioned a considerable literature, including H. Rigault, *Histoire de la querelle des anciens et modernes* (Paris, 1856); see also Richard Bentley (*infra*, VI). R. F. Jones, *The Background of the Battle of the Books* (Washington University Studies vii, 1920) and *Ancients and Moderns* (*supra*, III. 5), although going far beyond the late-seventeenth century controversy, provide the necessary setting for it.

Among books surveying the scholarship of the period are: E. F. Adams, *Old English Scholarship in England from 1566–1800* (Yale, 1917); D. C. Douglas, *English Scholars 1660–1730* (1939; rev. 1951); R. Wellek, *The Rise of English Literary History* (University of North Carolina, 1941).

8. Printing and Bookselling

The important seventeenth-century work on printing, J. Moxon's *Mechanick Exercises on the Whole Art of Printing* (1683-4), has been edited by H. Davis and H. Carter (1958).

A number of the bibliographical works cited above in I, such as *The Term Catalogues 1668-1709*, are indispensable here. For printers and publishers of the late seventeenth century there are H. R. Plomer's *Dictionary of the Booksellers and Printers ...from 1641 to 1667* (1907) and his companion volume for 1668-1725 (1922). For Scotland these may be supplemented by R. H. Carnie, 'Scottish Printers and Booksellers 1668-1775: A Supplement' (*Studies in Bibliography* xii, 1959; and ibid. xiv, 1960; xv, 1962). The section by Graham Pollard in *CBEL* ii dealing with 'Book Production and Distribution' is excellent, as is the supplement in vol. v by Cyprian Blagden. Among older accounts C. H. Timperley's *Dictionary of Printers* (1839) has much miscellaneous and curious information.

General studies include: F. A. Mumby, *Publishing and Bookselling* (1930; 4th ed. 1956); M. Plant, *The English Book Trade. An Economic History of the Making and Sale of Books* (1939); P. M. Handover, *Printing in London from 1476 to Modern Times* (1960); C. Blagden, *The Stationers' Company: A History, 1403-1959* (1960).

More closely related to our period are *The Life and Errors of John Dunton* (1705; ed. J. Nichols, 1818); L. Rostenberg, *Seventeenth Century English Publishers and Booksellers* (New York, 1962) and *Literary, Political, Scientific, Religious and Legal Publishing, Printing and Bookselling 1551-1700* (2 vols., New York, 1965); A. F. Johnson, 'The King's Printers, 1660-1742' (*Library*, 5th ser. iii, 1948); R. L. Haig, 'New Light on the King's Printing Office 1680-1730' (*Studies in Bibliography* viii, 1956); S. L. C. Clapp's papers on subscription publishing in the seventeenth century (*MP* xxix, 1931; xxx, 1933; *Library*, 4th ser. xiii, 1932); E. B. Murrie, 'Notes on the Printers and Publishers of English Song-Books, 1651-1702' (*Edinburgh Bibliographical Society Transactions* i. iii, 1938; cf. Day and Murrie, *supra*, II. 2); C. Blagden, 'Notes on the Ballad Market in the second half of the Seventeenth Century' (*Studies in Bibliography* vi, 1953); C. W. Miller, 'In the Savoy: A Study in Post-Restoration Imprints' (*PBSA* i, 1949); J. Alden, 'Pills and Publishing: Some

Notes on the English Book Trade 1660–1715' (*Library*, 5th ser. vii, 1952); R. S. Mortimer, 'The First Century of Quaker Printers' (*PBSA* i, 1949); A. N. L. Munby, 'The Distribution of the First Edition of Newton's *Principia*' (*Notes and Records of the Royal Society* x, 1952); R. M. Wiles, *Serial Publication in England before 1750* (1957).

Among studies concerned with individual printers are: C. W. Miller, 'Henry Herringman' (*PBSA* xlii, 1948); S. L. C. Clapp, *Jacob Tonson in Ten Letters by and about Him* (University of Texas, 1948); N. Hodgson and C. Blagden, 'The Notebook of Thomas Bennet and Henry Clements' (*OBS*, new ser. vi, 1953); J. Barnard, 'Dryden, Tonson, and Subscriptions for the 1697 Virgil' (*PBSA* lvii, 1963). See also Francis Kirkman, *infra*, VI.

For publishing outside London there are: F. Madan, *Oxford Books* iii (1931); J. Johnson and S. Gibson, *Print and Privilege at Oxford to the Year 1700* (1946) and *The First Minute Book of the Delegates of the Oxford University Press 1668–1756* (*OBS*, 1943); Sir S. C. Roberts, *A History of the Cambridge University Press 1521–1921* (1921); D. F. McKenzie, *The Cambridge University Press, 1696–1712: A Bibliographical Study* (2 vols., 1966); H. G. Aldis, 'A List of Books Printed in Scotland before 1700' (*Edinburgh Bibliographical Society* vii, 1904); J. Maclehose, *The Glasgow University Press 1638–1931* (1931); J. P. Edmond, *Aberdeen Printers, 1620–1736* (1886); E. R. M. Dix, *Books Printed in Dublin in the XVIIth Century* (5 pts., Dublin, 1898–1912); J. W. Hammond, 'The King's Printers in Ireland, 1551–1919' (*Dublin Historical Record* xi, 1950).

The essential parts of the Licensing Act of 1662 are printed in A. Browning, *English Historical Documents 1660–1714* (1953). Accounts of censorship include C. R. Gillett, *Burned Books* (2 vols., Columbia, 1932); F. S. Siebert, *Freedom of the Press in England, 1476–1776: The Rise and Decline of Government Controls* (University of Illinois, 1952) and 'Regulations of the Press in the Seventeenth Century' (*Journalism Quarterly* xiii, 1936); G. Kitchin (*infra*, VI, L'Estrange); J. Walker, 'The Censorship of the Press during the Reign of Charles II' (*History*, new ser. xxxv, 1950). The troubles of some newspaper printers and publishers are listed in IV. 2. The lapse of the Licensing Act in 1695 is discussed in L. Hanson, *Government and the Press 1695–1763* (1936). H. Macdonald has written on 'The Law and Defamatory Biographies in the Seventeenth Century' (*RES* xx, 1944).

V. THE BACKGROUND OF LITERATURE

This section comprises: (1) Political history and political thought; (2) Religion and religious thought; (3) Science and scientific thought; (4) Travel; (5) Social life; (6) Education and culture; (7) The arts.

1. POLITICAL HISTORY AND POLITICAL THOUGHT

The standard work of reference, Godfrey Davies, *Bibliography of British History. Stuart Period 1603–1714* (1928), now needs to be brought up to date, and a new edition is being prepared. To some extent Davies may be supplemented by C. L. Grose, *A Select Bibliography of British History 1660–1760* (University of Chicago, 1939).

Collections of contemporary materials include: *State Tracts ... Privately Printed in the Reign of King Charles the Second* (1689); *State Tracts: in two parts ... 1660–1689* (1692–3); *A Collection of State Tracts 1688–1702* (3 vols., 1705–7); A. Browning, *English Historical Documents, 1660–1714* (1953); D. O. Dykes, *A Source Book of Constitutional History from 1660* (1930); W. H. Dunham and S. Pargellis, *Complaint and Reform in England 1436–1714* (New York, 1938); *Crises in English History*, ed. B. Henning *et al.* (New York, 1949); W. C. Costin and J. S. Watson, *The Law and the Working of the Constitution, Vol. I, 1660–1783* (1952; repr. 1962); G. M. Straka, *The Revolution of 1688: Whig Triumph or Palace Revolution?* (Boston, 1963); J. P. Kenyon, *The Stuart Constitution 1603–1688: Documents and Commentary* (1966); G. Orwell *et al.*, *British Pamphleteers*, vol. i (1948); C. Hill and E. Dell, *The Good Old Cause* (1949), which brings out the significance of the Revolution of 1640–60; *The Notes which passed at Meetings of the Privy Council between Charles II ... and Clarendon* (Roxburghe Club, 1896); A. Bryant, *The Letters, Speeches and Declarations of King Charles II* (1935); R. Steele, *Tudor and Stuart Proclamations* (2 vols., 1910); Anchitel Grey, *Debates in the House of Commons, 1667–94* (10 vols., 1769). This list could be indefinitely extended by the inclusion of such sources as the *Journals* of the House of Lords and the House of Commons, the *Calendars of State Papers, State Trials*, etc. For these and other collections and for secondary materials, recourse may be had to the very useful short bibliography appended to Sir G. N. Clark's *The Later Stuarts 1660–1714* (1934; 2nd ed. 1956). There is a good deal of political information in Narcissus Luttrell's *Brief Historical Relation of State Affairs* (6 vols., 1857).

Some surveys of Europe are: *Cambridge Modern History*, vol. v (rev. 1961); D. Ogg, *Europe in the Seventeenth Century* (1925; 6th ed. 1952); Sir G. N. Clark, *The Seventeenth Century* (1929; rev. 1947; repr. 1961).

For English history Macaulay is still valuable, both for detail and general survey: his *History of England from the Accession of James II* should be read in Sir Charles Firth's edition (6 vols., 1913–15). Leopold von Ranke's *History of England* (6 vols., 1875) deals mainly with the seventeenth century. Twentieth-century histories include: Sir G. M. Trevelyan, *England under the Stuarts* (1904; 21st ed. 1949); Sir Richard Lodge, *The History of England 1660–1702* (1923); Sir G. N. Clark, *The Later Stuarts* (*supra*); D. Ogg, *England in the Reign of Charles II* (2 vols., 1934; 2nd ed. 1956; repr. 1963) and *England in the Reigns of James II and William III* (1955); I. Deane Jones, *The English Revolution . . . 1603–1714* (1931); M. Ashley, *England in the Seventeenth Century* (Pelican, 1952); C. Hill, *The Century of Revolution* (1961; repr. New York, 1966); J. R. Tanner, *English Constitutional Conflicts of the Seventeenth Century* (1928; repr. 1961); C. Roberts, *The Growth of Responsible Government in Stuart England* (1966).

More specialized studies include: G. Davies, 'The General Election of 1660' (*HLQ* xv, 1952), *The Restoration of Charles II, 1658–1660* (Huntington Library, 1955), and *Essays on the Later Stuarts* (Huntington Library, 1958); R. Bosher, *The Making of the Restoration Settlement* (1951); M. Beloff, *Public Order and Popular Disturbances 1660–1714* (1938); M. Lee, Jr., *The Cabal* (University of Illinois, 1965); K. Feiling, *British Foreign Policy 1660–1672* (1930), and *A History of the Tory Party 1640–1714* (1924; repr. 1951); K. H. D. Haley, *William of Orange and the English Opposition, 1672–4* (1953); F. K. Ronalds, *The Attempted Whig Revolution 1678–1681* (University of Illinois, 1937); Sir G. M. Trevelyan, *The English Revolution, 1688–1689* (1939); L. Pinkham, *William III and the Respectable Revolution* (Harvard, 1954); M. Ashley, *The Glorious Revolution of 1688* (1966); Sir Charles Petrie, *The Jacobite Movement: the First Phase,*

1686–1716 (1949); J. G. Muddiman, *The Bloody Assizes* (1929); Sir Edward Parry, *The Bloody Assize* (1929). For the activities of the Whig opposition and Whig republicans there is I. Morley, *A Thousand Lives: An Account of the English Revolutionary Movement, 1660–1685* (1954). Some other books on this topic are cited below under Political Thought. The literature of the Popish Plot is extensive, as may be seen from Narcissus Luttrell's *Popish Plot Catalogues* (see Luttrell, *infra* VI,). Among modern accounts of the plot are: Sir John Pollock, *The Popish Plot* (1903; repr. 1944); M. V. Hay, *The Jesuits and the Popish Plot* (1934); J. Dickson Carr, *The Murder of Sir Edmund Berry Godfrey* (1936); Jane Lane, *Titus Oates* (1949); Anna M. Crinò, *Il Popish Plot; nelle relazioni dei residenti granducali alla corte di Londra, 1678–1681* (Rome, 1954).

Biographies, etc., which throw light on the political scene include: Sir A. Bryant, *King Charles II* (1931; rev. 1955); C. H. Hartmann, *Charles II and Madame* (1934; repr., 1954, as *The King my Brother*), which gives the correspondence of Charles II and his sister, Henrietta-Anne, Duchess of Orleans; F. M. G. Higham, *King James the Second* (1935); M. V. Hay, *The Enigma of James II* (1938); F. C. Turner, *James II* (1948); N. A. Robb, *William of Orange: A Personal Portrait* (2 vols., 1962–6); S. B. Baxter, *William III* (1966). There are biographies of Mary II by N. M. Waterson (1928), M. Bowen (1929), and H. W. Chapman (1953); of Albemarle, by J. D. G. Davies (1936) and O. Warner (1936); of Shaftesbury, by W. D. Christie (2 vols., 1871), Louise F. Brown (New York, 1934), and K. H. D. Haley (1968); of Clifford, by C. H. Hartmann (1937); of Lauderdale, by W. C. Mackenzie (1923); of Arlington, by V. Barbour (Washington, 1914); of Danby, by A. Browning (2 vols., 1951); of Sunderland, by J. P. Kenyon (1958); of Thomas Bruce, Earl of Ailesbury, by the Earl of Cardigan (1951); of Jeffreys, by H. M. Hyde (1940), G. W. Keeton (1965), P. J. Helm (1966). For Clarendon, Buckingham, Temple, and Algernon Sidney, see *infra*, VI. Further material will be found in Clarendon's *Life*, Burnet's *History*, Reresby's *Memoirs*, ed. A. Browning (1936), Ailesbury's *Memoirs*, ed. W. E. Buckley (2 vols., Roxburghe Club, 1890), Roger North's *Examen* (1740). J. J. Jusserand's *A French Ambassador at the Court of Charles II* (1892) throws light on Anglo-French relations.

There are general histories of Scotland by P. H. Brown

(3 vols., 1899–1909) and Andrew Lang (4 vols., 1900–7), and a shorter one by Brown (1924; rev. H. W. Meikle, 1951). D. Nobbs, *England and Scotland, 1560–1707* (1952), takes Anglo-Scottish relations up to the Union, and G. Donaldson, *The Edinburgh History of Scotland*, vol. iii (1965), deals with the reigns of James V to James VII. W. C. Dickinson *et al.* compiled *A Source Book of Scottish History*, of which vol. iii (1954) covers the years 1567–1707, and P. H. Brown edited two collections, *Early Travellers in Scotland* (1891), and *Scotland before 1700 from Contemporary Documents* (1893). A. Mure Mackenzie's *Scottish Pageant 1625–1707* (1949) provides further contemporary documentation. For Wales there is Idris Jones, *Modern Welsh History from 1486 to the Present Day* (1934; 3rd ed. 1960); and for Ireland, there is a history by E. Curtis (1936; 5th ed. 1945), and E. MacLysaght, *Irish Life in the Seventeenth Century* (1939; rev. 1950).

A good general introduction to political thought is G. H. Sabine's *History of Political Theory* (New York, 1937; rev. 1950). Other works bearing on our period are: G. P. Gooch, *English Democratic Ideas in the Seventeenth Century* (1898; rev. H. J. Laski, 1927; repr. New York, 1959) and *Political Thought in England from Bacon to Halifax* (1915); H. J. Laski, *Political Thought in England from Locke to Bentham* (1920); *Social and Political Ideas of Some English Thinkers of the Augustan Age*, ed. F. J. C. Hearnshaw (1928; repr. 1967); J. W. Gough, *The Social Contract* (1936; 2nd ed. 1957); J. Bowle, *Hobbes and his Critics: A Study in Seventeenth-Century Constitutionalism* (1951); J. H. M. Salmon, *The French Religious Wars in English Political Thought* (1959); J. N. Figgis, *The Divine Right of Kings* (rev. ed. 1922) and P. Laslett's introduction to his edition of Sir Robert Filmer's *Patriarcha* (1949); L. G. Schwoerer, 'The Literature of the Standing Army Controversy, 1697–1699' (*HLQ* xxviii, 1965; and see *NQ* ccxi, 1966); W. H. Greenley, *Order, Empiricism and Politics: Two Traditions of English Political Thought* (1964).

Among studies of the activities and governing ideas of the Whig opposition are the following: Z. S. Fink, *The Classical Republicans* (Northwestern University, 1945; rev. 1962); G. F. Sensabaugh, *That Grand Whig Milton* (Stanford University, 1951), which traces the impact of Milton on Whig thinking; and 'Milton and the Attempted Whig Revolution' (Jones

Festschrift, supra, III, 1); P. Zagorin, *A History of Political Thought in the English Revolution* (1954); O. W. Furley, 'The Whig Exclusionists . . . 1679–1681' (*Cambridge Historical Journal* xiii, 1957); Caroline Robbins, *The Eighteenth Century Commonwealthman* (Harvard, 1959); J. R. Jones, *The First Whigs: The Politics of the Exclusion Crisis* (1961), and J. P. Kenyon (*History Today* xiv, 1964); B. Behrens, 'The Whig Theory of the Constitution in the Reign of Charles II' (*Cambridge Historical Journal* vii, 1941); C. A. Edie, 'Succession and Monarchy: The Controversy of 1679–1681' (*American Historical Review* lxx, 1965); F. Raab, *The English Face of Machiavelli, . . . 1500–1700* (University of Toronto, 1964); C. Hill, *Intellectual Origins of the English Revolution* (1965).

A standard work in economic history is E. Lipson's *Economic History of England,* vols. ii–iii (1931). More recent are Sir J. H. Clapham, *A Concise Economic History of Britain, from the Earliest Times to 1750* (1949); W. S. Reid, *Economic History of Great Britain* (New York, 1964); and C. H. Wilson, *England's Apprenticeship 1603–1763* (1965). Two other relevant books are Sir G. N. Clark, *The Wealth of England from 1496–1760* (1935), and H. Darby, *An Historical Geography of England before 1800* (1936). A useful collection of illustrative material is that by A. E. Bland *et al., English Economic History. Select Documents* (1919). More specialized studies are: W. C. Scoville, 'The Huguenots and the Diffusion of Technology' (*Journal of Political Economy* lx, 1952); J. K. Horsefield, *British Monetary Experiments, 1650–1710* (1960); J. E. Thorold Rogers, *The First Nine Years of the Bank of England* (1887); Sir J. H. Clapham, *The Bank of England: a History, Vol. I, 1694–1797* (1944); J. Giuseppi, *The Bank of England* (1966); Sir John Craig, *The Mint: A History of the London Mint from A.D. 287 to 1948* (1953); Sir Charles Oman, *The Coinage of England* (1931); L. Ming-Hsun, *The Great Recoinage of 1696–9* (1963); C. H. Wilson, *Profit and Power: A Study of England and the Dutch Wars* (1957); H. J. Habakkuk, 'English Landownership 1680–1740' (*Economic History Review* x, 1940); R. Davis, 'English Foreign Trade 1660–1700' (ibid. vii, 1954); W. R. Scott, *Constitution and Finance of English, Scottish, and Irish Joint-Stock Companies to 1720* (3 vols., 1911–12). For a contemporary account of dealings in stocks and shares, see Defoe's *The Villainy of Stock-Jobbers Detected* (1701).

For Scotland there are: J. Mackinnon, *The Social and In-dustrial History of Scotland to the Union* (1920); G. P. Insh, *Scottish Colonial Schemes, 1620–86* (1922) and *The Company of Scotland trading to Africa and the Indies* (1932); T. C. Smout, *Scottish Trade on the Eve of Union, 1660–1707* (1963). For Ireland: Alice E. Murray, *Commercial and Financial Relations between England and Ireland from the Period of the Restoration* (1903); G. A. T. O'Brien, *The Economic History of Ireland in the Seventeenth Century* (1919); M. J. Bonn, *Die englische Kolonisation in Irland* (2 vols., 1906); R. Bagwell, *Ireland under the Stuarts* (3 vols., 1906–16); R. H. Murray, *Revolutionary Ireland and its Settle-ment* (1911).

Among general histories of economic thought are those of E. Whittaker (1940) and E. Roll (1945; repr. Englewood Cliffs, N.J., 1956). For our period the most useful work is W. Letwin's *The Origins of Scientific Economics: English Economic Thought 1660–1776* (1963). Among other studies are: E. A. J. Johnson, *Predecessors of Adam Smith. The Growth of British Economic Thought* (New York, 1937); P. W. Buck, *The Politics of Mercantilism* (New York, 1942); C. B. Macpherson, *The Political Theory of Progressive Individualism: Hobbes to Locke* (1962); J. Viner, 'English Theories of Foreign Trade before Adam Smith' (*Journal of Political Economy* xxxviii, 1930); M. Beer, *Early British Economics* (1938). See also under Petty, North, Locke (*infra*, VI).

2. RELIGION AND RELIGIOUS THOUGHT

James Hastings's *Encyclopaedia of Religion and Ethics* (13 vols., 1908–27) and F. L. Cross's *Oxford Dictionary of the Christian Church* (1957) are comprehensive and reliable. Part of vol. v of H. Daniel-Rops, *L'Église des temps classiques*, has been translated by J. J. Buckingham as *The Church in the Seventeenth Century* (1963).

For Roman Catholicism there are *The Catholic Encyclopaedia* (15 vols., New York, 1907–12) and J. Gillow, *A Literary and Biographical History, or Bibliographical Dictionary of the English Catholics* (5 vols., 1885–1902; repr. New York, 1961). There are short accounts by E. L. Watkin, *Roman Catholicism in England* (1957), and D. Mathew, *Catholicism in England, 1535–1935* (1936). See also A. Curtayne, *The Trial of Oliver Plunkett*

(1953), and biographies of Archbishop Plunkett by D. Mathews (1961) and Fr. E. Curtis (1963).

For the Church of England S. Ollard *et al.*, *A Dictionary of English Church History* (3rd. ed., rev., 1948), is a standard work of reference. Two useful collections are R. Cattermole, *Literature of the Church of England* (2 vols., 1844), and P. E. More and F. L. Cross, *Anglicanism: The Thought and Practice of the Church of England, Illustrated from the Religious Literature of the Seventeenth Century* (Milwaukee, 1935).

Historical developments in the Church of England during our period are dealt with in the following: J. Stoughton, *History of Religion in England* (6 vols., 1882); W. H. Hutton, *A History of the English Church from the accession of Charles I to the Death of Anne* (1903); R. S. Bosher, *The Making of the Restoration Settlement: The Influence of the Laudians, 1649–1660* (1951); H. R. Trevor-Roper, 'The Restoration of the Church' (*History Today* ii, 1952); H. G. Plum, 'The English Religious Restoration, 1660–1665' (*PQ* xx, 1941); N. Sykes, *Old Priest and New Presbyter* (1956) and *From Sheldon to Secker: Aspects of English Church History, 1660–1768* (1959); G. R. Cragg, *From Puritanism to the Age of Reason . . . 1660–1700* (1950) and *The Church and the Age of Reason, 1648–1789* (1960); G. Every, *The High Church Party, 1688–1716* (1956); *From Uniformity to Unity, 1662–1962*, ed. G. F. Nuttall and O. Chadwick (1962); A. H. Wood, *Church Unity without Uniformity: A Study of Seventeenth Century English Church Movements* (1963).

There are lives of the following churchmen: Gilbert Sheldon, by V. Staley (1913); John Cousin, by P. H. Osmond (1913); William Lloyd, by A. T. Hart (1952); Thomas Tenison and Henry Compton, by E. Carpenter (1948, 1956); Nathaniel Crew, by C. E. Whiting (1940); Henry Aldridge, by W. G. Hiscock (1960). See also Burnet, Ken, Tillotson (*infra*, VI).

For the Non-jurors there are J. H. Overton, *The Non-Jurors* (1902); L. M. Hawkins, *Allegiance in Church and State* (1928); J. W. C. Wand, *The High Church Schism* (1951).

Among earlier accounts of Anglican thought are the following: J. Hunt, *Religious Thought in England* (3 vols., 1870–3; vol. ii for our period); J. Tulloch, *Rational Theology and Christian Philosophy in England in the Seventeenth Century* (2 vols., 1872; rev. 1874); E. A. George, *Seventeenth Century Men of Latitude* (New York, 1908); H. H. Henson, *Studies in English Religion in the*

Seventeenth Century (1903). Later works include: H. R. McAdoo, *The Structure of Caroline Moral Theology* (1949) and *The Spirit of Anglicanism: A Survey of Anglican Theological Method in the Seventeenth Century* (New York, 1965); T. Wood, *English Casuistical Divinity during the Seventeenth Century* (1952); A. W. Harrison, *Arminianism* (1937); T. P. Fenn, 'The Latitudinarians and Toleration' (*Washington University Studies* xiii, 1925); R. B. Schlatter, *The Social Ideas of Religious Leaders, 1660–1688* (1940), which is not confined to the Church of England; E. A. Burtt, *Religion in an Age of Science* (New York, 1929); R. S. Westfall, *Science and Religion in Seventeenth-Century England* (Yale, 1958); S. I. Mintz, *The Hunting of Leviathan: Seventeenth-Century Reactions to the Materialism and Moral Philosophy of Thomas Hobbes* (1962); D. P. Walker, *The Decline of Hell: Seventeenth-Century Discussions of Eternal Torment* (1964).

There is an extensive literature for the Nonconformists, beginning with Edmund Calamy's *Account of the Ministers . . . Ejected or Silenced after the Restoration* (1713), which may conveniently be read in A. G. Matthews, *Calamy Revised* (1934; rev. 1959), and Daniel Neal's *History of the Puritans* (4 vols., 1732–8; ed. J. Toulmin, 5 vols., 1793–7). The volumes of D. Masson's *Life of Milton* (1859–94) covering the years 1660–74 have lasting value for their summaries of controversies. The Savoy Conference as seen by Richard Baxter is recorded *in extenso* in his *Reliquiae Baxterianae*. Among modern works are: C. E. Whiting, *Studies in English Puritanism from the Restoration to the Revolution* (1931); A. H. Drysdale, *History of the Presbyterians in England* (1889); O. M. Griffiths, *Religion and Learning* (1935), a study of Presbyterian thought from 1662; H. G. Plum, *Restoration Puritanism. A Study in the Growth of English Liberty* (University of North Carolina, 1943); C. F. Mullett, 'Protestant Dissent as a Crime, 1660–1828' (*Review of Religion* xiii, 1949) and 'Toleration and Persecution in England, 1660–89' (*Church History* xviii, 1949); J. C. Spalding, 'The Demise of English Presbyterianism' (ibid. xxviii, 1959); G. R. Cragg, *Puritanism in the Period of the Great Persecution 1660–1688* (1957); J. T. Wilkinson, *1662—And After: Three Centuries of English Nonconformity* (1962); *From Uniformity to Unity 1662–1962*, ed. G. F. Nuttall and O. Chadwick (1962). See also G. F. Nuttall, *The Beginnings of Non-Conformity, 1660–1665. A Checklist* (1960).

For Quakerism the standard works are W. C. Braithwaite, *The Beginnings of Quakerism* (1912; rev. H. J. Cadbury, 1955) and *The Second Period of Quakerism* (1919; rev. 1961). Other works include: E. Russell, *A History of Quakerism* (New York, 1942); G. B. Burnet, *The Story of Quakerism in Scotland 1650–1850* (1952); A. Lloyd, *Quaker Social History 1669–1738* (1950). The literary and educational aspects of Quakerism are treated by Luella M. Wright, *The Literary Life of the Early Friends 1650–1725* (Columbia, 1932) and *Literature and Education in Early Quakerism* (University of Iowa, 1933). An essential bibliography is that of Joseph Smith, *Descriptive Catalogue of Friends' Books* (2 vols., 1867). R. A. Knox, *Enthusiasm: a Chapter in the History of Religion* (1950), deals especially with the seventeenth and eighteenth centuries, and includes the Quakers in its survey.

For the Congregationalists there is a recent history by R. T. Jones, *Congregationalism in England, 1662–1962* (1962). An earlier study is H. M. Dexter, *Congregationalism of the Last Three Hundred Years, as Seen in its Literature* (New York, 1880). For the Baptists, W. T. Whitley's *Baptist Bibliography* (2 vols., 1916–22) is being superseded by E. C. Starr, *A Baptist Bibliography* (Philadelphia, 1947, in progress). A. C. Underwood has written *A History of the English Baptists* (1947). For the Unitarians, there are E. M. Wilbur, *A History of Unitarianism: Socinianism and its Antecedents* (Harvard, 1945), and H. J. McLachlan, *Socinianism in Seventeenth-Century England* (1951) and *The Unitarian Movement in the Religious Life of England* (1934). There is a good account of the early deists in Sir Leslie Stephen (*supra*, III. 5), and a recent discussion by R. L. Colie of 'Spinoza and the Early English Deists' (*JHI* xx, 1959).

Among accounts of Scottish religious history there are: G. D. Henderson, *Religious Life in Seventeenth-Century Scotland* (1937); F. Goldie, *A Short History of the Episcopal Church of Scotland from the Restoration . . .* (1952); W. R. Foster, *Bishop and Presbytery: The Church of Scotland, 1661–1688* (1958); J. H. S. Burleigh, *A Church History of Scotland* (1960); D. Anderson, *The Bible in Seventeenth-Century Scottish Life and Literature* (1936).

Sermons of the late seventeenth century are not easy to come by in modern selections. Some are available in Cattermole (*supra*), H. H. Henson's *Selected English Sermons* (1939), and G. L. May's *Wings of an Eagle: An Anthology of Caroline Preachers* (1956).

Two St. Cecilia's Day Sermons were ed. J. E. Phillips (*ARS*, 1955). The standard critical work is W. Fraser Mitchell, *English Pulpit Oratory from Andrewes to Tillotson* (1932). C. F. Richardson's *English Preachers and Preaching 1640–1670* (New York, 1928) deals more with the preachers than with their sermons. There are relevant sections in C. Smyth, *The Art of Preaching* (1940), and in F. P. Wilson (*supra*, III. 2). R. F. Jones has a paper on 'The Attack on Pulpit Eloquence in the Restoration' (*JEGP* xxx, 1931; repr. in Jones *Festschrift*, *supra*, III. 1), and Helen W. Randall's 'The Rise and Fall of a Martyrology' (*HLQ* x, 1947) deals with the sermons preached on 30 January, the anniversary of Charles I's death. There is a bibliography, 'Pulpit Eloquence', by H. Caplan and H. H. King (*Speech Monographs* xxii, 1955). The first volume of Irène Simon's *Three Restoration Divines* (University of Liège, 1968) contains six sermons by Isaac Barrow, together with a long critical dissertation. A second volume will give selections from the sermons of South and Tillotson.

Among books which are difficult to classify in the above categories are: J. H. Overton, *Life in the English Church, 1660–1714* (1885); H. McLachlan, *The Religious Opinions of Milton, Locke and Newton* (1941); G. V. Portus, *Caritas Anglicana* (1912), which deals with the religious and philanthropic societies, 1678–1740; V. H. H. Green, *Religion at Oxford and Cambridge* (1964); R. M. Jones, *Spiritual Reformers in the 16th and 17th Centuries* (1914; repr. Boston, 1959). Some titles in Bush which are not repeated here are also relevant to the late seventeenth century.

3. SCIENCE AND SCIENTIFIC THOUGHT

H. F. Boynton's *Beginnings of Modern Science: Scientific Writings of the 16th, 17th and 18th Centuries* (New York, 1948) and N. Davy's *British Scientific Literature in the Seventeenth Century* (1953) reprint some of the scientific writings of the period. Collections of scientific correspondence were cited above in IV. 4. To these may be added *The Correspondence of Henry Oldenburgh*, ed. A. R. and M. B. Hall (3 vols., University of Wisconsin, 1966, in progress). The *Philosophical Transactions* of the Royal Society have been appearing since 1665.

F. A. Dudley *et al.* compiled *The Relations of Literature and Science: A Selected Bibliography 1930–49* (State College of

Washington, 1949); supplements to this have been appearing annually in *Symposium* since 1951.

Among histories of science and technology with special claims to consideration are: Sir W. C. Dampier, *History of Science and its Relations with Philosophy & Religion* (1929; 4th ed., rev., 1948); Sir H. Butterfield, *Origins of Modern Science* (1949; rev. 1957); A. C. Crombie, *Medieval and Early Modern Science* (New York, rev. 1959, with a useful bibliography); L. Thorndike, *History of Magic and Experimental Science, Vols. VII–VIII* (Columbia, 1958); A. R. Hall, *The Scientific Revolution 1500–1800: The Formation of the Modern Scientific Attitude* (1954; repr. Boston, 1956) and *From Galileo to Newton* (1963); L. W. Hull, *History and Philosophy of Science* (1959); Charles Singer, *A Short History of Scientific Ideas to 1900* (1937; repr. 1959); A. Woolf, *History of Science, Technology, and Philosophy in the 16th & 17th Centuries* (1935; rev. D. McKie, 1950; repr. New York, 1959); *A History of Technology, Vol. III: From the Renaissance to the Industrial Revolution c. 1500–c. 1750*, ed. Charles Singer *et al.* (1957); R. J. Forbes and E. J. Dijksterhuis, *A History of Science and Technology, Vol. I. Ancient Times to the Seventeenth Century* (Penguin, 1963); E. J. Dijksterhuis, *The Mechanisation of the World Picture*, trs. C. Dikshoorn (1961); *Science, Medicine and History: Essays . . . in Honour of Charles Singer*, ed. E. A. Underwood (2 vols., 1953); R. K. Merton, 'Science, Technology and Society in Seventeenth Century England' (*Osiris* iv, 1938); W. E. Houghton, 'The History of Trades' (*JHI* ii, 1941). The work of some later seventeenth-century scientists is set forth in various volumes of R. T. Gunther's *Early Science in Oxford* (1920 ff.) and *Early Science in Cambridge* (1937). M. 'Espinasse writes on 'The Decline and Fall of Restoration Science' (*Past and Present* xiv, 1958).

Among works dealing with particular sciences are: E. G. R. Taylor, *The Mathematical Practitioners of Tudor and Stuart England* (1954); M. Boas, *Robert Boyle and Seventeenth-Century Chemistry* (1958); C. E. Raven, *English Naturalists from Neckham to Ray: A Study of the Modern World* (1947); K. Dewhurst, *Dr. Thomas Sydenham, 1624–1689* (University of California, 1966); R. K. Merton, 'Some Aspects of Medicine reflected in Seventeenth-Century Literature, with special reference to the Plague of 1665' (Jones *Festschrift, supra*, III. 1); E. J. Russell, *A History of Agricultural Science in Great Britain, 1620–1924* (1966); G. E.

Fussell, 'Agriculture from the Restoration to Anne' (*Economic History Review* ix, 1938).

European scientific societies are the subject of M. Ornstein's *The Role of Scientific Societies in the Seventeenth Century* (University of Chicago, 1928), which may be supplemented by Harcourt Brown's *Scientific Organizations in Seventeenth Century France* (Baltimore, 1934). Sprat's *History of the Royal Society* (1667) is available in a modern edition by J. I. Cope and H. W. Jones (Washington University, 1958). T. Birch's *History of the Royal Society* (4 vols., 1756–7) is useful for its extensive quotation from the Society's minutes. Among other histories of the Society are those of C. R. Weld (2 vols., 1848) and Sir H. Lyon (1944); *The Royal Society: Its Origins and Founders*, ed. Sir H. Hartley (1960); Dorothy Stimson, *Scientists and Amateurs* (New York, 1948); Margery Purver, *The Royal Society: Concept and Creation* (M.I.T., 1967). R. H. Syfret discusses 'Some Early Reactions to the Royal Society' (*Notes and Records of the Royal Society* vii, 1950) and 'Some Early Critics' (ibid. viii, 1951), and writes on 'The Origins' (ibid. v, 1948), as do D. McKie in the volume edited by Sir Harold Hartley (*supra*), and M. H. Carré in *History Today* x (1960). A. R. Hall discusses sources for the early history of the Society (*History of Science* v, 1966). E. N. da C. Andrade has a paper on the *Transactions* (*Notes and Records of the Royal Society* xx, 1965), and there is some information in D. A. Kronick (*supra*, IV.2). M. B. Hall writes on 'Oldenburg and the Art of Scientific Communication' (*British Journal for the History of Science* ii, 1965), and W. E. Houghton, Jr., on 'The English Virtuosos in the Seventeenth Century' (*JHI* iii, 1942). John Ward's *Lives of the Professors of Gresham College* (1740) throws light on our period, as do Sir G. N. Clark's *History of the Royal College of Physicians* (2 vols., 1964–6), and *A History of the Worshipful Society of Apothecaries of London. Vol. I 1617–1815*, ed. E. A. Underwood (1963).

The impact of science on the life and thought of the period has been the subject of discussion from many angles, and only a few studies are listed here: J. B. Bury, *The Idea of Progress* (1920); A. N. Whitehead, *Science and the Modern World* (1925, etc.); E. A. Burtt, *Metaphysical Foundations of Modern Science* (New York, 1934; repr. 1954); J. H. Randall, *The Making of the Modern Mind* (1926; rev. ed. Boston, 1940); R. G. Collingwood, *The Idea of Nature* (1945; repr. 1960); *Roots of Scientific*

Thought, ed. P. P. Wiener and A. Noland (New York, 1957), a selection of articles from *JHI*; Sir G. N. Clark, 'Social and Economic Aspects of Science in the Age of Newton' (*Economic History* iii, 1937) and *Science and Social Welfare in the Age of Newton* (1937; 2nd ed. 1949); R. K. Merton, 'Some Economic Factors in Seventeenth-Century English Science' (*Scientia*, 1957); R. S. Westfall (*supra*, V. 2). Some books cited earlier in this section and in II. 5 are relevant here.

The impact of science on seventeenth-century literature has been traced by Marjorie Nicolson in a number of valuable studies which are listed by Bush, but most of her literary material is drawn from pre-Restoration times or from the eighteenth century. R. F. Jones's *Ancients and Moderns* is invaluable for its account of the development of the scientific movement in the seventeenth century, and his work on the influence of science on prose style is basic (cf. III. 2). Two recent studies are Marjorie Nicolson's *Pepys's Diary and the New Science* (University of Virginia, 1965), which ranges a good deal beyond Pepys, and her introduction to Shadwell's *The Virtuoso* (University of Nebraska, 1966). *Seventeenth Century Science and the Arts*, ed. H. H. Rhys (Princeton, 1961), has not much for our period. Some of the studies cited earlier in this section (e.g. by R. H. Syfret) and under 'History of Ideas' (III. 5) have a predominantly literary interest, as has F. P. Wilson's 'English Letters and the Royal Society' (*Mathematical Gazette* xix, 1935). A neglected work is C. S. Duncan's *The New Science and English Literature in the Classical Period* (Menasha, Wisconsin, 1913), which has recently been described as 'the pioneer in what has become a popular field'.

4. TRAVEL

The standard bibliography is E. G. Cox, *Reference Guide to the Literature of Travel: i. The Old World; ii. The New World; iii. Great Britain* (3 vols., University of Washington, 1935, 1938, 1949). For England there are a bibliography by G. E. Fussell and V. G. B. Atwater, 'Travel and Topography in Seventeenth-Century England: A Bibliography of Sources for Social and Economic History' (*Library* xiii, 1932), and G. E. Fussell's *The Exploration of England. A Select Bibliography of Travel and Topography: 1570–1815* (1935). Apart from William Dampier (*infra*, VI) there is no outstanding voyager in our period. Early collections include those of A. and J. Churchill (4 vols., 1704; v and vi, 1732; 6 vols., 1744–6; vii and viii by Thomas Osborne, 1745); John Harris (2 vols., 1705; 2nd ed. 1744–8); John Pinkerton (17 vols., 1808–14). Many early records have been edited for the Hakluyt Society, the Argonaut Press series, and the Broadway Traveller series. H. W. Troyer has edited *Five Travel Scripts* (Columbia, 1933), including Edward Ward's *Trips* to Jamaica and New England. The field of exploration is reviewed in E. Heawood's *History of Geographical Discovery in the Seventeenth and Eighteenth Centuries* (1912).

For European travel there are good accounts by J. W. Stoye, *English Travellers Abroad 1604–1667* (1952), and Clare Howard, *English Travellers of the Renaissance* (New York, 1914). For France, Constantia Maxwell's *The English Traveller in France* (1932) just takes in the end of our period. For Italy there is A. Lytton Sells, *The Paradise of Travellers* (1964), which deals with the Italian influence on English travellers in the seventeenth century: for Switzerland, G. R. de Beer, *Travellers in Switzerland* (1949): for Greece, T. Spencer, *Fair Greece Sad Relic* (1954); R. W. Ramsey, 'Sir George Wheler and his Travels in Greece, 1650–1724' (*Transactions of the Royal Society of Literature*, new ser. xix, 1942); J. M. Osborn, 'Travel Literature and the Rise of Neo-Hellenism in England' (*BNYPL* lxvii, 1963). For contemporary impressions of Poland, see R. South (*infra*, VI). Travel in China is discussed incidentally in W. W. Appleton's *A Cycle of Cathay* (Columbia, 1951). For Africa there is G. A. Starr, 'Escape from Barbary' (*HLQ* xxix, 1965). For the early exploration and settlement of America the reader is referred to the full listing in Bush (V. 4). R. A. Malt has an interesting account of Lionel Wafer, an associate of Dampier's (*Journal of the History of Medicine* xiv, 1959).

For the traveller in England there was, if he could afford it, John Ogilby's *Britannia* (1675), which was followed by his *Book of Roads* in the same year. Among native English travellers exploring their own country was Celia Fiennes, whose account of her peregrinations was published in 1888 as *Through England on a Side-saddle in the Time of William and Mary*; ed. C. Morris (1949). She is mentioned, along with others, in Joan Parkes, *Travel in England in the Seventeenth Century* (1925), and in Esther Moir, *The Discovery of Britain: The English Tourists, 1540–1840*

(1964). A foreigner's impression of England and the English was given soon after the Restoration by Samuel de Sorbière in his *Relation d'un voyage en Angleterre* (trs. *A Voyage to England*, 1709). A more friendly foreigner was Guy Miege, a Swiss who settled in England, and produced (1691) *The New State of England*, which he kept up to date with later editions. A contemporary guidebook to London by a foreigner is F. Colsoni, *Le Guide de Londres* (1693; ed. W. H. Godfrey, 1951). Impressions of German visitors are discussed by W. Robson-Scott, *German Travellers in England 1400–1800* (1953).

For the student of literature and of the history of ideas there are: G. Atkinson, *Les Relations de voyages du 17ᵉ siècle et l'évolution des idées* (Paris, 1926); R. W. Frantz, *The English Traveller and the Movement of Ideas* (University of Nebraska Studies, 1932–3), a well-documented and informative study; G. B. Parkes, 'Travel as Education' (Jones *Festschrift, supra*, III. 1), which deals with the English traveller in Europe, and 'John Evelyn and the Art of Travel' (*HLQ* x, 1947). P. G. Adams, *Travelers and Travel Liars* (University of California, 1962) lies mostly beyond our period.

5. SOCIAL LIFE

This section includes some general sources, but since London features so prominently in the literature of the period the main entry is concerned with books and articles dealing with various aspects of London life.

The annual volumes of Edward Chamberlayne's *Angliae Notitiae* (from 1669), Guy Miege's *New State of England* (from 1691), and Narcissus Luttrell's *Brief Relation of State Affairs* (*supra*, V. 1) throw much light on contemporary circumstances and social hierarchies. Among collections of original texts are: Andrew Lang, *Social England Illustrated. A Collection of XVIIth Century Tracts* (1903), and R. B. Morgan, *Readings in English Social History from Contemporary Literature* (1922). The diaries of Pepys and Evelyn are of primary importance, as are some of the collections of correspondence listed under IV. 4. See also *The Portledge Papers*, ed. R. J. Kerr and I. C. Duncan (1928). D. Hartley and M. M. Elliott, *Life and Work of the People of England . . . The Seventeenth Century* (1928), has many contemporary illustrations.

Among general works of modern research and comment are:
H. D. Traill and J. S. Mann, *Social England* iv (6 vols., 1893–7;
rev. 1901–4); *The Victoria History of the Counties of England*
(1900 ff.); G. M. Trevelyan, *English Social History* (New York,
1942, 1944) and *Illustrated English Social History* ii (1949); Sir
A. Bryant, *The England of Charles II* (1934); M. Ashley, *Life in
Stuart England* (1964); P. Laslett, *The World We Have Lost*
(1965), which deals with the social structure of pre-industrial
England in the seventeenth and eighteenth centuries; E. A.
Wrigley, *An Introduction to English Historical Demography from the
16th to the 19th century* (1966); J. Mackinnon, *The Social and
Industrial History of Scotland . . . to the Union* (1920).

Among foreign travellers who recorded their (not always
perceptive) impressions of England and the English were:
Samuel de Sorbière (*supra*, V. 4), and François and Henri
Misson, *Mémoires et observations* (The Hague, 1698; trs. 1718
as *Memoirs and Observations in his Travels over England*). For
French travellers in England see G. Ascoli, *La Grande Bretagne
devant l'opinion française* (2 vols., Paris, 1930). Other accounts
include L. Magalotti, *Travels of Cosmo III, Grand Duke of Tuscany*
(1821), describing a visit of 1669, and the *Lettres sur les Anglais
et les Français* (1725; trs. 1726) of B. L. Muralt, a Swiss
visitor.

Some special studies are: W. C. Sydney, *Social Life in England
1660–1690* (1892); Gladys Scott Thomson, *Life in a Noble
Household 1641–1700* (1937) and *The Russells in Bloomsbury*
(1940); C. Hole, *English Home Life 1500–1800* (1947); G. E. and
K. R. Fussell, *The English Countryman, His Life and Work A.D.
1500–1900* (1955); G. E. Fussell, 'Agriculture from the Restora-
tion to Anne' (*Economic History Review* ix, 1938); Sir J. C.
Drummond and A. Wilbraham, *The Englishman's Food. A
History of Five Centuries of English Diet* (1939); M. and C. H. B.
Quennell, *History of Everyday Things in England* ii (3rd ed., 1937);
J. Strutt, *The Sports and Pastimes of the English People*, ed. J. C.
Cox (1903); J. Ashton, *A History of English Lotteries* (1893) and
A History of Gambling in England (1898); Charles Cotton, *The
Complete Gamester* (1674); T. Lucas, *Lives of the Gamesters* (1714;
ed. C. H. Hartmann, 1930); J. P. Hore, *The History of New-
market and the Annals of the Turf to the end of the Seventeenth Century*
(3 vols., 1886); Alexander Smith, *History of the Lives and Rob-
beries of the most Notorious Highwaymen* (1714; ed. A. L. Hayward,

1926); R. W. Forsythe, *A Noble Rake. The Life of Charles, Fourth Lord Mohun* (Harvard, 1928); M. Petherick, *Restoration Rogues* (1951), including Colonel Blood, Bedloe, Mrs. Cellier, Fitzharris, etc.; *State Trials; The London Sessions Papers* (i.e. *The Whole Proceedings of the King's Commission of Oyer and Terminer*, from *c*. 1690 onwards); G. V. Portus, *Caritas Anglicana, or an Historical Inquiry into these Religious etc. Societies that flourished in England, 1678–1740* (1912); W. K. Jordan, *Philanthropy in England* (1959); D. Owen, *English Philanthropy, 1660–1960* (1964); A. Lloyd, *Quaker Social History, 1669–1738* (1950); E. D. Bebb, *Nonconformity and Social and Economic Life 1660–1800* (1935); J. Marlowe, *The Puritan Tradition in English Life* (1956); D. Marshall, 'The Old Poor Law, 1662–1795' (*Economic History Review* viii, 1937); C. Roth, 'Charles II and the Jews' (*Contemporary Review* cxlvii, 1935); F. de P. Castells, *English Freemasonry in its Period of Transition, 1600–1700* (1931). W. Notestein, *History of Witchcraft in England from 1558 to 1718* (Washington, 1911). For further titles on witchcraft, see Bush.

Some works on the life of women in the period are: Alice Clark, *Working Life of Women in the Seventeenth Century* (1919); Myra Reynolds, *The Learned Lady in England 1650–1760* (Boston, 1920); D. Gardiner, *English Girlhood at School* (1929); G. E. and K. R. Fussell, *The English Countrywoman: A Farmhouse Social History A.D. 1500–1900* (1953); C. Hole, *The English Housewife in the Seventeenth Century* (1953).

Studies of the Court are represented by numerous biographies of Charles II's mistresses, such as M. Gilmour's account of Barbara Villiers, Duchess of Cleveland, *The Great Lady* (New York, 1941), and J. H. Wilson's *Nell Gwynn: Royal Mistress* (1952). A very different view is obtained from W. G. Hiscock's *John Evelyn and Mrs. Godolphin* (1951). Among works contemporary with the period, Anthony Hamilton's *Memoirs of the Count de Grammont* gives a picture which is probably substantially true.

For some idea of life as it was lived in a noble household see Gladys Scott Thomson, *supra*, and the following books on great houses of the period: A. S. Turberville, *A History of Welbeck Abbey and its Owners. Vol. 1: 1539–1755* (1938); F. Thompson, *A History of Chatsworth* (1949); W. Addison, *Audley End* (1953); Lord Leconfield, *Petworth Manor in the Seventeenth Century* (1954). For one aristocratic country sport see Guy Paget, *The History of the Althorp and Pytchley Hunt 1634–1920* (1937). For less exalted life there are E. Trotter, *Seventeenth Century Life in the Country Parish* (1919), and some of the studies in W. Notestein's *English Folk. A Book of Characters* (New York, 1938). A more general study is Sir George Sitwell's *Country Life in the Seventeenth Century* (1901). M. Barton, *Tunbridge Wells* (1937), deals with a favourite resort.

For the clothes that English people wore, two old standard works are F. W. Fairholt, *Costume in England*, ed. H. A. Dillon (2 vols., 1896), and J. R. Planché, *Cyclopaedia of Costume* (2 vols., 1876–9). More recent are: I. Brooke and J. Laver, *English Costume from the Fourteenth through the Nineteenth Century* (New York, 1937); E. S. de Beer, 'King Charles II's own Fashion: An Episode in Anglo-French Relations 1666–1670' (*Journal of the Warburg Institute* ii, 1938); C. W. and P. Cunnington, *Handbook of English Costume in the Seventeenth Century* (1954); I. Brooke, *Dress and Undress: The Restoration and Eighteenth Century* (1958).

For London life, lively contemporary descriptions will be found in Ned Ward' s*London Spy* (1698–1700; repr. 1924; ed. A. L. Hayward, 1927) and Tom Brown's *Amusements Serious and Comical* (1700; ed. A. L. Hayward, 1927). Miss E. Jeffries Davies' 'London and its Records' (*History*, October 1921 and January 1922) is the work of a leading authority on London history. The London Topographical Society has reproduced a number of old maps. See, too, G. E. Mitton, *Maps of Old London* (1908), and N. G. Brett-James, *Maps of Seventeenth-Century London* (1929). R. J. Mitchell and M. D. R. Leys have written *A History of London Life* (1958). For the growth and development of London there are N. G. Brett-James, *The Growth of Stuart London* (1935), and P. E. Jones and A. V. Judges, 'London Population in the Late Seventeenth Century' (*Economic History Review* vi, 1936). H. B. Wheatley and P. Cunningham, *London Past and Present* (3 vols., 1891) is an admirable historical guide.

Defoe's *Journal of the Plague Year* (1722), although a work of fiction, is substantially correct in its facts about the Great Plague of 1665. F. A. Edwards (*NQ* cliv, 1928) deals with some of the contemporary accounts. The fullest discussion is that of W. G. Bell, *The Great Plague in London in 1665* (1924; repr. 1944); but see also H. G. Wright (*ESEA* 1953) and C. F. Mullett, *The Bubonic Plague and England* (University of Kentucky, 1956). For the Great Fire there are: W. G. Bell,

The Story of London's Great Fire (1920; repr. 1944); J. E. N. Hearsey, *London and the Great Fire* (1965); J. Bedford, *London's Burning* (1966). For the aftermath of the Fire there are: T. F. Reddaway, *The Rebuilding of London after the Great Fire* (1940; rev. 1943); Jane Lang, *Rebuilding St. Paul's after the Great Fire* (1956); *The Fire Court*, ed. P. E. Jones, vol. i (1966), dealing with the claims made after the Fire; H. Priestley, *London: The Years of Change* (1966).

Some account of early coffee houses will be found in the following: E. F. Robinson, *The Early History of Coffee Houses in England* (1893); W. R. Dawson, 'The London Coffee-Houses and the Beginnings of Lloyds' (*Essays by Divers Hands* xi, 1932); B. Lillywhite, *London Coffee Houses* (1963); R. J. Allen, *The Clubs of Augustan London* (Harvard, 1937); C. Wright and C. E. Fayle, *A History of Lloyds* (1928).

There are a number of books on the Post Office and postal services: J. C. Hemmeon, *The History of the British Post Office* (Harvard, 1912); M. Ashley's biography of William III's postmaster-general, *John Wildman* (1946); H. Robinson, *The British Post Office. A History* (Princeton, 1948) and *Britain's Post Office* (New York, 1953); T. Todd, *William Dockwra . . . : the Story of the London Penny Post, 1680–82* (1952); F. Staff, *The Penny Post 1680–1918* (1964). See also F. B. Relton, *An Account of the Fire Insurance Companies, also of Charles Povey* (1893).

Some miscellaneous London items are: F. W. Fairholt, *Lord Mayor's Pageants* (2 vols., Percy Society, 1843–4); E. F. Rimbault, *Old Ballads illustrating the Great Frost of 1683–4* (Percy Society, 1844); H. Morley, *Memoirs of Bartholomew Fair* (1859); C. L. Kingsford, *Early History of Piccadilly and Leicester Square* (1925); A. M. Hind, *Wenceslaus Hollar and his Views of London and Windsor in the Seventeenth Century* (1922); J. G. Southworth, *Vauxhall Gardens* (Columbia, 1941); W. S. Scott, *Green Retreats: The Story of Vauxhall Gardens 1661–1859* (1955); H. St. G. Saunders, *Westminster Hall* (1951); J. C. Hardwick's account of the murder of Thomas Thynne in 1682, 'The Thynne Affair' (*Cambridge Journal* iv, 1950–1). For Pope-burning processions see Sheila Williams and O. W. Furley (*supra*, III. 4).

An interesting view of manners and morals in the late seventeenth century may be obtained from Josiah Woodward's *An Account of the Societies for the Reformation of Manners* (1699).

6. EDUCATION AND CULTURE

Among writers on education of the late seventeenth century John Locke (*infra*, VI) is the most influential. General surveys include J. W. Adamson's *Short History of Education* (1919); S. J. Curtis, *History of Education in Great Britain* (1948; 4th ed. 1957); W. H. G. Armytage, *Four Hundred Years of English Education* (1965). For educational theory there is S. S. Laurie, *Studies in the History of Educational Opinion from the Renaissance* (1903). Contemporary or near-contemporary works on education are listed in *CBEL*, and there is a useful short bibliography appended to Sir Charles Mallet's chapter on Education in *Johnson's England* ii (1933).

More specialized are J. W. Adamson, *Pioneers of Modern Education 1600–1700* (1905); F. Watson, *The Beginnings of the Teaching of Modern Subjects in England* (1909) and *English Grammar Schools to 1660* (1908); M. L. Clarke, *Classical Education in Britain 1500–1900* (1959). The Baconian influence is traced in detail in R. F. Jones, *Ancients and Moderns* (*supra*, V. 3).

The educational problems of Roman Catholics and Protestant Dissenters have produced a considerable literature. For the Catholics there is A. F. C. Beales, *Education under Penalty: English Catholic Education from the Reformation to the Fall of James II* (1964). For the Protestant sects: F. Watson in *The Gentleman's Magazine* (ccxci, 1901; ccxiii, 1902); H. McLachlan, *English Education under the Test Acts 1662–1820* (1931); C. E. Whiting (*supra*, V. 2); Luella M. Wright (*supra*, V. 2); S. J. Price, 'Dissenting Academies, 1662–1820' (*Baptist Quarterly* vi, 1933); L. W. Cowie, 'The Conflict of Political, Religious, and Social Ideas in English Education, 1660–1714' (*Bulletin of the Institute of Historical Research* xxii, 1949); J. W. Ashley Smith, *The Birth of Modern Education: The Contribution of the Dissenting Academies, 1660–1800* (1954).

For the universities, M. H. Curtis, *Oxford and Cambridge in Transition 1558–1642* (1959), although based on an earlier age, is relevant to our period. For Oxford University, Anthony Wood's *Life and Times* (Wood, *infra*, VI) is indispensable. Modern works include: Sir Charles Mallett, *History of the University of Oxford* ii (3 vols., 1924–7); *Victoria County History of Oxford, Vol. III: The University of Oxford*, ed. H. E. Salter and Mary D. Lobel (1954); J. Foster, *Alumni Oxonienses, 1500–1714*

(4 vols., 1891–2). For Cambridge there are J. B. Mullinger, *The University of Cambridge* (3 vols., 1873–1911), which goes to about 1670; J. A. Venn, *Alumni Cantabrigienses, Part I. From the Earliest Times to 1751* (4 vols., 1922–7). W. T. Costello, *Scholastic Curriculum at Early Seventeenth-Century Cambridge* (Harvard, 1958) throws light on our period, as does Phyllis Jones, 'Scientific Studies in the English Universities of the Seventeenth Century' (*JHI* x, 1949). Other titles for both universities will be found in Bush, and some histories of public schools in Mallett, *Johnson's England* (*supra*). There are histories of Glasgow University, by J. D. Mackie (1954); of Edinburgh University, by A. Bower (2 vols., 1817); of Trinity College, Dublin, by J. W. Stubbs (1889), W. M. Dixon (1902), C. Maxwell (1946), H. L. Murphy (1951). For courses and teaching at Trinity, see R. B. McDowell and D. A. Webb, *Hermathena* lxix (1947).

The border-line between educational treatises and courtesy literature is not easy to define. Among works in our period which fall into one or other of those categories are: Obadiah Walker, *Of Education especially of Young Gentlemen* (1673), and Jean Gailhard, *The Compleat Gentleman; or Directions for the Education of Youth* (1678). Bibliographies of courtesy books include G. E. Noyes, *Bibliography of Courtesy and Conduct Books in Seventeenth-Century England* (New Haven, 1937), and V. B. Heltzel, *Check List of Courtesy Books in the Newberry Library* (Chicago, 1942). The best study is J. E. Mason's *Gentlefolk in the Making* (University of Pennsylvania, 1935). Some other titles will be found in Bush.

For libraries there are: W. D. Macray, *Annals of the Bodleian Library Oxford* (2nd ed., 1890); C. Sayle, *Annals of Cambridge University Library* (1916); *The English Library before 1700*, ed. F. Wormald and C. E. Wright (1958); T. Kelly, *Early Public Libraries: A History of Public Libraries in Great Britain before 1850* (1966).

7. THE ARTS

Two wide-ranging books, B. S. Allen's *Tides in English Taste 1619–1800* (2 vols., Harvard, 1937), and E. F. Carritt's *Calendar of British Taste 1600–1800* (1948), which is for the most part a collection of contemporary pronouncements, give a good idea of the taste of the period. Painting, sculpture, architecture, furniture, etc., are covered by M. Whinney and O. Millar's volume in the *Oxford History of Art, English Art 1625–1714* (1957) and by *The Stuart Period, 1603–1714*, ed. R. Edwards and L. G. G. Ramsey (Connoisseur Period Guides, 1957).

For painting there is a 'Bibliography of Seventeenth-Century Writings on the Pictorial Arts in English' by H. V. S. Ogden (*Art Bulletin* xxix, 1947), and an analysis of 'Seventeenth Century Literature on Painting' by L. Salerno (*Journal of the Warburg and Courtauld Institutes* xiv, 1951). Two useful catalogues are Mrs. R. L. Poole's *Oxford Historical Portraits* (3 vols., 1912–25) and D. Piper's *Catalogue of Seventeenth-Century Portraits in the National Portrait Gallery 1625–1714* (1963). For critical and descriptive accounts of painting there are: C. H. C. Baker and W. G. Constable, *English Painting of the Sixteenth and Seventeenth Centuries* (Florence and New York, 1930); E. Waterhouse, *Painting in Britain 1530–1790* (*Pelican History of Art*, 1953); H. V. S. and M. S. Ogden, *English Taste in Landscape in the Seventeenth Century* (University of Michigan, 1955); E. Croft-Murray, *Decorative Painting in England. Vol. I: Early Tudor to Sir James Thornhill* (1962). The relationship between poetry and painting in the period is dealt with by J. H. Hagstrum (*supra*, III. 1). For the portrait painters there are: C. H. C. Baker, *Lely and the Stuart Portrait Painters* (2 vols., 1912) and *Lely and Kneller* (1922); R. B. Beckett, *Lely* (1951); Lord Killanin, *Sir Godfrey Kneller and his Times, 1646–1723: a Review of English Portraiture of the Period* (1948); G. Reynolds, *English Portait Miniatures* (1952).

In architecture Sir Christopher Wren stands alone. His plans and papers will be found in the 20 volumes published by the Wren Society. Among studies of Wren, large and small, are those of G. F. Webb (1937), Sir J. Summerson (1953), V. Furst (1956), E. Sekler (1956). H. M. Colvin has compiled *A Biographical Dictionary of English Architects 1660–1840* (1954). Among earlier studies of English architecture is Sir R. Blomfield's *History of Renaissance Architecture in England, 1500–1800* (2 vols., 1897). An excellent modern study is Sir J. Summerson's *Architecture in Britain, 1530–1830* (1953; 2nd ed. 1958). Among other works are: R. Dutton, *The Age of Wren* (1951); H. A. Tipping, *English Homes*, iv. ii (2nd ed., 1928); O. Hill and J. Cornforth, *English Country Houses: Caroline 1625–1685* (1966); K. Downes, *English Baroque Architecture* (1966); M. D. Whinney, *St. Paul's*

Cathedral (1947); G. Dobb and G. Webb, *The Old Churches of London* (1942); M. Whiffen, *Stuart and Georgian Churches . . . outside London* (1947).

For interior decoration, furniture, etc., there are the following: R. Dutton, *The English Interior 1500–1900* (1949); M. Jourdain, *English Interior Decoration, 1500–1800* (1950); P. Macquoid and R. Edwards, *Dictionary of English Furniture* (3 vols., 1924–7; rev. 1954); R. W. Symonds, *English Furniture from Charles II to George II* (1929) and *Furniture Making in Seventeenth and Eighteenth Century England* (1955); Sir Ambrose Heal, *The London Furniture Makers . . . 1660–1840* (1953). H. A. Tipping has written on *Grinling Gibbons and the Woodwork of his Age* (1914), and D. Green on *Grinling Gibbons: His Work as Carver and Statuary* (1964). R. W. Symonds deals with the great clock- and watch-maker of the period in *Thomas Tompion: His Life and Work* (1952).

Books on sculpture include: R. Gunnis, *Dictionary of British Sculptors 1660–1851* (1953); Mrs. K. A. Esdaile, *English Monumental Sculpture since the Renaissance* (1927) and *English Church Monuments 1510–1840* (1946); H. Faber, *Caius Gabriel Cibber* (1926); M. Whinney, *Sculpture in Britain 1530–1830* (Penguin, 1964).

For gardens there are: A. M. Cecil, *A History of Gardening in England* (2nd ed., 1896); Sir R. Blomfield, *The Formal Garden in England* (1892; repr. 1936); B. S. Allen (*supra*); D. Green, *Gardener to Queen Anne: Henry Wise (1653–1738) and the Formal Garden* (1956); Helen M. Fox, *André le Nôtre, Garden Architect to Kings* (1963).

For music there is a standard bibliography, *The British Union-Catalogue of Early Music Printed before the Year 1801*, ed. E. B. Schnapper (2 vols., 1957), and a standard work of reference, *Grove's Dictionary of Music and Musicians* (5th ed., ed. E. Blom, 9 vols., 1954). Histories of music include: C. H. Parry, *The Oxford History of Music, Vol. III* (2nd ed., rev. E. J. Dent, 1938), which deals with the seventeenth century; E. Walker, *A History of Music in England* (3rd ed., rev. Sir J. A. Westrup, 1952); E. Blom, *Music in England* (Pelican, 1942); E. H. Meyer, *English Chamber Music* (1951); E. D. Mackerness, *A Social History of English Music* (1964).

There are a number of studies of Henry Purcell, including those of A. K. Holland (1932), Sir J. A. Westrup (1937), I. Holst *et al.* (1959), R. E. Moore (*supra*, III. 4), F. B. Zimmerman (*supra*, III. 4). Zimmerman has also compiled *Henry Purcell, 1659–1695: An Analytical Catalogue of his Music* (1963). Roger North, who was one of the best-informed musical amateurs of the period, wrote *Memoirs of Musick*, ed. E. F. Rimbault (1846) and *The Musicall Gramarian*, ed. H. Andrews (1925). E. D. Mackerness, in 'A Speculative Dilettante' (*Music and Letters* xxxiv, 1953), discusses North's comments on Restoration music. Among other studies with a musical interest are: W. J. Lawrence, 'Foreign Singers and Musicians at the Court of Charles II' (*Musical Quarterly*, 1922); E. F. Hart, 'The Restoration Catch' (*Music and Letters* xxxiv, 1953); Claude M. Simpson, *The British Broadside Ballad and its Music* (Rutgers University, 1966).

I. K. Fletcher has written on 'The History of Ballet in England, 1660–1740' (*BNYPL* lxiii, 1959).

VI. INDIVIDUAL AUTHORS

Elias Ashmole, 1617–92

Ashmole's chief work, *The Institution, Laws and Ceremonies of the Order of the Garter*, was published in 1672 (2nd ed. 1693). His *Antiquities of Berkshire* (3 vols., 1719) was reprinted with a brief memoir (1723). His *Memoirs* (i.e. his Diary) first appeared in 1717; they were edited, along with William Lilly's autobiography, in 1774, and by R. T. Gunther (1927). He has now been given the treatment of a classic by C. H. Josten, *Elias Ashmole: his Autobiographical and Historical Notes, his Correspondence, and Other Contemporary Sources Relating to his Life and Work* (5 vols., 1966; vol. i, a biographical introduction).

Mary Astell, 1666–1731

Mary Astell was the author of *A Serious Proposal to the Ladies for the advancement of their true and great interest* (1694), which ran into four editions; *Letters concerning the Love of God, between the Author of the Proposal to the Ladies and Mr. John Norris* (1695); *Some Reflections upon Marriage* (1700); and *Bart'lemy Fair: Or, An Enquiry after Wit* (1709). She was formerly credited with *An Essay in Defence of the Female Sex* (1669), but this piece is now thought to be by Mrs. Judith Drake, or alternatively by

'H. Wyatt' (see Macdonald, *Dryden*). She is discussed by Myra Reynolds (*supra*, III. 1.), F. M. Smith, *Mary Astell* (New York, 1916), and Ada Wallis, *Before the Bluestockings* (1930). J. E. Norton has compiled a bibliography (*Book Collector* x, 1961).

JOHN AUBREY, 1626–97

The only work of Aubrey's to be published in his lifetime was his *Miscellanies* (1696), containing an account of natural and unnatural phenomena (repr. 1857, 1890). His biographical collections were first published in *Letters written by Eminent Persons*, vol. ii (1813); the standard edition is that of A. Clark, *Brief Lives* (2 vols., 1898). A slightly smaller collection, *Aubrey's Brief Lives*, has been edited from the manuscripts by O. L. Dick (1949; repr. University of Michigan, omitting some additional material). There is a useful selection by A. Powell, *Brief Lives and Other Selected Writings* (1949), and another by J. Collier, *The Scandal and Credulities of John Aubrey* (1931), which has an interesting introductory essay. Aubrey's archaeological and topographical collections were published as (1) *The Natural History and Antiquities of the County of Surrey*, continued and edited by R. Rawlinson (5 vols., 1719); (2) *The Natural History of Wiltshire*, ed. J. Britton (1867); (3) *Wiltshire. The Topographical Collections of John Aubrey*, corrected and enlarged by J. E. Jackson (1862). His *Remaines of Gentilism and Judaisme* were ed. J. Britten (1881).

There is an excellent biographical study by A. Powell, *John Aubrey and his Friends* (1948; rev. 1963). Some facts were preserved in J. Britton's *Memoirs of John Aubrey* (Wiltshire Topographical Society, 1845). Miscellaneous information is supplied by R. T. Gunther (*Bodleian Quarterly Record* vi, 1931), and some letters between Aubrey and Locke have been published by M. Cranston (*NQ* cxcv, 1950; cxcvii, 1952). There is an appreciation by G. M. Young, *Last Essays* (1950).

PHILIP AYRES, 1638–1712

Ayres produced several translations and books in prose, including *The Voyages and Adventures of Captain Barth. Sharp* (1684), and *The Revengeful Mistress* (1696: prose fiction). He is remembered for his *Emblemata Amatoria* (1683; see *The Library* i, 1910) and his *Lyric Poems* (1687), both reprinted, with a biographical and critical introduction, in Saintsbury, vol. ii.

Ayres is discussed as a translator by Sir H. Thomas (*The Emblemata Amatoria . . . . An Essay*, 1910, and *Revue Hispanique* xlviii, 1920), and by Mario Praz (*MLR* xx, 1925).

JOHN BANKS, *c*. 1650–*c*. 1700

There is no collected edition of the seven plays. *The Unhappy Favourite: or The Earl of Essex* has been edited by T. M. H. Blair (Columbia, 1939). Comment on Banks is surprisingly meagre. The fullest account is that by H. Hochuli, *John Banks: eine Studie* (Berne, 1952). An earlier study is that of F. S. Tupper, *John Banks: a Study in the origins of Pathetic Tragedy* (*Harvard Summaries of Theses*, 1937); and there are short discussions in Nicoll (*supra*, III. 4), A. Sherbo, *English Sentimental Drama* (Michigan State University, 1957), and in other histories of drama. An adaptation of *Anna Bullen*, by James Ralph (*c*. 1735), was identified and discussed by J. M. Bastian (*HLQ* xxv, 1962).

ROBERT BARCLAY, 1648–90

Barclay published *A Catechism and Confession of Faith* (1673; frequently reprinted), and his fifteen propositions relating to Quaker tenets, *Theses Theologiae* (1675). *An Apology for the True Christian Divinity* appeared in 1678, with a dedicatory letter to Charles II, and was reprinted several times before the end of the century. E. P. Mather's *Barclay in Brief* (Pendle Hill, Pa., 1941) is a condensation of the *Apology*, and J. P. Wragge has edited some selections in *The Faith of Barclay* (1948). There is a Life by A. Kippis in *Biographia Britannica*, and another by W. Armistead (1802). The best account is that of M. J. Cadbury, *Robert Barclay, his Life and Work* (1912). His thought is discussed in histories of the Friends, and by L. Eeg-Oloffson, *The Conception of the Inner Light in Robert Barclay's Theology* (Lund, 1954). *Reliquiae Barclaianae* (privately printed, 1870) preserves some letters.

ISAAC BARROW, 1630–77

Only one of Barrow's sermons, 'The Duty and Reward of Bounty to the Poor' (1671), was published in his lifetime. His *Sermons preached on Several Occasions* and *Several Sermons against Evil-Speaking* appeared in 1678, and *Of the Love of God and our Neighbour in Several Sermons* and *A Treatise of the Pope's Supremacy* in 1680. His *Works* were edited in 4 vols. by John Tillotson (1683–9), and reprinted in 1716, 1818, 1830. The standard edition is *The Theological Works*, ed. A. Napier (9 vols., 1859). Napier undertook to restore the text, when possible, from the Barrow MSS. in the library of Trinity College, Cambridge; but his adverse criticisms of Tillotson's text were exaggerated and largely unjustified (see I. Simon, *English Studies* xlv, 1964). The fullest account of Barrow is P. H. Osmond's *Isaac Barrow. His Life and Times* (1944). He is discussed in Fraser Mitchell (*supra*, V. 2), and in Irène Simons, *Three Restoration Divines* (*supra*, V. 2).

RICHARD BAXTER, 1615–91

Among the most popular of Baxter's numerous writings during his own lifetime were two pre-Restoration pieces, *The Saint's Everlasting Rest* (1650; ed. W. Young, 1907) and *A Call to the Unconverted* (1657). His memoir of his wife, *A Breviat of the Life of Margaret . . . Charlton*, was published in 1681 (ed. J. T. Wilkinson, 1928). His long account of his own life and controversies was published after his death by his friend Matthew Sylvester as *Reliquiae Baxterianae* (1696); an abridged edition was published by Edmund Calamy in 1702 (with some additions, 1713), and there is a modern abridgement by J. M. Lloyd Thomas (1925; Everyman, 1931). Among other works reprinted in modern times are: *Chapters from Baxter's Christian Directory*, ed. Jeanette Tawney (1925); *The Poor Husbandman's Advocate to rich racking Landlords* (1691; ed. F. J. Powicke, *Bulletin of the John Rylands Library* x, 1926); *The Reformed Pastor* (1656; ed. J. T. Wilkinson, 1939). R. B. Schlatter prints selections from Baxter's political writings, with a critical introduction, in *Richard Baxter and Puritan Politics* (Rutgers University, 1959).

Among modern biographical and critical studies are those of F. J. Powicke, *A Life of Richard Baxter* (1924) and *The Reverend Richard Baxter: under the Cross* (1927); I. Morgan, *The Nonconformity of Richard Baxter* (1946); H. Martin, *Puritanism and Richard Baxter* (1954); M. Bottrall (*supra*, IV. 5); G. R. Abernathy, 'Richard Baxter and the Cromwellian Church' (*HLQ* xxiv, 1961); G. F. Nuttall, *Richard Baxter* (1966). He is discussed in E. Dowden (*supra*, III. 1), M. L. Wiley (*supra*, III. 5), and W. C. de Pauley (*Church Quarterly Review* clxiv, 1963). There are bibliographies by A. B. Grosart (1868) and A. G. Matthews

(1933). T. Rogers has compiled *The Baxter Treatises: A Catalogue of the Richard Baxter Papers (Other than letters) in Dr. Williams's Library* ('Dr. Williams's Library Occasional Papers' viii, 1959); and G. F. Nuttall has published 'A Transcript of Baxter's Library Catalogue' (*Journal of Ecclesiastical History* ii, 1951).

APHRA BEHN, 1640–89

The Plays were collected in two volumes (1702, 1716), and in four volumes (1724). The Novels came out in a series of editions from 1698 onwards. *The Plays, Histories and Novels* were ed. R. H. Shepherd (6 vols., 1871), and *The Works* (virtually complete) were ed. M. Summers (6 vols., 1915). There is an edition of *The Rover*, ed. F. M. Link (Regents Drama series, University of Nebraska, 1967); *The Emperor of the Moon* is included in *Ten English Farces*, ed. L. Hughes and A. H. Scouten (University of Texas, 1948). There is a collection of the Novels (not including *Love Letters between a Nobleman and his Sister*, 1684) by E. A. Baker (1905).

Biographical and critical studies of varying quality have been written by V. Sackville-West (1927), G. Woodcock (1948), Emily Hahn (1951); but no full or satisfactory assessment of her work is available. The most reliable account of her life is that given by W. J. Cameron, *New Light on Aphra Behn* (University of Auckland, 1961). Critical studies have been mainly directed at her novel *Oronooko* (1688), which is discussed by (among others) E. Bernbaum (*Kittredge Anniversary Papers*, Boston, 1913), J. A. Ramsaran (*NQ* ccv, 1962), R. T. Sheffey (*SP* lix, 1962). There is an interesting discussion of *Love Letters between a Nobleman and his Sister* by R. A. Day (*supra*, IV. 3). The plays are discussed by Nicoll (*supra*, III. 4), and by other historians of the drama.

RICHARD BENTLEY, 1662–1742

Bentley's Boyle Lectures, *The Folly and Unreasonableness of Atheism*, were published in 1693. His 'Dissertation upon the Epistles of Phalaris' was contributed to the second edition (1697) of William Wotton's *Reflections upon Ancient and Modern Learning*. The Hon. Charles Boyle, whose edition Bentley had attacked, replied with *Dr. Bentley's Dissertations on the Epistles of Phalaris . . . Examin'd* (1698: mainly the work of Bishop Atterbury), and Bentley answered Boyle in 1699. An incomplete collection of Bentley's *Works* was made by A. Dyce (3 vols., 1836–8), and his *Correspondence* was ed. C. Wordsworth (2 vols., 1842). Some additional letters have been published by E. Hulshoff Pol (Leyden, 1959). The standard Life is still that of J. H. Monk (2 vols., 1833), but R. C. Jebb's shorter account of Bentley (1882) gives a good critical survey of his life and work. There is a biographical study in J. S. Fletcher, *Yorkshire Men of the Restoration* (1921). A more recent account is that of R. J. White, *Dr. Bentley: A Study in Academic Scarlet* (1965).

H. W. Garrod writes on the Phalaris controversy in the Grierson *Festschrift* (*supra*, III. 1), and C. J. Horne in *RES* xxii, 1946. Further discussions will be found in books on Sir William Temple (*infra*, VI), and in books dealing with the Quarrel between the Ancients and Moderns. Various aspects of Bentley's scholarship are treated in *The Bentley Commemorative Lectures* (*Proceedings of the Leeds Philosophical and Literary Society*, 1963), in works on classical scholarship, and by J. W. Mackail, *Bentley's Milton* (Warton Lecture, British Academy, 1924).

CHARLES BLOUNT, 1654–93

Blount published in 1673 a short pamphlet, *Mr. Dreyden Vindicated* (a defence of Dryden against Richard Leigh's attack in *The Censure of the Rota*, 1673), and in 1683 *Religio Laici* ('written in a Letter to John Dryden, Esq.'). His *Appeal from the Country to the City* (1679) went through several editions (repr. in *A Collection of State Tracts . . . in the Reign of King Charles II*, 1689). Blount's various deistical and other writings were collected by Charles Gildon as *The Miscellaneous Works* (1695). He is discussed in P. Harth, *Contexts of Dryden's Thought* (University of Chicago, 1968). The successful practical joke that Blount played in 1693 on Edmund Bohun, the Licenser of the Press, is described by Macaulay in his *History of England*, ch. xix. There is a bibliography by J. S. L. Gilmour (*Book Collector* vii, 1958).

SIR THOMAS POPE BLOUNT, 1649–97

The elder brother of Charles Blount, Sir Thomas employed his considerable leisure in compiling from various sources his *Censura celebriorum authorum* (1690), and *De Re Poetica; or Remarks upon Poetry* (1694), which contains 'characters and censures of the most considerable poets', including some who wrote in

English. Blount also published *Essays on Several Subjects* (1691); the third edition (1697) has some additional essays.

THE HON. ROBERT BOYLE, 1627–91

Boyle's writings on religious subjects began with *Seraphick Love* (1659), and came to an end with the posthumous publication of *A Free Discourse against Customary Swearing* (1695). Among the most important of his numerous scientific writings are: *New Experiments Physico-Mechanicall, Touching the Spring of the Air* (1660); *The Sceptical Chymist* (1661); and *Some Considerations touching the Usefulness of Experimental Natural Philosophy* (1663), in which he set forth his views on the modern scientific movement. His discursive *Occasional Reflections upon Several Subjects* (1665) is the work that Swift parodied in *A Meditation upon a Broom-Stick*. Boyle's early prose romance ('By a Person of Honour'), *The Martyrdom of Theodora and of Didymus*, was not published till 1687. The *Works* were collected by T. Birch (5 vols., 1744; 6 vols., 1772). Both editions have a Life. His scientific writings, 'abridged and methodized' by P. Shaw, were published as *Philosophical Works* (3 vols., 1725). His *Theological Works* were epitomized by R. Boulton (3 vols., 1745).

Birch's *Life* (*supra*) was published separately in 1744. There are modern biographies by F. Masson (1924), L. T. More (New York, 1944), and M. S. Fisher, *Robert Boyle. Devout Naturalist* (Philadelphia, 1945). R. Maddison has compiled 'A Summary of Former Accounts of the Life and Work of Robert Boyle' (*Annals of Science* xii, 1957), and 'A Tentative Index of the Correspondence' (*Notes and Records of the Royal Society* xiii, 1958).

Boyle's work as a scientist is discussed in histories of science (*supra*, V. 3), and from various points of view by the following: J. F. Fulton, 'Robert Boyle and his Influence on Thought in the Seventeenth Century' (*Isis* xviii, 1932); P. P. Wiener, 'The Experimental Philosophy of Robert Boyle' (*Philosophical Review* xli, 1932); C. T. Harrison, 'Bacon, Hobbes, Boyle, and the Ancient Atomists' (*Harvard Studies and Notes in Philology and Literature* xv, 1933); D. Krook, 'Two Baconians: Robert Boyle and Joseph Glanvill' (*HLQ* xviii, 1955); M. Boas, *Robert Boyle and Seventeenth Century Chemistry* (1958); T. R. Pilkington, *Robert Boyle, Father of Chemistry* (1959). The impact of Boyle on seventeenth-century thought is discussed by R. S. Westfall *(supra, V. 2)*; H. G. van Leeuwen *(supra, III. 5)*; H. Fisch *(Isis* xliv, 1953; M. H. Carré *(History Today* vii, 1957).

There is an admirable bibliography by J. F. Fulton *(OBS, 1932)*.

ALEXANDER BROME, 1620–66

Two books of Brome fall within the Restoration period: *Songs and Poems* (1661; 2nd ed. with a prose commendatory letter, 1664; 3rd ed. 1668); and *The Poems of Horace* (1666; 3rd ed. 1680), which Brome edited, and to which he contributed. Some light is thrown on the other contributors by H. F. Brooks *(NQ* clxxiv, 1938) and W. J. Cameron (ibid. ccii, 1957).

BUCKINGHAM, GEORGE VILLIERS, DUKE OF, 1628–87

The Rehearsal was published in 1672, and frequently reprinted. The edition of 1675 has 'amendments and large additions', either by Buckingham himself, or with the assistance of his collaborators, Samuel Butler and Martin Clifford. There are editions by E. Arber (1869); M. Summers (1914); A. G. Barnes (1927, with Sheridan's *Critic*); C. Gale (New York 1960); G. Falle, *Three Restoration Plays* (New York, 1964). A *Key* was published by S. Briscoe (1704). Buckingham was also responsible for a successful adaptation of Fletcher's comedy *The Chances* (1682), and he wrote *A Short Discourse upon the Reasonableness of Men's having a Religion* (1685). His *Works* were edited by Tom Brown (2 vols., 1704; several reprints). The best study of Buckingham is that of H. Chapman, *Great Villiers* (1949), but there is interesting biographical material in J. H. Wilson, *A Rake and his Times* (New York, 1954). *The Rehearsal* is discussed by D. F. Smith *(supra, III. 4)*, and V. C. Clinton Baddeley *(supra, III. 4)*. E. L. Avery writes on its popularity on the stage for the next hundred years *(Research Studies,* vii, State College of Washington, 1939).

JOHN BUNYAN, 1628–88

Bunyan's first book, *Some Gospel-truths Opened,* was published in 1656; his last, *Solomon's Temple Spiritualiz'd,* in 1688. Between those dates he wrote a large number of books and pamphlets, of which only a few can be mentioned here. *Grace Abounding* (1666) was subsequently enlarged; the standard edition is that of R. Sharrock (1962). *The Pilgrim's Progress, Part I,* appeared

in 1678 (Noel Douglas facsimile, 1928; New York Facsimile
Text Society, Columbia, 1934). The first complete text is that
of the 3rd edition (1679). *The Pilgrim's Progress, . . . The Second
Part* appeared in 1684. The standard edition for both parts is
that of J. B. Whary (1928; rev. R. Sharrock, 1960); the edition
by G. B. Harrison (New York, 1941) has Blake's 29 water-
colour paintings reproduced for the first time. *The Life and
Death of Mr. Badman* was published in 1680 (ed. B. Dobrée,
World's Classics, 1928; ed. G. B. Harrison, 1928), and *The
Holy War* in 1682 (ed. J. Brown, 1887). *A Relation of the Im-
prisonment of Mr. John Bunyan* was first published in 1765 (repr.
R. Sharrock with *Grace Abounding, supra*). All of these are in
the Cambridge Classics series (1905–7). *A Book for Boys and
Girls* (1686, in verse) was reproduced in a facsimile edition by
J. Brown (1890).

A collected edition of Bunyan's *Works* was planned by his
friends, E. Chandler and J. Wilson, but only one folio volume
appeared (1692). A nearly complete edition was published in
2 vols., folio (1736–7). Another edition, adding 'The Divine
Emblems and Several Other Pieces', with a preface by George
Whitefield, was published in 1767, and an Edinburgh edition
in 6 vols. (1784). The editions by G. Offor (3 vols., 1852 and
1878) are the most convenient for general use.

There is a memoir by Offor, but the fullest account of Bunyan
is that of John Brown, *John Bunyan: His Life, Times and Work*
(1885; rev. F. M. Harrison, 1928). A Life by Southey appeared
in his edition of *The Pilgrim's Progress* (1830), which elicited a
review by Macaulay (*Edinburgh Review*, Dec. 1830; repr. in
Macaulay's *Essays*). The volume in the 'Men of Letters' series
is by J. A. Froude (1880). Among later books on Bunyan,
usually treating both his life and writings, are the following:
J. Kelman, *The Road, a Study of John Bunyan's Pilgrim's Progress*
(2 vols., 1912); G. B. Harrison, *John Bunyan, a Study in Personality*
(1928); W. Y. Tindall, *John Bunyan, Mechanick Preacher* (New
York, 1934; repr. 1964); J. Lindsay, *John Bunyan, Maker of
Myths* (1937); M. P. Willocks, *Bunyan Calling* (1943); H. A.
Talon, *Bunyan; l'homme et l'œuvre* (Paris, 1948; trs. 1951); V.
Brittain, *In the Steps of John Bunyan* (1950; American title,
Valiant Pilgrim); R. Sharrock, *John Bunyan* (1954); M. E. Hard-
ing, *Journey into Self* (1958: a psychoanalytic analysis); O. E.
Winslow, *John Bunyan* (New York, 1961).

Bunyan is discussed by E. Dowden (*supra*, III. 1); J. W. Mackail, *The Pilgrim's Progress* (1924); R. Bridges (*Collected Essays* xvii, 1934); Sir Charles Firth (*supra*, III. 1); E. Honig, *Dark Conceit: the Making of Allegory* (Northwestern University, 1959); R. M. Frye, *God, Man, and Satan* (Princeton, 1960). Aspects of his work are dealt with by H. Golder (*MP* xxvii, 1929); R. Sharrock, 'Bunyan and the English Emblem Writers', (*RES* xxi, 1945), 'Spiritual Autobiography in *The Pilgrim's Progress* (ibid. xxiv, 1948), 'Personal Vision and Puritan Tradition in Bunyan' (*Hibbert Journal* lvi, 1957); B. Haferkamp, *Bunyan als Künstler* (Tübingen, 1963: on *The Pilgrim's Progress*); U. M. Kaufmann, *The Pilgrim's Progress and Traditions in Puritan Meditation* (Yale, 1966). Interesting biographical light is thrown on Bunyan by *The Narrative of the Persecution of Agnes Beaumont in 1674*, ed. G. B. Harrison (1929).

There is a *Bibliography* (1932) by F. M. Harrison, mainly confined to first editions.

GILBERT BURNET, 1643–1715

Burnet's first work was *A Discourse* (1665) on the memory of Sir Robert Fletcher, father of the more celebrated Andrew Fletcher of Saltoun. His *Memoires of the Lives and Actions of James and William Dukes of Hamilton* (1677) was reprinted in 1852. The first two volumes of his *History of the Reformation* (1679, 1681) were followed by a supplementary Third Part, together with a re-issue of Parts I and II (1715). There was an abridgement of the first two volumes in 1682, and of the complete work in 1718–19. The two pieces most often reprinted in Burnet's lifetime were *Some Passages of the Life and Death of John Earl of Rochester* (1680), and *Some Letters* (1686), addressed to the Hon. Robert Boyle and giving an account of his travels in Switzerland, Italy, etc. Burnet also wrote Lives of Sir Matthew Hale (1682) and of Bishop William Bedell (1685), and *An Essay on the Memory of the late Queen* [Mary] (1695). Among his other works are a translation of More's *Utopia*, with an interesting preface (1684), *A Discourse of the Pastoral Care* (1692), and *Thoughts on Education* (first published in 1761; ed. J. Clarke, 1900). The first volume of *Bishop Burnet's History of his own Time* (1724) was followed by vol. ii in 1734, with the author's life 'by the Editor', i.e. the Biship's second son, Thomas Burnet. Later editions include that of M. J. Routh (6 vols., 1823; repr. 1833), and O. Airy (2 vols., 1897–1900; based on Routh, and not going beyond the death of Charles II). *A Supplement to Burnet's History* by H. C. Foxcroft (1902), uniform with Airy's two volumes, gives early drafts and some other unpublished material.

The standard biography is that of T. E. S. Clarke and H. C. Foxcroft (1907), which has a bibliography of Burnet's writings. (See also W. Rees-Mogg, *The Library*, 5th ser. iv, 1949, and R. J. Dobell, ibid. v, 1950.) H. W. C. Davis writes on Burnet in *Typical English Churchmen*, ed. W. E. Collins (1902). There is a valuable essay by Sir Charles Firth on Burnet as a historian (Firth, *supra*, III. 1), and a sympathetic account by Sir G. N. Clark (*Aberdeen University Review*, 1957). Burnet is also discussed by G. P. Gooch in *Courts and Cabinets* (1944), and in various works of historiography. There is an unpublished thesis on Burnet as a man of letters by R. J. Madden in the University of London Library.

THOMAS BURNET, 1635?–1715

Burnet's *Sacra Theoria, Libri duo priores* appeared in 1681, and was followed by his own English translation, *The Theory of the Earth* (1684), which ran to several editions before 1700, and to more in the eighteenth century. A further instalment (*Libri duo posteriores*) was published in 1689, and the English translation appeared in 1690. In 1692 he brought out his *Archaeologiae Philosophicae*, dealing with the Creation; and between 1697 and 1699 he issued a series of *Remarks* on Locke's *Essay concerning Humane Understanding*. His *Theory of the Earth* came under attack from several quarters, and Burnet wrote a number of replies. There is a modern reprint of the *Theory*, with an essay by Basil Willey (1965). Burnet's work is discussed by E. L. Tuveson, V. Harris, H. Meyer, H. Macklem, M. H. Nicolson (all *supra*, III. 5), and by H. V. S. Ogden (*ELH* xiv, 1947). For his connection with the eighteenth-century doctrine of the moral sense, see E. L. Tuveson (*HLQ* xi, 1948). Elizabeth Haller has analyzed Burnet's prose style in *Die barocken Stilmerkmale in der englischen, lateinischen, und deutschen Fassung von Dr. Thomas Burnet's 'Theory of the Earth'* (Berne, 1959).

SAMUEL BUTLER, 1612–80

The Bibliography of *Hudibras* is extensive and complicated. *Hudibras. The First Part* (1663) went through many contemporary editions. *Hudibras*. *The Second Part* is dated 1664, although, like the first part, it was published at the end of the year before the date on the title-page. An edition of Part I and Part II, with some alterations in the text, presumably by Butler himself, appeared in 1674. *Hudibras*. *The Third and Last Part* was published in 1678. Among later editions, that of 1704 has a Life of Butler; that of 1710 is the first illustrated edition, and Hogarth's plates appear for the first time in the edition of 1726. They were re-engraved for Zachary Grey's edition (2 vols., 1744), which is valuable for its notes. *The Posthumous Works* (1715–17, 1732, and 1734) contain chiefly imitative and spurious pieces in verse and prose; but in 1759 R. Thyer brought out two volumes of *Genuine Remains in Verse and Prose*. R. B. Johnson's revision (1893) of the Aldine edition of the *Poetical Works* gives useful bibliographical information, and has a section on the early writers of Hudibrastic verse. *Hudibras* was reprinted (1905) by A. R. Waller in the Cambridge English Classics series. For the same series he edited *Characters and Passages from the Notebooks* (1908), and R. Lamar edited *Satires and Miscellaneous Poetry and Prose* (1928). These last two volumes contain matter which had hitherto remained in manuscript, but some of the attributions in Lamar must be accepted with reserve. The standard edition of *Hudibras* is now that of J. Wilders (1967). Apart from *Hudibras*, the only verse published by Butler himself is the pindaric ode *To the Memory of the Renowned Du-Vall* (1671; ed. A. C. Spence with two other Butler poems, *ARS*, 1961).

Information about Butler's life is scanty. Some facts are recorded in Aubrey, Wood, the Life in the 1704 edition of *Hudibras*, and T. R. Nash, *History of Worcestershire* (1781–2). Some additional light has been thrown on his life by R. Lamar (*Revue anglo-américaine* i, 1924, and *Études anglaises* i, 1952); R. Quintana, 'The Butler–Oxenden Correspondence' (*MLN* xlviii, 1933); E. S. De Beer (*RES* iv, 1928).

Appreciations and discussions of Butler will be found in John Dennis, *Miscellanies in Verse and Prose* (1693; *Critical Works*, ed. E. N. Hooker, vol. i, 1939); Johnson; Hazlitt, *English Comic Writers*; E. Dowden (*supra*, III. 1); W. McN. Dixon (*supra*, III. 3); H. Craig, *Manly Anniversary Studies* (University of Chicago, 1923); J. T. Curtis (*PMLA* xliv, 1929); .D. Gibson, Jr., *Seventeenth Century Studies* (*supra*, III. 1); R

Quintana (*ELH* xviii, 1951); E. D. Leyburn (*supra*, III. 3, and *HLQ* xvi, 1953); W. P. Ker (*supra*, III. 1); W. S. Miller (*HLQ* xxi, 1958); J. L. Thorson (*PBSA* lx, 1966). There is a monograph by J. Veldkamp (Hilversum, 1923). E. A. Richards gives a useful account of Butler and his imitators in *Hudibras in the Burlesque Tradition* (Columbia, 1937).

HENRY CARE, 1646?–88

Care's most important work was his anti-Catholic periodical, *The Weekly Pacquet, Or Advice from Rome*, which ran, with several changes of title, from 3 December 1678 to 13 July 1683. He also wrote *Poor Robin's Intelligence* (March 1676–November 1677), and may have written *The Weekly Pacquet of Advice from Germany* (September 1679–February 1680). In the reign of James II he changed sides and wrote the semi-official *Publick Occurrences Truely Stated*, from 21 February 1688 until his death in August of that year. He was then briefly succeeded by Elkanah Settle. Care's various translations and pamphlets are of no great account, but he is credited with two popular writing books, *The Female Secretary* (1671) and *The Tutor to True English* (1687).

SIR JOSIAH CHILD, 1630–99

A New Discourse of Trade . . . By Sir Josiah Child (1693) contains all Child's published writings, and is practically identical with his *Discourse about Trade* (1689). There is a bibliographical account by T. H. Bowyer (*Library*, 5th ser. xi, 1956). Child's life and work are discussed by W. Letwin, *Sir Josiah Child, Merchant Economist* (Kress Library Publication xiv, Cambridge, Mass., 1963), which has a bibliography, including works of doubtful authorship and works incorrectly attributed to Child.

CLARENDON, EDWARD HYDE, EARL OF, 1609–74

Speeches and political pamphlets by Clarendon were published from 1641 onwards. *A Collection of Several Tracts*, containing a number of his essays, appeared in 1727 (repr. as *Miscellaneous Works*, 1751). His *Brief View and Survey* of Hobbes's *Leviathan* (1676) is one of the more effective of the numerous replies to Hobbes. Clarendon's *History of the Rebellion and Civil Wars*, with some passages omitted, was first published at Oxford (3 vols., 1702–4), as was his autobiography, *The Life of Edward*

Earl of Clarendon (1759). The best edition of the *History of the Rebellion* is that of W. D. Macray (6 vols., 1888). There is a selection from the *History* and the *Life*, ed. G. Huehns (World's Classics, 1955), and forty of Clarendon's characters are included in D. Nichol Smith's *Characters of the Seventeenth Century* (1918).

For an understanding of the relative value of the different portions of the *History* and *Life*, see Sir Charles Firth (*supra*, III. 1), and L. von Ranke's *History of England in the Seventeenth Century* (vol. vi, 1875). In addition to the somewhat pedestrian biography by Sir Henry Craik (1911), there is a detailed study by B. H. G. Wormald, *Clarendon, 1640–1660* (1951); an excellent book by A. Bosher, *The Making of the Restoration Settlement* (1951), covers much of the same ground. L. C. Knights reflects on Clarendon's *History* (*Scrutiny* xv, 1948; repr. in *Further Explorations*, 1965), and A. L. Rowse on the *Life* in *The English Spirit* (1944). There is a lecture by H. R. Trevor-Roper on Clarendon as a historian in *Milton and Clarendon* (William Andrews Clark Memorial Library, Los Angeles, 1965). For some light on Clarendon's relations with Charles II, recourse may be had to *Notes which passed at meetings of the Privy Council between Charles II and the Earl of Clarendon* (Roxburghe Club, 1896).

WILLIAM CONGREVE, 1670–1729

The first of a series of editions of Congreve's *Works* was published by Jacob Tonson (3 vols., 1710). A. C. Ewald edited the plays for the Mermaid series in 1887. Twentieth-century editions include those of M. Summers (*Complete Works*, 4 vols., 1923); B. Dobrée (2 vols., 1925–8); F. W. Bateson (New York, 1930); H. J. Davis (University of Chicago, 1967). There is an edition of *Incognita* by H. F. B. Brett-Smith (1922), and one of *Incognita* and *The Way of the World* by A. N. Jeffares (1966). There are editions of *The Way of the World*, ed. K. M. Lynch, and of *Love for Love*, ed. E. L. Avery (1967), in the Regents Restoration Drama series (University of Nebraska).

Criticism of Congreve begins with Dryden's verses 'To my Dear Friend Mr. Congreve' (1694) and Jeremy Collier's *Short View* (1698). Among eighteenth-century discussions are those of 'Charles Wilson' in *Memoirs of the Life . . . of William Congreve, Esq.* (1730); Voltaire in *Lettres sur les Anglais* (1734); Colley Cibber in his *Apology* (1740); and Johnson in *Lives of the*

Poets (1781). Nineteenth-century criticism is found in Hazlitt, Lamb, Macaulay, and George Meredith (in the works cited *supra*, III. 4), and in twentieth-century works on Restoration comedy (*supra*, III. 4). There are studies by D. Schmid (Vienna, 1897), and D. Protopopesco (Paris, 1924). Among recent discussions are those of Paul and Miriam Mueschke, *A New View of Congreve's 'Way of the World'* (University of Michigan, 1958); C. Leech, 'Congreve and the Century's End' (*PQ* xli, 1962); J. Gagen, 'Congreve's Mirabel and the Ideal of the Gentleman' (*PMLA* lxxix, 1964); K. Muir in *Restoration Theatre* (*supra*, III. 4). E. B. Potter writes on 'The Paradox of Congreve's *Mourning Bride*' (*PMLA* lviii, 1943), and C. R. Lyons on *Love for Love* (*Criticism* vi, 1964).

Biographical and critical studies include those of E. Gosse (1888; rev. 1924); D. Crane Taylor (1931); J. C. Hodges, *William Congreve the Man* (New York, 1941), *The Library of William Congreve* (New York, 1955), *William Congreve, Letters and Documents* (1964); K. M. Lynch, *A Congreve Gallery* (Harvard, 1951); B. Dobrée British Council, (Writers and their Work, 1963). The stage history of the plays is traced by E. L. Avery, *Congreve's Plays on the Eighteenth-Century Stage* (New York, 1951).

CHARLES COTTON, 1630–87

Cotton contributed a poem on the death of Lord Hastings to *Lachrymae Musarum* (1649), and published *A Panegyrick to the King* (1660). His burlesques of the first and fourth books of Virgil's *Aeneid* appeared as *Scarronides* (1664–5), and were frequently reprinted. Along with *The Wonders of the Peak* (1681) and *The Planters Manual* (1675) they were included in his *Genuine Works* (1715), which reached several editions. His best poetry is in *Poems on Several Occasions* (1689), which (according to his son's preface to Cotton's translation of *Memoirs of the Sieur de Pontis*, 1694) was published without consulting 'Mr. Cotton's relatives'. This volume, rearranged and with some additional poems, was edited by J. Beresford (1923), and there is a full selection, ed. J. Buxton (Muses Library, 1958). Cotton's poems are also available in Chalmers. His best-known prose writings are Part II of Walton's *The Compleat Angler* (1676), and his translation of Montaigne's *Essays* (1685). *The Compleat Gamester* (1674) is included in C. H. Hartmann's *Games and Gamesters of the Restoration* (1930).

An account of Cotton by William Oldys was published by Sir John Hawkins in his edition of *The Compleat Angler* (1760), and there is another account by Sir N. H. Nicolas in his edition of the same work (1836). In addition to C. J. Sembower's *The Life and Poetry of Charles Cotton* (New York, 1911), there are discussions by J. Beresford (*London Mercury* v, 1921) and M.-S. Røstvig (*supra*, III. 3). G. G. P. Heywood has written on *Charles Cotton and his River* (1928). T. Westwood compiled a list of his writings (*NQ* xxxiii, 1866), and there is an unpublished bibliography by J. A. V. Chapple in the University of London Library.

Thomas Creech, 1659–1700

Creech gained a considerable reputation from his *Titus Lucretius Carus. The Epicurean Philosopher, His Six Books De Natura Rerum Done into English Verse* (1682). To the second edition of this translation (1683) complimentary verses were contributed by Evelyn, Otway, Mrs. Behn, and others, and a few more were added to a third edition in the same year. His later translations of Horace and Theocritus (1684) and of Manilius (1697) added little to his reputation. Creech supplied the Life of Cleomenes for Dryden's tragedy of that name. His suicide occasioned a good deal of literary comment; e.g. *Daphnis: Or a Pastoral Elegy* . . . (1700) and *A Step to Oxford: Or, A Mad Essay upon the Rev. Mr. Creech's Hanging himself (as 'tis said) for Love* (1700). His *Lucretius* is discussed by G. D. Hadzits and by W. B. Fleischmann (*supra*, IV. 6). L. C. Martin pointed out a resemblance in *The Rape of the Lock* to a passage in Creech's translation (*RES* xx, 1944).

John Crowne, d. 1703?

Crowne's plays (omitting *Andromache, The Misery of Civil-War*, and *Henry the Sixth*) were poorly edited by J. Maidment and W. H. Logan (4 vols., 1873–7). *Sir Courtly Nice*, included by M. Summers in *Restoration Comedies* (1920), has been edited by C. B. Hughes (The Hague, 1965); *City Politiques*, ed. J. H. Wilson (University of Nebraska, 1967) is in the Regents Restoration Drama series. *The Destruction of Jerusalem, Part II* is available in *Five Heroic Plays*, ed. B. Dobrée (World's Classics, 1960). Crowne's prose romance *Pandion and Amphigenia* has never been reprinted, nor have his two heroic poems, *Doenids* (1692:

based on Boileau's *Le Lutrin*) and *The History of the Love between a Parisian Lady and a Young Singing-Man* (1692). The only extended account of Crowne is that of A. F. White, *John Crowne, His Life and Dramatic Works* (Cleveland, 1922), but E. Boswell (*supra*, III. 4) deals at length with his court play *Calisto*. His plays are discussed by Sir A. W. Ward, A. Nicoll, and other historians of drama (*supra*, III. 4). W. M. Peterson writes on sentiment in *The Married Beau* (*NQ* cxcviii, 1953).

JOHN CUTTS, BARON CUTTS, 1661?–1707

Cutts published *La Muse de Cavalier, or, An Apology for such Gentlemen as make Poetry their Diversion* (1685), and a volume of *Poetical Exercises* (1687). He may be read in S. S. Swartley, *The Life and Poetry of John Cutts* (Philadelphia, 1917). Some of his correspondence is available in *Letters of John, Lord Cutts to Col. Joseph Dudley* (Cambridge, Mass., 1886).

WILLIAM DAMPIER, 1652–1715

Dampier published *A New Voyage round the World* (1697), and *Voyages and Descriptions* (1699). These, together with *A Voyage to New Holland* (1703), are available in the edition of J. Masefield (2 vols., 1906). *A New Voyage* was edited by Sir A. Gray (1927; repr. 1937), *Voyages and Descriptions*, by C. Wilkinson (1931), and *A Voyage to New Holland*, by J. A. Williamson (1939). The best biography is that of C. Wilkinson (1939). W. H. Bonner, *Captain William Dampier* (Stanford University, 1934) discusses, *inter alia*, Defoe's debt to Dampier's writings. Recent accounts include those of J. C. Shipman, *William Dampier, Seaman-Scientist* (University of Kansas, 1962), and C. Lloyd, *William Dampier* (1966).

SIR WILLIAM DAVENANT, 1606–68

Most of Davenant's work belongs to the pre-Restoration period. He welcomed Charles II back to England with *A Poem, upon his Sacred Majesties Return* (1660). Besides writing a number of comedies, *The Rivals* (1668), *The Man's the Master* (1669), and *The Play-House to be Lett* (1673), he adapted *Macbeth* (1674), and, with Dryden, *The Tempest* (1670). His *Works* were published in 1673; the plays are available in the edition of J. Maidment and W. H. Logan (5 vols., 1872–4).

Davenant was attacked by Flecknoe in *Sir William Davenant's Voyage to the Other World* (1688; ed. A. K. Croston, *Theatre*

Miscellany, 1953). There are two full length studies: A. Harbage, *Sir William Davenant, Poet Venturer* (University of Pennsylvania, 1935), and A. H. Nethercot, *Sir William Davenant, Poet Laureate and Playwright Manager* (University of Chicago, 1938).

There is a critical edition of the *Macbeth* by C. Spencer (Yale, 1961), and he also reprints the play in *Five Restoration Adaptations (supra,* II. 3). Discussions of Davenant's versions of *Macbeth* and *The Tempest* will be found in books dealing with adaptations of Shakespeare, by H. Spencer, M. Summers, A. Nicoll, and others *(supra,* III. 4), and in H. Spencer *(PMLA* xl, 1925).

DORSET, CHARLES SACKVILLE, EARL OF, 1638–1706

Dorset's verse was printed in various poetical miscellanies, but may be read most conveniently in *The Works of the Most Celebrated Minor Poets,* vol. i (1749), and in the collections of Johnson, Anderson, and Chalmers. There is a selection by V. de S. Pinto *(supra,* II. 2). Some account of Dorset was given by Matthew Prior in the dedication of his *Poems on Several Occasions* (1718), and by Johnson in his *Lives of the Poets.* There is a checklist of the poems by H. A. Bagley *(MLN* xlvii, 1932), with additions by R. G. Howarth (ibid. l, 1935). The standard critical work on Dorset is that by Brice Harris (University of Illinois, 1940).

JAMES DRAKE, 1667–1707

Drake published *The Ancient and Modern Stages Surveyed* (1699), and a comedy, *The Sham-lawyer* (1697). He wrote a twice-weekly periodical, *Mercurius Politicus* (June–December 1705), and he was one of the translators of St. Évremond's *Miscellaneous Essays* (2 vols., 1692–4). There is an account of him in *Biographia Britannica.* E. E. Williams writes on 'Dr. James Drake and the Restoration Theory of Comedy' *(RES* xv, 1939).

JOHN DRYDEN, 1631-1700

Dryden's first published poem, 'Upon the Death of Lord Hastings', was contributed to *Lachrymae Musarum* (1649). His stanzas on the death of Cromwell were published, with poems on the same subject by Sprat and Waller, in 1659; and *To His Sacred Majesty* in 1661. His most important poems are: *Annus*

Mirabilis (1667); *Absalom and Achitophel* (1681); *The Medal* (1682); *MacFlecknoe* (1682: an unauthorized edition); his contribution to *The Second Part of Absalom and Achitophel* (1682); *Religio Laici* (1682); *Threnodia Augustalis* (1685); *The Hind and the Panther* (1687); *Eleonora* (1692); *Alexander's Feast* (1697). Some shorter pieces were written to accompany the poems or prose writings of others; e.g. Sir Robert Howard's *Poems* (1660), Walter Charleton's *Chorea Gigantum* (1663), Oldham's *Remains* (1684), and Anne Killigrew's *Poems* (1686). His chief verse translations were *Juvenal and Persius* (1693; with others); *Virgil* (1697); *Fables Ancient and Modern* (1700: renderings of Chaucer, Boccaccio and others).

Dryden's early poems and plays were mostly published by Herringman, but in 1679 he began his long connection with Jacob Tonson. He gave Tonson advice about contributors, and himself contributed to various volumes of poetical miscellanies, such as *Ovid's Epistles* (1680). An important series began with *Miscellany Poems* (1684), and was continued with *Sylvae* (1685), *Examen Poeticum* (1693), and *The Annual Miscellany* (1694). Two further volumes were added in 1704 and 1709, and the first four were reprinted with changes. In 1716 a new edition with more changes (including the insertion of Milton's 'L'Allegro') was published. The different editions of the Dryden–Tonson miscellanies (1684–1716) reflect the changing taste of the years in which they appeared.

There was an attempt at a collected edition in 1701, when two volumes of plays, the *Virgil*, the *Fables*, and *Poems and Translations* (4 vols.) were given a general title-page. The first complete edition is that of Sir Walter Scott (18 vols., 1808, 1821). Scott's edition was revised, without much of value being added, by G. Saintsbury (18 vols., 1882–92). This is now being superseded by *The Works of John Dryden* (the 'California' Dryden), of which the first volume, ed. E. N. Hooker and H. T. Swedenberg, Jr., was published in 1956. One volume of the poems and two volumes of the plays have so far appeared.

POEMS. In England the standard edition of the poems was for long that of W. D. Christie (1871, etc.). The edition of J. Sargeaunt (1910) was marred by the editor's too frequently expressed conviction that all earlier editors had been either careless or foolish; it has been replaced by a judiciously edited and well-annotated edition by J. Kinsley (4 vols., 1958). The text of Kinsley's edition, including the *Fables* but excluding the *Virgil*, is available in one volume (1962), as is the *Virgil* (1961). The best American edition is that of G. R. Noyes (Harvard, 1909; rev. 1950), which contains the *Virgil* and some of the critical prefaces, and is excellently annotated. There are various modern selections of the poetry; e.g. C. L. Day, *The Songs of Dryden* (Harvard, 1932); L. I. Bredvold, *The Best of Dryden* (New York, 1933); B. Dobrée (Everyman, 1934); P. Legouis (with French prose translations, Paris, 1946); G. Grigson (1950); D. Grant (Penguin, 1955); J. Kinsley (1963); R. Sharrock (1963); and selections of the poetry and prose by D. Nichol Smith (1925), D. Grant (1952), and W. Frost (1953).

DRAMA. Dryden wrote by himself, or in collaboration, twenty-eight plays, some of which went into many editions. These were bound in volumes and sold in this form during his lifetime. Two folio volumes containing all his plays were published in 1701; and an edition, with a short account of Dryden by Congreve, at last saw the light in 1717 (6 vols.). Other editions followed in the eighteenth century. In the present century M. Summers edited *The Dramatic Works* (6 vols., 1931–2), with an inaccurate text but with full annotation. Selections include those of G. Saintsbury (Mermaid, 2 vols., 1904), and G. R. Noyes (Chicago, 1910), and there are a few editions of single plays.

Several of Dryden's numerous prologues and epilogues were written for special performances and were published separately. Many were first printed in miscellanies such as *Covent Garden Drolery* (1672), and in eighteenth-century collections of prologues and epilogues. A few are given in A. N. Wiley's *Rare Prologues and Epilogues* (1940), and there is a complete modern edition of them by W. H. Gardner (Columbia, 1951).

PROSE. Most of Dryden's prose will be found in E. Malone, *The Critical and Miscellaneous Prose Works of John Dryden* (4 vols., 1800). Editions or collections of prefaces and dedications include the following: *Essays of John Dryden*, ed. W. P. Ker (2 vols., 1900; repr. 1926); *Dramatic Essays*, ed. W. H. Hudson (Everyman, 1912); *'Of Dramatic Poesy' and other Critical Essays*, ed. G. Watson (Everyman, 2 vols., 1962); *Literary Criticism of John Dryden*, ed. A. C. Kirsch (University of Nebraska, 1966). D. D. Arundell printed the *Essay of Dramatic Poesy* and other pieces in the Dryden–Howard controversy in *Dryden and Howard* (1929), and there is a similar collection by J. T. Boulton (1964). The

Essay, the *Defence of an Essay*, and the *Preface to Fables* have been edited by J. L. Mahoney (Indianapolis, 1965). Among separate editions of *An Essay of Dramatic Poesy* that of D. Nichol Smith (1900, etc.) is excellently annotated. There is a useful compilation by J. M. Aden of *The Critical Opinions of John Dryden* (Vanderbilt University, 1963). The non-critical prose has attracted comparatively little attention in modern times, but G. Davies edited *His Majesties Declaration Defended* (*ARS*, 1950). Dryden's letters were printed in the first volume of Malone, and have since been edited, with additions, by C. E. Ward (Duke University, 1942).

Hugh Macdonald's *John Dryden, a Bibliography of Early Editions and of Drydeniana* (1939) is an essential work of reference. Some additions were made by J. M. Osborn (*MP*, 1941, 1942). S. H. Monk compiled a *List of Critical Studies, 1895–1948* (Minneapolis, 1950). See also W. R. Keast (*MP* xlviii, 1951), and P. Legouis (*Études anglaises* xvii, 1964). *A Concordance to the Poetical Works* has been compiled by G. Montgomery (University of California, 1957).

The source of most of our rather scanty knowledge of Dryden is Malone's Life in *The Prose Works*, vol. i. This was in effect rewritten in a more attractive form by Sir Walter Scott for his edition of *The Works*, vol. i (ed. B. Kreissman, University of Nebraska, 1963). Information has been added from time to time by R. Bell, W. D. Christie, Sir Charles Firth, and others, and notably by J. M. Osborn, *John Dryden: Some Biographical Facts and Problems* (Columbia, 1940; rev. University of Florida, 1963). C. E. Ward's *Life of John Dryden* (University of North Carolina, 1961) assembles all the known facts and adds some more. Among articles with a mainly biographical interest are: L. I. Bredvold, 'Dryden, Hobbes and the Royal Society' (*MP* xxv, 1928); H. Macdonald, 'The Attacks on Dryden' (*ESEA* xxi, 1936); J. H. Wilson, 'Rochester, Dryden and the Rose-Street Affair' (*RES* xv, 1939); R. J. Smith, 'Shadwell's Impact upon Dryden' (ibid. xx, 1944); R. G. Ham, 'Dryden as Historiographer Royal' (*PMLA* l, 1935); J. H. Smith, 'Some Sources of Dryden's Toryism, 1682–1684' (*HLQ* xx, 1957); V. de S. Pinto, 'Dryden and Rochester' (*Renaissance and Modern Studies* v, 1961).

Criticism of Dryden is now very extensive. Among early general discussions are those of Johnson; Hazlitt, *Lectures on the English Poets* (1818); Macaulay (*Edinburgh Review* xlvii, 1828);

J. R. Lowell, *Among my Books* (1870); G. Saintsbury, *Dryden* ('Men of Letters', 1881). Discussions in the present century include those of A. W. Verrall, *Lectures on Dryden* (1914); M. van Doren, *The Poetry of John Dryden* (1920; rev. 1931; Indiana University, 1960); Sir Walter Raleigh (*supra*, III. 1); T. S. Eliot, *Homage to John Dryden* (1924) and *John Dryden: The Poet, the Dramatist, the Critic* (New York, 1932); B. Dobrée (*supra*, III. 4), *Variety of Ways* (1932) and *John Dryden* (British Council pamphlet, 1956); L. I. Bredvold, *The Intellectual Milieu of John Dryden* (University of Michigan, 1934); Sir Herbert Grierson (*supra*, III. 1); D. Nichol Smith, *John Dryden* (1950); A. M. Crinò, *John Dryden* (Florence, 1957) and *Dryden. Poeta satirico* (Florence, 1958); J. Sutherland, *John Dryden: The Poet as Orator* (1962); A. W. Hoffman, *John Dryden's Imagery* (University of Florida, 1962); W. Amarsinghe, *Dryden and Pope in the Early Nineteenth Century. A Study of Changing Literary Taste, 1800–1830* (1962); A. Roper, *Dryden's Poetic Kingdoms* (1965); E. Miner, *Dryden's Poetry* (Indiana University, 1967); K. G. Hamilton, *John Dryden and the Poetry of Statement* (University of Queensland, 1967); P. Harth, *Contexts of Dryden's Thought* (University of Chicago, 1968). Shorter discussions will be found in: P. Legouis (*Revue anglo-américaine* ix, 1932); B. Dobrée (*ELH* iii, 1936); J. Bronowski, *The Poet's Defence* (1939); C. S. Lewis, *Rehabilitations* (1939); R. L. Sharp (*supra*, III. 3); G. Williamson (*supra*, III. 1); E. Morgan (*Cambridge Journal*, 1953); J. Kinsley (*English Studies* xxiv, 1953); D. W. Jefferson, 'Aspects of Dryden's Imagery' (*Essays in Criticism* iv, 1954); L. Feder (*PMLA* lxix, 1954); R. A. Brower (A. D. McKillop *Festschrift, supra*, III. 1); McD. Emslie (*EC* xi, 1961); E. Miner (*PQ* xl, 1961; *SEL* ii, 1962); M. Price, *To the Palace of Wisdom* (New York, 1964). Some of the above essays are reprinted in two useful collections: *Dryden. Twentieth-Century Views*, ed. B. N. Schilling (Englewood Cliffs, N. J., 1963), and *Essential Articles for the Study of John Dryden*, ed. H. T. Swedenberg, Jr. (New York, 1966).

DISCUSSIONS OF INDIVIDUAL POEMS. 'Upon the Death of Lord Hastings': R. Wallerstein, *Studies in Seventeenth-Century Poetic* (University of Wisconsin, 1961). 'Epistle to Dr. Charleton': E. R. Wasserman, *The Subtler Language* (Johns Hopkins, 1959); S. A. Golden (*Explicator* xxiv, 1965). *Annus Mirabilis*: E. N. Hooker (*HLQ* x, 1946); B. A. Rosenberg (*PMLA* lxxix, 1964).

Absalom and Achitophel: R. F. Jones (*MLN* xlvi, 1931); E. S. de Beer (*RES* xvii, 1941; new ser. vii, 1956); R. Wallerstein (*HLQ* vi, 1943); G. Davies (ibid. x, 1946); J. Kinsley (*RES*, new ser. vi, 1955); I. Jack (*supra*, III. 3); C. H. Cable (J. Wilcox *Festschrift*, *supra*, III. 1); B. N. Schilling, *Dryden and the Conservative Myth* (Yale, 1961). *MacFlecknoe*: G. Thorn-Drury (*MLR* xiii, 1918); D. McKeithan (*PMLA* xlvii, 1932); H. F. Brooks (*RES* xi, 1935); R. J. Smith (*RES* xviii, 1942; xx, 1944); V. A. Dearing (*Studies in Bibliography*, 1954); G. B. Evans (*Harvard Library Bulletin* vi, 1953); I. Jack (*supra*, III. 3); T. H. Towers (*SEL* iii, 1963); G. McFadden (*PQ* xliii, 1964). *The Medal*: W. O. S. Sutherland (*Studies in English*, University of Texas, xxxv, 1955). *Religio Laici*: L. I. Bredvold (*supra*); E. N. Hooker (*ELH* xxiv, 1957); E. J. Chiasson (*Harvard Theological Review* liv, 1961); T. H. Fujimura (*PMLA* lxxvi, 1961); D. R. Brown (*MLR* lvi, 1961); V. M. Hamm (*PMLA* lxxx, 1965); J. W. Corder (ibid. lxxxii, 1967). 'To . . . Mrs. Anne Killigrew': R. Wallerstein (*SP* xliv, 1947); E. M. W. Tillyard, *Five Poems, 1470–1870* (1948); A. D. Hope (*Southern Review* [Adelaide], 1963); D. M. Veith (*SP* lxii, 1965). *The Hind and the Panther*: J. Kinsley (*RES*, new ser. iv, 1953); C. H. Miller (*JEGP* lxi, 1962); D. R. Benson (*SEL* iv, 1964); E. Miner (*supra*, and *BNYPL* lxix, 1965); P. Harth (*supra*). 'Epistle to Dr. Charleton': E. Wasserman (*JEGP* lv, 1956). 'Song for St. Cecilia's Day': J. A. Levine (*PQ* xliv, 1965). 'Epistle to . . . John Driden': J. A. Levine (*JEGP* lxii, 1964). The *Fables*: H. G. Wright (*RES* xxi, 1945, and *Boccaccio in England*, 1957); E. Miner (S. H. Monk *Festschrift*, *supra*, III. 1).

Dryden's translations are discussed in the following books and papers: J. M. Bottkol, 'Dryden's Latin Scholarship' (*MP* xl, 1943); H. M. Hooker, 'Dryden's Georgics' (*HLQ* ix, 1946); W. Frost, *Dryden and the Art of Translation* (Yale, 1953); L. Proudfoot, *Dryden's 'Aeneid' and its Seventeenth-Century Predecessors* (1960); M. B. Fleischmann (*supra*, IV. 6); R. A. Brower (*PQ* xviii, 1939; *PMLA* lv, 1940; and Ch. I. of his *Alexander Pope: the Poetry of Allusion*, 1959).

Among general discussions of Dryden's plays are: M. E. Hartsock, 'Dryden's Plays: a Study in Ideas' (*Seventeenth Century Studies, Second Series*, *supra*, III. 1); J. A. Winterbottom, 'The Place of Hobbesian Ideas in Dryden's Tragedies' (*JEGP* lvii, 1958).

HEROIC PLAYS AND TRAGEDIES. B. J. Pendlebury, *Dryden's Heroic Plays: a Study of the Origins* (1923); C. V. Deane (*supra*, III. 4); D. W. Jefferson, 'The Significance of Dryden's Heroic Plays' (*Proceedings of the Leeds Philosophical Society*, 1940); T. W. Russell, *Voltaire, Dryden, and Heroic Tragedy* (New York, 1946); M. E. Prior, *The Language of Tragedy* (New York, 1947); J. A. Winterbottom, 'The Development of the Hero in Dryden's Tragedies' (*JEGP* lii, 1953); W. Bleuler, *Das Heroische Drama John Drydens als Experiment dekorativer Formkunst* (Berne, 1958); S. C. Osborn, 'Heroical Love in Dryden's Heroic Drama' (*PMLA* lxxiii, 1958); T. H. Fujimura, 'The Appeal of Dryden's Heroic Plays' (ibid. lxxv, 1960); E. M. Waith, *The Herculean Hero in Marlowe, Shakespeare and Dryden* (1962); J. Gagen, 'Love and Honour in Dryden's Heroic Plays' (*PMLA* lxxvii, 1962); A. C. Kirsch, *Dryden's Heroic Drama* (Princeton, 1965), and 'Dryden, Corneille, and the Heroic Play' (*MP* lix, 1962); S. Zebouni, *Dryden: A Study in Heroic Characterization* (Louisiana State University, 1965); B. King, *Dryden's Major Plays* (1966). Some other relevant works will be found *supra*, III. 4. J. R. Moore has written on 'Political Allusions in Dryden's Later Plays' (*PMLA* lxxiii, 1958).

Among studies of the comedy are: N. B. Allen, *The Sources of John Dryden's Comedies* (University of Michigan, 1935), and F. H. Moore, *The Nobler Pleasure: Dryden's Comedy in Theory and Practice* (University of North Carolina, 1963). Other relevant studies will be found *supra*. III. 4,

DISCUSSIONS OF INDIVIDUAL PLAYS. *Sir Martin Mar-All*: F. H. Moore (MacMillan *Festschrift*, *supra*, III. 1). *The Indian Emperor*: D. MacMillan (*HLQ* xiii, 1950); M. W. Alssid (*SP* lix, 1962); J. Loftis (*PQ* xlv, 1966). *Tyrannic Love*: B. King (*RES*, new ser. xvi, 1965). *Aureng-Zebe*: A. C. Kirsch (*ELH* xxix, 1962); M. W. Alssid (*JEGP* lxiv, 1965). *Marriage-à-la-Mode*: B. King (*Drama Survey* iv, 1965). *The Spanish Friar*: P. Legouis (*Revue de la littérature comparée* xi, 1931); L. I. Bredvold (*University of Michigan Studies* viii, 1932). *All for Love*: F. R. Leavis (*Scrutiny* v, 1936); K. Muir (*Proceedings of the Leeds Philosophical Society*, 1940); R. Wallerstein (*RES* xix, 1943); O. Reinert (*The Hidden Sense*, ed. M.-S. Røstvig, Oslo, 1963). *The State of Innocence*: P. S. Havens (*Parrott Presentation Volume*, ed. H. Craig, Princeton, 1935); G. McFadden (*HLQ* xxiv, 1961); B. King (*SEL* iv, 1964). *Don Sebastian*: B. King (*Sewanee Review* lxx, 1962).

Amphitryon: A. L. Bondurant (*Sewanee Review* xxxiii, 1925). *The Secular Masque*: A. Roper (*MLQ* xxiii, 1962).

There are a few studies of Dryden as a prose writer; e.g. J. Söderlind, *Verb Syntax in John Dryden's Prose* (Uppsala, 1951, 1958); D. D. Brown, 'Dryden and Tillotson' (*RES*, new ser. xii, 1961); I. Simon, 'Dryden's Revision of the *Essay of Dramatic Poesy*' (*RES*, new ser. xiv, 1963) and 'Dryden's Prose Style' (*Revue des langues vivantes* xxi, 1965); J. M. Bately (*RES*, new ser. xv, 1964).

Some general studies of the criticism are: P. H. Frye, *Dryden and the Critical Canons of the Eighteenth Century* (University of Nebraska, 1907); J. H. Smith, 'Dryden's Critical Temper' (*Washington University Studies* xii, 1925); P. Legouis, 'Corneille and Dryden as Dramatic Critics' (Grierson *Festschrift*, *supra*, III. 1); H. Trowbridge, 'The Place of the Rules in Dryden's Criticism' (*MP* xliv, 1946); F. L. Huntley, 'Dryden's Discovery of Boileau' (ibid. xlv, 1947); J. M. Aden, 'Dryden and Boileau: the Question of Critical Influence' (*SP* l, 1953); G. G. Falle, 'Dryden: Professional Man of Letters' (*UTQ* xxvi, 1957); Max Nänny, *John Drydens rhetorische Poetik* (Berne, 1959); I. Lowens, 'St. Évremond, Dryden, and the Theory of Opera' (*Criticism* i, 1959); B. M. H. Strang, 'Dryden's Innovations in Critical Vocabulary' (*Durham University Journal* li, 1959).

DISCUSSIONS OF SEPARATE CRITICAL PIECES. *An Essay of Dramatic Poesy*: F. L. Huntley, *On Dryden's Essay of Dramatic Poesy* (University of Michigan, 1944); G. Williamson (*MP* xliv, 1946); D. T. Mace (*Journal of the Warburg and Courtauld Institutes* xxv, 1962). 'The Dramatic Poetry of the Last Age': H. Trowbridge (*PQ* xxii, 1943). The Preface to *Troilus and Cressida*: F. L. Huntley, *The Unity of Dryden's Dramatic Criticism* (Chicago, 1944). 'Heads of an Answer to Rymer': F. G. Walcott (*PQ* xv, 1936); G. Watson (*RES*, new ser. xiv, 1963).

RICHARD DUKE, 1658–1711

Duke contributed to two of Dryden's poetical undertakings, viz. *Ovid's Epistles* (1680) and *The Satires of Juvenal* (1693), and wrote satires on Titus Oates and William Bedloe (1680). A good deal of his verse was published in *Poems by the Earl of Roscommon . . . Together with Poems by Mr. Richard Duke* (1717). His collected verse is in Johnson, Anderson, and Chalmers. Duke's sermons are praised in Henry Felton's *Dissertation on Reading the Classics* (1713). The chief authority for his life is Johnson.

JOHN DUNTON, 1659–1733

Dunton's chief contributions to the literature of the late seventeenth century are: *The Athenian Gazette* (continued from No. 2 as *The Athenian Mercury*, 17 March 1690–14 June 1697); his autobiographical *A Voyage round the World* (3 vols., 1691); and *The Ladies Dictionary* (1694; see G. E. Noyes, *PQ* xxi, 1942). It is not always easy to distinguish between what Dunton wrote himself and what he only published. C. A. Moore's 'John Dunton: Pietist and Impostor' (*SP* xxii, 1925; repr. in Moore, *supra*, III. 1) gives a good account of Dunton as a publisher of religious books and pamphlets. Other information about his activities is provided by R. P. McCutcheon, 'John Dunton's Connection with Book-reviewing' (*SP* xxv, 1928); B.-M. Stearns, 'The first English Periodical for Women' (*MP* xxviii, 1930); A. C. Howell (*SP* xxix, 1932); G. D. Meyer, *The Scientific Lady in England 1650–1760* (University of California, 1955); P. M. Hill, *Two Augustan Booksellers: John Dunton and Edmund Curll* (University of Texas, 1958).

THOMAS DURFEY, 1653–1723

There is no collected edition of Durfey's numerous plays. The three parts of *The Comical History of Don Quixote* (1694–6) were reprinted in 1889; *A Fool's Preferment, Or, The Three Dukes of Dunstable* (1688) in 1917; and *Wonders in the Sun*, ed. W. A. Appleton (*ARS*, 1964). Durfey's preface to *The Campaigners* (1698) was reprinted, with an introduction by J. W. Krutch (*ARS*, 1964). Durfey's songs appeared in a series of collections between 1683 and 1720, culminating in *Wit and Mirth: Or Pills to Purge Melancholy* (6 vols., 1719–20; repr. 1876; ed. C. L. Day, 3 vols., New York, 1959). C. L. Day has edited a selection, *The Songs of Thomas D'Urfey* (Harvard, 1934). Durfey also wrote a number of burlesque, satirical, and panegyrical poems; e.g. *The Progress of Honesty* (1681), *Collin's Walk Through London And Westminster* (1690); *The Weesils* (1691).

The fullest account of his dramatic work is R. Forsythe's *A Study of the Plays of Thomas D'Urfey* (2 vols., Cleveland, 1916–17). K. M. Lynch discusses his contribution to sentimental comedy (*PQ* ix, 1930).

JOHN EACHARD, 1636?–97

The Grounds and Occasions of the Contempt of the Clergy (1670) ran through no fewer than ten editions in Eachard's lifetime; it provoked several answers, to which Eachard replied in 1671. His bantering attack on Hobbes, *Mr. Hobbs's State of Nature Considered* (1672; ed. P. Ure, 1958), was followed in 1673 by *Some Opinions of Mr. Hobbs Considered in a Second Dialogue.* There is a partial reprint of *The Grounds and Occasions* in E. Arber, *An English Garner*, vol. vii (1883). There were several collections of the *Works*, the latest in 3 vols. (1774). R. C. Elliott discusses similarities in style and tone between Eachard and Swift (*PMLA* lxix, 1954), and H. Macdonald writes on his bantering style (*ESEA*, 1947).

THOMAS ELLWOOD, 1639–1713

The History of the Life of Thomas Ellwood . . . Written by his own hand (1714) covers the years from his birth to 1683, but includes a supplement by Joseph Wyeth. The autobiography was frequently reprinted in the eighteenth century, and was edited by C. G. Crump (1900), and by S. Graveson (1906). His *Davideis. The Life of David King of Israel. A Sacred Poem, in Five Books* (1712) had several eighteenth-century reprints. Ellwood edited his friend George Fox's *Journals* (1690), and from 1660 onwards he wrote a series of pamphlets, many of them with picturesque titles. Comment includes B. S. Snell, *Ellwood, Friend of Milton* (1950), and J. M. Patrick, 'The Influence of Thomas Ellwood upon Milton's Epics' (*Essays in History and Literature Presented . . . to Stanley Pargellis*, Chicago, 1965).

EPHELIA

Female Poems on Several Occasions by this unidentified poetess appeared in 1679. Another edition, consisting of the sheets of 1679 with extra leaves containing poems by Rochester and others, was published in 1682. Edmund Gosse's suggestion (*Seventeenth-Century Studies*, 1883) that 'Ephelia' was the daughter of Katherine Philips has no evidence to support it.

SIR GEORGE ETHEREGE, 1634?–91

There were four editions of Etherege's *Works* between 1704 and 1735. The first scholarly edition is that of A. W. Verity (1888). The standard edition of the three comedies is that of

H. F. B. Brett-Smith (2 vols., 1927); a third volume for the poems and letters was projected, but never completed. *The Man of Mode* has been edited by W. B. Carnochan (Regents Restoration Drama, 1966). The standard edition of the verse is *The Poems of Sir George Etherege*, ed. J. Thorpe (Princeton, 1963); and there is a selection in V. de S. Pinto (*supra*, II. 2). *The Letterbook of Sir George Etherege* was edited by S. Rosenfeld (1928); see also her articles, 'Sir George Etherege in Ratisbon' (*RES* x, 1934), and 'The Second Letterbook' (ibid., new ser. iii, 1952).

Effective criticism begins with John Dennis, 'A Defence of Sir Fopling Flutter' (*Critical Works*, ed. E. N. Hooker, vol. ii, 1943). Since Etherege was not one of the four comic dramatists revived by Leigh Hunt in 1849, there is little nineteenth-century comment, and E. Gosse virtually rediscovered him in his *Seventeenth-Century Studies* (1883). V. Meindl followed with a monograph (Vienna, 1901). Etherege has more recently had full justice done him by J. Palmer, B. Dobrée, and others (*supra*, III. 4), and most notably by Dale Underwood, *Etherege and the Seventeenth-Century Comedy of Manners* (Yale, 1957), N. Holland, *The First Modern Comedies* (Harvard, 1959), and J. Powell in *Restoration Theatre* (*supra*, III. 4).

Biographical studies include one by B. Dobrée, in *Essays in Biography* (1925). Dorothy Foster contributes biographical information (*NQ* cliii, 1927; cliv, 1928; *RES* viii, 1932); E. Boswell (Ibid. vii, 1931). T. H. Fujimura has thrown light on 'Etherege at Constantinople' (*PMLA* lxii, 1956).

JOHN EVELYN, 1620–1706

Evelyn published a number of pamphlets, including *A Character of England* (1659; repr. in *Somers Tracts* vii, 1812, and *Harleian Miscellany* x, 1813); *Fumifugium* (1661; ed. R. T. Gunther, 1930; repr., with an introduction by Rose Macaulay, 1933); *A Panegyric to Charles the Second* (1661; ed. Sir Geoffrey Keynes, together with *An Apology for the Royal Party* (1659), for *ARS*, 1951); *Tyrannus or the Mode* (1661; ed. J. L. Nevinson, Luttrell Society, 1951). Evelyn's *magnum opus*, *Sylva*, was first published in 1664 (frequently reprinted, with various additions, during Evelyn's lifetime). His *Numismata. A Discourse of Medals, Antient and Modern* appeared in 1697. He produced several translations, including one of Lucretius, Book I, and two of French gardening books. Among posthumous publications are *The Life of Mrs. Godolphin*, first published by S. Wilberforce (1847), and frequently reprinted; the edition by H. Sampson (1939) gives the text in the Rosenbach manuscript. The text of *Londinium Redivivum* was first given in its entirety in *London Revived: Considerations for its Rebuilding in 1666*, ed. E. S. de Beer (1938). *Memoires for my Grandson* has been edited by Sir Geoffrey Keynes (1926).

The first version of Evelyn's diary to be published was *Memoirs illustrative of the Life and Writings of John Evelyn, Esq.*, ed. W. Bray (2 vols., 1818). A different edition with the same title appeared in the following year, and this was followed by a new selection, ed. H. B. Wheatley (4 vols., 1879), and by another, ed. J. Forster (4 vols., 1850–2; repr. Bohn's Library, 4 vols., 1859). The standard edition is that of E. S. de Beer, *The Diary of John Evelyn* (6 vols., 1955), based on a collation of all the manuscripts. The text of this is available in one volume (1959), with the annotation much reduced.

There is a bibliography of Evelyn's writings by Sir Geoffrey Keynes (1937). A number of his letters to Pepys were published by C. Marburg in *Mr. Pepys and Mr. Evelyn* (University of Pennsylvania, 1935). There are studies by Sir A. Ponsonby (1933), and by W. G. Hiscock, *Evelyn and Mrs. Godolphin* (1951), and *Evelyn and his Family Circle* (1955). Among articles mainly biographical are those of Sir Geoffrey Keynes, 'John Evelyn as a Bibliophil' (*Library* xii, 1931); M. Denny, 'The Early Program of the Royal Society and John Evelyn' (*MLQ* i, 1940); G. B. Parks, 'John Evelyn and the Art of Travel' (*HLQ* x, 1947); J. Underdown, 'John Evelyn and Restoration Piety' (*Sewanee Review* lxv, 1957); J. R. King, *Studies in Six Seventeenth-Century Writers* (Ohio State University, 1965).

THOMAS FAIRFAX, BARON FAIRFAX, 1612–71

A Short Memorial of the Northern Actions in which I was engaged, ed. Brian Fairfax, was published in 1699. There are various editions, including one by Sir Walter Scott in the *Somers Tracts*, vol. v (1811), and one in *Stuart Tracts 1603–1693*, with an introduction by Sir Charles Firth (1903). The correspondence of the Fairfax family is available in *Memoirs of the Reign of Charles the First*, ed. J. W. G. Johnson (2 vols., 1848), and *Memorials of the Civil War: comprising the Correspondence of the Fairfax Family*, ed. R. Bell (2 vols., 1849). There are biographies by C. R.

Markham (1870) and Mildred A. Gibb (1938), and an excellent short account by Sir Charles Firth in *DNB*.

THOMAS FLATMAN, 1637–88

Flatman published a volume of *Poems and Songs* (1674); later editions (1676, 1682, 1686) contain additional poems. The 1682 and 1686 editions form the basis of the text of the poems given in Saintsbury, vol. iii (1921), which contains a number of poems not collected by Flatman himself. More are to be found in F. A. Child's *The Life and Uncollected Poems of Thomas Flatman* (Philadelphia, 1921). See also P. Simpson (*Bodleian Quarterly Record* viii, 1937). There is a small selection, ed. J. R. Tutin (Orinda Booklets, 1906). Two prose pieces, *Montelion* (1661) and *Don Juan Lamberto* (1661), are attributed to Flatman. His connection with the political periodical, *Heraclitus Ridens* (1681–2), is discussed by T. F. M. Newton (*Harvard Studies and Notes in Philology and Literature* xvi, 1934).

RICHARD FLECKNOE, d. 1678?

Apart from his plays, of which only *Love's Kingdom* (1664) and *The Damoiselles a La Mode* (1667) were acted, Flecknoe published several small volumes of epigrams and 'portraits' in verse, miscellaneous poems, essays, and Theophrastan characters, usually including some of his previously published work in each new volume. *A Farrago of several Pieces* (1666) is typical of his medleys of verse and prose. *A Collection of the Choicest Epigrams and Characters* (1673) contains, oddly enough, a complimentary poem to Dryden. *A Relation of Ten Years Travels* (repr. 1665, as *A True Narrative*) has some biographical interest. Flecknoe's attack on Thomas Killigrew, *The Life of Thomaso the Wanderer* (1667) was ed. G. Thorn-Drury (1925). For his attack on Davenant, see Sir William Davenant (*supra*, VI). His *Short Treatise of the English Stage* is reprinted in Spingarn, vol. ii; and two of his characters are included in *Essays on Wit*, ed. E. N. Hooker (*ARS*, 1946). Biographical and critical studies have been written by A. Lohr (Leipzig, 1900), and by P. H. Doney (*Harvard Summaries of Theses*, 1931).

GEORGE FOX, 1624–91

A Journal or Historical Account of the Life, Travels, Sufferings, Christian Experiences, and Labours of Love in the Work of the Ministry of . . . *George Fox* was edited and corrected by Thomas Ellwood and other Friends, and published in 1694 with a preface by William Penn. An edition by N. Penney and T. E. Harvey from the original manuscript was published in 2 vols. (1911), and abridged by Penney (1924). The standard edition is now that of J. L. Nickalls (1952). N. Penney also edited *The Short Journal and Itinerary Journals of George Fox* (1925). There is an edition of the *Works* (8 vols., Philadelphia, 1831).

Biographies have been written by S. M. Janney (Philadelphia, 1853); A. C. Bickley (1884); T. Hodgkin (1896); H. G. Wood (1912); A. N. Brayshaw (1918); R. Knight (1922: a psychological study); H. Van Etten (Paris, 1923); R. H. King, *Fox and the Light Within* (Philadelphia, 1940); V. Noble, *The Man in the Leather Breeches: The Life and Times of George Fox* (1953); H. E. Wildes, *Voice of the Lord* (University of Pennsylvania, 1965). There is a study of Fox's wife by I. Ross, *Margaret Fell, Mother of Quakerism* (1949).

JOSEPH GLANVILL, 1636–80

Glanvill's best-known book today (chiefly because it contains the story of the Scholar Gipsy) is his first: *The Vanity of Dogmatizing* (1661; ed. J. Owen, 1885; ed. M. E. Prior, Facsimile Text Society, Columbia, 1931). It was revised by Glanvill and published as *Scepsis Scientifica* (1665). Further propaganda for the new science appeared in his *Plus Ultra* (1668; ed. J. I. Cope in facsimile, Gainesville, Fla., 1958), and his *Philosophia Pia* (1671). Glanvill also published *An Essay on Preaching* and *A Seasonable Defence of Preaching* (both 1678), *Essays on Several Important Subjects* (1676), and a vindication of the existence of witches and witchcraft (1667) best known as, *Sadducismus Triumphatus* (1681; the 1726 edition containing 'some account of Mr. Glanvill's life and writings'). *Some Discourses, Sermons and Remains* appeared posthumously, with a preface by Anthony Horneck (1681).

His work is fully discussed in F. Greensleet's *Joseph Glanvill* (New York, 1900), and J. I. Cope's *Joseph Glanvill: Anglican Apologist* (Washington University, 1956). He is also studied by J. Tulloch (*supra*, V. 2); H. Habicht (Zurich, 1936); H. S. and I. M. L. Redgrove, *Joseph Glanvill and Psychical Research* (1921); B. Willey (*supra*, III. 1); R. F. Jones; R. S. Westfall (*supra*, V. 3); M. L. Wiley; H. G. van Leeuwen (*supra*, III. 5) and other writers on science and religion in the period; M. E. Prior, 'Joseph Glanvill, Witchcraft and Seventeenth-Century Science' (*MP* xxx, 1932); R. H. Popkin, 'Glanvill as a Precursor of Hume' (*JHI* xiv, 1953) and 'The Development of the Philosophical Reputation of Joseph Glanvill' (ibid. xv, 1954); D. Krook, 'Boyle and Glanvill as Baconians' (*HLQ* xviii, 1955).

RICHARD GOULD, d. 1709?

Gould published various satirical poems and funeral eclogues between 1683 and 1700, and a volume of *Poems, chiefly consisting of Satyrs and Satirical Epistles* (1689; 2nd ed. 1697). His tragedy, *The Rival Sisters*, was published in 1696. Gould's *Works*, collected and published by his widow, Martha Gould (2 vols., 1709), include some work not previously printed. There is a monograph by E. H. Sloane, *Robert Gould, Seventeenth Century Satirist* (University of Pennsylvania, 1940). H. D. Weinbrot has pointed out some borrowings from Dryden (*English Language Notes* iii, 1965), and A. Nicoll (*supra*, III. 4) indicates the source of *The Rival Sisters*.

JOHN GRAUNT, 1620–74

Graunt's *Natural and Political Observations upon the Bills of Mortality* (1662) had reached a fifth edition by 1676, edited by his friend Sir William Petty (ed. W. F. Willcox, Johns Hopkins, 1939). Comment includes a paper by M. Ptoukha (*Congrès international de la population* ii, 1938), and a tercentenary address by D. V. Glass (*Notes and Records of the Royal Society* xix, 1964).

THOMAS GUMBLE, d. 1676

Gumble's *Life of General Monck* appeared in 1671. A translation by Guy Miege, *La Vie de General Monk*, was published in London in the following year. According to *DNB* some copies of this translation have a second additional title-page of 1712 'printed at Cologne', where the work was being sold to advance the cause of the Pretender.

HALIFAX, CHARLES MONTAGU, EARL OF, 1661–1715

Halifax's liveliest work is the attack on Dryden, *The Hind and the Panther Transvers'd* (1687), written in collaboration with Matthew Prior, and published anonymously. For a second unpublished poem by Montagu in reply to Dryden's poem, see H. M. Hooker (*ELH* viii, 1941). *An Epistle to . . . Charles Earl of Dorset* (1690), celebrating the victory of William III in Ireland, went through several editions. *The Works* (with a Life) were published in 1715, and the verse is available in Johnson, Anderson, and Chalmers. An unpublished Halifax MS. in the British Museum is described by J. D. Kern (*JEGP* xxxii, 1933). G. L. Anderson seeks to identify Sir Indolent Easie in Charles Gildon's *New Rehearsal* (1714) with Halifax (*PQ* xxxiii, 1954).

HALIFAX, GEORGE SAVILE, MARQUIS OF, 1633–95

Halifax published anonymously, and wrote (so far as is known) comparatively late in life. His publications are: *Observations upon a Late Libel* (1681; identified and ed. H. Macdonald, with a bibliography, 1940); *A Letter to a Dissenter* (1687); *The Lady's New-Years Gift: or, Advice to a Daughter* (1688; ed. B. Dobrée, 1927); *The Character of a Trimmer* (1688); *The Anatomy of an Equivalent* (1688); *A Rough Draft of a New Model at Sea* (1694); *Some Cautions Offered to the Consideration of Those who are to Chuse . . . Members . . . in the Ensuing Parliament* (1695). These, except *Observations upon a Late Libel*, and with 'Maxims of State' added, were published as *Miscellanies by the . . . Marquess of Halifax* (1700). *A Character of King Charles the Second: And Political, Moral and Miscellaneous Thoughts and Reflections* were published from his manuscripts (1750). The *Savile Correspondence* was edited by W. D. Cooper (Camden Society, 1858), and there are 'Some Unpublished Letters of George Savile to Gilbert Burnet' (D. L. Poole, *English Historical Review* xxvi, 1911). Some correspondence between his younger brother Henry and the Earl of Rochester has been published as *The Rochester–Savile Letters*, ed. J. H. Wilson (Ohio State University, 1941). There is an unpublished bibliography by M. B. C. Canney among the theses in the University of London Library.

The authoritative work on Halifax is that of H. C. Foxcroft, *The Life and Letters of . . . Halifax. With a new Edition of his Works* (2 vols., 1898; reviewed by Sir Charles Firth, *English Historical Review* xiv, 1899). Miss Foxcroft rewrote her Life, bringing it up to date, but omitting the writings, as *A Character of the Trimmer* (1946). The *Works* (omitting *Observations*) were edited by Sir Walter Raleigh (1912; the introduction repr. in Raleigh, *supra*, III. 1).

Comment on Halifax includes the following: H. Paul, *Men and Letters* (1901); G. P. Gooch, *Political Thought . . . to Halifax* (*supra*, V. 1); C. Whibley, *Political Portraits: Second Series* (1923); A. W. Reed (in F. J. C. Hearnshaw, *supra*, V. 1); B. Dobrée, *Variety of Ways* (1932); K. Klose, *George Savile . . . als Politiker und Staatsdenker* (Breslau, 1936); L. Stapleton (*JHI* ii, 1941); H. Trevor-Roper, *Historical Essays* (1957); V. Buranelli, *The King and the Quaker* (University of Pennsylvania, 1962); D. R. Benson (*HLQ* xxvii, 1964); F. Raab (*supra*, V. 1).

ANNE, LADY HALKETT, 1622–99

The Life of the Lady Halkett, with a dedication signed S. C., was published at Edinburgh (1701), and edited, as *The Auto-biography of Lady Halkett*, by J. G. Nichols (Camden Society, 1875). Two other pieces by her were published in 1701: *Meditations on the twentieth and fifth Psalm*, and *Meditations and Prayers*. She is discussed by M. Reynolds (*supra*, III. 1), and by M. Bottrall (*supra*, IV. 5).

ANTHONY HAMILTON, 1646?–1720

Mémoires de la vie du Comte de Grammont (Cologne, 1713) was frequently reprinted in Holland, and later in France. Horace Walpole printed a small edition in 1772. There is a modern annotated edition by C.-E. Engel (Monaco, 1958). The first English translation was made by Abel Boyer (1714). This was revised and improved by Sir Walter Scott (1811), and it is in this version that the *Memoirs* are still generally read. There are editions by A. Fea (1906); G. Goodwin (1908); P. Quennell (1931).

BENJAMIN HARRIS, d. 1714?

The Domestick Intelligence; Or, News both from City and Country ran from 7 July 1679 to 15 April 1681, with some minor changes of title. Besides publishing several other short-lived periodicals, Harris started on 6 June 1699 *The London Slip of News*, which became *The London Post* with the second number, and was still running in 1705. Harris has no entry in *DNB*, but he is noticed in *The American Dictionary of National Biography*. The chief authority for his career is J. G. Muddiman, *The King's Journalist 1659–1689* (1923; see also *NQ* clxiii, 1932); but there are also accounts of him by P. L. Ford, *New England Primer* (New

York, 1937), and F. Monaghan (*Colophon* xii, New York, 1932).

RICHARD HEAD, *fl.* 1660–80

The English Rogue described in the Life of Meriton Latroon (Pt. i, 1665) was the work of Head alone. Four other parts followed (1668–88), written either by Head, or by Francis Kirkman, or the joint work of both (repr. 1874, 1928). Head wrote *The Life and Death of Mother Shipton* (1667); *The Floating Island* (1673: describing low life in London under a fictitious disguise); *O-Brazile: or The Inchanted Island* (1675; ed. I. M. Westcott, *Seventeenth-Century Tales of the Supernatural, ARS*, 1958). He was also the author of *Proteus Redivivus or The Art of Wheedling* (1675). *The English Rogue* is discussed in F. W. Chandler (*supra*, IV. 3).

THOMAS HEYRICK, 1650–94

Heyrick's *Miscellany Poems* (1691) contains some unusual poetry, including his long 'pindaric' called 'The Submarine Voyage'. *The New Atlantis* (1687), an attack on Dryden and the Catholics after the publication of *The Hind and the Panther*, is of little account, but it reached a second edition (1690).

ROBERT HOOKE, 1635–1703

Hooke published a considerable number of lectures and papers, but the work by which he is known to the general reader is his *Micrographia: or some Physiological Descriptions of Minute Bodies made by Magnifying Glasses* (1665). This handsome volume, with Hooke's drawings of his microscopical observations, was edited by R. T. Gunther (*Early Science in Oxford* xiii, 1945). A volume of *Posthumous Works*, with a Life by Robert Waller, appeared in 1705. R. T. Gunther's *The Life and Work of Robert Hooke* will be found in *Early Science in Oxford*, vols. vi, vii (1930). Hooke's *Diary* (1672–80) has been ed. H. W. Robinson and W. Adams (1935). His work as an architect is dealt with by M. I. Batten in *The Twenty-fifth Volume of the Walpole Society, 1936–1937* (1937), and his interest in geography by E. G. R. Taylor (*Geographical Journal* lxxxix, 1937; xc, 1938). M. 'Espinasse gives a clear account of his many scientific interests and achievements in her *Robert Hooke* (1956; repr. University of California, 1962; see also her article in *RES* xiii, 1937), and A. R. Hall has published a tercentenary lecture,

Hooke's 'Micrographia': 1665–1965 (1966). Hooke is discussed by G. J. Whitrow (*Philosophy of Science* v, 1938), and E. N. da C. Andrade (*Nature* clxxi, 1953). There is a bibliography of his writings by Sir Geoffrey Keynes (1960).

CHARLES HOPKINS, 1664–1700

Hopkins wrote three almost unreadable tragedies in the lean period at the close of the century (1695–99). The first of these, *Pyrrhus*, had a prologue by Congreve; the second, *Boadicea, Queen of Britain*, is a late example of the rhymed play. Hopkins published in 1694 a volume of *Epistolary Poems on Several Occasions*, which includes some translations from Ovid's *Metamorphoses* and the *Elegies* of Tibullus. He produced some further translations from the *Metamorphoses* and *Heroides* in 1695, and from the *Ars Amatoria* in 1700. A volume entitled *Amasia* (1700) contains the bulk of his verse. For comment on Hopkins, see B. Maxwell (*RES* iv, 1928; on *Boadicea*), and A. E. Jones (*MLN* lv, 1940).

JOHN HOUGHTON, 1640–1705

A Collection of Letters for the Improvement of Husbandry and Trade came out irregularly in monthly parts from September 1681 to June 1683. It was succeeded by Houghton's weekly periodical, *A Collection for the Improvement of Husbandry and Trade*, 30 March 1692–24 September 1703. Parts of both of these were reprinted by R. Bradley in *Husbandry and Trade Improved* (4 vols., 1727). G. E. Fussell gives an account of Houghton (*NQ* cciii, 1958), and R. P. McCutcheon writes on him as an editor and book-reviewer (*MP* xx, 1923).

EWARD HOWARD, 1624–c. 1700.

There is no collected edition of the four plays published in Howard's lifetime. A fifth play, *The Change of Crownes*, banned by the King's order after the first performance (15 April 1667) and not printed, was edited by F. S. Boas from a manuscript prompt copy, with a descriptive account of Howard's various plays and poems (1949). Howard also wrote a much-ridiculed heroic poem, *The Brittish Princes* (1669), and another heroic poem, *Carolaides, or, The Rebellion of Forty One* (1689), which was perhaps spared for its subject. His *Poems and Essays* (1674) are discussed by F. S. Boas (*Contemporary Review* clxxiv, 1948).

A. J. Bull drew attention to a number of satirical poems on Howard preserved in a Bodleian MS. (*RES* vi, 1930). L. Bradner suggests that he may be the author of the anonymous *Spencer Redivivus*, 1687 (*RES* xiv, 1938).

JAMES HOWARD, *fl.* 1660–70

James Howard was the author of two fairly successful comedies, *The English Monsieur* (acted 1663; published 1674), and *All Mistaken, or The Mad Couple* (1672). Ethel Seaton showed (*TLS*, 18 Oct. 1934) that the first of those plays was acted as early as July 1663; and J. Sutherland (*NQ* ccix, 1964) offered some evidence (not accepted by J. Loftis, 'California' Dryden, ix, 1966) for dating *All Mistaken* in 1665, and therefore earlier than Dryden's *Secret Love*, from which Howard has been generally thought to have borrowed his gay couple.

SIR ROBERT HOWARD, 1626–98

Sir Robert Howard's first four plays appeared in print as *Four New Plays* (1665), without having had separate publication. *The Duke of Lerma* followed in 1668, and all five plays were republished as *Five New Plays* (1692). Howard's *Poems* (1660) were reissued in 1696. There is an edition of his successful comedy, *The Committee*, by C. N. Thurber (University of Illinois, 1921); and *The Great Favourite* (i.e. *The Duke of Lerma*) is given by D. D. Arundell in *Dryden and Howard* (1929), together with Howard's prefaces to this tragedy and to *Four New Plays*. Those two prefaces are also available in Spingarn, vol. ii.

Howard's life and writings are fully dealt with in H. J. Oliver's *Sir Robert Howard . . . A Critical Biography* (Duke University, 1963). His share in *The Indian Queen* is discussed by J. H. Smith (*SP* li, 1954), H. J. Oliver (*supra*), and by the editors of the 'California' Dryden viii, 19). A. Harbage gives reasons for believing that *The Duke of Lerma*, which Howard admitted to be an adaptation of an old play, was based on a tragedy by John Ford (*MLR* xxv, 1940).

LUCY HUTCHINSON, b. 1620

Memoirs of the Life of Colonel Hutchinson, ed. J. Hutchinson, was first published in 1806 (reviewed by Francis Jeffrey, *Edinburgh Review*, Oct. 1808). The best edition is that of Sir

Charles Firth (2 vols., 1885; rev. 1906). The *Memoirs* may also be read in a Bohn's Library edition (1846), and in an Everyman edition (1908), which includes the essay on Lucy Hutchinson by F. P. G. Guizot. Mrs. Hutchinson was also the author of *On the Principles of the Christian Religion*, ed. J. Hutchinson (1817). She is discussed by I. Warburg, *Lucy Hutchinson: das Bild einer Puritanerin* . . . (Hamburg, 1937); M. Reynolds (*supra*, III. 1); B. G. McCarthy (*supra*, IV. 3).

BENJAMIN KEACH, 1640–1704

Keach published *The Travels of True Godliness* . . . *in an Apt and Pleasant Allegory* in two parts (1683–5), and it quickly ran to many editions. Equally popular were some of his poems, *War with the Devil* (1674), *The Glorious Lover* (1679), and *Sion in Distress* (1681). Besides notices in the usual biographical sources, some account of him will be found in A. A. Reid's 'Benjamin Keach, 1640–1714' (*Baptist Quarterly* x, 1940); A. C. Underwood (*supra*, V. 2), and other histories of the Baptists.

GEORGE KEITH, 1638–1716

Among Keith's many Quaker publications were *Help in time of Need, from the God of Help* (1665); *The Deism of William Penn and his Brethren exposed* (1699); *The Standard of the Quakers examined* (1702: an answer to Robert Barclay's *Apology*). His *Journal of Travels from New Hampshire to Caratuck* appeared in 1706. A list of his writings will be found in J. Smith, *A Descriptive Catalogue of Friends' Books*, vol. ii, 1867. There is a biographical study by E. W. Kirby (New York, 1942). Marjorie Nicolson has written on 'George Keith and the Cambridge Platonists' (*Philosophical Review* xxxix, 1930).

THOMAS KEN, 1637–1711

Ken's *Works* were edited (with a Life) by W. Hawkins (4 vols., 1721). There was an edition of the prose works by J. T. Round (1838), and another by W. Benham (1889). There are biographies by W. L. Bowles (2 vols., 1830), by S. H. Plumptre (2 vols., 1888; rev. 1890), and by H. A. L. Price, *Thomas Ken: Bishop and Non-Juror* (1958). For his possible connection with Dryden's 'good parson', see J. Kinsley (*RES*, new ser. iii, 1952).

ANNE KILLIGREW, 1660–85

Poems by Mrs. Anne Killigrew came out posthumously in a quarto volume (1686), with a fine mezzotint portrait, and Dryden's poem 'To the Pious Memory of the Accomplisht Young Lady Mrs. Anne Killigrew, Excellent in the two Sister-Arts of Poesie and Painting'. There is a modern edition by R. Morton (Gainesville, Fla., 1967), and a few of her poems are in W. Kerr (*supra*, II. 2). She is noticed in such works as G. Ballard's *Memoirs of Several Ladies of Great Britain* (1742), T. Cibber's *Lives of the Poets of Great Britain*, vol. ii (1750); M. Reynolds (*supra*, III. 1).

THOMAS KILLIGREW, 1612–83

Most of Killigrew's plays fall in the pre-Restoration period. *The Parson's Wedding* (probably dating from 1639–40) was performed, perhaps for the first time, on 5 October 1664, and was published in Killigrew's folio volume of *Comedies and Tragedies* (1664). It can be read more conveniently in Robert Dodsley's *Select Collection*, ed. W. C. Hazlitt, vol. xiv (1876) and in M. Summers, *Restoration Comedies* (1921). This play is fully discussed by A. Harbage, *Thomas Killigrew, Cavalier Dramatist* (University of Pennsylvania, 1930), and by G. E. Bentley, *The Jacobean and Caroline Stage*, vol. iv (1956). W. R. Keast has a short discussion of 'Killigrew's Use of Donne in *The Parson's Wedding*' (*MLR* xv, 1950).

SIR WILLIAM KILLIGREW, 1606–95

Killigrew's *Pandora* (1664) was included, with *Selindra* and *Ormasdes* in *Three Playes* (1665). *Four New Playes* (1666) added *The Seege of Urbin* (ed. I. E. Taylor, University of Pennsylvania, 1946). Killigrew's prose reflections, *Mid-night Thoughts* (1681) were republished in 1684, with some additional material, and were followed by *Mid-night and Daily Thoughts. In Prose and Verse* (1694). Killigrew is noticed by A. Harbage, *Cavalier Drama* (New York, 1936). W. H. McCabe has a note on *The Imperial Tragedy*, which has been attributed to Killigrew (*PQ* xv, 1936).

FRANCIS KIRKMAN, *fl.* 1652–74

Kirkman added a 'sixth part' to *Amadis de Gaule* in 1652. He published a collection of drolls and farces in 1672, with the title of *The Wits; Or, Sport upon Sport* (ed. J. J. Elson, Cornell,

1932: see also W. J. Cameron, *NQ* ccii, 1957; cciii, 1958). Kirkman also compiled a catalogue of English plays which was appended to a translation of Corneille's *Nicomède* (1671), and which formed the basis of Langbaine's later catalogue. His narrative of Mary Carleton, *The Counterfeit Lady Unveil'd* (1673), is included by Spiro Peterson in a volume with that title, together with some other pieces of fictional biography (New York, 1961). Kirkman's own autobiographical narrative, *The Unlucky Citizen* (1673), has not been reprinted. His share in *The English Rogue* is noted *supra*, VI, Richard Head. There is a *Bibliography of Francis Kirkman . . . (1652–80)* compiled by Strickland Gibson (*OBS*, 1947), and interesting biographical material is presented by R. C. Bald (*MP* xli, 1943).

JOHN LACY, 1615–81

The Dramatic Works, ed. J. Maidment and W. H. Logan (1875), contain some biographical information, and there is a little more in F. S. Boas's edition of Edward Howard's *The Change of Crownes* (1949). Apart from brief notices in histories of the drama, Lacy's plays have excited little critical comment.

GERARD LANGBAINE, THE YOUNGER, 1656–92

Langbaine was an assiduous collector of dramatic literature. He issued catalogues of plays in 1680 (*An Exact Catalogue of all the Comedies . . .*) and in 1688 (*Momus Triumphans: or the Plagiarisms of the English Stage, exposed in a Catalogue . . .*). His *Account of the English Dramatick Poets* (1691), where his unamiable proclivity for detecting and recording plagiarisms is given full bent, was 'improved and continued' by Charles Gildon in 1698, as *The Lives and Characters of the English Dramatick Poets* (see G. L. Anderson, *NQ* cciii, 1958). There are annotated copies of the *Account* in the British Museum and the Bodleian (see A. Watkin-Jones, *ESEA* xxi, 1936).

NATHANIEL LEE, 1649?–92

Of Lee's thirteen plays (which include *Oedipus* and *The Duke of Guise* written in collaboration with Dryden) those most frequently reprinted were *Sophonisba*, *The Rival Queens*, *Mithridates*, *Oedipus*, and *Theodosius*. Collections of the *Works* appeared in 1687, 1694, 1713, 1722, 1734, and 1736. There is a modern annotated edition of the plays by T. B. Stroup and A. L. Cooke (2 vols., Scarecrow Press, 1954–5). There is an edition of *Nero* by R. Horstmann (Heidelberg, 1933); of *Constantine the Great* by W. Häfele (Heidelberg, 1914); and of *Lucius Junius Brutus* by J. Loftis (University of Nebraska, 1967). *Sophonisba* is included in *Five Heroic Plays*, ed. B. Dobrée (World's Classics, 1960).

Lee's plays have attracted attention from German scholars, e.g. A. Wülker, *Shakespeares Einfluss auf die dramatische Kunst von Nathaniel Lee* (Münster, 1934). They are discussed from a less specialized point of view by A. Nicoll (*supra*, III. 4), B. Dobrée |in *Restoration Tragedy* (1929), and R. G. Ham, who also contributes biographical information, in *Otway and Lee* (Yale, 1931). T. B. Stroup writes on '*The Princess of Cleve* and Sentimental Comedy' (*RES* xi, 1935), and A. Righter also considers this play in *Restoration Theatre* (*supra*, III. 4). The influence of Milton on Lee was examined by H. Fletcher (*MLN* xliv, 1929), and by G. B. Evans (*MLN* lxiv, 1949). There is a bibliography by A. L. McLeod in *Restoration and Eighteenth Century Theatre Research* i, 1962).

RICHARD LEIGH, b. 1649

Leigh wrote a pamphlet called *The Censure of the Rota* (1673), criticizing *The Conquest of Granada*, and a small book, *The Transproser Rehears'd* (1673), on Samuel Parker's side in the Marvell *versus* Parker controversy. Neither is of much importance. His *Poems upon Several Occasions* (1675) were edited by H. Macdonald (1947), with a biographical introduction considerably supplementing the meagre entry in *DNB*. P. B. Anderson put forward Samuel Butler, rather than Leigh, as the author of *The Transproser Rehears'd* (*SP* xliv, 1947).

ROBERT LEIGHTON, 1611–84

There were various collections of Leighton's commentaries, sermons, etc. from 1692 onwards. The best edition textually is *The Whole Works*, ed. W. West (6 vols., 1869–75), and there is another collection with the same title, ed. J. N. Pearson (New York, 1874). D. Butler provides a biographical account in *The Life and Letters of Robert Leighton* (1903). There is an interesting appreciation of him in Bishop Burnet's *History*, and E. A. Knox's *Robert Leighton . . . His Life, Times and Writings* (1930) gives a good estimate of him as author and preacher. He is discussed by J. Tulloch in *Scottish Divines, 1505–1872* (1883), and there are some interesting remarks by S. T. Coleridge, *Notes on English Divines*, ed. D. Coleridge (vol. ii, 1853).

SIR ROGER L'ESTRANGE, 1616–1704

L'Estrange's first recorded appearance in print was in 1646, and he continued to write, on the Tory side, until the Revolution. After 1688 he was mainly employed in translating. Of his many political books and pamphlets the following are among the most important: *No Blinde Guides. In Answer to a seditious Pamphlet of J. Milton's* . . . (1660); *A Plea for a Limited Monarchy* (1660); *The Relaps'd Apostate* (1661); *Considerations and Proposals in Order to the Regulation of the Press* (1663); *The Parallel, or, An Account of the Growth of Knavery* (1677: a reply to Marvell's *Account of the Growth of Popery*); *An Answer to the Appeal from the Country to the City* (1679); *The Reformed Catholique* (1679); *Citt and Bumpkin* (2 parts, 1680; Part I, ed. B. J. Rahn, *ARS*, 1965); *L'Estrange's Narrative of the Plot* (1680); *An Answer to a Letter to a Dissenter* (1687: a reply to Halifax); *A Brief History of the Times* (3 parts, 1687–8). He also wrote and published *The Intelligencer* (31 August 1663–29 January 1666), and *The Newes* (3 September 1663–25 January 1666). His *Observator* appeared from 13 April 1681 to 9 March 1687.

L'Estrange's translations include *The Visions of Quevedo, made English* (1667; frequently reprinted, most recently with an introduction by J. M. Cohen, 1963); *Five Love Letters from a Nun to a Cavalier* (1678); *Seneca's Morals by way of abstract* (1678; many subsequent editions); *Twenty Select Colloquies. Out of Erasmus Roterodamus* (1680; repr., with an introduction by C. Whibley, 1923); *The Fables of Aesop, and other Eminent Mythologists* (1692; a second part appeared in 1699, and both were frequently reprinted); *The Works of Flavius Josephus* (1702). L'Estrange also had a hand in *Terence's Comedies made English* (1694, etc.)

The only full-length study is that of G. Kitchin, *Sir Roger L'Estrange: a Contribution to the History of the Press in the Seventeenth Century* (1913), in which it is often difficult to see the wood for the trees. L'Estrange is discussed by C. Whibley (*CHEL*, vol. ix) in his section on 'Writers of Burlesque and Translators', reprinted in his *Literary Studies* (1919).

MARTIN LISTER, 1638?–1712

Lister, a zoologist of some distinction, published among other works *Historiae conchyliorum* (2 vols., 1685, 1692). In so far as he is now remembered by the general reader, it is for *A Journey to Paris* (1699; repr. in John Pinkerton's *Voyages*, vol. iv, 1809). William King's satirical skit on this, *A Journey to London in the Year 1698*, appeared in 1699. Lister is discussed in C. Maxwell's *The English Traveller in France 1698–1815* (1932).

DAVID LLOYD, 1635–92

Lloyd's most important work is *The States-men and Favourites of England Since the Reformation* (1665). This was reissued as *State Worthies* (1670), and was revised and enlarged by Sir Charles Whitworth (2 vols., 1766). Lloyd compiled another long work of less importance, *Memoires of the Lives, Actions, Sufferings, and Deaths of those Noble, Reverend, and Excellent Personages that Suffered by Death . . . in our late Intestine Wars . . .* (1668). Lloyd is one of the minor writers of the period who have attracted almost no critical attention, but his prose style would repay consideration.

JOHN LOCKE, 1632–1704

Locke did not publish anything until after the Revolution, and a mere list of his works with their dates of publication would give a misleading impression of his intellectual history. *Two Tracts on Government*, edited by P. Abrams and first published in 1967, comprise his earliest writings on political theory. *Essays on the Law of Nature*, edited by W. von Leyden and first published in 1954, was also early work. His first published work, *Epistola de Tolerantia* (1689), was translated into English by William Popple (1689), and was followed by *A Second Letter concerning Toleration* (1690), and by *A Third Letter . . .* (1692). *Two Treatises on Government* appeared anonymously in 1690, although written, at least in part, some years earlier. In the standard edition of P. Laslett (1959) there is a full discussion of the date of composition. *An Essay concerning Humane Understanding* also belongs to 1690; it was enlarged in 1694, and again in 1700. Early drafts of the *Essay* have been edited by B. Rand (Harvard, 1931), and by R. I. Aaron and J. Gibb (1936). Modern editions include that of A. C. Fraser (2 vols., 1894), the Bohn Library edition, the Everyman edition (re-edited by J. W. Yolton, 1961), and an abridged version by A. S. Pringle-Pattison (1924). *Some Thoughts concerning Education* (1693; 3rd ed. enlarged, 1699) was edited by R. H. Quick, and is also available in *The Educational Writings*, ed. J. W. Adamson (1912; rev. 1922). *The Reasonableness of Christianity* appeared in 1695; and Locke published *A Vindication* (1695) and *A Second Vindication* (1697). There is an abridgement by I. T. Ramsey (1958). From 1697 to 1699 Locke was involved in controversy with Bishop Stillingfleet and others over the *Essay concerning Human Understanding*. John Norris's *Cursory Reflections* upon the *Essay* were ed. G. D. McEwen (*ARS*, 1961).

Locke's French journals and other papers have been edited by J. Lough as *Locke's Travels in France, 1675–1679* (1953). *Some Familiar Letters between Mr. Locke and several of his Friends* appeared in 1708, and was followed by Lord King's *Life and Letters of John Locke* (1829); *Original Letters of Locke, Algernon Sidney, and Lord Shaftesbury*, ed. T. Forster (1830); *Lettres inédites de John Locke*, ed. M. Ollion (The Hague, 1912); *The Correspondence of John Locke and Edward Clarke*, ed. B. Rand (1927); and *Lettres inédites de Le Clerc à John Locke*, ed. G. Bonno (University of California, 1959). E. S. de Beer is preparing an edition of the complete correspondence. Locke's *Works* were first collected in three volumes (1714), and a list of the many subsequent editions will be found in *CBEL*. Selections include one by P. Laslett, *Locke on Politics, Religion and Education* (New York, 1965).

Among biographical and critical studies are those of Lord King (*supra*), H. R. Fox Bourne (2 vols., 1876), T. Fowler (English Men of Letters, 1880), A. C. Fraser (1890), S. Alexander (1908), H. Ollion (Paris, 1908), R. I. Aaron (1937; rev. 1955), D. J. O'Connor (Pelican, 1952), J. W. Yolton, *John Locke and the Way of Ideas* (1956). The standard biography is now that of M. Cranston (1957).

Books and papers dealing with special aspects of Locke and his work include C. Bastide, *John Locke, ses théories politiques et leur influence en Angleterre* (Paris, 1906); S. P. Lamprecht, *The Moral and Political Philosophy of Locke* (New York, 1918); J. W. Gough, *Locke's Political Philosophy: Eight Studies* (1950); R. Polin, *La Politique morale de John Locke* (Paris, 1960); H. McLachlan, *The Religious Opinions of Milton, Locke, and Newton* (1941); G. L. Cragg, 'The Religious Significance of John Locke' (*From Puritanism to the Age of Reason*, 1950; repr. 1960). D. G. James,

The Light of Reason: Hobbes, Locke, Bolingbroke (1949: excellent
on Locke); Sir W. Osler, *John Locke as a Physician* (1901); K.
Dewhurst, *John Locke (1632–1704): Physician and Philosopher*, which
includes an edition of the medical notes in Locke's journals
(Wellcome Historical Medical Library, 1963); G. Bonno, *Les
Relations intellectuelles de Locke avec la France* (University of
California, 1955); R. H. Cox, *Locke on War and Peace* (1960);
P. Laslett, 'John Locke, the Great Recoinage, and the Origins
of the Board of Trade' (*William and Mary Quarterly* xiv, 1957).

Studies with a literary bearing include B. Willey (*supra*,
III. 1, and in *The English Moralists*, 1964); K. MacLean, *John
Locke and English Literature of the Eighteenth Century* (Yale, 1936);
M. Kallich, 'The Association of Ideas and Critical Theory:
Hobbes, Locke, and Addison' (*ELH* xii, 1945); G. E. Smock,
'Locke and the Augustan Age of Literature' (*Philosophical
Review* lv, 1946); R. F. Brinkley, 'Coleridge on Locke' (*SP*
xliv, 1949); G. G. Pahl, 'Locke as a Literary Critic and Biblical
Interpreter' (L. B. Campbell *Festschrift*, *supra*, III. 1); E. L.
Tuveson, *The Imagination as a Means of Grace: Locke and the
Aesthetics of Romanticism* (University of California, 1960); R.
Hall, 'John Locke's Unnoticed Vocabulary' (*NQ* ccvi, 1960);
T. Redpath, 'John Locke and the Rhetoric of the Second
Treatise' (*The English Mind*, ed. H. S. Davies and G. Watson,
1964); R. L. Colie, 'John Locke and the Publication of the
Private' (*PQ* xlv, 1966).

H. O. Christopherson has compiled *A Bibliographical Introduction to the Study of John Locke* (Oslo, 1930). There is a useful
bibliography in Aaron (*supra*). W. von Leyden (*supra*) gives a
summary account of the Lovelace collection of Locke MSS.
in the Bodleian Library, and has also compiled 'A Summary
Catalogue of the Lovelace Collection' (*OBS*, new ser. vii,
1959). His articles in *Sophia*, Jan.–March 1949, and in the
Philosophical Quarterly, 1952, should also be consulted.

EDMUND LUDLOW, 1617?–92

Ludlow's *Memoirs* (3 vols., 1698–9) carry the nominal imprint of 'Vivay' on the title-page. There were several further
editions in the eighteenth century, and an incomplete translation into French was published in 1699. The standard English
edition is that of Sir Charles Firth (2 vols., 1894). Ludlow is
discussed by C. Robbins (*supra*, V. 1).

NARCISSUS LUTTRELL, 1657–1732

Luttrell's day-by-day chronicle of contemporary events was published as *A Brief Historical Relation of State Affairs from September 1678 to April 1714* (6 vols., 1857), after Macaulay had called attention to the MS. in All Souls College in his *History of England*. Excerpts from Luttrell's private diary of 1722–5 are given by P. Dixon (*NQ* ccvii, 1962). Sir F. C. Francis has edited *Narcissus Luttrell's Popish Plot Catalogues* in facsimile for the Luttrell Society (1956). J. M. Osborn discusses Luttrell as a collector (*Book Collector* vi, 1957).

SIR GEORGE MACKENZIE, 1636–91

Mackenzie's *Works* (legal, political, historical, together with various essays) were published at Edinburgh (2 vols., 1716–22). His 'serious romance' *Aretina* (1661) was not included in this collection; the preface to *Aretina*, 'An Apology for Romances', has been reprinted in *Prefaces to four Seventeenth-Century Romances*, ed. C. Davies (*ARS*, 1953). Mackenzie's *Memoirs of the Affairs of Scotland* were not published until 1821. There is a biography by Andrew Lang (1909), and a bibliography by F. S. Ferguson (*Transactions of the Edinburgh Bibliographical Society* i, 1936).

MARTIN MARTIN, d. 1719

A Late Voyage to St. Kilda (1698) went through several editions in the eighteenth century. *A Description of the Western Islands of Scotland* was published in 1703 (2nd ed. 'corrected', 1716). Both works were reprinted in J. Pinkerton's *Voyages*, vol. iii (1809), and have been edited by D. C. Macleod (1934).

ANDREW MARVELL, 1621–78

A full bibliography will be found in Bush. The following items have special reference to Marvell's post-Restoration satirical verse and to his prose. For the verse, problems of attribution are discussed by H. M. Margoliouth in his standard edition of *Poems and Letters* (2 vols., 1927; 2nd ed. 1952); P. Legouis, *André Marvell, poète, puritain, patriote* (Paris, 1928; trs. and rev. as *Andrew Marvell*, 1965); G. de F. Lord, in *Poems on Affairs of State*, vol .i. (*supra*, III. 2), in *BNYPL* lxii, 1958 (and subsequent discussions, lxiii, 1959), and in 'Satire and Sedition: The Life and Work of John Ayloffe' (*HLQ* xxix, 1966). The best commentary on the satirical verse and the prose is that of

P. Legouis (*supra*). There is some further discussion of the verse by J. Sutherland (*PQ* xlv, 1966), and by E. Miner (on *The Last Instructions to a Painter*, *MP* lxiii, 1966). Discussions of the prose or verse will be found in C. Robbins (*supra*, V. 1); C. Hill, 'Society and Andrew Marvell' (*Modern Quarterly* iv, 1946); D. Davison, 'Marvell and Politics' (*NQ* cc, 1955); D. Smith, 'The Political Beliefs of Andrew Marvell' (*UTQ* xxxvi, 1966).

PETER ANTHONY MOTTEUX, 1660–1718

Between 1695 and 1708 Motteux wrote a series of comedies, tragedies, operas, and dramatic entertainments, none of which is of much importance. His tragedy *Beauty in Distress* (1698) evoked some complimentary verses from Dryden. Motteux is remembered rather as the editor of *The Gentleman's Journal*, a monthly miscellany which he ran (and largely wrote) from January 1692 to November 1694, and as the translator of *Don Quixote* (4 vols., 1700–3). He also completed and revised Urquhart's translation of Rabelais (1694). In 1701 he published a collection of short novels, *A Banquet for Gentlemen and Ladies*.

There is a biographical and critical study by R. N. Cunningham (1933), and Cunningham also published a bibliography (*OBS*, 1933). D. Foster has written on *The Gentleman's Journal* (*PMLA* xxxii, 1917), as has R. Wieder, *Pierre Motteux et les débuts du journalisme . . .* (Paris, 1944).

WILLIAM MOUNTFORT, 1664–92

Six Plays Written by Mr. Mountfort (2 vols., 1720) include two by John Bancroft. Mountfort's best play was his comedy *Greenwich Park* (1691), but he also composed a farce, *The Life and Death of Dr. Faustus . . . With the Humours of Harlequin and Scaramouche* (1697), which is of some interest owing to the influence of the *commedia dell'arte*. Mountfort was the hero of the late seventeenth-century novel *The Player's Tragedy* (1693), based on his murder by Lord Mohun. His career as actor and playwright is the subject of A. S. Borgman's *The Life and Death of William Mountfort* (Harvard, 1935).

LODOWICKE MUGGLETON, 1609–98

Muggleton's *The Acts of the Witnesses of the Spirit* appeared posthumously in 1699. His other writings were mostly directed against the Quakers: a list of them will be found in Joseph Smith's *Bibliotheca-Anti-Quakeriana* (1873). The Life of Muggleton in *DNB* by Alexander Gordon is authoritative and sympathetic. For an account of the Muggletonians, see Gordon's papers in *Transactions of the Liverpool Literary and Philosophical Society* (1869, 1870).

MULGRAVE, JOHN SHEFFIELD, EARL OF (afterwards MARQUIS OF NORMANBY and DUKE OF BUCKINGHAMSHIRE), 1648–1721

Mulgrave's *Essay upon Satyr* was entered in the Term Catalogues for February 1680, but if an edition was printed no copy appears to have survived. It was published in *Poems on Affairs of State*, Part IV, 1689. His *Essay upon Poetry* was published in its first form in 1682, and *The Temple of Death* in 1695. His *Works* as 'Published by his Grace in his Lifetime' were printed by Edmund Curll in 1713. An edition of the *Works* undertaken by Pope, containing some interesting memoirs and an account of the Revolution of 1688 (2 vols., 1723), was frequently reprinted. For the publishing history of those early editions, see G. Sherburn, *The Early Career of Alexander Pope* (1934). Mulgrave's poetical works are in the collections of Johnson, Anderson, and Chalmers, and there is a selection of the verse in V. de S. Pinto's *Restoration Carnival* (New York, 1954). A selection of the verse and prose, entitled *Miscellanea*, was published by the Haworth Press (1933). Johnson's Life was for long the main source of information about Mulgrave, but some additional material has been added in recent years, e.g. by J. H. Wilson (*supra*, III. 1). M. Irvine discusses the identity of some characters in the *Essay upon Satyr* (*SP* xxxiv, 1937).

HENRY NEVILE, 1620–94

Nevile wrote *The Isle of Pines* (1668; repr. in *Shorter Novels: Jacobean and Restoration, supra*, IV. 3; and see A. O. Aldridge, *PMLA* lxv, 1950). His translation of *The Works* of Machiavelli (1675) was reprinted several times. In 1680 he published *Plato Redivivus, or a Dialogue concerning Government*, which also went into several editions. He is discussed by Z. S. Fink and C. Robbins (*supra*, V. 1).

Nevile is sometimes confused with Henry Nevil Payne, author of *The Fatal Jealousie* (1673; ed. W. Thorp, *ARS*, 1948), *The Morning Ramble* (1673), and *The Siege of Constantinople*

(1675). See W. Thorp, *Henry Nevil Payne, Dramatist and Jacobite Conspirator* (*Parrott Presentation Volume*, Princeton, 1935).

NEWCASTLE, MARGARET CAVENDISH, DUCHESS OF, 1623–73

This noble lady's numerous works began to appear, mostly in folio, in 1653, with *Poems and Fancies* and *Philosophical Fancies*. A volume of *Playes written by the thrice Noble, Illustrious and Excellent Princess, the Lady Marchioness of Newcastle* was published in 1662, and a further volume in 1668. Some stories in prose and verse, *Nature's Pictures drawn by Fancies Pencil to the Life* (1656), were followed in 1664 by *CCXI Sociable Letters*, and in 1668 by *The Description of a New World, called The Blazing World* (see K. Prasad, *Essays Presented to Amy G. Stock*, Rajasthan University, 1965). The work by which she is now chiefly remembered, her *Life* (1667) of her husband, the Duke of Newcastle, was edited by M. A. Lower (1872), and by Sir Charles Firth (1886; rev. 1906), and is available in an Everyman volume (1915). D. Grant has edited *The Phanseys of William Cavendish*, her suitor's poems and her letters in reply (1956), and has written a biography, *Margaret the First* (1957). See also B. G. MacCarthy (*supra*, IV. 3); G. D. Meyer, *The Scientific Lady in England 1650–1760* (University of California, 1955); and J. Gagen (*SP* lvi, 1959). There is a rather fuller bibliography in Bush.

SIR ISAAC NEWTON, 1642–1727

Newton scarcely comes into the field of English literature, and his influence on thought was felt more in the eighteenth century than in our period, although Richard Bentley supported his confutation of atheism by frequent references to the Newtonian laws in his Boyle lectures of 1692. Newton's *Philosophiae Naturalis Principia Mathematica* was published in 1687, and translated into English by Andrew Motte (1729). There is a revised edition of this, edited by F. Cajori (2 vols., University of California, 1962). The *Opticks*, written in English, appeared in 1704. There is a reprint of this, with prefatory and supplementary matter by Sir E. Whittaker *et al.* (New York, 1952). *Isaac Newton's Papers and Letters on Natural Philosophy* have been edited by I. B. Cohen *et al.* (Harvard, 1958), and there is a selection of his *Unpublished Scientific Papers*, ed. A. R. Hall and M. B. Hall (1962). A selection from his writings, *Newton's*

Philosophy of Nature, was made by H. S. Thayer (New York, 1953), and one from his *Theological Writings*, by H. McLachlan (1950). Three volumes of his *Correspondence* have been edited by H. W. Turnbull (1959–61).

The most complete account of Newton and his work was for long that of Sir David Brewster, *Memoirs of the Life, Writings and Discoveries* (1855). This has been superseded by the biography of L. T. More (New York, 1934), and by a memorial volume, *Isaac Newton, 1642–1727*, ed. W. J. Greenstreet (1927), which has a bibliography by H. Zeitlinger. R. de Villamil's *Newton: the Man* (1931) has a foreword by Einstein, and contains information about the books in Newton's library. There is also a biographical study by J. W. N. Sullivan (1938), and a portrait by E. N. da C. Andrade (1950). Sir John Craig's *Newton at the Mint* (1946) deals with that aspect of his career. There is a bibliography by G. J. Gray (1907). I. B. Cohen, 'Newton in the Light of Recent Scholarship' (*Isis* li, 1960), provides a conspectus of modern opinion.

Among studies with some general or literary interest are the following: H. McLachlan, *The Religious Opinions of Milton, Locke and Newton* (1941); E. W. Strong, 'Newton and God' (*JHI* xiii, 1952); Marjorie Nicolson, *Newton Demands the Muse* (Princeton, 1946: on the influence of the *Opticks* on eighteenth-century poetry); F. E. L. Priestly, 'Newton and the Romantic Concept of Nature' (*UTQ* xvii, 1948); R. Shackleton, 'Newtonianism and Literature' (*Literature and Science*, International Federation for Modern Languages and Literatures, 1954); R. W. V. Elliott, 'Isaac Newton's "Of an Universall Language"' (*MLR* lii, 1957); F. E. Manuel, *Isaac Newton, Historian* (Harvard, 1963: on Newton's views on ancient history, chronology, and corruptions of Holy Scriptures); D. Layton, 'The Motion of the Planets: Newton's Effect on English Thought' (*History Today* vii, 1957); H. Guerlac, 'Newton's Changing Reputation in the Eighteenth Century' (*Carl Becker's Heavenly City Revisited*, ed. R. O. Rockwood, Cornell, 1958; see also Guerlac's paper in *Aspects of the Eighteenth Century*, ed. E. R. Wasserman, Johns Hopkins, 1965).

JOHN NORRIS, 1657–1711

Norris published a volume of *Poems and Discourses* (1684), and *A Collection of Miscellanies* (poems, essays, discourses, letters) in 1687, which was reprinted several times. He also wrote various theological works and 'practical discourses', and he answered Toland's *Christianity not Mysterious* in *An Account of Reason and Faith* (1697), which ran through many editions. His philosophical *magnum opus*, *An Essay towards the Theory of the Ideal or Intelligible World*, appeared in two parts (1701–4). There is an edition of the *Poems* by A. B. Grosart (1871). His *Cursory Reflections upon . . . An Essay concerning Human Understanding* (1690) has been edited by G. D. McEwen (*ARS*, 1961). Comment on Norris includes Sir Leslie Stephen (*supra*, III. 5); F. J. Powicke, *A Dissertation on John Norris* (1894); F. I. Mac-Kinnon, *The Philosophy of John Norris of Bemerton* (1910); J. K. Ryan (*New Scholasticism* xv, 1940). His poetry is sympathetically discussed by M.-S. Røstvig (*supra*, III. 3), and by G. Walton (*supra*, III. 3).

JOHN OGILBY, 1600–76

Ogilby was an industrious translator of the classics. His *Virgil* appeared in 1649, and was republished in royal folio with plates by Hollar (1654), and in octavo (1665). In 1658 he published a fine folio edition of the Latin original, embellished with over 100 illustrations. The *Virgil* was followed by an *Aesop* (1651); a second part, with some fables of his own, appeared in 1669, including 'Androcleus, or the Roman Slave' in 31 parts, and 'The Ephesian Matron' in 17 parts. A photographic reprint of 'The Second Edition' of 1668 has been edited by E. Miner (*ARS*, 1965; see also M. Eames, 'John Ogilby and his Aesop', *BNYPL* lxv, 1961). Ogilby's translation of the *Iliad* came out in 1660, and that of the *Odyssey* in 1665. In his later years he compiled and supervised the publication of books on geography and topography and a number of maps. The first (and only) volume of his *Britannia* ('An Illustration of the Kingdom of England and Dominion of Wales, by a Geographical and Historical Description of the principal Roads thereof, printed on one hundred copperplates') was undertaken at the desire of Charles II, and published in folio in 1675; and an *Itinerarium Angliae, or a Book of Roads* appeared in the same year. (See Sir Hubert Fordham, *Library*, 4th ser. vi, 1925; S. L. Clapp, *MP* xxx, 1933; Janet R. Wadsworth, *Manchester Review*, 1961–2, who gives a bibliography of maps and roadbooks in the Manchester Reference Library). A modern bibliography of Ogilby's complex publishing activities is badly needed. F. Bowers deals with editions and issues of Ogilby's coronation *Entertainment* (*Papers of the Bibliographical Society of America* xlvii, 1953), and E. Halfpenny amplifies Ogilby's account of those proceedings (*Music and Letters* xxxviii, 1957). The influence of Ogilby's *Virgil* on Dryden's translation is discussed by H. M. Hooker and by L. M. Proudfoot (*supra*, Dryden), and that of the *Aesop* on *The Hind and the Panther* by E. Miner (*supra*, Dryden).

JOHN OLDHAM, 1655–83

A few of Oldham's poems, e.g. *Garnet's Ghost* and *A Satyr against Vertue* (both 1679) were published separately and anonymously. His *Satyrs upon the Jesuits: Written in the Year 1679* appeared in 1681, to be followed by *Some New Pieces* (1681), *Poems and Translations* (1683), and *Remains of Mr. John Oldham in Verse and Prose* (1684). These, or later editions, are often found bound up together. An edition of *The Works* (1684) was frequently reprinted, and an edition of 1722 in 2 vols. has an anonymous Life. The *Compositions in Prose and Verse* were ed. E. Thompson (3 vols., 1770), and his *Poetical Works* (omitting some pieces) were ed. R. Bell (1854; repr. with an introduction by B. Dobrée, 1960,). There is a collection in the Bodleian (MS. Rawl. Poet. 123), chiefly in Oldham's handwriting, of poems by himself and poems by others which he admired. H. F. Brooks, who is preparing an edition of the poems, has compiled a bibliography (*OBS*, 1936). W. M. Williams discusses the *Satyrs upon the Jesuits* (*PMLA* lviii, 1943; *ELH* xi, 1944), and C. R. Mackin, Oldham's satirical technique in these poems (*SP* lxii, 1965). D. M. Vieth writes on *A Satyr against Vertue* (*PQ* xxxii, 1953).

ORRERY, ROGER BOYLE, EARL OF, 1621–79

Orrery's plays (mostly tragedies) were published before 1700 either singly, in pairs, or in a collection of *Six Plays* (1694). *The Dramatic Works* (2 vols., 1739) omits the comedy *Mr. Anthony*. There is a sound modern edition of *The Dramatic Works* by W. S. Clark (2 vols., Harvard, 1937). *Mustapha* is included in *Five Heroic Plays*, ed. B. Dobrée (World's Classics, 1960). Orrery's romance *Parthenissa* appeared in six parts (1654–69). He wrote *English Adventures* (1676: prose fiction), and *A Treatise of the Art of War* (1677). A collection of his

State Letters was published in 1742. The Preface to *Parthenissa* is included by C. Davies in *Prefaces to Four Seventeenth-Century Romances* (*ARS*, 1953).

Orrery's plays are surveyed by E. Siegert, *Roger Boyle, Earl of Orrery, und seine Dramen* (Vienna, 1906). K. M. Lynch considers 'Conventions of Platonic Drama in the Heroic Plays of Orrery and Dryden' (*PMLA* xliv, 1929), and L. J. Mills, 'The Friendship theme in Orrery's Plays' (*PMLA* liii, 1938). *Parthenissa* is discussed, with varying degrees of protest, in histories of the English novel (e.g. Raleigh, Baker, *supra*, IV. 3), and by T. P. Haviland (*supra*, IV. 3). C. W. Miller discusses the editions (*Studies in Bibliography* ii, 1949–50). K. M. Lynch has recently published a well-documented biographical and critical study, *Roger Boyle, first Earl of Orrery* (University of Tennessee, 1965).

THOMAS OTWAY, 1652–85

Don Carlos (1676), *The Orphan* (1680), and *Venice Preserv'd* (1682) were among the most popular plays of the late seventeenth century. A quarto volume of *The Works of Mr. Thomas Otway* appeared in 1692, consisting of separate quarto editions of nine tragedies and comedies bound together. *The Works* (2 vols., 1712), containing the plays, poems, and love-letters, were several times reprinted (in 3 vols., 1757, 1768). An 1812 edition has a Life of Otway 'enlarged from that written by Dr. Johnson', and an 1813 edition by T. Thornton has 'Notes, Critical and Explanatory, and a Life of the Author'. *The Complete Works* were ed. M. Summers (3 vols., 1926); the standard edition is *The Works*, ed. J. C. Ghosh (2 vols., 1932). The 'Mermaid' selection, ed. Roden Noel (1888), contains *Don Carlos, The Orphan, The Souldiers Fortune, Venice Preserv'd*, and the love-letters. C. F. McClumpha edited *The Orphan* and *Venice Preserv'd* (Belles Lettres ser., Boston, 1909); *Venice Preserv'd* was ed. I. Gollancz (1899), and is available in Wilson (*supra*, II. 3).

Effective criticism of Otway begins with Johnson's Life. There are discussions of the plays in E. Gosse, *Seventeenth-Century Studies* (1883); B. Dobrée, *Restoration Tragedy* (1929); R. G. Ham, *Otway and Lee* (Yale, 1931); Gisela Fried, *Gestalt und Funktion der Bilder im Otway und Lee* (Göttingen, 1965); and T. B. Stroup (D. MacMillan *Festschrift*, *supra*, III. 1). In *Next to Shakespeare* (Duke University, 1950) Aline M. Taylor deals with the history of *The Orphan* and *Venice Preserv'd* on the London stage. Special studies of *Venice Preserv'd* include those of J. R. Moore (*PMLA* xliii, 1928); Aline M. Taylor (*Tulane Studies in English* i, 1949); D. R. Hauser (*SP* lv, 1958); R. E. Hughes (*NQ* cciii, 1958); W. H. McBurney (*JEGP* lviii, 1959); W. van Voris, (*Hermathena* xcix, 1964); G. Gillespie (*Comparative Literature* xviii, 1966).

SAMUEL PARKER, 1640–88

Parker's most important work, *A Discourse of Ecclesiastical Politie* (1670) led to a number of replies, including Marvell's *The Rehearsal Transpros'd* (1672). Parker answered Marvell with *A Reproof to the Rehearsal Transprosed* (1673). His *History of his own Time*, written in Latin, was first published in 1728, in an English translation by T. Newlin. There is an account of Parker's appointment as President of Magdalen College in J. R. Bloxam, *Magdalen College and James II, 1686–1688* (Oxford Historical Society, 1886).

SIMON PATRICK, 1626–1707

Patrick's most interesting works are *A Brief Account of the new Sect of Latitude-Men* (1662; ed. T. A. Birrell, *ARS*, 1963); *The Parable of the Pilgrim* (1664; frequently reprinted); and *A Friendly Debate between a Conformist and a Non-Conformist* (1669), with *A Continuation . . .* (1669) and *A Further Continuation . . .* (1670). Patrick left an autobiography in manuscript, which was edited by T. Chamberlayne (1839). His *Works*, ed. A. Taylor (9 vols., 1858) contain the autobiography, and are well annotated. He is discussed in J. H. Overton, *Life in the English Church 1660–1714*, and in other works of that nature.

WILLIAM PENN, 1644–1718

Several of Penn's numerous works were widely read in his own day. These include *The Sandy Foundations Shaken* (1668); *No Cross, No Crown* (1669; ed. N. Penney, 1930); and *Some Fruits of Solitude* (1693; ed. E. Gosse, 1901; ed. J. Clifford, 1905). *A Collection of the Works of William Penn* was edited by J. Besse (2 vols., 1726). *The Select Works* (1771) were reprinted several times, and there was a *Selection* by I. Sharpless (1909). *William Penn's Journal of his Travels in Holland and Germany* was edited by J. Barclay (1835), and *My Irish Journal* was edited by I. Grubb (1952).

Besides the accounts of Penn in histories of the Friends there are numerous Lives, including *Memoirs of the Private and Public Life of William Penn* (2 vols., 1813), by Coleridge's friend, Thomas Clarkson. Later biographies are those of W. H. Dixon (1872), J. Stoughton (1882), J. W. Graham (1916), M. R. Brailsford (1930), B. Dobrée (1932), C. E. Vulliamy (1933), W. I. Hull (Swarthmore College, 1936), and C. O. Pearce (Philadelphia, 1957). See also W. I. Hull, *Eight First Biographies of William Penn in seven languages and seven lands* (Swarthmore College, 1936), and L. V. Hodgkin, *Gulielma, Wife of Penn* (1947). Penn's relations with James II form the subject of V. Buranelli's *The King and the Quaker* (University of Pennsylvania, 1962), and J. E. Illick's *William Penn the Politician* (Cornell, 1965) deals with his relations with the English government.

SAMUEL PEPYS, 1633–1703

Pepys's *Diary* was first deciphered by the Rev. J. Smith and published in part, together with some of his correspondence, by Richard, Lord Braybrooke (2 vols., 1825). A new and fuller edition from the manuscript, but still with some omissions, was produced by the Rev. Mynors Bright (6 vols., 1875–9). The whole diary, 'except some passages which cannot possibly be printed', was edited by H. B. Wheatley from the Mynors transcript (10 vols., 1893–9). *Everybody's Pepys*, ed. O. Morshead, gives an abridgement of the complete text; and other abridgements include one in the Everyman series (1953), and one by J. P. Kenyon (1963). A new edition of the whole diary, freshly deciphered by W. Matthews, and under the general editorship of R. Latham and W. Matthews, is now in the press. Pepys's *Memoires relating to the State of the Royal Navy of England* were published in 1690 (repr., with an introduction by J. R. Tanner, 1906). His *Account of the Preservation of King Charles II after the Battle of Worcester* (dictated to Pepys by the King in 1680) was published by Sir D. Dalrymple (1766), and has been often reprinted, most recently in an edition by W. Rees-Mogg (1954). W. Matthews has edited *Charles II's Escape from Worcester: A Collection of Narratives Assembled by Samuel Pepys* (University of California, 1966). There is an edition of *The Tangier Papers* by

E. Chappell (Navy Records Society, 1935). Some of Pepys's letters are included in *The Life, Journals, and Correspondence*, ed. J. Smith (2 vols., 1841). Among subsequent collections are two by J. R. Tanner, *Private Correspondence and Miscellaneous Papers* (2 vols., 1926), and *Further Correspondence* (1929); *Letters and Second Diary*, ed. R. G. Howarth (1932); *Shorthand Letters* ed. E. Chappell (1933); *The Letters of Samuel Pepys and his Family Circle*, ed. Helen T. Heath (1955). Further correspondence will be found in the Calendars of State Papers (Domestic), 1660–81, and in various Reports of the Historical Manuscripts Commission.

The standard Life is that of Sir Arthur Bryant in 3 vols.: *Samuel Pepys, the Man in the Making* (1933); *The Years of Peril* (1935); *The Saviour of the Navy* (1938). Comment on Pepys is extensive. J. R. Tanner's *Mr. Pepys. An Introduction to the Diary, together with a Sketch of his Later Life* (1925) is well suited to the general reader. Pepys is discussed by Lord Ponsonby in *English Diaries* (1922) and in a volume in the English Men of Letters series (1928); J. Drinkwater, *Pepys, his Life and Character* (1930); C. Marburg, *Mr. Pepys and Mr. Evelyn* (University of Pennsylvania, 1935); P. Hunt, *Samuel Pepys in the Diary* (University of Pittsburgh, 1958); J. H. Wilson, *The Private Life of Mr. Pepys* (New York, 1959); C. S. Emden, *Pepys Himself* (1963); M. Willy, *English Diarists: Evelyn and Pepys* (British Council, Writers and their Work series, 1963).

Among specialized studies are those of J. R. Tanner, *Samuel Pepys and the Royal Navy* (1920); E. Chappell, *Samuel Pepys as a Naval Administrator* (1933); W. Matthews, 'Samuel Pepys, Tachygraphist' (*MLR* xxix, 1933) and 'Pepys's Transcribers' (*JEGP* xxxiv, 1935); McD. Emslie, 'Pepys's Songs and Songbooks in the Diary Period' (*Library*, 5th. ser. xii, 1967); H. McAfee, *Pepys on the Restoration Stage* (Yale, 1916); E. N. da C. Andrade, 'Samuel Pepys and the Royal Society' (*Notes and Records of the Royal Society of London* xvii, 1963). M. H. Nicolson's *Pepys's Diary and the New Science* (University of Virginia, 1965) ranges beyond Pepys to some of the experiments conducted by the Royal Society, and the attacks made upon its activities.

There is a descriptive catalogue of Pepys's library, *Bibliotheca Pepysiana*, ed. J. R. Tanner *et al.* (4 parts, 1914–40). H. E. Rollins edited *The Pepys Ballads* (8 vols., Harvard, 1929–32) and a selection of black-letter broadside ballads, *A Pepysian*

Garland (1922), mainly from the Pepys collection. L. M. Goldstein discusses 'The Pepys Ballads '(*Library*, 5th ser. xxi, 1966).

SIR WILLIAM PETTY, 1623–87

Petty's *Treatise of Taxes and Contributions* appeared in 1662, and reached a fourth edition in 1685. His *Essay concerning the Multiplication of Mankind* (1682) was followed by *Another Essay in Political Arithmetick* (1683) and *Two Essays in Political Arithmetick* (1686). In 1690, after his death, appeared *Political Arithmetick*, written apparently fifteen years earlier (repr. in *An English Garner*, ed. E. Arber, vol. iii, 1909). Petty's *Economic Writings* were collected and edited by C. H. Hull (2 vols., 1899). Letters and miscellaneous pieces, published as *The Petty Papers* (2 vols., 1927), were edited by the Marquis of Lansdowne, who also edited *Petty–Southwell Correspondence, 1676–1687* (1928).

There is a good deal of biographical information about Petty in Aubrey, Wood, Pepys, and Evelyn. A *Life* (1895) by his descendant, Lord Edmond Fitzmaurice, makes use of the family papers at Bowood. There is a more recent study by E. Strauss, *Sir William Petty: Portrait of a Genius* (1954). Brief discussions of Petty's work will be found in the standard histories of political economy. He is given full treatment by W. L. Bevan, *Sir William Petty: a Study in English Economic Literature* (Baltimore, 1894); M. Pasquier, *Sir William Petty: ses idées économiques* (Paris, 1903); W. Mueller, *Sir William Petty als politischer Arithmetiker* (1932); and W. Letwin (*supra*, V. 1). A general assessment has been made recently by K. T. Hopper (*History Today* xv, 1965).

EDWARD PHILLIPS, 1630–96?

The dictionary compiled by Phillips, *The New World of English Words* (1658), is discussed by De W. T. Starnes and G. E. Noyes (*supra*, IV. 1). His *Theatrum Poetarum: or a compleat Collection of the Poets . . . particularly those of our own Nation* was published in 1675. It was edited by Sir S. E. Brydges (1800); the Preface was reprinted in Spingarn, II. For discussions of Milton's possible hand in this work (first suggested by Thomas Warton), and for other relevant comment, see E. N. S. Thompson (*MLN* xxxvi, 1921); W. Albrecht, *Ueber das 'Theatrum poetarum' von Miltons Neffen Edward Phillips, 1675* (Leipzig, 1928); H. Fletcher (*JEGP* lv, 1956); R. G. Howarth (*MLR* liv, 1959);

and S. Golding (*PMLA* lxxvi, 1961). Phillips's Life of his uncle, John Milton, together with a Life ascribed to his brother, John Phillips, will be found in Helen Darbishire, *The Early Lives of Milton* (1932).

WALTER POPE, 1630?–1714

Pope's *Memoirs of Du Vall* appeared in 1670 (repr. *Harleian Miscellany* iii, 1809). His best-known poem, 'The Wish', was first published in H. Playford's *The Theatre of Music* (1685), and is usually referred to as 'The Old Man's Wish'. *Moral and Political Fables* ('done into measured prose intermingled with rhyme') appeared in 1698. Pope also wrote a *Life of Seth* [Ward] *Lord Bishop of Salisbury* (1697); it has been edited for the Luttrell Society (1961), with a biographical and critical introduction by J. B. Bamborough.

THOMAS PORTER, 1636–80

Porter wrote four plays, the best of which are a tragedy, *The Villain* (1663), and a comedy, *The Carnival* (1664). There is no collected edition. Although Porter is briefly discussed in histories of the drama (e.g. A. Nicoll, *supra*, III. 4, and A. Harbage, *Cavalier Drama*, New York, 1936), he has attracted less critical attention than he deserves.

EDWARD RAVENSCROFT, 1644–1704

The most popular of Ravenscroft's twelve plays, *The London Cuckolds* (1682), had reached a fourth edition by 1697; it is reprinted in M. Summers, *Restoration Comedies* (1921). *The Anatomist, or the Sham Doctor* (1697) is reprinted in *Ten English Farces*, ed. L. Hughes and A. H. Scouten (University of Texas, 1948). There is no collected edition of Ravenscroft. Comment, apart from histories of the drama, is mainly confined to the sources of Ravenscroft's plays (e.g. E. T. Noyes, *MLN* xlvi, 1936; R. E. Parshall, *RES* xii, 1936), but there is some more general discussion in L. Hughes, *A Century of English Farce* (Princeton, 1956). His life and work are covered in an unpublished thesis by N. Petterson in the University of London Library.

JOHN RAY, 1627–1705

Some of Ray's works were written in Latin, and would in any case be outside the scope of this volume. His *Catalogus Plantarum*

Circa Cantabrigiam (1660) was the first local English flora: some passages giving the localities of plants are in English. His *Observations . . . Made in a Journey Through Part of the Low-Countries* (1673) contains detailed accounts of what he saw. He published the English version of his friend Francis Willughby's *Ornithology* in 1678. His *Miscellaneous Discourses Concerning the Dissolution and Changes of the World* (1692) is one of the many books in the late seventeenth century in which the origin of the Earth is discussed. Besides his books on botany and zoology, Ray published *A Collection of English Words not generally used* (1674, 1691), and *A Collection of English Proverbs* (1670, 1678), to which new material was added in several editions after Ray's death. His *Wisdom of God manifested in the Works of the Creation* (1691) went into many editions. His *Persuasive to a Holy Life* (1700) is less interesting. Ray's *Philosophical Letters* were published by W. Derham in 1718, and his *Select Remains* (with a Life by Derham) in 1760. His *Correspondence* (1848) and *Memorials* of him (1846) were published by the Ray Society.

C. E. Raven's *John Ray* (1942) gives a full and admirable account of his life and works. Ray is discussed by B. Willey (*The Eighteenth-Century Background*, 1940; repr. Columbia, 1961); H. Meyer (*supra*, III. 5); R. S. Westfall (*supra*, V. 2). There is a bibliography by Sir Geoffrey Keynes (1951).

SIR JOHN RERESBY, 1634–89

Reresby's *Memoirs* were first published in 1734, and there was an edition of *The Travels and Memoirs* in 1813. The standard edition of the *Memoirs* is that of A. Browning (1936), which includes some of Reresby's letters. There is a biographical study in J. S. Fletcher, *Yorkshire Men of the Restoration* (1921).

ROCHESTER, JOHN WILMOT, EARL OF, 1647–80

Rochester's first known poem, 'To His Sacred Majesty', written when he was a fellow-commoner of Wadham College, appeared in a collection of University poems, *Britannia Rediviva* (1660). Some of his poems were printed in other miscellanies during his lifetime, others circulated in manuscript, and a few, e.g. *A Satyr against Mankind* (1675), were published separately. The first collected edition of his *Poems on Several Occasions* was that said to be 'printed at Antwerpen' (1680). In 1691 an edition including the tragedy of *Valentinian*, and described as one which might 'not unbecome the Cabinet of the severest Matron', was published by Jacob Tonson, with a preface by Thomas Rymer. Early eighteenth-century editions put out by Edmund Curll add a good deal of obscene verse, not necessarily or certainly by Rochester. The 'Antwerpen' edition has been edited by J. Thorpe (Princeton, 1950). Modern collected editions include those of J. Hayward (1926), and V. de S. Pinto (Muses Library, 1953; rev. 1964). The establishment of the canon has always been a difficult problem. There is a bibliography in J. Prinz, *John Wilmot, Earl of Rochester, his Life and Writings* (Leipzig, 1927). D. M. Veith, *Attribution in Restoration Poetry: A Study of Rochester's Poems of 1680* (Yale, 1963) provides a full discussion of the Rochester canon and of various textual problems.

Valentinian (altered from the tragedy by Fletcher) was first published in 1685, with the important preface by Robert Wolseley (repr. Spingarn II). The obscene play *Sodom* exists in several manuscripts; it was privately printed by L. S. A. M. von Romer (Paris, 1904), and there is a recent Paris reprint (1957), and one with an introduction by A. Ellis (North Hollywood, California, 1966). There is no reliable evidence for or against Rochester's authorship of this piece: R. M. Baine (*RES* xxii, 1946) attributes it to Christopher Fishbourne. *Familiar Letters*, by Rochester and others, were edited by Tom Brown and Charles Gildon (2 vols., 1697; repr. 1699, 1705). The letters that passed between Rochester and Henry Savile have been edited by J. H. Wilson, *The Rochester–Savile Letters, 1671–1680* (Ohio State University, 1941).

Biography begins with the funeral sermon preached by Robert Parsons, and Burnet's *Some Passages of the Life and Death of . . . Rochester* (both 1680), Wolseley's Preface to *Valentinian* (1685), and Rymer's Preface to *Poems . . . On Several Occasions* (1691). There is further information in Aubrey, Wood, and Johnson. J. Prinz published some anecdotes in his *Rochesteriana* (privately printed, Leipzig, 1926), and a biographical and critical study (*supra*). There is a full-length study by V. de S. Pinto, *Rochester. Portrait of a Restoration Poet* (1935; rewritten as *Enthusiast in Wit*, 1962). Pinto has also edited an account of the 'Alexander Bendo' escapade, *The Famous Pathologist . . . By*

Thomas Alcock and John Wilmot, Earl of Rochester (1961). There are also biographical studies by C. Williams (1935) and Jane Lane (1950), and biographical information in J. H. Wilson (*supra*, III. 1), in Wilson's 'Rochester, Dryden and the Rose-Street Affair' (*RES* xv, 1939) and 'Rochester's "A Session of the Poets"' (ibid. xxii, 1946), and in L. Hook (*MLN* lxxv, 1960).

Among critical studies are those of Pinto (*supra*, and in *Transactions of the Royal Society of Literature* xii, 1934, *ESEA*, new ser. vi, 1953, and the J. M. French *Festschrift, supra*, III. i); F. Whitfield, *Beast in View* (Harvard, 1936); K. B. Murdock in *The Sun at Noon* (New York, 1939); G. Williamson, 'The Restoration Petronius' (*University of California Chronicle* xxix, 1927); F. L. Huntley (*PQ* xviii, 1939); E. Giddy (*Études de lettres*, ser. 2, vii, 1964); R. Berman, 'Rochester and the Defeat of the Senses' (*Kenyon Review* xxvi, 1964); H. Erskine-Hill, 'Rochester: Augustan and Explorer' (Pinto *Festschrift, supra*, III. 1); Anne Righter (*Proceedings of the British Academy*, liii, 1968). Rochester's *Satyr against Mankind* has attracted more attention than any other of his poems. Among discussions are those of J. F. Crocker (*West Virginia University Studies* iii, 1937); J. F. Moore (*PMLA* lviii, 1943); F. Bruser (*UTQ* xv, 1946); T. J. Fujimura (*SP* lv, 1958); C. F. Main (J. M. French *Festschrift, supra*, III. 1). J. Auffret has discussed 'Rochester's Farewell' (*Études anglaises* xii, 1959), and P. Legouis has written on 'Rochester et sa réputation' (ibid. i, 1937).

ROSCOMMON, WENTWORTH DILLON, EARL OF, 1633?–85

Roscommon's only well-known poem, *An Essay on Translated Verse* (1684), was 'corrected and enlarged' in the second edition of 1685 (repr. Spingarn III). This and other pieces are available in *The Miscellaneous Works of the late Earls of Rochester and Roscommon* (1707; many later editions), and in the collections of Johnson, Anderson, and Chalmers. The best edition is *Poems by the Earl of Roscommon* (1717), which also contains the poems of Richard Duke and Mulgrave's *Essay on Poetry*. There is biographical information in the preface to Elijah Fenton's edition of Waller (1729), in Johnson, and in C. Niemeyer (*RES* ix, 1933; *MLN* xlix, 1934; *SP* xxvi, 1939). Some of his poems are sympathetically discussed by D. M. Stuart (*English* i, 1936), and by M.-S. Røstvig (*supra*, III. 2).

SIR PAUL RYCAUT (or RICAUT), 1628–1700

The Present State of the Ottoman Empire was first published in 1668, and had reached a sixth edition by 1686. It was translated into French, Polish, and Italian within a few years, and into German in 1694. In 1680 Rycaut published *The History of the Turkish Empire from 1623 to 1627* (a continuation of *The General History of the Turks* by Richard Knolles), and *The History of the Turks, Beginning with the Year 1679* in 1700. He also translated *The Critic* (1681) from the Spanish of Baltasar Gracián.

THOMAS RYMER, 1641–1713

Rymer translated Rapin's *Réflections . . .* as *Reflections on Aristotle's Treatise of Poesie* (1674), and wrote *The Tragedies of the Last Age Consider'd* (1678) and *A Short View of Tragedy* (1693). His preface to the first of those, together with sections of the other two, will be found in Spingarn II. All three works were edited by C. A. Zimansky, *The Critical Works of Thomas Rymer* (1956). *An Essay concerning Critical and Curious Learning* by 'T. R.' (1698), sometimes attributed to Rymer, is not accepted as his by Zimansky, but he has edited it separately for the Augustan Reprint Society (1965). Rymer's heroic tragedy *Edgar* (unacted) was published in 1698. His great work of historical scholarship, *Foedera*, a collection of state treaties in 20 vols., which he did not live to complete, began to appear in 1704.

From Macaulay onwards reactions to Rymer as a literary critic have been in general hostile. His critical views are discussed by A. Hoffherr, *Thomas Rymers dramatische Kritik* (Heidelberg, 1908), by G. B. Dutton (*PMLA* xxix, 1914), and by G. Saintsbury, J. W. H. Atkins, A. Maurocordato, and other historians of criticism (*supra*, IV. 7). There is a sympathetic account of his work as a scholar in D. C. Douglas (*supra*, IV. 7).

SIR CHARLES SEDLEY, 1639–1701

Many of Sedley's verses were printed anonymously in H. Kemp's *Collection of Poems* (1672). Poems, speeches in the House of Commons, and some other writings were collected by W. Ayloffe as *The Miscellaneous Works* (1702), and there were two further collections in 1707 and 1722, adding a good deal of spurious matter. Sedley contributed to a translation of Corneille, *Pompey the Great* (1664), and wrote two comedies, *The Mulberry Garden* (1668) and *Bellamira* (1687), and a tragedy, *Antony and*

Cleopatra (1677). *The Poetical and Dramatic Works* (2 vols., 1928) were edited, with a bibliography, by V. de S. Pinto, who also published a biographical and critical study in 1927. Pinto includes some of Sedley's verse in *Restoration Carnival* (1954) and in *Poetry of the Restoration* (1966), and he discusses his work in *The Restoration Court Poets* (British Council, Writers and their Work, 1965).

ELKANAH SETTLE, 1648–1724

Settle's nineteen plays (mostly tragedies and operas) have never been collected. The most celebrated of them is *The Empress of Morocco* (1673), the first English play, as Pope pointed out, 'that was ever printed with cuts' (i.e. plates); it is included in Dobrée's *Five Heroic Plays* (*supra*, II. 3). The Preface to *Ibrahim* was edited by H. Macdonald (Luttrell Society, 1947). Settle's semi-fictitious work, *The Notorious Impostor* (1692), has been edited by S. Peterson, together with *Diego Redivivus*, which may also be his (*ARS*, 1958); and Peterson has included another Settle piece, *The Complete Memoirs of . . . Will. Morrell* in a collection, '*The Counterfeit Lady Unveiled*' *and other Criminal Fiction of Seventeenth-Century England* (New York, 1961). Settle clashed with Dryden in *Notes and Observations on the Empress of Morocco Revised* (1674), and in *Absalom Senior* (1682; repr. in *Anti-Achitophel* (*1682*): *Three Verse Replies*, ed. H. W. Jones, Gainesville, Fla., 1961). For further contacts between the two men, see H. Macdonald's *Bibliography* of Dryden. Dryden's relations with Settle are discussed by R. G. Ham (*MP* xxv, 1928), and the implications of his quarrel with Settle on the genesis of *MacFlecknoe* by G. McFadden (*PQ* xliii, 1964) and A. Doyle (*SEL* vi, 1966). Settle's Whig pamphlet, *The Character of a Popish Successor*, ran through several editions in 1681.

There is a bibliography in the only full-length study, F. C. Brown, *Elkanah Settle: his Life and Works* (University of Chicago, 1910), and some addenda by E. G. Fletcher (*NQ* clxiv, 1933). Settle is of interest to book collectors on account of the fine armorial bindings in presentation copies of his poems. (See W. E. Moss, *Book Collector's Quarterly* xiii, 1934.)

THOMAS SHADWELL, 1642?–92

Contemporary copies of Shadwell's plays were collected and published as *The Works* (1693). In 1720 James Knapton and

Jacob Tonson brought out an edition of *The Dramatick Works* (4 vols.), dedicated by his son, Sir John Shadwell, to George I, with a prefatory 'Account of the Author and his Writings'. M. Summers edited *The Complete Works* (5 vols., 1927). Four of the plays (*The Sullen Lovers, A True Widow, The Squire of Alsatia, Bury Fair*) were edited by G. Saintsbury (1903) for the Mermaid series; *Epsom Wells* and *The Volunteers* by D. M. Walmsley (Boston, 1930); and *The Virtuoso* by M. H. Nicolson and D. Rodes (Regents Restoration Drama, University of Nebraska, 1966). Shadwell collaborated with Dryden and Crowne in *Notes and Observations on the Empress of Morocco* (1674). An attack on Dryden, *The Medal of John Bayes* (probably by Shadwell), appeared in 1682. He may also be the author of *The Tory-Poets: a Satyr.*

A. S. Borgman, *Thomas Shadwell: his Life and Comedies* (New York, 1928), gives a full account of his career. There are considerable discussions of the operatic version of *The Tempest* (W. J. Lawrence, *Anglia* xxvii, 1904; D. M. Walmsley, *RES* ii, 1926; G. Thorn-Drury, ibid. iii, 1927; H. M. Hooker, *HLQ* vi, 1943; C. E. Ward, *ELH* xiii, 1946). Shadwell's use of Hobbes is considered by T. B. Stroup (*SP* xxxv, 1938); his satire on the virtuosi, by C. Lloyd (*PMLA* xliv, 1929); his impact upon Dryden, by R. J. Smith (*RES* xx, 1944); 'Shadwell, the Ladies, and the Change of Comedy', by J. H. Smith (*MP* xlvi, 1948); his social satire in *Timon*, by P. F. Vernon (*Studia Neophilologica* xxxv, 1963); and *Timon* and the Duke of Buckingham, by G. Sorelius (ibid. xxxvi, 1964).

WILLIAM SHERLOCK, 1641?–1707

Sherlock's most celebrated work, *A Practical Discourse concerning Death* (1689), ran rapidly through many editions. His *Vindication of the Doctrine of the Trinity* (1690) was attacked by various divines and other writers, including Robert South (see South *infra*). His second thoughts about the Revolution of 1688, *The Case of the Allegiance due to Sovereign Powers* (1691), provoked many replies, and Sherlock published two defences of his position in the same year. This controversy is discussed by C. F. Mullet (*HLQ* x, 1946). There is some comment on Sherlock in S. T. Coleridge's *Notes on English Divines*, ed. D. Coleridge, vol. ii (1853).

THOMAS SHIPMAN, 1632–80

Shipman wrote a rhymed tragedy, *Henry the Third of France* (1678), with a preface in defence of rhyme. A small volume of his verse, *Carolina, or Loyal Poems* (1683), was edited by his friend Thomas Flatman after his death. It contains, *inter alia*, some verses on a performance of *The Conquest of Granada* at Belvoir in 1677. In addition to the brief biography of him in *DNB* there is an account by V. de S. Pinto in the *Transactions* of the Thoroton Society of Notts. vol. liii, 1950.

ALGERNON SIDNEY, 1622–83

Sidney's *Discourses concerning Government* were edited by John Toland (1698). There is an edition of *The Works* (1772). *Letters to the Hon. H. Saville* were published in 1742, and further correspondence will be found in *Letters and Memorials of State* (ed. A. Collins vol. ii, 1746); and in T. Forster, *Original Letters of Locke, Algernon Sidney* . . . (1830). Accounts of Sidney's trial were published in 1683 and 1684, and later in the various editions of *State Trials*. The fullest account of Sidney is that of A. C. Ewald, *The Life and Times of Algernon Sidney* (2 vols., 1873). Later comment includes that of F. J. Zwierlin (*Thought* xiii, 1938); J. H. Salmon, 'Algernon Sidney and the Rye House Plot' (*History Today* iv, 1954); and that of Fink and of Robbins (*supra*, V. 1.). There are a few remarks in Coleridge's *Notes, Theological, Political, and Miscellaneous*, ed. D. Coleridge (1853).

ROBERT SOUTH, 1634–1716

Several of South's sermons were published separately in the early years of the Restoration, and in 1679 came the first of many collections, *Sermons Preached upon Several Occasions*. A volume of *Posthumous Works*, containing memoirs of his life and writings, sermons, and the interesting 'Account of his Travels in Poland', appeared in 1717. Collected editions of the sermons continued to appear in the eighteenth and nineteenth centuries, and there are several selections. His two devastating attacks on William Sherlock, *Animadversions upon Dr. Sherlock's Book* . . . (1693) and *Tritheism Charged upon Dr. Sherlock's new notion of the Trinity* (1695), were both published anonymously. W. M. T. Dodds has printed some unpublished letters between South and Sherlock, and discussed their quarrel (*MLR* xxxix, 1944). There is a bibliography of South's publications by the same writer among the unpublished M.A. theses of the University of London.

Comment on South is sparse. W. C. Lake writes on 'South the Rhetorician' (*Classic Preachers of the English Church*, ed. J. E. Kempe, New York, 1877), and N. Mattis discusses his rhetorical theories and practices (*Quarterly Journal of Speech* xv, 1929); S. Spiker writes on the figures of speech in his sermons (*RES* xvi, 1940). There is a more general discussion by J. Sutherland (*Review of English Literature* i, 1960). Irène Simon will shortly publish a selection from the sermons of South and Tillotson in *Three Restoration Divines*, vol. ii (University of Liège) she discusses South in the introduction to vol. i. (167).

THOMAS SOUTHERNE, 1659–1746

Eight of Southerne's ten plays, beginning with *The Loyal Brother* (ed. P. Hamelius, Liège, 1911), were published as *The Works of Mr. Thomas Southerne* (2 vols., 1713). *The Spartan Dame* (produced in 1719) was added to another collected edition in 1721, and *Money the Mistress* (produced in 1726) was reprinted in *Plays written by Thomas Southerne, Esq.* (3 vols., 1774), together with a Life by T. E[vans]. *Oronooko* is available in *Five Restoration Tragedies*, ed. B. Dobrée (World's Classics, 1928). J. W. Dodds, *Thomas Southerne, Dramatist* (Yale, 1933), is the chief authority for his life and work. There is a perceptive discussion in Nicoll (*supra*, III. 4). More specialized studies include C. Leech, 'The Political Disloyalty of Thomas Southerne' (*MLR* xxviii, 1933). The source of *The Fatal Marriage* (which became well known on the Continent through French and German translations) is discussed by P. Hamelius (ibid. iv, 1909), and M. Summers (ibid. xi, 1916).

THOMAS SPRAT, 1635–1713

Sprat's verses on the death of Cromwell appeared, along with those of Waller and Dryden, in *Three Poems upon the Death of his late Highness Oliver, Lord Protector* (1659). His most celebrated poem, *The Plague of Athens*, went into seven editions between 1659 and 1700. Sprat's poetical works are available in the collections of Johnson, Anderson, and Chalmers. *The History of the Royal Society of London* (1667) was reprinted several times in the eighteenth century (the edition of 1702 being 'corrected'), and there is a facsimile of the first edition, ed. J. I. Cope and H. W.

Jones (Washington University, 1958). Sprat's *Observations on M. de Sorbier's Voyage into England* (1665) was reprinted three times in the next twelve years. His description of a conspiracy to implicate him in a supposed Jacobite plot, *A Relation of the Late Wicked Contrivance of Stephen Blackhead and Robert Young*, reached three editions in 1693. Sprat was persuaded by Charles II to relate the story of the Rye-House Plot: *A True Account and Declaration of the Horrid Conspiracy* . . . (1685) had reached a sixth edition by 1696. His well-known 'Account of the Life and Writings of Mr. Abraham Cowley' accompanied editions of Cowley's *Works* from 1668 onwards. Sprat's *History of the Royal Society* is more often quoted or summarized than discussed, but there is some critical assessment by A. Rosenberg (*Isis* xliii, 1952). H. Fisch and H. W. Jones consider the influence of Bacon on the *History* (*MLQ* xii, 1951), and Jones has also supplied some much-needed biographical information (*NQ* cxcvii, 1952).

SIR ROBERT STAPYLTON, 1605?–69

Stapylton wrote three plays, of which the most successful was *The Slighted Maid* (1663). The *Works, Dramatic and Other* were published in the same year. Among the 'other works' were several translations, including one of Juvenal (1647), *Dido and Aeneas* (1634: a version of *Aeneid* IV), and one of Musæus, *The Loves of Hero and Leander* (1645).

GEORGE STEPNEY, 1663–1707

Stepney (a Platonic pattern of the minor occasional poet) contributed a translation of the eighth satire to Dryden's *Juvenal* (1693). This has been edited by T. and E. Swedenberg from a manuscript in Stepney's hand (University of California, 1948). Stepney published a volume of *Poems* (1701). His collected verse is to be found in *The Works of the Most Celebrated Minor Poets* (1751), and in Johnson, Anderson, and Chalmers. The chief authority on the career and moribund reputation of Stepney is Johnson, but he has been given a new lease of life by H. T. Swedenberg, Jr., 'Stepney, my Lord of Dorset's Boy' (*HLQ* x, 1946).

EDWARD STILLINGFLEET, 1635–99

Stillingfleet's *Works* were collected in six volumes (1707–10), with a Life by Richard Bentley. Collections of his sermons had been appearing from 1669 onwards. Among his most important writings are *Irenicum, a Weapon-salve for the Churches Wounds* (1661); *Origines Sacrae* (1662; 7th ed. 1702); *A Rational Account of the Grounds of Protestant Religion* (1665); *The Unreasonableness of Separation* (1681); *Origines Britannicae; or the Antiquities of the British Churches* (1685). In the late 1690s Stillingfleet was involved in controversy with Locke (see W. Dahrendort, *Lockes Kontroverse mit Stillingfleet*, Hamburg, 1932). S. T. Coleridge, *Notes on Stillingfleet* (ed. R. Garnett, 1875) deals with *Origines Sacrae*. There is a short account of Stillingfleet by J. W. H. Nankivell (1946: repr. from *Transactions of the Worcestershire Archaeological Society*); and he is discussed by J. Tulloch (*supra*, V. 2), and by W. C. de Pauley, *The Candle of the Lord: Studies in the Cambridge Platonists* (1937).

HENRY STUBBE, or STUBBES, 1632–76

Stubbe attacked Joseph Glanvill, Thomas Sprat, and the Royal Society in *The Plus Ultra reduced to a Non Plus*, in *Legends no Histories*, and in *Campanella revived, or an inquiry into the History of the Royal Society* (all 1670). He also launched attacks on Hobbes, Harrington, Baxter, and others; and in *Rosemary and Bayes* (1672) he answered Marvell's *The Rehearsal Transpros'd*. In his less pugnacious hours he wrote Latin verse, and translated from the Italian. There is some biographical information in Wood's *Athenae Oxonienses*, and in the Supplement to *Biographia Britannica*. He is noticed in books and articles dealing with the early years of the Royal Society (*supra*, V. 3), and by C. F. Mullet, 'Physician *vs.* Apothecary 1669–1671' (*Scientific Monthly* xlix, 1939).

NAHUM TATE, 1652–1715

Tate wrote nine plays, mostly tragedies, including his version of Shakespeare, *The History of King Lear* (1681; repr. by C. Spencer, *supra*, II. 3). His very successful farce, *A·Duke and No Duke* (1681) may be read in L. Hughes and A. H. Scouten, *Ten English Farces* (University of Texas, 1948). The 1693 edition contains a preface concerning farce, which is discussed by S. A. Golden (Wilcox *Festschrift*, *supra*, III. 1). Tate published a volume of *Poems* (1677), and wrote, in collaboration with Dryden, the larger and feebler portion of *The Second Part of Absalom and Achitophel* (1682). Among his other writings are

Panacea: A Poem upon Tea (1700), and a number of occasional poems, and he collaborated with Nicholas Brady in a well-known metrical version of the Psalms (1696). He also wrote the libretto of *Dido and Aeneas* (1680; repr. in facsimile, 1961), and edited two poetical miscellanies, *Poems by Several Hands* (1685), and *Miscellanea Sacra* (1696; with additions, 1698). A full bibliography of his numerous publications will be found in *CBEL*.

Tate's version of *King Lear* is treated sympathetically by C. Spencer (*SEL* iii, 1963), and is discussed by H. Spencer, *Shakespeare Improved* (Harvard, 1927), by W. M. Merchant, *Restoration Theatre* (*supra*, III. 4), and by T. D. Duncan Williams (*Studia Neophilologica* xxxviii, 1966). J. Black writes on its stage history (*Restoration and 18th Century Theatre Research* vi, 1967). Tate is discussed by E. K. Broadus, *The Laureatship* (1921), and in other works on that subject, and more fully by H. F. Scott-Thomas (*ELH* i, 1934).

JOHN TATHAM, *c.* 1610?–64

Most of Tatham's work belongs to the pre-Restoration period. His only important play is *The Rump* (1660), which was given a renewed lease of life when Mrs. Behn rewrote it as *The Roundheads* (1681). Tatham's *Dramatic Works* were collected by J. Maidment and W. H. Logan (1879). He also wrote a number of civic pageants between 1657 and 1664, and published two volumes of verse, *Fancies Theater* (1640) and *Ostella* (1650). For his dramatic writings, the best account will be found in G. E. Bentley, *The Jacobean and Caroline Stage*, vol. V (1956).

SIR WILLIAM TEMPLE, 1628–99

Temple's popular *Observations upon the United Provinces of the Netherlands* appeared in 1673 (ed. Sir G. N. Clark, 1933). His essays were published in *Miscellanea. The First Part* (1680), followed by *The Second Part* (1690), and *The Third Part* (published by Jonathan Swift, 1701). The contents of the above volumes, together with a few poems, a large number of letters, and the separately published (1695) *Introduction to the History of England*, were collected in 2 vols. as *The Works of Sir William Temple* (1720), and frequently reprinted. His *Early Essays and Romances* were edited by G. C. Moore Smith (1930). There are several selections of the essays, including one by J. E. Spingarn (1909), and another by S. H. Monk (University of Michigan, 1963).

An Essay upon the Original and Nature of Government (1680) has been edited by R. C. Steensma (*ARS*, 1964).

Memoirs of the Life and Negotiations of Sir William Temple were written by Abel Boyer (1714), and a character of him by his sister, Lady Giffard, was published after her death (1728). The fullest biography is T. P. Courtney's *Memoirs of the Life, Works and Correspondence* (2 vols., 1836), which was the occasion of Macaulay's acid review. Later studies include C. Marburg's *Sir William Temple: a Seventeenth Century 'Libertin'* (Yale, 1929), and H. E. Woodbridge's *Sir William Temple: the Man and his Work* (New York, 1940). C. B. Macpherson has considered Temple as a political scientist (*Canadian Journal of Economics and Political Science* ix, 1943), and D. C. Douglas deals briefly but sympathetically with him as a historian (*supra*, IV. 5). The famous letters written by Dorothy Osborne to Temple before their marriage were edited by G. C. Moore Smith (1928).

HENRY TEONGE, 1621–90

The Diary of Henry Teonge was first published, with biographical and historical notes, by Charles Knight in 1825. There is a modern edition by G. E. Manwaring (1927).

JOHN TILLOTSON, 1630–94

There were several gatherings of Tillotson's sermons published during his lifetime. The first collected edition is that of R. Barker (14 vols., 1695–1704), and the best is that of T. Birch (*The Works*, 3 vols., 1752). There is a selection of the sermons (ed. G. W. Weldon, 1886), and in *The Golden Book of Tillotson* (1926) J. Moffat gives extracts from his works, together with a sketch of his life. Biographical accounts begin with the funeral sermon preached by his friend Gilbert Burnet (1694). A *Life* was compiled in 1717 by Francis Hutchinson from the minutes of Edward Young. T. Birch wrote a full biography for his edition of the *Works*, which was also published separately, and there is a good short Life in *Biographia Britannica* (1763). The auction catalogue of Tillotson's library was published as *Bibliotheca Tillotsoniana* (1695). Tillotson's preaching is discussed by W. Fraser Mitchell, and by other writers on pulpit oratory (*supra*, V. 2), and there is a full, but occasionally misleading account in L. G. Locke's *Tillotson: A Study in Seventeenth-Century Literature* (Anglistica ser., Copenhagen, 1954).

D. D. Brown deals with the text of the sermons (*Library*, 5th ser. xiii, 1958), and discusses the influence of Tillotson on Dryden's prose style (*RES*, new ser. xii, 1961). Irène Simon will shortly publish a selection from the sermons (see South, *supra*).

SIR SAMUEL TUKE, *c.* 1620–74

The Adventures of Five Hours was published in 1663, and a 3rd edition (revised) in 1671. Both versions are given by A. E. H. Swaen in his edition of the play (Amsterdam, 1927), together with an English translation of Tuke's Spanish source. There is an edition by B. van Thal and M. Summers (1927). Tuke's source, *Los Empeños de Seis Horas*, is discussed by A. Gaw, *Sir Samuel Tuke's Adventures of Five Hours in relation to the Spanish plot and to Dryden* (Baltimore, 1917). Tuke also wrote *A Character of Charles the Second* (1660). E. S. de Beer supplies some biographical information (*NQ* clxi, 1931).

JOHN TUTCHIN, 1661?–1707

Tutchin published a volume of *Poems on Several Occasions* (1685), a number of occasional poems, pindaric and otherwise, and a verse attack on several bishops, *The Tribe of Levi* (1691). He also published *A New Martyrology: or, The Bloody Assizes* (1689), which became in the 5th edition (1705) *The Western Martyrology*. Tutchin is best remembered for his anti-Dutch poem *The Foreigners* (1700), which provoked Defoe's more famous reply, *The True-Born Englishman*, in the following year. *The Foreigners* is included by S. Peterson in a small gathering of *Selected Poems, 1685–1700* (*ARS*, 1964). Some account of his early life is given in *Rabshakeh Vapulans* (1691), an answer to *The Tribe of Levi* (*supra*). G. A. Aitken's biography in *DNB* is well documented. Some light on his later career as writer of *The Observator* will be found in J. Sutherland, *Defoe* (1937), and J. R. Moore, *Daniel Defoe, Citizen of the Modern World* (University of Chicago, 1958).

WILLIAM WALSH, 1663–1708

Walsh's *Works in Prose and Verse* were published in 1736, and his poems are in the collections of Johnson, Anderson, and Chalmers. Dryden contributed a preface to Walsh's prose *Dialogue concerning Women, being a Defence of the Sex* (1691). His

'Letters and Poems Amorous and Gallant' were printed in vol. iv of Jacob Tonson's *Miscellany Poems* (1716). Letters and poems in the Bodleian Library were described in the *Bodleian Quarterly Record* vii, 1934, by Phyllis Freeman, who also gave an account of recently discovered letters between Walsh and Dryden (*RES* xxiv, 1948), and of two further manuscripts containing seven unpublished poems and part of an essay on critical and curious learning (ibid., new ser. viii, 1957).

NATHANIEL WANLEY, 1634–80

Wanley's curious and naively erudite compilation, *The Wonders of the Little World: or, A General History of Man* (1678) was reprinted several times in the eighteenth and early nineteenth centuries. L. C. Martin collected and edited *The Poems of Nathaniel Wanley* (1928), and also wrote a critical study (*ESEA* xi, 1925). Many of Wanley's letters are in the British Museum (Harl. MS. 6430).

SIR PHILIP WARWICK, 1609–83

Warwick was the author of two works, both published posthumously: *A Discourse of Government* (1694), and *Memoires of the Reigne of Charles I* (1701). The *Memoires* were later edited by Sir Walter Scott (1813).

SAMUEL WESLEY, 1662–1735

A volume of verse, *Maggots* (1685), was published by Wesley while he was still at Oxford. *The Life of our Blessed Lord. An Heroic Poem* appeared in 1693, with a prefatory discourse on heroic poetry. *An Epistle to a Friend concerning Poetry* (1700) was edited by E. N. Hooker (*ARS*, 1947), together with the discussion on heroic poetry mentioned above.

HENRY WHARTON, 1664–95

Wharton's *Anglia Sacra* was published in 2 vols., 1691. A third and unfinished part appeared in 1695. Under the pseudonym of 'Anthony Harmer' he published a sharp attack on Bishop Burnet, *A Specimen of some Errors and Defects in the History of the Reformation* (1693). He was entrusted by Archbishop Sancroft with the publication of the Remains of Archbishop Laud, and lived long enough to edit two volumes. The first of these, *The History of the Troubles and Tryal of William Laud. Wrote by himself* . . . came out in 1695, and a second volume of *Remains* was published by his father (1700). There is an assessment of Wharton in D.C. Douglas (*supra*, IV. 5).

ROBERT WILD, 1609–79

The celebrated *Iter Boreale*, a poem on General Monck's march from Scotland to London, was published in 1660, and was frequently reprinted. Later editions of 1661 and 1668 contain additional poems. There is a collected edition of *The Poems of Dr. Robert Wild*, ed. J. Hunt (1870).

JOHN WILSON, 1627?–96

Wilson's successful comedy, *The Cheats*, went into four editions between 1664 and 1693, and there is a modern critical edition by M. C. Nahm (1935), whose 'John Wilson and "Some Few Plays"' (*RES* xiv, 1938) provides some information about his writings. *The Dramatic Works*, ed. J. Maidment and W. H. Logan (1874) gives all four of Wilson's plays. There is a study by K. Faber, *John Wilson's Dramen* (Wiesbaden, 1904), and F. S. Boas deals with *The Cheats* and censorship (*Shakespeare and the Universities*, 1923). Wilson also wrote several pieces on constitutional law, some miscellaneous verse, and a translation of the *Moriae Encomium* of Erasmus (1668).

WILLIAM WINSTANLEY, 1628?–98

Winstanley was an industrious plagiary and compiler of books, of which the following are among the more interesting: *England's Worthies* (1660); *The Loyall Martyrology* (1665); *The New Help to Discourse* (1669; many editions); *The Lives of the Most Famous English Poets* (1687). This last has been edited in a facsimile reproduction (Gainesville, Florida, 1963) by W. R. Parker, who has elsewhere assessed the value of this work (*MLQ* vi, 1945). Winstanley probably had some hand in the *Poor Robin* almanacs from 1664 onwards.

ANTHONY WOOD, 1632–95

Wood's *Historia et Antiquitates Universitatis Oxoniensis* (2 vols., 1674) was edited by John Gutch in an English version (3 pts., 1792–6). Gutch also edited from the Wood MSS. in the Bodleian Library *The History and Antiquities of the Colleges and Halls in the University of Oxford* (2 vols., 1786–90). Wood's *magnum opus, Athenae Oxonienses. An Exact History of all the Writers and Bishops Who have had th.ir Education in the University of Oxford, from 1500–1690,* appeared in 2 vols. (1691–2), was reprinted (1721,) and was edited by P. Bliss (4 vols., 1813–20). Wood's autobiographical and miscellaneous manuscripts are available in A. Clark, *The Life and Times of Anthony Wood* (5 vols., 1891–1900), which includes an account by the editor of the Wood papers in the Bodleian Library. There is an abridgement by L. Powys (1932; repr. World's Classics, 1961). Wood also put together a sort of Oxford jest-book, published in 1751 with the title of *Modius Salium.* His general reliability is discussed by J. M. French (*PMLA* lxxv, 1960).

WILLIAM WOTTON, 1666–1727

Reflections upon Ancient and Modern Learning was published in 1694. The second edition of 1697 contains Bentley's 'Dissertation upon the Epistles of Phalaris', and to the edition of 1705 Wotton added 'A Defence of the Reflections, with Observations upon The Tale of a Tub'. Wotton also published *The History of Rome from the Death of Antoninus Pius to the Death of Severus Alexander* (1701); two volumes of *Miscellaneous Discourses relating to the Traditions and Usages of the Scribes and Pharisees* (1718); and *A Discourse concerning the Confusion of Languages at Babel* (1730). R. C. Olson discusses Wotton in 'Swift's Use of the *Philosophical Transactions* in Section V of *A Tale of a Tub*', (*SP* xlix, 1952). For discussion of Wotton's connection with the Ancients and Moderns controversy, see J. H. Monk's *Bentley*, vol. I (1833), and Richard Bentley, *supra*, and J. B. Bury, *The Idea of Progress* (1920). There is an account of his precocious educational development in Henry Wotton's *Essay on the Education of Children* (1753; written in 1672).

JAMES WRIGHT, 1643–1713

Wright published *The History and Antiquities of the County of Rutland* (1684), and an epitome in English of Dugdale's *Monasticon* (1693). His pleasant *Country Conversations* (1694; repr. 1927), and *The Humours and Conversations of the Town* (1693; ed. in a facsimile reproduction by B. Harris, Gainesville, Florida, 1961) show his lighter side. Wright's *Historia Histrionica: an Historical Account of the English Stage* (1699) was reprinted in Dodsley's *Select Collection of Old Plays* (1744, vol. xi), and reproduced in facsimile by C. W. Ashbee (Reprints, No. 28, 1872).

WILLIAM WYCHERLEY, 1641–1716

The Works of the Ingenious Mr. William Wycherley (2 vols., 1713) was followed by several later eighteenth-century editions. In 1840 Leigh Hunt published *The Dramatic Works of Wycherley, Congreve, Vanbrugh and Farquhar,* which Macaulay fell foul of in *The Edinburgh Review* (January, 1841). Wycherley's four comedies were edited by W. C. Ward (Mermaid series, 1888), and recently by G. Weales (New York, 1966). *The Complete Works* (including the letters and verse) were edited by M. Summers (4 vols., 1924). *The Posthumous Works,* ed. Lewis Theobald (1729), contains poems, a collection of maxims, and a memoir by Richardson Pack. *The Posthumous Works, Vol. II,* ed. A. Pope (1729), gives a different text of some of the poems, and supplies the Wycherley–Pope correspondence (which can also be read in *The Correspondence of Alexander Pope,* ed. G. Sherburn, vol. i, 1956). There is a full account of those two volumes by V. A. Dearing (*PMLA* lxviii, 1953). Wycherley's two most popular comedies, *The Country Wife* (1675) and *The Plain-Dealer* (1677), were edited together by G. B. Churchill (Boston, 1924). *The Country Wife* has been edited by U. Todd-Naylor (Smith College, 1931), and by T. H. Fujimura (Regents Restoration Drama, University of Nebraska, 1965), and is available in several small selections of Restoration drama. *The Plain-Dealer* has been edited by L. Hughes (Regents Restoration Drama, University of Nebraska, 1967).

A brief memoir by George Granville, Lord Lansdowne, was first published in *Letters of Wit, Politics and Morality* (1701), and there is biographical material in C. Gildon, *Memoirs of the Life of William Wycherley* (1718); John Dennis, *Critical Works,* ed. E. N. Hooker (2 vols., Baltimore, 1939–43): Joseph Spence, *Anecdotes* (1820; ed. J. M. Osborn, 2 vols., 1966). H. P. Vincent (*Harvard Studies and Notes in Philology and Literature* xv, 1933) first cleared up the problem of Wycherley's second marriage, and he has also thrown light on Wycherley's 1704 volume of *Miscellany Poems* (*PQ* xvi, 1937).

Nineteenth-century critics of Wycherley include Hazlitt, *Lectures on the English Comic Writers* (1820); Lamb, 'On the Artificial Comedy of the Last Century', *Elia* (1823); Leigh Hunt and Macaulay (*supra*). Wycherley is discussed in most of the twentieth-century books of dramatic criticism listed *supra*, III. 4. He is treated at length by C. Perromat, *William Wycherley. Sa Vie — son Œuvre* (Paris, 1921); W. Connely, *Brawny Wycherley* (1930); Rose A. Zimbardo, *Wycherley's Drama, A Link in the Development of English Satire* (Yale, 1965). There is a short study by P. F. Vernon (British Council, Writers and their Work, 1965). The reputation of *The Country Wife* and *The Plain-Dealer* is dealt with by E. L. Avery (*Research Studies of the State College of Washington* x, xi, xii, 1942–4). On *The Plain-Dealer* there are papers by A. H. Chorney (Lily B. Campbell *Festschrift*, *supra*, III. 1); K. M. Rogers (*ELH* xxviii, 1961); Rose A. Zimbardo (*SEL* i, 1961). There are articles on Wycherley by G. B. Churchill (*Schelling Anniversary Papers*, New York, 1923); E. E. Williams (*MLN* liii, 1938); and T. W. Craik (*English Studies* xli, 1960). J. Auffret has written on 'Wycherley et ses maîtres les moralistes' (*Études anglaises* xv, 1962).

JAMES YONGE, 1646–1721

Yonge, a naval surgeon, published some medical writings. He has recently been resuscitated by the publication of his journal preserved in the Plymouth Institution, *The Journal of James Yonge (1646–1721)*, ed. F. N. L. Poynter (1963).

INDEX

Some minor names and incidental references are omitted. Main entries are in bold figures. An asterisk indicates a biographical note. Topics in Sections IV–V of the bibliography are listed.

Translations : Dryden 193-4